Power Failure

The Political Odyssey of a Pakistani Woman

Power Failure

The Political Odyssey of a Pakistani Woman

SYEDA ABIDA HUSSAIN

OXFORD
UNIVERSITY PRESS

OXFORD
UNIVERSITY PRESS

Oxford University Press is a department of the University of Oxford.
It furthers the University's objective of excellence in research, scholarship,
and education by publishing worldwide. Oxford is a registered trade mark of
Oxford University Press in the UK and in certain other countries

Published in Pakistan by
Ameena Saiyid, Oxford University Press
No.38, Sector 15, Korangi Industrial Area,
PO Box 8214, Karachi-74900, Pakistan

© Oxford University Press 2015

The moral rights of the author have been asserted

First Edition published in 2015

All rights reserved. No part of this publication may be reproduced, stored in
a retrieval system, or transmitted, in any form or by any means, without the
prior permission in writing of Oxford University Press, or as expressly permitted
by law, by licence, or under terms agreed with the appropriate reprographics
rights organization. Enquiries concerning reproduction outside the scope of the
above should be sent to the Rights Department, Oxford University Press, at the
address above

You must not circulate this work in any other form
and you must impose this same condition on any acquirer

ISBN 978-0-19-940157-4

Typeset in Adobe Garamond Pro
Printed on 55gsm Book Paper

Printed by VVP

Dedication

To the memory of my parents;
and to my children, Umme Kulsum, Sughra, and Abid

Contents

Acknowledgements ix

1. Power Failure 1
2. A Chapter Closes 36
3. My Journey Begins 77
4. Upheaval 127
5. Grass-Roots Politics 164
6. National Assembly, At Last 219
7. In Opposition 277
8. Pakistan's First Woman Prime Minister 318
9. 'Madam Ambassador' 378
10. Washington D.C. 417
11. America Elects a New President 470
12. Back to Basics 504
13. Winner Turns Loser 538
14. Musharraf Usurps Power 585
15. Nawab Akbar Bugti's Assassination 623
16. Benazir Bhutto's Assassination 652

Epilogue 694
Index 699

Acknowledgements

My deepest gratitude to my friend Sara Suleri who told me that I could and should write my story without the help of any professional writers. When I sent her my manuscript, I was immensely encouraged by her observation that she found the text 'enthralling'. My friend Ayesha Jalal, with her acute sense of the meticulous, kept encouraging me to complete my text and to improve it, and painstakingly assisted me to do so. My friend Hamida Khuhro was equally supportive, helpful, and encouraging; as was Abbas Rasheed.

My thanks to Maheen Pracha for doing a professional read of my manuscript and for helping me with some corrections. I am also grateful to Ali Imran who helped to make me computer literate enough to type out my narrative on my laptop and to gradually discover the world within the box.

I would also like to thank Fakhar, my partner of forty-five years, for his patience, perseverance, and tolerance of taking almost a year out of our lives to prioritize the writing and completion of my narrative. Halfway through my writing, I contacted Ameena Saiyid regarding the possibilities of Oxford University Press publishing my work. She evinced immediate interest and encouraged me to complete my narrative and send it to her editorial board. I am grateful to Nadia Ghani and Hassan Rizvi for their cooperation and support.

Most of all I would like to thank the many thousands of people of Jhang to whom I belong and who I have always felt belong to me.

They have been, in the final analysis, the fundamental source of my inspiration, providing me with the capacity to refresh my spirit and recover myself from the setbacks that life inevitably brings. I've enjoyed writing most of all about them, and sharing with my readers glimpses of our culture and heritage.

Syeda Abida Hussain

1

Power Failure

Perhaps it was thus to be that writing would become a force of necessity prompted by prolonged failure of power and governance, inducing me to write a personal, anecdotal account of missed opportunities. As I begin to write, I cannot help feeling a sense of an intertwining of personal and national destiny in what will necessarily be an account of missed opportunities: my own and those of my country. Certainly my country's history would have been quite different had our leaders been less self-serving and our institutions stronger. Almost from the outset, state power was exercised in a manner that served only to erode it. Greater circumspection and lesser commitment to power as an end might have helped reduce our involvement in the great games that were being played out in neighbouring Afghanistan, starting in the late seventies, which bedevilled us for decades, continuing right up into the twenty-first century.

Spanning a period of forty years, Pakistan, a young nation with an old civilization, and the potential to lead the Muslim World, ceased progressing as a modern state, with militant and extremist groups emerging out of religiosity rather than religion onto its political landscape. How and why this came to be has been the subject of much discourse and debate, with many scholarly treatises written on multiple aspects of the issue. Some have traced the roots of the issue to our history, some have located them in the poverty and inequity of our societal construct, while others have dwelt on the many conspiracies spawned by individuals, both at the national as well as international level, who merely sought to serve what were often their perceived short term aims and objectives. As an individual, I found myself caught up, quite unwittingly, in the vortex of these issues, from time to time, with my life often under threat, and my career in politics interrupted, even prematurely curtailed. Towards the twilight of my life, reliant on personal notes and diaries and a reasonably functional memory, I thought of recording the events that resonated with me, in which I had some part to play and that indirectly shed some light on why my country and I suffered prominent power failure.

So where should my narrative begin?

I am a year older than Pakistan, one of midnight's children, born to privilege and a contingent sense of entitlement. I grew up in a united, albeit post-colonial, Pakistan, a country with two segments, an East Pakistan and a West Pakistan, carved out of what were the prime portions of our subcontinent, the Indus valley, and the delta of the Brahmaputra. My parents and grandparents were born and raised in colonial India, and educated in colonial institutions. My grandfather on my father's side was heir to a large estate in the heartland of Punjab, handed down to him by twelve generations of forebears. He was a student of Aitchison College in Lahore, popularly known as 'Chiefs College', where he spent a decade, enrolling in 1889 and obtaining a Diploma in 1899. My grandfather on my mother's side was a self-made man, modestly educated, but successful at business—starting out in Ferozepur, moving onto Lahore in the late 1920s; he was able to send his older sons to the Central Model School and his youngest to Aitchison College when his business expanded; while his daughters studied at Queen Mary's.

My parents sent me to an International school for girls in Switzerland as soon as I finished with my 'O' Levels at school in Lahore, to pursue my 'A' Levels at Montreux. I was thrilled at the prospect, not knowing at the time that I owed what was considered to be a unique privilege by my peers, to Tahir Ayub Khan, the youngest son of President Ayub Khan. In the summer of 1962, Tahir and I had met at my aunt Sarwat's home in Murree. Tahir came with his sister Jamila and brother-in-law Amirzeb of Swat State. I noticed Tahir looking at me admiringly, and he appeared keen to chat. Unbeknownst to me, he expressed to his father his interest to marry me. Ayub Khan, aware of the deep friendship between my father and Nawab Kalabagh, the then Governor of West Pakistan, sent a proposal through the latter seeking my hand in marriage for his son Tahir. My father declined, telling Nawab Kalabagh, apparently quite firmly, that he should have dealt with it himself rather than coming to father—and should have conveyed to Ayub Khan that there was no question of my father agreeing, as he was certain to marry his only child to someone within his own family; and moreover, he had scant respect for Ayub Khan's usurpation of power. Apparently, close on the heels of Nawab Kalabagh's visit, Lady Viqar un Nissa Noon, wife of the deposed Prime Minister, Malik Sir Firoz Khan Noon, who was Prime Minister at the time Ayub Khan's coup d'état, dropped by to see my parents. Aunty Vicki (as Lady Viqar un Nissa was called) was a great friend of my mother. She informed my parents that Ayub Khan was enraged at their refusal of his son's marriage proposal, hence, it would be wise to send me away to school overseas for a few years, until the incident blew over.

The nexus between privilege and power had already been established. Ayub Khan, unlike my father, may not have been to the bungalow born, but having flourished as an officer in the

British Indian Army, his children grew up with privilege and entitlement, and therefore perhaps failed to understand why anyone would refuse such an honour.

The Swiss school my parents chose was administered by Roman Catholic nuns. It comprised of forty-eight students, belonging to various nationalities: from the Americas, Africa, Europe, and Asia. We learnt as much in the classrooms as we did from our peers. We were taught French, could opt to prepare for the Baccalaureate or 'A' Levels, and were offered a variety of courses ranging from painting to ceramics, cuisine and couture; we could learn to play the violin or the piano, and take courses in psychology or comparative religion. Our teachers were Swiss and French, and we were at Mourgins, staying in chalets from January to March to study in the evenings and ski during daytime. In the spring and summer, we were taken for excursions to different parts of Switzerland, to Austria, Germany, Italy, and Spain. At the end of my first year, I visited Florence with a small group of eight students and accompanied by a teacher. Florence was a magical city. I discovered a girls' school there located in a classic Tuscan villa just off the Viale Michael Angelo. I decided that when I completed my 'A' Levels at Montreux, I would plead with my parents and convince them to send me to Florence for at least a year. Savouring a cappuccino at the Piazza della Republica, opposite the Uffizi and close to the Berninis in the Galleria, I felt like I had dwelt here in another life, and had an extraordinary feeling of belonging. When I finished my Swiss schooling, my parents came to fetch me and I successfully managed to persuade them to visit Florence. They were sufficiently charmed by the place to accede to my request of studying in Florence.

My year in Florence gave me a sense of style and helped me forge lifelong friendships with two English girls, Mandy Haggenbach and Patsy Lyons. I took a course in the History of Art and Architecture with Professor Gori-Montanelli, and learned to draw in the Atelier of Signorina Simi. I accessed the studio of the great Florentine maestro of his time, Pietro Annigoni, and pottered around while he did a sketch of me, which he then presented to me, declaring that I was better looking than Gina Lollobrigida. Since by this time, Annigoni was quite elderly, I thought that he was making this statement because he could not see properly! Emilio Pucci was all the rage in the world of fashion at the time and Gucci was already the last word in bags and shoes, along with Ferragamo—all of them illustrious Florentines. My friend Patsy's parents, Sir Jack and Lady Lyons, came from London to visit her and allowed me to tag along with them to the fashion houses and meet with young Antinoris and Corsinis in their Palazzos. I wore chiffon saris and was made much of wherever I went. Most people commented that I looked like an exotically dressed young Italian. All this attention had a head-spinning effect on me; I wanted my year in Florence to last forever. But all too soon, the summer was upon us and it was time for me to return to my own country and to my family.

In June of 1965, I was back home in Pakistan after a three-year stint in Europe, and now hoped to go to Cambridge, which would be another three years. Only nineteen years old at the time, I would still be graduating at the right age. But life scripted it for me quite differently, as I was to find out later.

Besides being a political leader of his time, my father was also an enthusiastic farmer and horse breeder, and would often spend July and August in Karachi to race his horses. I was happy to be in

Karachi instead of being isolated up at Cliffden, our family farm in the Murree hills. Karachi was a peaceful city at the time, with flourishing business houses and a fairly slick social life. The Karachi Race Course was a fashionable place to be seen on Sundays, with the Haroons and Hidayatullahs, Chinoys and Rahimtoolas, Dossas and Dadas, and Sonny Habibullah, my father's dear friend, always in the Stewards Box, where we would all be seated. These families all belonged to the Bombay business elite, and were among the founding families of Pakistan. My father was racing his horses with great success that summer, and almost every Sunday, I would lead a winner or two in the paddock, walking by his side. We were much photographed, focused on, and entertained. Daily lunches and dinners were held in the homes of politicians and friends. Notable among them were A. K. Brohi, Pakistan's most eminent lawyer and former High Commissioner to India; M. A. H. Ispahani, our first Ambassador to the United States, Kazi Fazalullah, prominent politician from the Larkana district of Sindh; Haji Moula Bux Soomro, whose brother, Allah Bux Soomro, was minister of Sindh before Partition, and Mohammad Ayub Khuhro, who had been a cabinet colleague of my father. Mian Mumtaz Daulatana, former chief minister of Punjab, like us had a place in the hills, but he also spent a part of his summer in Karachi everyone found him a fascinating conversationalist. His daughter Shahida was a friend and both our families were frequently entertained by the Khuhros. M. A. Khuhro, Mian Mumtaz Daulatana, and my father had been colleagues in the first West Pakistan Assembly after the formation of One Unit in 1955, and they would discuss endlessly whether the formation of the Republican Party was unavoidable or otherwise, of what ought not to have happened and at what point Ayub Khan started plotting his coup. M. A. Ayub Khuhro's older daughter Hamida and I bonded and we became lifelong friends.

I once accompanied Hamida to a get-together in the pleasantly Bohemian apartment of Yasmeen and Sohail Lari where I met Timmy Bokhari, who typified 'desi' elegance. I was very taken in by her and we became friends, our lives intertwining interestingly in the years ahead. Because of my training in art at Florence, I was keen to meet Sadequain, who had won an award at the Biennale in Paris, and was told he would be exhibiting at the Karachi Arts Council shortly, when Sadequain himself walked in. He looked at me quizzically above the glasses perched on the tip of his nose, as I gushed over him, telling him how proud I was as a Pakistani learning about the acclaim that he had won in the art world of Paris. At my insistence, my father bought two of his paintings, although he valued the work of our classicists, Abdur Rahman Chughtai and Ustad Allah Bukhsh a shade more. My own paintings that I had brought with me from Florence were purchased by the Khuhros and Ispahanis.

And while I was busy discovering and forging friendships with Karachi intellectuals and socialites, my father insisted that I take time out to visit Mohtarma Fatima Jinnah, whom he described as the 'heroine' of Pakistan. I had a vivid recall of Miss Jinnah arriving on my sixth birthday party at 'Nasheman', the large sprawling bungalow of my maternal grandparents on Davis Road in Lahore. I was deeply impressed with her courage in contesting against Ayub Khan in the presidential elections of 1965, the first Muslim woman to contest for the highest office at the time.

Calling on Miss Jinnah was the first dampener that came my way since my return home to Pakistan. On a windy morning in late July, my mother and I arrived at Mohatta Palace, having made an appointment with the Mohtarma. We rang the front door bell for the longest time. The door was finally opened by Miss

Jinnah herself—she led us into a sitting room which was dark and stifling. 'Open the latches of the window, Kishwar,' she said, addressing Mother by her name, 'you and your daughter are taller and stronger than I am.' We rushed to do her bidding and as the louvred teak windows opened and the light and air entered the room, I was taken aback to see how old and frail she looked.

'Chandi (my nickname) has just come back from school in Switzerland and Italy, and Abid was very keen that she should come and pay her respects to you,' said my mother deferentially.

'Child, stretch for that bell, so my deaf old servant can bring you some tea or *limoo paani* (lemonade), if you prefer. Kishwar, as you can see, my sofas have loose covers on because I seldom have visitors. They all go to see my half-sister, Shireen Bai, these days, since she has an "in" with Ayub Khan's government. Had my brother foreseen all this, would he have struggled so hard for the creation of Pakistan? Would he have wanted a country without a constitution, without justice, where skilled sycophants become powerful, while people with integrity and dignity start falling behind? If this was what Pakistan was to become, then making Pakistan was a foolish mistake.' I felt a chill sweep over me and wanted to get away from this dark conversation as soon as possible, but to add to my dismay, when I recounted this to my father on our return from the visit, he said, 'I understand how Miss Jinnah feels. When Huseyn Shaheed Suhrawardy and I faced our EBDO (Elected Bodies Disqualification Order) trials, we had similar misgivings. We were, after all, among the founders of Pakistan. I was a young and minor player at the time, but Suhrawardy was the architect of the eastern wing of our country and the Usurper declared us all unfit to represent, after having abrogated the Constitution which was framed by the founders of our state, and then dictating a constitution that disenfranchised the people. With the military in power here, India has an added advantage and will seek to score over us in some way.'

Sure enough, by August, our newspapers started carrying stories of 'infiltrators' entering Kashmir. At a dinner in the home of Ishaat Habibullah, the younger brother of Sonny Habibullah, the discussion centred around who could be behind the 'infiltrators'. The consensus was that it was Ayub Khan. Jahanara Begum, our hostess, whose brother, Sahibzada Yaqub Khan was a well-known officer in the Pakistan Army, looked very troubled when my father suggested that this could lead to an Indo-Pakistan war.

The 1965 Indo-Pak War broke out within nine weeks of my return home, interrupting my reverie abruptly. My father thought the Indians would cross the international border either from Rajasthan or Wagah, and told my mother to start packing for our return to Punjab. The Indian Army aimed for Wagah on the 6th of September, and my father rushed to the railway station returning with tickets for a coupe carriage on the Chenab Express destined to depart for Shorkot, in District Jhang, the same evening.

Aboard the train, we heard the sirens screaming as the train came in for a prolonged stop at Sammasatta. My cousin Iffi was with us, along with his sister Zarina, who was called 'Bia'. Mother kept fussing about the tiny lavatory, while I kept fussing over my hairdo! Father would listen in on the station master's transistor radio and inform us of the advance of the Indians and our holding onto Lahore. He was agitated and I could not understand why, because the war seemed far off and remote to us in Sammasatta! Meanwhile, Uncle Babar Ali, my mother's youngest brother, along with my mother's sisters-in-law, nephews, and nieces from Lahore, were ensconced in Shah Jewna House, our home in the town of

Jhang, along with some Pakistan Tobacco Company executive's wives and children. Jhang was the name of our district, and the district headquarter town was also called Jhang. The district had two sub-divisions or tehsils: Chiniot to the north, and Shorkot to the south. We disembarked at Shorkot and drove into Jhang town. As we entered the house, my father said: 'The more the merrier! Kishwar, organize the rooms and if there is a spill-over, some of us will move to Shah Jewna.'

'There will be no need for that because you and I and Chandi can move into the storage rooms in the courtyard,' said my mother. Storage rooms—what an outrage, I thought!

'Do not forget, Chandi, your country is at war,' said Father, face reading as usual. Mother shifted furniture around and managed to make the storage rooms fairly acceptable. On day six of that somewhat short war, I walked out of the refurbished storage rooms of my home, a grand colonial bungalow built by my grandfather at the end of the nineteenth century.

The house has served as a protective womb for me throughout my life. This bungalow, occupied by my grandfather when he was appointed Honorary Magistrate of Jhang district in 1900, had a wide-arched porch with a deep verandah in the front and in the rear end of the sprawling house. The ceilings were high, with a passage running from the front door to a lounge which opened onto the rear verandah, the sitting and dining rooms on either side of the passage, and four bedrooms, two opening onto the front verandah, two onto the rear. It was known as 'Shah Jewna House', named after our village, Shah Jewna, which in turn was named after our fifteenth-century forebear, Pir Shah Jewna. The house was located in the Civil Lines area, near the district courts. I emerged out of the rooms rearranged by my mother for us, wearing a sari with my hair teased into an elaborate chignon. Everyone around, cousins, aunts, and friends, looked at me—some smiled—some looked askance. 'You are not quite in Paris,' said my cousin Tariq Ali. And suddenly I knew I had landed where I truly belonged, I was in Punjab's heartland where the two great rivers, Jhelum and Chenab, meet. Europe and its culture seemed very far away.

I belonged to the Punjab, and Punjab belonged to me: its flatlands and its colour, emerald green and saffron yellow fields, and its meandering rivers, the Jhelum and the Chenab, its handsome people with burnished brown skins, wearing magenta and purple lungis, the hot bright sun. The sages, Saints, and Sufis embedded in this land, an intrinsic part of my heritage.

And now my country, a locale of peace, was suddenly at war. At night the sirens would wail occasionally as our new airbase at Shorkot came under threat. Everyone would be glued to their transistors, and many of us started knitting pullovers in khaki wool for our soldiers. Father donated a hundred thousand rupees, a small fortune at the time, to the government's defence fund, but he was critical of Ayub Khan for getting us stuck in a war he was clear we could not win. Every time he would say this, there would be an argument.

> Look, I am only an honorary Colonel, but when I was preparing to become a recruiting officer during World War II, I read a bit on warfare, and I am enough of a politician to know that India will not concede on Kashmir. We cannot conquer India, we will only bleed ourselves financially and our economic progress will come to a standstill.

Father was a common-sense person who spoke with clarity and conviction and it was hard to disagree with him. 'Young Pakistanis must never forget that Pakistan was created for economic reasons,' he would emphasize. He was a staunch supporter of Fatima Jinnah and was imprisoned two days prior to the presidential elections date. He was handcuffed and paraded in the precinct of the district courts, presumably to intimidate the electors who were the so-called 'basic democrats', the overwhelming majority of whom had pledged to vote for the sister of Quaid-i-Azam Muhammad Ali Jinnah, the Founder of Pakistan. As word spread of the Ayub administration's crude attempt at intimidation of my father, who was Jinnah's ardent supporter and the youngest member of his team in the Legislative Assembly of undivided India, my father's supporters, in the town of Jhang as well as in the surrounding villages, started marching toward the district courts. Threatened by a rapidly increasing crowd jeering and shouting outside his office, the deputy commissioner informed the commissioner who consequently informed the Governor, the Nawab of Kalabagh, Amir Mohammad Khan.

The Nawab Kalabagh (as he was known) and my father, Abid Hussain Shah, had been Wards of Court and fellow students at Aitchison College and were taken for summer holidays together to Simla by a common tutor. The Nawab ordered my father's immediate release and Fatima Jinnah won the vote in Jhang against Ayub Khan. This was the only district in Punjab that she won. She had, of course, scored in the city of Karachi, but lost in East Pakistan. According to my father, Maulana Bhashani, the political leader of the then East Pakistan sold out on Fatima Jinnah and the Combined Opposition Parties (COP) that was supporting her. Ayub Khan had impressed Bhashani because of his overtures of friendship with China; Maulana Bhashani was left-leaning and pro-China.

After the elections, Father filed a case against the district administration for rigging in the elections. He engaged Mian Manzoor Qadir, an eminent jurist, as his lawyer. His cousin and brother-in-law, Uncle Mubarik Ali Shah, was co-petitioner. They won the case, but while subordinate officers were sentenced to a jail term, the deputy commissioner and superintendent of police were let off the hook and only sentenced till the rising of the court. The lawsuit had cost a fortune, said my mother, but my father derived pride and satisfaction from the reality that this brought the rigging in the presidential contest on record and the judgement given became a precedent for the future.

As the war raged, my father dwelt lengthily on the finer points of the lawsuit. 'I wish you had been with me in the court room, your keen mind would have appreciated the sharp points highlighted eloquently by Manzoor Qadir. You would also have valued the forceful logic of Barrister Mahmud Ali Kasuri who had filed a similar petition.' I understood from my father's keenness to apprise me of all that happened in my years of absence from home that he was urging me to grow up and be serious, which I was; even though looking good at the time was a major concern, it was not necessarily a priority.

Uncle Amjad Ali, my mother's eldest brother, was Pakistan's Permanent Representative at the United Nations. We moved for a ceasefire at the UN. Why we were seeking a ceasefire when the Pakistani media of the time was propagating victory for us was baffling. My father's dispassionate indictment of why we had ended up at war in the first place had now begun to resonate with the community of war escapees sheltered temporarily at Shah Jewna House.

Mother, persuaded that her elder brother, whom she so looked up to, would be speaking for us in the Security Council, herded us all onto the veranda to hear the speech on her transistor radio. But it was Pakistan's dashing young foreign minister who spoke and rejected the Polish resolution. Mother was disappointed and said Zulfikar Ali Bhutto's voice was much too high pitched.

'Who cares?' said I. 'He sounds terrific. I want to meet him.'

'So do I,' said cousin Popety.

Popety and I were classmates of the same age and great chums. Mother frowned at us as if to suggest we were being disloyal to our Uncle Amjad Ali.

Pakistan declared a ceasefire when the Russians moved into the game and, in a sense, the contours were delineated for a new Great Game to be played out between the Capitalist World and the Communists. The killing fields designated to be the sparsely-populated, arid, platitudinous terrain of our neighbouring Afghanistan.

Father was a great horse lover. He captained the Aitchison College tent-pegging team as a student; after his release as a ward of court, coming into quite a bit of money, he started what became a lifelong pursuit of buying horses. In British India, when the owners of large estates were orphaned as children, their properties were managed by the local administration, headed by a British officer who was head of what was named the Court of Wards. My father remained a Ward of Court until he reached the age of twenty-one.

Nine years later, 1946 became a landmark year in his life. It was in this year that he took his seat in the Legislative Assembly in Delhi as a young and enthusiastic Muslim Leaguer, and voted for Partition, thus becoming one of the founders of Pakistan. It was also in this year that he established the Shah Jewna Stud and Livestock Farm on a portion of the land he had inherited. And I, his only child, was born in that same year.

Twenty years later, when he was enjoying considerable success as a horse breeder, his attention was diverted by the rising tensions around us, and our house in Lahore became an increasing hub of political activity. The assertion of Mohtarma Fatima Jinnah that the military ruler Ayub Khan had no right to abrogate the Constitution, framed after some difficulty by the leaders of East and West Pakistan to forge a consensus, resonated with public opinion, and Fatima Jinnah, backed by the Combined Opposition Parties, was expected to win the election, but the Bhashani betrayal made Ayub Khan triumph momentarily. Defeating the icon of Pakistan was not a simple matter and the prevailing mood of disdain led Ayub Khan towards engaging in the disastrous military adventure in Kashmir, which embroiled us in a costly and fruitless war with our powerful neighbour. Not only were we set back in economic terms, we also managed to leave the rather more politicized eastern wing of our country deeply troubled regarding issues relating to its security. Our articulate Bengali brethren questioned the costs incurred on the defence establishment of Pakistan with the bulk of the spin-off benefits accruing to Punjab, while East Pakistan remained undefended.

As early as February 1960, shortly after we had moved into our new house that my father had built in Gulberg, Lahore, H. S. Suhrawardy came to the city to establish the National Democratic

Front (NDF) and was my father's most honoured house guest. The NDF was established in the reception room of our house and was joined by a handful of those political leaders who did not collaborate with Ayub Khan. The NDF later morphed into PDM, or Pakistan Democratic Movement, as the demand for restoration of democracy intensified. My father emerged as a veteran advocate for the need to revert to a democratic dispensation and won wide respect for his efforts, although this made my mother's businessmen siblings somewhat nervous. My mother, intensely loyal to her brothers, tried to argue, but my father was firmly committed to the view that the nascent entrepreneurial community was errant in its support to military dictatorship and would eventually lose out to Indian entrepreneurs who had thrown their full weight behind the development of political parties, under the able stewardship of Jawaharlal Nehru. Clearly my father was a visionary on the subject and understood that this military-industrial complex would cost Pakistan dearly.

Although heavily supported by the Americans, Ayub Khan found it difficult to balance himself after the stalemated 1965 War, and his talented Foreign Minister, Zulfikar Ali Bhutto, sensing the popular mood, skilfully controversialized the Tashkent Declaration (1966) which was not much different from the earlier rejected Polish Resolution. Cutting his umbilical cord from his mentor, Ayub Khan, Bhutto moved unerringly towards popular leadership.

Zulfikar Ali Bhutto came to call on my father after his dismissal from the cabinet of Ayub Khan. He was undecided, he said, on whether to join the Tehrik-e-Azaadi party of Mian Mumtaz Daultana or the Awami League of Sheikh Mujibur Rahman or strike out on his own. My father suggested that he join Mujibur Rahman to serve the interests of provincial integration. We were in our house in Lahore and I was anxious to make an impression on this dashing visitor in a white suit and with considerable panache, so I asked a couple of questions which Bhutto answered with a twinkle in his eye. 'My daughter is very keen on politics and reads quite a lot,' said my father, looking a trifle embarrassed at my eagerness to join in the conversation. Then Bhutto asked him where he was going to be in the coming weeks and when my father said that he was taking my mother and me to London for the summer, Bhutto said he was going to London as well, and would seek an opportunity to meet us there.

After the coup d'état of 1958 and the sending into exile of President Iskander Mirza by Ayub Khan, whenever my parents and I were in London, Mother would always call her good friend Naheed Khanum, the Iranian wife of Iskander Mirza. When she did so in the summer of 1968, Naheed Khanum invited us for dinner, informing us that Bhutto would be coming and also the Raja of Mahmudabad.

Raja Mahmudabad and my father had been friends since they were colleagues in the Central Legislative Assembly of undivided India. Both of them never tired of telling the story of their very first encounter in Delhi in 1946. When the Legislative Assembly was called into session, Quaid-i-Azam summoned a meeting of the Muslim League Assembly Party. Raja Mahmudabad was seated next to the Quaid when my father entered the room. 'Ameer, I told you that you are not the youngest member of my Assembly. The youngest member has just joined us. Abid Hussain Shah, were you not born in the middle of 1915? I seem to recall the year from your application for our party nomination.'

'Yes, Jinnah Sahib. I was born in July 1915,' said my father.

'Abid come forward and meet your colleague Ameer, my young brother, just a few months older than yourself, without whose generosity I would never have managed to resource our effort to reach out to all the Muslims of India.'

'Please do not embarrass me Jinnah Bhai', said Raja Mahmudabad. The Quaid was Jinnah Sahib to my father while he was Jinnah Bhai to Raja Mahmudabad. Apparently when the two young men embraced, the one from Oudh and the other from the Punjab, they both noticed that they wore a Dur-e-Najaf agate set in silver on the third finger of their right hands, obtained by their respective mothers from the Marjah at Najaf-e-Ashraf in Iraq. From that moment, a friendship was ignited which endured through their lifetime, across many national boundaries and ethnic and linguistic divides.

Naheed Khanum and President Iskander Mirza lived in London in a charming flat in Prince's Gate, just off Exhibition Road. The dinner was splendid. Uncle Sonny Habibullah and Aunty Attia, my parents' dearest friends, were there, along with their daughter Shama. Safia Afkhami, Naheed Khanum's daughter was stunning, as was Shama. They were both a few years older than me. Shama was a Cambridge graduate and Safia was an Oxford graduate and I was in awe of both of them, but my confidence was greatly boosted by my friend Sulaiman, the only son of Raja Mahmudabad who was at the time at Pembroke College, Cambridge. Sulaiman and I bonded because we were both so adored by our respective parents that we recognized each other's burden, and we also shared an irrepressible sense of humour. When Bhutto Sahib started narrating the story of Ayub Khan's nervousness during the 1965 war and General Musa Khan's near panic, Sulaiman and I stopped chatting and listened to Bhutto with rapt attention. I was fascinated, but Sulaiman said he was disgusted by Bhutto's disloyalty to the man in whose cabinet he had served for so long. 'After Ayub Khan had gotten rid of his brilliant foreign minister, what loyalty could he be owed?' I argued, but my friend Sulaiman, a purist, remained unconvinced.

We met Raja Mahmudabad often that summer. My father was very keen that he should return to Pakistan and focus on an effort to provide leadership to the Pakistani people, but Raja Sahib had set his heart on developing a Muslim congregation centre in London and was beginning to plan what came to be the Islamic Centre in Regents Park. I kept suggesting to my father that he consider the Bhutto option, but he had reservations similar to Sulaiman's and would not forget that Bhutto had served as Secretary General of the Ayub Khan Muslim League when the presidential elections had taken place in 1964.

From London, my parents and I went to Holland. We had never been to Holland before and planned this visit because my father wanted to look at the system of dykes: as a keen farmer, he sought to increase his knowledge of irrigation systems. My mother wanted to go because she loved flowers and wanted to see tulip fields, and I was happy for the opportunity to feast my eyes on the Rembrandts in the Rijks museum.

We were in Amsterdam when my father complained that he suddenly felt extremely uncomfortable and unwell. Mother was hysterical. I telephoned my friend Anetje Jorgensen who had been at school with me at Montreux, Switzerland. Anetje's kindly father drove us to a nearby hospital. My father was given a preliminary check-up. His basic indicators were fine, the doctor prescribed some sedatives, but when we were back in the hotel, my father remained fretful which was so unlike him. Cutting our visit short, we returned to London; we did not meet Bhutto again, and were home a fortnight earlier than had been planned.

Father, whom I used to address as 'Ganji', a diminutive for 'Agha Jan', which is how all my cousins addressed their fathers, spoke to me for the first time about my marriage. Who I would marry was the most favoured topic of discussion among my aunts, cousins, and friends. I enjoyed talking about it, and had frequent crushes, but knew that I could not marry without my father's approval, and he would not consider anyone outside of a Bokhari Syed suitor. I loved my father far too much to displease him. But I did enjoy playing the role of Tragedy Queen, nonetheless. It reduced the envy of those around me. Soon enough my father broached the subject of my marriage with me. It was a touching moment, causing a lump in my throat. 'Chandi, while I hate the thought of letting you go, when I felt unwell in Amsterdam, pondering over what would become of my family if I disappeared suddenly, I decided I had to speak with you seriously regarding your future. I very much desire grandchildren and feel the time has come for you to get married.'

'But what about my going to Cambridge?' I asked him tremulously. He opted not to hear my question and gave me a choice of cousins, but I knew he was partial to Fakhar, who had lost his father when he was six years old. Pir Imam Shah Bokhari of Qatalpur, named after his forebear, was a descendant of Pir Shah Shaikh Ismail, a cousin of Pir Shah Jewna, with a common progenitor, Hazrat Jalaluddin 'Surkh' Bokhari. Pir Imam Shah was a graduate of Aligarh and married my mother's older sister: my aunt Fakhra, who bore him five daughters in a row followed by three sons. Fakhar Imam was the eldest of the sons. His father, Pir Imam Shah, died of renal failure at the age of thirty-seven.

Aunt Fakhra hence became a thirty-year-old widow, having been left with a fertile and generous piece of land by her husband, but with eight children to rear by herself.

Father respected Aunt Fakhra greatly and would say that she is as dignified in her widowhood as his mother, my 'Daadi', Ghulam Sughra, had been in hers. I wondered how all these details were relevant to me. Except, I did secretly find Fakhar devastatingly attractive. He was also well educated. Aunt Fakhra had sent Fakhar to Prep School and then to Public School in England, after which he opted to go to university in America. At a time when well-off Pakistanis tended not to think beyond Oxford or Cambridge, Fakhar decided to apply to the University of California to study agriculture. Graduating from U.C. Davis in 1966, Fakhar returned home and went to Qatalpur to farm and further develop the land for himself and his siblings. Unlike my other cousins, he neither hung around me, nor would he bother to attend social events in Lahore. He was as focused and serious at age twenty-three as he has been all his life, right up till today!

'What have you decided?' Mother asked me.

'I don't know, Baji.' (Like my cousins, I would call my mother 'Baji'). While everyone is talking politics, Fakhar is boring enough to be sitting for the Central Superior Services (CSS) exams, which makes him act superior. And he is a hopeless dancer!' I declared to Mother.

'Well I think you are simply being coy,' said Mother, and I wondered how she had become so savvy suddenly and said so to her. She said, 'I know you darling, like all mothers know their daughters. There must be absolute honesty between us; it is a question of your happiness. Your father and I have no right to be selfish so he has agreed to allow you to go out with Fakhar. Afsar Qizilbash and her husband will take you to a party and Fakhar will drive you home afterwards. Also, your father and I will be away in Jhang for two weeks and Fakhar can come to call on you every day so that you can get to know each other.'

'And Fakhar has agreed to all this?' I asked, as my heart pounded. Mother nodded, her eyes twinkling.

'Baji, I did not know you were such a schemer!'

'I am incapable. It was my friend Tahira [Mazhar Ali] who planned it all,' said Mother gently, a stickler for accuracy.

My parents went off to Jhang. Afsar and Raza came to fetch me. I had dressed with care and felt that everyone noticed my arrival when I entered the party. Fakhar was there. He took his time, approached me eventually.

'You look great,' he mumbled shyly.

'May I take you home?' he said.

'So soon,' I whispered, as our eyes locked, my legs seemed to carry me out of the door of their own volition. Fakhar parked the car not far from our gate. 'Will you come to see me tomorrow?'

'If you want me to,' he replied.

Fakhar came every day and we would sit in the verandah of our 7-F.C.C. home in Gulberg and chat all day. I began to marvel at how much knowledge he had accumulated. I would tease him about becoming a musty bureaucrat and he would assure me that although he would definitely do his CSS Academy training, he was not sure he would take up his commission to serve in the government. 'They pay a pittance as salary, although there are benefits and privileges. I would earn so much more growing cotton.'

'So why are you bothering with the exam?' was my query.

'Because it is a challenge; because I want to give myself the option; and because the bureaucracy in this country is so damn powerful that nobody can get anywhere without them. Besides I am reading books I may otherwise not have delved into, on the emergence of Pakistan and the sociology of our people. My foreign education taught me a lot but there are gaps in my knowledge nonetheless.' The answer was typical of Fakhar, practical and straightforward, rather like my father.

We disagreed on many issues, particularly when it came to the United States. I looked upon them as Imperialists, while Fakhar simply contended that we were living in the American century, and that it was the US that set the pace of events.

One day I asked him why he wanted to marry me. 'Do I?' he queried.

I started crying.

'Why do you come here every day if you don't want to marry me? I do not look like the back of a bus, and I am smart. And *I* have to decide whether *I* want to marry you!' I said, my voice shrill.

'No, Chandi,' Fakhar replied. 'We both have to decide. You are spoilt and demanding, and I may not be able to measure up to your expectations.'

'I have no expectations except that you love me—and love my father and mother. You must know that my father is looking for a son as opposed to a son-in-law. And you will have to agree to live with us.'

'Loving you is not the problem, I have loved you since you were nine and I was twelve, and I love your mother and your father. But living in your house, losing my identity ... and then everyone knows you, while I have only a few friends.'

'You have been in love with me all this while; why did you never tell me! You were always so aloof when you came home for your holidays. I would quarrel with you to provoke you into saying something. I suppose I too must have been in love with you all this time.' Reaching out for Fakhar's hand with its warmth enveloping me, I knew then that we would walk through life together.

It was decided that we would get married on 6 February 1969. To ensure that the date was auspicious for us, Father sent Syed Shabbir Shah (Shahji) all the way to the Grand Ayatullah Mohsin ul Hakim at the Hauza in Najaf, Iraq, for 'Istikhara' (supplication for right guidance). Shahji used to come to our house every Thursday and pray for our wellbeing as a commitment he had made to my Daadi before she had passed away in 1960. As soon as Shahji returned with positive news, my parents announced the date to the extended family. Everyone was not happy. I felt some waves of jealousy swirl around me.

Father planned a grand wedding, even though by now the political climate against the Ayub regime had started heating up, and he was quite immersed in meetings and demonstrations of the PDM (Pakistan Democratic Movement), of which he was an active member. He took time off from his political activities to focus on planning my wedding. A series of elaborate events were planned in detail, for after all, I was his only child. Father decided that week-long wedding festivities would commence in Shah Jewna and would conclude in Lahore. Fakhar being the eldest son in his family was also in a situation where his mother and sisters were going all out to plan festivities. Meanwhile Fakhar had qualified his exam and was now a probationer in the Finance Services Academy.

Our wedding was truly splendid. My dearest English friends, Mandy Haggenbach and Patsy Lyons, flew in from London and drove down to Shah Jewna to join in the festivities. Our wedding dinner that my parents hosted at our Gulberg residence in Lahore, was attended by all the significant leaders of the country—ranging from the left-wing gurus of the time across the political spectrum—to the religious right, including Maulana Maudoodi. Nusrat Bhutto came with Malik Ghulam Jillani. Zulfikar Ali Bhutto had been incarcerated by the tottering Ayub administration at the time.

Three days after my wedding, I went out into the first demonstration staged by women, which included the wives and daughters of all the PDM leaders: Tahira Mazhar Ali and her group of progressive women workers; Begum Maudoodi and her Mansura supporters; women journalists; students; lawyers led by Rabia Kari; and women labourers. As we marched down Jail Road towards the Governor's House, I savoured my first taste of liberation when we were shouting anti-Ayub slogans. The next day, I flew off with Fakhar for our honeymoon to Dacca (Dhaka), Bangkok, and Hong Kong.

When Fakhar and I returned home two weeks later, Mother had left for Hajj (annual pilgrimage) to Mecca, and Father was in Shah Jewna for Eid ul-Adha. Fakhar and I joined him there. I was standing with my father looking at the horses at his Stud Farm, while Fakhar was sent off by him to look at the mango garden.

'Are you alright, Chandi *baita*?' my father queried gently.

I was. There was a song in my heart, and I now wanted to go to Qatalpur. The road to Qatalpur was ten miles of *kacha* (dirt road) along the bank of their canal. Fakhar's ancestral *haveli* (mansion) was beautiful but in a state of disrepair. His farm was less developed than ours at the time. He assured me that he would get the road built as soon as he could access the commissioner of Multan as a government servant, because bureaucrats primarily helped each other. He agreed with me that this was not how it should be and that the District Councils established by Ayub Khan were a hoax. The bureaucracy had too much power and that the old system of district boards should be revived and elected representatives should deal with local development issues. I shared with Fakhar that I was concerned about my father; he had looked a little pulled down to me, but Fakhar assured me that he had not noticed any difference.

We returned to Lahore, and Fakhar went back to the Academy. He would be gone all day while I wished for him to be with me. When my mother returned from Hajj, she was agitated to see my father. She felt he had lost weight and insisted he undergo a medical check. It transpired that my father had developed diabetes. He was fifty-three years at the time and was unperturbed by the news, since diabetes ran in the family. He started taking medication for it, and said that the weight loss made him feel lighter. He became increasingly busy with political meetings and frequent demonstrations. People would now gather outside the Lahore High Court for processions and would then go onto the Mall. Mother and I would follow Father in another car. He would drive into the High Court precincts while we would park opposite to it, in front of Nabi Bux, a general store which had been there since my childhood.

It was there that we met Nawab Akbar Khan Bugti for the first time. He was tall, lean, and handsome, and drove a Chevrolet, which he parked near our car. He saw my mother and greeted her very respectfully, but did not look in my direction. As he strode across the Mall to join the demonstrators, my mother told me that just after I had left for Switzerland, Nawab Akbar Khan had come to see my father. He wanted my father to speak to Nawab Kalabagh regarding the release of his sister who had been imprisoned by the Military in Dera Bugti. Although Nawab Kalabagh was appointed Governor of West Pakistan since the coup, my father had never visited him at the Governor's House despite their profound friendship. He went to see him on Akbar Bugti's request. Nawab Bugti sat with my mother in our house while my father was gone. He returned within half an hour and told Bugti that when Father gave his name at the gate, the Governor sent for him immediately. He was waiting in the porch when my father alighted from his car. Declining to enter the rooms, Father had spoken to him while standing in the verandah. He had simply said to the Nawab, 'Bhaiya, if Akbar Khan is Governor in the future and detains your sister in Kalabagh, how would you feel?'

Nawab Amir Mohammad Khan (Nawab Kalabagh) responded: 'Tell Akbar Khan to return home. His sister will be released before he reaches Dera Bugti,' and she was.

As the demonstrations mounted pressure on the Ayub administration, the political leadership of the time demanded that Ayub Khan convene a round-table conference of all political leaders. My father told Nawabzada Nasrullah Khan that the demand ought to be that Ayub hand over power to the Speaker of the Assembly. Nasrullah Khan had emerged in what my father always referred to as the Basic Democrats, or B.D. Assembly, and joked with him a great deal, as they had been classmates at the Government College, but was always mindful that Nasrullah Khan was not consequential enough to have been disqualified under the EBDO.

The R.T.C or Round Table Conference was convened and aborted because the politicians demanded the release of Mujibur Rahman who had been accused of treason in the Agartala Conspiracy Case. The Bengalis agitated against the Ayub administration more aggressively, and this provided the GHQ of the Pakistan Army with the excuse they needed for a second military intervention.

General Yahya Khan declared Martial Law in April 1969, abrogating the Constitution dictated by Ayub Khan and announcing elections on the basis of adult franchise under a Legal Framework Order (LFO).

No sooner was the Proclamation Order announced, our house in Lahore started to fill up with friends and relatives—everyone congratulating my father on the riddance of Ayub Khan. Even those of my mother's siblings and cousins who had been fans of Ayub were turn-coating in the classic Punjabi tradition of riding the bandwagon. So they must have been disappointed when my father spoke and reminded the gathering that there was really no cause to celebrate because one 'usurper' had been replaced by another. He also reflected that if the new man blundered we could lose East Pakistan. At this, one of my mother's cousins observed that we would be well rid of the Bengalis. My father lost his temper at her: 'If this is to be our attitude, then we do not deserve to remain an independent country! Then maybe Maulana Abul Kalam Azad was right and Jinnah Sahib and all of us were wrong. You realize if we lose East Pakistan, we could also lose West Pakistan! None of us should forget this, least of all you Lahoris who benefit hugely from the creation of Pakistan,' my father seldom raised his voice but on this occasion he did.

Not long after Yahya Khan took over the reins of power, the Director of the Intelligence Bureau N. A. Rizvi, came to call on my father to ask him to join the cabinet that General Yahya was contemplating to form. My father declined by saying that he had waited a decade and had contributed in the struggle for the restoration of democracy. He was happy that General Yahya had announced his intent to hold elections and had abrogated the Ayub Constitution and re-enfranchised the Pakistani people. Father then informed Rizvi that he did intend to contest elections, but he would rather enter the government through the front door rather than through any back door channels. He emphasized that he did not have a personal grudge with Ayub Khan but he was against his usurpation of power. Similarly, he did not consider Yahya Khan's coming to power through a military coup to be any different. Father then suggested to Rizvi that General Yahya should consider Sardar Abdur Rashid in his stead. Subsequently, Sardar Abdur Rashid, who hailed from Peshawar, was inducted in his cabinet by Yahya Khan as Interior Minister.

Father had been appointed in the Central Government of Pakistan as Minister for Food and Agriculture in 1954, and for a short while as Education Minister, serving in the Cabinets of Chaudhry Mohammad Ali and Huseyn Shaheed Suhrawardy. After the creation of the One Unit (1954), he had joined the cabinet of Dr Khan Sahib, as Minister for Communications in the West Pakistan Government, as had Sardar Abdur Rashid with whom he forged a deep and enduring friendship. My father admired Dr Khan Sahib greatly and always contended that had it not been for the boycott of the Referendum by Khan Abdul Ghaffar Khan and his Redshirts for the accession of the North-West Frontier to Pakistan, the Muslim League would have failed to carry the Referendum and there would have been no Pakistan. After Punjab's Governor Mushtaq Ahmed Gurmani's moves against Dr Khan Sahib, that forced the latter's resignation, my father had insisted that Sardar Abdur Rashid be made Chief Minister of NWFP (now Khyber Pakhtunkhwa) to prevent the Pushtuns from abandoning their support for the One Unit. His contention was that it was the removal of Sardar Abdur Rashid from the office of Chief Minister and his replacement by Nawab Muzaffar Ali Khan Qizilbash, a move orchestrated by shadowy figures, which set the stage for the intervention by Ayub Khan. Malik Sir Firoz Khan Noon was Prime Minister. Both offices being held by Punjab was designed to inflame Bengali sentiment as well as cause annoyance in the Frontier. My father believed that the Ayub Khan's coup had been scripted and subsequent events certainly did not follow a course that may adequately have disproved his contention.

As the Yahya regime settled in, a major excitement came my way. I received an invite to the International Conference for Women to be held in Helsinki in June of 1969 and was sponsored by the United Nations. The invitation came to me through the Anjuman Tarraqui Pasand Khawateen of which I was a donor and to which I had attached the Abid Welfare Society, an income-generating project for rural women which I had initiated in Shah Jewna in 1966. Assessing that women in our rural communities had outstanding traditional skills of weaving and embroidery, I developed a program that grew and spread rapidly in several villages, and bonded me with humble and hard-working rural women.

Travelling to Moscow, onto Helsinki and after the conference, stopping by at London to look up my friends was an exciting prospect. Fakhar was going for a tour of Pakistan with his Academy probationers and he was as enthused about his impending travels as I was about mine, since he would be visiting all the important civil and military institutions of Pakistan.

My first international conference was unforgettable. There were three of us from Pakistan: me, Rashida Patel who represented the All-Pakistan Women's Association, popularly known as APWA, and Begum Habibur Rahman who represented a refugees' welfare organization. The conference was chaired by Valentina Tereshkova, the first woman cosmonaut, but the star of the conference, in my view, was a young Vietnamese warrior who worked on the staff of General Giap (1911–2013) of the Vietnam People's Army.

The conference lasted the usual three days with a day to discover Helsinki, which I was visiting for the first time. The Indian contingent to the conference included Hamida Habibullah, Uncle Sonny's sister-in-law. Her husband, 'Bubbles' Habibullah, a junior military officer in the British Indian Army, was the youngest of the Habibullah brothers. He had decided to remain in India after Partition, while his two older brothers, Sonny and Ishaat, had opted for Pakistan. The Habibullah family belonged to Lucknow, and were a classic example of a family split by the Partition of India and the creation of Pakistan in 1947. Aunty Hamida had been to Lahore for the Horse Show in the fifties, and had known me as a child. General 'Bubbles', and everyone called him that, was a polo player and also a show jumper and of course he happened to be the first Commandant of the Indian Military Academy at Kharakwasla. I communicated with Aunty Hamida, now a member of the Rajya Sabha, only briefly. Cognizant of my

Pakistani ethos, not wanting to seek untoward proximity with an Indian representative, despite the background of family friendship, I made a studious effort to stick to Rashida Patel, forging a lasting friendship with her.

No sooner had I reached London, when mother called to say father would be joining me in London, as he had shed more weight and the doctors at Lahore and Karachi had recommended that he proceed to London for a detailed medical investigation. I was staying with my friend Patsy who was recently married also, and living in a beautiful house in Cadogan Place. We booked my father at the Wilbraham, a lovely old fashioned hotel, which was right round the corner, and went to fetch him from the airport. He looked distinguished as always, and as he walked towards us in his dark brown suit, Patsy said to me that he looked so well it was nonsensical to suggest that he could be ill. 'He is not,' I said, more to assure myself than her, 'But no harm in getting a check up.'

My father had an appointment with Dr Sir Francis Avery Jones, a Harley Street specialist, who recommended detailed investigations after examining him. Patsy's parents invited us for dinner, and her mother repeatedly told my father that he looked a picture of good health and the specialist was only recommending hospitalization so the bill goes up. Nonetheless, my father checked into the Central Middlesex Hospital and was admitted for a full one week, undergoing all sorts of tests and scans.

I accompanied my father when he went to see Sir Francis with the results of the investigations. 'Well, Colonel, in my opinion you are suffering from an acute pancreatitis. The chances of a malignancy cannot be ruled out, but if we were to open you at this stage, we may or may not be able to locate any growth. Let me prescribe you medication. Eat meals free of fat, drink a lot of clean water, walk, and work. If, however, you develop a jaundiced condition, fly out to us immediately.' My father and I went horse racing after this, to Newmarket, to Goodwood, to Doncaster. He bought a couple of broodmares before we returned home together. We were in Shah Jewna briefly. The weather was dreadfully humid and father dropped some more weight, causing Mother and myself considerable anxiety and we retreated to the cool weather of the Himalayan foothills, to our summer estate at Bansragali near Murree, which was known as Cliffden Farm.

Mother fussed over my father's diet, conspiring endlessly with the cook to whip up recipes that comported with the doctor's dietary instructions and yet were appetizing enough for him to eat with relish and recover some of the weight he had lost. In the meanwhile, we would laze on deck chairs in the garden or go for short rambling walks on the estate. He would talk about horses; about his encounters with those people who had impressed him; about his disappointment with much of what had emerged in the State which he had helped to sponsor. 'The tragedy of Pakistan has been that very small men came to fill very big shoes. The will of the people has never been allowed to prevail because popular politics would have cut second-rate civil servants and some military officers down to size,' he would say.

'But government officers and their families have no sense of this. They tend to put the blame for what goes wrong on politicians,' I countered.

'You are right. The establishment of Pakistan has subsumed the powers and rights of the people and yet shows neither embarrassment nor shame in this regard. This is why we are not measuring up to our goals as a State. And if Yahya Khan blunders, we will end up losing one half of our country, because in the ten long years of Ayub Khan's misrule, the Bengalis have been systematically alienated. The likes of East Pakistan Governor Abdul Monem Khan (1962–1969) have triggered deep resentment against what the Bengalis identify as a Punjabi army.'

In the ensuing days, Sardar Rashid came to Cliffden to see my father and told him: 'Abid, you must come and talk to Yahya Khan. He is open to persuasion. He does have some pernicious influences around him, but your ability to state matters precisely and logically would help him to achieve some clarity. If he calls you, I hope you will agree to meet with him.'

My father replied: 'Yes, I will drive down to Rawalpindi if his office calls me and I will give him the best advise I may have to offer. I consider this to be my patriotic duty. I have been telling Chandi that I fear we are failing as a State, and if a word of caution from me can help the current military leadership to alter course, why would I not proffer such advise?' A couple of days later the office of the CMLA (Chief Martial Law Administrator) called and Father drove down to Rawalpindi.

When he returned to Murree, he looked tired. The conversation had been disappointing. He felt that Yahya Khan was out of his depth. He said,

> I told him that I had come with goodwill. We happened to share a Fiqh. I suggested that he learn to trust Sheikh Mujibur Rahman. Mujib will want to be Prime Minister and you should not have any qualms. Z. A. Bhutto could be Deputy Prime Minister. He is ambitious and better educated and would take over from Mujibur Rahman eventually. But you must cede power to the Bengalis if you want to maintain the Federation of Pakistan. Do not forget that the Bengalis were left unprotected in the 1965 war and the Indians have been fanning their sentiments of perceived deprivation. If the

Bengalis remain neglected, India will capitalize and a rupture of the two wings of our country will erode the Two-Nation Theory on which Pakistan is based, and the western wing of our country will also become vulnerable. But I am afraid all this was too complicated for Yahya Khan, who, in his simple soldiering mindset, failed to grasp the political reality that I was seeking to apprise him of. I fear for the future of Pakistan. It has definitely fallen prey to those that may not mean harm, but have limited understanding.

We returned from Murree with my father looking marginally better. Friends and family frequented our house at Lahore in large numbers, everyone offering friendly advise on what his health regimen should involve. My father would focus on the ongoing unrest in the country and Yahya Khan's options, but he started losing weight again and in early November 1969, he walked out onto the verandah of our Lahore home and asked me and my mother to take a look at his eyes that had turned unmistakably yellow. He had developed the dreaded jaundiced condition that Sir Francis Avery Jones had warned us about. No time was to be lost; we had to leave for London immediately. Mother turned to me for arranging the travel logistics, while she did the accounting and packing. Uncle Wajid Ali, my mother's brother, offered to accompany us. Within three days, we were in London where it was cold, grey, and miserable. Sir Francis saw my father in his Harley Street clinic consulting rooms the very next day, and sent him immediately to Dr Gummer who was a surgeon, and whose clinic was next door to his.

My father looked grim and listless, with his topcoat hanging on his thinned out frame; he was just not the strong, robust father I had known all my life. Suddenly he was a sick man and a helpless look had entered his jaundiced, dimmed eyes. Dr Gummer said he would operate on him at his London clinic the very next day.

2

A Chapter Closes

The clinic ambulance came to the White House Hotel where we were staying, a couple of furlongs away from the clinic. My father smiled at me as I held his hand to assist him, 'Chin up, Chandi *baita*' he said, his wan smile causing my eyes to mist over. Increasingly he would add '*baita*', meaning son, to my name. He was wheeled into the operation theatre, while I crouched by a wall outside, my face bathed in tears. A kind nurse put a hand on my shoulder, guided me to the elevator and suggested I rejoin my family in the waiting hall, as the surgery was likely to take over an hour. The waiting hall was full of visitors and flowers. Mother sat with her brother Wajid Ali, and her friend Nahid Iskander Mirza. Malik Sir Khizar Hayat Tiwana, former Chief Minister of undivided Punjab, cutting a swathe in his jodhpurs with a matching twill flared achkan to top them, was being lionized by my friend Patsy's parents, Sir Jack and Lady Lyons. My friends, both Mandy and Patsy, rushed towards me, both of them in tears seeing my agony. In a quiet corner, Uncle Sonny Habibullah and Aunty Attia, his wife standing beside him. Present also were Lal Khan, my father's subordinate from his recruiting officer days, who had subsequently migrated to England, and Zulfiqar Noon from Jhang who had recently migrated to England and had obtained a job in the British Government's medical service. The visitors in the waiting hall were in many ways a microcosm of the diverse circle of friends of our tiny three-member family and a reflection of the lives touched by my father's immense reservoir of warmth and affection.

Uncle Wajid and I went over to the Surgery—time moved slowly—and finally Dr Gummer came out.

'I did the best I could,' he muttered. After thanking him profusely, Uncle Wajid led me back to the waiting hall and assured my mother that the surgery had been a success. Dr Gummer was satisfied with the results and was hopeful that his patient would soon recover his health. Everyone around us began to congratulate us, and although I was also swept away by my uncle's bluff, I remained anxious. While my mother slept soundly, lulled into sleep by her brother's assurances, I was up all night. The surgeon's dour expression printed on my mind's eye kept me awake.

The following morning, I rushed to Dr Avery Jones's clinic, and pleaded with his secretary to allow me to see him for five minutes. Waiting about an hour, which seemed like forever, as a patient exited, Sir Francis came out and took me into his office. He looked at me with great compassion and said,

> Your father has developed pancreatic cancer. It was probably the size of a common pin when we scanned him and we may well not have found it then. Dr Gummer cut out as much as he could and did a short circuit on his bile duct. Your father will have to undergo radiation which will give him some more time. Radiation is a new and difficult process. Although he is going to suffer discomfort, the radiation will restrict the growth of the cancer. When we scanned your father, we discussed with him the possibility of putting him through radiation as a precautionary measure but he declined it vehemently at the time.

I asked: 'How much more time will he gain from radiation therapy?'

Sir Francis replied, almost is a whisper: 'I cannot say. Cancers often throw lesions after which they tend to move rapidly.' His voice was soft and compassionate. The conversation was not easy for either of us. Sir Francis continued, 'Your question is a difficult one for me to answer. Your father appears to be an exceptionally strong-willed individual and if he puts up a good fight he could last a while. He would have to keep himself busy and deeply engaged with his interests to fight off the pain, because the pain could be severe. We would of course prescribe strong medication to help him cope with the pain, but it would be debilitating nonetheless.' At the doctor's mention of pain I felt a spasm shoot through my abdomen.

'Would the radiation not stave off the pain, doctor?' my voice now breaking.

'No, the radiation will not prevent pain. In the years ahead we may be able to find better solutions, but you will have to accept your father's terminal condition in order to help him cope. He seems immensely reliant on you.'

Blinded by tears, I left the doctor's office. His secretary armed me with tissues to wipe the tears off my face and led me to a passage which connected to the clinic. I dreaded having to face my mother. What would I say to her? Could I tell her that the person she lived for was dying? I remained in the passage for a long while. At that moment, it dawned on me with sharp, painful clarity that the sun-filled chapter of my life was ending. The insouciance of what I had known, the warmth of total paternal protection, the joie de vivre which I had assumed to have been my birthright, was gone in one fell swoop. My focus on my own development, pursuit of art, literature, and music, interest in fashion, flair for amusing conversation, all ceased to be relevant. The ensuing time would revolve around medical appointments, the enduring smell in my nostrils would be that of ether, I would have to live beyond myself and find within myself the capacity to cope. I could not hope to turn to mother for help. I would have to help her to deal with her man with an altered status, she knew him only as a provider of love, as an indulgent partner, and a compassionate friend, and now she would see him as a vulnerable and sick person who would need her to nurse him. Would she have the capacity to live beyond herself? I knew instinctively that I would have to bear the load and also look after my mother whose grief would disable her from managing the real or the practical. She would not be able to be substitute as head of the household; I would have to learn to make decisions. First and foremost, I would have to do whatever it would take to somehow make my father well again.

With this determination gripping me, I entered my father's hospital room. Mother was deeply engrossed in prayer.

I decided to seek Patsy's father's help in obtaining a second medical opinion and in establishing contact with specialists at Mount Sinnai hospital in New York, which I had heard was the Mecca of oncology. I went to Patsy's house to meet her father, Sir Jack Lyons. He phoned a friend in New York who had access to a Mount Sinnai specialist. The friend asked for my father's detailed medical report. I called Sir Francis' secretary who had the report ready for me the following day. Patsy's father sent the report by urgent air mail to his friend in New York, for us to obtain a comprehensive comment from Mount Sinnai specialists within a week. In the meanwhile Sir Jack suggested that we should also send a copy of the report to the Royal Marsden Institute, London, that specialized in cancer research and obtain their opinion as well.

The week went by excruciatingly slowly for me. Meanwhile, my father was recovering reasonably well from his surgery. Every day he would get numerous visitors and phone calls which I would handle. One of these calls was from Sheikh Mujibur Rahman, who pronounced his name as *Muzeebur Rahman*, hence, for a moment I did not understand. He was calling from the London airport and was on his way back to Dacca (Dhaka). He said that he had just got the news that his friend Colonel Syed Abid Hussain Shah was in hospital, and asked me to convey his good wishes. He went on to inform me that my father was considered to be a friend by the Bengali people and his struggle against Ayub Khan was appreciated by them. He would pray for his speedy recovery as he was sorely needed to play an active role in the politics of our country. I assured our caller that I would convey his message to my father. Little did I know that he would not be flown in to Dacca as he hoped: his flight would be diverted to Rawalpindi and he would be incarcerated, while my father battled to regain his health.

Fakhar would call every day and enquire if I wanted him to come. I had quite forgotten that I was married and felt that Fakhar's presence would perhaps be intrusive, so I told him to hold on and if we were to go to New York, he could fly out there.

The response from Mount Sinnai was not encouraging, nor the one from the Royal Marsden. Sir Francis Avery-Jones came to call on my father and stayed a long while. He tried to be reassuring and said that my father had mended well and could now move to a flat in the vicinity and continue his treatment from there, coming to the clinic when required. My father said he would take the radiation for no more than a month and when the final check-up allowed him to travel, he would fly home via Meshed in Iran, where he would like to pay homage at the Imam Reza Shrine and pray. Mother did not intercede on the radiation issue. The decision seemed to have been taken by him irrevocably. Clearly he did not want to prolong his life at the cost of his dignity and, I was unable to make him relent.

We moved into a flat off Baker Street. Mother complained of a stomach ache and I had to settle us all in singlehandedly, pampering my mother as I went along and maturing with every minute that was ticking, ever so conscious that my father was watching and willing the strength into me. Just two days later, Mother woke up soaked in blood and hysterical. My father looked pale and drained but he aided me with calling for the ambulance, and helped me in getting Mother changed and into the ambulance. As we were driving away, Father, with a wan smile on his face, and his now shockingly thin arm raised in a gallant gesture, looked visibly drained of strength and energy. At that moment, I understood with a flash of clarity which of my parents I was losing.

Mother was wheeled into the clinic—there was a quick diagnosis—she had uterine fibroids. She was given local anaesthesia and curettage, and was back in the hospital room within an hour. When I returned to the flat, armed with groceries and the good news of Mother, I found my father lying slumped on his bed with his arms folded tightly across his stomach. The expression on his face was of pure agony. Dropping the groceries, I rushed towards him and asked:

'Are you in pain?'

'I am in acute pain, *baita*.'

I felt the familiar knot in my stomach. I pleaded with him to swallow the painkillers which the doctor had prescribed but he refused, and insisted that he would fight off his pain with his will. When I argued that the pain would exhaust him, he responded that the exhaustion would induce sleep. My father had always been my hero but at this point, with his dignified determination, his stature reached celestial heights for me. I thought it was heroic of him, and when I told him so, he attempted a smile. My pressing his feet seemed to soothe him, and although sleep eluded him, he bore the pain in silence, courageously and manfully. I tried to cope and take care of him as best as I could. All this while I could sense myself undergoing a change, a steeliness seeping inside me.

Mother was back from the hospital after three days. She kept giving me chores. When Father told her that I had taken care of him in her absence and that I had not been eating or sleeping much, she was pleased. It meant a lot to her that my father should not miss having a son, not that she ever voiced her thoughts, but I knew, as we all know the elemental desires of those we are closest to.

Raja Mahmudabad came to see my father, and insisted that he cook a meal for us in his flat above the makeshift Islamic Centre in Regents Park, where he was involved in getting a teaching and congregation centre constructed for the British Muslim community. It was now ten days since Father had been out of hospital and five days since Mother had returned to the flat.

We ordered a taxi and arrived at the Islamic Centre. Sulaiman, Raja Mahmudabad's son, was at the entrance to receive us. With the ineffable courtesy that hallmarks the Mahmudabads, he took my parents up in the somewhat rickety elevator in what must have been a grand mansion once, but was in a current state of disrepair. The Raja would not spend a shilling from the fund for the Centre on his personal comfort. Moreover, the building was destined for demolition once the Centre was built. Raja Sahib cooked a delicious chicken curry with prunes, without using any oil, only yoghurt. The Raja and my mother became engrossed in a discourse, with the Raja giving detailed recipes of dishes that Mother could cook for Father that would be tasty and also fulfil the doctor's dietary instructions.

All this while, Agha Hassan Abidi, who had founded the BCCI Bank in Luxembourg was also present. He continued to sit on the floor next to the Raja because he had migrated from Mahmudabad to Pakistan and seemed to have the most profound respect for his former Ruler.

We were now preparing to leave London and I was talking to the travel agent regarding our return home via Tehran and Meshed, in Iran, when Patsy called to say that Prime Minister Edward Heath was coming to dine with her parents the following evening at a small, informal dinner. Her parents kindly invited me also, and had sent my name to protocol as a close friend of their daughter.

'But how can I leave my parents alone?' I asked her.

Patsy replied: 'Don't be stupid Abida, they will manage without you for a few hours; in any case I have already spoken to both of them and they are delighted that you will be meeting the British Prime Minister, but you are not to discuss the politics of Pakistan with Edward Heath. He is probably sick of politics by the evening. In any case, what he has in common with my parents is music. Galina Vishnevskaya and Vladimir Rostropovich are coming, she will sing while he will play the cello. It will be a rare treat, I promise you!'

Patsy had spoken to my parents when I was out for grocery shopping and had asked my mother not to say anything as she would persuade me herself. I told her that it was nice of her to think of me but I could not leave my parents alone in the condition that my father was in. Patsy chided me and said that I had a life to live; at which I retorted that my father was my life! The thought of losing him was unbearable! By now, I was weeping.

Father, although, he understood my emotions, mentioned Patsy's call and urged me to go for the dinner. As I was arguing with him that I did not feel like going, my friend Sohail Iftikhar, son of my father's good friend Mian Iftikharuddin, who had owned the leading newspapers in Pakistan until they were taken over by Ayub Khan, telephoned and invited me to accompany him for a Bharat Natyam dance performance by a celebrated Indian dancer at the Wigmore Hall, for which he had tickets. The hall was close to where we were lodged. I told Sohail that I had an invitation to a dinner for Prime Minister Heath at my friend's house and I might be going. Sohail Bhai trashed Heath for being a colourless Tory but said that he would give an arm and a leg to hear Vishnevskaya in a private concert. He then volunteered that he would spend the evening with my parents and give the tickets for the dance performance to friends. Before Sohail Bhai passed away, bowing out on family and his large circle of friends, a mere three years later, he chastised me for having stood him up for Edward Heath!

We flew out of London for Tehran a few weeks later. My father visited Sir Francis Avery-Jones the day before our departure, but he met with him alone and assured us that the doctor was satisfied with his progress. In the airplane he suffered severe pain, and declined to eat, only sipping on apple juice, while mother polished off whatever was on his tray and hers. Her hearty appetite was back and I was grateful to Allah that at least one parent was well recovered. It was bitterly cold when we landed at Tehran and the airport was not as well heated as Heathrow Airport in London. Father's pain seemed to worsen the few hours that we had to spend at Tehran airport before flying out to Meshed.

Mother kept chastising me for not having organized a night's stopover at Tehran, quite forgetting that it was her idea that we fly to Meshed at the earliest. 'Kishwar, it was my insistence that we fly onto Meshed as soon as possible,' said my father, typically protective of both of us.

Mother prayed with great intensity as we reached Meshed which was even colder than Tehran. The hotel, called the Iran Hotel, was modest by western standards and the heating was nominal. Father observed that this was evidence of the exploitation of the Anglo-American oil companies. This was precisely why Mossadegh had so much support and that Raza Shah was a fool not to see through the machinations of the British and American authorities, who pumped less oil for the people in whose lands they were mining than for the comfort of their own people, who were provided Iranian oil in plenty and at cheap rates.

My parents settled into their room, which was large and bare but for the beautiful carpet. My room was smaller, on the opposite side of the hallway. Finally Father said he felt like dinner, so we went down to the hotel dining room and feasted on beautiful Irani saffron rice and chicken and lamb kebabs. He ate heartily after many weeks and Mother declared that there would be a '*mojiza*', a miracle at Meshed, and the first sign was that his appetite had been restored, but he expressed anxiety about his capacity to digest the food. All three of us were anxious to offer prayers at the Shrine of Imam Reza, the sixth Imam, whose lineage was directly from the Holy Prophet through his daughter, Bibi Fatima who was married to the Prophet's first cousin Ali, the fourth of Caliph of Islam.

We decided we would go to the shrine at noon the following day and offer our *Zuhr* (afternoon), *Asr* (late afternoon), and *Maghrib* (evening) prayers there. I had been to Meshed with my parents for the first time as a six-year-old, and then again when I was nine and twelve years. Each time, while entering the courtyard of the shrine, I had been struck by the magnificence of the monument. In my childhood perhaps it was the scale that awed me, now it was the symmetry, the glory of the turquoise tiles and the opulence of the inset, enormous gilded doors along with the gilded dome. The shrine was serene, at the same time opulent, the air around it translucent, worshippers thronging towards the giant gilded portals. Ganji (Father), Baji (Mother), and I looked up at the magnificent chandeliers in the outer hallway and down at the exquisitely crafted tiles on the walls, cornices, and archways. '*Subhan Allah*' Praise be to Allah—my parents kept intoning. After a bit, I joined them. We went further inside, and when the shrine became visible before us, the call to prayer, a magnificent '*Azaan*' penetrated my senses. All three of us offered our prayers on elegant prayer mats placed on the cool and beautiful floor. As I prostrated myself, I wondered how worshippers coped when it became colder. It was November and I was shivering, as was Father, despite the heavy top coat and fur hat he was wearing. Baji interrupted her prayers and said, 'Why don't both of you return to the hotel while I continue with my prayers and join you later?'

'Will you manage to find a taxi and return to the hotel by yourself, Kishwar?' Father enquired tenderly. Tears started rolling down my face and I looked away.

As we mounted the staircase of the Iran Hotel, Father held his stomach tightly with one hand; the knuckles of his other hand on the stair rail turned ashen white. Seeing him contorted in pain, tears started streaming down my face. Turning towards me, he said, 'I think I will manage to sleep for a while, I feel exhausted. You also look like you could do with some sleep, Chandi.' He then went into his room and I went into mine.

Sleeping the sleep of the dead, I woke with a start to hear gentle knocking on my door. I leapt to the door and saw Father standing there. He looked suddenly cheerful and the light was back in his eyes. 'Come into my room, I have great news to share with you,' he said to me. He went and lay down on his bed, propping himself against his pillows and ushered me to a chair next to the bed.

> Chandi, when I was a student at the Government College, Lahore, I came across a verse of Hafiz, the great Persian poet, which in Farsi was:
>
> > *hargiz na merde anke dilash zinda shud be ishq*
> > *sabat ast bar jarida alam dawam e ma*
>
> and translated would mean 'a heart which is filled with love never dies, its love permeates the universe.' When I came back from the shrine and lay down on my bed, I succumbed to deep sleep after many weeks. And in my sleep while dreaming, I heard the incantation of this verse of Hafiz followed by a verse which was so clear and vivid that I woke up and penned it down, so here it is:
>
> > *Abid fikar me kun, kay anjaamat qarib ast*
> > *Zaamin shud ast bakshish farda imam e ma*
>
> You understand, *baita*, that I should not fear since my end is as near as the Imam Zaamin i.e. Imam Reza who is the guarantor of

my deliverance! Why are you crying Chandi? I thought you were courageous and smart. I thought your Daadi, my late mother, had taught you that to be a Shia means to know how and when to die. We all exit one day, but how fortunate am I to know my end is near and deliverance is at hand. I am no ascetic but as my flesh reduces, I approach my end emaciated and hopefully expiated. And by the grace of Allah and His Loved Ones, I am relieved of my pain. Chandi *baita*, I feel no pain, so I can now live the days that are left to me in a meaningful manner. It will begin with my teaching you about your lineage and legacy. No better place for you to start this process of learning than at Meshed.

Each word that he uttered in that hotel room remains deeply etched in my mind. And this became the source of my own well of courage and capacity that I have drawn on through the more than four ensuing decades of my life. When Mother returned from the shrine, she found Father and me sitting in the hotel lounge watching on television with rapt attention, the funeral of Jamaal Abdel Nasser (1918–1970), who served as the second President of Egypt from 1956 up to the time of his death. Mother came and sat beside me and whispered, 'I think your father looks much better. It is a *mojiza*. He will be cured!' I hugged her, and she also became absorbed in watching the grand funeral of a man the world has today forgotten.

'Jamaal Abdel Nasser was a great Egyptian, a great Arab, and a great Muslim leader of a decolonizing world. The measure of a man is truly known on the day of his funeral. If ordinary folk flock of their own volition, it means whoever is to be interred was an outstanding human being and a generous spirit,' observed my Father. Mother agreed; and I wondered. But today I would agree with them both.

In the coming days, we visited the shrine daily and spent several hours there. Mother would pray fervently and devoutly. I would lean my back against the tiled walls and contemplate. My eyes feasted on the beauty of the shrine, the symmetrical perfection of the architecture and design, the fusion of colour with the dominant turquoise offset by an intense cobalt blue and richly deep sepia. I would think of Fakhar, I started yearning for his warmth and I had this deep urge to bear a child that my father could see.

The year 1969 had started on the highest possible note for me: I was married to the cousin of my choice. My forehead was adorned by a diamond 'teeka' which was truly magnificent and given to me by Fakhar's mother. And there was my handsome father in his Shahpuri achkan standing proud and tall with his white turban wound around his gold cap; the turban tied, as always, by himself, unquestionably the finest looking figure in the gathering according to everybody, particularly my English friends, Mandy and Patsy, who had flown down for the wedding, as mentioned earlier. The magic of my wedding was overtaken by the collapse of Ayub Khan's power the same year, and my father's deteriorating health.

It was hard to believe that the gaunt figure who returned with us from Tehran was the same person who, a mere eighteen months earlier, was the elegant host who had been receiving guests at his daughter's wedding. When we returned to Lahore, visitors would come in large numbers every day to inquire after my father's health at our home. My mother, hospitable by nature, would be catering the guests one moment, and fretting over my father's health the next. It irritated me that the demands of our culture were such that people who came to be solicitous required to be fed, but when I voiced my observation to Mother, she retorted that I was spoilt and selfish and ought to be more gracious and also grateful that so many people were coming to inquire about my father's health. Moreover, this was a source of strength and comfort to her. Father, too, seemed to derive comfort from his visitors, specially the folk who came from Jhang. But he would tire easily, and when his face contorted with pain, I would feel the dreadful pain return in my own stomach. In a way my pain was a consolation to me that I was somehow sharing my beloved father's pain.

I was grateful for Fakhar's warmth. And for his tears shed in unison with mine; for his silent capacity to understand my pain; and for his tolerance of my determination to bear it alone. Fakhar informed me that due to my father's deteriorating health, he had decided to resign from the government and join the corporate sector. While I was away in England, he had met the American head of Dawood-Hercules, an American-managed fertilizer company, the largest one to be set up in Punjab to date. Fakhar had been offered the package of a top professional and had accepted the offer. I was proud of Fakhar being so highly evaluated and it dawned on me that a major decision needed to be taken by my father as well. I also knew that I would have to help him in taking that decision.

Fakhar informed me of his decision to accept the handsome offer he had received from the CEO of the American-managed Pakistan-US joint venture fertilizer company and acquire some experience in the corporate sector. This was the largest company to be set up in the Punjab, and I was happy for Fakhar for achieving this distinction at such a young age. All of this had materialized during my absence in London and I was relieved that Fakhar would be based at Lahore, and by my side during this excruciatingly difficult time. It also dawned on me that I would now have to help my father take the major decision that he had been mulling over since a few days, as in the meanwhile events in Pakistan were leading us inexorably towards general elections. General Yahya Khan's deadline for announcing a Legal Framework Order (LFO) was approaching. Father was looking and feeling marginally better. Should he contest elections himself? Could his health take it? What weighed with me most was what Sir Francis had advised, that he be kept as busy as possible, his attention focused away from his health, his diet appropriately controlled, and his strong will at work should continue. As long as he was not complaining of pain, leading a normal life would help him fight the cancer and his urge to live would be optimized. Hence I broached the subject with him when we were alone.

'Ganji, I think you should contest elections from the platform of the Pakistan Peoples Party (PPP). Zulfikar Ali Bhutto is going to every nook and corner of Pakistan and young people are flocking towards him. Perhaps you should meet Bhutto Sahib again.'

My father replied: 'Well, I am feeling better and my weight has been somewhat stable these past couple of weeks. I was thinking of going to Karachi for the Quaid-i-Azam Gold Cup Race meeting. You and your mother will be with me, and yes I could meet Bhutto while I am there. But before that I was thinking of meeting with my political friends in Punjab, many of whom also struggled for restoration of democracy and who are currently politically non-aligned, to discuss our future course of action. Bhai Mubarik Ali Shah was telling me that his sons are pressing him to join Qayyum Khan because they say he has the backing of General Yahya. But Bhai Sahib had the goodness to tell them that he will go along with whatever I say. So I am glad you have motivated me, I will make a list of friends right away, and tell my staff to issue invitations for a meeting here at the house a week from now.'

'Since our back garden is filled with the gentle warmth of the December sun, we shall have the meeting in the afternoon.' Mother was pleased to see Father energized, and got busy with organizing for the tea. Her father, Sir Syed Maratib Ali, was the favoured caterer of the British Indian Army for which he had earned knighthood. Hence hospitality came naturally to my mother. She had clearly inherited this outstanding capacity from her father. Sadly, my genetic code did not favour the propensity, at least not in the earlier passage of my life.

The turnout at my father's political event was better than what he had expected. When he welcomed his guests, he spoke with clarity and courage, expressing his determination to fight his illness and to fight for his health while concurrently mounting a struggle for the health of the country, in the creation of which he and his cousin, Mubarik Ali Shah, had contributed.

After paying his tributes to his father-in-law (who was also Mabarik Ali's father-in-law), Syed Maratib Ali, along with his sons Syed Amjad Ali and Syed Wajid Ali for their generous contributions to the State Bank of Pakistan at the time of Independence, he acknowledged the presence at the meeting of Khan Mohammad Arif Khan, Nawabzada Iftikhar Ansari from Jhang, who had stood by him in the struggle for restoration of democracy. He acknowledged also the presence of politicians who were from different districts of Punjab, namely, Ch. Mohammad Hussain Chatha from Sheikhupura, Amir Abdullah Khan of Rokhri from Mianwali, Ch. Zahur Illahi from Gujrat, Sardar Ahmed Ali from Kasur, Sardar Mohammad Khan Leghari from Dera Ghazi Khan, and Makhdumzada Syed Hassan Mahmud from Rahim Yar Khan.

My father then dwelt on the alienation of the Bengalis and the issue of national integration and of the phone call he received from Sheikh Mujibur Rahman while he was recuperating from his surgery at the London Clinic. He emphasized the importance of democracy in keeping Pakistan united, and suggested that if all his friends, associates, and family were to consider joining the Awami League (AL), this would guarantee the continuance of Pakistan. The other options he mentioned were the Pakistan Peoples Party (PPP), the National Awami Party (NAP), the Pakistan Muslim League (PML) led by Mian Mumtaz Daultana, and the Pakistan Muslim League (PML) led by Abdul Qayyum Khan. He concluded his statement by announcing that his final decision would be determined by the advise offered by his friends and family who were present. Some voiced their support for the Daultana Muslim League and some for the Qayyum League, but there were no takers amongst these gentlemen for the liberal new parties led by relatively young leaders: Sheikh Mujib in East Pakistan; and Zulfikar Ali Bhutto and Khan Abdul Wali Khan in West Pakistan. The meeting concluded with a consensus that in view of his excellent linkages and friendships in all the regions of Pakistan, my father and his Jhang group contest elections as Independent candidates and provide the consensus base to the future Assembly. I was disappointed with the decision as was my mother, who favoured Wali Khan and the National Awami Party (NAP), but my father was pleased and enthused and he even gained a little weight as we prepared to leave for Karachi.

When my father had flown in from Delhi to Karachi at the time of Independence (1947), he lodged at the Central Hotel on Victoria Road. He would always recall how humid the city was and how he longed to move into a more spacious place. When he had mentioned this to the hotelier, the latter had told him that he knew of a property dealer who was seeking a buyer for a spacious residence located on Victoria Road. The very next day my father went to see the bungalow on 18-Victoria Road. It was situated in a large compound which was over an acre. My father paid the dealer one lac rupees, half the price of the property, as advance. He then wrote to his *munshi* (secretary) at Shah Jewna in Jhang to sell a piece of land that he owned in Mandi Shah Jewna and send him the remaining amount so that he could take possession of the bungalow. But before the sale could be effected, Uncle Amjad Ali wired in the money to my father, suggesting that because they would be setting up their main business offices at Karachi, they needed a residence there as well, and since my father only needed a place to stay during Assembly sessions, he could always live in the bungalow he had purchased as his own.

Meanwhile, Jinnah Sahib had told the members of his Constituent Assembly that he would order the building of a new Capital for Pakistan at Malir, in the hinterland of Karachi and had exhorted his Muslim Leaguers to buy land at Malir, so that its development could be initiated. Hence my father decided to let his in-laws buy the 18-Victoria Road bungalow, and instead bought, with that one lac, twenty-five acres of property in Malir. Whenever he recalled the incident there would be a note of regret in his voice since he felt that he should have sought the bungalow.

Father narrated this story to Bhutto when called on him at 18-Victoria Road. The conversation was convivial until Bhutto Sahib said, 'Colonel Sahib, join my party. You will see I am going to go from the street to the palace!' While I was agog hearing this sharp thought thus expressed, my father's forehead became furrowed.

'I do not follow your language, Zulfikar Ali. You see, while you were in proximity to Ayub Khan's palace, I was struggling with a handful of friends for the restoration of democracy. When I was handcuffed for supporting Mohtarma Fatima Jinnah, you were steering Ayub Khan's Muslim League. But twelve years is a long time. I am now in my fifties, you are a good bit younger and the youth seem to be with you. Further down the road, perhaps my daughter and son-in-law will join you. My cousin Mubarik Ali Shah and I along with our associates of Jhang have decided to remain Independent for the time being. My health has not been good, but I will contest and Zulfi Bokhari, my cousin's son who was your colleague in the 1962 Assembly, and whom you know, will be my covering candidate. Unfortunately my daughter is under-age, otherwise she would be my covering candidate.'

In a flash it became evident to me and also my mother that my father was setting the course for my future.

On our return to Lahore, Mother suggested that I spend some time with Fakhar, since she would be going with my father to Jhang, as he would be spending all his time there as the elections were now only three months away. Knowing that I would be reluctant to be away from my father, Mother suggested that I could follow them in a couple of weeks. It was evident that she wanted me to start a family which was my desire too, and nature having its ways, I discovered within a few days that I was already with child. It made me happy to think that my father would be able to hold my baby in his arms. And when Fakhar drove me down to Jhang a couple of weeks later, I could not wait to tell my mother. She passed on the news to Father, who held my hand, and with a twinkle in his eyes said, 'May you have many more.' This statement did not amuse me. Sensing it, Father quickly changed the topic. He told me that he had decided to sell a chunk of his land, about three hundred acres for a million rupees, a hefty amount at the time. This sum of money would take care of the cost of his election and his medical care, in case he had to suddenly fly out to see his doctors. I became immediately apprehensive and asked him if he was feeling any pain or discomfort.

'So far so good.' He said. 'Tomorrow you will come with me to Shah Jewna, along with your mother so that I can show you that this land is in Mauza Ramana, closer to Mandi Shah Jewna, and while it is good land, it yields poor income.' When we drove to our farm the next day, passing by ripening wheat fields, with my father at the wheel and me sitting beside him, I observed flocks of sparrows taking flight out of the wheat fields, and asked him that with the birds devouring grain, how could the land yield good income. Father stopped the car, and looked me gently in the eye.

'Never forget Chandi, that the produce of the land will always depend on how many you are sharing it with, from ants to birds to fellow humans.' That was my father, large-hearted and generous to a fault. Those who are still around of those times will always recount anecdotes of Abid Hussain Shah's immense generosity. This was the wonderful father that I was losing. And like my mother, I began to pray intensely every night for a miracle to happen that would spare my father's life.

But as the tension accumulated inside me, the foetus developing in my womb reacted. I was rushed to Lahore but I aborted. Dr N. A. Seyal, who was treating me, was from Jhang. When my father came to take me home, along with Mother and Fakhar, Doctor Seyal told Father: 'Colonel Sahib, your daughter will be fine. She has suffered a simple miscarriage. She is young and healthy and will bear you several grandchildren. But *you* do not look good to me. Do look after yourself.'

'Thank you, Dr Sahib,' Father said. 'You are right, I have not been well, but I will try to carry on to see my election through and to hold at least one grandchild in my arms.'

I noticed a tear rolling down my father's face, and I felt a severe spasm again, similar to the one that I had experienced while I was aborting, and I collapsed in the car.

We returned to Jhang a few days later, and Fakhar, having taken time off from work, also came with us. Shah Jewna House in Jhang started buzzing with pre-election activity. Every day large numbers of people would arrive from all over the constituency which covered the entire Jhang tehsil. I would pore over the map of the district and the three tehsils which were the three National Assembly constituencies, with Chiniot tehsil marked in pink; Jhang in green; and Shorkot in yellow. I would also devour the details efficiently recorded in the district gazetteer, a 1939 edition which my father had given me which I found fascinating, with a wealth of information provided in it. From it, I understood that each tehsil had several police precincts, or *thana*s. Jhang tehsil, divided by the River Chenab, had three *thana*s on the east bank and two on the west bank, namely, Kotwali Saddar, Mochiwala, on the town side; Qadirpur Massan across the river on the Shah Jewna side; and 18-Hazari across the Trimmu Barrage.

There was controversy on the issue of who would be my father's running mates in the two provincial constituencies. Father favoured Taqi Shah from Qadirpur-Massan, while my cousin Iffi was encouraging Wajid Ali Shah. In the town, my father's running mate was Nawabzada Iftikhar Ahmed Ansari, and in Saddar-Mochiwala my father favoured Mehr Zafarullah Bharwana while Major Mubarik Ali was inclined towards Mehr Jahangir Bharwana.

Khan Arif Khan was contesting the National Assembly constituency from Shorkot and wanted Akhter Abbas Bharwana as his running mate, while Major Sahib was favouring Shamsul Haq Bharwana. Fakhar would sit silently alongside my father, never commenting on issues that he recognized were not a part of his turf. At night, he would update me briefly of the ongoing events. I longed to sit out on the verandah with my father but when I mentioned it to my mother in the presence of Aunt Surraya, she was emphatic in opposing the idea, stating that in Jhang, women of the family had to observe purdah (veil). I told her that I thought this was rank hypocrisy, since none of us were in purdah in Lahore, a mere three hour's drive away, so why should we be expected to observe purdah here at Jhang?

Frowning at me, my mother gestured that I follow her into her room. She chastised me for having been discourteous to her elder sister. She reminded me that we may own the Shah Jewna House, but my father was extremely close to his cousin who occasionally helped in looking after the bungalow which he looked after as his own. Now that I was grown up and married, I should never make any family member of his feel that this house did not belong to them.

'But what does this have to do with the hypocrisy on Jhang-specific purdah?' I exclaimed! I realized being the only child, with one parent ailing, I was going to be facing a lot of 'what is thine is mine' attitude from relatives, some of whom struck me as being predatory and discriminatory.

Father started campaigning, and we would breakfast together, before he set off each day. He would encapsulate the main events of the previous day, dwelling enthusiastically on how in village after village, women would lay ginned cotton on the path for him to walk on so his feet would not tire, and how they would mob him with handfuls of sugar for him to bless as he was their 'Sohna Pir', their handsome spiritual guide! Mother and I were consoled that the colour was coming back to his face—and he was eating better—and said he was feeling better.

Then one day, Father came home looking pale as a sheet and visibly upset. He told us that he was in Bagh, a small surburban town just outside the Jhang municipal limits, when he encountered a cavalcade of mullahs behind the car of Ghulam Haidar Bharwana, his rival candidate who was on a Jamiat-e-Ulema ticket. The mullahs were shouting 'Shia Kaffir', in other words, Shias are heretics. I did not understand. My father explained that the Jamiat-e-Ulema had opposed the creation of Pakistan, and had declared Jinnah Sahib 'Kaffir-e-Azam' (the Great Heretic), but after Partition (1947) they were subdued. Now if they were going to raise sectarian and divisive slogans, they would cause irrevocable damage to Pakistan. He said,

> What is deeply disturbing is that Ghulam Haidar Bharwana is hardly a model Muslim. We have been friends and I know him to be profligate in his conduct. So, if being born Sunni is in itself a virtue, then we will devalue the ethics of our religion from the public platform, which will have dreadful consequences for our social development as a nation. I have asked Iftikhar Ansari to organize a jalsa in Jhang city, in order to stress upon these points to our supporters and help them to counter this pernicious propaganda.

As the mugginess of the monsoon faded away, a dreadful cyclone struck East Pakistan and Yahya Khan delayed elections till December 1970. My mother felt relieved. She thought that we should take a month off, get my father out of the tail end of the heat of summer, fly to London for him to see his doctor, and return in time for the last lap of the election campaign. Father agreed and off we went to London again, the three of us. We had four good weeks in London, and while we were there, Former President Iskander Mirza passed away. My mother spent a lot of time with his wife and her friend Naheed, while my father and I made several trips to Newmarket to buy a stallion. He settled on a horse which had been bred in France, and consulted with his friend Madame Couturie on the telephone regarding the pedigree. I had a long chat with Madame Couturie, at whose chateau, Le Mesnil, I had spent a magical summer when I was at school in Switzerland. She was concerned about my father's health, and very keen to have us over at her place in Normandy, but Father said he was now preparing to return home as he had an election to fight. I felt that he was going through the bother of making a new equine acquisition so that he could show me the paces on all of what went into buying and then breeding horses successfully.

Our three weeks in London went by smoothly. The bland and healthy diet of English food, broth and soups, and thin strips of tender roast beef seemed to suit my father's palate and digestion. We had Dr Avery-Jones over for dinner at the old fashioned and quite charming hotel, St. Ermin's near Victoria Station, which he had recommended that we lodge in because of the wholesome food served at the hotel restaurant. We all enjoyed our meal. Sir Francis was really pleased with the progress of his patient.

'Colonel, you do not tire while you are campaigning for your election?' Sir Francis queried gently.

'The truth is, I do,' said my father. 'But I am so mentally engaged in the process that it keeps my mind focused away from my debility.' Sir Francis looked at me with great kindness, I thought he was conveying a 'well done!' to me, and felt consoled.

We returned to Jhang and to the elections that were now only a few weeks away, but my father was most distressed to find that in his absence, while a lot of his money had been spent, his campaign was in total disarray. The sectarian story had reached a hiatus, with Iftikhar Ansari and Zafarullah Bharwana, his Hannafi running mates, pleading helplessness while Uncle Mubarik Ali Shah accused them of only soliciting their own votes. Meanwhile, my cousin Iffi was now openly supporting Wajid Ali Shah, who was married to Fakhar's sister, Mano, which created all sorts of complications for me. My father understood this, and when my mother tried to make a pitch for Wajid, my father told her categorically that he would not help Wajid because he apprehended that this would marginalize me in Shah Jewna and consequently in Jhang. He had understood that nobody wanted to cede space to his only child because they believed that as a woman, I had less right to my patrimony than they might have had to theirs, although as Shias they ought to be supportive of a woman's right to her patrimony.

Then to compound my father's concern regarding the intrigue building around him, because of his failing health, his cousin, late Khizar Hayat Shah's son, Mohammad Ghaus arrived to harass Father regarding his step-sister Maryam, who had been left in my parent's care and custody by Khizar Hayat Shah before he died way back in 1958. Ghaus, like his father had been a school dropout but, unlike his father, was reputed to be mentally unstable. He married a woman from Lahore, had three children in rapid succession, set them up in a house in Lahore, and lived in Shah Jewna, enslaved to a family of servants. Both his uncle, Mubarik Ali Shah, as well as my father had little to do with him. They both disapproved of his selling more than half of the eight hundred acres of land which he had inherited—wasting the money from the proceeds—and always eyeing his step-sister's land, making the occasional effort to usurp her crops.

One day, Ghaus barged into the Shah Jewna House, and told my father, 'Everyone is saying you are suffering from a terminal illness, so why don't you hand over Maryam's custody to me?'

'For the same reason that your father did not leave her in your custody. After all, you were a mature man when your father died. When I pass on, my wife will look after Maryam,' said my father. This emotional outburst cost Father three pounds of weight loss overnight, and myself a bitter and sleepless night. Observing my restlessness, Father suggested that I go for election campaigning to the town with Nawab Iftikhar's wife and daughter. I draped myself in a big chaddar and arrived in this house which was charming and old and in the main bazaar of Jhang. Nawab Iftikhar's daughter Talat and I became friends. She was a few years younger than me; was chatty, perky, and very politically oriented. Talat gave me a spare burkah or outer garment to put on, which I hated, although, it did give me a feeling of anonymity.

Nawab Iftikhar's wife, Talat, and I, along with a group of women supporters, stepped on to the street. The people around us did not seem to notice us. We walked through a labyrinth of alleys and arrived at a large open space in what was known as 'Marzipura' where people were gathering for the jalsa that my father was coming to address. The crowd swelled and the women were hustled to stand or sit near the side of the stage. When he arrived, accompanied by Nawab Iftikhar, heavily garlanded but looking gaunt and thin, Talat kept asking me if he was sick, and tears rolled down my face. I was grateful for the privacy which the burkah provided. The stage secretary raised slogans for the unity of Pakistan, for democracy, for Nawab Iftikhar, and for my father, and then a crescendo of '*Shia-Sunni Bhai Bhai*' (Shia-Sunni are brothers). These slogans became the theme for Nawab Iftikhar's brief speech.

My father spoke at length. When he was speaking colour came back on his face. He spoke of how the popular vote would be sending him, if he scored a majority, into what would be a Constituent Assembly, to frame a new Constitution for Pakistan. And this Constitution would restore Jinnah's Pakistan back to the Pakistani people, and wash away the stains of the dictatorship that had usurped the rights of the people for more than a decade. He said:

> If you do not send me to this forum, you will by default be sending Ghulam Haider Bharwana who knows as much about these matters as the local police station in-charge that he spends the major part of his day in dealing with. If you prefer him merely because he was born a Sunni, while I was born a Shia, then a day will come when this thinking will consign us back to 'Akhand Baharat' or reunification with India. And I would fear for all of us if that were to come to a pass. Either we ought not to have created Pakistan, now that we have, we must make it succeed for our own sakes and for our future generations, who will curse us if we leave them a legacy of failure.

Today when I hear my father's tape-recorded speech, it sounds prophetic to me. His voice and wisdom make me miss his presence profoundly. As the days of electioneering dragged on, I heard and observed many painful things around me. While we were canvassing in the labyrinthine alleys in the mohallah's (neighbourhoods) of Jhang, I heard a street urchin shout 'Abid Murdah!' (Death to Abid!). It was as though I had been pierced by a dagger; the moment is etched in my memory.

Polling day arrived at the end of the bleak month of December. At the polling stations of Jhang city, where I went in my burkah with some women supporters, I saw women canvassing for Bharwana. His electoral symbol was 'key'. Their rhetoric was that if they stamped on the 'key' on the ballot paper, it would ensure their entry into Heaven! This absurd propaganda quite amazingly seemed to be taking effect. When I tried to assert that this was nonsense I was shouted down by most women present there. They began to dub me as a heretic, shouting 'Shia Kaffir!' in a chorus. At another polling station, on seeing me, a group of boys started shouting 'kaffir! kaffir!' At that moment a well-dressed man appeared, and the boys ran away. I was informed that he was the Deputy Commissioner, and he reacted against sectarian slogans. Clearly we were losing in the city, but my father had anticipated this. I kept reassuring myself that his leads in Mochiwalla, Saddar, Qadirpur, Massan, and Athara Hazari would balance our losses in the city.

Alas! This was not how the results emerged. Father did score handsomely across the river but in Mochiwalla and Saddar he went down. We lost the election and I realized that life would be ebbing out of him now. His heroic spirit would inevitably be breaking down. Feeling totally crushed, my spirit bruised, body ached; a constant reminder of the sickness that gripped my heart. I had to get a hold of myself, to struggle, to live beyond myself, to prevent myself from wallowing in self-pity, and to force myself to soldier on, to be the son that Father never had.

Father addressed his dejected supporters who crowded the front garden of the Shah Jewna House. 'Do not blame yourselves or each other. The cause of my defeat clearly was my failing health. And I say to the only child I leave behind, as I say to all of you who are like my family, do not hold any of this against the people of Jhang. They have been misled and the events of the future will make them acknowledge this reality in the fullness of time.' The crowd cheered him enthusiastically as he made his way back from their midst, erect, with the aura of great dignity, a hallmark of his presence. 'Pir Colonel Abid Hussain Zindabad!' I cheered along with the crowd, standing in the doorway of the house.

As he entered, Father called out to Mother: 'Kishwar, pay all outstanding bills while I rest for a while; I feel exhausted. Tomorrow let us proceed to Lahore, so that I can consult with my doctors. Chandi *baita*, try and call Sir Francis Avery-Jones and ask him if he can come to visit me in Lahore, and if he agrees, then arrange for his flight here.' His instructions to his attendants and to his family were always so precise and cogent. I wondered how I would manage when he would not be there to guide me with his clear-cut instructions. I mentioned this to him when we had settled him back at the house in Lahore.

'Do not worry Chandi, I am already writing out detailed instructions on what is to be done for your mother, for you and Fakhar, and for Maryam, who has been my responsibility, although, I have noticed that she has not been much help to you or Kishwar during my illness. Perhaps she has been beset by her own fears lest she be consigned to her unkind step-brother.'

Dr General Mohyuddin, and Hakim Said came to see my father from Rawalpindi and from Karachi. Both left instructions on diet and medicines, both allopathic and homeopathic. Mother dedicated all her time to meticulously following both sets of instructions, while I tracked Sir Francis Avery-Jones who agreed to being flown in to Lahore at the end of January 1971.

Our house in Lahore was a hub of visitors coming to inquire after my father's health. Mother's siblings were around all the time, as were most of my cousins, and my Daadi's brother, nephews, and nieces. Constantly surrounded by family and friends, while their warmth was sustaining, I felt terribly alone with my grief, the depth of which nobody, not even Fakhar, could really share. Perhaps my mother's grief was even deeper than mine, but she did not seem to want to lean on me; clearly she did not want to weaken my resolve. She would read out the newspapers to Father every morning, and all three of us would fret about the nasty turn events were taking in East Pakistan. Father apprehended that we were heading towards dismemberment. It was in this atmosphere that Sir Francis arrived at our house in Lahore. He sat long hours with my father every day, and the rest of his time he spent talking to me.

On the fourth day of his visit, Sir Francis said to me that he would like to talk to my father in mine and Mother's presence, before his departure. He then went on to ask me if I had any queries. I asked him if he could medically explain why my father felt no pain. I thought it was the strength and miracle of faith, which was why I continued to hope that Allah would spare his life, but what could this mean in the medical sense?

Sir Francis explained:

> While it is a reality that your father is in a condition of acute pain, his will interposes and prevents his brain from recording the message of pain. You understand that it is the brain that records all messages that are then transmitted to the body. But tell me, at whatever stage nature deprives you of your father's presence, what would you do to contribute towards improving the health needs of the people that your father deeply cares for? Would you consider setting up a Trust Fund

to resource a medical facility in your home town? I think that would be a befitting tribute to your father, who deserves to be remembered for his greatness. In my long medical career I have treated many outstanding men and women, but I feel honoured to have known a man as courageous as your father.

'Yes, Sir Francis, I will do as you suggest, and thank you for gracious comments.' I was crying, as he patted my hand gently.

The following day, Sir Francis sat by my father's bedside, and Mother and I were also present in the room. He told Father that he would be leaving for the airport shortly for his flight back to London. He had had a comfortable stay with us and would always remember the hospitality he had received. He had particularly valued his instructive conversations with his patient on Islamic history and on the martyrdom of the family of the Holy Prophet of Islam. Addressing my mother and me, Sir Francis informed us that my father had told him that in about a month's time it would be Muharram, the month of commemoration of the martyrdom of Imam Hussain and his family at Karbala. My father would desire to return to his birthplace, and we should not attempt to prevent him from undertaking the journey.

Buoyed by his doctor's visit, Father started eating somewhat better, and Mother and I prayed fervently for the restoration of his health. As we ploughed through the chill of February, I started feeling nauseous again, and quietly underwent a pregnancy test. I was expecting, and could not contain my excitement, so I rushed to tell Mother, who informed Father immediately. He called me and said that he felt he may not have the good fortune of seeing his grandchild but he was grateful to Allah for the knowledge that his progeny would carry on. If it were a boy, he would want him named after his father, and if a girl, he would think of a girl's name and let me or my mother know later.

Father's condition suddenly took a turn for the worse. My mother told him that Muharram was round the corner, and would he like to travel to Shah Jewna? 'I know tomorrow is likely to be the 1st of Muharram. I think I would like to go home to Shah Jewna on the fifth of Muharram.

Meanwhile, the National Assembly of Pakistan had been summoned to meet on 3 March 1971, which concurred with the fifth day of Muharram. On the 1st of March, mother was reading out the headlines in the newspapers to Father when I entered their room.

'Convening of Assembly postponed', she read. After a few moments my father spoke. His voice was frail, but distinctly audible. He addressed my mother.

'Kishwar, this is the end of the Pakistan that you and I have known.'

This was the last sentence Father ever spoke; it was a prophetic sentence. I somehow understood that life was ebbing out of him. Calling doctors suddenly seemed so futile, but nevertheless, I did call a doctor. By the time he came, my mother's entire clan had converged, informed by Fakhar. Mother was standing by the side of Father's bed, constantly praying. The doctor was taking Father's blood pressure which clearly was not rising. I had positioned myself at the bottom of Father's bed. I saw him place his hands on top of his bedsheet, wearing his rare gold agate ring from Najaf which he had worn since his childhood. I could see the vein in his neck which was pulsating ever so slowly, and then suddenly, audibly, he uttered 'Ya Ali!', and his vein stopped pulsating.

A CHAPTER CLOSES

In the early hours of 3 March 1971, my magnificent father was gone.

As the day dawned, Maulanas arrived to perform Father's death rites. His coffin was laid in a cot and taken out in the front garden where a large crowd, several hundred strong, had collected for his Namaz-e-Janaza. I stood at the bottom of the garden, while Mother was held back by her sisters. The Namaz ended, the crowd started moving away, the cot was carried by Fakhar and my uncles, and placed in an ambulance cortege. I tried to climb up into it but was led gently by Uncle Wajid Ali and Uncle Mubarik Ali onto the front seat of my car with Maryam, Mano, and Popety in the back, while Mother was eased into her car with her sisters Sarwat and Sitwat, and our friend Bunny Said, who was trying to calm her down. My car was immediately behind the cortege, and Mother's car was behind mine as we exited out of our Gulberg home: 7-F.C.C.

We drove out slowly and a long line of what must have been more than fifty cars of friends and family followed. Crossing the River Ravi, the cortege picked up speed, and I was anxious that Father's wish to reach his birthplace on the 5th of Muharram be honoured. But about forty miles out of Lahore, as we reached the outskirts of Sheikhupura to turn left towards Lyallpur (now Faisalabad) and from there onto Jhang, my grandmother, Daadi Ghulam Sughra's entire Bhatti Rajput clan had turned up from Jalalpur Bhattian, Pindi Bhattian, and Sangla Hill. The cortege was surrounded by mourners, Mian Sher Alam Bhatti, my Daadi's surviving younger brother, his sons from Jalalpur, his nephew from Pindi Bhattian, three nephews from Sangla, their kinsmen and serving people, accompanied by dhols, traditional drums, beating out the sounds of mourning with people chanting a dirge, mourning the demise of the Makhdum and Pir of Shah Jewna, the great and grand Colonel Abid Hussain Shah, who had brought honour to his Rajput family as he had brought honour to Shah Jewna. Traffic at this crossroad stopped for well over half an hour. The crowd swelled and joined the mourning and wailing. Mian Sher Alam found my car and placed his hand gently on my head. I alighted from my car as a mark of respect for my father's elder whom he had been so fond of.

As we moved on from Sheikhupura to Lyallpur (Faisalabad), with the cars and busses of the Bhattis joining the funeral procession, which now comprised probably more than a hundred vehicles, it was already noon, and I was fretful. Driving through Lyallpur city we slowed down again, and outside the Markazi Imambarah on Jhang Road, a large crowd, comprising of my father's friends and admirers, had gathered from the city and its environs. A multitude of people were beating their heads and wailing. Dozens of vehicles joined in the funeral entourage. We moved onto the Jhang Road and picked up speed, mourners had gathered at Nawan Lahore and Painsra which slowed us down. They would join the procession. This was all amazing even for me, and once we crossed into the peripheries of Jhang, it was as though every man, woman, and child around from the entire region were on the road, with their own drums, mourning and wailing, women beating their breasts, men beating their heads. All the clans of the region: the Kalyas, Bhojias, Nangas, Umranas, Rimas, Joppus, Khanuanas, to mention a few, along with the Baloch, and the Nauls had come in thousands to pay their respects. For them, the cortege would pause briefly, crowds running alongside and then hopping onto busses and even trucks. As we reached the outskirts of Jhang, thousands were standing on both sides of the road, body to body, it was a spectacle that left me and my cousins truly amazed. My cousins kept repeating that how could one individual mean so much to so many people. They were mourning him as if they had lost someone of their own.

On the crossroad before entering the town, from the road coming in from Chiniot came the great Jat clans of the Sipras, the Jappas, the Chaddhars, and most of all, the Bharwanas chanting above the entire cacophony: 'Abid Hussain Zindabad! Ghulam Haider Murdabad!' The chant of the Bharwanas placed a bit of balm on my torn heart. Thousands of vehicles and more than a hundred thousand people were all heading in the direction of Shah Jewna House. As the cortege entered the Civil Lines area, with the seemingly endless queue of vehicles behind it, the roadside was packed with more mourners coming in from the direction of the Toba Road and Gojra Road. The cortege was now making very slow progress through the density of the crowds of mourners who kept joining in. There were waves of humanity around the cortege. As we turned towards the Shah Jewna House, the cortege halted and Uncles Mubarik Ali and Wajid Ali, my cousins Iffi and Zulfi, and Fakhar lowered my father's casket onto scores of waiting shoulders. The casket was then carried with the crescendo of a mournful wail accompanying it into the compound of the house. Meanwhile, family retainers were pushing my car forward to the rear of the house from whence women were surging out. I was dragged out of my car and the thousands of women packed into, and spilling out of the rear courtyard, were surging towards me, falling on me, asphyxiating me. I could not breathe, and felt that I was going to die, when suddenly a huge woman emerged to rescue me. Pushing away the surging crowd, she yelled, 'Are you all mad, can you not see you are constricting the poor child? First you kill her father by giving your dirty votes to that filthy Haideroo, and now you want to snuff the life out of the only light he has left behind! Is this your expression of remorse, you dirty scum!' The gigantic woman lifted me out of there and put me gently onto my feet, and beating everyone back, saved my life.

'Who are you?' I asked her.

'I am Mai Soobaan Balochni, widow of Allawal Baloch, nambardar. I am a retired school teacher and I know these ignorant fools. But they did not mean to harm you, they will love you as they loved your father. It was their ignorance that made them believe that stamping on that wretched key symbol, they were buying their way to heaven.'

'Thank you, Mai Soobaan, I will never forget you.' I said as I gratefully drank the glass of water she had magically produced. I was concerned for my mother, and pushed my way through the women till I found her inside the house in the corridor leading out to the front door. She looked amazingly serene.

'Chando, remember that your father said to you at Meshed, a great Muslim is acknowledged by the scale of his funeral. I was more privileged than I understood at the time. I was sharing thirty-two years of my life with this great Mussulman, the great humanist that was your father. I am glad they are now taking him for another Namaz-e-Janaza to the Islamia High School grounds, where Haji Azizul Hassan, a dear and scholarly man, will lead the prayer. It is befitting that the prayer here was led by Allama Naseer Hussain, our Shia scholar and in the large grounds of Islamia School the prayer will be led by an eminent Sunni, and a suitable riposte for the bigots who dragged him down.' I kissed my mother's face, now bathed in tears and she kissed mine with ineffable sweetness, as she said to me, 'We have each other, and all this vast reservoir of his memories to motivate us and to inspire us to accomplish all that he did not get the time to achieve.' And we held onto each other for a long moment.

It was after the *Maghrib* (evening) prayers that our funeral procession embarked on the final lap of its journey. As we crossed the Chenab, the last line of red in the sky seemed to bid us adieu, as though the dying sun could accompany us no further. Turning the corner at Chund to move onto the road to Shah Jewna, we could see the headlights of the vehicles behind stretching back and melting into the rear horizon. Shah Jewna was still a couple of miles away when the road on either side started to line up with men, offering my father a final salute. The cortege stopped at the gates of the Imambarah, where Father had sought to be buried. Mother and I entered the Imambarah from the side entrance, and went to stand in the verandah near the corner where his grave had been dug. As his coffin was brought in slowly through the densely crowded compound, I noticed the Deputy Commissioner standing next to a pretty young woman, who could only be his wife. She was weeping copiously. As the box of the coffin was lowered and opened, the shroud was brought out into the grave by Allama Naseer Hussain, a tall, sturdy man with a kindly face. He was the first to lower himself in the grave, and was followed by Khan Arif Khan Sial and Amir Abdullah Khan Niazi, both my fathers' life-long friends and associates. They placed my father's coffin gently onto the floor of the grave. And as they were heaved out of the grave, the grave diggers started shovelling earth to cover the shroud, which was rapidly disappearing from our view. My mother fainted at the sight, and was carried by her family to our *Haveli*, our ancestral home, while I stood in the verandah till the mound of the grave had been delineated and water poured onto it. The men were now all drifting away, but I stood there, with Fakhar beside me, numbed by the realization that I would never see my father again, except perhaps in my dreams. I was suddenly utterly bereft. I had lost my mentor, my friend, my Father!

We mourned him for the customary forty days. Condolence callers would start arriving early in the morning, and leave late at night. And the wailing never stopped. The crowd at his *Qul*, the customary prayer gathering on the third day of the death, was unprecedented. As were the prayers that were held every Thursday till the *Chehlum*, prayer gathering after forty days of death. My father's *Chehlum* was the largest gathering that the region had ever known.

I had called in Father's staff the day after the burial and assigned them their duties. All visitors' names were to be recorded and I would send out letters of acknowledgement to whoever had come for the *Chehlum*. Uncle Mubarik Ali suggested that the letters be sent out by him, but Mother vetoed this with remarkable sang-froid and nobody dared question her. The matter was settled. Mother and I would carry my father's legacy as best we could. This created a fissure between my Aunt Surraya, Uncle Mubarik Ali and their family, which added to my mother's sense of loss; less to mine. I was too busy making notes of whatever I thought noteworthy and receiving callers coming to condole. Visitors who made the greatest impression on me were Haji Maula Bux Soomro, accompanied by his young grandson Mohammad Mian, who came from Shikarpur, Kazi Fazalullah from Larkana, Nawab Akbar Khan Bugti, who came from Dera Bugti, Khan Saadullah Khan, Dr Khan Sahib's son who came from Utmanzai, and Malik Khizar Hayat Tiwana who came every Thursday from Lahore. All the gentry of the Punjab were there as were tens of thousands of humble folk, all of whom earned my deep respect. And what I can never forget are the scores of men and women, which included my Aunt Fakhra, Fakhar's mother, who read the Quran day and night besides my father's grave, and my Lebanese friend Tarfa Salaam Saigol who sent a car laden with flowers to be placed on the grave.

After the *Chehlum*, my mother returned to Lahore and I flew to Karachi, to sell horses at the annual sales at the Karachi Race Club, where I suffered a threatened miscarriage, and was confined to bed for ten days. My friend Timmy and her sister Pappu Afzal Khan moved me from 18-Victoria Road to their home, and looked after me till I stabilized. Fakhar came to Karachi immediately, and formed an enduring friendship with Afzal Khan and his family. Raja Mahmudabad arrived from London and came to visit me. He sat with me a long while grieving Father's death with me. He himself was not in good health, and I feared he did not have long to go.

The doctor who was taking care of me in Karachi promised me that he would come to Lahore for the delivery. It boosted my level of confidence. By now I was missing my mother intensely. Hence after expressing much gratitude to Timmy and Pappu, Fakhar brought me home to Lahore, accompanied by my friend Bunny who had been sent by my mother.

Sleeping beside Mother one late April afternoon, I saw my father in so vivid a dream that I woke up with a start, with his voice still echoing in my ears. He looked well and happy, in robust health, and dressed elegantly in his white bush-shirt and trousers. He said to me, 'Chandi *baita*, if you have a daughter you are to name her Umme Kulsum, after the daughter of Hazrat Ali and Bibi Fatima, who had a happier life than her sister Bibi Zeynab.'

My father never saw my children, but he named my first born who arrived in this world exactly six months to the day after he had passed on. As my mother held Umme Kulsum in her arms, she smiled for the first time in more than two years.

3

My Journey Begins

Through the summer of 1971, events in East Pakistan continued to deteriorate. My mother, Fakhar and I did not retreat to the hills that summer. We remained in Lahore and my mother kept lamenting that not only had her life's partner left her, one half of her country was also leaving her. She was critical of Zulfikar Ali Bhutto conniving with Yahya Khan after having led the Pakistan Peoples Party (PPP) to victory in West Pakistan. Uncle Mazhar Ali Khan and Aunty Tahira, who were daily visitors to our home, endorsed her point of view, but I would argue in support of Bhutto, on the grounds that it was Yahya Khan who was in the driving seat and who had ordered military action in East Pakistan.

Towards the end of summer, Khan Abdul Wali Khan was visiting Lahore. At a lunch at Uncle Mazhar Ali and Aunty Tahira's, Mother told Wali Khan that I was a great fan of Z. A. Bhutto, and that, much to her chagrin, I wanted to join his party, the PPP. Wali Khan told her that he thought it was inevitable that East Pakistan would secede and that Bhutto would become premier of what would be left of Pakistan, and if I wanted to join his party, my mother should not discourage me; the sooner I did so, the better it would be. He said that I would be an asset to Bhutto and he was politician enough to honour me.

So the very next day, I called on Begum Nasim Jahan, a prominent representative of the PPP, obtaining from her a membership form that I filled in. Hence, I became a member of the Pakistan Peoples Party (PPP) on September 1970, thereby embarking on my own political journey.

At this point I realized that if I was going to seriously follow a career in public life I would need to be a graduate at least, so I obtained the required course of studies and applied to the Punjab University to sit my exam as a private candidate for a Bachelors' degree in Political Science and Economics. The examination hall was at the Lady Maclagan School, and it was unbearably hot there. My Political Science and compulsory papers went off well, but I was in the middle of my Economics paper when I had to rush out of the hall and was throwing up violently. The invigilators prevented me from re-entering the hall, and advised that I take my compartment exam later in the year, after the delivery of my baby. Pakistan dismembered by year's end, and I failed to graduate until many many years later.

Before this tragic development, towards the middle of November 1971, when Umme Kulsum, whom everyone had bestowed the diminutive of Umku, was six weeks old, Mother and I and baby Umku set off for Jhang. After a few days at Shah Jewna and trying to get a handle on our farm issues, we came to Jhang and were installed in the Shah Jewna House when we got the news on BBC radio that Dacca (Dhaka) had fallen, Indian troops were in control and the proud Pakistan Army had ignominiously surrendered to the Indian Army. Forty thousand of our soldiers had laid down their arms, along with twenty thousand paramilitary forces. My father had been so right; it was the end of the Pakistan that even I had known.

Zulfikar Ali Bhutto was handed power before the year ended. When I met him, he was kind—and said to me that he was going to nominate me as a member of the Punjab Assembly on a women's reserved seat—in acknowledgement of my late father's contribution towards democratic causes.

In February of 1972, I took oath as Member Provincial Assembly (MPA) of the Punjab, and felt somewhat vindicated when people came from Jhang to say to me that they were glad that the light of my father's home would keep glowing and its doors would remain open. I realized that not only would my father's path be a hard one to follow, many censorious eyes would also monitor every move I made. The journey ahead would be rough, but after all the pain had been endured, and the determination and capacity to forge ahead had developed within me.

I went to Islamabad to thank Begum Nusrat Bhutto for her husband's kindness to me. She was very affectionate and supportive, and warned me that some party members might make things difficult for me due to jealousies, but assured me that if the situation for me became too unpleasant, she would always be there to comfort me. She then asked for my advise on how she should style her hair and on how she should do her eye make-up, complementing my eyes, and declaring that I reminded her of Elizabeth Taylor! I thought she was simple and adorable; I felt that I had found a friend in her.

Not long after becoming an MPA, I was pregnant again. The discovery made me happy. Fakhar and Baji (Mother) were both overjoyed when informed. I had taken to wearing baggy *kurta*s and *shalwar*s (loose trousers) made out of *khaddar* (hand-loom cloth) woven by the weavers of Shah Jewna, who had been organized by me as part of the income-generating project I had set up several years earlier. These weavers had set to work and succeeded in resurrecting a dying traditional skill. Hand-spun yarn, hand-made vegetable dyes, with different tones in the warp and weft of the fabric, making an interesting texture, and my outfits triggered what evolved gradually into a line of fashion. And out of the trunks stored in my late Daadi's rooms, I pulled out old silk *dupatta*s (scarves) to cover my head with. Being mildly myopic provided me an excuse for shielding my eyes behind large round glasses. All of this was part of a calculated attempt on my part to dress down and not draw attention to my physical presence. I had not as yet lost the weight I gained from my last pregnancy; with the second pregnancy, it started piling again. But my spread was comfortably camouflaged by the baggy *kurta*s.

With the start of the budget session, it was expected that I deliver my debutante, or maiden speech. Malik Meraj Khalid, a dear man, was our Chief Minister. He was a fluent speaker, as was Allama Rahmatullah Arshad who led the Opposition. Hanif Ramay, the Finance Minister, and Dr Abdul Khaliq, the Education Minister, were frequently on their legs on the side of the Treasury, during our first session, while Haji Saifullah and Tabish Alwari were oratorical and verbose from the Opposition benches. Everyone spoke in Urdu with ease and confidence. The Speaker, Sheikh Rafiq occasionally resorted to English but mostly in the context of legal terminology. So when on the second day of the budget debate, he informed me that he would be calling on me to speak the next day, I was paralyzed at the thought of conveying all I had to say in Urdu. I wrote out my speech in English and tried to rehearse an Urdu version at home before Fakhar and Baji.

'Chando, I like the content of your statement, especially your opening sentences regarding the tragic loss of East Pakistan, but you will murder the speech in Urdu. So I would stick to English if I were you,' was Mother's advise. 'But I will be heckled by Tabish and Saifullah.'

'You can deal with the heckling by reminding the honourable members that the Rules of the Punjab Assembly allow for bilingual discussion and debate,' said Fakhar, settling the issue for me.

Mother came to hear my very first speech in the first Assembly I represented in. I was very conscious of her presence in the gallery and desperately sought to do her proud. Hence, even though my knees quivered like jelly, I forced my voice to ring out. I spoke in English and amazingly nobody heckled me. There was considerable desk thumping and as I looked up at my mother: she nodded and smiled in unmistakable approval. Both Leaders of the House and Opposition had thumped their desks: Ramay, Tabish, and Saifullah and many others sent me 'well-spoken' chits: and my father's friends, Makhdumzada Hassan Mahmood, Amir Abdullah Khan Rokhri, Colonel Aslam Khan Niazi, Mir Balakh Sher Mazari, and Nawab Sadiq Hussain Qureshi came and patted me on my head. Even the Speaker sent me a note saying that my late father would have been proud of me. As I drove home from the Assembly that day, it seemed to me that my colleagues would henceforward take me seriously on this forum.

Close on the heels of this feel-good moment, came a time of deep personal anguish again. Chairman and President of the Pakistan Peoples Party, Zulfikar Ali Bhutto, my leader whom I admired so much, announced Land Reforms. While listening to his address to the nation, it dawned on me that I would be losing a sizeable portion of my farmland, my personal interest coming into direct conflict with the reforms that Bhutto announced. My father had inherited 5,300 acres of land. He had lost 800 during the time of Ayub Khan's land reforms; given away 500 acres to a family Trust; sold 1,000 acres and had invested the proceeds in my maternal family's group of enterprises; and had sold his most valuable 300 acres to build his large and beautiful house in Lahore. His less valuable 300 acres were sold to cover the costs of elections and his medical care. In his written directives to Mother and me, he had asked us to give away a hundred acres to his retainers who had served him well, and whom he thought would continue to serve us equally well. Time proved him right. He left me with 2,000 acres of well-developed prime and productive land. Bhutto's land reforms were to deprive me of more than one-third of my ownership. Mercifully, under the land reform law itself, having surrendered 600 acres to the government, I was able to lease the remaining 600 acres according to a relevant proviso in the law if I maintained on half the area the livestock and equines which I had previously maintained on the whole. Nonetheless, in surrendering 600 acres of prime irrigated land, I was surrendering a small fortune. The capital value of this land today would exceed a couple of billion rupees! But I grit my teeth and decided that with Mother to help me, we would work hard enough to make up for the lost income within a couple of years; which we managed to do.

The fact that I owned more land than any one of my kinsmen made me a target of envy, jealousy, even vindictiveness. Since we were Shias, my being the sole heir to my father's property was not disputed legally but many of them tried to squeeze me out of the environment by being needlessly critical, and in some cases even censorious. I turned a blind eye and deaf ear to their negative propaganda, their barbs, and their relentless effort at needling and provoking me, carrying on with my struggle to achieve recognition and respect, determined that my gender cease to be viewed as a handicap.

In November of 1972, exactly thirteen months after the birth of Umku, I was blessed with a second daughter whom we named Sughra, after my Daadi, whose only grandchild I had been. Having always yearned for a sister, it gave me great satisfaction to hold my two baby girls in my arms. Mother had been hoping and praying for a grandson—when the second granddaughter was born, she tried hard to contain her disappointment. She dreamt of my father, who indicated to her that good fortune had entered his home. There were now two girls, whereas previously there had only been one. The dream consoled my mother, who took enthusiastically to the raising of her granddaughters.

Mother's taking over the looking after of my daughters freed me to carry on with my political work full time, enabling me to make rapid progress, winning support in Jhang. I was determined to establish the fact that given the opportunity, a woman could work twice as hard as a man. I also decided that in the future I would contest general elections and seek to win by popular vote.

Discovering individual personalities of the folk who would come to visit me was riveting. I sent for Mai Soobaan Balochni, who had miraculously lifted me up from the suffocating crowds at my father's funeral. She became my chaperon as well as my guide. Not only was she a mine of information, but she could also be very amusing and would frequently send me into peals of laughter. She hated my being attentive to her kinsman, Jamal Khan Baloch, who was left-wing and a 'kissan committee' worker. Soobaan insisted that he was pretentious and ordinary. Both my new-found Baloch friends were in their early fifties and their incipient rivalry taught me that much of politics was premised on rivalries.

Besides Soobaan, I resorted frequently to consulting with Malik Riaz, one of my father's retainers who managed a business that my father had established in the town of Jhang, which was a distribution company for Pakistan Tobacco and several other products, known as A. H. Syed & Co. Malik Riaz informed me that Fateh Khan Patoana was someone my father rated very highly and whose advise he often sought on local matters. I thought to do the same and found that Fateh Khan was indeed a wealth of information on the 'who's who' of the district. Fateh Khan would visit daily, invariably accompanied by an odd-looking fellow called Mian Fuzail Chela. Mian Fuzail had a strangely crooked face. He told me that when he was a young man his rival kinsman had tried to kill him over a dispute on water. His adversary had attacked him with a hatchet that gashed part of his head and face. Blood spurted out and he had been thrown into a canal and left to die. But Allah had willed it otherwise, and Mian Fuzail survived. However, the village apothecary who stitched Mian Fuzail's face failed to do a good job, which resulted in a crooked face! I marvelled at the good humour with which Mian Fuzail narrated the story of his affliction.

'So what happened to your attacker? Was he sent to jail?' I queried.

'No, I killed him,' said Mian Fuzail, quite cheerfully. I was aghast, as it gradually dawned on me that under a placid surface lurked a violent society, working with which would be difficult in the extreme. When I said as much to Soobaan, she assured me that this was not violence, and that it was enjoined in the Quran that you take an eye for an eye and a tooth for a tooth.

'But Soobaan there are laws that govern us and these comport with Quranic injunctions. We must all follow the law. We cannot dispense law as we please. We have the courts to dispense justice,' I insisted.

'The Courts follow the police and the police report in favour of those that have the capacity to bribe. Men like your father could prevent that, and people will expect the same from you. My cousin Mapal Khan needs your help. His son was murdered and he has taken the matter to court. You must help him. He will be coming to see you.' Soobaan informed me.

Mapal Khan Baloch was a tall, sturdy, and handsome man. Soobaan looked at him with adoration. It did not take much to notice that there was closeness between the two. He was accompanied by a tall, dark, and incredibly beautiful woman who looked like a middle-aged version of the African princess, Elizabeth of Bagaya. This was Mapal Khan's wife. She looked intently at me and in a deeply imperial voice, said, 'Proud daughter of Pir Abid Hussain, your father was my murshid (spiritual guide) and you will become my murshidzadi (female murshid) if you help me to avenge the wasted blood of my son. He was young and innocent and did not deserve to pay for the sins of others. My name is Daulaan, and I beseech you for all I am worth, and pray that you are kind-hearted and fair-minded, even as your father was before you.'

I was deeply moved and yet disturbed by her plea. What if the court erred, would Mapal and Daulaan hold it against me? And how could I influence the court? The people and their way of life, so unquestioningly based on a series of traditions, were compelling, but many of the practices and traditions were cruel and needed to be departed from. Did I have the capacity to launch a reform mission, or should I simply stick to what was reasonable and doable, using my personal moral compass to guide me and seek Mother's advise from time to time? To retain goodwill and credibility would not be easy, under the weight of these antiquated traditions and customs.

As I was gradually getting a grip on my new life as a public representative, summer was upon us. Although my little girls were thriving under the loving care they received from their grandmother, they would cling to me noticeably when they saw me, which tugged at my heart. So I decided to spend a few weeks at a stretch with them and with Fakhar and Mother, in the hills at Cliffden Farm, in the cool air of Murree.

Cliffden brought with it an enormous reservoir of memories of my late father. Mother had wonderful photos of him at different stages of his life put up in all the rooms and did not appreciate it when the conversation veered away from reminiscences of the time we had shared with him. The monsoons of 1973 were unusually generous and everyday Fakhar would predict flooding. And sure enough, by the end of August, floods hit Jhang and Multan in a major way. Leaving Umku, Shugu, and Baji was a wrench but Fakhar and I drove down to Islamabad and caught the Fokker flights operating to Multan and Lyallpur (now Faisalabad). I had instructed Malik Riaz to bring my father's jeep, which was kept garaged at the Shah Jewna House, to the airport to fetch me. While landing, it seemed that we were descending over a large lake. There was water everywhere, even on the runway.

It took us several hours to reach Jhang, making all sorts of detours to get around the inundated areas. Grateful for my father's old jeep, knowing I would never have it made in a car, we finally entered Jhang after five hours. Getting into the compound of my house was a complicated exercise, as the streets of Jhang were flooded. Malik Riaz informed me that when the Trimmu barrage banks were breached a few days ago, motor launches were plying around the district courts.

Drawing on my childhood memories I recalled the flood of 1952, when Mother and I remained in Murree and my father went down to Jhang. My Daadi was in Shah Jewna and to get word of his welfare across to her and to hear from him, she had to send Namdar, a competent swimmer, who floated across the waters with a *mashk* (goatskin water bag) tied around his waist, to buoy him up and carry him across the water. Daadi never tired of telling me the story, when I would sit on her lap as a child, of how the flood waters had reached our *haveli* and entered the cellar, which had caused fissures in the new building in the compound which my father had erected before bringing his bride, my mother, from Lahore to Shah Jewna. She would particularly enjoy telling me about Namdar and his float across the bloated River Chenab bringing her news of her son. I recalled also my father talking about the relief work he had undertaken for the flood affectees.

Fateh Khan, Malik Riaz, and Mai Soobaan, my consigliere, informed me that if I sought to do relief work, I should visit the relief camps set up by the district administration in the school buildings of the Satellite Town, which my father had established for Jhang when he was Minister in the West Pakistan Government. They warned me, however, that reaching the camps would be tricky, that I would find a terrible stench around the area and the humidity level would be uncomfortably high. I was not exactly a comfort addict, and was irritated with my advisers for their all too obvious attempt to discourage me. I hopped into the jeep, making the trio pile in behind me. As we headed towards the camps, our vehicle ploughing through water that seemed to be as high as the wheels, I noticed the sunlight glittering on some strange-looking strands in the water. When I queried from my companions what these could be, they replied in unison that they were snakes! For once I was truly terrified and pulled my feet off the floor of the jeep and close to my chest, which made Soobaan guffaw heartlessly. Finally we reached the relief camps, and as I alighted out of the jeep, an awful stench hit my nostrils, and I threw up on the roadside, with Soobaan holding my shoulders and looking just slightly more sympathetic. Some district officials were distributing food as I went to the women and children, handing out hundred rupee notes. My ten thousand rupees were exhausted in no time and there were hundreds of folk who were left.

I got used to the stench and worked long hours in the camps for several days, when the Deputy Commissioner called to inform that Prime Minister Zulfikar Ali Bhutto was arriving the next day to visit our relief camps. He would land in his helicopter near the camps, do a quick round, then address a gathering of the flood affectees, after which he would fly on to the Trimmu headworks and then onwards to Multan. I was expected to receive him in the line-up at the helipad, not far from the Satellite Town relief camp.

The entire administration of Sargodha division, along with all the MNAs and MPAs, lined up at the helipad and an Assistant Commissioner went down the line, handing garlands of marigolds and red roses to all the elected members. When he reached me, standing towards the tail end of the line, I asked him what the garlands were for? 'For the Quaid-e-Awaam,' he responded, as though taken aback by the question. I was appalled by this crude attempt at sycophancy. The Prime Minister was coming to empathize with and provide relief for those devastated by the flood, in the line of his duty. Why was the bureaucracy trying to convert this into a political rally? I said as much to the Commissioner who responded by saying that the chopper was coming in to land and we could pursue the discussion later!

Bhutto alighted from the helicopter wearing a Mao cap, and a white safari suit. Everyone garlanded him, except me. Noticing this, he took off all the garlands. 'This is not an occasion for garlands,' he said loudly. He then lowered his voice and asked me gently, 'Is that you Abida? You look terrible. What is the matter?'

'I have been working in the relief camps, Prime Minister, and the condition of the folk here is dreadful,' I answered.

'Where are they? Show me,' and he started striding forward briskly with the Governor of Punjab, Ghulam Mustafa Khar, walking alongside him. I had to run to keep up with them, with the rest of the crowd following a few paces behind. As we reached the women and children, the stench hit us and Bhutto brought out his handkerchief perhaps to hold it up to his nostrils, but when he heard the cry of the women for help, his eyes brimmed with tears and he kneeled to draw the children near him into his arms, wiping their grubby little faces with his handkerchief. At this moment he reminded me of my father whom I had often seen making similarly humane gestures towards the poor and the humble. 'Abida,' Bhutto Sahib called out to me, 'tell me what these women and children need most urgently.'

'Prime Minister, they need soap, detergents, anti-bacterial and cleaning stuff, basic utensils, summer clothing and slippers, and dry rations like biscuits, flour, rice, and edible oil. What they *are* getting are mostly old quilts and warm clothing, along with old boots and shoes, truck loads of which are being sent by the well-off from Lahore and Lyallpur. The local administration and the well-off folk of Jhang have been contributing cooked food but the clamour is for dry rations because people want to start returning to the localities from where the water is receding.' I made my long statement breathlessly; I was heard intently.

'Bajwa!' the Prime Minister called out to Commissioner Sargodha.

'Make a note of what our young representative has said and get a truck of soap in to these people right away, and also all the other stuff that is required. Now let us go to where the men are assembled.' I was amazed to see that a huge dais had been erected, and the flood affectees had gathered there. A horde of policemen were also standing in guard. As Bhutto clambered up the makeshift stairs by the side of the dais, the PPP president of Jhang, Umar Hayat Sial, was bellowing slogans through a megaphone: 'Quaid-e-Awam Zindabad!'

Bhutto strode up to him, took the megaphone away from him and shouted: '*Chamcha! Baith Ja*!' (sit down, you sycophant!) Sial was not to be deterred. He picked up another megaphone and shouted '*Mujhe Quaid-e-Awam ka chamcha honay pe fakhr hai*,' (I am proud to be sycophant to the leader of the people!) is what he said.

'*O chamcha*! (spoon) I do not need you. I know how to eat with my hands!' countered Bhutto. The crowd loved this exchange, and 'Jeay Bhutto! Jeay Bhutto!' (Long Live Bhutto!) slogans went on for quite a while. This was Z. A. Bhutto, the great populist. I was happy for having shared the moment, and never tired of repeating the narrative to my friends and family on my return to Lahore when the waters receded.

Not long after the floods were behind us, Zulfikar Ali Bhutto legislated for the people of Pakistan a Constitution which stood the test of time, even though he sponsored seven amendments to it in three years. The basic structure of the Constitution was sound enough for it to have endured. Later amendments mauled it, but nonetheless, the 1973 Constitution has served as guarantor for the Federation of Pakistan for forty years.

Meanwhile, my mother had busied herself in establishing the 'Syed Abid Hussain Memorial Trust Hospital' at Jhang. After my father's death, Mother and I had set aside a sum of one-and-a-half million rupees (which in today's terms would be more like one hundred and fifty million rupees) to develop a health facility for the women and children of Jhang. We requested Begum Nusrat Bhutto to come for the inaugural and she did. Women poured in and packed the hospital compound in thousands and Begum Bhutto commented to me and Mother that she had never addressed such a large gathering of women before. She was generous in her praise as my mother walked her around the wards and the operation theatre. She lauded Mother's hard work and philanthropic efforts, and was very impressed by the Shah Jewna House, when we took her there for lunch. Her husband called her while we were at lunch and she told him what a tremendous women's *jalsa* it was that we had asked her to address; how wonderful the hospital was; and what a beautiful house we had in Jhang. Begum Bhutto had taken the Fokker flight from Islamabad airport to Lyallpur. I was at the airport to receive her in my mother's pale blue Mercedes, which was the last car that my father had bought for her before we lost him, but the Governor had sent his newer, larger black Mercedes for her. Begum Bhutto asked me to accompany her in the car as we drove into Jhang. When she left Shah Jewna House, she was driving straight back to Lahore to join her husband who had informed her that he would be there in the evening. When she was departing, Begum Bhutto embraced me affectionately and said, 'Chandi, I am so impressed with you and your mother. You have really honoured your late father's memory so well. I am proud to have you in our party.'

Not long after this, Dr Mubashar Hassan sent for me. I was charmed by the simplicity of his residence in main Gulberg.

He said to me, 'Abida, you know that the PPP has decided to launch a People's Works Programme. I heard you talking about an income-generating programme you have initiated for the women of your village, and I have received impressive feedback from my relatives who live in Jhang. I want you to write a proposal for expanding this programme throughout the country. After I have vetted your proposal, we will set up a committee under the chairmanship of Begum Nusrat Bhutto for its implementation and you will be associated with the committee.'

I was delighted to hear all this and wrote up a proposal within a few days for Dr Mubashar's approval. Shortly thereafter I got a call from Begum Bhutto's secretary inviting me to a meeting at the Prime Minister's House at Rawalpindi.

When I arrived for the meeting, I was taken aback by the lack of formality. I was shown into a small sitting room, where I was joined by Iffat Khurshid Hassan Meer and Sadia Pirzada. Begum Bhutto entered the room, saying that since she was not feeling well, she did not get time to look at the document sent by Dr Mubashar. Therefore, could I explain to her the details. I briefed the ladies on the proposal.

What I had proposed was that in every Union Council of Pakistan, an income-generating unit be set up for teaching cutting and sewing to women of the locality, and in every tehsil headquarter, a designer and social welfare worker be installed to liaise with these units, provide them with material and designs to stitch *kurta*s and *shalwar*s for local as well as for export purposes. At every district headquarters, a marketing centre should be established for these products, which would be based on our traditional crafts, but adapted for modern usage.

Begum Bhutto asked Iffat and Sadia their opinion and in the ensuing discussion it was decided that we set up a training, design, and marketing centre under the Directorate of Social Welfare at Lahore and get our party workers to bring indigent women in for training. After a month's training these women should be provided with fabric and design. They should embroider and stitch caftans, *kurta*s, and *shalwar*s. Once that is achieved, their products should be exhibited at a fashion show which should be held at the Lahore Fort with the Sound and Light Show that had been recently installed there with the help of the French Government. The invitees could include officials of the Export Promotion Bureau, diplomats, and the local gentry. This would launch the programme effectively and the setting up of income generating units on a large scale would then be a natural follow-up.

During my vacations, a decade previous, at the Chateau Du Mesnil, with Madame Jean Couturie in France, the famous horse breeder, and my late father's good friend, I had been to the 'son et lumiere' spectacle at the Chateau de La Lude, in the neighbourhood of Le Mesnil, which had turned out to be an exhilarating evening for me, and I remembered it vividly. I was accompanying the Comte and Comtesse de Tarragone, son-in-law and daughter of my kind hostess, who took me with them into the Chateau to meet with the family and their house guest, Princess Irene, in whose honour there was to be a special display of fireworks, since she was Danish royalty, at the end of the sound and light show. That magical evening, still fresh in my memory, became the benchmark for me when I set out to organize our presentation at the Lahore Fort.

Nabi Ahmed Khan was the scholarly curator of the Lahore Fort. He conversed with me on history as he walked me around the Fort day after day. He gave me a fascinating book to read on this exceptional monument that he seemed to be utterly devoted to. He was most excited at the prospect of meeting with Begum Sadia Pirzada so that he could hand her the memorandum that he had laboriously prepared for her spouse, the Minister of Education and Culture, Abdul Hafeez Pirzada, in which he solicited for the desperately needed resources for urgent repair and restoration work of his beloved monument. He motivated me to urge Sadia to visit Lahore.

My mother was happy to have Sadia as her house guest because her late father-in-law, Abdus Sattar Pirzada and my father had been Cabinet colleagues and friends. We decided to have our guests drive up through the 'haathi pol' gate, the elephant walkway that led up to the Diwan-e-Aam of the Lahore Fort, and our fashion show would be held down the walkways of the fountain court behind the Diwan-e-Aam, or people's entrance. Watching me work, Nabi Ahmed Khan suggested to me gently that I should strive to be elected MNA (Member National Assembly) in the future, and that I should ensure that Archaeology and Culture be brought under one ministry, and that I should head that ministry! I hugged him and told him that that this was exactly what I was going to struggle to achieve!

The fashion show was a resounding success. Our lead model did us proud. On display were caftans in *rilli* (patchwork), *kurta*s in khaddar (handloom), richly embroidered with silk and *tilla* (gold). The music was a fusion of eastern and western as was the ambiance, with a large number of diplomats and their wives and the Lahore gentry applauding. Begum Nusrat Bhutto read out the speech I had written for her. After welcoming the guests, she outlined the purpose of the project that was launched nationwide: the unemployed and the under-employed women of Pakistan should be able to generate income. Begum Bhutto was generous in her compliments to me.

The success of the evening cemented our friendship. But Bhutto Sahib became displeased with me and I was summoned by him to explain why I had attended a meeting in 'Kisaan Hall' to listen to Mir Ghous Bux Bizenjo and Nawab Khair Bux Marri's speeches. He failed to understand what interest I could have in Baloch nationalist leaders and I could not fathom why he was objecting, until he dismissed their government in Balochistan a few months later.

After the passage of the Constitution, Zulfikar Ali Bhutto's next major moment came with the first Islamic Summit which he decided to hold in Lahore in 1974. General N. M. Raza was Chief of Protocol and was assigned the task of selecting private homes where the heads of Islamic countries would stay. Thirty monarchs, presidents, and prime ministers were expected to attend the summit. Ten were to be lodged in the Government House and the State Guest House, and twenty in private residences whose owners would have to vacate their homes. General Raza called my mother to ask whether she could lend her residence to the State for a week—and she readily agreed—as did her brothers, Uncle Wajid Ali and Uncle Babar Ali, and also her sister, Aunt Sarwat. Ours was the only family in Lahore that gave up four homes, others giving a home or two each. My mother, the babies, Fakhar, and I moved into Aunt Fakhra's spacious home, across the road. Two-year-old Umku would perch on the shoulders of Allah Ditta, our old chauffer, and watch the Prime Minister of Lebanon's motorcade drive out of our home every morning, clapping her little hands when the motorcycles of the military police revved up with their blue lights flashing, while baby Shugu slept peacefully in her cot. I would be rushing off to the television station because the French wife of a government employee and I were the only two francophone women who passed the visual test that Pakistan Television had been able to get hold of, to read the French bulletins for the Conference, which was conducted in Arabic, English, and French. Nusrat Bhutto telephoned me and said she had seen me on television, and was complimentary as always. She invited me to a select luncheon at the Governor's House thrown in honour of the spouses of the heads of state who had opted to accompany their husbands unexpectedly.

At the lunch, I was seated next to the latest wife of President Muammar Gaddafi of Libya, a great hero of the Muslim World at the time. Madame Gaddafi spoke in Italian, which was distinctly more sketchy than mine, and was a rather masculine-looking woman, therefore, it came as no surprise when she informed me that she had been a leading member of her husband's team of bodyguards. What I appreciated nonetheless was that she was candid and fiercely proud of having been a working woman. Her dress was hideous, saffron yellow, short, a fraction above her knees, under which she wore gleaming white vinyl long boots. I caught Begum Bhutto's eye looking at these amazing boots. She winked at me while I worked hard on suppressing a giggle.

'How is it going, Chandi?' Begum Bhutto asked me, her voice free of its usual anxiety. I replied:

> Prime Minister Bhutto has emerged as the undisputed leader of the Muslim World, Begum Sahiba. Pakistanis feel proud that we are led by a modernist who can hold his own against any world leader and effectively advocate all just causes of Muslims. Palestine, Kashmir, fair prices for our raw materials, including energy, respect, and recognition for our overseas work force, all the vital issues emerging out of the decolonized Muslim world.

Nusrat Bhutto seemed satisfied and happy with my reply. The Summit ended, and the visiting heads were beginning to depart when we got a message from protocol that the Prime Minister of Lebanon, who had been lodged in our house, wanted to meet with us before he left, and that we must bring with us the little girl whom he had noticed clapping for him every morning. Hence, Mother, Fakhar, little Umku, and I walked across the road to our house. We would have also taken baby Shugu along with us, had she not been fast asleep in her crib.

The Lebanese Prime Minister was wearing a bright red Fez cap, and received us in the formal and somewhat grand reception room of our home. He was utterly charming, and made Umku sit in his lap, while he apologized with great courtesy for having inconvenienced us. Mother assured him that it was an honour for us to have been able to make this modest contribution in the service of the Muslim Ummah. Umme Kulsum kept trying to get his attention by tugging at the tassel of his fez and lisped in her pigeon Punjabi, 'O King with the red hat, please go away. I love your red hat but I will not be going away with you!'

Mother narrated the episode for years afterward with the exclusive pride of a grandmother.

A few months later, Bhutto Sahib dismissed the majority government of Balochistan led by Sardar Ataullah Mengal and replaced Governor Ghaus Bux Bizenjo with Nawab Akbar Khan Bugti. The National Awami Party—Jamiat Ulema-e-Islam coalition government in the Frontier province resigned. When Leader of the Opposition in the National Assembly, Khan Abdul Wali Khan and Deputy Leader, Maulana Mufti Mahmud protested on the floor of the House, they were led away, arrested, the NAP banned, and Wali Khan as the head of this Party, was charged with treason, and alongwith the Baloch party leaders that included Mir Ghaus Bux Bizenjo, Nawab Khair Bux Marri, and Sardar Ataullah Mengal. They were detained in a Hyderabad jail in Sindh. Prime Minister Bhutto came under severe criticism for this high-handed action. My mother was vociferous in condemning him for turning dictatorial, and assessed correctly that this would be the beginning of Bhutto's downfall.

Shortly thereafter, Bhutto embarked on his 'meet the people' tour of the Punjab. By this time Hanif Ramay was the Chief Minister of Punjab, who called to inform me that the Prime Minister was scheduled to visit Jhang during his tour of the province, and had expressed his desire to stop at my house for tea.

While I was really excited at the prospect of the Prime Minister visiting Shah Jewna House, Mother was less than enthusiastic. I ended up organizing the event all by myself, assisted by Fakhar, who arranged for the army band to come in from the Corps Headquarters at Multan, while I urged Sher Afzal Jaffery, the celebrated poet of Jhang, to compose a poem especially for the event. The ample front lawn of the Shah Jewna House was covered in an immense marquee, and the list of invitees included my late father's closest friends and associates. I requested Khan Arif Khan to sit on the sofa next to the Prime Minister and Chief Minister Hanif Ramay, while I would sit on the other side of the Prime Minister. But when Bhutto Sahib arrived, all order broke down— everyone left their seats and rushed towards the edge of the red carpet which had been laid from the porch, through the front lawn and up to the dais, and some young Khokhar lads shouted 'Quaid-e-Awaam Zindabad!' and 'Pir Colonel Abid Hussain Zindabad!' and the entire gathering cheered and clapped. Bhutto Sahib raised his hands clapping, as he strode briskly down the red carpet towards the dais. Sher Afzal Jaffery stood beside the dais and recited his lovely poem in which he referred to me as Pir Abid Hussain Bokhari's only daughter, as capable as seven sons!

Bhutto Sahib gazed at me for a long time and then enquired: 'Who built this house, Abida? On how many acres does it stand and do you own the whole of it?' I informed him that my grandfather, Makhdumzada Pir Syed Raje Shah Bokhari had built it in 1900, and it had devolved on my father, who was his only child when he passed on, and since I was my father's only child, this house now belonged to me, and that its compound is spread over nearly three acres of land. I felt, somehow, that Bhutto Sahib was not pleased to hear any of this, declaring that his house in Larkana was bigger.

'How much land did your grandfather have?' was his next question.

When I answered; he said his grandfather had more.

This troubled me, because he now sounded displeased, which made me react foolishly, by asking him whether I should continue to work in his party or opt out.

'Opt out of what? Abida, you are an intelligent girl. You cannot leave me. When I no longer need you, you will know!'

Tea was being served, Bhutto Sahib did not eat anything, took a few sips of tea, stood up, jumped off the dais, shook hands perfunctorily with Fakhar, and a few others and strode back towards his car, with Governor Ghulam Mustafa Khar a step or two ahead of him. Khar sat at the wheels, Bhutto Sahib sat beside him, Hanif Ramay and the Military Secretary scrambled in the back seat, and they drove off. Just before hopping into the car, Bhutto shook my hand briefly and limply. He mumbled a thanks and they were gone. It was such a contrast to Begum Bhutto, who, when she was leaving Shah Jewna House just two years earlier, departed with effusive warmth and gratitude. I felt disappointed and let down.

My disappointment did not last long, however, because at the end of his tour of our province, the Prime Minister hosted a dinner for all the Senators, MNA's and MPA's of the Punjab at the Governor's House in Lahore. I dressed down, as I always did for any political event, wearing a pale blue plain *shalwar-kameez*, with a matching chiffon *dupatta*, while all the other women legislators were formally and some even gaudily dressed. Prime Minister Bhutto walked briefly towards us, offered us a collective greeting, and went off to be seated at a high table at the end of Darbar Hall, while the rest of us stood around the buffet tables at the opposite end of the large and beautiful mahogany-panelled room. The dinner did not last long and we went to wait in the porch for our vehicles while the Prime Minister and the Governor disappeared into the less formal rooms of this grand relic of the Raj.

I was resigned to a longish wait in the porch as first the ministerial flagged cars were called, followed by those of the Senators and MNAs, when the ADC (Aide-de-Camp) of the Prime Minister clambered down the grand stairway and headed towards me, and said that the Prime Minister was calling me. I felt conspicuous and embarrassed as I climbed up the stairway with scores of eyes watching my ascent. The ADC led me through the outer verandah of the main floor towards the rooms that led to the Prime Minister's suite at the far end of the verandah. As he held the door open for me, I stumbled into the sitting room in which Bhutto was sitting, in a winged leather chair by the fire place, puffing his cigar. Mustafa Khar was sitting opposite him, and stood up as I entered. Bhutto ushered me towards the sofa next to the chair where Khar had been sitting. I sat on the edge of the sofa, somewhat intimidated.

'So Abida, what do you think of my government?' asked Premier Bhutto. I made a herculean effort so that I sounded composed and responded,

'Prime Minister, your government has done some very good things and it has also had some limitations and suffered some setbacks.'

'Setbacks? Alright, tell me about the good things before you start recounting my failures,' said Premier Bhutto, with an unmistakably bemused expression, which gave me the sense that he was baiting me.

I took a deep breath and replied: 'The great thing you have done for all of us is that you have held us together after the dismemberment of the two wings of our country. You have erected a base for a new Pakistan. You have prevented us from feeling like absolute failures, and got our prisoners of war from India back. You have given heart and courage to poor and oppressed Pakistanis. Also, you have given us a Constitution premised on Provincial Autonomy so that we never divide again. Finally, you have provided direction to the Muslim world and emerged as its leading voice.'

'And what are the negatives that I have done … what have been my failures?' he asked in a gentler tone.

I avoided mentioning Balochistan, apprehensive of drawing his ire and said, 'You initiated your reforms too rapidly and have not been able to consolidate any single reform. Your Land Reforms have been so poorly implemented that, having surrendered twelve hundred acres of land, I feel like a fool because nobody else that I know has bothered to surrender much land, and are retaining their farms having made back-dated mutations in names of relatives and retainers and even children that are not yet born! Your Education Reforms have generated panic among the missionaries who fear being milked by functionaries of the education departments, and the newly-created Ministry of Religious Affairs bureaucracy. Did we need a Ministry for Religious Affairs?'

Without giving me an answer, Bhutto turned towards Mustafa Khar and said, 'Mustafa, did you hear what Abida said about Land Reforms?'

Ghulam Mustafa Khar said, 'Sahib, I agree with Abida Bibi. Did I not tell you that this Sheikh Rashid cannot control the *patwaris*, or lowest revenue functionaries, because they all know he was a *patwari* himself.' Bhutto Sahib did not respond to this and turned to me again, asking me what, at the time, was a truly unexpected question.

'Tell me Abida, should I make Urdu the official language for Pakistan and do away with English? If I make the change it will be gradual. If I am replaced by someone like Maulana Mufti Mahmud, the change will be abrupt and uncomfortable for Pakistanis like you or I who have been trained in English.'

'But Prime Minister, Maulana Mufti Mahmud or his ilk will not replace you in a million years, so I fail to understand why we should alter our existing linguistic arrangements.' I was young and inexperienced enough to not fathom at the time what awaited us further down the road, but Bhutto Sahib clearly had anticipated the rise of the religious right. His last question to me was, 'Abida, you are very westernized. How does a girl like you manage in

Jhang? I wondered about this when I visited your house there. You see I have an interest to know because I have sent my daughter, Pinky, to Harvard and Oxford and sometimes I wonder how she will manage after me in Larkana.'

'The value of a good education is that it teaches one to become not less but more adaptable, Prime Minister. I have no problem managing in Jhang. I belong there. I love the land and the people. I have broken with tradition in some ways and upheld it in other ways. It is a male-dominated society but women like me will prove that if women work hard enough, we can elevate ourselves to achieve and score.'

Bhutto Sahib then placed the cigar in the ashtray, arose, held his hand out towards me, shook my hand politely and in a congenial voice said: 'Abida, thank you for coming. I have enjoyed talking to you. I am going to take you with me to the Soviet Union. Nusrat cannot come, so Pinky will be accompanying me and I want her to get to know you.'

I felt quite elated as I walked down the grand stairway of the Government House and into my car.

Agha Shahi was Foreign Secretary and called me shortly thereafter to inform me that I would be accompanying the Prime Minister to the Soviet Union on a two-day visit to Moscow. He informed me that Moscow in November would be cold, hence I should travel with warm clothes. The Chief of Protocol, Colonel Ismail, was to provide me with further information. Around 1966, when my father was living, Agha Shahi had visited our house with Uncle Amjad Ali when we had held a Qawwali. I was hoping he would remember that event, now that I was a serious young representative.

The protocol office sent for my passport. Before marriage, my maiden name, Abida Hussain, was written on my passport. Just before my wedding, Father had asked me for my passport, saying that he would have to get my name changed since Fakhar and I would be travelling after our marriage. I wanted to retain my maiden name also. Hence, it was decided between my father, Fakhar, and me, that the new name on my passport and all other documents would be, 'Syeda Abida Hussain'.

Colonel Ismail was very tickled by my refusal to be referred to as 'Begum' and on my insistence that my name in the list of delegates should be as is written in my passport. Colonel Ismail was one of many Pakistani men I encountered in the workplace who found it awkward not to be able to call me 'Begum' or 'Mrs' and address me as 'Syeda', which is what I would invariably suggest they do, pointing out that in the Islamic tradition a woman always carried her father's name and that the marital status definition was a part of our colonial legacy. He was not helpful to me on issues of dress code either. I decided to ask Sadia Pirzada who was accompanying her husband Abdul Hafeez Pirzada as member of the delegation. She told me that we would be warmer and more comfortable in trouser suits, but the dress code requirement was our national dress, therefore we would have to manage in saris, shawls, and topcoats, and suffer frozen legs!

The list of delegates accompanying the Prime Minister included Hafeez and Sadia Pirzada, Rafi Raza, Raffay Fareedi, Yahya Bakhtiar, Mir Balakh Sher Mazari, Taj Langah, an MNA from Sheikhupura (I had not heard of him before or since), Mrs Khursheed Haidar, and Agha Shahi from the Foreign Office. And, of course, Zulfikar Ali Bhutto's daughter, Benazir Bhutto, who was to join us at Moscow airport where she was flying directly from England.

A few days later, with Prime Minister Zulfikar Ali Bhutto leading his delegation, we were airborne for Moscow. The Member Parliament from district Sheikhupura, a middle-aged and homely looking man was the only stranger for me in the delegation, with Sadia, Khursheed Haidar, and me being the only three women aboard the aircraft. The Prime Minister and his cabinet colleagues occupied the front half of the airplane, while the rest of us delegates along with the foreign office functionaries were in the rear half.

Colonel Ismail, while chatting with each of us, handed all the delegates a small booklet of instructions. He explained painstakingly to all of us that the limousine allocated to every delegate had a number, which was the number on the front of each booklet. We were to remember the number and sit only in the limo with the number allocated to us. Since Mir Balakh Sher Mazari and I were the two MPAs in the delegation, we were to share a limo; the MNA from Shiekhupura and Taj Langah, who was a member of the Central Executive Committee of the PPP were to share another limo, and the four of us would be lodged in the Rossiya Hotel, along with Foreign Office personnel, including Agha Shahi, Khurheed Haidar, and Raffay Fareedi. The Prime Minister and Benazir Bhutto, Sadia and Hafeez Pirzada, Rafi Raza, and Yahya Bakhtiar were to reside in the State Guest House. After a few hours of rest, the parliamentarians and the party official Langah, would call on the Supreme Soviet Committee in the Kremlin; return to the hotel; and an hour later be back at the Kremlin to attend the banquet that was to be hosted by Soviet Prime Minister Alexei Kosygin for the Pakistani Prime Minister Zulfikar Ali Bhutto.

'Tight schedule! Not much time to change saris! Maybe you should have brought your britches along!' said Colonel Ismail in his jokey style, addressing me. As a horseman he had seen me riding around at the Lahore Polo Ground through my childhood and my teens, but I was mortified at his remark, as the MNA and Taj Langah looked at me balefully. My being a horsewoman confirmed me as a 'feudal'. As our aircraft touched down at Moscow it was pouring with rain and sleet, it was windy and freezing cold. I had a fashionable, black cape over my silk, *ajrak* (a form of block print) printed sari, and my warmest shawl around my neck, but as I got down from the plane, the wind swept through my clothes. I tried to cover my head with my shawl in the manner Sadia had done, but it flew away. Some gentleman managed to catch it just in time, handing it to back me as we entered the airport building, where it was warm but crowded with humanity. I saw a tall young woman who I knew was Benazir Bhutto, and an equally tall middle-aged woman, the immaculately turned out spouse of our Ambassador in the Soviet Union at the time, Begum S. K. Dehlavi. In a somewhat dishevelled state, I was just beginning to get into a conversation with Mazhar Kazi, who had introduced himself. He was complimenting me on my *ajrak* sari, when the entire crowd started moving towards the exit of the reception area. As the limousines pulled up, there was a big scramble, with everyone trying to get out of the rain as fast as possible. I was trying to locate the number of my limo when Rafi Raza saw me, opened the door of his limo that he was sharing with Yahya Bakhtiar, and both gentleman urged me to hop into their vehicle to prevent me from catching a chill in the freezing rain.

'But what about my car?' and just then I saw Mir Balakh Sher Mazari, and waved out to him, while Rafi lowered his windshield to holler that Balakh Sher should follow our car. Even if

Balakh Sher had heard Rafi Raza, there was no way for him to communicate this to the chauffer and persuade him to change his direction. Rafi Raza assured me that they would get off at the State Guest House and then the chauffer would drop me off at my hotel, the Rossiya. I settled down to a convivial conversation with my car companions, who informed me that the Russians were demanding too high a price for the Pakistan Steel Mills project and that both of them were going to ensure that the legal contracts for the project be carefully worded to secure maximum advantage for Pakistan. We seemed to be driving out of the city and entering a forest. The cars pulled up in front of a large ornate villa. Alighting from the vehicle, Rafi was trying to remonstrate with the reluctant chauffer to take me to the Rossiya Hotel but this impassive looking fellow kept shaking his head when Prime Minister Bhutto turned around and called out to Rafi. I slithered myself down on the seat of the limo, terrified lest Premier Bhutto notice my 'not-required' presence. Rafi Raza swiftly went towards Bhutto and disappeared into the villa. I kept hoping that Rafi would return or request someone with clout from among our hosts to get me dropped at the hotel so that I could catch up with the rest of the delegates. But Rafi had obviously forgotten my existence and the clock was ticking. I looked woefully at the chauffer through the rearview mirror.

'Hotel Rossiya, Spasiba,' I pleaded to the chauffer, and forced myself to burst into tears. This resulted in due effect. He revved the car and sped me to the Rossiya. As I entered the hotel lobby, my colleagues were already assembled. This time I was in the designated limo with Mir Balakh Sher, and we drove to the Kremlin.

I had visited Moscow and Leningrad with my parents in the summer of 1964 and a decade later nothing had changed, hence I was able to, fairly efficiently, give Mir Balakh Sher a guided tour, remembering the River Neva, Gorky Prospect, St. Basil's Cathedral, and the Red Square. I remembered my father and felt the old familiar stab of pain. We walked through long corridors of a Stalin-era building, and were guided into a large reception room where we were seated. Taj Langah and Chaudhry Sahib, the MNA from Sheikhupura, started arguing vociferously, mercifully in Punjabi, as to who was leader of our four-member group. I pointed out that it was obvious that we were all leaders, Langah Sahib was the Party leader, Chaudhry Sahib was the National Assembly leader, Mir Sahib was the Provincial Assembly leader, and I would have to claim to be a woman leader. This drew a laugh from all and we entered the adjoining room to meet with four members of the Supreme Soviet: three men and one woman. It turned out that our guide was the interpreter, who spoke fluent English, Urdu, and even Punjabi. At the end of the stilted and formal conversation, punctuated by a series of smiles, we hit an awkward patch when we stood to toast friendship between 'the great people of the Soviet Union and the great people of Pakistan' holding up our glasses of tea when Chaudhry Sahib demanded vodka! I was aghast as was Mir Balakh Sher, but then we were the 'feudals', while Taj Langah had already announced himself and his vodka swivelling mate, Chaudhry Sahib, as the 'proletariat'.

Finally, I was in the room allotted to me at the Rossiya, which was a huge and hideous hotel. On my first visit to Moscow, my parents and I had stayed in the Ukraine, a grand old building, fraying at the edges but with large, spacious rooms. I thought of my father again and felt the old pain return. The pain of his loss had never really left me, it only embedded itself deeper inside me, and occasionally a remembrance would sharpen its edge. I pulled all the clothes out of my box and dumped them on one of the two beds, undecided on what to wear, as I retreated into the bathroom for a shower which was very shoddy. Grumbling to myself and wondering whether this was the downside of Communism or whether I was just unlucky in getting this room with a squalid bathroom, I dressed up as best as I could, concentrating on my eye make-up and draping myself in a gold sari.

When I entered the reception room to join the Prime Minister, and the rest of the delegates, Sadia Pirzada, looking ravishing, came up and led me towards Benazir, who was again dressed in black. She had a severe outbreak of acne, a thin fringe hiding her generous forehead, and a somewhat gaunt face, but she was magnificently tall and slender. We had barely exchanged greetings, when the ADC appeared by Benazir's side and led her to her father. The rest of us fell in line of protocol behind our Prime Minister and his daughter, as we walked down a stairway into a large and cavernous banquet hall that was an exquisite Byzantine chapel, now absorbed into the Kremlin, with beautiful brass candelabras illuminating the mosaic on the walls and ceiling, and an L-shaped banquet table arranged alongside the walls. The room was splendid and opulent, not quite communist in its appearance.

Prime Minister Kosygin and his daughter were seated in the centre of the table, but I could not see them because I was in the cusp of the L-shape, with a large Soviet gentleman to my left obstructing my view of the main table. Both Prime Ministers made lengthy speeches, that were heard in pin drop silence. When the speeches were over, dinner was served, and the room suddenly filled with the din of convivial chatter and laughter.

Air Marshal Nur Khan, who was now Chairman of PIA (Pakistan International Airlines), was sitting on my right. This was the first time that I was seeing him with our delegation, he explained that he had been in the cockpit most of the time on our flight to Moscow.

Nur Khan spoke of my father, recalling our lunch together with him when he was Governor of West Pakistan, just five years previous and said what a great loss my father's death had been for the country. My eyes brimmed with tears. One of the Russians seemed to have noticed this and handed me a tissue to dab my eyes. He started chatting with me in near perfect Urdu as well as English, informing me that in the Soviet School of Diplomacy it was mandatory to be fluent in at least three languages other than Russian, and before being promoted as director of any section, a fourth language added to the repertoire ensured promotion. He was a director and 'Hindustani' was the fourth language that he had sought to learn. I reminded him politely that the language was called 'Urdu', but he refuted my contention brusquely saying that the major language of Hindustan is more naturally referred to as 'Hindustani'.

It reminded me of an earlier moment, when visiting Moscow with my parents, Pakistan's Ambassador Salman Ali had invited us for dinner and had told us that when the U-2 aeroplane had flown out of the American airbase at Badaber, Peshawar, on 1 May 1960, he was summoned by the Soviet Head, Nikita Khruschev, who threatened that the next time an American spy-plane was caught over Soviet airspace, having flown out of Peshawar, he, Nikita, would ensure that Peshawar would go up in a smoke-cloud the size of Hiroshima! Monsieur le Directeur's struck me as being in the mould of their erstwhile Soviet leader Nikita. After dinner the

Prime Ministers began leaving, and everyone followed suit; I never did get to see Prime Minister Kosygin's daughter.

The following morning, I was required to arrive at the State Guest House to accompany Benazir Bhutto for a tightly scheduled round of activities. There was no hot water in the bathroom so I had to subject myself to a freezing cold shower, and decided to record a vociferous protest with Aunty Tahira and Uncle Mazhar upon my return. If Communism and proper plumbing were incompatible than how would Communism improve the quality of life in the Indian Subcontinent, I wondered, driving in the limousine from the Rossiya to the State Guest house.

I was shown into a sitting room by a svelte and cheery middle-aged woman who shook my hand warmly, helped me out of my topcoat, while she acknowledged me by my name and I presumed her to be our interpreter for the day. Begum Dehlavi was already seated and rose as we entered. I greeted her deferentially and told her that I knew her son Saeed who was by far the most gorgeous-looking young man in Pakistan. Begum Dehlavi smiled and the interpreter laughed. At this point Sadia Pirzada entered the room, kissed Begum Dehlavi, the interpreter, and me on both cheeks, and, with her usual warmth and effervescence, said, 'Pinky (Benazir) is obviously not ready. My husband was rushing me, fretting that I was late and everyone would be waiting.'

'Please be seated, ladies. Let us have some hot tea, while we wait for Miss Bhutto,' said the interpreter, ringing the bell and ordering tea. Another svelte-looking Russian woman who had responded to the bell, but did not quite look like a waitress, joined our circle.

Addressing the senior Russian lady, Sadia said, 'Your Excellency, you speak perfect English, so if you and Miss Bhutto will allow me, may I take our Embassy car with your interpreter shopping to GUM [main department store of the Soviet Union], while all of you visit the University and the Armoury Museum, both of which I saw along with my husband on our last visit to Moscow. I will join you for lunch.' I wondered why Sadia was addressing her as 'Excellency' and ascribed it to Sadia's usual effervescence. Miss Bhutto walked in, dressed in her long black outfit yet again.

'Sorry to keep you waiting, I hope not for too long,' she said, also addressing the senior interpreter, who told her that Sadia would be visiting GUM while we would be at the University and at the Museum, and we would regroup for lunch.

'Begum Dehlavi, would you like to accompany Begum Pirzada? I am sure you will be bored in our company,' said Benazir Bhutto, in a somewhat imperious tone, as we exited from the villa and walked up to the cars. Benazir Bhutto entered the long black Zil limousine, with the interpreter ushering me onto the seat beside her, while she sat herself opposite us in the sedan. I saw Sadia and Begum Dehlavi sit in the car behind ours, while the second interpreter popped into the front of our vehicle, and we set off with a pair of outriders on motorbikes piloting us and another couple of cars behind us. I felt very grand and said so, chattering and laughing with the interpreter, while Benazir Bhutto maintained a stony silence. Throughout our visit to the University and the Museum, I kept narrating anecdotes of my visit to Moscow with my parents as a tourist, making my companions constantly burst into laughter, with my humorous ancedotes.

'You are so amusing. I now understand why Mummy loves you,' said Benazir, her ice finally melting. As for the Russian woman, she laughed so much that she was wiping tears from her eyes when we pulled up at the big souvenir shop in the front end of the Rossiya. While I bought babushka dolls for Umku and Shugu, Benazir said she had no interest in buying any souvenirs, as her rooms at Oxford were already crammed with stuff.

'We have half an hour before lunch, according to the itinerary, so may I suggest that we go up to my room, where we can relax for a bit,' I offered. 'Why not, if you would like a rest?' said the interpreter, looking at Benazir Bhutto, who, I thought, nodded a little hesitantly. As we were approaching my room, I warned the ladies that they would have to overlook the untidiness. I also requested our interpreter to call the hotel staff and ask them how I could get my lavatory to work more efficiently and how I could obtain some hot water for a shower later in the evening. She asked if she could go into my bathroom to check. She addressed both issues by pushing two levers that I had not been able to handle!

While freshening up, we laughed and joked some more, and were soon back in the limo on our way to lunch. Benazir asked me what young men in Pakistan were like. I told her that there were not many who combined a good education with good looks, and there were certainly some who would gravitate around her when she returned home. She said she had not met anyone half-way decent at Harvard or Oxford, except a few weedy types who would not leave her alone.

'That is because you are the Prime Minister's daughter. When your father ceases to be PM, all the decent guys will be available, because you are well educated and attractive, but while he is in office, every scummy bloke will try to approach you. That is the price you pay, I am afraid, for being the daughter of the most important man in our country.' Although I said all this with affection and empathy, she seemed to have resented my statement and responded curtly.

'You are a member of my father's party and are daring to suggest he will no longer be Prime Minister.'

I said, 'Please do not misunderstand me, I am a huge fan of your father, and he will always remain a great leader but he cannot remain a Prime Minister always! My own father was a minister for a few years only, but he remained a leader until he died.'

Benazir lapsed into a stony silence and I wondered why. Fortunately nobody was privy to this conversation, because the interpreter had seated herself in the front of the car and kept up a steady stream of conversation in Russian with an audio contraption, while Benazir Bhutto and I had been speaking sotto voce.

At lunch, there were two large tables, with Benazir seated between Professor Gankovsky and our interpreter, while I was at the second table, with women members of the Supreme Soviet. Sadia, who joined us, asked me how our morning had been. I told her we had a jolly time, while she seemed to have enjoyed her shopping spree. After the late lunch, we adjourned to our respective lodgings and had got some time to rest before we proceeded to the dinner which our Prime Minister was hosting for the Soviet Prime Minister, in return hospitality.

We were assembled in a large, modern lounge that opened onto a vast dining hall, which was quite bare, and I was asking Khursheed Haidar and Agha Shahi why we had chosen this unattractive locale for our dinner, when both Prime Ministers walked in along with Benazir Bhutto and our friendly interpreter, quite dashingly dressed. Hafeez and Sadia followed, I asked Sadia if she had noticed the diamond solitaires our interpreter was wearing in her ears.

'Interpreter? Have you lost your mind, Chandi, that is Prime Minister Kosygin's daughter!'

'OH MY GOD! How could I have made such a huge mistake? But nobody introduced her to me, and she was so informal and friendly.' As I was whimpering to Sadia, Galena, for that I recall was her name, saw me, came up and hugged me affectionately.

'Excellency, I am so mortified. When we met this morning you did not mention that you were Prime Minister Kosygin's daughter. You were so warm and welcoming that in fact I wondered why Begum Pirzada addressed you so formally and Miss Bhutto did not let on either. I am truly ashamed of myself, please do forgive me,' I pleaded.

'Forgive you for what? Thank goodness you were relaxed and such good fun to be with. You made us laugh so much that I even told my father what a pleasant day I had with you, and I will remember it. Please call me Galena, for we are friends now.'

Her warmth and kindness touched me but my face continued to burn with embarrassment while the national anthems were played. We then entered the banquet hall. I was seated at the far end of the table next to Air Marshal Nur Khan again, who noticed my flushed face and enquired whether I was feeling alright. I confessed my blunder to him—he laughed and told me to not to dwell upon it. If the Russian lady was not offended, it did not really matter, he assured me.

As the dinner ended and we rose from the tables, our Prime Minister gestured towards me to step forward. As I went up to him Prime Minister Kosygin, who was standing beside him, enveloped me in a truly Russian-style bear hug, and addressing Bhutto, said,

'Excellency, you leave this pretty girl here to conquer Soviet hearts and cement the ties between our countries!'

'Excellency, representative Abida is here with us for her good work for our party and for our country and not for her good looks, so I would have to take her back to her work,' replied Prime Minister Bhutto, and although his words were kind and protective, he did not look pleased.

Seated in the aeroplane for our return journey, awaiting the boarding of our Prime Minister, I received a large and beautiful bouquet of orchids and lilies-of-the-valley with a card which read, 'From your friend Galena. I hope our paths will cross again.'

Rafi Raza and Agha Shahi came to chat with me when we were airborne and asked me about the bouquet and when I gave them a rundown of the previous day, they informed me that the PM was displeased. Since it had been an honest mistake on my part, I asked them why was the PM displeased.

'My dear girl, have you not understood that the Bhutto's do not appreciate anyone else getting attention?' said Agha Shahi, and I felt disappointed.

Oil prices had shot up in the world market which led to inflation, and when I was next in Jhang, I was taken aback when I heard most of my visitors complain about the high cost of living and everyone presumed that now that I had even travelled with Zulfikar Ali Bhutto, I could intercede with him to ensure that he take measures to protect the downtrodden who loved him dearly, against the vicissitude of rising prices. My enumerations of his achievements were beginning to fall on deaf ears and I felt perturbed. So when I was next in Lahore I went to call on Sheikh Rafiq, Speaker of the Punjab Assembly; Malik Meraj Khalid, who had been Chief Minister and I knew him to be a dear and humble person; Hanif Ramay, who had well honed oratorical skills; and Dr Mubashar Hassan who was the party ideologue with whom I felt most comfortable. I told them that people had begun to be critical of our government. While they seemed to have the same awareness, none of them encouraged me to air my opinions and all of them warned me that I could be misquoted and misrepresented, and if Bhutto heard that I was expressing any form of concern, he would not be pleased.

My aunts and uncles, cousins, Mother and even Fakhar were critical of the economy going downhill, and of Bhutto becoming intolerant. I thought that their criticism flowed from their resentment at losing some of their industrial enterprises which had been nationalized, but it bothered me that my friends, all liberals and progressives, had started taunting me about my 'autocratic' party leader.

By now it was early 1976. I had established myself as a political entity in the environment of my district. I still missed my father a great deal and talked about him frequently to Mother and to my people in Jhang, who would tell me that I had worked as tirelessly as my late father would work, and that I should prepare to contest the next election by popular mandate. So with my sights set on election year, I was increasingly spending more time in Jhang. Fakhar had quit his job at Dawood Hercules and was spending much of his time in Qatalpur and Multan to carve out a political place for himself, also with an eye to the next elections which he hoped to contest.

In early spring, I was contacted by the US Consul General at Lahore informing me that the US State Department ran a programme for young leaders worldwide whom they invited to acquaint them with life in the United States of America, and that he had recommended my name for this Overseas Visitors Programme. I was pleased to get the opportunity as I had only been to the US only once before, in 1964, with my mother, to visit Uncle Amjad Ali who was Pakistan's Permanent Representative at the time. We had spent ten days in New York and five days in Washington D.C. after which I had gone back to school in Europe, my interest in America somewhat kindled. And this State Department Programme offered a visit to five major cities so I opted for Boston, New York, Washington D.C., New Orleans, and San Francisco.

Arriving at Boston, I lodged with Kitty Galbraith whom I had met the year previous, courtesy of Begum Nusrat Bhutto when Kitty had visited Lahore and stayed at our house. Kitty drove me to Vermont to see their family home set in the Vermont woods, which, in the fall was incredibly beautiful. Her son, Peter, was teaching at a college nearby and his wife, Ann, had been Benazir Bhutto's roommate at Radcliffe. I went for an exhilarating ride in the woods with Ann who rode bareback, while I barely managed to hold onto my saddle.

Returning to Boston, I spent a couple of days in the Galbraith home on Francis Street, Cambridge, where I got into a heated argument with Hannah Pappaneck on our 'excesses' committed in East Pakistan and what was by now Bangladesh. Even though there was merit in what she said, I did not like hearing it from a foreigner, especially since her spouse Dr Gustav Pappaneck had set up the Five-Year Plans for Ayub Khan's government which had tilted the balance in favour of West Pakistan, according to the Bengalis. I also had a very challenging discussion with Professor John Kenneth Galbraith who kept emphasizing the inherent strengths of India while pointing out some of the weaknesses of Pakistan, suggesting it would be hard for us to catch up with India.

Arriving at Washington D.C., I stayed with our Ambassador Sahabzada Yaqub Khan and Tuba Begum who were good friends of my family. He gave me a detailed briefing on Kashmir as I had an appointment with Senator Sparkman, Chair of the Foreign Relations Committee.

Capitol Hill was awesomely impressive, but when I met Senator Sparkman, he gave no time beyond the pleasantries to hear me; instead he was hugely complimentary on my appearance, declaring that he would like to introduce me to his friends. Most unexpectedly, he led me onto the floor of the House where he introduced me as a young Representative from 'Italy, I mean Pakistan!', he said. I could not believe this was happening and only wished I had a camera to record the moment. Exiting out of the building, I shared an elevator ride with the handsome young Senator Edward Kennedy who said, 'Hi! Representative from Italy, I mean Pakistan.' And we both laughed.

New Orleans did not make as exciting an impression as anticipated, but for my visit to a sugar plantation, which was introduction to corporate agriculture in the U.S. However, San Francisco bowled me over and I now understood why Fakhar was so enamoured of this city. Returning home a month later, I had to confess that my anti-imperialism had been somewhat watered down.

Three months later, Begum Bhutto called me to a meeting at the Government House, Lahore. It was late spring and the lawns of the Governor's residence were interspersed by glorious flower-beds of bright pink petunias and tall white gladioli. I was shown into a lovely sitting room with bay windows, directly below the one in which I had chatted with her husband just a few months ago. All the prominent women workers of the PPP were present. Begum Bhutto yawned and said that this weather always made her sleepy. I stifled my own yawn in empathy and tried to concentrate on the proceedings. Begum Bhutto informed us that as Chair of the 'Shoba Khawateen', the women's wing of the party, she had decided to get party elections conducted, setting a precedent thereby for elections in the party as a whole. Since next year was to be election year, the party needed to be geared up for the contest. I raised a question regarding the danger of all the disputes within the party engulfing the election of the women's wing, but half a dozen voices asserted that there was no danger of this and everyone seemed to be struggling to please the 'First Lady'. I was assigned the task of being in charge of the polling of women workers of Sargodha division, which comprised of districts Mianwalli, Sargodha, Lyallpur (Faisalabad), and Jhang. Polling was to be conducted at the District Council Hall at Lyallpur. Nargis Naeem, MNA, was given the responsibility to ensure mobilization of the women from all four districts to Lyallpur.

Arriving at the District Council Hall of Lyallpur, which is a magnificent colonial building, on the due day, I was instantly plunged into chaos and pandemonium. Thousands of women, most of them dragging a squalling brat or two with them, tried to mob me. They were all complaining and some were cursing.

'Where is our *roti, kapra, aur makaan* (food, clothing, and shelter)? We want jobs for our brothers and sons! This inflation is killing us!' was the common refrain. Nargis Naeem had become totally hoarse trying to persuade the women to line up in a queue. Finally, when some order was restored, I shouted through a microphone that PPP workers must not be disloyal to their Quaid-i-Awaam, who had taken factories from the wealthy, so that more jobs could be generated. He had taken more than two million acres from rich landowners like myself and distributed this land among more than two hundred thousand tillers. He had given everyone ownership of the land on which village homes were built, and had broken the powers of the rich landowner. He had taken over schools making education free for children of poor folk, and he had regularized wages for teachers. He had made medicines cheap by introducing generic formulae. He had brought all the rulers of the Muslim world together under one roof. He had given Pakistan a Constitution which made every Pakistani equal, men and women, in the eyes of the law, and he had brought ninety thousand prisoners back from India. Were these achievements not enough in four years? I asked. But my question was answered by incoherent replies. The votes were finally cast and counted. Conveying the results to Begum Bhutto's office, and having written a detailed report which I sought to hand over personally, I asked to see her.

She summoned me to Rawalpindi. I made a clean breast of whatever I had seen and heard from party workers, which made Begum Bhutto sigh and look the other way while she gave me the following response. 'Chandi, you are a nice girl and I would normally believe whatever you say, but everyone else has reported that the elections went off well and that the workers are happy with the party and the leadership. And even the Intelligence reports confirm this view. Anyway, thank you for taking all this trouble, and now run along—Begum Kulsum Saifullah is coming to call on me.'

All this rankled with me so I went back to Dr Mubashar. 'Why can you not understand, Abida, that this is the reactionaries and the rightists hitting back with their propaganda? The rise in oil prices has nothing to do with us. We have to deal with the consequences, and the rise in prices plays into the hands of those for whom we are a threat, because we are a force for change. The Establishment, which is the civil and military bureaucracy, seeks status quo and are resistant to change. My only worry is that our party Chairman is playing into the hands of the Intelligence agencies and they are never to be trusted.'

In late spring, I discovered I was pregnant again. I had finally shed the weight that had accumulated with my earlier pregnancies and was tired at the thought of becoming fat again. Mother was thrilled. 'Baji, what if I produce a third little girl?'

She replied, 'My Allah is Just. He took away my Abid from me. I have not wronged Him. He will place a baby boy in my arms so that I can hear the name "Abid" around me again. Have faith Chando.' I knew that my mother was pious and pure hearted and I tried to keep my faith strong along with hers.

However, before I started ballooning, there was an invite for me from the Prime Minister for a banquet that he was hosting at the Governor's House at Lahore for Dr Henry Kissinger and his wife Nancy. The newspapers had been full of Bhutto seeking to purchase a reprocessing plant from France. The French had taken the down payment for the plant from Pakistan. Bhutto had announced that after India had tested its atomic capability in 1974, it was clear that India was in pursuit of building a nuclear bomb, and since Pakistan's plea on this score had been ignored by the nuclearized nations of the world, Pakistan had the right to seek to protect itself. Our newspapers were speculating that Secretary of State Kissinger was coming on behalf of the US to persuade Bhutto not to pursue the acquisition from the French. I thought that since France was one of the five nuclearized nations of the world, it was ridiculous that the Americans should seek to persuade us, when they could not persuade the French not to make the sale. I was confident that Bhutto would be able to handle Henry Kissinger deftly.

We had an early monsoon that year. It poured and poured with rain. My friend Shahid Hamid was Director General, Lahore Development Authority. He told me that the office of the Prime Minister had ordered him to widen and carpet the road between the airport and the Governor House, but he was more concerned about the roof of the Governor House which had a tendency to leak when it rained heavily. Thanks to this warning, I did not make an elaborate chignon with my hair, and stuffed a scarf into my evening bag. I was looking forward to meeting Benazir again, who I was told would be present at the banquet. We had been assembled for well over an hour in the reception rooms, while our Prime Minister, his family, and the Kissingers remained with each other in a separate salon. Finally, we were told to take our seats at the banquet tables in the Darbar Hall and the Bhuttos and the Kissingers walked down the beautiful teak stairway that descends directly into the hall from the minstrel's gallery. National anthems of both countries were played by the band perched on the opposite side of the gallery, while all eyes were on the tall and willowy Nancy and the equally tall and willowy Benazir, who looked so much better in the gold dress she was wearing here at Lahore than the black she had worn in Moscow.

I was at quite a distance from the head of the table, tried to catch Benazir's eye but got no acknowledgement, though I did get a smile from Begum Bhutto. I was seated between General Raza, who was now the Chief of Protocol, and General Imtiaz Warraich who was the military secretary to the Prime Minister.

As soup was being served, raindrops started plonking into the soup dishes and onto our heads. When I asked the generals on either side of me whether the roof had been mended to protect us from the downpour outside, they assured me it had, particularly around the area above the main table, but the rest of us would get a little wet, they informed me cheerfully.

Bhutto stood up to speak. Addressing Dr Kissinger he made an extraordinary speech. He mentioned the tomb of the Sufi Saint that lay buried under the smaller dining room adjacent to this banquet hall, implying that Punjab, which was the largest and most populous province of our country, was the land of Sufis and Saints who preached the message of peace and love. It was for this message that they were revered and their tombs were never obliterated. Punjab, he said, was the land of love and love legends, and its people made love to their rivers and to each other. In this land of peace, nobody could doubt that the peace of the region would ever be disturbed, but if the enemies of this land were armed with lethal weapons, then these people would seek protection through reprocessing or any other means. Dr Kissinger responded in a gruff and heavily accented voice, warning that some means of seeking protection could prove dangerous for Pakistan, and we could be made into a horrible example.

Deeper into the summer, vacationing in Murree with Baji, Fakhar, Umku, and Shugu, walking, playing 'Scrabble', chatting with my cousins and Aunty Vicki, who was often with us, and eating to my heart's content, I started piling on weight again. Aunty Vicki or Begum Viqarunissa Noon, as she was widely known to be, always told my mother that she would have to share me with her as her surrogate daughter. Vicki was a colonial remnant, tuned into the power structures of Karachi–Lahore– Rawalpindi–Islamabad, and my mentor. Mother and she were good friends and she had been extremely considerate and affectionate to my mother when she lost my father. Although, Mother and Aunty Vicki were poles apart in many ways: Mother being naive and philosophical while Aunty Vicki was shrewd and practical, but both women had force of character. Vicki tried to teach me the ropes with regard to the 'who's who' of the civil and military bureaucracies and expected me to teach her how to paint her eyes and how to use contemporary cosmetics. I thought it was a fair exchange. Aunty Vicki did not like Zulfikar Ali Bhutto and was convinced that the Kissinger visit was heralding his downfall. She was not proven wrong. I would argue with her that Bhutto had emerged as the voice of the Muslim World and would make us into a nuclear power and she would counter argue that he would not get away with it. While Mother focused on his arrogance and Fakhar on his economic mismanagement, I would stand up for him, but some of the criticism made would impress the point home even with me, and sometimes while mounting counter arguments I would sound somewhat garbled, even to myself. What I found impossible to defend was the alleged 'Hyderabad Conspiracy Case' and the subsequent military action ordered in Balochistan.

Khan Abdul Wali Khan, as the Leader of the Opposition in the National Assembly, along with his Baloch colleague, Mir Ghaus Bux Bizenjo were skilled orators and men of substance, the natural alternative leadership to that of the Pakistan Peoples Party. They were critical of Zulfikar Ali Bhutto, and were penalized for their criticism by being dubbed as traitors, accused of smuggling arms from Iraq to Balochistan to support the creation of an independent Balochistan. The charge did not quite convince, but it became a cause of action for the dismissal of Sardar Ataullah Mengal as Chief Minister of Balochistan. The very people who had facilitated

Z. A. Bhutto's passage of the Constitution in 1973, were declared 'traitors' in 1976 and put on trial, incarcerated in a Hyderabad jail, accused of perpetrating an 'insurgency' in Balochistan and conspiring to dismember Pakistan. The conspiracy was, in fact, against Bhutto. The 'Hyderabad Conspiracy Case' as it came to be known, turned out to be the beginning of the end for Bhutto. The intelligence agencies had convinced Bhutto that the Leader of the Opposition in the National Assembly, Khan Abdul Wali Khan, and his National Awami Party (NAP) members were traitors and ought to be tried under Article 6 of the Constitution that they themselves had voted in, a mere three years ago. For a man of Bhutto's intellectual calibre not to spot the trap laid for him was nothing short of the tragic. And he seemed to have isolated himself, with two police officers serving as his only eyes and ears, namely, Saeed Ahmed Khan and Masood Mahmood, the latter having created the Federal Security Force (FSF), which allegedly became an instrument to terrorize dissidents and opponents. Many ugly stories were circulated regarding the oppressive measures taken by the FSF by force; most of them may well have been grossly exaggerated. But it was the incarceration of his opponents that many of Bhutto's most ardent admirers found difficult to defend.

Pre-Partition: Muslim League Assembly Party, Legislative Assembly of India, 1946. Seated, 4th from left, Quaid-i-Azam. Standing, 1st row, 5th from left, Syed Abid Hussain Shah.

Muslim Students League, Govt. College, Lahore. Quaid-i-Azam with Syed Abid Hussain seated to his left and Syed Innayat Ali to his right (1938).

Independence Day Dinner 14th Aug. 1947. Quaid-i-Azam Mohd. Ali Jinnah, Lady Edwina Mountbatten next to him, and Lord Louis Mountbatten shaking hands with Member Constituent Assembly Syed Abid Hussain Shah.

Abida Hussain, 'Chandi's' 6th birthday, attended by Mohtarma Fatima Jinnah at Lahore, 1952. Next to Chandi is her mother, 'Baji', Begum Kishwar Abid Hussain.

Dinner hosted by Maulana Abul Kalam Azad for Syed Abid Hussain Shah in Dehli 1954. Left side, Syed Abid Hussain Shah, Minister for Education, next to Jawaharlal Nehru, with Aliya and Mohd Ali Bogra next to him, and Naheed Iskander Mirza and Raja Ghazanfar Ali Khan, H.C. for Pakistan at Dehli.

Cabinet of Central Government of Pakistan, 1954. H.S. Suhrawardy with Syed Abid Hussain Shah beside him. Gen. Ayub Khan and Gen. Iskander Mirza seated at the far end, with Mohd. Ali Bogra at right end.

Premier Chou en Lai of the People's Republic of China on his first visit to Pakistan, Lahore 1956. Minister-in-Waiting Syed Abid Hussain Shah's ten-year-old daughter Chandi presents Premier Chou en Lai a bunch of roses.

Syeda Abida Hussain having received the Quaid-i-Azam Gold Cup from Mohtarma Fatima Jinnah after the victory of her filly 'Montreux'. Jockey Arif Rasheed and Habib Ibrahim Rahimtoola Chairman Karachi Race Club are also in the picture.

4

Upheaval

My son Abid was born on 9 December 1976. Two nights before his birth I was fretful because of having overshot my date of delivery. Sleep eluded me till the early hours of the morning. Finally dropping off to sleep, I had an extremely vivid dream. I saw Zulfikar Ali Bhutto with a noose around his neck, hanging from the mango tree in the front garden of our house in Lahore. A group of soldiers holding bayonets were looking up at him. I woke up with a start, roused Fakhar, and narrated my dream to him. He looked incredulous, and went back to sleep. Getting out of bed, I went to Mother's room and lay down beside her on her bed. She was awake.

'What is it, Chando?' she asked me gently, stroking my hair. When I narrated my dream to her, she forbade me to mention it to anyone. 'You will endanger yourself if you do. Bhutto is in danger and he has become dangerous. Masood Mahmood and his organization are said to be out of control. Please be careful and do not talk too much. Forget your dream, take a hot bath, you will be going into labour shortly.'

Abid's arrival in the world brought much rejoicing to our house. Everyone we knew came or called to congratulate us and Mother. And a few days later, the Assemblies were dissolved and fresh elections were fixed for March of 1977. Umku and Shugu were suddenly insecure and visibly jealous of the new arrival. I spent a lot of time assuring them that I loved them dearly. They kept asking me if similar celebrations were held when they were born! Both the girls were school-going by now. We had decided to send them to the Lahore American School which had the nicest Kindergarten and I also wanted that my children should acquire co-educational schooling with a strong science base.

The girls had their Christmas break from school and when Abid was two weeks old, all of us drove down to Shah Jewna, so that my mother could finally take a son and heir to my father's resting place.

Meanwhile, I threw myself into hectic political activity, networking with all the people who were well disposed towards me. Jhang District now had five National Assembly constituencies, one of which was where Ghulam Haider Bharwana would be contesting from. I wanted to contest against him and thought it would be prudent to convey to my cousin Zulfiqar Bokhari who had recently announced that he was joining PPP. He could contest from N.A. 69, which included Shah Jewna, while I would contest from N.A. 67 opposing Haider Bharwana, and if my cousin Iftikhar Bokhari wished to contest a provincial constituency along with his brother, I would not need to be in conflict with my cousins in an electoral fight. This would be hurtful to my mother as well as their mother. The Bokhari side of my cousins were not too keen on my pursuit of politics, but their sister, Zarina, who was called 'Bia', was very close to my mother. She agreed that if we did not come into direct confrontation with each other, it would be ever so much better for the image of the Shah Jewna clan. So I wrote a letter to Zulfikar Ali Bhutto, Chairman of the Pakistan Peoples Party (PPP) seeking the party nomination from N.A. 67, Jhang 2. I mentioned in my letter that I had worked extremely hard and reached out to large numbers of voters in this area and was confidant that I would carry the constituency successfully for PPP.

It quite honestly never occurred to me that Bhutto, the modernist, could possibly have a gender bias and would toss my papers aside on the grounds that I was a woman! Therefore it came as a profound shock to me when the PPP nominations were announced and my name did not feature at all on the list. Instead the virtually unlettered Haider Bharwana was awarded the nomination from N.A. 67, while my cousin Zulfiqar Bokhari was to be PPP candidate from N.A. 68. And to compound the mess, N.A. 69 was awarded to Faisal Saleh Hayat, the twenty-four-year-old son of my kinsman, Mohammed Ghous, who had been one of my relentlessly difficult relatives, with Iftikhar Bokhari as his running mate in the province. Nobody had ever seen Faisal Hayat in Jhang. His mother had been estranged from his father for years and lived in Lahore with her three children, none of whom had any particular scholastic achievements to their credit. So how did an under-age candidate suddenly feature in the list of the PPP? It transpired that Faisal Saleh Hayat's mother's younger sister's husband, a Punjabi civil servant who she was very close to, was posted as Commissioner Larkana—Bhutto's home district—and had endeared himself to the Prime Minister by keeping Bhutto's 'talented' cousin Mumtaz Ali Bhutto in restraint. Without doubt, it was at his sister-in-law's behest that the Commissioner put in the application of Faisal Saleh Hayat, neglecting to mention that Hayat was under-age. The law required that candidates for the Legislature had to be twenty-five years of age in order to seek election. But obviously, the Commissioner appeared to have little patience for the law. Not only did he manage to get the PPP nomination for Faisal Saleh Hayat in Jhang, he also obtained a provincial constituency in Lyallpur (Faisalabad) district for his brother, Javed Kharal, much to the consternation of PPP workers of that locality. For added measure, he deeply obligated his sister-in-law by managing to connive, it was rumoured, with a compliant district administration in Jhang in obtaining a false birth certificate for young Faisal, in which the year of his birth was written a year previous to the actual year of his birth.

When the matter was brought to Bhutto's notice, I got a call from the Secretary to the Prime Minister, who told me that the Prime Minister had ordered that I file my papers as covering candidate for Faisal Saleh Hayat. I told him that I would only do so on the condition that I be then allowed to contest the elections if I am able to prove through documentary evidence that the ticket holder of the party was under-age. He said that he would convey my message to the Prime Minister. I rushed to Lahore, went to Aitchison College where I knew Faisal Saleh Hayat had been a student, and obtained from the Principal, the Aitchison College Year Book, which indicated that Faisal Saleh Hayat was born in 1953, and was therefore twenty-four years old in 1977. I filed my papers before the Assistant Commissioner, who was the Returning Officer, but on the day of the scrutiny of papers, the Assistant Commissioner, Jhang gave more weightage to what appeared to be a bogus birth certificate and passed Faisal Saleh Hayat's papers. Appalled and disgusted, I withdrew my papers and left for Lahore, having been politically marginalized by my party; my five years of struggle having come to naught.

Mother tried to console me as did Fakhar, in whose constituency the PPP nomination for Kabirwala in District Multan, had gone to Iqbal Haraj, an unlettered landowner. The political landscape was changing rapidly. All the political parties in opposition to the

PPP had galvanized themselves into an alliance called the Pakistan National Alliance or PNA. The PNA was led by nine party leaders who were given the appellation in the media of 'Nine Stars', which included Begum Nasim Wali Khan, wife of Khan Abdul Wali Khan, who was languishing in jail in Hyderabad. Nasim Bibi was in her forties, an exceedingly handsome Pushtun woman, very traditional, draped always in a white cotton chaddar, and with a gift for oratory. When the National Awami Party (NAP) was banned, on behalf of its incarcerated leadership, Nasim Bibi had persuaded Sardar Sherbaz Mazari, who had been elected as an Independent candidate to the outgoing National Assembly, to lead the regrouped NAP workers under the platform of a new party named the National Democratic Party (NDP). Sardar Sherbaz Mazari was the younger brother of Mir Balakh Sher Mazari who had been my colleague in the outgoing Punjab Assembly. Sardar Sherbaz had been a classmate of my cousin Zulfiqar Bokhari at the Aitchison College in Lahore and also of my cousin Asad Ali, popularly known as 'Sheru', Uncle Amjad Ali's eldest son. Way back in 1960, Sardar Sherbaz had visited Shah Jewna accompanied by his wife Surraya and his two little boys Sher Azam and Shehryar. My father had taken a great liking to Sardar Sherbaz and whenever my parents and I visited Karachi, we would always have a meal with the Mazaris. So when the PNA bandwagon rolled into Lahore, in the early leg of the election campaign, the NDP leaders visited with us and told us that they would be addressing a rally in Gol Bagh the following day. Nasim Bibi had been drawing crowds already.

Aunty Tahira Mazhar Ali, Mother, some friends, and I decided to go to Gol Bagh to hear Nasim Bibi speak, and also to get a sense of what the PNA was about, since the alliance was a mix of progressives and reactionaries. A multitude of humanity was thronging the Gol Bagh venue and our car could not proceed beyond the Zamzama Square. Most people were walking there, while some were on bicycles. There were not too many cars. The turnout of women was poor. This was a lower middle class crowd, the kind of crowd that I would have expected to see at a PPP rally. So what was going on? I asked my friends. They thought this was the result of Bhutto having turned authoritarian, for having had too much reliance on the bureaucracy and the police, and for having promised more than he could deliver. But above all, for having treated his political opponents unfairly, as my mother opined.

We managed to walk into the compound of the Town Hall, with Aunty Tahira as a veteran political worker leading the way. The stage on which the 'Nine Stars' were seated was far away from where we were. All we could see beyond was the enormous crowd, but we heard all the speeches quite clearly through the public address system, with one loudspeaker mounted on a pole quite close to where we stood. I had very mixed feelings listening to one speaker after another, with all of them lashing out at Bhutto, who I still somewhat admired. And then Begum Nasim Wali Khan's name was announced and she came to the centre stage to speak. Her voice rang out and the words flowed mellifluously from her throat. She spoke of the tolerance required for the establishing of a democratic order. She spoke of the rights of the smaller provinces and of the need to rein in the chauvinism which was the legacy of military rulers. She spoke of the importance of social justice, equity and the Rule of Law. She did not sound personal or rancorous. She did not mention the detention of her husband or the ban imposed on their party. She spoke with passion and her language was eloquent and graceful. Hearing her speak, I felt as though I had a calling to follow perhaps a woman leader, who would not undermine my gender or question my ability to be as competent as a man. The consensus among my friends was that they had not heard a better speech. And as Nasim Bibi wound up, a youthful voice raised slogans for the 'plough', the electoral symbol of PNA. The crowds were shouting: 'This plough of ours will win the day! For the sake of the Prophet, it will win the day! For the sake of the Caliph Ali, it will win the day! For the sake of the Martyrs it will win the day!' The rhythm of the slogans, with their distinctly Shia flavour, sent tingles down my spine. By the time we left the rally and were walking towards our car, which was parked well over a mile away, my friends and I were chanting the 'plough' slogan. Such is the power of crowd chemistry. The crowd in Gol Bagh had radiated strong chemistry.

The PNA campaign went on gaining momentum and political commentators started asserting that although the PPP would win the election, Z. A. Bhutto was not going to have the walkover which everyone had earlier expected. I followed the campaign through the newspapers since Pakistan Television (PTV) showed only the rallies of the PPP candidates. But it was more by word of mouth that we heard about the growing cavalcades of the PNA and the decline of the PPP. I continued to have mixed feelings and dreaded having to return to Jhang with no role to play in the elections. But it was my father's sixth death anniversary on the third of March and my mother and I planned to be in Jhang from the first.

Polling day had been scheduled for 7 March 1977. When we arrived in Jhang, with the children in tow, mother decided to carry on to Shah Jewna with Umku, Shugu, and baby Abid, while my plan was to stay overnight in Jhang in order to keep myself informed on the local atmosphere of the elections from my stalwarts.

Fateh Khan Patoana told me that Jamal Khan Baloch, the progressive lawyer who prided himself on being a Socialist, and who was one of my frequent visitors at the Shah Jewna House, and Mai Sooban's nemesis, had a son, Zaffar Jamal, who had been head of the Jamiat-e-Tulaba, the student wing of the Jamaat-i-Islami, a case of deep ideological differences between a father and a son. Zaffar Jamal had been fielded by the PNA against Faisal Saleh Hayat. Both candidates were young and unknown in the area, but the house which had been bought, from a local resident in the Civil Lines area, around the corner from the Shah Jewna House, for Faisal Saleh Hayat's mother, was rumoured to have a direct telephone connection to the Commissioner, Larkana. It was believed that the Commissioner would call the superintendent of Police at Jhang every morning from Larkana, urging him to mobilize the police in N.A. 69, and instructing them to round up people and threaten them that if they did not vote for Faisal Saleh Hayat, they would be in trouble. Fateh Khan thought that this was a shame because no member of the Shah Jewna clan had ever solicited votes through government employees before, and this unhealthy practice had been introduced by Faisal Saleh Hayat's uncle, because he was the son of a low-ranking police functionary himself. This information was a surprise for me. My kinsman Mohammed Ghous's brother-in-law was the son of an SHO! This appeared to be an effective model of social mobility.

'And is Zaffar Jamal not protesting?' I asked.

'Of course he is but the district administration is turning a deaf ear,' said Fateh Khan, adding, 'Your cousin Zulfiqar is not involving the police, so he may need your help, and I would suggest you stay neutral since the PNA has fielded Nawab Iftikhar Ahmed Ansari, your father's good friend and erstwhile running mate.'

Fateh Khan's warning was timely. I received a phone call from Mumtaz Ali Bhutto, the Prime Minister's 'talented cousin' informing me that he was in Jhang and would like to call on me. I told him he was welcome; he arrived within minutes, driving in from Bokhari House, the residence of my cousins, which was just down the road. Mumtaz Ali Bhutto was probably a dozen years older than me, a smooth talker with something of a reputation.

'Why are you not helping your cousin Zulfi in the election?' he asked me, as I poured the tea. I replied:

> Well, I had applied for a party nomination from N.A. 67, but you gave that nomination to Haider Bharwana, an uneducated boor. And in N.A. 69 I was told to file my papers as a covering candidate to Faisal Saleh Hayat who is under-age, and then I withdrew my papers, because his were unlawfully upheld, and now he has the SHOs commandeering votes for him, I am told. What kind of an election is this? Why are you gentlemen so desperate to win? Even if you were to fail in winning a majority, the PNA is a disparate alliance and bound to fall apart. So you would be in Opposition only for a very short while, after which you could team up with two of the relatively progressive parties in this alliance and form a coalition government. Anyway, disappointed with my party, for which I had been working so hard these past five years, I had retreated to Lahore, because of not having any role in this election. The only reason for my return is because on the third is my fathers *barsi* (death anniversary).

Mumtaz Ali Bhutto seemed to have heard me out carefully. However I was taken aback by his response. 'My cousin [Zulfikar Ali Bhutto], and our party leader has done some things which will catch up with him the moment he relinquishes his hold on power. So he cannot afford to lose power even for a day.' And I sensed that Mumtaz Bhutto, who appeared to be quite bright, was referring to Bhutto's directives of carrying out the military action in Balochistan when Mumtaz spoke of 'some things'.

When I arrived at Shah Jewna, Aunt Surraya, Mother's eldest sister, was there with her. As anticipated, Mother and I were both very conflicted. We could not refuse her if she asked for help for her sons, which she was clearly going to, and we would be embarrassed vis-á-vis Nawab Iftikhar, who had stood by us after my father's death, if we moved against him. Politics, I was beginning to discover, was all too often a game of exceedingly difficult choices.

On 7 March 1977, the polls were swept away by Pakistan Peoples Party (PPP). A great roar of '*Dhandli*' (cheating) rose up from the PNA the following day. The allegation was that the polls had been rigged, and the PNA announced a boycott of the provincial polls which were held on 10 March. My mother and I returned to Lahore to take Umku and Shugu back to school, and as we entered Lahore, we found that traffic was being diverted from Shahdara because the PNA had taken to the streets and a mammoth rally was proceeding from the Data Darbar towards Mall Road. The atmosphere was thick with smoke and the smell of burning tyres. The children were terrified and baby Abid would not stop howling. After we had entered the city, it took us well over an hour to reach home.

Mother thought that Bhutto could salvage himself and the situation if he were to announce re-polling. But I had made the tough decision to resign from the PPP. Bhutto was going down and my instinct for survival was dictated by the emerging steely side of my character. I wrote a letter to Bhutto, conveying to him my decision, mentioning my disappointment at having been overlooked despite my selfless work for the party, and stating that perpetrating illegality by including an under-age candidate to favour a dishonest bureaucrat was a denial of what I had thought the PPP stood for. Travelling to Islamabad, I visited Yusuf Buch, who was Bhutto's Special Assistant and a family friend, and requested him to hand over my letter to Bhutto.

When I returned to Lahore the next day, Bhutto telephoned me, telling me that he had kept a seat reserved for women open for me. Expressing my regret, my response was emotional. I told him that it was humiliating, given that I had been running around for years, gearing up to deal with a popular mandate, and had no interest in a seat reserved for women. 'You broke my heart, Sir,' I blabbered. Always acute in his articulation, Bhutto responded, 'You think that I am going to lose power, Abida, but I am not going to lose power. It will be alright. This hullabaloo will die down. You wait and see.' I was sorry that he opted to ignore the hurt and embarrassment that had been caused. Had he acknowledged it, I may have found it difficult to refuse him.

The National Assembly was summoned. Z. A. Bhutto took oath as Prime Minister and swore in a new Cabinet. For a few days, it looked as though things would settle down, but the demonstrations continued, and the turning point came when the Punjab Assembly was summoned and the police were rough and high-handed with women demonstrators.

Begum Nasim Wali Khan was in Lahore and came to stay with us. Her NDP workers and office bearers were in and out of the house, and I would chat with them and they would urge me to join their party. The PPP seemed to have gone on the wrong side of the people. The NDP was a small party flowing from a legacy of nationalist and progressive politics, with strong roots in Frontier and Balochistan but little known in the Punjab. Nasim Bibi had great popular appeal, and if she were to tour the districts of the Punjab, it would gain popularity and I would contribute to its growth and development. I was tempted at the thought of playing a creative and normative role, but was undecided. However the brutality perpetrated at Charing Cross with professional women, allegedly from the red light area of Lahore armed with batons and bricks attacking a women's demonstration outside the Punjab Assembly, contributed in making up my mind, my mother, funnily enough, expressed her reservations. Mother's political opinions always carried weight for me.

I said to her: 'Baji, you have always admired the Red Shirts, what are your reservations now?'

'You are interested in electoral politics and Punjabis are very often close-minded. Some newspapers have for so long projected Abdul Ghaffar Khan and his family as "traitors" that I do not know if they will ever be able to win seats in the Punjab. Besides, I had my reservations about Bhutto, but he seems now to be victim of the same bureaucracies that nurtured him earlier. You cannot help him but perhaps you should not disassociate from his Party at this juncture.' My mother had a soft heart and was extremely principled, which is what had clearly endeared her so deeply to my father that he defied all convention and honoured her as though she were mother of the sons she had failed to bear. I asked Begum Wali Khan how she saw events unfold.

'Bhutto will have to talk to us, i.e. the PNA. And we will demand a fresh election, under a neutral administration. He may score a majority in a free and fair election, but he will face a strong Opposition in the next Assembly and he is certain to lose in Frontier and Balochistan. We are meeting today, all the PNA leaders, in the home of Chaudhry Zahoor Illahi, round the corner from your house. Would you like to accompany me and hear it all for yourself? Baji, would you mind my taking Chandi Bibi with me to our meeting?' Mother said it was up to me and I was dying to go. Zahoor Illahi came from humble origins. He would seek to always extend great courtesy to all prominent post-Independence Punjab politicians, including my father, becoming a facilitator and message carrier for them all. He latched onto Ayub Khan by asserting himself in the 'Convention' Muslim League, but fell afoul of Nawab Kalabagh, as well as of Bhutto, who would lampoon him and ridicule him.

Chaudhry Zahoor Illahi was extremely courteous to me when I entered his house accompanying Sardar Sherbaz Mazari and Nasim Bibi. I was introduced to Prof Ghafoor, Chaudhry Ashraf of the Khaksar Tehrik and Maulana Mufti Mahmud. Nawabzada Nasrullah Khan patted me on the head and Malik Wazir Ali representing Air Marshal Asghar Khan, exchanged pleasantries. I was the only young person in the room, and felt privileged to be in the company of so many leaders. Then Pir Pagaro walked in, along with Makhdumzada Hassan Mahmood, who hugged me and said, 'Abida is going to join my Party.' At this Professor Ghafoor pointed out that the constituency I was interested in was in the quota of the Jamaat-i-Islami.

'We will swap it with you,' said Uncle Hassan Mahmood. 'We will give you any constituency of your choice in our quota in the Punjab, except mine, of course.'

'But yours is the one we want!' came the retort from the kindly-looking Professor; after this healthy banter, everyone started settling down to the proceedings. When we returned home, Sardar Sherbaz Mazari suggested gently that the NDP (National Democratic Party) could swap a seat in their tiny Punjab quota which was in Okara where the Jamaat-i-Islami probably had a stronger candidate, with my constituency in Jhang, if I wanted to contest election from the platform of the NDP.

'Chandi Bibi, I do not doubt that you will win the constituency because of the great goodwill your father left behind and because of your courage in seeking to maintain his legacy. I have seen how hard you work and how many people from Jhang visit your home on a daily basis and how helpful you are to them. So think about contesting on our party ticket.'

'Sardar Sahib, I would never have walked away from the PPP if they had not discarded me because of my gender and in denial of their own manifesto. But if your offer is serious, let me think about it. It seems to me that it is becoming difficult for Bhutto to survive. Although I am essentially a Bhutto admirer and have worked hard for people in my district, my feet are not as yet planted firmly enough in the political reality of Jhang for my detractors not to obliterate me if I make any major miscalculation at this stage. What attracts me to your party is that your agenda is liberal and progressive as PPPs, and Nasim Bibi's presence ensures that your party would not carry any gender bias. So I thank you profoundly for offering me an appealing alternative to think about.' Sherbaz Mazari was like an elder brother, so I thought I could be totally frank with him.

Events hurtled by rapidly. In Jhang everyone was agog with the punches that young Faisal Saleh Hayat was managing to pull. People who had dared to oppose him were being arrested; third division matriculates were being appointed at lucrative government posts. The local administration was being virtually run by the Commissioner, Larkana. The Deputy Commissioner at Jhang was allegedly being harassed by him—with the demand that he should report that I was growing prohibited crops on my land—so that police cases could be registered against me. My farm employees were accused of stealing water from the canal; my farm manager, a retired major, Sarfaraz Khan, was forced to obtain bail before arrest and I had to stay put in Jhang and seek legal help from lawyers who had the courage to come to my rescue—and there were not many of those around. Mother kept reminding me of the warning that she had given me to lay low as Bhutto could be dangerous if he felt himself endangered in any way. But I had not done anything to merit attention and would tell her that I was too small a fry to count, and that Bhutto was probably unaware of these details of harassment that his minions were subjecting to whomsoever they had a threat perception from.

Nonetheless, those were bewildering and troubling times for me. I yearned for my father's protection and would often cry myself to sleep but would try and keep up a bold demeanour when visitors would come to the Shah Jewna House. My romance with being centre of attention in Jhang seemed to have come to an abrupt end. Having managed to get court orders of temporary relief, I returned to Lahore to keep myself apprised of the dramatic and day-to-day developments in our country. The popular reaction to the Bhutto regime seemed to be widespread and by June, Bhutto, appearing to be considerably weakened, engaged in talks with the Opposition. His last televised address to the Nation betrayed his panic and the next day General Zia ul-Haq, Chief of Army Staff, intervened; imprisoned Bhutto; and declared himself Chief Martial Law Administrator on 5 July 1977.

The reaction to Z. A. Bhutto's removal was mixed. The bigwigs of the country, those whose businesses had been nationalized in particular, the civil and military bureaucracies, and their connections rejoiced, some overtly, others covertly. His supporters, the humble folk in the countryside, along with the urban petit bourgeoisie, to whose aspirations Bhutto had lent his strong voice, were aggrieved at his removal but had no capacity to express their sentiments out of fear of the Martial Law. The more sincere among the PPP urban workers, who had been pushed aside earlier by the *cordon sanitaire* of opportunistic police personnel and civil servants, who had constantly been around their leader, sulked in their homes and failed to react. There were no demonstrations, the streets fell silent.

It was hot and oppressive in Lahore. Baji and the children were at Cliffden in Murree, and Fakhar and I joined them there. Bhutto had been taken to the Governor Punjab's residence in Murree and was being held there under detention, while Hafeez Pirzada, Ghulam Mustafa Jatoi, and Mumtaz Ali Bhutto were detained in the School of Military Intelligence at Cliffden Camp, just up the hill from our Cliffden Farm. The PNA leaders were also detained and lodged at the Punjab House just below Pindi Point. Among them were Sardar Sherbaz Mazari, Nawabzada Nasrullah Khan, and Air Marshal Asghar Khan. Begum Nasim Wali Khan came from her summer home in Swat to stay with us for a few days at the Cliffden Farm. We discussed politics morning, noon, and night. Like my mother, I was now of the view that if there was a re-poll, the situation could saved. But if the politicians started to demand fresh elections, we could regress to a 1971 type of situation and prolonged uncertainty could become a threat to what was left of the country.

Sherbaz's wife, Surraya Mazari sent a suitcase full of clothes and books for her husband to Cliffden, with a note addressed to me requesting that I ensure delivery of the suitcase to Sardar

Sherbaz at the Punjab House where he was detained. I took this opportunity to voice my thoughts to the leaders that I might be able to access at the time. Nasim Bibi had heard me out but she did not comment much, understandably so, since her priority was to secure the release of her husband and his co-accused from the hellish prison of Hyderabad where temperatures were raging above forty degrees centigrade. Sardar Sherbaz agreed with me on my observations. He was sitting with Nawabzada Nasrullah Khan and Professor Ghafoor in a large and grubby lounge of the Punjab House that was the property of the Punjab Government in Murree. But Nawabzada Nasrullah Khan, puffing away on his customary hubble bubble or *hookah*, differed.

'My dearest niece,' he addressed me with the utmost courtesy which hallmarks the gentry of Southern Punjab. 'We have considered the option you suggest but, you see, if we are to form the government after the elections, we must have suitable candidates who could then run the affairs of State. When we forged an election alliance, all our energy was consumed by allocation of quotas to the nine parties that I brought together single-handedly. Asghar Khan was particularly difficult and many tickets were allotted to virtual lamp posts. So what is required is a re-election, not re-poll, to enable each party to select appropriate people that can then run the government in a healthy manner.'

And while Professor Ghafoor was agreeing with the Nawabzada, I could hear my father's voice ringing in my ears. He was sitting with Nawabzada Nasrullah Khan and Arif Khan Sial in the verandah of our Gulberg home in Lahore. It was sometime in 1968 and he was saying: 'You old Ahrari, so long as you are around with your constant refrain of 'healthy' politics, normal politics will keep eluding us!' My father's tone had been bantering and affectionate and I had wondered what he had meant. And now it was the same gentleman, my father's old classmate from Government College, Lahore, sitting in front of me all these years later, lecturing me on healthy politics, and I thought of the good old French adage, *'La plus ça change, la plus c'est la même chose'* (the more it changes, the more it is the same). When I tried to argue back, Nawabzada excused himself by saying that he had other visitors to attend to, while Professor Ghafoor and Sardar Sherbaz told me that their information was that Zia's visit with Bhutto at the Governor's House in Murree had not gone well and the chances of a re-poll were minimal. There would be a re-election in September/October and the Jamaat-i-Islami had agreed to swap the Okara constituency with the NDP so I could contest from N.A. 69 on an NDP ticket. I asked them what would become of Bhutto, and both gentlemen were of the view that Bhutto's fate was in his own hands. If he cooperated with General Zia, he would justify his own overthrow, and if he took him on, he would suffer, they opined.

'I would hate to be in Bhutto's shoes. He is faced with a Hobson's choice,' said Sardar Sherbaz Mazari.

'Politics seems to be a series of tough choices. Bhutto Sahib was not fair to me personally but I do feel aggrieved on his behalf for having been Prime Minister one minute and detenue the next, which does not bode well for the democratic process. And General Zia looks sinister,' I said to Sardar Sherbaz as he escorted me towards the cottage that Air Marshal Asghar Khan was lodged in. I wanted to see him as well. Gohar Ayub Khan was sitting with the Air Marshal. I voiced my thoughts regarding the re-polls to him too. But the Air Marshal was as dismissive of it as Nawabzada Nasrullah had been.

I returned to Cliffden and tried to read a story to Umku and Shugu. Umku asked me what would happen to Bhutto, and Shugu chimed in that the servants were saying that Zia would give Bhutto *'phansi'*, at which both my daughters (five and four years old at the time) wanted to know what *'phansi'* meant. Mother and I looked at each other askance, and then Mother explained to my daughters very gently that the word meant hanging. To our astonishment the children seemed to understand and both began to howl; it became a chore for us to make them stop crying. Zia announced elections, saying that the election process had been given the name 'Operation Fairplay' and that he would personally ensure fairplay during this process. Fakhar applied to the Tehrik-e-Istiqlal for a party nomination from Tehsil Kabirwala, where Qatalpur is located. He was turned down for being a 'feudal'.

Reactive to Bhutto, Asghar Khan failed miserably in constituency politics. Although a good and decent man and favoured by certain sections of the haute bourgeoisie in our urban centres, Asghar Khan could never get through to the ordinary and humble folk in his own locality and the Establishment was never interested in helping him either, because he was militantly against corrupt practices, and our officers, both civil and military, had learnt to enjoy incrementally high standards of living, although, there were some honourable exceptions. Ayub Khan had legitimized corruption by making his own family rich. Bhutto was born rich, but looked the other way when officers sought to become rich who were 'useful' for him. Nobody wanted an Asghar Khan who was dismissive of tradition, community, and locality and who had a retired bureaucrat, Malik Wazir Ali, who was not people friendly either, as his ideologue. I told Fakhar that he was better off contesting as an independent candidate and even if he did not win in the coming election, he could lay a base for the next one, provided we remained on the democratic track. The fashionable argument at the time was that the army had come to put the nation back on track and would pull out after the elections. I did not believe this would be the case, convinced that with the passage of each day, Bhutto would be seen as a menace by Zia. I feared for Bhutto.

By August, armed with an NDP nomination from the PNA platform, I returned to Jhang. My heart was heavy. I still admired Bhutto, but I also respected Begum Nasim Wali Khan and the detenues of Hyderabad jail. Hence, I entered N.A. 69, speaking about the manifestos of the PPP and NDP being similar, focusing on the rights of the people. My constituents did not seem to be interested in any political party. They only recognized me as the daughter of Abid Hussain Shah. Some called him Makhdum Abid Hussain Bokhari, some referred to him as Pir Abid Hussain Shah, while majority of them simply called him Colonel Sahib. I became Bibi Abida or Mai Sain or Murshidzadi. I felt comfortable with Abida Hussain and would encourage them to call me that. Initially it did not work but eventually it did, at least with the women. For the men I came to be Bibi Sahiba, but for the women I was Abida Hussain.

I would set out in what was now my Willy's jeep and I had rented a Toyota car that would follow. The constituency was divided by the rivers. I would cross the Trimmu Barrage where the Jhelum falls into the Chenab River, and would head out towards the Thal desert. I would stop at Wasu Astana from where two well-known local politicians would accompany me as we entered Kachchi, a long, fertile green belt which stretched some thirty miles to the upper end of the constituency, to the border of Khushab, with the sand dunes of the Thal on one side and the Jhelum River on the other. The villages were close to each other, surrounded by clumps of date palms that stood tall against the deep blue sky, with their dark green leaves and deep red bunches of dates peeping from below. I had started valuing the verses, or 'kaffis' as they were known locally, of Baba Ghulam Fareed and kept intoning his celebrated lines:

Uchiaan uchiaan lal khajooraan (tall date palms with red fruit)

Naal patar unhaan dai saavvai (and leaves of deep green)

The fields were carpeted with lush green fodder and buffaloes, cows, and sheep ruminated contentedly. Kachchi had a Biblical quality, a peaceful pastoral society, densely populated with Baloch and Sial clans, living cheek by jowl more or less harmoniously. The men all wore white turbans, mostly white *kurta*s and vividly coloured *lungi*s (loin cloth). The women always had their heads covered in bright *dupatta*s, with gaily printed cotton *kurta*s and *lungi*s but *shalwar- kamiz* had caught up with the children. I loved this locality, which had Kot Shakir as its central point, a large community starting in the sand dunes and straggling down close to the river. Wherever I went, the people were warm and welcoming and would turn out in large numbers to see me, specially the women, with their numerous children, of course. They all recalled my father who was something of a legend for being the Pir who gave them a road into Thal and a High School at Kot Shakir. I would solicit their votes and they would say they could not refuse a lady from the Holy Prophet's lineage, but when I would remind them that there were many who claimed that lineage, they would respond cheerily that I had reached them first and that I was the only child that Abid Hussain Shah had left behind and that I was befittingly seeking to be his son. Living near-Spartan lives, with no electricity and largely rudimentary infrastructures, these folk struck me as being remarkably astute.

One day, my little cavalcade got caught up in a dust storm. We were driving through the desert, up the Khushab road, towards Mari Shah Sakhira, a dramatically beautiful and ancient community built on the sand which was compacted and stable but had dunes all around it, when the sky started darkening and suddenly the visibility became zero. There was dust all over me; in my eyes, nostrils, mouth, and ears. My consigliere, Fateh Khan, Mian Fuzail, and Soobaan who were always with me in my jeep or car, were hollering at me to cover my face and wrap my chaddar around my head. Barely able to breathe, I felt I was choking and thought I was going to die. But the storm abated as rapidly as it had risen and as I unwound my chaddar to dust it off, I saw a beautiful falcon perched on a thorny scrub close to my jeep. The falcon's eyes were shut, it first opened one eye, then the other, gave me an intent stare, then spread its wings, taking flight, circling slowly in the air, widening the circle, and gradually gaining height till it was a mere speck in the once again deep blue sky. I thought of Leonardo da Vinci and what I was taught by Signorina Simi during my year at Florence regarding his observation of hawks and falcons, which were behind his drawings of a flying machine, and I longed for a sketch pad and charcoal between my fingers before the images faded from my mind's eye.

Another day, we ran out of fuel. Malik Riaz had miscalculated. We were bailed out by one of my supporter's cars that was passing by, who gave us some extra fuel he was carrying, while I raved and ranted at Malik Riaz. When we arrived at Shah Jewna House, before I could complain to Mother, Malik Riaz tendered his resignation to her. She chastised me gently. I was furious with my mother who calmed me down and said, 'Chando, you are making enough enemies around you without adding the people who serve us to that list. I suggest you apologise to Riaz.' And I did. She also informed me that Sardar Sherbaz Mazari had called her from Lahore where he had come for a PNA (Pakistan National Alliance) meeting. Mother's observation was that the elections were going to be postponed because of the popular opinion that Bhutto was winning the election and the military man who had seized power could not afford that. So, in all probability Zia ul-Haq would postpone the elections.

I decided to leave for Lahore, along with Mother, to receive Sardar Sherbaz Mazari. Fakhar also left his campaign and came to join us. The PNA leaders reached Lahore as did Zulfikar Bhutto, whose followers turned out in full force and clashed with a PNA procession on Jail Road, where Maulana Shah Ahmed Noorani of the Jamiat-e-Ulema Pakistan and Javed Hashmi, a student leader of the Jamaat-i-Islami, were dragged out of their vehicles and roughed up by PPP workers.

Zulfikar Ali Bhutto went to the residence of his former Chief Minister, Sadiq Hussain Qureshi, in Shadman Colony, across the canal from our house, and a huge crowd gathered there. Fakhar went to see what was happening and returned to inform us that Bhutto had stood on the rooftop of Qureshi's house, and through the loudspeaker had shouted that he would skin General Zia ul-Haq while the crowd roared their approval.

The lines were drawn—the dye was cast—elections were postponed. Zulfikar Ali Bhutto was arrested on a murder charge for having ordered the firing on Ahmed Raza Kasuri, who was a maverick MNA of the PPP in the now defunct National Assembly.

In the firing, Ahmed Raza's father, Mohammed Ahmed Khan Kasuri, had been killed.

I was dejected. The polls had been a mere fortnight away and I was confident of winning, looking forward to working towards the development of my constituency and to sitting in the same National Assembly that all the leaders of Pakistan would be in. Instead there was to be a murder trial against ZAB (as Bhutto was often so called) with the entire nation going into a kind of limbo, as it were. Meanwhile, General Zia indicated that the Hyderabad Conspiracy Case would be addressed and that justice would be meted out. This ensured that the NDP leaders maintained silence after their initial demand that a fresh date for elections be announced. Sardar Sherbaz Mazari and Begum Nasim Wali Khan were in Lahore when they received a call from the General Headquarters (GHQ) inviting them to visit with an election cell that had been set up by General Zia. After due deliberations with their party colleagues, they decided to drive up to Rawalpindi, and asked me if I would like to accompany them. It was decided that we go early in the morning, attend the meeting, and drive back to Lahore the same evening.

When we reached the GHQ building to which we had been directed, it took several minutes before our car was allowed through the huge iron gates, and Sherbaz Mazari complained of the military's arrogance towards civilians. Inside the compound we were directed towards a modest looking building, and when we entered the small outer office, a homely looking young officer asked us for our identification papers. Sherbaz Mazari was most irritated and said that we had come in response to an invitation, and if we could not be met with due courtesy then we would be happy to go back. Abid Zuberi from Karachi was also with us.

As we were walking towards the exit, Zuberi saw an older officer entering the room and apprised him of the situation. This officer said that he had been sent by General Faiz Ali Chishti to receive us and that he was sorry not to have been at the entrance. He apologized profusely, hence, we decided to follow him through the corridor into the small and modest room that General Chishti, Corps Commander Rawalpindi, occupied. Two other officers were in the room with General Chishti: General (retired) Rao Farman Ali and Lieutenant General Jamal Said Mian.

General Chishti welcomed us, and apologized for the boorishness of the officer who had asked for our identification papers. The mere fact that he knew convinced us that the offence was intended, a typical ploy to keep us politicians in our place, Nasim Bibi observed afterwards. Rao Farman Ali did the talking.

> It is easy enough for the Pakistan Army to take over the running of the country, since it has happened twice already, but once it intervenes, it is not easy for it to get out. Look at what happened to us in East Pakistan. We were bogged down, although we were anxious to get out. Therefore, General Zia ul-Haq has mandated us to offer you to join the Cabinet and to find a way for the army not to embroil itself further. You could then take responsibility for steering the ship of the State and the army can go back to the barracks.

Nasim Bibi spoke gently but firmly and Sardar Sherbaz Mazari endorsed her view. 'Thank you, General Sahib. Although we appreciate your being forthright and perhaps cognizant that it is not the job of the army to run the government, we come from a strictly democratic tradition. I cannot speak for the rest of the PNA which is a loosely-structured alliance, but we in the NDP cannot join the government through backdoor channels, prior to being elected. If some of our colleagues in the PNA wish to join you we would not seek to impede them, but we would suggest that you announce a schedule for election as soon as may be possible.'

General Farman Ali replied: 'The CMLA (Chief Martial Law Administrator) also wants to conduct a free and fair election as soon as possible, but he is firmly of the view that the Hyderabad case and the Kasuri case ought to be adjudicated on a priority basis as these matters would become election issues and that could endanger a smooth process for the election.'

The gauntlet had been thrown. The rest of the meeting was mere small talk. We left the GHQ in less than an hour and drove back to Lahore on the Grand Trunk Road.

With the elections going into indefinite delay, most of the PNA parties decided to send a representative into the Cabinet of Zia ul-Haq. The NDP remained an exception. And in February of 1978, Khan Abdul Wali Khan and his associates in the former National Awami Party (NAP) were released from the Hyderabad Jail, after four years, absolved of the charges of treason which had been laid at their doorstep. This trumped-up case, in many ways distorted the destiny of Pakistan, depriving its people of the progressive leadership of not only Zulfikar Ali Bhutto, but also that of Khan Abdul Wali Khan, Ghous Bux Bizenjo, Ataullah Mengal, Khair Bux Khan Marri, and Akbar Khan Bugti.

Wali Khan, Ghous Bux Bizenjo, and Haji Ghulam Ahmed Bilour came to Lahore shortly thereafter and were my mother's very honoured guests. Mother invited as many people as she could think of and was successful in putting Majid Nizami (owner of the widely read Urdu daily, *Nawai Waqt*) together with Wali Khan Sahib, which went a long way in reducing the animus of *Nawai Waqt* for the 'red shirts'.

After my father's death, bit by bit, Mother had found herself a new life. She travelled and read extensively, and surrounded herself with all the young intellectuals of the day, whom she would invite frequently to have meals with her. She was disappointed when they reflected reservations regarding Wali Khan's inability to overcome his bitterness against Zulfikar Ali Bhutto, which disappointed me as well. Abdul Wali Khan was a great orator and when he embarked on a tour of the Punjab in March 1978, I accompanied him, which was a learning experience for me. It did disappoint me that he was implacable whenever Bhutto was mentioned and never forgave the fact that Bhutto cooperated with General Yahya Khan on the postponement of the National Assembly convening on 3 March 1971. He cited as evidence the reality that Bhutto had flown back from Dacca (Dhaka) in the same airplane as Yahya, while the rest of the MNA's elect from West Pakistan, including himself, had to find their way back on their own. Nonetheless, when I tried to speak in favour of Bhutto, he would ward me off by saying that although he appreciated my speaking up for a man who had been kind to me, I should be aware that I was speaking for a man who had been cruel to others. He would then cite the case of Attaullah Mengal's son who had been brutally killed, and of his own son Asfandyar who had been deprived of a proper education because he had to flee from home to Afghanistan, because not only was his father unjustifiably charged with treason, additionally, an attempt was made to implicate Asfandyar in the assassination of Hayat Muhammad Khan Sherpao, Bhutto's young stalwart in the Frontier.

Not long after Wali Khan's tour of the Punjab concluded, Begum Nusrat Bhutto came to Lahore, and attempted to demonstrate near the Liberty Market roundabout in Gulberg. A sizeable crowd had gathered which was subjected to baton charge. Begum Bhutto was hit on the head and left with a gash. The following day's newspapers were filled with photographs of her collapsing, with blood trickling down her forehead. Mother and I were aghast and wanted to go and see her, so along with Aunty Tahira, we went to the Khagga House that Begum Bhutto had rented. The house was cordoned off by the police and we were barred entry. Farooq Ahmed Khan Leghari came to see me. He had joined the PPP not long after his father, Sardar Mohammad Khan Leghari's death in 1972, resigning his commission from the civil service, and was appointed Minister in the Federal Cabinet by Bhutto in March of 1977. Farooq was like an older brother to me, and when he suggested that I should return to the PPP and stand by Nusrat and Benazir Bhutto, I was sorely tempted, but my survival instinct impeded me.

I told him, 'Zia ul-Haq is brutal. And Fakhar and I are not quite on our feet as yet. My kinsmen, and his, would hound us, and we would not be able to do much for the Bhutto ladies in any case. And now that I have joined the NDP and Begum Nasim Wali Khan has been kind to me, it would be extremely awkward for me to backtrack. But I do hope and pray that it goes well for the Bhutto family and they come out of their crisis without further harm or humiliation. I hope you understand, Farooq Bhai.' He assured me that he did, which made me feel better.

At about this time, events in neighbouring Iran had taken an even more dramatic turn. On 11 February 1979, Shahanshah 'Aryamehr' Raza Shah Pahlavi of Iran had been overthrown in what appeared to be a genuine revolution and Ayatollah Khomeini had become the Supreme Leader of Iran.

As we headed towards summer, Mother and I decided to sell 250 acres of our land, and transferred the money to my mother's bank account through people from Jhang who we knew and who were settled in England. We then left for London, taking Umku and Shugu with us, while baby Abid was left behind with our family 'ammah' who had raised me and my girls, under the watchful eye of Fakhar and his mother. We bought a spacious three bedroom flat in Empire House, at Thurloe Place in Knightsbridge, which was a five minute walk from Naheed Iskander Mirza's flat in Ennismore Gardens. Mother thought that we would rent the flat out in the winter months and keep it for ourselves in the summer, and this would provide a safety net for the children's higher education in the times ahead. She was convinced that with Iran having undergone a revolution, and with Afghanistan also in a state of flux, Pakistan could go in any direction with a tyrant like Zia ul-Haq at the helm of affairs.

With my friend Mandy's help, we decorated the flat, and prepared to let it out. The Wali Khan's also came to London for a few weeks, and agreed that our region was full of incertitude. Mother took Umku and Shugu back to Pakistan and Fakhar flew out to join me for a few weeks. I had invested quite a bit of money with Uncle Babar Ali in a new company he had set up, 'Milkpak', and Fakhar was mulling over setting up a similar but smaller unit at Kabirwala, so he was engaged with its planning and made good friends with Mandy's husband, Ronald Clarkson, who was a successful businessman. We also saw a lot of Sulaiman Mahmudabad who would assert that India was the only stable state in our region, but Fakhar always argued that Pakistan would stabilize and that he had faith in his country and its future. I found Fakhar's belief reassuring. We returned home after renting out the flat.

By now the Bhutto trial was seriously underway and had the entire nation mesmerized. Bhutto had been shifted to the Kot Lakhpat Jail at Lahore. Huge arguments raged in our house and in all the salons of Pakistan. Maulvi Mushtaq, the Chief Justice of the Lahore High Court, where the case was being heard, was reputed to have an animus for Bhutto and most people were convinced that he would sentence Bhutto harshly. Whenever my mother heard such comments she would say 'tauba', look stricken, and state, 'Allah alone has the right to take life. Bhutto must not be sinned against more than he sinned. We as citizens ought to build some pressure on the courts.' Her eldest brother, Amjad Ali, who was devoted to her, would tell her that military rulers did not allow, nevermind defer to, the pressure of citizens, and Zia would want a noose around Bhutto's neck rather than his own. This would cause my mother to shudder and invariably make my eyes turn moist.

Chief Justice Maulvi Mushtaq pronounced the death sentence for Zulfikar Ali Bhutto. The sentence sent shudders down Pakistani people and PPP worker's spines. Jahangir Badar, Qayum Nizami, Ghulam Abbas, and other young PPP stalwarts were punished with lashes at the Shadman Park, where, according to the newspapers, thousands gathered to watch. The brutalization of our state had well and truly been started, causing deep concern to all conscientious citizens.

An appeal was filed in the Supreme Court. Yahya Bakhtiar and Hafeez Pirzada were to defend Zulfikar Ali Bhutto before a nine-member Bench, presided by Chief Justice Anwar ul Haq. Hafeez Pirzada was visiting Lahore and my mother expressed the desire to see him, and suggested that I invite him for lunch. We also invited Major General Shah Rafi Alam, whose father had been a good friend of my father, along with friends who were lawyers, and their wives. The lunch was pleasant enough, with Hafeez confident of his case. His contention was that it was unprecedented for the Apex Court not to grant relief in a case of abetment. Among our friends who were present were some well known barristers and they all agreed. But General Rafi remained gloomy, and eventually muttered his disagreement. Hafeez said he knew the court and Rafi retorted that he knew the army. This placed a pall over the gathering and the lunch ended on a sombre note, with Mother looking deeply dejected.

The Supreme Court Bench comprised seven judges: four from Punjab and one each from Sindh, the North-West Frontier Province (Khyber Pakhtunkhwa), and Balochistan. When the Apex Court took up Bhutto's appeal, it was assessed that the Sindh, Frontier, and Balochistan judges would seek to uphold the appeal. The question was, would one of the Punjab judges differ with the Chief Justice, who was likely to concur with the army. Most people expected Justice Nasim Hasan Shah to support the Sindh and Frontier judges. It shocked me that people spoke of the Apex Court being riddled with ugly self-serving politics. My father used to say that we would need at least twenty years of undiluted democracy for the Judicature to become truly independent. But in the decades past we had seen the fall of our first military dictator, the rise and fall of our second military dictator, and the secession of one half of our country, after which we lived through the rise and fall of our first populist leader, and now we were with our third military dictator. I wondered if we would achieve a stable democracy in the next ten years.

Meanwhile, the Appeal was heard and concluded towards the end of 1978. It stood rejected in a split judgment, with the Sindh and Frontier judges upholding the Appeal and all five Punjab judges turning it down, sustaining the death penalty for Zulfikar Ali Bhutto, voice of the impoverished and the downtrodden of Pakistan.

Calls for clemency for Bhutto poured in, addressed to General Zia ul-Haq from all over the world. Pesident Demirel of Turkey made a personal visit to plead for clemency for Bhutto, as did Sheikh Zayed, the Ruler of Abu Dhabi, and Yasser Arafat of the PLO (Palestenian Liberation Organization). Three PPP workers torched themselves on fire outside the Assembly Chambers of Lahore and millions of Pakistanis sent telegrams and letters begging for mercy for Bhutto.

On a balmy afternoon in the last week of March 1979, mother and I went to watch a polo game to cheer ourselves up. My cousin Shahid Ali had called to say he was playing in the final rounds of the top tournament of the season. Mother spotted General (retired) Jehanzeb, who was reputed to have been a friend of ZAB and had also been a friend of my late father's. Mother wanted to talk to him and waved to him. He came over to us. In her forthright way, she asked him what General Zia was going to do and said she fervently hoped that he would grant clemency to Bhutto.

'No, Begum Sahiba, Zia is going to reject all appeals for mercy. He sent me to talk to Nusrat Bhutto as he knew I was a friend of theirs, with the message that if she and her daughter would agree to leave the country, he would lock Bhutto up in some rest house and spare his life but Nusrat did not agree, saying that she could not trust Zia to keep his word. I know Zia well enough to know that he will now get the verdict of the court implemented.' Tears welled up in Mother's eyes. After quietly saying goodbye to

General Jehanzeb, she got up and started walking away from the polo field with me following behind her. As we sat in our car, we clung to each other, deeply saddened. The buzz that Bhutto would be hanged was doing the rounds. I felt waves of nausea sweep through me and told my mother and Fakhar that I wanted to get away, so I left for Jhang. Driving on to Shah Jewna and after sitting a long while beside my father's grave, when I entered the *haveli*, women started pouring in, asking me if all was well, wondering why I had arrived suddenly.

'They are going to hang Bhutto!' I wailed and all the women joined me loudly. We squatted on the floor and mourned in the traditional manner, as is done when an honoured and revered family member passes away. A couple of hundred women and an equal number of humble village men sat with me mourning for Bhutto—the people's man—till there was light in the sky.

The following morning, I was wandering around in my cotton fields when one of my farm employees came running to tell me that the radio broadcast had just announced that Bhutto had been hanged and his body had been flown to Larkana and buried at night. Hence on 4 April 1979, Zulfikar Ali Bhutto was hanged in what was a shocking miscarriage of justice, which many began to describe as a judicial murder.

Climbing into my car I asked my driver to speed me to Jhang. I wanted to know if there would be a protest in the town and to call friends in different parts of the country to find out how people were reacting. As we entered the town I asked the driver to drive me through Shaheed Road, the main bazaar of Jhang, to see if the shutters were down. Alas! Not only were all the shops wide open, it was business as usual and the radios were belting forth a medley of popular film songs. Sad and sickened, I drove past my Bokhari cousin's house, which appeared to be quiet and normal, with a few cars parked in the driveway, then past the house that had been purchased through an odd transaction for Faisal Saleh Hayat, which did not appear to have a soul in sight. I then drove into the Shah Jewna House where my sympathisers were waiting for me, a couple of dozen folk, looking gloomy and distressed. 'There ought to have been a *Ghaibana Namaz Janaza* for *Quaid-e-Awam*', pondered Soobaan. 'If you had been a son, you would have had a prayer in your front garden at least. But your relatives who were with PPP have gone into hiding!' The men sitting around seemed to share her cynicism. My cousin Zulfiqar Bokhari had protested when Bhutto was a detenue, and so had Faisal Saleh Hayat, which he cashed in on later. But on the 4th of April there was no protest to speak of in Jhang.

The press informed us that Nusrat Bhutto had been flown to Karachi where she would be kept confined to her home at 70-Clifton for the period of her '*iddat*' (Islamic period of mourning for wife), while Benazir had been imprisoned. There were photographs of mourners queuing outside the Bhutto residence in Karachi, going in groups of twos and threes to pay bereavement calls to Begum Nusrat Bhutto who had been widowed in her late forties. I called my friend Timmy in Karachi and flew from Lyallpur (Faisalabad) to Karachi the next day to condole with Begum Bhutto whom I truly wanted to console. Soobaan was dying to come with me and it was only when I told her that PIA may not agree to take her on board because of her enormous weight that she laid off!

Timmy was at the airport to receive me. I insisted that we drive straight to 70-Clifton before going to Timmy's sister's place at 9-A-Clifton. There was no one outside the Bhutto residence except about a dozen policemen and half a dozen plain-clothes men. Our car was stopped by the police well outside the gate. I got out of the car and said I had come to condole with Begum Bhutto. The policeman called one of the plain-clothes men who asked for my identification and then told me somewhat discourteously that visitors were not allowed, but I could record my message in the Visitor's Book. I told him as unctuously as I could that I had come all the way from Jhang, and could I not see Begum Bhutto for at least five minutes? He shook his head firmly in the negative. I wanted to argue with him, but Timmy restrained me, and I asked for the Visitor's Book, which was procured from the police cabin, outside the gate of the Bhutto family residence. I wrote a long paragraph, and Timmy wrote a condolence message as well.

'Are you sure this Visitor's Book will reach Begum Bhutto?' I asked of the odious plain-clothes man. 'Sure, sure,' he responded off-handedly, but I was not sure at all.

A decade later Benazir informed me that they were not shown any Visitor's Book or letters or telegrams that came at the time of her father's hanging. I returned to Lahore the following day to find that most people were already beginning to discuss newer realities, dropping the names of the brigadiers and generals that were known to them, which nauseated me.

General Zia ul-Haq, however, had become an international pariah and all assistance to Pakistan was cut off in 1977. But then Zia got lucky. Soviet troops entered Afghanistan to stabilize the 'Saur Revolution' which had been essentially a coup perpetrated by left-wing officers in the Afghan Air Force who installed Nur Mohammad Tarrakai, head of the 'Khalq' or People's Party, as the President of Afghanistan. The coup makers had bombarded the Presidential Palace of Daud Khan, younger brother of King Zahir

Shah, who had, a few years earlier, deposed the King and had installed him self as President. But Daud was a Mohammedzai Durrani and the tribal consensus on the Durranis maintained. Nur Mohammad Tarrakai failed to carry the tribes who declared him 'Kaffir', or heretic, because he was a well-known socialist, influenced by the Soviet Union, while the Kabul oligarchs were West leaning and the tribal folk deeply circumspect of religion. Tarrakai did not fit into either the tribal or the traditional nationalist paradigm, therefore a tribal revolt sparked off against him in the early days of his regime. He was then replaced by a fellow Khalqi who was younger and more vigorous, called Hafeezullah Amin. Amin did not last the course either, and was replaced by the leader of the 'Parcham' or National Party which stood more for Pushtun nationalism than socialism, called Babrak Karmal. Babrak was an acolyte of Baccha Khan and well known to Khan Abdul Wali Khan. But he was not acceptable to the Tajiks or Uzbeks in upper Afghanistan—the areas bordering Uzbekistan, Tajikistan, Kyrghizistan—all these located in the underbelly of the Soviet Union. Therefore when Babrak was severely challenged, Soviet leadership decided to send the Red Army into Afghanistan.

The Western world reacted sharply, accusing the Soviet Union of aggressing against a neutral state. Pakistan thus became a 'Front Line' state and Zia ul-Haq a crucial tool for Western interests.

From then onwards, for nine years, Zia ul-Haq was given a free hand by Washington to manage Pakistan. The US also provided him two squadrons of high performance jet fighters, F-16s, which were reputedly far superior to the MiG jets which the Soviet Union had been supplying to India. Economic assistance followed military assistance and the US Congress legislated an aid package of $1.3 billion to the Zia regime—superseding all pro-democracy and anti-nuclear laws in the US that Bhutto stood for—forgotten by the western world. Clearly a connection seemed to have been assumed in the capitalized western world between the Shia Revolution in Iran and the arrival of Soviet troops in Afghanistan. Pakistan as a 'Front Line' state was required to prevent the Soviet juggernaut from reaching the warm water ports of the Arabian Sea and the Persian Gulf. Pakistan became a crucial American ally in the Capitalist's fight against Communism. The Pakistan Peoples Party was subdued as were all the other political parties that were demanding a return to democracy. Instead Zia ul-Haq promised that he would conduct local elections on the basis of adult franchise, which would be followed by parliamentary elections on the basis of proportionate representation. Student and labour unions had been banned, and the press had been muzzled. All discussion and debate was reduced to conversations in drawing rooms and in tea shops on roadsides. The quiescent business community started hailing the Zia regime and the farm community was left to its own devices. Religion became a major focus and religious rituals were emphasized at the level of the state for the first time. As Bhutto entered the realm of legend, Zia increasingly became the living reality. Pakistan slid from being a forward-looking liberal state into a conservative, ritualistic one.

5

Grass-Roots Politics

By May 1979, a row, which had been simmering between the Baloch leaders of the National Democratic Party (NDP) and Khan Abdul Wali Khan since their release from Hyderabad Jail the previous year, broke out in the open. Sardar Sherbaz Mazari and my mother, who had goodwill on both sides, made an honest and dedicated effort during the marriage of Asfandyar Wali Khan to try and prevent the row from escalating. I was totally bowled over by Nawab Khair Bux Marri, who was quite the most beautiful man I had ever seen, while Sardar Ataullah was elegant and precise, and the third in the Baloch trio, Mir Ghous Bux Bizenjo, eloquent and persuasive. Along with Khan Abdul Wali Khan, they presented an admirable calibre of leadership, and being in command of two provinces, together they would have an outstanding chance of scoring handsomely in the remaining two. Their split would deprive Pakistan of a cogent and capable leadership. But as the gulf between them widened, it seemed to me that too many people around these leaders had an axe to grind and were fanning the flames of discord, resultantly and sadly the NDP ended up splitting. I was deeply dejected, since I had assumed that my association with the second political party I joined would be an association for life. Mir Ghous Bux Bizenjo became the founding President of the Baloch National Party (BNP) and very kindly invited me to join, while Khan Abdul Wali Khan suggested I join the Awami National Party (ANP). Sardar Sherbaz Mazari opted out and the NDP stood dissolved. It was hard for me to refuse Bizenjo, and even harder to turn down Wali Khan. I told both leaders that since the split had come along ethnic lines, being a Punjabi, I needed time to resolve the issue in my mind, and for the time being would like to remain independent. As it turned out, I did not join any political party for fifteen years.

About two months later, Zia ul-Haq announced local elections on a non-Party basis, and it so happened that I qualified, as did Fakhar. Fakhar and I had so often discussed the importance of grass-roots democracy and now we were with an opportunity to try our luck and seek to seize the opportunity of providing local leadership. Mother took the children up to Cliffden and Fakhar and I went to Multan and Jhang respectively to start networking and gearing up for the elections. When the schedule was announced, with the contingent rules, it turned out that the constituent unit for membership of each District Council would comprise four Union Councils, which was about a third the size of a Provincial Assembly constituency and in the case of Jhang District Council this came to twenty-eight popularly mandated members. Four weeks were given for the election to membership of the District Council, filing of nomination papers, scrutiny of papers and withdrawals in the first week, campaigning for three weeks and balloting on the thirtieth day. The same procedure applied to the Union Councils. After the election of membership on the basis of the popular vote, the members notified as elected would elect members on 'special interest seats'—one member to represent farmers, one member to represent labour, one woman member, and one member to represent the religious minorities. After the 'special seat' elections, three weeks were to be given for election to Chairmanship, with the Chairman to be elected by the members from amongst themselves. There would also be a

Vice Chairman who would be delegated powers by the Chairman. The powers of Chairman as laid out were to be extensive, making the elected Chair of the District Council responsible for all development functions in the district.

My constituency comprised Ratta, Shah Jewna, Maharwali, and Pabbarwala Union Councils and I was familiar with the lay of the land because of the 1977 aborted election, during which I had campaigned vigorously in quite a few places in this area. I started working the main communities a couple of weeks ahead of the official campaign, determined that I would reach as many voters as I possibly could in order to understand appropriately their developmental requirements. I spoke to my mother and the children on the telephone every day and mother was fretful lest cousin Iffi decided to take me on directly. She asked me to come down to Lahore and discuss the matter with Bia, as my cousin Zarina was called, who was as fretful as her at this prospect. I wanted to see Bia, who shared a house with her younger brother Iftikhar, popularly known as 'Iffi' at the time. Having missed my children terribly. I could not bear to leave the house and my children alone again, so I asked Bia to come by immediately as I planned to return to Jhang the same evening. Bia came and informed me that Iffi was determined to oppose me and was planning to spend on the election the money that he had saved to build a house for himself, his wife, and three children, as well as one for Bia and her two children. She said she was fed-up of living in rented homes and wanted a place of her own. Hence if I did not contest the election, Iffi would not do so either, and their homes would be built.

I said to her: 'Bia, I love you dearly and hate the thought of your being uncomfortable, but I do not understand why you cannot prevent Iffi from using your resources and proceed with the construction of your house. I am committed to contesting this election because I believe in Local Government, just as my father did, and I want to build on his record as Chairman District Board. There is a parliamentary election coming up just after the local election and Iffi can contest that and I promise not to oppose him in those.'

'I am not as tough and brave as you are, Chandi, nor as empowered. I will try and suggest to Iffi that he should avoid a clash with you, but I am afraid he may not hear me.'

'Bia, please tell him from me that I am all geared up for this election. I am campaigning already and I feel people are inclined to vote for me. If I lose to Iffi it will not be the end of the world for me, but if he loses to me it will be tragic, because I would hate for him to be hurt any further.'

I returned to my campaign in a sombre frame of mind and was given the bad news that Ghazanfar Abbas of Ratta had sent a message for me: that I should not visit Panj Giraeen which was a sizeable community a short distance away from my farmland, since this village was a part of Ghazanfar Abbas's late father's estate. That may have been so in the past but that land had been sold and some of it alienated under Land Reforms. In any case how could anyone curtail any candidate from visiting any locality. I thought Ghazanfar Abbas was being absurd and had clearly been put up to it.

Anyhow, I was not to be deterred. So I sat in my jeep with my employees, the duo known as Ameer and Zameer, and Soobaan in the back, myself in the front and Ameer's brother Nazar, who was my driver, at the wheel. I drove through my farm, looking at the cotton crop which had just started flowering, and was now on the dirt track leading towards Panj Giraeen, when Nazar suddenly rammed the breaks of the vehicle. On either side of the road ahead of us were a couple of dozen men holding up axes, with their heavy looking blades glinting in the sunlight.

It was a 'tharrha', in our locality a squad formed to threaten an adversary. 'Bibi, I suggest we turn around and go back', said Ameer, his voice quavering.

'We shall do no such thing. If you are scared, you and Zameer may jump off the jeep and run back to Dosera. I shall carry on. Okay Nazar, either you press down hard on the accelerator or you jump out as well. I will drive the jeep myself!' I said in a raised voice. Looking stricken, Nazar nonetheless did as he was told, and the two at the back did not jump out either. The vehicle shot past the men with axes, blowing huge amounts of dust onto them, which had certainly not been calculated, but it helped ensure momentary inaction and we were already inside the village. 'Where is Bakhaan Khokhar's house?' I asked a passer-by who looked as though he had seen a ghost. He pointed towards a door nearby. I jumped out of the jeep and ran inside Bakhaan's compound. Her old mother arose from a traditional stool we call *pirhi*, and Bakhaan came out into the compound from inside.

'Bismillah! Bismillah! What a blessed day that Bibi Abida should cross my threshold.' Bakhaan called out in a loud voice, dragging a charpoy forward and quickly laying a *khes*, a colourful bed-cloth across it, ushering me to be seated. By this time Soobaan lumbered in looking dazed, and asking for a glass of water! As Bakhaan's mother fetched Soobaan the water, I called out in a loud voice to all outside who may have been listening.

'This is a free country, where anyone can go anywhere they choose, provided they remain within the law. Nobody can stop anybody to canvass for votes during election, and I have come to ask my sister Bakhaan and her clan, the proud Khokhars of this land for their votes.'

Slowly, Bakhaan's cousins, aunts, and uncles started trickling into her compound and then children started swarming around. The clan's elder then invited me into his home nearby, and before long there were a few dozen folk demanding my attention. Soon it was the business of election as usual. Later, Ghazanfar Abbas sent one of his employees inviting me to visit Ratta whenever it was convenient for me.

I understood that I had won the election that day. And my friend Bakhaan made it possible for me. Like me, she was also the only child. She had eloped with Salehon Shah who was a Shah Jewna Syed. Bakhaan had a daughter and was living with Salehon Shah in his village which was not far away, but she feared that one of her kinsmen would kill her and pin the blame on her father to get his land. Over this issue she had come to visit me a couple of years previous and sought my help. I had called her parents and persuaded them to forgive her and allow her to return to her home. After some initial reluctance, they had agreed. I then managed to persuade Salehon Shah to let her go on the condition that his daughter would remain with him. He was already married to his cousin and had four sons from his first wife. His wife said she would raise the girl as her own and Bakhaan could come to visit her whenever she desired. Salehon Shah's first wife was relieved that Bakhaan would not be crowding her space any longer, and as the mother of sons, her consolation was that she was the *real woman* in Salehon Shah's life. Bakhaan was sad to give up her little girl but more comfortable and secure in her own home. She did not seem to care for Salehon Shah enough to regret his being out of her life. She never married again although she was very beautiful and had no shortage of suitors. To this day she remains my friend and visits me several times a year. Her parents died a while back. She now farms her land and says that Bibi Abida taught her to be an independent woman!

My cousin Iffi did file his nomination papers against me. This grieved my mother and his mother and their other siblings, so when I won against him, there was not much rejoicing around me, although, I was personally delighted at having broken the gender barrier with the popular vote. Fakhar also won his membership of the Multan District Council and was fortunate to have siblings who were so thrilled that they all came to Jhang to congratulate me.

But the big fight was still up ahead for both of us. We were candidates for Chairmanship of our respective District Councils and were pitted against heavyweight adversaries. Sardarzada Zaffar Abbas of Rajoya in my case; and Makhdum Hamid Raza Gillani in Fakhar's case. I was only thirty-three years old at the time, while Zaffar Abbas was in his late forties. He had been elected MPA in 1977, and had been President of the Jhang Bar Association a few times. He had a convivial personality and was widely viewed in our district as having cronies everywhere. Rajoya was located in Tehsil Chiniot and the Syeds of Rajoya, also Bokharis, descendants of Pir Daulat Shah, had long rivalled the Syeds of Shah Jewna. It was therefore assessed that I was up against a tough fight, particularly because my cousin Iffi was in hectic support of Zaffar Abbas and spending money like water, as had been feared by his sister Bia. I had decided to take Malik Mumtaz Nissoana, who was from

Chiniot, as my Vice Chairman candidate, and was strategizing my campaign for Chairmanship, when General Zia ul-Haq announced a postponement of the parliamentary elections that were to have started by this time.

While visiting my children, who were back from the hills and in Lahore with Mother, the Commissioner Sargodha telephoned to inform me that the Governor of Punjab and Martial Law Administrator, General Sawar Khan, would be visiting my farm in a few days. I asked the Commissioner as to who might have invited him for such a visit, as I certainly had not, and was told that the visit had been suggested by the Governor's advisor on agriculture, Dr Bhatti. Bhatti was a maize specialist who worked for an edible oil company before becoming gubernatorial advisor. He used to visit our farm and encouraged us to grow maize for the corn oil company that employed him. The Commissioner suggested that I leave for my farm immediately. I agreed to be there the following day. The Commissioner told me that he would also come a day before the Governor's visit, to ensure that suitable arrangements had been made. I wondered what arrangements were required. Welcoming the Commissioner when he arrived, I asked him what arrangements were required for a farm inspection. He indicated that we would need to erect a *shamiana* (tent) and a dais for the Governor to be seated on along with the others. After my welcome address, perhaps the Secretary of the Livestock Department and the Commissioner could say a few words, which may then be followed by a presentation of the livestock: horses and the cows.

At this, I retorted: 'You must be joking, Commissioner. First of all I have not been told anything nor have I invited the Governor. He has decided to come out presumably either out of curiosity, or in his perceived line of duty. Secondly, this is not going to be a mini enactment of a horse and cattle show. And finally, where on earth would I place the *shamiana*, not in a paddock surely?'

'Wherever you wish, but there has to be a *shamiana*,' responded the Commissioner rather pompously. The Deputy Commissioner parroting what the Commissioner was saying, hence, there was no point in turning to him for rescue. Despite my vociferous arguing, officialdom had their way. Eventually agreeing to a small *shamiana* at the entrance of the main yard of the stud farm building, I successfully resisted the formal speeches and dais, conceding to place the desk from my office, with its smart green felt cover, and the chairs from out of the office, in a row behind the desk. The Governor could be seated in the middle behind the table, with the Secretary beside him, and the Commissioner next to him on the other side. I would be seated next to the Commissioner, while the Deputy Commissioner could go next to the Secretary. The Commissioner approved of the seating order, it seemed to please him that I had ranked myself below him, although, he added, that since the Deputy Inspector General of Police would also be coming, he would be seated next to the Secretary while the Deputy Commissioner and Superintendent of Police could be seated next to him. The Governor's aide de camp would be next to me. When I asked him why police officers were coming, the Commissioner informed me that it was a matter of protocol. When the Governor went anywhere, senior officers of the administration that included police personnel, were required to be present in accordance with the rules of government.

'What a perfect waste of public money! And this Governor is not even constitutionally appointed. He is a Martial Law Administrator (MLA). Let the military manage his protocol, why do civil servants have to debase themselves?' I thought I had made a legitimate observation, but the Commissioner reacted as though he had heard profanity.

'Well, Begum Abida, perhaps you could repeat your observations to the Governor. ... And what would you propose to do, once we are seated?'

'The stallions would be led out of their stalls and shown, and I would present their pedigrees. Then we would cross the yard, and I would show the visitors the broodmares in their stalls, and then walk through the second yard to see the yearlings and the feed stores, after which we could walk out onto the paddocks to see the broodmares with foals at foot, and then we could drive down to the dairy farm. A walk around the dairy farm, and a glance at the crops, and we would be done in just over an hour. And yes Commissioner, I would tell the MLA that I find civil servants shockingly obsequious before military authority and also that civil and military officers should be careful with public resources and not waste money on silly protocol.'

'What you say to him is up to you, but kindly ensure that the Governor is served cold drinks and tea when he arrives and please be punctual. As for the programme which you have laid out, if the Governor agrees to it, that will be fine by us. Please do discuss it with him when he is seated.' The Commissioner sounded surly, clearly offended with me.

General Sawar Khan arrived on the dot, his motor cycle outrider and military police jeep kicking up huge clouds of dust as they turned onto the short driveway leading to the main Shah Jewna Stud Farm building. The General alighted from the Mercedes behind, along with Dr Bhatti, who looked as pleased as the

Cheshire cat, and General Sawar Khan, a tall and strikingly handsome man with a genial expression. We exchanged greetings at the entrance and as I was welcoming him, he strode around the yard and went and sat in the first chair, ushering me to sit beside him, and ordering the phalanx of officialdom accompanying him, brusquely, to sit down.

'What a magnificent place this is and what wonderful trees. They would be hundreds of years old. Tell me, Abida Bibi, who runs this place? Is Fakhar Imam Sahib here?' Despite my intent of abhorring Bhutto's hangman's cohort, I could not help liking this erect and handsome soldier, also because he dispensed with the silly 'Begum Sahiba' bit. I informed him that Fakhar was in Multan preparing to contest for the slot of Chairman District Council Multan, and that I managed my farm myself. Upon my instructions to the head groom, the stallions were then brought out. As the horses were being paraded, I rattled off their pedigrees, and then suggested we walk around to look at the mares and the young stock.

'I would be happy to walk around, stretch my legs, after that drive down from Lyallpur (Faisalabad) which took over an hour. Who handles the technical and veterinary side of this farm?'

'I plan the breeding tables myself, while Mukhtar Shah does the veterinary care. General, I was telling our Commissioner that in my opinion, government servants should spend public money sparingly and not waste it on protocol, particularly these days, when it is a military government, but I find that our civil servants hesitate to amend the requirements of protocol. What would be your comment?' I looked obliquely at the Commissioner at the end of my statement. The General laughed and turned to the Secretary of Livestock, Brigadier Ijaz Hussain.

'What was I telling you Ijaz, we waste too much time and money on this nonsense of protocol. Abida Bibi is absolutely right. Let us now look at your broodmares and then I am very interested in your cows. Bhatti was telling me that you have this cow that milks a phenomenal amount, I want to see her.' As we moved towards the livestock, the Commissioner looked distinctly uncomfortable.

Not long after the Governor's departure, I was back in my *haveli* when I was informed that Pir Amir Sultan, member-elect of Jhang District Council had come to see me. This big and quaint-looking gentleman informed me that I did not need to come to his home at Mirak Sultan near Shorkot, to ask for his vote as he had himself come to Shah Jewna to offer his vote to the daughter of Pir Abid Hussain Shah and the daughter-in-law of Pir Imam Shah. But he invited me to come to Mirak to break bread with his wife and children and requested for a date from me so that he could get a befitting feast prepared.

This set the pace for my campaign, criss-crossing the district, being feted everywhere, I managed to scoop up fifteen members who pledged support within a fortnight. Next came the moment to decide my panel of special interest members. It was easy enough to select the farmer, labour, and minority candidates—but I had a hard time finding a suitable woman who would be considered electable—and eventually settled on the wife of Jamal Khan Baloch, much to Soobaan's chagrin. When my group of fifteen supporters collected at Shah Jewna House to proceed to the District Council Hall, the younger members seemed to be very curious regarding Begum Jamal Khan's appearance. Since she was middle-aged and homely looking, I quietly suggested to her that she keep her *burka* on till after the election for fear of disappointing her electors. We were with a majority of three and with four special interest votes being added to my total, I would have a comfortable lead for my chairmanship and could relax a bit. We drove confidently to the District Council Hall. The ballots were cast, but when counted, three of my members were elected, although, my farmer member was defeated, which came as a shock. However, still with a comfortable majority of five in hand, we returned to Shah Jewna House fairly triumphantly. As the members seated themselves for a discussion on what may have happened, Dilawar Khan Chaddhar, who had been an MPA colleague of mine, and was now a member of my Council, went inside and fetched the Holy Quran from a table in the hallway where it was always kept and placed on it on his head, declaring that he swore by the Holy Book that he had voted for all four members of my panel and urged that all members take similar oath so that the guilty one be identified or all would remain suspect.

'Please stop!' I said. 'It is only an election. The vote is voluntary. There is no coercion required in this matter.' But they opted not to listen to me and the Holy Quran was passed from head to head. I was terrified. Someone had lied through the most serious oath a Muslim can take and that too in my house, which made me feel really wretched. But the very next day, the culprit revealed himself. Haji Azizul Hassan, who had led my father's funeral prayers, came to see me and informed me that a gentleman had come to see him to ask what '*kufara*' or penance was required to be paid for taking false oath on the Holy Quran. The gentleman had been elected Member District Council and his family name was Bharwana! I requested Haji Sahib to keep the matter to himself as I would still need that vote. Like Haidar Bharwana, this kinsman of his was feckless, bogus, and overtly religious, a complete '*munafik*' or hypocrite, who is denounced most frequently in the strongest words in the Holy Quran. My cousin Iffi challenged my victory over him in the contest for membership. Fortunately the Court gave a hearing before the contest for Chairmanship. I decided to engage Shahid Hamid who had resigned from government service and set up a law practice, while Iffi engaged S. M. Zafar, a seasoned and eminent lawyer who commanded a hefty fee. On the day of the hearing, I entered a chamber of the Lahore High Court for the first time. I was alone with my Counsel while Iffi was accompanied by a bus-load of supporters. Zafar's argument was that seven polling stations were irregularly constituted and the votes cast at these should therefore be declared null and void. I was confused, at which point Shahid said, 'Conceded, Your Honour, but if you total the votes of the remaining polling stations, the respondent is still the winner.' Pocket calculators were brought out, the result sheet examined, my lawyer's arithmetic established as accurate, and the petition against me was dismissed. When I thanked Shahid, he laughed and said he had been ably assisted by S. M. Zafar who had failed in his arithmetic!

On election day for Chairman, I walked into the District Council Hall to find that not only were my Bokhari cousins and Faisal Saleh Hayat in the cavalcade of Zaffar Abbas, but Nazir Sultan of Bahu Sultan, Mohammad Ali Shah of Rajoya and Haidar Bharwana were also there. I asked Mohammad Ali Shah what I may have done to offend him. His wife had been in school with me and Zaffar Abbas was his local rival. He laughed and said, 'Bibi, if you win, the whole of Punjab will think all of us in Jhang wear bangles!' Wearing bangles was a taunt flung in Punjabi at men who were accused of being effeminate.

The ballots were cast and counted and I won the chairmanship of Zila or District Council, Jhang. The male bigots of Jhang would be looking good in their bangles, I thought to myself. Despite them,

I had managed to become the first woman in Pakistan to Chair a local council. Meanwhile, there was a tie between Fakhar Imam and Hamid Raza Gillani, who each got an identical number of votes. Hamid won the toss but Fakhar obtained a Stay Order from the High Court on the grounds that Hamid's proposer was not duly qualified. This meant that Fakhar's Chairmanship would be in limbo for a few months until the case was decided in the court.

Mother and the children arrived in Jhang, and when I took the children into the District Council Hall, all three of them, awed by the ornate chair that I would be sitting on during my council meetings, wanted to sit in the chair concurrently! And folk in Shah Jewna rejoiced when we went to my father's resting place in the Imambarah. On the beat of dhols, there were slogans of *'Puttar Banrh Wikkhaya Hai!'* (you have proven yourself to be a son). But happy as the moment was, I knew there was a daunting task ahead of me. Doing a man's job in this misogynist culture was not going to be easy. The challenge of development was monumental, but I was determined to work at top speed and pull my district out of its backwardness. I plunged in headlong, going to my new office the very day I was notified, to get myself apprised of the budgetary details of the institution and to schedule the inaugural meeting of my Council.

Leaving my house the following morning, I saw a jeep, which looked fairly new, parked in my driveway and a couple of new gardeners working on the lawns outside. I called the gardeners and asked who they were and who had asked them to work in my garden. They informed me that they were Zila Council employees and that Mukhtar Butt, who was the District Engineer, had sent them. Telling them that I had not asked Engineer Butt for gardeners, and that my own gardener was enough, they were told to return to the Council. Then a bearded, unkempt-looking fellow appeared who introduced himself as Ismail, the Zila Council driver who had brought the Chairman's jeep, which had been earlier in the usage of the Deputy Commissioner. I kept the jeep and rode in it to the Zila Council premises, in assertion of my legal right to use the vehicle. I was led into an office, which was a little cubby hole adjacent to the Council Hall. The hall had been built by my late father when he chaired what was then known as the Jhang District Board. He was the first elected chair of this board. The chief officer, Tareen, and the District Council engineer, Mukhtar Ahmed Butt followed me into the office. Tareen informed me that he was the brother-in-law of the naval chief, which explained his uppity body language, while Butt, with a bushy grey beard, informed me that he had had long years of service as an engineer. He had been in Jhang for only a year. Since his home was in Sheikhupura, he had mostly worked in Lahore. The *sous-entendu* of both officers was that they were at a sufferance to be serving in a backwater like Jhang. I understood this to mean that they were unlikely to be cooperative and compliant.

I asked them if there was anyone around from my father's times and they sent for the head clerk, who appeared to be ancient, with shaky upper dentures and thick lens spectacles. He told me with great pride that my late father had recruited him and taught him everything, thereby probably conveying to me that he was above reproach. Behind him stood a frail looking, very dark and wizened fellow who introduced himself as Humayun Girwah and said that he was my father's devotee. He had been appointed *chaprasi* (orderly of sorts) and served as his door keeper, saying that he missed him ever so much even today. I asked him to be seated and addressed him as 'Mehr' Humayun, which made him grin from ear to ear, and I knew that Humayun would be one man who could be trusted.

The resource base of the Zila Council stood at three crores, or thirty million rupees. Twenty-five million was held in securities and five million in the Personal Ledger Account of the chairman, previously operated by the Deputy Commissioner, who also had access to 'octroi' tax which accrued to the District Council, and brought in as much as the rest of the council's income. But now the government had recently announced that the 'octroi' charges stood withdrawn from the districts. The annual revenue receipts stood at fifteen million of which half went into salaries and establishment costs, while fifteen million was the development budget for the district, which, of course, was a pittance. Looking at the numbers I resolved to double the income as well as the development outlay within the first year and told the Zila Council staff to prepare for the inaugural meeting of the Council, as the Council's mandate would be required to raise additional levies and to delineate a revised development program.

Not being used to working at a cracking pace, I encountered considerable resistance from Tareen and his subordinates, who were clearly unable to pull their weight, and I therefore decided that Tareen would need to be replaced, while an internal readjustment could be made on the head clerk, pending the decision, until the Zila Council inaugural meeting. My first *ijlaas* or meeting went off smoothly, because in my address to the members I assured them that those who supported me, as well as those who opposed me, had equal rights as members and I would remain strictly neutral in the performance of my tasks and equitable in the allocation of development funds. Moreover, I would be accountable to my council.

After this I took them into confidence regarding my intent of making additional levies to improve tax collection and to double the development programme. I was cheered by the entire House and given a unanimous vote of confidence. Sardarzada Zaffar Abbas made a graceful speech, saying that with a proud legacy behind me, I could be trusted to manage the resources of the council judiciously and that he would urge me to hold the annual Zila Council *mela* or fair in the early spring, suggesting the month of February as opposed to March. His motion was carried and as the meeting culminated, I settled down to work tirelessly, taking in the recommendations of all the members for the revised development programme, prioritizing the upgrading of primary schools to middle schools and middle schools to high schools, building thirty miles (ten per tehsil) of additional rural roads, bringing electricity to thirty (ten per tehsil) new villages, and adding as many healthcare and veterinary dispensaries as resources would allow, ensuring a minimum of one each per tehsil.

Seeking an appointment with the Governor Punjab, I visited General Sawar Khan to request him to inaugurate my District Council *mela* of Jhang at the end of February, and to revert the 'octroi' income back to the District Councils. My invitation to the fair was readily accepted. 'Abida Bibi, may I ask you a personal question?' querried the General. 'You are chairing an important District Council, one of the largest in the Punjab, and our reports are that Syed Fakhar Imam is likely to obtain the chairmanship of Multan, which is the largest District Council in the Punjab, and you happen to be married to each other, so pardon my asking, but how on earth will you stay in touch with each other?'

While he was talking, I was looking at a letter that was lying on General Sawar's desk. It was the letter that Hazrat Ali (Prophet Muhammad's [PBUH] cousin and son-in-law) had written to

Malik Ashtar, and which my father had made me memorize as a teenager. I laughed and responded, 'Exactly as I have done over the last eleven years since I got married to Fakhar Imam. We are not constantly tied to each other, you know. We spend about half the month together and the rest of the time we work at Jhang and Multan respectively. Now with our new responsibilities we are likely to spend about ten days in the month together. We would probably be too busy to notice each other's absence. Not being with my children is more of a deprivation. But then I have a commitment to my late father's memory, and there is always a price to be paid for carrying a commitment.'

'Thank you for the explanation. Your father would have been proud of you. I look forward to your *mela*. I hope you will be bringing your beautiful horses and cows to it. Some of the best Sahiwals I have seen, better than at Jahangirabad. I told this to Subah Sadiq Wattoo who claims to have the best and he is sitting on government land, while you are on your own land reform farm. In fact, the six hundred acres resumed from you would be better off returned to you. If you apply for it, we could consider returning it to you.'

'Thank you, Sir. I will apply when there is a duly elected government in place. I look forward to receiving you at Jhang, but what about the "octroi"!' He told me he would look into that as he did not quite follow the issue. As I exited from the Governor's office, the military secretary was standing by the doorway, with a rosy-faced young man beside him, who was carrying a large box of *mithai* (sweets). Seeing me into my car, the military secretary informed me that this was Mian Nawaz Sharif as though I would know who he was, I had never heard the name before and did wonder.

General Sawar's chopper landed at the police lines. As I went up to receive him I experienced a surreal moment. The last time I was at this helipad it was Zulfikar Ali Bhutto who had clambered down the steps of the chopper, in a Mao cap and white safari suit, seven years previous, and now it was a taller, more erect figure in khakis with a hat and a stick, albeit with a benign face under the hat. Sitting in the Governor's car, we drove to the Mai Heer Stadium situated across the railway line from the helipad. I had taken the stadium project in hand to get a high and sturdy brick wall constructed, along with a grand entrance gate and new stands. The gate had been completed while the wall and stands were under construction. I was briefing the Governor on this when we arrived and were received by a huge, cheering crowd. As we alighted, the impassioned rhythm of dhols accompanied by *shehnai* (eastern flute) greeted us. A host of white pigeons were released to fly up above our heads and melt into the bright blue sky.

My members had lined up on both sides of the dais with the Commissioner, Deputy Inspector General of Police, Deputy Commissioner, and Superintendent of Police besides them. I effected introductions and led the Governor up on the dais where our National Anthem was played, the flag of Pakistan unfurled, and we moved to the ornate red velvet sofas laid out in the front row of the stadium. Bearers in white sherwanis and smart white turbans, led by my friend Mehr Humayun, promptly served freshly squeezed orange juice, and I sought my guest's permission to present the welcome address. The 'Sipaas Naama', or dedicated tribute, had been nicely written by the best calligrapher in Jhang and beautifully framed by the best frame maker in Chiniot. I read partly from the text and partly spoke extempore, since I was by now comfortable in the role of a public speaker. The applause, as I enunciated plans for the development of Jhang, was deafening.

I spoke of the proud culture of our land of Jhang and of the two rivers which flowed through it, the Jhelum and the Chenab, of its love legends, of Heer and her Ranjha, of Mirza and his Sahiban; of its great Sufis, Bahu Sultan, Shah Jewna, Shah Shaikh Ismail, Shah Daulat, Shah Zinda, and Noori Gul Imam; of its skilled craftsmen, the wood carvers and metal workers of Chiniot, the *lungi* (loin cloth) weavers and *khussa* (rural shoes) makers of Jhang; and the lacquer turnery workers of Shorkot. I spoke of its great equestrian tradition of tent-pegging, pig-sticking and polo. I spoke of its farm potential and of its contribution to the economy of Punjab and Pakistan, and I lamented how little it got back from the State. But, I asserted, we were now determined to make a push for development and to take our district forward so that we would cease to be known as a 'backward district' and begin to be cited as a model of progress and as one of the better-developed localities of Pakistan.

The Governor responded to my twenty-minute speech with brevity, announcing a million rupees grant for our council, assuring us that he would support better funding for Jhang. He complimented the people of Jhang for being forward looking enough to have chosen the most dynamic person in the district as their chairman, and who was the only woman elected to this office in Pakistan. He also said he would put up my request to the Federal Government for reverting the 'octroi' tax back to the District Councils. As we came back to our seats, a pair of beautifully mounted horsemen in full regalia galloped in from the far end of the stadium to seek formal permission to begin the show. Assent given, the cavalcade started, with a battery of dhols and *shehnai*, followed by the *dharees*, the local version of bhangra dancers in brightly coloured *lungi*s, white *kurta*s, and vividly coloured waistcoats with turbans to match. Their exuberance made everyone tap their feet and cheer them. The dancers were followed by the horses and stallions from Shah Jewna, prancing proudly behind the blue and gold S. J. (Shah Jewna) banner, and then came the dancing horses of the local clans. The equines were followed by the bovines. A second Shah Jewna banner came in view with my Sahiwal bull, 'Bahadur', behind it, with his dark hump and deep red torso shining in the sun. Behind him came the very best cows and some heifers. The next banner was that of the Sial Farm of Shamshir Khan Sial who had also brought some fine-looking bulls and cows, after which came the Gillani Farms banner with better than average stock, and finally the Kot Amir Shah banner with what were not like the better quality of pedigree animals. The cows were followed by the wonderful buffaloes of the Lakhnanas, who were reputed to own the finest Nili-Ravi buffaloes in Punjab, and then came the cows, Dhanni, Sindhri, and Sahiwal breeds, and the buffaloes of many individual farmers, whose names were announced individually. Tailing the bovines were herds of Lohi and Kajli sheep and some magnificent goats from Thal. And finally came the camels from Thal, with their curved necks and high stepping hooves moving to the rhythm of the dhols.

These were followed by the tent-pegging teams of Jhang, Sargodha, and Toba Tek Singh. The names of the teams were announced as they filed past each team was cheered by the stands that were now filled to capacity, which meant that the *mela* attendance had exceeded our expectations and broken previous records.

As the cavalcade ended, tea was served, with the bearers bringing tall silver stands laden with sandwiches, patties, and pastries. The commissioner gave me an approving look as if to suggest that I had done it properly this time, and I flashed him a friendly smile. While tea was being served, the inimitable *dharees* and bhangra dancers, the 'maachi' clan of Jhang, moved up before the dais, dancing right up to where we were seated, and the two little boys in front bent so far backwards that their heads touched the ground. People got up to shower ten rupee notes on them and the boys now bent so low forward that they started to pick up the notes by their teeth. I stopped them because it was terribly unhygienic even though it showed how supple their young bodies were. The tent-pegging then started, with singles to begin with, then doubles, and finally teams of four. 'There is no sight in the world to equal the beauty and excitement of a team of four tent-peggers on black, shiny steeds with their silver trappings glinting in the sun, their elegant style of balancing themselves in their exquisite handcrafted saddles, often passed down from generation to generation, as they charge down towards the pegs, and no thrill bigger than when they lean forward and with stunning accuracy to lift the pegs on the tip of their lances.' I gushed to the Governor. He agreed with me, smiling affably.

'Abida Bibi, one day you will be a Minister and you should take Culture and Tourism as your portfolios. You would be good at promoting all this for Pakistan to the world.' This was the second time such a suggestion was coming my way. But for the moment I was immersed in living my culture, my heart beating in unison with all the folk who were enjoying the *mela* along with me. The finale came with the dancing horses and the two master trainers of the Punjab, both men were the pride of Jhang, both vying with each other to make their horses dance as skilfully as any ballet or Bharat Natyam dancers. These tall and handsome men were Ghulam Mohammed Pathan and Mumtaz Bikaneri. The crowd showered hundred rupee notes on the dancing horses and on the *sawar*s (horsemen).

The Governor stayed an hour beyond his schedule, until the aide de camp reminded him that the chopper needed visibility to take off. I thanked him and suggested he give away just a few prizes before leaving. That over, accompanied by my councillors, we led him to the exit and returned to the pavilion to watch the rest of the tent-pegging and give away the remaining prizes. As I walked down the steps, the crowd gave me a standing ovation, cheering, 'Bibi Abida Zindabad!' and some voices rang out: 'Colonel Abid Hussain Zindabad!' Tears rolled down my face. At that moment I forgot the fatigue of the many days of gruelling hard work it had taken in the preparation of this event. I had been exacting on every detail and my staff and members had risen admirably to the occasion. The chief officer had been replaced by an excellent man called Minhaas, and Butt, the engineer, and I had developed a working relationship despite his beard and his tendency to pray multiple times a day instead of the required five! Throughout this time, I had remained conscious of the fact that my father had been a founding member of the National Horse and Cattle Show in the 1950s, and there was therefore a standard to live up to.

A few months later, there was a change of Governor in Punjab. General Sawar Khan went up as Vice Chief of Army Staff, and General Ghulam Jilani Khan was appointed Governor and Martial Law Administrator (MLA). It was May and sizzling hot. I went to Lahore to look in on the children and catch up with my mother, also thinking of making the new Governor's acquaintance, to follow up on the request I had made of his predecessor for enhanced funding for the development of my district, and for reverting the 'octroi' tax back to us. I called his private secretary somewhat reluctantly because I had a negative impression of General Jilani. Not only was he the officer who had led the evidence against Khan Abdul Wali Khan and the Baloch leaders in the Hyderabad Conspiracy Case, he was also allegedly the intelligence officer who had informed General Zia ul-Haq that Bhutto was going to replace him and appoint his military secretary, Imtiaz Varaich, in his place, which allegedly made Zia intervene and declare Martial Law. The Governor's private secretary continued to be Mr Hameed, whom I had known him since my childhood, from the time when my father was in the West Pakistan Cabinet and Mushtaq Gurmani had been Governor. When I called, he said he would give the Governor the phone. 'Oh no, Hameed Sahib, don't bring him on the phone. Get an appointment for me for a visit.' As I was speaking another voice came on the phone: 'Jilani speaking, Begum Abida. You can come any time. Come right away, if you like. I have the Secretary Local Government coming shortly so that will be useful. I will see you first. He can wait. So how long will you take to get here?' I was somewhat amazed at this and said I would be with him in half an hour. When I told Mother, she said that she did not think well of this man and cautioned me to be careful, saying that he had been an intelligence officer perhaps for too long.

I was totally disarmed when, driving into the porch of the Governor House, a short, slight man in white trousers and a pale blue shirt, wearing slippers with their back straps open, stepped forward, and opening the door of my car, said, 'Ah! Begum Abida, nice to see you. I am Jilani.' What a strange man, I thought to myself. Ghulam Jilani Khan was short, balding, and greasy looking. He sounded utterly insincere. An odd-looking fellow, he seemed such a contrast to his predecessor.

He led me onto the front lawn and held a chair out for me under a garden umbrella. He asked me if I found it too hot, moving the pedestal fan close to my chair. I told him I was fine, as it was early evening and the sun was beginning to come down. 'I do not much care for air conditioning, having been a soldier all my life. I love to sit out on this beautiful big lawn. Won't be a Governor all my life, so may as well enjoy it while I can.' He had parked himself opposite me and slouching in the cane chair, gave me a broad smile. 'So, what shall we talk about?' he asked me enthusiastically.

'Well, I wanted to see you about providing more funds for the development of my district.'

'Will be done. What else? I hear you are a painter. I believe you studied Art in Florence. I studied dance and music at Shantiniketan, you know, Tagore's Academy in Bengal. This was pre-Partition, of course.' He gabbled on.

I went back to Jhang and immersed myself in work. Although I did take a couple of weeks off to be with my mother, Fakhar, and the children during the summer, but for the most part I was busy in Jhang, working at a gruelling schedule daily, from 8 a.m. to 10 p.m. I was determined to double my revenue receipts and to monitor my development programme so as to ensure that the sluggish and corrupt *thekedari*, or contract system, picked up speed and efficiency. Fakhar's case was still pending in Court. He gave me hard-nosed advise when I consulted him on issues relating to bureaucracy that were bothering me. While we were at Cliffden in Murree, Aunty Vicki Noon came up and suggested that I ask Agha Shahi, who was now Foreign Minister, to include me in the UN Delegation that would be going to New York in early September. The thought of going to the United Nations electrified me, so we persuaded Agha Shahi to come up to Cliffden for lunch. Mother understood that I was not comfortable soliciting on my own behalf, even though, I did it for all and sundry all the time, so when Agha Shahi came up, Mother asked him what was the criterion for selecting a delegate for the UN General Assembly Session.

'Technically, Begum Sahiba, public representatives from the federating units are recommended by the government, therefore, under the current dispensation whoever the CMLA and his MLAs may choose to nominate shall go.'

'And you find that kosher, Shahi Sahib?' I interjected.

'Well, young lady, under Martial Law, every order must be deemed as kosher. Let me tell you I am impressed with your usage of typical New Yorker terminology. You would do well as a delegate, but I could only support you if the Governor of Punjab nominates you.' Agha Shahi spoke in his exclusively measured manner, while cleaning out his pipe and fumbling with his match sticks.

'I would rather not solicit the Governor of Punjab, but you are a friend, so you can ask him if you like. That way I would incur no obligation to military authority.' Shahi then opted to change the subject and I thought that was the end of the matter, but towards the middle of August, when I was back in Jhang, Agha Shahi called to say that he was going to be in Lahore the following day and was to call on the Governor, who was hosting a dinner for him. The Governor had asked him who else he should invite and Agha Shahi had given Fakhar's and my name.

We arrived for dinner and found General Jilani sitting with Agha Shahi in the front lawn. He bounced up to greet us enthusiastically. The dinner table for four people was laid out on the lawn, with the candelabra on the table lit already, attracting an incredible number of moths. Agha Shahi was drawing on his pipe as usual, while our host quizzed Fakhar on the progress of his case. I wondered if Shahi had mentioned the UN matter to Jilani before our arrival. As we sat down for dinner, Shahi raised the issue. Jilani laughed and said, 'New York will be more interesting than Jhang, Begum Abida, but who will manage your Zila Council in your absence?'

'Jhang, for me, is more interesting than New York. But since I am at the learning stage, the UN experience is likely to add to my knowledge. I have started implementation of my council's programme and the monitoring will be supervised by members of the council and my vice chairman. The rules also allow me to nominate an acting chairman if the chair is away for three months,' I answered.

'Done. I am impressed that Begum Abida finds Jhang so interesting. But if the Foreign Minister wants her in his delegation, it is fine by me.' To register my appreciation for the decision taken, I made the gentlemen laugh, regaling them with stories of my previous two visits to New York, the first one with Uncle Amjad Ali, whose idea of entertainment for his sister and niece was to take us for a walk in Central Park, and whose economizing with everything was legendary. I narrated the story of my visit with Dr Zbigniew Brzezinski in 1975 who kept telling me that America's primary interest was India because of it being the world's largest democracy, and Pakistan could only be important if we stuck close to the Shah of Iran, and five years later it was as though the Shah was ancient history. I told them of how Senator Sparkman, Chairman of their Foreign Relations Committee, had kept saying, 'You sure are young and pretty, let me introduce you to my friends,' instead of listening to a word of what I had to say regarding the Kashmir issue, over which I had been painstakingly briefed by Sahibzada Yaqub Khan, our Ambassador in Washington at the time. The Americans were amusing, but the UN would be fascinating because it would mean meeting people from all over the world, and lobbying for my country, I opined. The gentlemen agreed.

Shortly thereafter, Agha Shahi informed me that I should be prepared to leave for New York by the middle of September and would return by the middle of December. Leaving the children for two months was a real wrench, but Fakhar was gearing up for his installation as Chairman of the District Council in Multan, and I knew he would be deeply immersed in work with his new duties, and probably barely notice my absence.

We were a twenty-member delegation that arrived in New York for the 35th session of the UNGA (United Nations General Assembly), which included retired Chief Justice Hamoodur Rahman, Miangul Aurangzeb of Swat, Jam Amir Ali from Sindh, and three District Council Chairmen, other than myself, from Peshawar, Sahiwal, and from Vehari. At the time, Ambassador Niaz Naek was our Permanent Representative, and Agha Shahi as our Foreign Minister headed the delegation.

I camped for a few days with my friend Nasra Hassan, who worked in the Angolan Mission at the time and had a charming one bedroom apartment in Beekman Place, which was an easy ten-minute walk to the UN building. I then moved into a one bedroom rental of my own in Beekman Towers, around the corner from Nasra's place. I was allocated the Third Committee, the Humanitarian and Social Affairs Committee, which was popularly known as the 'Women's Committee' since it worked on the 'soft issues' of inter-state relations. My advisor from the Pakistan Mission was Shaukat Fareed, whose cousin Nigar Ahmed had been my closest friend at school. Shaukat's wife Marina had my friend Rubina Khan staying with her. Rubina had been working with Ford Foundation in Guyana and was now in New York for interviews for a job at the UN Secretariat. Between Nasra, Rubina, and Shaukat Fareed tutoring me, I obtained a reasonable insight into the workings of the UN system and, through a series of conversations with delegates and representatives of diverse African, South American, and East Asian countries, my views on Third World political assertion, and on the Non-Aligned Movement confirmed and matured. I spent long hours nattering with Yousaf Buch, who was now speechwriter for Secretary General Kurt Waldheim, on the plight of the Kashmiris, and with Agha Shahi on the nascent revolution in Iran and its implications for us as the neighbouring state and of the significance of a Socialist state bringing instability to Afghanistan. And I learnt to read the extensive papers put out by the Status of Women Commission and became friends with its Chair, Lucille Mair, who was an impressive Jamaican. Ambassador Tarzi of the PLO (Palestinian Liberation Organization) struck me as being the most active Representative whom I observed hectically networking in the Delegates Lounge on a daily basis. My fascination with the UN was, however, tempered by a Berber delegate of the Polisario Front whose comment on the UN was that this organization only served the interests of our former colonial rulers and imperial America who used it to make independent-minded and spirited leaders of developing countries regurgitate their anger and ventilate their thoughts so that they could either be bought out or marginalized by the intrusive and 'friendly' advise of 'donors', to ensure that they retain their status of 'First World' while we continue as developing countries without ever becoming fully developed, and remain the 'Third World'.

About halfway through the General Assembly session, Ambassador Niaz Naik informed us that General Zia ul-Haq was coming to

New York to address the General Assembly, and our delegation would be received by him when he came to the Mission to solemnize the marriage of Tayab Siddiqui, a foreign service officer currently posted at Washington D.C., who, we were informed, had been in our embassy in Jordan at the same time when Zia ul-Haq took a military delegation there. The two had ended up being good friends. This was touted by the officers at the Mission as Zia's greatness. He had remembered his friend, even after having climbed to the dizziest heights of power. In sycophancy, our bureaucrats are hard to beat. When we were introduced to Tayab Siddiqui, to my dismay, I found some of my fellow delegates with political backgrounds fawning over him as well. Feeling that I did not belong in any of this, I suggested to Ambassador Naek that I should be excused from attending this wedding ceremony, but was told by him that since Zia ul-Haq's wife will be accompanying him, being the only woman in the delegation, I would be conspicuous in my absence, as the list of invitees had already been sent to all relevant quarters in Pakistan.

I had met Begum Zia when her husband was Corps Commander in Multan. I was in Multan with Fakhar sometime in 1976, and had been invited to tea by Begum Allah Nawaz Tareen, whose house was in our neighbourhood, and had found myself seated on a sofa next to a rather homely-looking lady on the one side; and a perky, attractive one on the other. So I chatted with the perky lady, believing her to be the corps commander's wife, only to discover, just as we adjourned for tea, that the homely and quiet one was General Zia's wife, while my new found friend was Shahida Ejaz Azeem, whose husband was then the Division Commander, and was now our Ambassador in Washington. At least I would have the identities right this time, I thought to myself.

When the CMLA arrived at the Mission, we were herded into the committee room. The furniture had been removed, the floor nicely polished, and this was now to serve as the reception room for the gentlemen, while the bride and all the women were to be in the second largest room on the premises, which I was not allowed to access until the entourage had arrived. When the visiting delegation emerged, and as I was about to slip across to the 'ladies side' as everyone described it, seeking to avoid General Zia, Ambassador Naek stepped forward and said, 'Would the Pakistan delegation kindly follow us into the office, where the President of Pakistan will address you.'

General Zia ul-Haq sat at the desk, with Niaz Naek beside him, while we were ushered into our chairs, ten on either side of the room, in two rows of five each. Everyone seemed to be anxious to be in the front rows, hence, it was easy enough for me to slither into the back row. After a lengthy recitation from the Holy Quran, Zia started speaking, and all the while his eyes seemed to be scanning the room. His articulation was polite, the language pedestrian. When he finished, Justice Hamoodur Rahman asked for an increase in the daily allowance of the delegates which was $100 per day. I thought this was embarrassing, and as Zia ul-Haq directed Ambassador Naek to double the allowance, he looked straight at me and said, 'How are you Abida Sahiba? You will now be able to speak more often on the telephone to Syed Fakhar Imam, who is working very hard on his District Council. I was in Multan the other day and he made an excellent presentation on his development plans for the district.' Although he was probably trying to be courteous, I thought he was trying to humiliate me indirectly for being absent from my district, or did he think I needed taxpayer's money to make phone calls to my husband? In any case, I did not appreciate being singled out and was even considering some sort of response, when he got up, was surrounded by everyone, with several of the men being unctuous to him, as he shook hands with everybody and started walking out of the room, with my colleagues following suit.

I was not exactly feeling on top of the world going in to join the ladies. Begum Shafiqa Zia ul-Haq was seated on a sofa next to the bride, and I was led to the chair beside her. As we exchanged greetings, she held my hand and in Punjabi said, '*Kurriye*, young girl, have we met before?' This was quite disarming. She was simply dressed and seemed to be a straightforward person. I told her we had met in Multan and that I was Fakhar Imam's wife. This made her lean towards me and whisper, 'I have met Fakhar Imam. He is such a handsome and well-educated young man, I liked him very much. He told me that you visit Multan rarely. But Multani women are very dangerous. Are you not afraid of leaving him alone so much in that city?' she asked sympathetically.

'Begum Sahiba, I am a working woman, and currently elected to Chair the Jhang District Council. I have no siblings and my late father died at a relatively young age, leaving me not only his material assets but also a set of social as well as political obligations and a contingent mass of responsibilities to deal with. Meanwhile, Fakhar, whose father died when he was young, since he grew up, has had his mother and several sisters and brothers to look after. Our work is centred in two separate districts, but our children go to school at Lahore and are looked after by my mother, who is also Fakhar's *khala* (maternal aunt). So Fakhar commutes between Multan and Lahore, while I commute between Jhang and Lahore, and we spend about half the month together. Now I am in New York with the delegation and will not be seeing my children and Fakhar for another six weeks. But you know, I feel that if Fakhar

Imam is going to prefer some woman over me, then to hell with him!' After my lengthy assertion, I thought I had conveyed the message clearly and must have satisfied Begum Zia's curiosity. Her response came as a surprise.

'You know, when cantonment wives tell me that I should not let my husband travel alone, I tell them the same. If my man is stupid enough to prefer a woman over the mother of his children then it will be his loss and he will come to regret it, and like you I also say, then to hell with him!' I could not help liking Shafiqa Zia.

The following day, General Zia arrived at the UN to address the General Assembly. During his address, someone stood up from the Visitor's Gallery and shouted, 'Zia ul-Haq, killer of Palestinians, murderer of Bhutto!' The heckler was led out by security guards. Meanwhile, Zia ul-Haq did not so much as flinch and continued with his speech. I thought he had nerves of steel, my animus towards him somewhat diluting.

After General Zia's departure from New York, everyone at the Mission relaxed and some of the delegates started taking trips to other cities, which had become affordable with the enhancement of our allowances. I had taken a few thousand dollars of my own which I was using to pay for the expensive one bedroom apartment that I had rented in Beekman Towers. By now my money was also depleting. It was becoming colder so I went and bought myself a black mink coat. What shocked and disgusted me was that some of the officers at the Mission and their wives talked to me with more respect when they saw my coat. It mattered far less to them that I was the only woman to be elected Chair of a District Council and more that I was rich enough to buy a fur coat. I then understood from their reactions that our foreign service folk become so disconnected from the realities of the country they represent that the only kind of Pakistani they value is either someone in power or someone with pelf. Hence, as soon as the UNGA session ended, I was ready to return home, my curiosity regarding the UN and our diplomats laid to rest.

Umku, Shugu, and Abid were delighted with the toys I took for them while Fakhar simply said, 'I missed you.' Mother was pleased that her brother, Uncle Amjad Ali, that she so looked up to, had a good word to say about me, of how active a delegate I had been. Immersed in the warmth of family reunion, my dedication to Jhang was tested, and I had to will myself away from my nest in Lahore. But when I settled down to resume work at the District Council, I learnt that my two month absence had dealt a severe setback to the work that I had set in motion before leaving for New York. My vice chairman was embroiled in domestic problems and had nominated an acting chairman from among the members who had created near chaos, and I found myself having to burn the midnight oil to get the affairs of the council back on track. But I understood at the time that hard work lends itself very often to making effective solutions, and promising myself and my colleagues that I would not disappear on them again for more than a few days at a time, I soldiered on, determined to make my council the top performing local council in the country, with Fakhar Imam now giving me stiff competition from District Council Multan.

One day in early February, with Fakhar in Multan and me in Jhang, while chatting on the phone, we decided to meet up and do a joint inspection of the roads which we were constructing in the vicinity of our adjoining Tehsils: Khanewal and Shorkot. As our vehicles pulled parallel, Fakhar opened the door of his Zila Council jeep which he was driving and asked me to hop in and also get my district engineer into his jeep. We were in Shorkot and headed towards a road which was being constructed under my supervision. Fakhar was quite critical of the quality of the work and kept addressing my engineer as he pointed out the flaws, which irritated me considerably. Suddenly his vehicle came to a standstill. Fakhar looked at me sheepishly and said that his jeep had run out of gasoline and we would have to shift into my vehicle! I felt elated! And my moment of triumph was short-lived, for the very next day Fakhar called to say that he had received a call from the MLA (Martial Law Administrator) telling him that CMLA (Chief Martial Law Administrator) wanted to see him in Islamabad, with the possibility of offering him a Cabinet position. 'Oh dear! Fakhar, I hope you will refuse it. You cannot join a military government. We are democrats, do not forget.'

'Sure,' said Fakhar, 'If I am made the offer I shall say that I have just got into my stride in my District Council and would rather work at the local level.'

'Please stick to that, Fakhar, Zia will only be using you. He has to shed the Ministers who sat with him through the Bhutto execution. It is logical that he should try to take in fresh faces that look and smell better.' I was so perturbed that I left for Lahore to ask Mother to caution Fakhar but he was untraceable. His staff at Multan said that he had taken the flight to Rawalpindi and they had no further information. He had not called me for two days, which was very unusual. We put on television news, and mercifully, there was nothing there. On the third day, Fakhar called to say that he would be taking oath shortly as Minister for Local Government and Rural Development. I was unhappy, even though I understood that for the majority, being appointed on a ministerial position meant a lot to them. I also knew that

Fakhar would do well on the assignment because of his diligence and knowledge. I told the children that their Papa had become a Minister and sent them across the road to their grandmother's house where I knew that Fakhar's mother and sisters would be celebrating. Fakhar's family were apolitical and saw politics as most people do, as a pursuit of public office, while my mother and I understood politics to be the pursuit of an ideal.

The children returned from their grandma's house flushed with excitement and soon enough all the aunts, uncles, and cousins were arriving to congratulate me and Mother, after having congratulated Fakhar's mother. Everyone kept asking me why I had not gone to Islamabad for the oath taking, and I told them all that Fakhar had not asked me to come because he knew I disapproved of his joining a military regime. Most of my relatives were critical of my attitude, cynical about Bhutto, reminding me that he too had been minister in a military government, and questioning of the validity of democracy. Despite losing half our country, the well-heeled seemed to have learnt very little and almost conferred preference to military autocracy over the democratic process, reminding me that in a way, I too had lent myself to it, giving precedence to local development over rigid adherence to a return to the parliamentary democratic process.

Umku, by now a precocious ten-year-old, returned from school the following day looking disturbed because her classmates had decided that her dad had become a priest, since they saw in the dictionary that a minister is a priest! And then Nasra Hassan arrived from New York and militated with me that we both go to Islamabad to visit with the 'Minister', as she said her curiosity was getting the better of her and she wanted to see what the trappings of ministerial office precisely were about. Umku and Shugu wanted me to go and check out whether their Papa had become a priest! So, Nasra and I flew in to Islamabad. Fakhar was at the airport to receive us. We spent a couple of days together, laughed and joked a great deal, visited a few friends, and returned to Lahore without having seen any appurtenances of the ministerial office. Fakhar had been given a rather battered old car and was lodged in a somewhat crummy set of rooms in the officers' hostel, and his office was in a house in F-6-3, which was being renovated. He assured us that the next time we came he would be better organized, but Nasra was going back to the US and I still had a lot of work to catch up on in Jhang.

A few weeks later, Al-Zulfikar, allegedly an organization created by Zulfikar Ali Bhutto's sons, Mir Murtaza and Shahnawaz Bhutto, hijacked an airplane and flew it into Kabul. As a result of this incident, General Zia announced a further set of draconian laws that were utterly outrageous. I telephoned my friend Nigar Ahmed and we decided to visit Fakhar in Islamabad to ask him to resign in protest. By now Fakhar had shifted into a suite of rooms at the newly constructed Sindh House. Nigar and I were both appalled by the grandeur of the building and the luxury of the rooms but we could not help but admire the stunning view of the Margalla Hills from the large French windows of the sitting room of the suite that Fakhar was occupying. Both of us urged him to resign. The one good thing that Zia had done was that he had not abrogated the 1973 Constitution, but had held the Articles relevant to fundamental rights and the democratic dispensation in abeyance. Now, by promulgating a Revision of Constitution Order, he had created an instrument to deface the Constitution at will. We argued with Fakhar that he should not go along with this and it would be befitting for him to walk out of the Cabinet and tender his resignation. Fakhar heard us out carefully and assured us that he would not be part of this Cabinet unduly, that he would resign on a point of principle and we should have faith in his ability to choose the appropriate moment. 'I will not let you girls down, I promise. For the moment I am working on amendments to the local government laws with a view to facilitate the functioning of the local councils and I will be touring in all four provinces to consult with the mayors, chairmen, and the local officials, and Chandi you can join me on these tours whenever you wish, not as my wife, but as my colleague.' This was a sop that I fell for. Nigar was staying with her parents and I decided to spend a few days with Fakhar and meet with some of his Cabinet colleagues and their spouses. Also Gulzar Bano, Secretary of the newly created Women's Division called me and suggested a meeting in connection with a Women Councillors Convention which she was planning, in coordination with the Ministry of Local Government and Rural Development.

Gulzar Bano was the most senior woman in the Civil Service of Pakistan and the first woman to be appointed Secretary to Government. She also wrote poetry—some of her poems, worthy of admiration. Visiting her office was a real pleasure, and I was excited at the prospect of encountering women elected to different local councils throughout the country. She told me that since I was the only woman elected to chair a council, I would be the convenor of the conference; she would be the conducting officer; and Fakhar Imam as the Minister in-charge would be the Chief Guest. It would take her two months to prepare for the event. I informed Fakhar after my meeting with Gulzar Bano that maybe he should hold off his resignation till after this Conference! And when I met Begum Arbab Niaz, whose husband was also a Minister, and told her that I wanted my husband to resign from this military government soon after the proposed Women

Councillors Convention, she remarked that I was a strange girl wanting to drag myself and my husband back to our villages. She never wanted to go back to their village because Islamabad was so much nicer. It came as a shock to me that anyone should prefer Islamabad over their village.

The women's convention gave me an excuse to visit Islamabad each time I went from Jhang to Lahore, and like Begum Niaz I started liking the place, but not more than where my roots were. Islamabad was a small town, quasi-rural at the time. I took the children with me for their spring break. They loved Sindh House and the sandwiches that Fakhar would keep ordering for them. Abid was a handful, but the girls were no trouble at all, and it was lovely for us to be together. Fakhar told me that he wanted to move into a house and would I like to go out with Razi Abbas, his private secretary, to look for a suitable house. I saw several houses and chose a simple single-storied house in sector F-7/2. Fakhar suggested we move the children to Islamabad, but thinking that it would break my mother's heart, I also reminded Fakhar that if he were then to resign, it would only cause an unnecessary disruption in the education of our children.

I decorated the house with cane furniture and simple wooden sofas painted white and upholstered in off-white embroidered khaddar from my weaving and embroidery project at Shah Jewna. I brought my Daadi's old brass urns from the Shah Jewna *haveli* and filled them with tall ferns plucked off the roadside between Jhang and Islamabad, and I hung plain off-white cotton curtains along the French windows of the living room. The décor came together quite well, light and cheerful and altogether different from the *sarkari* official style of the time, based on heavy carved furniture and velvet upholstery with velvet drapes in deep pink, lime green, or turquoise.

Fakhar wanted to host a big dinner for some of his cabinet colleagues and federal secretaries, but I suggested that we host half a dozen small sit-down dinners instead, making an interesting mix of people at each dinner, so that discourse on national issues could be encouraged, since everyone in Islamabad was tight lipped on crucial questions raised by sensible people everywhere else in Pakistan—questions pertaining to where the country was heading. So we embarked on a social agenda which led to our developing friendship with Ijlal and Shireen Zaidi, Ejaz Naek, Roedad Khan, and Agha Shahi, among the civil servants; and Ilahi Bux Soomro; Mahmood Haroon, Arbab Niaz, and Mir Ali Ahmed Talpur among the politicians, who had been around since my father's time; and Zafarullah Jamali, who was of our generation. My conversation always focused on development issues in rural Pakistan and the importance of reverting back to democracy. 'When are we going to have elections?' was the standard question I would pose. The response would invariably be a shrug, a smile, or silence. Fakhar would remind me gently that my question caused embarrassment to most people. So I would return to Jhang and the issues of my Zila Council, stopping en route always with my mother and my children.

Fakhar decided to call a Local Government Convention, bringing together all the Mayors of the Corporations and Chairmen of the District Councils of Pakistan. General Zia ul-Haq inaugurated the conference which was held in the auditorium of the State Bank building and which was where the National Assembly used to sit in the seventies. Zia read out a speech emphasizing the importance of 'Grass-Roots Democracy'. He sat on the podium in what was the Speaker's Chair, with a chair placed on either side, one occupied by the Minister Finance, Ghulam Ishaq Khan, and the other by Minister Local Government, Fakhar Imam. Secretary of Local Government Muzaffar Hussain, who ironically had also been Secretary National Assembly in the past, conducted the proceedings. The Governor/MLAs: Lt. General Ghulam Jilani Khan from Punjab, Lt. General S. M. Abbasi from Sindh, Lt. General Fazle Haq from the Frontier, and Lt. General Rahimuddin Khan from Balochistan, were seated in the Speaker's Gallery, a level below the podium, but at a higher level than the floor of the auditorium. After Zia, all those named above spoke, and finally, two hours later, the Mayors of Karachi, Lahore, Peshawar, and Quetta were called to the podium to speak, followed by two Chairmen District Councils from each province. From Punjab, I was one of the two who spoke. I demanded that 'octroi' duty that had been withdrawn from the District Councils be restored, primary schools be placed under District Councils, and the Khairwala Drainage Scheme, which had been awaiting implementation for several years, be resourced forthwith, to rescue a fertile tract in the districts of Sargodha, Faisalabad, and Jhang from waterlogging and salinity. My speech drew prolonged applause from my colleagues. When the conference concluded, Ghulam Ishaq Khan complimented me on my speech and said that the 'octroi' duty could not be restored to us, since it had become a part of the provincial budget, but he could recommend to the provincial government's that the inter-district movement on certain goods be allowed as a local levy, which could, if efficiently collected, bring in almost as much as octroi. And he would try and find funds for the drainage scheme mentioned. He then said that he had the privilege of working with my father whose demise had been a loss to the nation. On hearing this I warmed up to him, recalling that my late father, too, had regard for him as an honest and dedicated servant of the state.

On an invitation by the UNICEF, Princess Anne was on a visit to Pakistan as head of the 'Save the Children Fund'. Fakhar, as Minister of Local Government, and Rural Development, was Minister-in-Charge of the visit. General Zia hosted a dinner for the Princess at his modest residence, the Chief of Army Staff House of the time, which was smaller than the one occupied by Ayub Khan or Yahya Khan, and where Z. A. Bhutto and Begum Bhutto had also lived for five years after Bhutto had been handed power initially as CMLA. It was a warm evening, and the guests were ushered onto the front lawn of the house where the Princess was introduced to all of us by the Pakistan representative for UNICEF. While introducing me, Zia informed the Princess that I was a horsewoman, so it was not surprising that Princess Anne looked towards me at the end of the presentation, telling me how nice it was to meet a horsewoman here. She then asked me whether I preferred hunting or hurdling, looking straight at me with laughter in her eyes. I glanced around the garden and said, with as straight a face as possible, but with the laughter doubtless in my eyes as well, 'Not much to hunt here, Your Highness, and I stopped hurdling a while back. I breed horses now: thoroughbreds, bloodlines imported from England, Ireland, and France.' She said that I would get on famously with her mother.

We were led indoors for dinner and seated at a table which seemed too large for the room it was in. The protocol in Zia's days was that husbands were seated next to wives. I had Fakhar sitting on my right and General K. M. Arif on my left, with his wife next to him. Begum Arif had short hair so I assumed her husband would be more liberal than General Zia who sat at the head of the table, flanked by his wife and the Princess.

'When are we going to see elections to Parliament, General?' I addressed my question to K. M. Arif.

'Perhaps after you have completed your first term of local government,' was the polite response.

'But that would be after another two years and take us into 1984, while people have been waiting since 1979, and that is a long time,' I said.

'Not really. It is just enough time to ensure that a second term is secured for the local councils so that democracy is properly implanted at the grass-roots,' he answered. 'Does it not make you feel bad that you have broken your promise to the people of this country? You had said that local elections would be followed by parliamentary elections,' I added, perhaps a trifle testily.

'They will be.' He responded evenly, while Fakhar kicked me under the table and whispered in my ear that I had obtained the answer to my question and should not belabour the point. Suddenly, I felt suffocated and could not wait for the dinner to end.

Next, King Hussain and Queen Nur of Jordan visited Pakistan. Fakhar was told that he would be minister-in-waiting to the King and I would be required to be lady-in-waiting to the Queen. I returned to Islamabad for two whirlwind days. Queen Nur was bright and beautiful—a Princeton graduate—she would lead the conversation and the King would hang on every word she uttered. I took her to our Institute of Folk Heritage, which we could rightfully be proud of. The Queen asked many questions, which

Uxi Mufti, the Executive Director of the Institute that was also known as 'Lok Virsa' handled competently.

On my next visit to Islamabad I decided that I would not be a mere Begum Minister, but would use my access to do something creative. I met Uxi Mufti again, this time in Vicki Noon's home, who was chairing the Pakistan Tourism Development Corporation at the time. Uxi invited me to visit Lok Virsa, for a more detailed visit. Uxi and I got on like a house on fire and dreamed up the Crafts Council of Pakistan which collaborated with Lok Virsa to launch a folk festival which took Islamabad by storm and centred me with the diplomatic corps of the time. We structured the National Crafts Council and got it recognized as an affiliate of the World Craft Council and I was unanimously elected its first Chair, and was succeeded two years later by Zari Sarfaraz. We organized a gathering of master craftsmen from all over Pakistan, which led to a revival of many of our dying traditional skills and crafts of unmatched quality.

Meanwhile, General Jilani had set up a Provincial Council which comprised Mayors and Chairmen of District Councils and District Headquarters Municipal Chairmen. This council would meet at Lahore for a quarterly review of the development programmes of the Local Councils. The venue selected by the MLA ironically was the Chamber of the Punjab Assembly, and as a former member of that Assembly. I deeply resented the misuse of this Chamber by an ad hoc body called the Provincial Council, created through an edict, with no legal sanction behind it. Jilani would sit in the Speaker's Chair and conduct the proceedings chattily and informally. He had also inducted a cabinet into which he had sought to rope me in, but I had declined politely. He installed in his cabinet a motley crew of men and women that included Mian

Salahuddin and Nawaz Sharif to represent the Kashmiri clans of Lahore, he said. He would bait Mian Salahuddin to provide comic relief and guffaw at his gaffes, which was deeply offensive. Mian Salahuddin was an affable and genial gentleman with a wonderful background, and Jilani's attitude towards him caused me considerable resentment. The ministers would be seated in the front row and the chairmen in the second and third rows. Fakhar would attend some of these meetings in his capacity as Chair of Multan District Council, and sit quietly in the back. During one of these Provincial Council meetings, Khan Abdul Wali Khan happened to visit Lahore and was staying at our house, as usual. A police jeep detailed to follow him wherever he went would remain parked outside our gate.

The Provincial Council was convened for two days. On the second day of the meeting, while Wali Khan was in still in town, Fakhar returned to Islamabad before the meeting adjourned. I was chatting with a colleague, as we were wending our way out, when the Military Secretary to the Governor/MLA approached me, and said that the Governor was waiting to see me in his chamber. As I entered, the Governor stood up from the long table of what used to be the Chief Minister's Committee Room. With him was the then Secretary to Governor, a civil servant.

'Ah! Begum Abida. Come and sit down. I wanted to take up this matter of the strange situation outside your Lahore residence. I have two police jeeps there, one to escort your husband's ministerial vehicle, and the second one to follow an opposition leader, Wali Khan, who I believe is staying at your residence. This is not on Begum Abida, not on at all.'

'I do not understand what you wish to say, General. Fakhar and I live with my mother and Khan Abdul Wali Khan is her honoured guest. He and his wife always stay with us when they visit Lahore, and it is good of him to ignore the fact that Fakhar is in the cabinet of a military government which he opposes, in principle, as a die-hard democrat.'

'Look here Begum Abida,' said Ghulam Jilani Khan in a curt voice, 'I have served in the Frontier, even in Sindh and Balochistan. They are nothing—these *chotte subay wallas* (these folk of the smaller provinces). Punjab is Pakistan, never forget that.' He banged his fist on the table. I could not believe what I had just heard. I looked towards the secretary, whose face was impassive. And my anger flared; my short fuse well and truly alighted. 'Pakistan is Balochistan and Frontier and Sindh and Punjab. And nobody should forget that, General, not after what we did to East Pakistan.' My voice was loud and clear and I stood up to leave. Jilani looked up at me incredulously and I noticed froth appearing at the corners of his pink mouth as I marched out of the room, running down the grand stairway and the front steps and into my waiting car, my body trembling with anger and fear, cognizant that we were under Martial Law, and there could be consequences. When I told Mother, she hugged me and said that she was proud of me, but also warned me that from now henceforward, I would be in the path of danger. I told her of my having signed up for the China course with the Administrative Staff College, which would keep me out of harm's way for at least a month.

The China course involved two weeks of daily sessions at the Staff College from breakfast till dinner, and reading up on China, along with attending lectures delivered by people with experience of China. After this was over, we would spend a fortnight in the People's Republic of China, visiting Beijing, Guangzhou, Shanghai, and Gweilin. We were then to fly back to Beijing and return to Islamabad. We were to study the 'four modernizations' undertaken by the Chinese authorities, in what was the cusp of the Mao era and the Deng era. It was a fascinating time to visit China, with those denounced earlier as 'revisionists' now at the helm of affairs, and with everything that had gone wrong being blamed on the 'Gang of Four'.

I loved China. I loved my interpreter, Mr Li, I loved eating Peking Duck in the 'Peking Duck' restaurant in one of the alleys of the old part of the city, Beijing (formerly Peking). I loved the children in the playschool of the commune outside the city, in the heartland of the Han Chinese, who flew readily into the arms of visitors. I admired the intensive utilization of land where vegetables or fruit trees were planted even on the water courses. I loved the boulevards of Beijing and Tiananmen Square, the succulent cuisine of Guanzhou and the pre-Revolution flavour of Shanghai, where the major reminder of regimentation came in the form of callisthenics performed like street theatre early in the morning in the narrow streets of the old city, before the teeming workforce entered their workplaces. We met endless numbers of Chinese officials and asked endless questions. In Shanghai I also had the liberating experience of being able to offer Friday prayers in a mosque in the Jamaat or congregation alongside the men. I have always taken the message of Islam to have been a liberating force for women, poorly interpreted through history, to end up constricted by a predominantly misogynist culture, so it pleased me to no end when the Chinese Imam insisted that I stand at the start of the line of the Jamaat, fifteen that we were: fourteen male civil servants and myself. I was totally comfortable with this, while my colleagues looked awkward, with the exception of three men who took my praying alongside of them in their stride. I returned from China with these outstanding civil servants, Ahmed Sadik,

Kanwar Idrees, and Sheikh Fareeduddin as my friends, and we continued to remain friends. I learnt a lot in China and am able to comprehend their current level of success, because of having caught a glimpse of the foundation being laid more than three decades previous.

After my rough conversation with Jilani, I felt that Fakhar's ministerial lark would not last, so I decided the time had come for me to buy a house in Islamabad. I had toyed with the idea since the late seventies and we were now into 1982. I discussed the matter with my mother and she agreed that upon selling some land and dipping into the savings we had and adding them to the land proceeds, we could buy a house which would be easy maintenance. Fakhar had declined to get a plot which was offered to him by General Zia, next to a plot allotted to A. K. Brohi. Ilahi Bux Soomro was allotted a plot also. When Ilahi Bux heard from Fakhar that he had declined the plot offered to him by Chairman CDA (Capital Development Authority), Ilahi Bux asked us whether we would mind if he had the plot marked out for Fakhar allotted for himself, and the one marked for him for his brother, Ahmed Mian Soomro.

Mahmood Haroon also took a plot and I was horrified that all these wealthy gentlemen thought nothing of becoming beneficiaries of subsidized real estate at the cost of the exchequer. I expressed my thoughts to Khwaja Rahman, who was a great friend of Ilahi Bux Soomro and brother-in-law of Mahmood Haroon, who looked me straight in the eyes and said, 'I will agree that it would not be nice to ask for a plot as a favour, but if it is being offered then not to take it is stupid, because a refusal of this type does not come into any record.' But I did not agree with Mannaji, as Khwaja Rahman was popularly known, sold a hundred acres of land and bought myself a house Sector F-7/3 in Islamabad. And I was proud of being 'stupid'. But certainly Mannaji was right in so far as there being no distinction made between those politicians who seek to do the correct thing, as opposed to those who do not bother, nor any acknowledgement from the public either.

Having been able to complete my projects within the first four years of my tenure as chair of Jhang Zila Council, I therefore knew I would sail through my second election on the basis of my performance, but was concerned for Fakhar. He did not realize that as Minister he was expected to achieve miracles by his supporters and would be likely to hit problems when he returned to his district. I suggested to him that he should resign from the Ministry which would relieve him of the burden of incumbency, but his cousin Khawar, who was present when I made the suggestion, shot down the idea, saying that although Fakhar's prospects were grim, if he were to quit the ministry, his defeat would be a certainty. So, as anticipated I won my election, securing a second term as Chair of the Jhang District Council, while sadly Fakhar lost his election by one vote. The minute I heard he had lost, I sat in my car and sped down to Multan. En route, I thought of persuading him to resign, but by the time I reached Fakhar's Multan house, he had already resigned, and the announcement had gone out to the media. Fakhar's resignation created a great stir. The newspaper editorials eulogized him for taking a principled position and withdrawing from the Federal Cabinet after having lost his local election by one vote. His siblings were dejected, as were his supporters, with the exception of Javed Hashmi, who agreed that Fakhar Imam had now centred himself for leadership. And my mother was so proud of him that she drove all the way down to Multan to congratulate him. Fakhar was reluctant to leave Multan, but a couple of days later, he got a letter from CMLA/President, reprimanding him for releasing his resignation to the Press before tendering it in person to his appointing authority, and asking to see him. Fakhar was glum as we were driving into Islamabad, but he cheered up when all our friends came to laud him for what he had done. And we were both relieved that we were in our own home and the only thing that needed to be surrendered was his car and the official telephone. We wondered if we should rent out the house and consulted with Aunty Vicki, who was always at hand to help us along. She thought we should keep it, as there would be an election sooner rather than later, and we would need it then.

We went back to our respective districts: Fakhar to focus on the affairs of Kabirwala Dairy, a milk-processing plant which he had set up and was now seeking to sell as it was not doing too well; and me to concentrate on the developmental work that I was doing for Jhang.

Zia ul-Haq's regime was coming under challenge, as the dust settled on the local elections. Benazir Bhutto had been exiled to London, and Begum Nusrat Bhutto was mostly confined to her home in Karachi, but a broad-based front comprising all the major political parties had been formed, the MRD or Movement for Restoration of Democracy, was led by Nawabzada Nasrullah Khan, Khan Abdul Wali Khan, Air Marshal Asghar Khan, and Ghulam Mustafa Jatoi, representing the Pakistan Peoples Party (PPP), JUI, and included several other smaller parties. The MRD launched a movement demanding a repeal of Martial Law and a restoration of the democratic process. This was by now a familiar pattern in our national life: autocratic rulers challenged by democratic movements.

As the movement started picking up steam, Congressional delegations from the US that visited Pakistan to support the

Afghan resistance also started stressing the importance of the democratic process. Inside Afghanistan, the Mujahideen groups of Islamic dissidents from mostly Arab countries, along with some Sudanese, were brought in to bolster the Afghans who had taken up arms against the Soviet troops that were now in Afghanistan to assist the Afghan government. A coordinated effort by Turki al Faisal, who headed the Saudi intelligence and General Hamid Gul who headed the Pakistani Inter-Services Intelligence or ISI, under the guidance of the CIA, seemed to be giving the Red Army a difficult time. American visitors to Pakistan sounded increasingly confident that the Soviets would withdraw out of Afghanistan under the pressure of the Mujahideen. But the view of the establishment in our country seemed to be that the Soviets would remain in Afghanistan for a long time, and America would have to give Pakistan increasing amounts of money in assistance, and ultimately when Pakistani soldiers in covert operations were able to give the Russians a defeat and maybe even drive them out, America would remain grateful to us for a long time.

Meanwhile, the influx of refugees from Afghanistan had run into the millions and by 1984, the estimated number had exceeded five million refugees. Our population, at the time, stood at around ninety million, so this huge number of refugees was exceeding five per cent of our total population. Hundreds of tent villages had grown around Peshawar, Mardan, Nowshera, and in Punjab, initially around Pindi/Islamabad and Murree and then through Attock, Chakwal, and Khushab down to Mianwalli.

Tens of thousands of Afghan men were now leaking into the Pakistani work force, the majority of them entering the private transport business and squeezing out local enterprise. The Afghan refugees also brought with them a culture of guns and drugs and a few hundred of them claiming kinship with Pir Gillani, who was a prominent exile figure patronized by the ISI and the CIA, turning up in Jhang. They bought a few modest-sized homes in the Satellite Town area of Jhang city and encroached on a couple of acres of public land adjacent to their homes. The matter was brought to my notice and I suggested to the Chairman of the Municipality, Shaikh Iqbal, that he get the encroachment cleared, but he informed me that the Superintendent of Police was refusing to cooperate. When I questioned the superintendant as to why he was not proceeding against a blatant encroachment by foreign nationals, he informed me that he would proceed, provided I could help him face the flack from higher authorities. Assuring him I would seek to do so, I was impeded by a call from Mir Afzal Khan, a personal friend of ours, asking me in his ineffably courteous way not to press on the matter of encroachment by the Gillanis. Mir Afzal also told me that I should start preparing for elections which were round the corner.

However, what was announced in 1984 was not an election but a referendum. It was a strangely worded referendum, seeking affirmation of the voter as a good Muslim, to endorse Zia ul-Haq as President. In other words whoever did not endorse Zia as President was not a good Muslim. The wording of the referendum met with much cynicism and criticism, but it did not deter the Zia administration.

Within a few days I was summoned as Chair of Zila Council, Jhang to the rest house of Zila Council Toba Tek Singh to meet the Deputy Martial Law Administrator of the time, Major General Ghulam Mohammed. The Mayor of Faisalabad was there, along with the Chairman of the Zila Council Faisalabad, a transporter known as Nazeer Kohistani because he owned the Kohistan

Transport Company, who had allegedly bought his chairmanship by gifting a dozen members of his District Council with brand new Toyota cars, which was considered scandalous at the time. The Chairman of Toba, a newly-created district, was acting as host. We were seated facing the general, with a table between him and ourselves, and a few junior officers, presumably his staff, sat behind us. The general tossed out a brief lecture on the importance of continuity for Pakistan, with a major theatre of war going on next to us in Afghanistan of the multiple virtues and capacities of General Zia and his indispensability to the nation and of the importance of an eighty per cent turnout in the referendum. At the end he stated, magnanimously, that the voters would be absolutely free to vote as they wished. Even if they opted to vote against the President, they would in no way be impeded from doing so, but, of course, he was confident that the overwhelming majority would repose their trust in the President. And he called on us elected leaders of our districts and of Faisalabad city to ensure eighty per cent mobilization. I had to make a huge effort not to laugh. Nazeer jumped up as soon as the general finished. 'I will ensure eighty-five per cent turn out, Sir,' he proclaimed. The Mayor was quiet but the Deputy Mayor, Sidique Salaar, boomed, rolling up his sleeve, 'I will ensure a ninety per cent turnout.'

'And I will achieve a hundred per cent presence of voters and they will all vote for our Mard-e-Momin, or man of faith', said the Chairman of Zila Toba.

'And what about Jhang, Begum Sahiba?' queried the general politely.

'Well, I cannot beat a hundred per cent can I? With due deference to the claims of my colleagues, I do not seek to mislead you, General. The voter turnout at the very best will be about twenty per cent. People go out to vote when there is a contest. In the absence of contest there is little interest and there is no way that any of us can coerce the very people who have voted for us, since we are dependent on them for our own votes. In any case we were all elected in a non-partisan local election and are not members of the government, so we have no obligation to carry out instructions from a higher authority.' As I finished I heard the officer behind me say, albeit in a low voice, 'By God, this woman deserves to be shot!' I reacted. Standing up, and addressing the General, I said, 'Your officer behind me is making threatening observations. You had better restrain him.' Whereupon the General told the officer to leave the room, but did not demand an apology from him, as may have been appropriate.

In the wake of a visibly unsuccessful referendum, because of the abysmal voter turnout, at the end of 1984, General Zia ul-Haq announced parliamentary elections on non-party basis. The electoral rules promulgated stated that only those individuals could seek election to National Assembly and Provincial Assemblies who were not members of an existing political party. You could contest if you renounced your membership. Since neither Fakhar nor I were members of any party at the time, we were happy to gear up for the contest. The MRD member parties decided to boycott this election, but many of their members renounced membership and went ahead to participate in the first parliamentary elections after an unprecedented gap of eight long years.

Prime Minister Zulfikar Ali Bhutto with MPA Syeda Abida Hussain at Jhang, Sept. 1972.

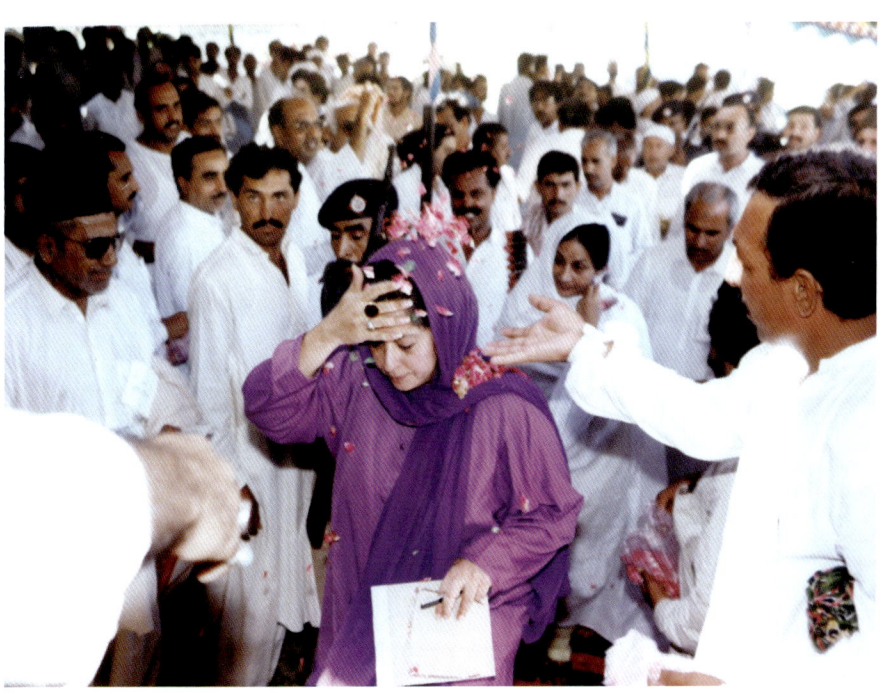

Syeda Abida Hussain at an election rally 1985 at Jhang. Abida Hussain was candidate from N.A. 69, Jhang III.

Islamabad, May 1991: H.R.H. Princess Diana of Wales being received by Syeda Abida Hussain, Minister-in-Waiting to Princess Diana. Standing beside Abida is spouse Fakhar Imam, Minister of Education.

Islamabad, 1991: H.R.H. Princess Diana of Wales with President Ghulam Ishaq Khan and Minister-in-Waiting to H.R.H Syeda Abida Hussain.

Washington D.C. 1991: Dinner hosted by Ambassador Abid Hussain of India, standing far right. Syeda Abida Hussain Ambassador of Pakistan is surrounded by SAARC and some ASEAN Ambassadors.

Washington D.C. 1992: Ambassador Abida Hussain of Pakistan with President George Herbert Bush of USA.

Washington D.C. January 1993: Ambassador Abida Hussain meeting President William B. Clinton with First Lady Hillary Rodham Clinton standing beside him.

December, 1996: Presidency of Pakistan. Interim Cabinet of 1996, Govt. of Pakistan. Minister Abida Hussain seated between Prime Minister Meraj Khalid and President Farooq Leghari and the rest of the Interim Cabinet.

Washington D.C. 1997: Minister Abida Hussain on a visit to Washington D.C. with Senator Carol Mosely Brown. Seated alongside is Ambassador Riaz Khokhar of Pakistan.

Islamabad, Presidency, March 1997: After oath-taking of Syeda Abida Hussain in the Cabinet of Prime Minister Nawaz Sharif. President Farooq Leghari and Prime Minister Nawaz Sharif both pour tea for Abida Hussain.

President Farooq Leghari administering oath to Syeda Abida Hussain and other ministers in the Cabinet of Prime Minister Nawaz Sharif, March 1997.

Bonn, Germany, 1998: Minister Abida Hussain with Dr Anne Marie Schimmel, renowned German Sufi scholar.

Minister for Population, Syeda Abida Hussain with Minister Koizumi of Japan, who went on to become the Prime Minister of Japan.

6

National Assembly, At Last

Throughout my election campaign from N.A. 9 Jhang III, I remained in high spirits. I knew I would win by a wide margin. My cousins all boycotted, convinced that the parliamentary elections would go the way of the referendum. The elections were conducted on a non-party basis but anyone could contest by renouncing their party affiliation, as in the local elections.

The voter turnout was healthy enough to confer legitimacy on the process, and I scored an easy victory, winning by a margin of more than thirty thousand votes. I was the only woman to win in the general elections and would be the first woman in Pakistan to take oath alongside 114 male members who had been elected. Fakhar was elected from his home constituency in Kabirwala, so we also became the first married couple to be mandated by popular vote.

We had barely finished with our rounds of gratitude, when we were called by the Governor/MLA to come to Lahore to attend a reception that he was hosting, after which we would be meeting the Chief Martial Law Administrator (CMLA).

Fakhar and I reached Lahore simultaneously. Accompanying me was my father's old friend, Arif Khan Sial, who had won from Shorkot. Our house in Lahore was inundated with callers. All sorts of people came to solicit our votes for the Senate and for the seats reserved for women. The three of us also had six running mates who had been elected, and our own supporters were eyeing

Senate seats. Many of our visitors were among those who did not identify themselves with a constituency but belonged to the urban elite, who failed to understand the value of belonging to a specific locale, when it came to their personal interest. Dr Mahbubul Haq, who had worked long years in the World Bank being one of them, turned up, accompanied by my Uncle Babar Ali. Fakhar and I were amused to see our high-minded friend grovelling in front of Khan Arif Khan, who expressed surprise when Mahbubul Haq informed him that he was a blue blooded Punjabi who would protect the rights of the Punjab in the Senate.

'Dr Sahib, we thought you were a Bengali who advocated Land Reforms on the pattern of Bengal. The rights of Punjab are appropriated by the military and bureaucracy. We need Senators that live among our people and who will protect them from Punjabi officers. But now you have come with the youngest brother of Begum Abid Hussain, whom I, and my family, revere. With Babar Ali as your recommendee, we will have to consider your request.' Both Mahbub and my uncle looked hugely embarrassed. Mahbub was followed by Wasim Sajjad, my former classmate's Azra's husband, who wanted us to explain the run-off system of voting for the Senate. He was followed by Colonel Mukhtar Hussain Kirmani from Shergarh, who tied with Wasim when the votes were counted and with whom he had a run-off in which Wasim prevailed. Fakhar's friend Khalid Mahmood brought General Jilani's protégé, Mian Nawaz Sharif who had been elected MPA and wanted our support as Chief Minister. Sylvat Sher Ali Khan, a family friend, older than me, and Raafia Tarik Rahim, another family friend, who was my age, also came to ask for our votes for the seats reserved for women. I told them both that since Attiya Inayatullah had come all the way to Jhang, spending a day on the campaign trail with me, and Mrs Nisar, whose husband was a civil servant and had come also to Jhang along with Arif Khan Sial who pleaded support for her, I had committed my first and second options to them but I would give my third option to Sylvat Sher Ali, and my fourth option to Raafia. Fakhar told Raafia that he would give his first option to her and his second option to Sylvat who we would address as 'Apa', or elder sister.

The reception at the Governor's House was out in the front garden, teeming with the newly elected members from all over the Punjab. As we entered the garden, General Zia ul-Haq in his immaculate white *sherwani*, with General Jilani similarly clad, greeted us affably and I could have sworn that Jilani slurred his usual form of greeting: 'Mizaaj-e-Sharif' (a polite form of a 'how do you do') which sounded more like 'Nawaz-e-Sharif', who he was visibly favouring as the potential Chief Minister. When Khalid Mahmood had brought the emerging tycoon and now clearly budding politician, Nawaz Sharif, with him, Khalid had done all the talking, soliciting support for his friend who came across as a typical businessman, but not quite as a man of the people. However, rumour had it, he had supplied the building material for the house Jilani was constructing in Lahore cantonment, in readiness for his retirement.

Within half an hour the MNAs were required to be assembled in batches of our respective administrative divisions and led into the main reception room of the Governor's House where Sahibzada Yaqub Khan appeared on the side of Jilani and Zia ul-Haq, with General Zia soliciting votes for Sahibzada Yaqub Khan. While I was wondering about this obvious attempt at regimentation, a short bespectacled member from Faisalabad, stood up and addressed General Zia:

> You have stated yesterday, according to the headlines of today's newspapers, the handpicked members of your irrelevant 'Majlis-e-Shoora', your nominated Assembly, were better than us, but you do not know us. You are meeting most of us for the very first time today. And it is the height of arrogance for you to claim superiority of your nominees over those voted for by the people of Pakistan. Therefore, it is my demand that you apologize to the nation before proceeding any further.

Les Generales, as Sahibzada Yaqub Khan would say, looked taken aback, which encouraged me to take the floor next.

> While endorsing what my colleague has said, we would support Sahibzada Yaqub Khan because he refused to resort to indiscriminate firing in East Pakistan and because he is a distinguished Pakistani diplomat today, not because we are obligated to do so. A non-partisan Parliament will not hold water, inevitably there will be a Treasury and an Opposition and all of us as members would be accountable only to the people of Pakistan.

As I resumed my seat General Zia apologized, and through us, he said, to our electors. Meanwhile I noticed that Jilani picked up a file from the table beside him, opening a page which he showed to Sahibzada Yaqub who smiled, while Jilani also chuckled, looking towards me and towards the member from Faisalabad, Chaudhry Shafiq. When our meeting ended, with several members having made duly sycophantic statements, and we were filing out, the telling file with a page open was on the table, I looked down and against Shafique and my name he had inked 'Potential Rebels', proving himself in my eyes to be the spy master he was reputed to be.

As we were driving to the National Assembly which was still in the premises of the State Bank building, while the new Parliament

House was being furbished, I asked Fakhar what seat number he had been allotted, and understood immediately that, since after taking oath we would be electing the women on seats reserved for our gender, the Assembly Secretariat in its wisdom had decided to seat me alongside the quota ladies, as I had been given Seat Number One, while the male members were to be seated in alphabetical order.

'Stay calm,' counselled Fakhar, sensing that I was already spoiling for a fight. There were many effusive exchanges of greetings with our new colleagues, government officials, and journalists, as we entered the premises of the Assembly, ascended the escalators, and entered the House. I went straight up to the Secretary National Assembly, Aminul Haq, and asked him why he had seated me next to the quota ladies that we would be voting in. I was popularly mandated and hence should be seated as other mandated members. The secretary, in classic bureaucratic fashion, sought to pass the buck and mumble his way out, making a vague reference to the Acting Chief Election Commissioner who was to chair the opening session and administer oath to us, until we elected our own Speaker, the following day. But with considerable experience of dodgy officialdom at the provincial as well as local level behind me, I was not to be fobbed off by the secretary. Upon my insistence, he asked me if I wanted to be seated next to Syed Fakhar Imam which only made me laugh.

'Mr Secretary, I can sit with my spouse as much as I want in our home, but in the House of the People I have a right to be seated like all other representatives regardless of gender or personal relationship. I hope I make myself clear.'

'Give me a few minutes,' he said. As the bells were rung for the House to be called to Order, a minion of the secretary brought me my seat number. I walked up the fifth aisle and found my seat in about the middle of the aisle, not the most advantageous seat, which would have been seat number one, which I had not wanted. On the other hand, this one was more or less, in accordance with the alphabetical order and I found myself seated next to Syed Zaffar Ali Shah from Sindh. We took oath collectively swearing to uphold all the laws of Pakistan, and then each member had to go up and sign the Register after which we were to cast votes for the twenty women members. Shortly after the names started being called out, and as I was seeking to acquaint myself with the member from Nawabshah seated next to me, to my utter dismay, the Shah asked me not to mind if he changed his seat as all his colleagues from Sindh would joke with him for being seated next to the only elected woman.

'Is being a woman a joke, Shahji?' I asked him, trying to keep the hurt out of my voice.

'We Sindhis are a very traditional people. Please do not take it ill. Perhaps you would prefer sitting next to Syed Fakhar Imam.' He shuffled off before I could frame an answer. I observed him going up to the secretary's desk who was smiling as he looked down at the list of members. The next person the secretary sent up to sit next to me was Shah Turaabul Haq, a cleric from Karachi, whom I greeted, he greeted me back, and looked away.

'Maulana, I am not conscious of my feminity, so I hope you will not be either, and look upon me as a fellow member.' He did not respond and started walking down the aisle towards the secretary. Understanding that he, too, would ask for a change of seating, looking around the chamber, my eye fell on a member, who looked very young. He was seated at the end of the hall, in the parallel row. I left my seat, walked up to the rear end of the hall and across, down the aisle to where he was sitting. The name on the desk was, Salahuddin Saeed. I greeted him and told him he looked like the youngest member of the Assembly and not quite twenty-five. He was from Mansehra.

'Begum Sahiba, would you like to sit down? In exactly two weeks' time I shall be twenty-five. You see my opponent was a lady, Begum Oughi. Do you know her? If she finds out that I am two weeks short on age before I take oath, she will rush to the Court and get a stay order.'

I assured him I was not likely to inform his rival, but if he wanted to ensure it, he would have to sit next to me, and I narrated my saga to him which made him laugh heartily.

'Begum Sahiba, I will request the secretary, very courteously, that he should move me to the seat next to you which is parallel, and in the 'S' row. You will have made your point, and I will get a better seat.'

Smart kid, I thought, and walked down the aisle, and up to my seat, while Salahuddin went to talk to the secretary. En route, I stopped to greet Air Marshal Nur Khan, who had been elected from Mianwali and was standing next to (retired) Air Commodore Khaqan Abbasi, elected from Murree. Both of them had been well reputed airmen and were now, interestingly, grounded in the house of the people.

'Khaqan and I were just coming to chat with you, Abida Bibi. Khaqan is a friend of Zia, while I do not care for him as you may be aware of. I was telling Khaqan that if we accept Zia's nominee, Khwaja Safdar, as Speaker tomorrow, we will look like spineless jokers, and no different to that nominated Majlis-i-Shoora which Safdar presided at Zia's behest. So we were discussing who we should put up as candidate for Speaker in the election tomorrow and we thought of you. As you are the only woman elected, your taking on Zia's man will hit the headlines worldwide.'

'Thank you Sir, but considering the members are reluctant even to sit next to me, not too many will vote for me. But they might vote for Fakhar Imam. And if we are going to take on General Zia, then let us try to win the Speaker's election. If we succeed, it will hit the headlines everywhere in any case.'

'Yes, good idea, let us talk to Fakhar Imam,' said Khaqan Abbasi. As we walked up to Fakhar where he was standing, we found Anwar Aziz and Amir Hussain, both from Sialkot, and local rivals of Khwaja Safdar selling the same idea to Fakhar, who suggested that we talk around to other colleagues, and in the tea break assemble in the cafeteria. About twenty members—that included Abdul Hamid Jatoi from Sindh, Mir Ahmed Nawaz Bugti from Balochistan, and Fateh Mohammad Khan from Swat—all of whom had known my father—joined us. The decision was taken that Fakhar contest against Khwaja Safdar in the Speaker's election the following day. All members of the National Assembly, including the twenty women and five religious minority members we were electing today would be the electoral college of the Speaker and the vote would be by secret ballot. Fakhar suggested that we meet at our Islamabad house in the evening, and each of us should try to bring a few additional members along and then develop a strategy for the vote the following day. Both of us anticipated that General Zia's people would mount pressure on the elected members before the vote, and we wanted to be certain of those who would stand by us.

When the voting for the women members and the religious minority members ended, and their oaths were taken, all members were informed that they had been asked to the Presidency where the President/CMLA would address them. This was the first time that we were visiting the grand edifice which is our Presidency, which had not as yet been occupied since its recent completion, and found it a sterile and impractical building with four lifts to herd us all up into an enormous hallway. Entering a large hall, we were ushered into chairs which had our names pinned on the back of each chair. Predictably, I was seated up in the first row, next to Fakhar, but before us was Illahi Bux Soomro, who looked pleased as punch, anticipating that he would be nominated Prime Minister. General Zia walked in in full military regalia: medals, sash and all. He was followed by two young aides de camp, and seated himself on the dais facing us. Immediately after recitation from the Holy Quran, Air Marshal Nur Khan stood up, and addressing General Zia, he spoke, 'The time has come for you to lift Marshal Law.' Nur Khan's tone was not polite.

'Sir, rest assured I will. But allow a little time for the Parliament to settle down. And now, Honourable members, I request you to endorse my nomination of the Prime Minister of Pakistan. After careful consideration, I have decided on Mohammed Khan Junejo, who is a fine gentleman, and despite being a Sindhi, is such a good man that he has married only once.' Everyone seemed to be taken aback since the buzz was that he had decided on Ilahi Bux Soomro. Poor Soomro seemed crestfallen. Air Marshal Nur Khan stood up and began to leave. General Zia also got up, and while many members flocked towards him, some went towards Junejo, while we started heading out, along with Ilahi Bux.

The day we had arrived from Lahore to Islamabad, my old friend Raana Sheikh and her husband Najmuddin Sheikh, who was Joint Secretary in the Foreign Office at the time, had invited us for dinner. They lived in the government residences in F-6/2, and as we drove into the street, we saw a long queue of cars.

'Raana and Najmuddin seem to have invited lots of guests, and you had told me it was going to be a small informal dinner,' Fakhar observed, as we were walking into their driveway.

'Well maybe the numbers grew because we are two members and you know what this town is like. I suspect we will be socially in demand for a while,' I responded. As we reached the entrance door, Shaikh Anwar Zahid, who had been designated Secretary to the Prime Minister was standing at the entrance receiving guests. We had come to the wrong house! We apologized but Zahid insisted that we come in for a while since we would know most of his guests. Sure enough, as we entered his sitting room, we found Ilahi Bux Soomro present, surrounded by all the important secretaries to government, along with their wives, being feted as the Prime Minister elect. Making our escape to Najmudddin's place a few minutes later, we found a few friends gathered there which included the Military Secretary to General Zia, Mahmud Durrani. When I told Raana that we had walked into the wrong house, Mahmud doubled over with laughter over our mistake, and said, 'But the real joke is that these bureaucrats are dining with the wrong Prime Minister.' We tried to make Mahmud elucidate his observation but he kept laughing and would say no more, so Raana and I decided that he was only joking. And now, as we walked out of the Presidency with Ilahi Bux Soomro looking disconsolate, we knew better.

Eighty-four MNAs collected at our house that evening. Addressing the gathering, Fakhar said if he was going to take a stand then he would not back off regardless of any pressure that may be mounted. Khan Arif Khan Sial sounded sceptical but Arif

Jan Hasani from Balochistan, and Mumtaz Tarar from Mandi Bahauddin stated emphatically that since it was to be a secret ballot, there were a sizable number who were assembled here, therefore, it would not be difficult to withstand any pressure. Raja Shahid Zaffar from Rawalpindi suggested that I approach all the women members who had been elected, while Fakhar visit the members who were not present, to add to our strength, and guard against any slippage. Chaudhry Akhtar Ali from Sialkot, who had earlier served as Chairman District Council, had brought Sajida Nayyar Abidi with him. She had been directly elected as Member District Council, so she accompanied me to lobby with the women. We first went to Attiya Inayatullah, who I had voted for. After that we went to Afsar Qizilbash who was like an older sister to me; then to Aunty Vicki's house to talk to Malik Nur Hayat Noon; and on to Sylvat Sher Ali Khan and then to Raafia Tarik Rahim, all of whom were close family friends. They were all spontaneously supportive and all thought that Fakhar would make an outstanding Speaker, because although he was young he had the required gravitas.

Next we visited Bilquis Nasruminallah, the widow of a civil servant and the niece of Justice Safdar Shah, who had written the note of dissent in the Bhutto case. We then visited Mrs Nisar, whom I had given my second option to. Both ladies were supportive. We then went to Nur Jahan Panezai from Balochistan who was about my age. She was enthusiastic and supportive. We went to Rehana Mashadi who was rather vague; not like Apa Nisar Fatima who was forthright enough to tell me that she would not like to displease General Zia ul-Haq, and whose candour I appreciated.

Although some of these women did not seem to be from pampered backgrounds, all of them were comfortably middle class. I regretted not having had the wit to ask Mai Soobaan to file her papers. She would have been a more authentic representative of the average Pakistani woman and would have made her presence felt in the Parliament. Our last two visits were with the two most glamorous women members of our Assembly: Kulsoom Saifullah from the Frontier; and Salma Ahmed from Karachi, who were totally supportive. Sajida Nayyar planned to file for the Punjab Assembly which was to be summoned shortly. She assured me that she would telephone all the other women members first thing in the morning, and tell them that we were winning hands down. She was confident that we would get their support. This would ensure our securing at least eighteen out of the twenty women's votes for our independent candidate for Speaker, Fakhar Imam.

After dropping Sajida off, I returned home past midnight, to find Salman Farooqui, whom I had interacted with when he was Secretary Local Government in Sindh and Fakhar was Federal Minister Local Government. At that time I had received an invitation to accompany the minister on a tour of Sindh in my capacity as Chair of District Council Jhang. I had never driven through Sindh before. Salman had organized an efficient five-day tour, taking us through Hyderabad, Sehwan, Dadu, Larkana, and Nawabshah, all the while addressing district councils and municipalities everywhere we went.

And now Salman Farooqui was sitting in our house in Islamabad along with an odd-looking fellow, whom Salman introduced as Brigadier Imtiaz. Salman told me that he was now an Additional Secretary, posted in the Secretariat of the incoming Prime Minister, and along with his companion had come to see Syed Fakhar Imam.

'My husband does not seem to be home as yet. It is very late. Can I take a message? He will probably wake me up when he returns,' I said to the visitors.

'If you do not mind, Begum Sahiba, we will wait for Shah Sahib to return. We have an important message to deliver to him. But your servant seems to be up, so could we encroach on your hospitality and ask for some tea. You look very tired so please do not feel obliged to sit with us,' Salman replied. It was clear they were not going to share the message with me, so I ordered tea and went up to my bedroom to sleep, as I was truly exhausted after what had been a long and tense day. But sleep eluded me so when Fakhar came in, I was awake.

'What did Salman Farooqui want, and who was the odd-looking Brigadier with him?' I asked Fakhar.

'He is an ISI officer, popularly known as 'Billa', as Salman mentioned. I was meeting him for the first time. He said that General Zia wants me to give up the Speaker's slot, since he has listed me up as finance minister. Did I not tell you they would mount pressure? I refused point blank so now they will probably knock on every door of the MNA's Hostel. I could lose the election, and they certainly aren't going to make me finance minister after that.'

'This is not pressure, this is bribery. You would make a sound finance minister, but they don't mean it. The press is touting Dr Mahbubul Haq who is favoured by the Americans. I think you will win the vote InshAllah. The majority of the women are going to vote for you. And if you lose, you can lead the Opposition, which will be much more interesting.'

'And who will sit behind me in the Opposition?'

'I certainly will and there will be a few others like Rahim Bux Soomro and now even Illahi Bux Soomro, Abdul Hamid Jatoi, Mir Ahmed Nawaz Bugti, and Khan Arif Khan. Now let us sleep. We have another long day ahead of us.'

'I have to visit Raja Afsar who has a house nearby at 9 a.m. and then a few others in the Hostel, who were asleep by the time I reached them, and will come to the Assembly directly. Be sure to reach punctually at 11 a.m.' Fakhar was snoring within minutes but I hardly slept.

In the morning, Fakhar had a hurried breakfast, and was out of the house—punctual as always. I was dawdling over yet another cup of coffee when the doorbell rang and Nawabzada Abdul Ghafoor Khan of Hoti walked in.

'Sorry to barge in, but you are like a niece to me. Your father was like an older brother and my older brother Amir Khan's dearest friend.'

'Yes I recall, Uncle Amir Khan.' I welcomed him. 'Please come in, Sir. What can I do for you? I hope you will join me for a cup of coffee.'

'Yes, thank you. Let me come straight to the point. General Zia ul-Haq has sent me to request you to persuade your husband to change his mind. Both of you have a great future. God has blessed you with everything, but if you defy the CMLA you will regret it. You will be looked upon as anti-military and they will never forgive you.'

'Nawabzada Sahib, I am not against the Army as an Institution. It is *my* army since I pay taxes. Their job is not to run the country but to protect it. General Zia had come only for ninety days and he is still here in power after eight years. It is time for him to go gracefully.' My statement was made in as firm a voice as possible.

'You know Abida, when you were a little girl and I came to your house once with my brother, you came and sat on my lap, and you are refusing me now?' he pleaded.

'Well Sir, it is too bad that I have grown up. I apologize deeply, but I really must prepare to leave for the Assembly now.' We both got up, and I saw him out of the front door as courteously as was possible.

When I entered the Assembly Hall, almost everyone was seated but I could not see Fakhar. Ilahi Bux Soomro informed me that he had been standing with Fakhar when a message came that the CMLA wished to speak to Fakhar, who said that he would take the CMLA 's telephone calling Acting Chief Election Commissioner, Justice S. A. Nusrat's office. I found my way to the relevant office, but by the time I reached, Fakhar was coming out.

'What did he say?' I asked Fakhar.

'Repeated what the brigadier said last night. I told him I was sorry but had made up my mind, and it was too late to make a change now.'

We returned to the hall and shortly thereafter voting began. I noticed Salik sitting in the furthermost corner of the President's Gallery. When Fakhar was minister and I was visiting him in Islamabad, Fakhar had gone to an official dinner which had finished early. He had returned accompanied by someone who he introduced to me as Brigadier Siddique Salik, Press Secretary to General Zia ul-Haq.

I had said to him, 'Some job you have, Brigadier. Do you write all those dull speeches that the General keeps inflicting on the nation, hectoring us to be good Muslims all the time? Now why do I feel like we have met before?'

'We have met before. In fact I have been to your beautiful home in Lahore.' Fakhar looked surprised at his remark, hearing it for the first time.

'Really. And when was that?' I had asked him.

Salik had said, 'I came with the NAFDEC group, Khwaja Shahid Hussain and Jamil Dehlavi to discuss the filming of 'Blood of Hussain' in your village. I was a young major at the time.'

'You know, I had no idea, nor did Shahid Hussain, what Jamil was up to. I thought he was doing a love story, a modern day Heer Ranjha.'

'Yes I know. He took everyone for a ride,'

'Salik Sahib, are you MI or ISI?' I asked.

Fakhar was frowning at me, but Salik was smiling.

'If you can read in Urdu, I will just bring you a book which lying in my car. If you care to go through it you may find the answer to your question.' He brought his book titled, '*Hama Yaraan Dozakh*', which translated literally would mean 'friends with hell'. He handed it to me and kept chatting genially for a while before taking his leave.

I read Salik's book through the night, which was a truly gripping account of his time in solitary confinement in an Indian jail. I was still reading the book when Fakhar woke up in the morning. And Fakhar and I became friends with Salik. I understood that he was fiercely patriotic and would do anything in the perceived interest of our country and I think he also came to understand, and perhaps value, the nationalist in me.

All this was going through my head as the votes were being cast in the Speaker's election and I decided that if Fakhar were elected, Salik could take Fakhar to see General Zia to water down his annoyance. Despite my hubris, I understood that we had courted danger. General Zia was a military dictator after all. He had nominated the Chairman Senate, the Prime Minister, and he had nominated a Speaker. If his nominee was defeated, his Prime Minister candidate could fail to obtain a Vote of Confidence which could complicate matters for Zia beyond his point of endurance which needed to be averted, and we had no better conduit than Salik, who was with Zia every single day. As the vote count ended there was pin-drop silence in the House. The result was announced. Syed Fakhar Imam was elected by a margin of fifteen votes over Khwaja Mohammad Safdar. Everyone thronged around the new Speaker elect; most of the women however thronged around me. Members from Sindh, Frontier, and Balochistan were the happiest, as well as those from the Punjab who had issues with Khwaja Safdar. Anticipating that many of our friends and colleagues would be visiting us at home, I tried to get home early. I knew also that my mother would be coming from Lahore and would be bringing the children, and I could not wait to see my trio.

As I made my way out of the Hall, I encountered Salik, and asked him to get an appointment with his boss for Fakhar as soon as possible. Figuring out whether Salik looked happy or displeased was difficult, because it was never easy to read his face.

The house filled up rapidly. I was organizing cold drinks and tea when Fakhar arrived, greeted everyone assembled, with his usual courtesy, and then disappeared into the study. When Ijlal and Shireen, and Roedad Khan arrived, I went to call Fakhar from the study and found him poring over the Rules of Business. 'I am looking up the procedure for removal of Speaker. I will not be allowed to remain Speaker for long,' said Fakhar, when he saw me enter. I threw my arms around him.

'We will face the situation when it develops. Let us enjoy the moment. I met Salik as I was leaving the Assembly and asked him to set up a meeting between yourself and General Zia.'

'Salik was there? I did not see him. Where was he sitting?'

'He was seated in a corner of the gallery. Our friends are here so let us join them.' They were all delighted. And then Sahibzada Yaqub Khan and Tuba Begum arrived along with Aunty Vicki, who informed me that my mother was on her way. And as more and more friends came, Roedad Khan Sahib took me aside and looking intently at me he said, 'Chandi Begum, do not forget, the best days of your Assembly are already behind you.'

'Khan Sahib, this Assembly has made a great beginning. It will now proceed to repeal martial law and rid us of the Revision of Constitution Order.'

'I hope you are right, but as events unfold, kindly remember what I have just said.'

Salik came to see us the following morning and informed us that after Mohammad Khan Junejo obtained his vote of confidence, the Speaker would be required to read out the Prorogation Order for the first session of the Assembly, which the President had already signed. He hoped that I would support the Prime Minister for the vote of confidence. I told him that I was not going to rise to oppose and since it was a voice vote it would doubtless be carried, whether I said 'Aye' or not. Salik then told Fakhar that General Zia would see him in the evening. The visit was brief; Fakhar was home earlier than I had expected.

Fakhar informed me that Zia had strange ideas about how he wanted the Assembly to be managed. He kept suggesting that plenary sessions would only yield rowdyism and most of the business ought to be worked through the committees, and that the role of Speaker would be crucial in the management of the committees. The Speaker would be working closely with him. Clearly he had no interest in the classic Parliamentary form, and wanted the Revision of the Constitution Order to become a permanent part of the Constitution, retaining the key role for himself, while the Prime Minister would be reduced to being a mere cipher. This would yield a hybrid between the Presidential and Parliamentary forms of government, a neither here nor there arrangement, arbitrary, and therefore temporary. Fakhar told him that he ought to consider giving the Parliamentary form a chance, in which the committees would develop perhaps more gradually, but legislation would have to be enacted in the House. He mentioned that the Finance Bill or Budget would need to be moved within eight weeks. The members would have to be consulted in their choice of committees and their consent would be required to make adjustments, if some committees were more in demand than others. Apparently Zia lost interest in Fakhar's attempts at outlining the fundamental concept of Legislature for him. So Fakhar decided to take his leave, at which Zia looked relieved. Altogether, Fakhar spent half an hour with Zia.

As he was seeing him out, he informed Fakhar that he would be administering oath to the cabinet tomorrow, after the Prime Minister's vote of confidence and would see him there, and also that he was summoning a Joint Session the following day for one sitting. And the next session would come a few weeks later, in May, which would be the Budget Session, followed by another working session, so he seemed to have worked out the legislative calendar, at least for the time being. On listening to Fakhar's narrative, it was apparent to me that we would have trouble ahead. Fakhar was not likely to take the sop of being crucial and working closely with Zia—who, being a military dictator, could move against Fakhar. But we needed to cross that bridge when we came to it. For the moment we had to get back to our base. I had my District Council to manage and Fakhar had his constituents whom he would need to satisfy. They would doubtless be thinking that he could deliver the moon and the stars for them since he had been elected to the high office of Speaker, as voters always have a high level of expectations.

Prime Minister Junejo obtained his vote of confidence the following day, and made a lacklustre speech which indicated that he was no orator—his style was diffident—and his language ordinary. As successor Prime Minister to Z. A. Bhutto, this was indeed a come down for my country. I articulated this thought randomly to colleagues while walking out of the House. One of them reacted and said I ought to be more circumspect of the Prime Minister. I was irritated and retorted that we must now not wish to become *'chamchas'* or acolytes of the Prime Minister, who was, after all, only the first among equals, and a nominee at that. We were heading towards the cafeteria and at this point I saw Ghulam Ishaq Khan, now Chairman Senate. I walked up to him and said, perhaps in a somewhat agitated voice, that I wished

Ghulam Ishaq to know that in my opinion, the establishment of our country was giving us—the freshly elected representatives of the people of our country—a long rope with which to hang ourselves. We had started our innings with a worn-out Prime Minister who already seemed to be acquiring sycophants around him. Moreover, he did not appear to be capable of tackling the multitudinous and complicated issues that our country was facing, both internally and externally. Therefore, as politicians we may well manage to hang ourselves with the long rope extended to us. I was communicating all this to him for the record, so that he is aware that not all of us were bereft of the capacity to comprehend the situation.

Ghulam Ishaq Khan, having served as finance minister in General Zia's cabinet for five years, had smoothly transitioned from civil servant to politician, and was clearly the leader of the civil bureaucracy. He was elected Senator from NWFP (now Khyber Pakhtunkhwa), after which he was nominated Chairman Senate—a heartbeat away from the Presidency. As a doyen of the civil as well as military bureaucracies of my country, Ghulam Ishaq's stature was tall. He was reputed for his honest work ethics and fiscal transparency.

When I had communicated my emphatic opinion to him, Ghulam Ishaq seemed taken aback. His face looked flushed but he responded in a measured tone, choosing his words carefully: 'The long rope will allow us all the opportunity to give a good account of ourselves and if all of us, or at least the majority of us, comport to the laws of the land and do not consider ourselves above the law, and if we look after the interests of Pakistan above our personal interests, no rope will hang us and democracy will take root.'

'Agreed. But then this must apply across the board, to the civil and military bureaucracies as much as to those who are popularly mandated,' I responded and moved away.

The National Assembly was called back into Session in May. At the end of the first sitting, the ensuing calendar of sessions was announced by the Speaker. Fakhar looked handsome and sounded efficient and said we would adjourn for a tea break and had been requested to assemble in the cafeteria where the CMLA/President would also join us.

'Any idea what he wants now?' I asked Minoo Bhandara who lived on his Murree Brewery estate in the neighbourhood of the GHQ (General Headquarters). Bhandara, who was a Parsi, had been elected by us as representative of the religious minorities. Minoo paid due taxes, and was well regarded and well informed since he played golf with powerful generals of the time. He had a ponderous manner of speaking and by the time he had begun to frame an answer to my question, we were approaching the cafeteria.

To our surprise, in the cafeteria, chairs had been laid out in rows on one side of a large table and three chairs facing the row of chairs. Sylvie Apa, Raafia, and I sat together. Neither of them much cared for General Zia, despite Sylvie being the wife of a retired general, and Raafia, the daughter of one. This bonded us together as a like-minded trio.

When all the seats had been filled up, General Zia ul-Haq walked in, in his full military regalia. He was accompanied, of all people, by Pir Pagaro and Prime Minister Mohammad Khan Junejo, and a devotee of Pir Pagaro, was following a few paces behind. General Zia greeted us all in his usual courteous style, sounding almost deferential towards us 'honourable members'. At this point, I remembered my father telling me that Mardan Shah II, Pir Pagaro V, had come to see him in the early sixties, seeking to buy some horses and asked my father to choose two of the best colts which he had bred and was selling. My father had chosen for him a bay colt and a chestnut. Pir Pagaro told him that he would name them 'Kingree 1' and 'Kingree 2', whereupon, my father politely suggested to him that it would be more suitable to name the chestnut 'Kingree', presumably the name of his home and the bay 'Lakiaree', the name of Pir Pagaro's village. This vignette did not make me think highly of the gentleman facing us.

Addressing us, General Zia began:

> I have requested Pir Sahib Pagaro Sharif to withdraw from his position as President of the Muslim League and further requested him to confer this position on our new Prime Minister, the very Honourable Mohammad Khan Junejo, and he has kindly agreed. So now I request all of you, Honourable Members, in whom the people of Pakistan have reposed their faith and trust, to join and strengthen the Muslim League, the party of the great Quaid-i-Azam, the Founder of our Nation, whose motto emphasized Unity, above all, so I would hope that all of you will remain united before your new leader. Now may I ask you all to raise your hands in support of the Prime Minister and set a unique example in the world of total unity.

This was General Zia ul-Haq at his unctuous and simplistically self-serving best. I was hoping that not a single hand would be raised, but alas! It was a vain hope—majority of hands shot up—which included an overwhelming majority of the men and all the women, less Sylvie Apa, Raafia, and me. I was craning my neck to see who did not raise their hands up. I could not do a proper count but the ten members who were affiliated to the Jamaat-i-Islami did not raise their hands, along with a few Baloch, a few Sindhis, a few Pushtuns, and a few Punjabis. Through the thicket of raised hands, it seemed that only about forty of us out of a House of two hundred and forty would not join the 'King's Party'. The ten members of the Jamaat-i-Islami were, of course, directly supportive of their like-minded General Zia, who had signboards put up on the main roads of all the major cities of the country enjoining all citizens to offer their prayers, perform the pilgrimage or Hajj, give Zakat or charity—in other words become better Muslims by reading signboards! Talk about pedestrian thinking. When Soobaan first saw the signboards, she observed that Zia could not be very intelligent if he had not understood that we are as Muslim as we desire to be and he cannot force us to be more Muslim than that; my learned and compassionate mother questioned why the spirit of our faith escaped him. Instead of making him ensure that we were deterred from killing, cheating, stealing, or breaking our word, he was emphasizing only the rituals through his dictate. These signboards devalued our faith, according to Mother and her many intellectual friends who were mostly liberal scholars.

Press reporters mobbed us as we exited the cafeteria, asking as many members as they could, who had decided to join the 'King's Party' and who had not. When they accosted me, I told them that, having been elected as an Independent, it was befitting for me to honour my mandate by remaining Independent. In my opinion, those who sought to alter their mandate ought to seek re-election.

The finance committee of the House of which I had become a member, met the following day, as did all the other committees in order to elect our respective chairs. I was relegated to the status of member as I was the only Independent in what I thought would be a crucial committee, the chair was now naturally a member of the new King's Party. I demanded that we discuss our proposals for incorporation in the budget but Salma Ahmed, Member of the Finance Committee was with us, and said that there was no point wasting time on discussion as the budget would be presented in a day or two, so we should send our proposals to the finance minister as she had done already. And the chairman adjourned the meeting, in instant agreement with her. 'That was quick work Eenie,' this was how Salma was popularly known. 'I have been really slow in comparison to you.' Eenie tossed her stylishly curled, perfumed, and pomaded hair, and beamed her pouty smile at me. Casting a cursory glance over my own shoulder, I saw all the gentlemen following us, eyeing her shapely back with unmistakable admiration.

Dr Mahbubul Haq, having added a Senatorial feather to his many feathered hat, presented the first Budget of the 1985 Assembly. His speech was flowery, with many a poetic flourish and copious quotes from Faiz. But the statistics he rattled off sounded more fictional than factual to me. The upshot of his lengthy statement appeared to suggest that borrowing was healthy and not being able to spend at speed was unhealthy, that government needed to emulate the private sector. He kept repeating the buzz words that were beginning to gain currency in the Bretton Woods Institutions at the time, 'poverty alleviation' and 'sustainable development'. What I found really offensive was when, in a truly patronizing tone of voice, Mahbubul Haq said, 'And now I come to that part of the Budget which will be most popular among my Honourable colleagues. I have set aside a very substantial sum of money to be allocated to the Honourable members for development of infrastructure in their constituencies.' When the desk thumping subsided, I knew that the Speaker would not let me disrupt the budget speech of the finance minister, so I shouted from my seat as loudly as I could, and everyone heard me, though my statement did not become a part of the record.

'But that is the task of the elected local councillors. Our job in legislature is to enact laws that ensure that provincial governments pass down at least thirty per cent of federal funding to the local councils.' My statement was, however, shouted down by many and the whole of it heard by only a few sitting in my vicinity. Later in the evening, Fakhar told me that I should have waited to make the point in my Budget speech. 'But,' I said 'if two hundred members are going to participate in the Budget debate, who will reflect on the fine points of every speech?' Fakhar responded that this was precisely the task of the finance minister, to pick up the relevant criticism made by members and respond to it in his winding up statement.

'Mahbub was performing for the Gallery at least as much as for the House. Had you been finance minister, you would have sat through every speech and made copious notes. But Mahbub will only want headlines on a daily basis, which he will get by chatting up reporters in the cafeteria. He will certainly be making banner headlines in the morning. The press appeared to be lapping up his speech. I am certain they understood the Faiz much better than the fictional data that Mahbub presented.'

My turn came on the third day of the debate. Making my submission by expressing the thought that, as far back as my conscious memory went, we were merely repeating our mistakes, instead of learning from them. As a proud Pakistani I was now hoping that we would at least have the capacity to make some new mistakes that we could then seek to learn from. If I were to make a budget speech today, twenty-eight years later, I would repeat the same thought. My second thought articulated was, that in the successful parts of the world, the foreign policy of prospering nations determined the strategic contours and defence policy of that nation, while in Pakistan it was the defence policy which determined the foreign policy of our nation, and that this had resulted from three episodes of military rule. My next thought pertained to my conviction that the Constitution required an Amendment that would obligate the provincial governments not only to empower the elected local governments, but also pass down at least one-third of the federal grants to the local councils, which should then be utilized in consultation with the members of parliament. This would be a much better way of securing the participation of all elected representatives in development functions, and allow the existing and time tested local bureaucracy emerging out of the Local Council Service to utilize the resources with minimum slippage and maximum supervision. I further elucidated my contention suggesting that the way the finance minister had pitched it would only create another layer of federal bureaucracy with minimal supervision leading to maximum slippage, and in due course the reputation of the elected representatives would come under question and our capacity to question government employees on graft and inadequate performance and to hold them accountable, which was the basic reason why we were elected, would be severely compromised. Pretty soon this would lead to government employees holding the elected representatives to account, thereby, defeating the entire purpose of democracy.

Although I had no crystal ball, only perhaps some foresight, but should any researcher, one day, bother to delve into the Assembly record of debates, some of my statements may appear to be prescient. And had Dr Mahbubul Haq lived longer he may have agreed that the development funds for MNAs and Senators became a veritable albatross around the neck of a succession of Parliaments.

The Budget debate only yielded a few fiery and critical speeches by members from the smaller provinces and even fewer 'rebellious Punjabis'. We would congregate at our house every evening. About a dozen of us who were politically on a similar wavelength would have a meal together and chat about everything under the sun. Fakhar would adjourn to our bedroom and library upstairs after dinner, saying that he had to prepare for the following day's session. I would invariably ask him what was there to prepare and why could he not remain with us for a bit of chatting or *gup shup*, but he would only smile mysteriously and start mounting the stairs. Therefore, I was just as stunned as all my other colleagues when, as the debate concluded, Fakhar, from the Speaker's Chair, threw a veritable bombshell, holding, 'Martial Law Illegal and without Lawful Authority'.

The Speaker's Ruling made history. This was the first quasi-judicial ruling that declared martial law illegal while it was still in effect. Previous Supreme Court rulings in the Dosso case and the Asma Jillani case had been announced post facto, which was why Justice Munir's notion on the Law of Necessity had so far remained prevalent. Speaker Fakhar Imam had ruled that since the money expended on the administering of martial law was not reflected in the Budget presented in the House, the administering of martial law was without any lawful authority whatsoever. The initial shock over, some of us thumped our desks till our hands hurt and Abdul Hamid Jatoi stood up to eulogize the Speaker for his courageous Ruling. On the other hand, Mohammad Khan Junejo, who later claimed credit for a repeal of martial law, looked distinctly morose and remained utterly silent. After the passage of the Budget, the

House adjourned *sine die*, only to be called back into Session just a few days later.

It was blazingly hot. Our summers are designed to test the patience of saints, for ordinary mortals it is very trying, and very difficult to maintain good humour. Fakhar breakfasted hastily, looked tense, but when I asked him what the order of business of the day would be, he answered briefly that we would find out when we reached the House. He left in the ramshackle Mercedes which had been allotted to the Speaker. Chairman Senate's office apparently wanted to order a new Mercedes and for which a query had been put in with the Speaker's office, but Fakhar had ordered a modest new Toyota, stating that he did not wish to strain the budget of the Assembly. Hence the Chairman Senate did likewise, but the new car was taking its time in arriving. I worried that the old car may break down again as it had done a few days earlier, when we were driving to the airport together, and we had hitched a ride with a joint secretary who had the courtesy to stop when he saw us standing by the roadside. He was in a brand new Toyota, naturally provided to him by the government, and we mentioned that a similar vehicle had been ordered for the Speaker. The joint secretary protested that the Speaker should have ordered a car befitting of his status, mentioning that the Speaker of the National Assembly ranked fourth in the Warrant of Precedence, taking us to be green horns, in typical bureaucratic fashion, assuming that we would we have no awareness of this. Fakhar responded courteously to him, 'My friend, some of us have to try and lead by example,' he said.

Worrying lest my worthier half be stranded again, I sacrificed my second cup of coffee which I savoured every morning seated opposite my favourite Ijazul Hassan painting of Lilies, which was hung on the wall of our dining room, I rushed out and hopped into my car to follow Fakhar who might need another rescue. Fakhar's car had managed to speed forward, and got him safely to the Assembly ahead of me. He was already seated and *Tilawat* (recitation of the Holy Quran) had started when I reached my desk, and picked up the Order of the Day. I was horrified to see that as Fakhar had feared, it was a Constitution Amendment Bill which sought to incorporate the infamous Revision of Constitution Order (RCO), in toto, into the Constitution of Pakistan. My former colleague from the Punjab Assembly, Haji Saifullah, now a Member of the National Assembly, who was an ace on parliamentary procedures, sat in my vicinity, 'Haji Sahib, this RCO will deface the Constitution entirely. What should we do?' I exclaimed to him.

He replied authoritatively, 'When the Law Minister stands to introduce this terrible Bill, we shall rise to oppose it, and try to get as many members as we can to oppose it along with us. I will raise two important questions for the consideration of the Speaker and keep him engaged in discussion for as long as possible and you, Begum Sahiba, try to influence as many as you can to rise and oppose the Bill. Tell them that each member will be able to raise amendments to the amendment, and we will drag this on for months until the whole Nation is standing by us, and Zia ul-Haq will never get away with it.'

I found Haji Saifullah convincing as always, and proceeded to lobby, undertaking a considerable amount of legwork, reaching out to as many members as I could. As I explained to member after member that the Prime Minister had given assent to a Bill that would strip him entirely of any consequential power, some of them looked incredulous, some sheepish, the majority disbelieving.

The two questions that Haji Saifullah raised concerned the legality of the CMLA continuing in his office once martial law had been held to have been illegal; and the legality of Mohammad Khan Junejo's membership who had been elected as an Independent as there was a Bar on political parties, and he had now become head of a party before the removal of that Bar. A lively engagement ensued between the Speaker and Haji Saifullah. And as tension mounted in the House, I discontinued my lobbying effort and came back to my seat, wondering what the Ruling from the Chair would be. Saifullah's arguments were powerful and logical and if sustained by the Speaker could send us all packing. We were still under martial law and Zia had sent Bhutto to the gallows without flinching, hence, he could dissolve the Legislature equally peremptorily. Clearly the same thought must have crossed Fakhar's mind, so having heard Saifullah out, he announced that he would reserve Judgement on both questions raised, and would discuss the matter further before giving a Ruling. He then called out Iqbal Ahmed Khan, the Law Minister, and asked him to move his Bill. Observing our movement on the floor from the vantage point of the Speaker's chair, he would obviously have understood that the Bill would be opposed.

Iqbal Ahmed's voice quavered as he introduced the Eighth Amendment Bill to the Constitution of Pakistan. The Leader of the House did not look up at all and seemed to be in a deep scrutiny of his toe nails. And, thirty-two members of the National Assembly of Pakistan stood up in opposition to the Eighth Amendment Bill.

Haji Saifullah Khan from Rahim Yar Khan, Dr Sher Afghan Niazi from Mianwali, Dr Shafiq Chaudhry from Faisalabad, and I wrote up more than eighty Amendments and obtained signatures from thirty-two colleagues that included: Air Marshal Nur Khan, Rahim Bux Soomro, Abdul Hamid Jatoi, Mir Ahmed Nawaz Bugti, Mir Balakh Sher Mazari, Mir Arif Jan Hassani, Fateh Mohammad Khan, Saalem Khan Khalil, Shaikh Rashid Ahmed, Javed Hashmi, Raja Shahid Zaffar, Ch. Mumtaz Tarar, Khan Arif Khan Sial, Syed Nusrat Ali Shah, Sardar Assef Ahmed Ali, Minoo Bhandara, Raafia Tarik Rahim, and Sylvat Sher Ali Khan Pataudi, along with the ten members of the Jamaat-i-Islami, including Liaquat Baloch and Hafiz Salmaan Butt.

We managed to filibuster the Bill for forty-four days, having a judicious Speaker in the Chair was a big advantage, many of us communicating almost daily. We needed to remain focused lest the Speaker cut us off for being repetitive or irrelevant, but giving us all the time in the world so long as we conformed to the rules. The Treasury benches would remain largely quiet, a couple of mild hecklers who would occasionally interrupt, as would a pair of Maulanas, both from Karachi, both affiliated to the Jamiatul Ulema-e-Pakistan (JUP), but their interventions invariably came when Jamaat members would speak, their favoured target being their rival religious party, the Jamaat-i-Islami. The press gave us good coverage, surprisingly no lawyers came forward to proffer any advise or assistance, except M. Bilal from Rawalpindi, however, no big gun lawyer contacted us as we struggled to restore the Constitution to its original form. Those forty-four days will remain enshrined in our Legislative record, for none of the fourteen Amendments to the Constitution have been as deeply or as thoroughly debated on the floor as the Eighth Amendment was.

During the course of the debate, those of us who had opposed the Amendment would meet at the end of each sitting in a room behind the Assembly Hall and Haji Saifullah would brief us on procedural details for the following day, and the behind the scenes conversation that Iqbal Ahmed Khan, Law Minister was carrying on with him. He would laugh a lot and refer to his interlocutor as 'Silver Fox' who, he would inform us, was secretly really pleased that we were doing his job for him struggling to get the Prime Minister's powers reverted to him, and he would assure us that sooner or later General Zia ul-Haq himself would talk to us. And sure enough, on the forty-fifth day after the introduction of the Eighth Amendment, he informed us that we had been invited to the State Guest House to meet with the CMLA, but not more than twenty of us should be there. He proposed the names of two Jamaat representatives and eighteen of the rest of us, from the four federating units of our country. Everyone among the larger group agreed on the names, and at the appointed hour we set off for Rawalpindi. Upon arrival, we were shown into a gloomy room, with ten chairs ranged in a row and another ten chairs opposite, with three chairs set out, facing the two rows.

The CMLA walked in wearing his uniform, looking solemn, he greeted us stiffly, without his customary smile. Accompanying him were Iqbal Ahmed Khan, and to my great surprise, Dr Mahbubul Haq. General Zia began the conversation with a precise lecture on the salient features of the power clauses of the Government of India Act of 1935, the Indian Constitution, the 1956 Constitution of Pakistan, and the unamended version of the 1973 Constitution of Pakistan. He had obviously been competently briefed and he told us categorically that in lieu of our agreement on indemnity, he was willing to withdraw those clauses of the proposed Amendment on which we reached consensus. He suggested the names of Mahbubul Haq and Haji Saifullah, who he said could sit together to draft a proposed Amendment which would then be circulated to all the members of the Assembly and ought to be passed unanimously. He further stated that in the event that we did not agree with the proposed draft of Saifullah and Mahbub, he was confident that his chosen Prime Minister would get it passed by the two-third majority of those who had joined his party. Some of us started arguing, but while he heard us, none of our arguments seemed to have any effect. The dictator had shown his iron fist, and walked out of the room, leaving Iqbal Ahmed Khan and Mahbubul Haq to deal with our cumulative wrath. Both men sought to assure us that they would not let us down, and the forty of us would be shown the draft before it was circulated to members of the ruling party. Disappointed, we returned to our respective premises in Islamabad, feeling that we had been had, some of us questioning whether Saifullah might have sold out on us.

Saifullah called us all to put up to us the draft he suggested we agree to. Abdul Hameed Jatoi flatly refused, saying that we simply could not give indemnity to all of Zia ul-Haq's actions of the last eight years in order to empower Mohammad Khan Junejo who was a convenient tool for dictators. He suggested that we simply refuse to be part of this Eighth Amendment.

'But, worthy Jatoi Sahib,' chimed in Dr Sher Afghan Niazi in his inimitably Punjabified English, 'while I laud you from bottom of my heart, Zia has told us that he will get the Amendment passed anyway. So if he is going to concede that he will allow deletion of the relevant Article under which National Security Council would be constituted which would indeed be a Supra Constitutional Body, the spirit of the 1973 Constitution would remain intact. So I propose that we offer a vote of thanks to Haji Sahib for his struggle, and give our consent so that the House may be summoned and the Amendment passed. Our voters are cursing us for our prolonged absence from our constituencies.'

'Our voters in Sindh will curse us even more if we return home having bailed out Zia and his stooges. Let us get out of this cubby hole and go to the Speaker's office. We owe him a great deal. Without his wisdom and cooperation we would not even have reached this point. Saifullah you would have been guillotined and failed to emerge as the Cicero of this Assembly.' Putting Saifullah and his stooge Sher Afghan in their place, Jatoi Sahib strode out towards the Speaker's office while the rest of us followed.

Sher Afghan was a veritable joker, who would send Raafia and me into peals of laughter, and I would tell Raafia that at some point we would have to record a list of Sher Afghan's gaffes and jokes. When we reached the Speaker's large, simply furbished, and well-lit office, Fakhar greeted us all warmly and enthusiastically, embracing all the gentleman, with Jatoi Sahib joking that he should also embrace his wife, and Fakhar looking shy and embarrassed. Fakhar informed us that the law minister had requested for an evening session and had informed him that a consensus had been achieved and the Bill would be passed unanimously, whereupon Mir Ahmed Nawaz Bugti observed that this was presumptuous of the law minister. Fakhar told us that we had all put up a really fine show of resistance to the amendment as it had been originally proposed, and he had tried his best to give us all the time that we had requested for, and that there was no previous legislative record of such a lengthy debate after the passage of the 1973 Constitution.

The seven previous Amendments had been very lightly debated and even the fourth Amendment did not enter a third week of debate, while the current one had crossed six weeks. He went on to inform us that now that our list of proposed Amendments stood exhausted, our filibustering having ended, there was no further cause for him to deny the law minister's request for a late session that evening. He had just been examining the text of the agreement reached between Haji Saifullah and the minister of finance, according to which the President had the power to dissolve the Legislature, hence, his sword would hang over the Legislature. In any case, Fakhar pointed out, even without the agreement, the ruling party had the required two-third majority. So we would have the option of opposing the Amendment, in which case a call for Division would be given, but the Jamaat members had reached the same agreement with the law minister, as Haji Saifullah had with the finance minister, so our number would not exceed twenty-two members. He emphasized that he was not making any suggestion, clarifying that it was not his place to do so, but that he was merely apprising us of what was in his notice.

On hearing all this, Saifullah asserted to the Speaker that while we were all highly grateful to the Speaker for all the patience and wisdom he had demonstrated, he, i.e. Saifullah, wanted to point out he had in no way compromised on the principle of sovereignty of the legislature as the relevant article applicable to Dissolution, Article 58(2) sub-section (b) made the provision justicible, and the Supreme Court would have to be fully satisfied as to the causes of dissolution before upholding such an order. Saifullah further argued that in a way, this provision would block the path for a further military intervention.

Rahim Bux Soomro from Sindh contended that this argument did not necessarily hold ground, as there were always enough compliant judges from Punjab to ensure that non-democratic orders could be upheld. Rahim Bux Soomro's manner was mild and modest but his thinking was invariably strong. Mir Ahmed

Nawaz Bugti suggested that we could consider abstaining, and simply not come for the late-night session, which appealed to me and which I decided to act upon. Another colleague was very agitated and expressed his apprehension that Zia ul-Haq could also order his tanks to surround this Parliament. My opinion was that nothing could be put past Zia if he felt pressured, but it was now time for us to go home. From now henceforth, each decided themselves what they had to do: whether to return to the Assembly or stay at home.

I was heavily misquoted later by a colleague who I took to be a friend. In our gossipy culture, friends will often cause more damage to one's reputation than detractors. Needless to say, this colleague of mine went to the late night Assembly session, while I stayed home as did seven of our other Independent colleagues. One of the ministers telephoned me to ask whether I would be coming to the Assembly, but I told him that I had decided to abstain.

Eight honourable members of the 1985 Assembly did not sign the Assembly register when the Eighth Amendment to the Constitution of Pakistan was passed, and I was proud to be one of them. The others, needless to say, were mostly from the smaller provinces.

The Eighth Amendment gave indemnity to all of Zia ul-Haq's orders including the Law of Evidence and several other discriminatory laws. My conscience remains clear that I did not vote for this amendment. Tragically even up to the Eighteenth Amendment to the Constitution of Pakistan, these retrogressive orders indemnified in the Eighth Amendment have never been repealed.

Mother and the children were up in the hills, so as soon as the session concluded Fakhar and I went to see them. By now the girls were in their early teens, and Abid a precocious nine-year-old was rearing to travel. Mother used to take them to interesting destinations for holidays abroad every year, and they had been harassing their 'Baji Amma' for another trip. But Mother had not been feeling well, so Fakhar and I decided to take them for a fortnight to Bangkok, Manila, and Hong Kong.

The newspapers were advertising a Philippine Airlines package tour which seemed promising, so we booked it for ourselves, paying from our private resources. The children were most excited, asking a million questions about everything. When we entered the lounge to depart from the Karachi airport, our cousin Fakir Ayaz was also there. He told us that since he had the agency or manifest for Philippine Airlines, when he saw our names on the list of passengers, he had rushed to the airport to tell us that he was going to be in Manila with his wife and two sons by the time we got there. The Chairman of Philippine Airlines was a great friend of Imelda Marcos and he could take us to visit the 'Iron Butterfly'. 'I must show them that I, too, have a talented cousin!'

Jooma (Fakir Ayaz's childhood nickname) lived up to his word. When we reached the Philippines, accompanied by the immaculately dressed and good-looking Philippine Airlines Chairman, and Jooma passing himself off as Speaker Imam's aide, we went through layers of security before entering the Malacañan Palace. Climbing up a grand mahogany stairway, we entered a large wood panelled hall, reminiscent of the Darbar hall of Governor's House in Lahore. Ranged on either side of the hall were two long rows of generals of the Philippine army. 'Has something unusual happened?' I inquired.

'No,' responded the airline chairman, 'All the senior generals of our army come every morning to pay their respects to Madame Marcos. As our President is sick, the First Lady runs the government.' So saying, he nodded perfunctorily at the generals and led us into a small spherical room which was also panelled in burnished mahogany, with a skylight in the middle of the domed roof, and the light poured down onto a magnificent floral display of breathtakingly beautiful orchids. The chamber was also well chilled, and in my thin and casual *shalwar-kameez* was shivering, when a strong scent wafted into the room and Imelda Marcos entered, wearing an elaborate white traditional gown with huge stiff mounted sleeves, her face full of make-up, her hair done up in an enormous complicated hairdo. She looked every inch the iron lady she was reputed to be. She beamed her smile at Fakhar, revealing a set of perfect teeth, and addressing him as Mr Speaker, she gushed all over him, exclaiming how young and handsome he was. She added that her husband was also young and handsome when he was Speaker of our House of Representatives, which was when she had first seen him. Of course, she was only a little girl at the time. He became President later and had always been very popular, especially since she had married him. But alas! He was sick now, so she had to receive his callers. Since he was still popular, she informed us, a lot of people came and they all prayed for him, even the poor peasants, she had been told. Imelda Marcos then fluttered her heavily mascaraed eyelashes at Fakhar and said to him that she hoped he would be President of his country soon and replace that dictator general that we had as President. She went on to say that it was really nice to have met with the young Speaker from Pakistan. All this while, she had not let go of Fakhar's hand or taken her eyes off him!

Fakhar responded formally and courteously that it had been a pleasure for us to have been received by the famous Madame Marcos, and we were grateful to the able Chairman of Philippine Airlines, who had given us an excellent briefing on economy, and who arranged this visit. Fakhar mentioned to Imelda Marcos that he was there with his wife, who was also a Member of Parliament, and that we, on a private visit—a short family holiday. He then introduced cousin Fakir Ayaz (Jooma) as the representative of the Philippine Airlines in Pakistan, and me. Imelda turned perfunctorily towards Jooma and barely glanced at me. Jooma attempted to speak but she was not listening, and shook my hands limply while winking at her Chairman friend, sailing past us into the grand outer hall where the generals had been waiting for her. We were ushered out to the stairway and back to the Manila Hotel where we were staying.

Ironically, a couple of years later, I was back in Manila as member of an international observer mission for elections oversight, and went with the group to the Malacañan Palace to be shown Imelda Marcos's wardrobe and her countless pairs of shoes! By then, Corazon (Cory) Aquino was President (1986–1992), and was living in a modern, elaborate new palace in the same compound. When we went to call on her, each of us was given a 'Cory doll' to remind us of the great leader we were to meet! At the time the rollercoaster of power in the Philippines appeared as stomach-churning as ours, but in due course of time theirs seemed to have settled down to a duller routine while we continued to spiral up and down.

On our return home from our vacations, Abid reported to Baji Amma (Mother) that he enjoyed Bangkok, and the floating market and the Sampan Ride and in Hong Kong he loved the big rollercoaster ride the best. But he did not enjoy himself in Manila where his parents did not take him with them to meet Imelda, because he really wanted to see why everyone called her an iron butterfly! Umku and Shugu also complained that they had missed obtaining Imelda's autograph.

The next session of the National Assembly found an empowered Prime Minister Junejo, exuding more confidence, receiving large number of callers, all the MNAs seeking to meet him in his chamber, which was just off the lobby, opposite the main entrance to the Assembly Hall. A young bilingual journalist who spoke rapid fire Urdu and English, and wrote for the *Far East Economic Review*, accosted me and asked when I would be calling on the Prime Minister. I told him I had no intention of so doing because I had nothing to say to him.

The journalist told me that he could not help overhearing my saying to Begum Sylvat Sher Ali that the Prime Minister should call a conference of all the political leaders outside the Parliament who had boycotted the non-party elections, before lifting martial law and seek their support in maintaining order, to give democracy a chance to stabilize. He thought this was an excellent idea and should be put across by someone dynamic like myself directly to the Prime Minister. Taken aback by all this, I told him that first of all, I did not like being addressed as Begum Sahiba. Being a working woman, I felt it was more appropriate if I was addressed as either Syeda Abida or simply Abida Hussain. Secondly, I observed that he was the first blue jeans wearing 'chattar, chattar', Urdu speaking journalist that I had ever met. I asked him who he was since he had not bothered to introduce himself. He told me cheekily that he was popularly known as H. H., as in Hussain Haqqani, suggesting that he would like it better if I called him by his initials. His prompt reply was accompanied by a mischievous smile and a leprechaun look.

Laughing, I proceeded in the direction of the escalators, while Haqqani joined the tall and handsome MNA from Khushab, Malik Naeem Awan, and the short and heavy-set Siddique Kanju from Lodhran, both of whom were with the 'King's Party'. I overheard Naeem comment to Haqqani, 'If she were a couple of inches taller, I would really fancy her!' Stopping dead in my tracks, I spun around, outraged and looking straight at Naeem retorted, 'If you were to lop four inches off your head maybe then someone might fancy you!' Naeem and Kanju looked embarrassed and chastened. In due course of time, however, all three of us ended up as friends, since both Naeem and Kanju were smart enough to understand that women at work did not appreciate unwanted attention in their workplace. As I turned around to walk away again, the military secretary who was coming out of the Prime Minister's chamber, approached me. He informed me that some of my Independent colleagues were with the Prime Minister already and the Prime Minister desired me to join them. It would have been unnecessarily rude for me to refuse; I was also curious about which of my Independent colleagues were with him, and for what reason. So I followed the military secretary.

When I walked into the Prime Minister's chamber I was taken somewhat surprised to see Nusrat Ali Shah, whose father had been my father's childhood playmate, whose friendship was like a part of my inheritance, Sardar Aseff Ahmed Ali, whose father had been a political affiliate of my father, Ch. Mumtaz Tarar whom I had known from my early District Council days, Javed Hashmi, Fakhar's supporter from his Multan District Council, and Javed Hashmi's friend Senator Tarik Chaudhry, who had become our friend as well, and was distinguished for his hearty sense of Punjabi humour. Our independent friends appeared to be mingling comfortably with Iqbal Ahmed Khan, Law Minister; Yasin Wattoo, Finance Minister; and Hamid Nasir Chattha also a Minister, who was our age group, while the Prime Minister, Iqbal Ahmed, and Yasin Wattoo were a generation older, remnants of the Ayub era.

I settled into a chair and came straight to the point. 'Prime Minister, since you have announced your intent of repealing martial law at the start of 1986, which is a mere three months away, I am wondering how you will cope with the law and order situation, since the leaders and supporters of the political parties, who boycotted the non-party election, are bound to regroup and launch an agitation. As soon as martial law is lifted, I would urge you to call a conference of all these leaders to seek their cooperation in allowing democracy to take root, and allow this Parliament to function for another three years, and then you could consider calling an election one year earlier as a quid pro quo for their cooperation.'

Before Junejo could frame an answer, Nusrat Ali said that there was no need to take all those leaders so seriously when the voters had paid no heed to their call for a boycott. The others seemed to agree with him. The Prime Minister asked if there was anything else that the members wished to say, but Mumtaz Tarrar said that we primarily came to request development resources for our constituencies, and since he had given an assurance that there would be no discrimination against those who had not joined his party, we would request him to remain true to his intent, and would now leave him with his ministers. All the gentlemen shook hands, and we exited from the chamber. I asked Mumtaz Tarar why none of our friends had mentioned the meeting to me, and he answered that since I was still chairing the District Council, this meeting may not have been a priority for me.

When Martial Law was declared in 1977, Pakistan had lost membership of the Inter-Parliamentary Union (IPU). The IPU was to meet in Mexico for its annual Congress, and Speaker National Assembly (Fakhar) was sent an invitation, close on the heels of martial law being lifted, for Pakistan to revive its membership in the IPU. The Speaker's office proposed a delegation and sent the file to the Prime Minister's office. The Prime Minister made several changes in the names proposed by the Speaker, which was his prerogative, but irritating nonetheless. However, the Speaker had proposed that although his spouse was invited, since I happened to be a Member of Parliament, I would pay for my own ticket and the delegation would have the benefit of one extra delegate without causing any burden to the exchequer, and to this the Prime Minister had given his assent.

After Fakhar was elected Speaker he had received a flurry of invitations from Speakers of the Parliaments of different countries, and had kept them pending. After the repeal of Martial Law, the Junejo Muslim League had amended the Rules of Business of the Assembly and reduced the requirement of sittings. The new legislative calendar had been announced and with the session prorogued, there was a window of two months before the next session. So Fakhar decided that, after the IPU meeting in Mexico City, he would accept the invitation of the Speaker of the Brazilian Parliament and take some members of the same delegation on to Brazil. On our return from Brazil, Fakhar would avail of the invitation of the Speaker of the British House of Commons which was extended to him and his spouse only. Hence after Brazil, the

NATIONAL ASSEMBLY, AT LAST

delegation would head home to Pakistan while Fakhar and I would stop over for a few days in London as guests of Speaker Weatherill of the House of Commons, the 'mother' of all parliaments.

I was really excited at the prospect of my first visit to Central and South America. I had lost touch over the last twenty years with my Latina friends from my school days, but was determined to trace them out. After all, two decades earlier, whoever was sending their daughters to Swiss and Italian schools would be from well-known families and not difficult to trace out, just as I was not difficult to trace out for foreign friends who visited Pakistan.

It was a really long flight which took us from Karachi to Mexico City. En route we broke journey, and stayed overnight at Tampa, Florida, where we were pleasantly surprised to meet Nayyar Mehfooz, Fakhar's batch mate from the academy, who had joined the police service and was posted at Florida by our anti-narcotics force. We spent a long evening together and he threw light on the corrupt practices he encountered in the state government of Florida and even in US federal institutions. 'Shahji, they are every bit as dishonest as we are, but they work harder and are more efficient than we are.' Never having worked in the US, we believed Nayyar, and told each other afterwards that this was useful information, something to be kept in mind.

We landed at Mexico City airport and were received by Ambassador Amir Usman and his first secretary, Masood, both diplomats were Pushtun. Masood informed us that he was also the second as well as the third secretary, and the Embassy had a modest budget and was short on personnel. Driving us from the airport to our hotel, Ambassador Usman urged Fakhar to take it up with the government, on our return, that either we should not have an Embassy or it should be properly resourced. Fakhar assured him that on his return he would be sending a report on his visit to the Prime Minister and would mention the Ambassador's request, along with his own recommendation. Meanwhile, I asked Masood whether he knew any glamorous Mexican women around my age, giving him the names of some of my Mexican friends from my school days in Montreux and at Florence, but none of the names resonated with him, however, he said he had one very social friend who knew everybody worth knowing in Mexico City, and he would run these names by her, if I could list them up. We had a free day before the start of the IPU meeting. Quite early in the day Masood rang me and said that his friend knew one of my friends and gave me the telephone number of Gaby de la Lama, who I called up immediately.

'Ola! Gaby, this is Abida Hussain from Pakistan. I hope you remember me. I am in Mexico City, and would love to see you.'

'Abida, in Mexico! Dios mio! I cannot wait to see you. Where are you?' I gave her the name of the hotel. She said it would take her half an hour to reach me, and asked for the number of my suite. My cost conscious spouse had told Aminul Haq, Secretary National Assembly, who was a member of the delegation, that he would forego his entitlement to a suite, a double room was good enough for the two of us, since the IPU invite did not cover costs, there was no need to burden our government with unnecessary payments. Our room was small, so I told Gaby that I would meet her in the lobby, she asked whether we would recognize each other after all these years, and said she was bringing her teenaged daughter along. I assured her that while I had put on a considerable amount of weight, my face was still the same and I would be wearing my Pakistani clothes, so recognition would be no problem. We spotted each other, simultaneously, after much hugging and kissing and mutual reassurances that we looked no different, both had merely enlarged somewhat, Gaby introduced me to her daughter, who was a replica of her mother in her teens, except taller. I wanted Gaby to meet Fakhar who joined us in the lobby and led us into the coffee shop of the hotel where some of our delegates were seated at a table together.

Masood had organized a day of sightseeing for the group. Gaby wanted to take me to her house, so Fakhar suggested that I go with my friend, while he would tour the city with the delegation. Gaby's house was a lovely, custom built and compact hacienda-style home, the style which caught up with UAE construction companies some three decades later, and in Pakistan a few years after that. Gaby gave me a choice of either going to a nice restaurant for lunch, or she could fix a sandwich/salad lunch at home, and I opted for the latter. While Gaby pottered around her immaculate kitchen, I chatted with her daughter, who had her mother's voice. I had the unusual experience of regressing into my teens, communicating with a girl who was about the age that Gaby and I were when we had first met.

A lovely table was set, and over the delicious and ample meal that my friend had produced, I asked Gaby about all the other Mexican girls who had been with us in the Villa Miramonte at Montreux, starting of course with Gaby's sister, Chatta, who was a beauty, and who I recalled always greeted everybody with an enthusiastic 'Hola linda!' Chatta apparently was happily married, with two children and was currently travelling in Australia. I was sorry to have missed seeing her. Patti Quintana was around, had become a famous dietician and was going to call us up soon; the two Lizzaraga sisters had migrated to the United States, as had the Dolores who lived in Acapulco, and Dolores Gomez Kopp, who had been with me at Le Fleuron in Florence as well, had finally become the Californian she always wanted to be.

Meanwhile Patti called and invited us both for lunch. We fixed an appointment for my last day in Mexico City, as the following three days I would be busy in the Conference. Patti and I lunched in a beautiful restaurant with a terrace and a lovely arbour overhead. Patti looked as young as ever. Her skin glowed and she was very slender. I ate heartily as usual, while Patti ate sparingly. She told me that when she was in her mid-twenties she had become very ill, and for eight years had been in and out of hospitals. Tired of conflicting medical opinions, she took to reading on foods and nutrition, inventing a diet for herself which cured her and now she was a recognized dietician with a growing following and a publication on diets which was already in its second edition! Her theory on diets was based on detoxification of the system by eating only fruits and raw or boiled vegetables for six weeks and then reverting to a sparse normal diet, with very little meat or poultry, very little oil, and not much of dairy product. The diet sounded worse than death to me and when I said as much, Patti laughed, telling me that I must not take my health for granted, should lose weight and try out her diet for a few days. If I felt better and lighter, I would want to continue it. When I returned home, I did try Patti's diet, but did not get past the first day!

I found the IPU conference fascinating. To rub shoulders with Parliamentarians from all over the world was an experience to be cherished. Fakhar was asked to chair a session and when he announced that Pakistan had restored a democratic order after an interregnum of eight years, he was greeted by a thunderous round of applause. I chaired a sub-committee meeting on the importance of women's representation and maternal/child health care. The tea/coffee breaks were convivial and animated; as were the lunches and dinners, the most memorable one being a special lunch arranged on the terrace of the spectacular Museum of Modern Art that the Mexicans were extremely proud of. It is at this museum that Diego Riviera and Frieda Kahlo paintings are housed. We feasted our eyes on them; the memory has remained etched in my mind. We were also taken to Acapulco for a half-day trip, and to look at an Aztec pyramid. Everywhere we went we were serenaded by Mexican minstrels, with their banjos, guitars, colourful ponchos over their white baggy shirts and trousers and wonderful wide sombreros. Whenever they struck up 'Guantanamera' Fakhar and I would sing along, much to the consternation of our fellow delegates, except for General (retired) Majeed Malik, who enjoyed himself, although he was considerably older than us. Fakhar stood out as a youthful Speaker, popular with the ladies, while I thought I was not short on popularity myself. Rehana Mashadi, looked disapproving sometimes, and would always keep her head covered demurely. Although when the minstrels serenaded her, she would go into peals of laughter. Hence all of us, in our own ways enjoyed our five days in Mexico.

We discovered that Senator Mohammad Ali Khan of Hoti had quite a sense of humour, and in his own quiet way, so did Aminul Haq. When Ambassador Amir Usman hosted a dinner for us on our last evening in Mexico, and I narrated my saga of how no male colleague wanted to sit next to me in the National Assembly because I was a woman, he even managed to laugh heartily.

Our next destination was Brazil. The flight to Brasilia was along one, with a stopover at Rio for a flight changeover. I was exhausted and without thinking checked in my unlocked vanity case with the rest of our luggage. Foolishly, I had brought some old valuable pieces of jewellery with me, which was in the vanity case. It all got stolen, probably at the Rio airport. When we finally reached our hotel room in Brasilia, I discovered my loss, and as a result, spent the night sleepless and anxious. Although I had lost my most precious father, and six hundred acres of very valuable land, those losses had been beyond my control; this loss was my fault and it rankled me for some days.

Ambassador Khairi and his wife received us at the airport and he had the same complaint as our Ambassador in Mexico, that he was under-staffed and under-resourced, and could the Speaker take up the matter with the government on his return to Pakistan. Fakhar gave Ambassador Khairi the same assurance as he had to his counterpart in Mexico.

Brasilia was set on an undulating plateau, reminiscent of the Potohar Plateau on which Islamabad is built, but without the hills in the background. Both capital cities, Brasilia and Islamabad, were built from scratch around the same time. The Brazilian Parliament was an architectural marvel, with the Upper House situated under a convex dome, while the Lower House was atop a spire with a concave ceiling, symbolizing the state and the people.

We attended a session of their senate and heard some fiery oratory in Portuguese, with earphones giving us a faltering English translation. The Chairman of the Brazilian Senate hosted a grand banquet for us. Fakhar wore a white *achkan*; I wore a silver embroidered pale turquoise sari and really missed my jewellery. The conversation centred on Afghanistan and the Soviet occupation, with Pakistan being a front-line state. The Chairman of the Brazilian Senate was exceptionally well-informed. He commented that the Afghans had a history of tribal wars, and having been destabilized, were not likely to settle down easily, nor would the refugees return soon, and we would be left carrying their burden for a long time.

The next morning we were taken to look at the agriculture around Brasilia, an immense corporate sugar plantation which could rival the one that I had seen in the North American south a decade earlier. The fields were filled with dark molasses out of the sugar mill nearby. There was an equally immense corporate dairy and poultry venture, with feed mills, milk processing units, and a huge slaughter house on the premises.

The following day we left for São Paolo, and visited a jet aircraft manufacturing plant. The Brazilian economy seemed to be galloping along, and it was impossible to imagine that this rapid growth would hit an economic maelstrom in the future. I made a serious effort to track down my friend Solange from my Swiss school days, who was from São Paulo, but pulled a blank. We left São Paolo after two days, having met many officials and financiers, but without any personal souvenir of this crowded metropolis.

As we flew into Rio de Janeiro, the breathtaking beauty of the city made me forgive whoever may have stolen my jewellery. Rio captivated me so much that I said to Fakhar that an oceanic miracle would be desirable which pushed South America closer to South Asia. I would then buy myself an apartment in Rio to compensate for the apartment that he had made me sell in London, before we took oath in the Assembly, because it was not legal for a Pakistani to hold property overseas at the time. The law was amended five years later, but my law-abiding husband had, at the time, made me sell my flat in a hurry and at a throwaway price in an attempt to become a role model in a country where the more rules you break the higher you ascend in leadership.

As guests of the Brazilian Parliament, we were lodged in an old fashioned European style hotel along the ocean front called 'The Majestic'. Rehana Mashadi thought the hotel was old and mouldy but I loved it. That evening, the Chairman of the Brazilian Senate and our host had also come to Rio and was hosting a dinner for us. Fakhar, Majeed Malik, and Senator Hoti went for a walk along the Copacabana Beach, while Rehana and I went into our respective rooms for a nap. Fakhar came back looking happy, saying the beach was really full, lots of women in skimpy bikinis. 'Just as well Rehana did not go. She seems quite prudish.'

We were taken to a popular restaurant by our host. It was very big, with a stage elevated along one end of the dining hall. The Brazilian Senate Chairman told us we would watch an outstanding performance of Brazilian dancers there. The show started en course of an elaborate meal, with briefly clad dancers, with elaborate plummage, making their white, as well as dark, near perfect bodies undulate provocatively, which made Rehana 'hai!' and 'haw!' non-stop, while she giggled away. It was actually a fabulous show, Fakhar thanked our kind host, and through him, his government, for a memorable visit to his beautiful country.

On our return flight, Senator Hoti, Rehana Mashadi, and Majeed Malik thanked Fakhar profusely. We parted at London airport—they flew back home—while we were received with full protocol of the Speaker's office, and driven to the Carlton Towers Hotel.

After a morning meeting with some members of the House of Commons, we were invited for lunch by the British Foreign Secretary at the Lancaster House. Many questions were bombarded at us regarding the possibilities of Benazir Bhutto's return to Pakistan. Speaker Weatherill hosted a dinner for us at the Speaker's residence which was within the Houses of

Parliament. It was a splendid seated dinner for twenty-four, in a beautiful panelled dining room, the guest list carefully planned by the Speaker's ultra-efficient secretariat. It included the former Headmaster of Clifton, the Public School where Fakhar had been a student, who was currently a Don at Queen's College, Oxford; his house master, who was the current headmaster at Clifton; our friends, Mandy and Ronald Clarkson, and Patsy and David Maude Roxby; along with some leading MPs, both Tory and Labour, who had considerable knowledge of South Asian politics and profound interest in Afghanistan. They were all immensely interested in the phenomenon of the 'Red Army' getting bogged down in Afghanistan. The MP seated next to me predicted the withdrawal of Russian troops in haste, and sounded to me like General Hameed Gul who had given us an 'in-camera' briefing session on Afghanistan just before martial law was lifted, telling us that the Soviet Union would break up and the Russians would be confined to the 'Kingdom of Muscovy'. I quoted this to the MP who informed me that this was exactly what American and British Intelligence sources were saying. I now understood why General Hameed Gul, head of our military intelligence at the time, had sounded so convinced.

The Speaker and his wife also invited us to their house in the country for the weekend. We were driven to their place on Friday, in the late afternoon, and informed by our host and hostess that Winston Churchill MP junior, as the Americans would say, and his wife, would be joining us for dinner. Over a cup of tea, Mrs Weatherill gossiped a bit regarding Winston's involvement with another woman which had hit the newspapers and caused considerable stress to his marriage. She also told me that we would dress formally for dinner, adding that every weekend they hosted a dinner for six, usually combining an MP couple with civil servants or military officers. Since her husband had served in the British army before he joined politics, he was always keen to ensure good social relations between officers and politicians.

Winston looked amazingly similar to his father, Randolph Churchill, had his mother, Pamela Harriman's bright blue eyes, and was exceptionally good looking. His wife, on the other hand was ordinary, though pleasant, and her conversation revealed depth, while his was full of amusing banter. The dinner discussion centred on Afghanistan. Fakhar mentioned that the Afghan refugees in our country had now exceeded three million and were penetrating our social fabric to a dangerous level. I spoke of the 'stinger missiles' that Dr Marie Broxup, a strategic studies scholar at Oxford, whom I had met in London in the summer of 1984, had mentioned would give the Mujahideen a crucial advantage over the Soviets increasingly trapped in Afghanistan. Speaker Weatherill, himself a soldier/statesman in the Churchillian tradition, was confident that the Soviets would retreat out of Afghanistan, taking a leaf out of British experiences in the Afghan Wars. He emphasized the importance of Afghanistan remaining a 'Buffer State', the recurring refrain of all Anglo-American diplomats posted in our country at the time. After dinner, Winston suggested that since their countryhouse was nearby, very close to Chartwell, his grandfather's home, if we had not seen it, he and his wife would be happy to take us there the next day, and would come to pick us up mid-morning. We were both delighted at the prospect of visiting Sir Winston Churchill's retreat in the company of his grandson.

Driving us down to Chartwell, Winston explained that by the end of his second tenure as Prime Minister, his grandfather, Winston Churchill, was fairly broke. The Marlboroughs (Churchill belonged to the aristocratic family of the Dukes of Marlborough), tended to be spenders. His great-grandfather, Winston informed us, had managed to save his estate by marrying an American heiress. His grandfather had inherited reasonably well, but spent a fortune on his travels in India and Africa and on race horses. Sir Winston Churchill was, however, left with Chartwell, before he became Prime Minister. After the Second World War, since Britain itself went broke, his grandfather was never really able to recuperate financially, and after he ceased to be Prime Minister for the second time, he willed Chartwell to the National Trust, with the proviso that he and his wife be allowed to live in it till their deaths. 'Now Chartwell spins hundreds of thousands of pounds for the National Trust, a few hundred thousand people from within the Britain as well as from all over the world, pay three pounds each to visit Churchill's home.'

'My late father bought a horse called Le Pretendant at a sale in Newmarket in 1960, which had belonged to your grandfather,' I told Winston, who was taken aback.

'What an extraordinary coincidence! Was that not the horse that won the Churchill Stakes?'

'Yes, indeed it was. He was a great horse, auctioned for a song at Newmarket because of a lump on his nose which was believed to be cancerous, which disappeared in a couple of years after my father bought him. He stood at our Stud farm in the Punjab and sired many good horses for eighteen years. My father wrote a letter to Sir Winston asking if he had a photograph of himself leading in Le Pretendant when he won The Churchill Stakes, and got a fairly prompt response from his secretary to say that when she read the letter out to your grandfather, he had instructed her to send a photograph of Sir Winston by Cecil Beaton which he signed personally a year before he died. My father passed away in 1971 and your grandfather's portrait remains among our prized possessions.'

'Hang onto it. It is probably the only personally signed famous photograph of my grandfather by Cecil Beaton in your country.'

There was already a long queue at Chartwell, and as Mrs Churchill informed us, it was likely to become longer by the afternoon. But we did not have to wait in the queue. Winston paid for the tickets for all of us, and one of the caretakers took us outside of the cordon. This was the only concession made for the grandson and his guests. We went through all the rooms downstairs. They were elegant and homely in a quiet way, after which we went upstairs, where Lady Winnie's room was at one end of the house and Sir Winston's at the other end. Her room was pretty, with floral chintz curtains, a skirted dressing table and bedcover to match, while his room was small and Spartan, with a simple iron bed by the wall facing windows that looked out on the garden, a simple table across the bed with a large dent cut into the middle of the table.

'Do you notice the dent?' Winston asked. 'This was to accommodate his belly. My grandfather spent the last passage of his life soaking in that bathtub.' The bathroom door was ajar; we could see an outsized bathtub, a table with a basin, and a large commode. 'His only luxury was hot water for his bath. He would soak in his bath till the water turned cold, and then wrap his bathrobe around himself and climb into bed. He read in the bath and wrote in his bed hence the dented table.'

What fascinated me most were the two letters displayed in the hallway one on which the simple letterhead read, 'Prime Minister', and the text addressed to Field Marshal Viscount Montgomery more or less was an order to Montgomery: 'Montgomery, you are hereby ordered to take Africa', and was signed, 'Winston Churchill'. Juxtaposed with this was the response to this letter, with an equally simple letterhead which read, 'Africa Command' addressed to Prime Minister with more or less the text, which stated: 'In compliance with orders of the Prime Minister, reporting, I have taken Africa,' and was signed, Montgomery. The explanatory plaque below the letters simply stated that both letters were couriered. I wondered whether our correspondence between Prime Ministers and Army Chiefs was this simple. Could I, as MNA, access the command letters written by Ayub Khan to Akhtar Malik or Yahya Khan? Of course not.

At the end of the visit hosted by Speaker Weatherill, Fakhar flew home while I decided to stay on in London for reunion with my friends, Mandy and Patsy. Fakhar called me from Islamabad to say that Haji Saifullah was pressing him to take up the question he had raised regarding the legality of Mohammad Khan Junejo's membership to the National Assembly. Fakhar had kept the judgement reserved, but Saifullah wanted to obtain an opinion or else he said the Court could pass a stricture. I urged Fakhar not to react for a few days. Then Haji Saifullah called me up, asking me to convince Fakhar to hold on. But when I called Fakhar to pass on Saifullah's message, he told me that he had said something before and now was saying something else.

Fakhar had decided to go along with the dictate of the Constitution. The Constitution stated that if a question is raised with the Speaker regarding the legality of membership of any individual elected, the Speaker shall refer the matter to the Chief Election Commissioner. Fakhar felt the word 'shall' left him no discretion, and he had pended the matter long enough. I rushed back home, but before I landed in Islamabad, Fakhar had already referred the matter to the Chief Election Commissioner (CEC). It was clear to me that a dirty intrigue had been launched, perhaps at Zia ul-Haq's behest, by the proverbial 'hidden hands', to trap Fakhar, with several of those members who pretended to be our friends being involved. And as Munir Niazi wrote in his powerful Urdu poem, 'on whose hands do I see the stains of this heinous crime, when the entire town is wearing gloves.'

7

In Opposition

Fourteen months after the majority of the Members National Assembly of Pakistan had elected Fakhar Imam as Speaker, a Special Session of the Assembly was summoned and a motion of 'No Confidence' against the Speaker was moved by the law minister. Fakhar had anticipated it from the outset and so had I, especially after Fakhar's Ruling against Martial Law. But when the hit actually came, it brought back the old knot of pain in the pit of my stomach that had faded away in the last few years and left me with a hubris resulting from people occasionally referring to me as 'bionic woman'. In my twenties, I had hurt for my father and now at the start of my forties, I was hurting for the father of my children.

Fakhar's face was impassive, as the motion was read out. He vacated his Chair immediately, and the Secretary of the Assembly announced a week's recess, before the Motion was to be put to a vote, which again would be by secret ballot.

A large number of colleagues came to our house. Fakhar revealed considerable sang-froid, telling everyone that he was expecting it, saying that he would be following, the illustrious footsteps of Maulvi Tamizuddin. I betrayed my anguish as our friends tried to console me, with Air Marshal Nur Khan concluding that Fakhar had given the Assembly credibility and conducted it impeccably, and whoever had voted for him would surely vote to retain him, and there would be others who would join as well, because it was a secret ballot, the motion would not carry. Abdul Hamid Jatoi agreed partially with Nur Khan, adding that this would apply to the members from Sindh, Frontier, and Balochistan, but he feared that if Zia ul-Haq took an interest, then the majority from the Punjab would do his bidding.

When the Assembly reconvened, the orders of the day indicated that the law minister would make a short statement followed by statements by two speakers for the Motion, after which the Speaker under 'No Confidence' would address the House, at the end of which the members would vote. As we reached the Assembly, we saw General Zia ul-Haq's motorcade in the driveway. On entering the Hall, Fakhar was led to the front bench of the aisle and was seated next to the Prime Minister. The bells were rung. The law minister was on his feet, looking somewhat sheepish, perhaps because he was an old enough political worker to have been in agreement with my 'long rope' theory, and had understood that the unravelling of this Parliament had begun. He obediently stated that the Ruling Party, the Muslim League and its members, found the conduct of the Speaker biased against the Prime Minister and in questioning the legality of the membership of the Honourable Prime Minister, the Speaker was virtually seeking to dislodge him. So saying, he resumed his seat and to my great amazement, the two members who spoke in support of the motion were none other than General (retired) Abdul Majeed Malik and Rehana Mashadi, who had been with us in Mexico and Brazil not so long ago, both Punjabis, both new entrants in the political game: Majeed Malik elected from Chakwal, and Rehana on a quota seat for women. In his speech, Majeed Malik accused Fakhar Imam of such deep bias against the Prime Minister that when his wife ridiculed the Prime Minister, he never bothered to contradict her, and she also stated openly that Fakhar Imam deserved to be Prime Minister because in her opinion he was more able than the Honourable Prime Minister. At this, several members stood up to protest but their microphones were switched off. However, Abdul Hameed Jatoi's stentorious voice rang out: 'She is an honourable member in her own right, popularly mandated, who did not join the King's Party of her own volition and, furthermore, I agree with her that Fakhar Imam is more able than Mohammad Khan Junejo.' At this several members of the King's Party stood to counterattack, and in the din that ensued, Rehana Mashadi's mike was switched on. Rehana shouted into the mike that the House should know about the Speaker of the Islamic Republic of Pakistan—that he took a delegation to Brazil—and she was witness to him and his wife going to night clubs to watch scantily clad men and women dancing. They had dragged her along with them, even though she kept protesting. Moreover, the Speaker's wife was always trying to persuade her to keep her *dupatta* off her head and this couple brought shame to the Islamic Republic. And as the Honourable member Majeed Malik had said, this couple were continuously planning to overthrow our beloved and popular Prime Minister. I felt nauseous, the bile rising up to my throat, finding it difficult to comprehend this level of treachery.

Then Fakhar rose to speak and there was pin drop silence. He reminded the members that we had been elected in a non-party election, furnishing affidavits that we were not members of a political party at the time of filing nomination papers. When we took oath as members of this August House we took oath as independently-elected members. The Honourable Prime Minister, after being nominated by the then CMLA (Chief Martial Law Administrator), General Zia ul-Haq, obtained a unanimous vote of confidence from a non-partisan House. Subsequently, a new version of the PML (Pakistan Muslim League), led by him was registered with the Election Commission, which is when the Honourable Member from Rahim Yar Khan, Haji Saifullah, had raised the question regarding the legality of Junejo's membership. By reserving judgement on the question, Fakhar went on to say, he had given ample time to the Prime Minister to comport with the requirement of the law and had tried to show the way out to the Honourable Law Minister: that the Prime Minister relinquish his office nominating a colleague in his place for what would not be more than six weeks, resign his membership, and seek re-election from his constituency in Sanghar. Unfortunately, the worthy Prime Minister had not opted for the correct course, thereby denying himself the opportunity to stand on high moral ground. And had the question raised not had legal basis, why would the Law Minister have piloted an Amendment with retrospective effect to provide legal cover to the members who had joined the Ruling Party? Therefore, as Speaker he had no option but to follow the letter of the Constitution which stated that, 'should a question arise on the legality of membership of the Prime Minister, the Speaker shall refer the matter to the Chief Election Commissioner.' Fakhar then pointed his finger at the Prime Minister, who as per usual was holding his head in his hands. In a loud voice, Fakhar reminded the Prime Minister that he had given assent to General Zia ul-Haq's RCO (Revival of Constitution Order) being moved as the Eighth Amendment Bill to the Constitution of Pakistan which conferred all powers of the Executive to the President and rendered the Prime Minister's office virtually powerless. And had it not been for twenty-two Independent members, including Haji Saifullah, and the ten members of the Jamaat-i-Islami, who had themselves registered prior to the elections, opposing the Bill, and himself as Speaker allowing the lengthiest debate in our legislative history, the Parliamentary character of the Constitution would not have been reinstated, nor would the Prime Minister have had his power as Executive restored to him.

Addressing the members Fakhar ended his speech on a poignant note, reminding us that while Chairman Senate, the Prime Minister, and the Ministers of Finance and Foreign Affairs, were all presidential nominees, the Speaker was elected by the House, and remained indebted to the Honourable Members, whose confidence he had tried his best to honour and uphold. He was proud of the fact that he had played a consequential role in empowering the Parliament which had become the focus of considerable attention both within as well as outside of Pakistan. Therefore his conscience was clear that he had not defaulted in any way in the discharge of his duties, and he expected the Honourable Members to vote according to the dictate of their conscience, setting all expediencies aside. He reminded us that we should seek to be role models for our electorate and give precedence to principle above all personal considerations.

The applause that greeted Fakhar's oration was thunderous, with the Press Gallery giving him a standing ovation. A large number of members went to his desk to congratulate him and many flocked to my desk as well. Encouraged by this, I went up to a few of those colleagues who had been enthusiastic supporters when Fakhar was being elected Speaker, a few were evasive, some laudatory, but when I approached Malik Sarfaraz from Sheikhupura, he said, 'I must come clean with you and tell you that General Zia arrived in his chamber early this morning and summoned at least fifty of us from the Hostel. We were shown into his chamber individually, and he repeated the same two sentences to all of us: if we tried to save our Speaker by voting for him and he were re-elected, then Zia would take it as an indication of their loss of trust in him and he would be constrained to dissolve the Assembly and announce elections within ninety days, and we could go back and face our electorate. However, if we voted out Fakhar Imam, we would not only save the Prime Minister in whom we reposed our trust at his request, we would also save our Assembly. Those of us who discussed the matter amongst ourselves decided to save the Assembly. General Zia ul-Haq was in uniform and deadly serious. While the others may not tell you, I thought I would prepare you so that you are not too disappointed. I am proud of Fakhar Imam, we all are, everything he said was absolutely true, but we are pragmatists, especially those of us who belong to Punjab.' I thanked Malik Sarfaraz for his honesty.

The votes were counted. Ironically, Fakhar had polled seventy-two votes, and ceased to be Speaker. It was clear to me that it would be Mohammad Khan Junejo next, who was too myopic to see it just yet. Zia ul-Haq had planned to rule the Parliament. The Speaker who had stood in the way had to be removed. The clout that his uniform carried remained effective.

The new Parliament House stood completed and the ensuing Session was summoned in its permanent precinct. Hamid Nasir Chattha was elected Speaker by the Junejo Muslim League. Eighteen of us constituted an Independent Parliamentary Group, and elected Syed Fakhar Imam as Leader of the Opposition. The ten Jamaat-i-Islami members also sat on Opposition benches, adjacent to our Independent Parliamentary Group, which came to be popularly known as the IPG, while the Jamaat-i-Islami sat behind their own Parliamentary leader, Syed Asad Gillani.

Fakhar led the Opposition as admirably as he had conducted the House. To make an Assembly successful, the roles of Speaker,

Leader of the House, and Leader of the Opposition are crucial. The 1985 Assembly is well remembered by all those who have observed the seven Parliaments that have ensued in the last twenty-eight years. The prevalent view among them being that all those issues that have relevance and meaning in our country today were raised in the 1985 Assembly by the small and effective Opposition, and all the errors and excesses of the Majority Party of that time have been repeated by all governments that have come thereafter.

The first Private Members Bill that was entered in the Assembly secretariat was moved by me. It was an environment protection bill which focused on seeking to save the Houbara Bustard from extinction. Speaker Fakhar Imam had admitted my 'Banning of Gaming of the Houbara Bustard Bill, 1985' to the Committee for Food and Agriculture which constituted a sub-committee for environmental protection. The sub-committee would not meet and my bill was deferred again and again. Speaker Chattha, to temper my onslaught from the floor against the Minister in-charge, Kazi Abid, told the minister to examine my bill without further delay. Speaker Chattha always looked apprehensive whenever I asked for the floor and I decided to mark the advantage. When the sub-committee met with the Minister in the chair, I presented my arguments which were countered by the aging minister, who was in his seventies and who, by way of response reminded me that he had been my father's colleague in the West Pakistan Assembly thirty years ago. I told him that while I valued my association with him through my father in a strictly personal sense, it had no relevance for the matter under consideration. Kazi Abid then said that my bill would have negative impact on our Foreign Policy as it would impair relations with the UAE (United Arab Emirates). I was waiting for him to field this argument. 'Clearly Kazi Sahib, you were inattentive and failed to hear my opening statement when I introduced the bill, and your Ministry has failed to brief you appropriately. Healthy inter-state relations are based on mutuality. The UAE rulers have no respect for, and give no rights to Pakistanis who go to work there, while we bend over backwards for them. I think it is deeply regrettable that while we do not issue shooting permits to our own people for gaming of the Houbara, we issue permits for up to five hundred birds to these Arab gluttons, who have cleaned out this extraordinary migratory bird from their own spaces, and are now busy cleaning it out of Cholistan and Thal, a part of which is in my constituency.'

Kazi Sahib was stumped by my argument, and in trying to mount a counter argument ended up saying, 'As you have stated, Syeda Sahiba, the Houbara is a migratory bird, but it is only the male that migrates. The females remain home in Siberia, I believe.'

'Kazi Sahib, you seem to be confusing the Houbara with our migrant workers in the Gulf States who leave their wives and children behind in their homes. The female Houbaras surely do not stay in their Siberian homes in Burkas!' I was laughing, and even the Secretary, as well as the Joint Secretary from the Ministry of Foreign Affairs, could not suppress their quiet laughter. The minister turned down my bill in haste thereafter, but I was determined to keep my bill on the floor every day for as long as I could, and prevent it from being voted out. I lobbied IPG colleagues to speak on my bill every Tuesday to prevent it from being talked out for more than two years. By the time it was voted out by the Treasury, at least the newspaper-reading public was sensitized to the issue. Further down the years, Kazi Abid's daughter became the first woman Speaker in our country.

I moved several Private Members Bills, including an important one on preservation and protection of national monuments and heritage buildings, not having forgotten my friend Ahmed Nabi Khan, of the Lahore Fort. But none of my other bills got the attention in the media which my Houbara Bill elicited, perhaps because it was the first Private Members Bill moved after a legislative gap of eight years.

The Budget debate for 1986 was opened by leader of the opposition, Syed Fakhar Imam, who pointed out that the most major head under which public money was spent, after debt re-servicing, was defence; the budgetary documents dismissed this considerable cost in two lines, and since the inherent power of Parliament vested in its control of the money bill, the budget was, in a sense, incomplete because it made no explanation of detail costs incurred on the second largest expenditure head. I took Fakhar's argument further by demanding specifically that the Budget of the intelligence agencies be placed on the table of the House so that the members could subject it to individual scrutiny.

I was rewarded for my pains in making a speech which ensured the establishing of the Saudi-funded Sipah Sahaba emerging in my home town of Jhang not long thereafter. I also questioned the wisdom of our continuing support to the so-called Afghan 'Jihad'. I stressed upon the fact that it was not our war, and why were we involving ourselves in a conflict in our neighbouring country, with our country getting inundated with an influx of refugees from Afghanistan who were not even grateful for our opening our doors to them and sharing our bread with them. I demanded that the Afghans be limited to camps in specified areas near the Afghan border and not spread out throughout the country, and further suggested that we examine the implications for Pakistan if the Soviet Union did indeed walk out of our neighbouring country, lock, stock, and barrel. Needless to say what rolled most easily off the tongues of the King's Party affiliates, when they were forced to focus on strategic questions, was the term 'Ummah' (Muslim Brotherhood). The Ummah being behind us, it was logical that we farm out our brains to our good friends, the Americans, who, in their wisdom, were helping us to secure not only 'Strategic Depth in Afghanistan' but who were also being generous enough to give us 1.3 billion dollars of economic assistance and allowing us to buy a squadron of high performance fighter jet aircrafts called F-16s. In front of them the MIGs that the Indians were procuring from the Russians were no match.

My further question, raised in cut motions, was that if we were getting so much assistance from the Americans, then where were we spending our own allocations on defence, and why were there no details provided as questioned by Leader of the Opposition in the Demand for Grants that had been placed before us.

While the Budget Session was going on, I decided to make a brief weekend visit to Lahore to attend the parent/teacher conference that was held at the end of the academic year at the Lahore American School, where our three children were studying. I was catching a Fokker flight and was about to board the coach which ferried passengers from lounge to aircraft, when someone shouting '*Hatto*! (Out of the way!)' pushed me so hard that I stumbled. Recovering myself I turned around and looked at a tall lean Pushtun with a black turban straight in the eye.

'How dare you push me? Are you Pakistani? You look Afghan. Pakistani men do not go to Afghanistan to push women, so what gives you this right in my country?' He did not deign to respond to me, but one of the three men with him, probably the one who pushed me, announced the black turbaned Pushtun's name, 'Commander of the Faithful, Engineer Gulbuddin Hekmatyar', and they proceeded to seat themselves in the coach. I was furious, and decided to protest with the US Ambassador, and to highlight the incident in the Assembly. I did both.

When I brought the incident in the Assembly, nobody seemed to be interested except Liaquat Baloch who proclaimed that Gulbuddin was a dedicated 'mujahid' and the push was clearly inadvertent so he apologized on behalf of the 'Hizb-e-Islami', Hekmatyar's party.

At a dinner hosted by the US Ambassador, Dean Hinton, I protested to him that American support to the Mujahideen ought to ensure that their leaders confine themselves to Afghanistan, instead of wandering around in the interior of Pakistan. Ambassador Hinton appeared interested in my narrative, but said this was a matter for the Government of Pakistan to take up with the Mujahideen leaders. He informed me that Congressman Charlie Wilson would be in town shortly and would ask us around to meet with him. He further informed me that Congressman Wilson was friendly with all the leaders of the Afghan resistance but of the two engineers, he preferred the Tajik Ahmed Shah Masud to the Pushtun Gulbuddin Hekmatyar. The irony was that both engineers had been students in Peshawar. Patricia Hinton, the gorgeous Nicaraguan wife of the Ambassador, on hearing all this, put her arm around me and told me that she sympathized with us since this Afghan adventure that we had gotten involved with could really mess up our country. This only affirmed my existing views.

Driving into Jhang at the end of summer, I noticed prominent graffiti, 'ASS' in large letters, with 'Anjuman Sipah Sahaba' written in smaller letters below it. It seemed to be common knowledge that the Deobandi Maulvi, Haq Nawaz, had established this group. He was being supported by some local transporters and businessmen and also by the Saudis. I wondered what interest the Saudis would have in a remote place like Jhang, unless it was motivated by those elements that had involved us in the Afghan Jihad.

Our employee, Malik Riaz, happened to be a Shia. He came to see me, trembling and quaking, and informed me that graffiti in bold letters had been painted on his front door. The words were 'Shia Kaffir', and under it was written, Anjuman Sipah Sahaba ('Association of the Warriors of Companions of the Prophet'). I was still chairing the District Council, and from my office called the Superintendent of Police, to ask if he was aware of this provocative graffiti. He told me that the Deputy Commissioner had issued orders that the graffiti should be removed and also summoned a meeting of the district peace committee to which Maulvi Haq Nawaz and some of his associates, as well as some Shia members of the committee, which included my employee, Malik Riaz, had been invited, and everyone would be duly cautioned that maintaining peace was an imperative, and whoever disturbed the peace would be dealt with in accordance with the law. I also told him that I had information that automatic weapons seemed to be proliferating in our district as was heroin trafficking, to which he reminded me that Jhang was not an island and this twin menace was spreading everywhere thanks to the Afghan refugees coming in increasing numbers into our country, and infiltrating everywhere. I asked him whether their wandering freely outside of their camps was because they were being protected by elements in our establishment, at which he remained quiet signalling the end of our conversation.

Before the Assembly went into summer recess, several of my IPG colleagues and I raised the issue of the Afghan refugees increasingly becoming a problem, proliferating guns and narcotics everywhere; but the Treasury members would merely mumble some weak and garbled responses. Tired of these dodgy answers, as Prime Minister Junejo walked into the House for one of the concluding sessions, I took the floor and, quoting from Shakespeare's great comedy, 'Twelfth Night', said,

> Some are born great, some achieve greatness, and some have greatness thrust upon them. Prime Minister, if you do not wish to fall into the last category, then I demand a comprehensive statement from you on the floor of the House on the increasing proliferation of weapons and narcotics in our country.

I was interrupted by King's Party loyalists and prevented from continuing. Some of my colleagues were beginning to resist the tolerance for democratic expression.

Meanwhile Prime Minister Margaret Thatcher arrived for a two-day visit to Pakistan. Fakhar and I were invited to a banquet at the Presidency in her honour. When Fakhar was introduced to her she shook his hand very warmly, and gave him a wide smile. She told him that Speaker Weatherill had spoken highly of him, adding that his losing the Speaker's office to become Leader of the Opposition in his first legislative term will provide him excellent experience for government in the future. Standing beside Thatcher, General Zia looked sombre, almost dour, but when she turned to me to say I must be proud of my husband, to my great surprise General Zia spoke up, telling Prime Minister Thatcher that I had been popularly elected in my own right. I could not fathom why General Zia was being nice to me, having no clue as to what was in store.

The ten-year lease on my farm, resumed under land reforms, had run out, and I had applied to the Chief Land Commissioner for an extension, but despite the proviso built into the law which gave me the right of first refusal, without any due notice from the government, I was asked to vacate my farm.

Shahid Hamid, my friend and legal adviser suggested I engage S. M. Zafar who was a seasoned and well-known senior lawyer, to file a writ petition which was marked before a division bench of the Lahore High Court comprising Justice Zia Mahmood Mirza and Justice Fazli. The former was senior and well reputed, while the latter was one of the personal advisers of the Ittefaq Group, Chief Minister Nawaz Sharif's business house. Advocate General was Khalil Ramday, also formerly an Ittefaq Group adviser. Fortunately for me, S. M. Zafar's arguments prevailed and Justice Mirza announced a stay-order in my favour. But ignoring the orders of the court, the Chief Minister directed the Jhang District administration to seize my land.

A tremendous drama ensued. While I rushed to my farm, members of the IPG created a big noise in the Assembly, with the sergeant-at-arms physically removing Javed Hashmi, who tended to be aggressive, out of the chamber. Fakhar and our IPG colleagues came to give me moral support, and my farm was filled with supporters from all over Jhang, Fakhar's supporters from Kabirwala, men, women, and children from Shah Jewna and the surrounding villages, did a round-the-clock sit in on the farm. The media covered the episode extensively and as we faced off with the police, S. M. Zafar filed a contempt suit against the chief minister and his government.

When the case was fixed for the hearing, my counsel and the advocate general informed the court that they had agreed on an out of court settlement. My lease was extended and the attempt to punish me postponed, but the message had been delivered that lampooning those momentarily anointed could lead to financial penalties, as the strong arm of the state was unsparing.

I was deeply obligated to our IPG colleagues who had come down to Shah Jewna to express solidarity when my farm was under siege of the Punjab police, so when we returned to Islamabad, we would get together often around meal times, and Dr Sher Afghan Niazi would invariably provide us with comic relief when we tired of discussing Junejo's newfound arrogance. Quoting Hazrat Ali, the fourth Caliph of Islam, he said to me one day, 'Bibi Sahiba, those who eat too much and talk too much never achieve anything.'

'Why are you telling me this, Dr Sher Afghan?' I queried.

'It is obvious Bibi Sahiba, because you eat too much and talk too much!' He sent us all into peals of laughter. And he would also keep reminding us that while many Pakistanis committed the Holy Quran to memory, and earned the title of 'Hafiz', he was the first Pakistani to commit the Constitution to memory, so he deserved to be called 'Hafiz'. Some of our colleagues would bait Dr Sher Afghan and then roll with laughter when he would speak of Punjabis being great warriors. 'It is nonsense that Punjabis lay arms before invaders or enemies. General "Tiger" Niazi was unlucky. You place a regiment under my command and I will conquer Delhi!' Sher Afghan would say, causing much merriment. My friends outside our small circle of MNAs would refer to Sher Afghan as my court jester.

Fakhar and I were also popular with the diplomatic corps and were frequently invited to diplomatic dinners. We became good friends with the Ambassador of the Republic of Germany, Gerd

Berendonk and his wife Friedel as well as with the British High Commissioner, Dick Fyjis Walker and his wife Gaby—friendships that lasted down the years.

Towards the end of April 1986, Benazir Bhutto returned to Pakistan. Our common friend Peter Galbraith informed me that the Chair of the Senate Foreign Relations, Senator Clairborne Pell, had urged the US Government to persuade General Zia to allow her return. General Zia could bully whoever he wished in Pakistan, but he could in turn be bullied, or 'persuaded', by his American friends to do their bidding.

Benazir Bhutto landed at Lahore airport, drawing a mega crowd. My friend Raafia was very taken in with her, as was her husband, Khwaja Ahmed Tarik Rahim. Along with Sylvie Sher Ali and Sardar Asseff Ahmed Ali, they suggested that Fakhar, as Leader of the Opposition and head of the IPG, host a dinner at Islamabad for Benazir Bhutto. We agreed, and Sardar Farooq Ahmed Khan Leghari, who was Secretary General of the PPP at the time, came from his house, which was around the corner from ours, to work out the dinner details. We decided that it should be an informal, get-to-know-each-other event. There were seventeen of us, since Haji Saifullah by now had joined the Junejo government, and we could seat twenty-four on the terrace in the back of our house, so BiBi, as Benazir Bhutto was known, could bring along seven of her colleagues. Farooq told Fakhar that Benazir would like him to make a formal speech but he would need to take the text for her approval; then she would send the text of her reply for his approval. I penned out a simple statement on Fakhar's behalf, telling Fakhar that she could say what she pleased and this exchange of texts would only lend formality to a situation which ought to be kept informal in order to facilitate a working relationship between the

Opposition inside the Assembly and outside of it. Farooq agreed, but the story of the dinner started spinning out of his control and ours. All sorts of characters entered the picture and eventually we ended up hosting the dinner at the Intercontinental Hotel in Rawalpindi which belonged to PIA. Air Marshal Nur Khan, as former Chairman, got us a reasonable 'corporate' price, for what ended up as a dinner for two hundred people!

Benazir walked in looking almost bridal, wearing very formal attire. A video camera was focused on her as she entered the dinner. She looked spectacular, and spent quite a while greeting her party members. She then came towards us. It was as though the Pakistan Peoples Party (PPP) were hosting the dinner and we were irrelevant. A banquet table had been set up at the end of the garden. Benazir made a collective acknowledgement of all of us, as Fakhar seated her in the middle of the table. He sat on her right with Raafia seated between him and Farooq Leghari. Ilahi Bux Soomro, Jahangir Badar, and other colleagues were seated on the same side. Air Marshal Nur Khan sitting next to Benazir on the left side, with Sylvie Apa, Abdul Hameed Jatoi, Mir Ahmed Nawaz Bugti, Aitzaz Ahsan, Rahim Bux Soomro and some of our younger colleagues.

A podium had been set up at an angle, toward the far end of the table from us.

Fakhar stood up, and spoke extempore. He welcomed Benazir on behalf of himself and his colleagues, acknowledging the IPG members by name. He said that they looked forward to working with the PPP and its leadership for the advancement of democratic causes. He then demanded a release of all political prisoners, and emphasized the importance of all democratic forces joining hands for creating an enabling environment for the protection of the human rights for all citizens of Pakistan, regardless of their creed or ethnicity. And he appealed to the international community to ensure a return of the Afghan refugees to their homeland.

Benazir gave a lengthy fifteen minute response, starting with a quotation from Iqbal, which she could not articulate properly so she called Farooq Leghari to come up and help her with it. She then went into the saga of the sacrifices and sufferings of PPP workers. She read assiduously from her text and hardly looked up. When she resumed her seat, she turned to Sylvat Sher Ali and asked her if she enjoyed being a member of the Assembly.

'Yes I do, very much. I feel I am learning a lot,' Sylvat responded.

'In that case, I am sorry you may not have an Assembly to go back to tomorrow,' was the somewhat surprising observation made by Benazir Bhutto.

'Why, what is happening tomorrow?' asked Sylvie.

'Because of us, because of this evening, Zia and his generals would be shivering in their shoes. The report of this huge dinner must have reached them already and they are likely to dissolve the Assembly tonight.'

'I am afraid I do not agree with you. It will take much more than this for Zia to start shivering,' Sylvie Sher Ali countered. Whereupon Benazir turned to me, 'And what do you think, Abida,' Finally, she had recognized me.

'I agree with Begum Sher Ali. I think we will have a session of the Assembly as per routine tomorrow. Zia may try and dump Junejo and bring in an even more supine Prime Minister, but not just yet. After a few months maybe.' I responded, while BiBi abruptly turned her head away and began to focus in the other direction. I was most disappointed with Benazir's lack of political acumen. She had become a great star, larger than life, almost, with the privilege of boasting a truly dramatic curriculum vitae, but she had clearly failed to understand how weak politics had become, and how, with US assistance, because of their presence in Afghanistan, the military had strengthened.

Of course the Assembly was in session the following day and it was as though our dinner for BiBi had gone unnoticed. A few weeks later she launched a movement, claiming that the 'doves of democracy' had alighted on the shoulders of the people of Pakistan and the people should rise to materialize democracy. The attempt at rallying a mass movement flopped, but it did embolden Mohammad Khan Junejo.

The following year, in 1987, Benazir Bhutto married Asif Ali Zardari, son of Hakim Ali Zardari who belonged to Nawabshah. Hakim Ali had been an MNA when I was an MPA, and I had known him since the mid-seventies. When he joined the NDP (National Democratic Party), I had introduced Hakim Ali Zardari to my friend Timmy Bokhari who had married him in the early eighties. One of my closest friends, hence, was now the mother-in-law of Benazir Bhutto. Benazir's glamorous wedding photographs rendered her into more of an international star, her doves of democracy flying away for a while.

Politics, I had learnt was not only a game of tough choices; it was also an adventure into the realm of cause and effect. Prime Minister Junejo actually started acting prime ministerial. He banned the use of luxury vehicles by senior civil and military personnel; put a bar on the president's foreign travel allowance; enlarged his own discretionary fund with which he ordered one and two room homes to be built for one widow in every Union

Council through contractors appointed through his own office. This was a hastily conceived and poorly implemented programme which created an unfortunate precedent, which in turn dogged the exchequer down the years.

In a murky backdoor move, Junejo overlooked General K. M. Arif as Vice Chief of Army Staff, appointing the less known General Mirza Aslam Baig as Vice Chief instead, and he started supporting the Geneva Peace Process which was designed to allow the Soviets safe and easy passage out of Afghanistan.

Meanwhile, in Eastern Europe, the coordinated efforts of Polish politician, human rights activist, and subsequently President of Poland (1990–1995), Lech Walesa, and Pope Paul VI, head of the Catholic Church (1963–1978) had started to bear fruit. The Soviet troika of Alexei Kosygin, Nikolai Podgorny, and Leonid Brezhnev which had lasted the course, ended with the back-to-back deaths of the first two and the failing health of the third, who remained in office for a while, but was replaced by Konstantin Chernenko, who, after a brief period at the helm of affairs, was replaced by Yuri Andropov, former head of the KGB. Splits within the Soviet Politburo were focused on heavily by the western media. In our neighbouring Afghanistan, Babrak Karmal had been replaced by Mohammad Najibullah (1987–1992) The Mujahideen, ably assisted by the Pakistan Army, seemed to be gaining ground.

We, the Opposition in the National Assembly, demanded a debate on the Geneva Accords of 1988 over the settlement concerning Afghanistan. The debate opened with Sahibzada Yaqub Khan making a short statement. As I read through the brief points of the proposed Accord which had been placed on our tables, I pounced on the clause of 'positive symmetry'. This clause suggested that for a period of two years, during which time the Americans would guarantee a ceasefire by the Mujahideen, while the Soviets would keep sending in weapons to the Afghans who were backing them, who would otherwise fear a slaughter; in turn, the Americans would carry on arming the Mujahideen who would otherwise fear the same fate.

In my speech I spoke with all the vehemence at my command. Because of my passionate manner, I would often be described as 'angry Abida' by the press, a description which dogged me through the years. And of course it angered me when I felt that our oligarchs all too often made blunders or were wilfully greedy, which went palpably against the interest of the people of Pakistan. I asked the Foreign Minister, for whom I had the highest personal regard, whether arming the opposing factions of Afghans would not lead them to kill each other to the last Afghan. Would this not make, by now five million Afghan refugees, a permanent liability on Pakistan? Should we not be demanding 'negative symmetry' along with the ceasefire? Afghanistan was weaponized enough; more weapons being given to the Afghans would mean more weapons proliferating inside Pakistan. And how would it serve our interests to agree with these accords, which would provide the Soviets with a fig leaf and the Americans a claim to victory, but it would only encumber us with liabilities.

I had barely finished speaking when the House was adjourned. The Foreign Minister had no time to make a formal response, but as I was leaving, he came up to me, and putting his arm around me, he said, 'Chandi Begum, you hit the nail on the head. This positive symmetry is what Zia ul-Haq is deadly opposed to, so for once you are in agreement with him!' And as confirmation, Siddique Salik called to say that General Zia had asked him to convey to me that he had heard my speech in his chamber and had appreciated it.

'I certainly did not speak for his benefit, Salik,' I said. 'All of you are such snoops anyway. But does this mean that General Zia is failing to cut ice with the Americans?'

'He has invited you and Syed Fakhar Imam to a small dinner at the old Presidency. He is hosting it for Senator Laurence Humphrey who is the leading supporter of the Afghan Jihad in the US Senate, and hopes that you will attend. You may find the answer to your question during the course of the dinner,' Salik replied.

I told Fakhar that we should not lend ourselves to being used by Zia ul-Haq, but Fakhar said we should do whatever is in the interest of Pakistan, and there would be a substantial reason behind Zia putting his personal animus aside to invite us, and using Salik as conduit.

'You have a strong and convincing point of view and should put it across to Senator Humphrey.'

Hence, Fakhar and I arrived at 'Bachan Nawas', a famous Hindu home on Rawalpindi Mall. After Partition, it had become evacuee property, and then taken over by the Pakistan Army. Initially used as a residence, it was converted into a State Guest House. Subsequently, it became the first venue of Fatima Jinnah Women's University.

It was a singularly beautiful structure and a visual pleasure to be in. The gathering was frighteningly small: four Americans, the Senator, an officer with him, the Ambassador Sahibzada Yaqub Khan and his wife Tuba Begum, General K. M. Arif and his wife, Fakhar and me, and the host and hostess: General Zia ul-Haq and his wife.

General Zia made a lengthy statement on all the help we had rendered during the Jihad and how we expected American friendship to be maintained under all circumstances. General Zia then quoted Chinese Premier Chou En-Lai, repeating what he had told Dr Henry Kissinger when Kissinger flew in great secrecy from Islamabad to Beijing. Premier Chou had counselled Kissinger never to blow the bridge he had just used for a crossing, but to keep using it. The bridge of course was Pakistan. He sounded almost as though he was pleading, which I found quite revolting, but also troubling, because the thought crossed my mind that maybe he knew more than what we were aware of.

The Senator did not say more than 'great fight you have been putting up'. I was seated next to the Senator and repeated to him what I had said earlier in the Assembly about the Geneva Accords, and my fear that the Afghan refugees would become a permanent liability for us, as they would not find bread easily in their own war-torn country.

'You are mistaken Ma'am. They will have a huge amount of work to do in the rehabilitation of their country. They will return as soon as the Russians start pulling out, which will start as soon as the Accords have been inked.'

'But Senator, the refugees have grown used to easy living. They get free food rations, their women do not work in any case except for some cooking and washing, and the men peddle narcotics and guns. If we sign these Accords, you and the Russians will be out and we will be left alone to clear the debris.'

'If Pakistan does not ink the accords it will be a pity, but the accords will go through anyway. In any case, your Prime Minister thinks differently. He told me so when we met earlier this evening.' So saying, Senator Humphrey turned to chat with Begum Yaqub

Khan who was sitting on his other side. There is nobody to beat the Americans when they decide not to hear you.

On our way home Fakhar and I agreed that Zia was not himself that evening, the stormy clouds had begun to gather on his horizon, but we hoped it would not go badly for Pakistan. It was clear to us also that Junejo had out foxed his benefactor.

On 12 April 1988, the Geneva Accords were signed with considerable fanfare. Earlier, Mahbubul Haq had been replaced by Yasin Wattoo, and now Sahibzada Yaqub was replaced by Zain Noorani who was elevated from rank of Minister of State to full-fledged Foreign Minister. Junejo, aided and abetted by powerful interests, had become his own man.

Salik came to thank us for joining his boss's dinner for Senator Humphrey, and confided to us that Zia had discussed grooming Fakhar Imam and Abida Hussain as the power couple to take on Benazir Bhutto who would inevitably return to Pakistan and would have to be politically countered, but was dissuaded by his Director Military Intelligence, General Hamid Gul. He said that our background, education, and training was sound, but because we were Shias we would cause immense annoyance to the Saudis. Zia ul-Haq abandoned the idea and was then persuaded by General Jilani to pick up Nawaz Sharif instead and groom him for leadership.

Rumours were afloat in the Assembly cafeteria that Zia was going to replace Junejo with his old friend Khaqan Abbasi.

In May of 1987, the Ojhri Camp disaster occurred. There was an ammunition dump at Ojhri that was in the vicinity of Chaklala, between Rawalpindi and Islamabad where there was an explosion, as a result of which munitions and rockets expelled in all directions.

It was as though an awful thunderclap had hit Islamabad. Khaqan Abbasi happened to be driving his vehicle on the Constitution Avenue of Islamabad with his eldest son sitting with him, when a rocket fell on his car, as a result of which Khaqan was killed and his son incapacitated for life.

When we heard the news, we went to Khaqan Abbasi's house which was close to ours. Begum Abbasi was there, whom we had met before, but we were meeting their daughter Sadia for the first time, and it was clear that she found it hard to believe that the incident was an accident.

The following day the Ojhri Camp disaster was hotly debated in the National Assembly. Participating in the debate I demanded that, since we had lost millions of dollars worth of ammunition and hundreds of Pakistani lives, including an honourable colleague, those responsible for this criminal negligence be held to account forthwith. I went on to demand that the worthy premier, who was no longer a fledgling and had finally come into his own, must ensure that action is taken, not only on low-ranking functionaries but also against senior officers who were in-charge of the responsibility of maintaining the ammunition dump.

Salik again called us and wanted to meet Fakhar and me urgently. We told him we were home and he could come over, but he said that we always seemed to have visitors and also that our house was bugged. I had suspected that our house was bugged but the confirmation was nonetheless unpleasant. Salik had shifted from Rawalpindi Cantonment into his own house in Islamabad. We went to his house, wondering what all this cloak and dagger was leading up to.

Salik welcomed us into his simple home. He shut the doors and windows of his sitting room, pulled the curtains and said, 'If heads are to be rolled then should it not be the officer precisely in control of the ammo dump. Why should the entire Army be blamed?'

'Quite right,' I said, 'but how would we know unless an inquiry is held?'

'The inquiry will never name the former DG (Director General) ISI and the present Joint Chief of Staff. I am not pointing any fingers, just giving an example.' Salik had given himself away, or maybe we were being set up, I wondered. But what he said next winded even Fakhar.

> We no longer know friend from foe. You both know that I have not always agreed with my chief, but he is my chief and if he orders, I obey. It is not up to us to reason why, for us, it is to do or die. I am always with my chief. So should anything happen to me, I will request you both to keep an eye on my family. The reason I am asking both of you is because I have known very few people with your level of humanity and fellow feeling. Sahifa my eldest daughter will need to get married. She could then look after her mother and younger siblings. I encashed my provident fund to build this house, and this is all I will be leaving behind apart from twenty-five acres along the border, which could be sold to build an annex that my family could live in. They could rent out the main house that will generate the income for them to live on.

'Come on, Salik. I cannot believe that a hard boiled character like you is suddenly becoming soft and being stalked by mundane fears. Zia ul-Haq may well go, and it is time. He has overshot even Ayub Khan's tenure. But you are a professional and will salute the next chief.'

'Yes, possibly, provided we are spared the violence. But Abida Bibi, you are forgetting that you became tolerant towards me fairly early in our acquaintance when I told you that I work for Zia ul-Haq because we have an affliction in common. We are both parents to a daughter with special needs. And you had won me over when you had said that maybe God had given us an opportunity in answer to the prayers of the special children of this land, because now at least institutions were being established for them by the State.' As Fakhar stood up and, we took our leave, Salik gave Fakhar a big hug, and surprisingly, me a warm handshake. We never met him after this.

Next morning Ijlal Haider Zaidi, who was now Secretary Defence came to see us and asked me if Salik had mentioned Akhtar Abdur Rahman in connection with Ojhri. I was taken aback. For once, Fakhar was quicker than me and observed that Salik's house was probably bugged. The brouhaha over Ojhri died down, the Assembly adjourned, Junejo set off for a junket to East Asia, and we went back to our constituencies. I had not contested for a third term as Chair of Jhang Zila Council towards the end of 1987. It would have meant seeking support of Chief Minister Nawaz Sharif and I really was not inclined to do that, so I distanced myself from the local tug of war in Jhang, focusing more on the maintaining of sectarian harmony. The ASS, now renamed the Sipah Sahaba ('Army of the Companions of the Holy Prophet'), had refreshed its graffiti but otherwise were lying low. After networking with my supporters, I returned to Lahore to help Mother prepare for her journey with the children. She was taking them to Egypt for a cruise down the Nile from Alexandria to Luxor and then onto Istanbul; and a second cruise on the Bosphorus. I wished I could have been a part of this excitement, but the Budget session was due and Fakhar and I thought we would catch up with the children later in the summer, in London.

However, in a surprising and dramatic move, General Zia ul-Haq dissolved the Assembly, invoking Article 58 2b of the Constitution. Fakhar and I returned to Islamabad. An Interim Government was announced, with Aslam Khattak appointed as the Senior Minister. No Prime Minister was named. Uncle Aslam as we called him, came to see us and asked Fakhar if he would like to join the Cabinet but the proviso attached was that if the elections were delayed, then Zia ul-Haq had directed his Senior Minister to obtain a guarantee from Fakhar Imam that he would not resign, as he had done so in the past by walking out of General Zia's Cabinet. Fakhar declined the guarantee and both of us urged Uncle Aslam to ensure that the elections were held freely and fairly.

Before we returned to our respective constituencies to start preparing for a second round of elections to the National Assembly, some of our IPG colleagues arrived at our house to discuss whether we should contest elections form the platform of the PPP (Pakistan Peoples Party) or whether we should remain Independent. Both Fakhar and I were inclined to remain Independent, while Raja Shahid Zaffar and Mumtaz Tarar wanted to join the PPP. Javed Hashmi and Dr Shafiq Chaudhry thought that the Islami Jamhoori Ittehad, or IJI, which was in the process of being formed, and which would include the Muslim League, the Jamaat-i-Islami, and some other parties could be asked to accommodate us as an Independent Group. Fakhar and I thought that we could consider this but first we would return to our constituencies and consult with our local supporters, keeping our options open for the time being.

When I reached Jhang, I was planning to contest from my previous constituency, i.e. N.A. 69. But on my very first morning at Shah Jewna House, I was besieged by visitors from the town. There was a large delegation which comprised of Sher Afzal Jaffery, our popular poet, Manzur Akbar Haideri, my late father's stalwart who brought along with him Allama Nayyar, leader of the Barelvis, or mainstream Sunni Muslims and opposed to the strict Wahabi school of religious belief, and a crowd people from the city, who informed me that Maulvi Haq Nawaz, of the militantly Wahabi Sipah Sahaba, had announced his intention of contesting from N.A. 68, which included the city and about forty per cent of the rural area surrounding it. He was more than likely to win the constituency and the only person who could defeat him was me. While this delegation was with me, an equally large group of Bharwanas and Bhojias, along with Liaquat Sipra and Afzal Chaddhar who had been members of my district council, and my strong supporters, from N.A. 67 also arrived saying that I would have an easy victory against Maulvi Rahmatullah in this constituency. So we caucused through the day and I told everybody that I needed a day or two to reflect. I consulted with my mother on the telephone and she informed me that my cousin Iffi had decided to contest N.A. 69, and if I could avoid a direct clash with him, I should do so. I also swung through a few villages in the rural end of N.A. 68 as well as communities of N.A. 67. I was greeted with great enthusiasm everywhere I went. Having thought the matter through, I decided to contest from N.A. 68 and N.A. 67. If I managed to get rid of the sectarian menace of Maulvi Haq Nawaz, it would restore harmony to the town of Jhang and also vindicate my father's defeat of 1970. I also thought that if Benazir was contesting from four constituencies, why couldn't I contest from two? Initially, my supporters from N.A. 69 were disappointed but then reconciled to the situation, because they agreed that if I could win from the district headquarters it would be advantageous for them as well. My decision having been made, it further occurred to me that encumbering myself with running mates could be difficult; therefore it would better for me to focus only on soliciting my own votes as an independent candidate.

In August I heard that Fakhar's eldest sister, Paro, had been taken ill, so I rushed to Lahore to look in on her. Fakhar's mother, my Aunt Fakhra had passed away in January 1988. Fakhar had been deeply dejected when he lost his mother, and remained profoundly grieved for a long time, internalizing his pain. I would try to console him that although she passed away relatively early, at age seventy-two, she had lived long enough to see all eight of her children married, and less Paro, all of them with children. And most of all she had seen Fakhar become a national figure and do her proud. When we congregated around Paro in their late mother's room, Fakhar looked really depressed and I knew that he was thinking of his mother. It was then that Fakhar received a phone call from a friend in Multan who told him that the C-130 that was flying Zia ul-Haq to Bahawalpur had crashed. It was lying in the bed of the Indus, not far from Multan, and reports were that there were no survivors. It was 17 August 1988.

'If Zia ul-Haq is dead, we must go to Islamabad to condole with his family, he had come to condole for my mother,' Fakhar said, so we left for Islamabad. A large number of friends and foreign journalists poured into our house. Reactions were mixed. The C-130 took down with it not only Zia, but also Akhtar Abdur Rahman, the recently appointed US Ambassador, Arnie Rafael and some other military personnel, which also included our friend Siddique Salik. Recalling his conversation a short while earlier, we went to his house to console his family. General K. M. Arif was there.

Ghulam Ishaq Khan, Chairman of the Senate, had been announced Acting President, and General Arif observed that Zia was fortunate, he went while still in uniform, and Ghulam Ishaq Khan would be a befitting President for Pakistan. Both Fakhar and I agreed with him.

Zia ul-Haq's funeral was to be held at the Faisal Mosque and he was to be buried in the outer ground of the mosque. That day we were woken up early by an inordinate amount of noise of traffic. Our street was a quiet street, which was one reason I had chosen to buy this house, so what was happening?

Fakhar was up before me, as always, and in the shower. I went out onto the terrace outside our bedroom and saw not only an endless number of buses, brimming with passengers but also an equally endless queue of pedestrians, all wearing caps and all with beards. Around mid-morning Emma Duncan, the British journalist, arrived to say that most of the streets around the Margalla Road end and near the Faisal Mosque were choked. It seemed that Zia ul-Haq's funeral would be immense, and was likely to include huge number of Afghans. Some friends, mostly civil servants, also dropped by and Fakhar decided to go along with them to the funeral, while I decided to tag along with Emma, not because I was grieving but because I was curious. My driver managed to get us to the funeral.

It certainly was a huge funeral. Attendees included a large number of Afghans as I had anticipated, although there were more Pakistanis, mostly military personnel. Majority of the crowd though was distinctly right wing. George Schultz, the then

Secretary of State, represented the US Government, and with him was Robert Oakley, the new US Ambassador to Pakistan.

Nawaz Sharif became the head of the Islami Jamhoori Ittehad (IJI). Ijlal Zaidi suggested that Fakhar should meet him and if his opponent was going to be on a PPP ticket, it could be useful to remain Independent but on IJI's symbol since it was going to get a lot of publicity. He also suggested to me that for me the IJI would be a protection against the Sipah Sahaba because Jamiat Ulema-e-Pakistan (JUI) was a component of the IJI and that would split the Deobandi vote. I told him that it suited me to contest two constituencies and if the IJI was agreeable to give me nominations from both constituencies, it may make sense, otherwise I was comfortable contesting exclusively as an Independent. My development work as Chair of the District Council would stand me in good stead for the forthcoming general election.

Fakhar went to Lahore where the IJI meeting was convened by Nawaz Sharif to discuss nominations for the elections, while I headed back to launch my campaign in Jhang. I filed my papers from N.A. 68 as well as from N.A. 67 as an Independent candidate. In N.A. 68, Maulvi Haq Nawaz filed from the platform of Sipah Sahaba; my cousin Syed Zulfiqar Bokhari filed as nominee of the PPP; and Riaz Hashmat Janjua, who had been a member of my district council, also filed as an Independent. In N.A. 67, Maulana Rahmatullah filed as a candidate of the IJI. Fakhar had informed me the day previous that Nawaz Sharif had said that I could take the IJI nomination for N.A. 68, but N.A. 67 had been promised to Maulana Rahmatullah because he had joined the Muslim League. This did not bother me in the least, and I turned down the nomination of the IJI for N.A. 68, advising Fakhar to go Independent as well, but he said he had been given the ticket he had asked for and his running mates had been accommodated as well, hence, he could not pull out now. I tried to argue with him that courtesy was not a requirement in politics, and one had to look out for one's own interest but he did not listen to me. He regretted it when Nawaz Sharif changed the nomination of his running mate at the last minute, which cost Fakhar his election.

My campaign in N.A. 67 was a wonderful experience. The PPP candidate did not feature, and Ghazi Salahuddin of Sial Sharif withdrew, so the fight was between Maulana Rahmatullah and me, and it was an imbalanced fight. I had developed a network of roads in the Bhowana/Mochiwala area and had all the large villages electrified. The Khairwala drainage scheme, which had materialized as a result of my effort, had saved thousands of acres of farmland in this constituency from waterlogging and salinity, and I had taken all middle schools up to high school level, hence, almost every union council now had a high school. All people seemed to show their gratitude and I received more hospitality than I could handle.

I would enter this constituency at 10 a.m. and leave by 5 p.m. In every village, people would be gathered in large numbers, both men and women. I would first chat with the men and then with the women and counsel them on avoiding paying bribes to the police and trying to resolve their disputes through their own *panchayat*s or village councils. I would also urge them not to marry their children off in their teens and refrain from wasting money at shrines or giving hand-outs to 'Pirs'. Often they would try to give me hand-outs but I would laugh and turn down their offerings. I would also discuss prices of agriculture produce. Our discussions were interactive. To the women, I would advise them on issues of health, hygiene, and family planning. I would tell them if their first born was a boy and the second born a girl, then they ought not to have more children, and ensure good food and a proper education for the two. For those who had two daughters to begin with, a third try for a son would be in order. I would quote my own example, and tell them that if the first two children were boys then a third attempt for a girl was also desirable. But going beyond having three children was absurd. Invariably some woman would say, 'And what about those that have three daughters, what should they do?'

'Those of you who are Ahl-e-Sunnah know that our Holy Prophet had four daughters, so are you not content with what he was content with? And in the case of those who are Shia as my father would say, since he had only me as his child, that the Holy Prophet was his role model and a daughter was good enough.' But at the end of my statement, invariably an argument would ensue, with the older women disagreeing while the younger ones endorsing my point of view.

As the demographics of the locality indicated a decade later, my advise to my voters on the advantages of having a small family did have some impact. This was a fertile area, the land ownership largely confined to small land holdings, clean homes with courtyards that would invariably have an indigenous Punjab *neem* or *shisham* tree, and doorways or compound walls embellished with mud plaster and painted over in white and indigo. I loved these simple homes and would exhort the owners never to tear them down. Every family owned a few buffaloes, and all the women wore pure gold ornaments, very decorative, relieving the simplicity of their apparel.

I would head out of the rural communities of N.A. 67 and into those of N.A. 68, but when I entered the town of Jhang, tension would start mounting. During the middle of the campaign, driving past Mohallah Kappyan in the city one evening, I saw a well-lit *jalsa* in an open space, just off the road with a huge number of Sipah Sahaba banners on every electricity pole in the street. Using public property for political propaganda was in violation of electoral rules, so I made a note of it to report to the District Returning Officer, and told my driver to park the car in the shadows not far from the amplifiers so I could hear what the Sippah Sahaba speakers were saying.

To begin with, a quasi-musical religious incantation poured forth, then when the music revved up, a bunch of young lads with hairy chins or scraggly beards, mounted the stage and went into a war dance, tossing their heads, flailing their arms about, and chanting 'Shia Kaffir, Shia Kaffir, Kaffir Kaffir, Shia Kaffir!' (Shias are idolaters) in perfect rhythm, to the beat of drums. Then, some prominent-looking character took the microphone, the dancers forming a circle at his feet, and taking my name, announced that in voting for Maulana Haq Nawaz the voters of Jhang would not only ensure for themselves a key to heaven, but would also set aside the profligate woman from Shah Jewna who was a heretic and did not deserve to live, and casting a vote for her would be tantamount to inviting the wrath of Allah and burning in the fires of hell.

I was deeply troubled hearing this speech, and determined now to focus more on my campaign in N.A. 68. I had looked upon politics as a mission to serve the people of my country. My sense of religion was to endeavour to be truthful, honest, and generous with my time and my resources. The venomous outpouring that I had heard was beyond my comprehension. I was troubled enough to forego sleep, to block the feel-good factor that coasting around in rural communities had been bringing me.

I would spend the evenings campaigning quietly, going door to door in the impoverished *mohallah*s (neighbourhoods) of the town, returning home late at night, and setting out early in the morning, day after day. My mother fretted about me and said I would fall ill.

Sure enough, in the last week of the campaign, I woke up with a dreadful pain in my lower abdomen. The lady doctor, Dr Majeeda, from the Abid Hussain Memorial Hospital came to see me, and said that it appeared to be an attack of appendicitis. The X-rays bore her diagnosis out. She recommended immediate surgery. I told her I would go in for surgery after the election, now only a few days away. She said that since my appendix was seriously inflamed, if it burst, it could cause complications. I pleaded with her that she must not tell my mother and assured her that I would will my appendix not to bother me for another ten days and requested her to prescribe me pain killers so I could get by. Dr Majeeda helped me out and spared my mother the anxiety. The appendicitis attack passed and eventually I underwent the surgery a couple of years later.

My campaign ended on a high note. I led a twenty-hour cavalcade, with about a hundred vehicles pitched in by my supporters from both constituencies, as we swung through the main arteries of N.A. 67 and N.A. 68. A day before polling, when I was giving out forms and voter lists to my polling agents, I warned all my agents to lie low at the polling stations within the urban limits and to allow the Sipah Sahaba to feel they were winning the election, otherwise I feared they would resort to violence. I had understood by now that I was going to win both elections, and all that was required was that order was maintained.

Sylvie Sher Ali had come down from Lahore for my polling day. My mother was in Shah Jewna to support her nephew, my cousin Iffi Bokhari against Faisal Saleh Hayat. I had indicated to some of my supporters that they could support Faisal Saleh Hayat, who was on a PPP ticket, if they wanted to. Iffi was the IJI candidate and had joined the Muslim League and my mother and my cousin Maryam, who had been brought up by my mother, were supporting him as best they could.

I decided to remain home on polling day, the children went out with Sylvie Apa to the polling stations in the town and I urged them to be careful. They returned to the house and Sylvie Apa said that at several of the polling stations which they had visited, I had no polling agents and there were long queues in the camps of the Sipah Sahaba outside the polling stations and I had no camps. 'Maulvi is winning,' eleven-year-old Abid kept shouting. 'Chando, do something!' was Umku and Shugu's refrain, with Sylvie Apa in agreement with them. I assured them that I would contact whoever I could in the administration, and calmed them down. I told them to go and visit some polling stations in the rural area surrounding the town.

They returned in the late afternoon, feeling more cheerful and also hungry. While they were having a good tuck-in my mother arrived from Shah Jewna, dejected because she thought Iffi was losing, but relieved that at least the contest was not between him and me. 'Baji Amma, we are winning!' was Abid's new slogan, but the girls were nervous, urging their brother to be quiet till the results started coming. They armed themselves with paper and pens and, as my polling agents started arriving with the results, Umku and Shugu sat on either side of me helping me with the calculations. At that moment, the realization came to me that my children were growing up so fast and that I had given so little time to them.

The results from Mochiwalla were coming in fast, I was sailing ahead of Rahmatullah and from the rural areas of Saddar, I was pulling ahead of Haq Nawaz. The dhols started beating in Shah Jewna House, but then the dhols of the Sipah Sahaba also started to beat in our neighbourhood as they were winning the town.

The results from Bhowana were coming in, and I was winning there as well. The girls totalled away and Abid was carried out by my supporters to join them in the bhangra. I beat Maulana Rahmatullah by 24,000 votes, winning N.A. 67. Gradually the drums in the neighbourhood fell silent. I won N.A. 68 by a margin of 8,000 votes from Maulana Haq Nawaz Jhangvi, founder of the Sipah Sahaba, an undoubtedly militant organization.

Mother came out onto the verandah to inform that Pakistan Television (PTV) had announced my victory from two constituencies. She asked me to come inside for a moment, hugged me warmly and said to me 'Chando, I am so proud of you.' This was the first time my mother had said this to me, and I could not handle it. 'Baji, please scold me or criticize me. I am more used to that!' I whispered to her, wiping my tears and hugging her tightly. And then I thought of Fakhar. I called him, pleading for silence around me. 'Fakhar, what is your election result?'

'I have lost to Iqbal Haraj. Congratulations. I hear you have won.' There was a stab in my heart. The girls wanted to know their Papa's result. When I told them, they became very quiet.

I left my supporters, and withdrew indoors to call Fakhar again. Abid crept quietly into the room which he shared with his sisters. I found him sitting there, weeping silently for his father.

The national results were in: surprisingly the PPP had failed to win a majority, as had the IJI, with the IJI trailing about thirty seats behind the PPP. The new sensation was the Muhajir Qaumi Movement, who had swept urban Sindh: fifteen seats, their acronym, MQM, making every muhajir doubtless feel proud everywhere in Pakistan. The JUI, Jamaat-i-Islami, and a sizeable block of Independents, along with the MQM would determine government formation. In other words, given our political culture, the ball of government was fairly and squarely in the court of Acting President Ghulam Ishaq Khan, doyen of the Establishment. I wanted to be with Fakhar, but was too exhausted to travel that night and thought I would go with the children the following day. Having slept the sleep of the dead for a few hours, fairly early in the morning, I was woken up by my friend Timmy's phone call saying how sorry she was that Fakhar had lost, which had clouded all the other victories for her, and that Hakim Ali Zardari wanted to talk to me. Hakim Ali said he had spoken to his son, Asif Ali Zardari, who wanted Fakhar to be their Governor in Punjab. Telling him that although the message would be passed on to Fakhar immediately, I was not certain he would accept, I called Fakhar and told him, 'Fakhar, Hakim Ali just called me. They want you to be Governor of Punjab, and I think you should accept.'

'Chandi, you are being impetuous as usual. I have lost to a PPP candidate, and have no interest in becoming Governor. The PPP has not even won a majority. They are probably only interested in securing your vote,' said Fakhar.

'In any case, Fakhar, I will have to resign from one constituency and you could come in on a bye-election, so you will only miss a session, maximum two, of the Assembly. After all I have no other candidate.' Fakhar has always been deeply principled, so his answer did not surprise me.

'I have only lost an election. My score of votes has been respectable. If Nawaz Sharif had not changed the IJI ticket for one of my running mates at the last minute, I would have won. In any case, I have to nurse my constituency and you have to nurse yours, so I am telling you here and now that I will not contest your bye-election, but I will accompany you to Islamabad when you go to take oath.' I knew that Fakhar would not change his mind. The year 1988 had been such a dreadful year for him. Not only had he lost his mother whom he truly revered; he had also lost his second parliamentary election. When I told him that Baji, the children, and I were coming to Multan to be with him, he said that he was going to Qatalpur to sit by his mother's resting place, and then to his constituency to express his gratitude to his voters, reminding me that I would have to do the same in mine, which would take several days, by which time we would be leaving for Islamabad. He spoke to the children on the phone, telling them he was just fine, would win his next election so they should not worry about him, celebrate their mother's victory, and go back to school.

My supporters had started pouring in with the inevitable dhols, *shehnai*s, and dancing horses. A stage had been erected by our employees in the front garden and Muneer, a local folk singer who sang lovely *tarana*s (patriotic songs) throughout my campaign, performed while thousands of my supporters drifted in and out of the house. My mother came out and sat on the dais for a short while, happy for me but also a trifle sad because all three of her nephews had lost. She ordered a ton of *mithai* (sweets) for everyone and *deg*s, or large cauldrons of *pullao* (rice cooked with meat), taking the children back to school the following day.

Having struggled in the Opposition had cost us, the IPG was history. The majority of our colleagues lost, the five survivors out of the original seventeen, other than myself, were split, with Mumtaz Tarar, Shahid Zaffar, Sher Afghan Niazi, and Salahuddin Saeed going to the PPP; Sheikh Rasheed to the Muslim League; and I was left alone as an Independent. As Opposition, we had done our legislative duty, raised all the right issues, effectively filibustered the Eighth Constitutional Amendment, brought due focus on the Afghan refugees and our meddlesome Afghan policy, refused to take plots and benefitted only to the extent of what was then a meagre allocation of allowances. None of us left the Assembly richer than the day we had entered it.

It was clear that our voting public was lacking in political education and that poor reporting in our state-controlled audiovisual media was much to blame. The print media was marginally better. Of the English press, the dailies like *Dawn* and *Muslim* were good, but English readership was limited. Of the Urdu press, the readership was much larger, and the Urdu daily *Jang* tended towards pro-establishment views, while the *Nawai Waqt* more broadly held a pro-democracy stance. Regardless, voters, especially in Punjab where sixty per cent of our national constituencies were contained, tended to focus on local issues and were often caught by the 'who is winning syndrome'. Thus, pervading attitudes at the time made little to no distinction between authoritarianism, the politics of cult, and pursuits of the democratic way.

8

Pakistan's First Woman Prime Minister

When Fakhar and I drove into Islamabad, the schedule for the convening of the Assembly had been advanced by a few days. The election to the office of President ought to have preceded the nomination of the Prime Minister, however, this was turned around and the Prime Minister would be named, after which the President would be elected, which would be followed by the Prime Ministerial nominee's election as Leader of the House. We understood from this change in the schedule that Ghulam Ishaq Khan was seeking to secure his position, so that he would be unanimously elected, while Benazir Bhutto probably wanted to secure her nomination for Premiership before her Party voted for Ghulam Ishaq Khan. Our assessment was confirmed in the very first evening of our arrival in Islamabad.

Fakhar and I had been invited to dinner by the newly appointed US Ambassador, Robert Oakley and his wife, Phyllis. Phyllis was a career diplomat herself and had been the White House spokesperson before her husband was assigned the job to succeed the late Arnold Rafael at Islamabad. We were greeted warmly by our hostess, who was an attractive woman, and who led me by the hand towards the chief guest: the visiting Assistant Secretary of State. As she made the introductions, I was amazed to see Happy Minwalla, Ambassador Jamshed Marker's brother-in-law and owner of the Metropole Hotel in Karachi, standing with his arm around the Assistant Secretary. We greeted each other and I asked Happy what he was doing in Islamabad.

'I am here to broker a marriage, a political marriage, that is, between the Acting President and the lady he should nominate as Prime Minister.'

'You mean me, of course!' I turned to the American and said, 'You know that Happy is quite experienced in the marriage department, being marriage prone himself, I gather he remarried recently.' Happy grinned from ear to ear, looking like the cat's whiskers, and I understood that the Americans were ensuring the deal between Ghulam Ishaq Khan and Benazir Bhutto.

Sure enough, a few days later Benazir or BiBi, as she was increasingly being referred to, was nominated Prime Minister of Pakistan by Ghulam Ishaq Khan. After her nomination, he was to be elected as the President. I received two important phone calls after these announcements were made. The first one was from Ghulam Ishaq Khan requesting me for my vote. I told him, in as courteous a voice as I could muster, that just before his call, Ahmed E. H. Jaffer had dropped by to see. He informed me that since he had been a colleague of my late father in the Central Legislative Assembly of Undivided India, he considered himself to be one of the Founders of Pakistan, and had requested me to sign his nomination forms as his proposer, as I was the only offspring of those thirty-two founding fathers who had been elected to this Assembly. Ahmed Jaffer told me that he had no illusions about being elected; his motivation for filing his papers for the office of President was to teach young Pakistanis a lesson in history. I had proceeded to sign his nomination papers as proposer, thereby endorsing his attempt to seek to be elected President. It would be dishonourable if I were now not to vote for him. To this Ghulam

Ishaq Khan responded by saying, 'You were absolutely right in proposing his name. Had I been in your place I would have done the same, and it is correct that you vote for him.'

The second phone call that I received was from Benazir Bhutto. 'Abida, this is BiBi. Mummy said that I should come to see you, but I am so busy I do not have time to scratch my head. So I am calling to ask for your support. Mummy talks about you often, she really loves you.'

'Please convey my profound regards to your mother. I will seek to pay my respect to her whenever she has time. But, BiBi, may I suggest to you that you should reconsider forming government. You won the largest block of seats so Ghulam Ishaq has done the correct thing in nominating you, but you can always call on the next largest party to field a candidate. Islamabad is a treacherous and slippery wicket, you should get a handle on the situation first and perhaps form the government a few months later, in which case you can certainly count on my support.'

'Well Abida, my party's Central Executive Committee did discuss what you have suggested but then the view that prevailed was that our workers had suffered so much, now that we have an opportunity to compensate them we must not make them wait any longer. Thank you for your advise, and I hope we will keep talking.'

'Thank you for calling, and I will always be just a phone call away.'

In August 1988 Ghulam Ishaq Khan was elected with a resounding majority. Ahmed Jaffer obtained three votes. He did teach us a history lesson, which in my opinion was that we really had no interest in history. When I had moved a Resolution in the 1985 Assembly proposing that a road in Islamabad be named after

Raja Mahmudabad, who worked tirelessly towards the creation of Pakistan, the reaction of most members was, 'who was he?' and the proposed Resolution had fallen by the wayside. One of my deepest regrets is that there is no road in our country named after my father. Whenever I have attempted to get a road allotted by his name, my attempt has been thwarted, either by some petty bureaucrat or by some thieving politician in the ascendant.

Benazir Bhutto was definitely the most glamorous Prime Minister in the world to have taken oath on 2 December 1988. She wore a green satin *kameez* with a white *shalwar*, the colours of the Pakistan flag, with a white chiffon *dupatta* draped over her head. I appreciated the symbolism. The same evening, she hosted a reception for all members of Parliament at the State Guest House in Rawalpindi, which was a large rambling building, around the corner from a bungalow of similar architecture that had been occupied for four and a half years by her late father, Zulfikar Ali Bhutto when he was Prime Minister.

Kulsum Saifullah had been re-elected on a quota seat. Her son, Anwar Saifullah was married to Ghulam Ishaq's daughter, Samina. Kulsum Apa rang to ask me if I was attending Benazir's dinner and suggested that we drive down together to Rawalpindi, and chat on the way. Rawalpindi and Islamabad were twin cities: it took half an hour to get from the residential areas of Islamabad to the cantonment area of Rawalpindi, and Kulsum Apa was enjoyable company, hence, I was happy to share the ride with her. She was her usual glamorous self, elaborately coiffed, and dressed in vivid colours. Kulsum Saifullah was my mother's age but while my mother had aged considerably, Kulsum Apa looked the same as she did six years earlier when we had travelled to Sri Lanka together to attend a meeting of the Asian Crafts Council.

Kulsum Saifullah was sugary, almost bordering on sycophancy, towards everyone she encountered. Resultantly she had everyone eating out of her hands, but would complain that the only person who was impervious to her charm was her crusty 'samdhi' or son's father-in-law, Ghulam Ishaq Khan. I had grown fond of her. Widowed young, I respected Kulsum Apa for having been an admirable single parent and for having struggled her way up in life despite being a part of the arch conservative Pushtun culture.

I said to her as we swung into the porch of the State Guest House: 'Kulsum Apa, our young and beautiful Prime Minister probably suffers from a swollen head already, so please try not to add to it by flattering her too much.'

'You stay by my side and you will hear for yourself, I will not flatter her.' She squeezed my hand and we entered the bungalow laughing. Benazir was standing near the doorway to greet us, and Kulsum Apa gushed away, 'Your mother was the most beautiful First Lady we had and my very dear friend, and you are the most beautiful Prime Minister and the whole world is proud of you.' Benazir drawled a 'Salaam' in our direction, and as we moved forward because of the queue behind us, I noticed that Benazir had wiped the make-up off her face. She looked tired and less glamorous but contented. Meanwhile Kulsum Apa whispered in my ear, 'She did not look good without the make-up.'

'You flattered her nonetheless!' I whispered back.

'When I mentioned her mother, she did not seem to like it. I hear there is trouble between them because Nusrat wants her son, Murtaza, back and Benazir is understandably reluctant because he is a declared terrorist. Poor Nusrat, I would hate to be in her shoes,' said Kulsum Apa.

The line of guests had diminished. After she had finished with them, Benazir ambled in our direction.

'Abida, we have some friends in common who recommend that we work together, so I would like to ask you to join my Cabinet. Sahibzada Yaqub Khan has agreed to be my Foreign Minister, and I would give you a portfolio of your choice.' I understood that Sahibzada Yaqub's choice must have been part of the deal brokered by President Ghulam Ishaq Khan, so I wondered which friends we had in common that she was referring to.

'Thank you BiBi. It is gracious of you to suggest it, but I was not with your party in your years of struggle, and it would be unfair on those that were in it if I were to now hog a ministry. As I mentioned when you telephoned, I will always be there for advise, should you seek it.' When Kulsum Apa and I were driving back she commented that she had heard that Mohammad Khan Junejo had offered me a Ministry at the outset of the previous Assembly and I refused. Now I had refused Benazir, so did I want to remain in Opposition permanently, like Nawabzada Nasrullah? I joked with her and said to her that since she always wanted to be in the Government, maybe I should do the opposite and always stick with the Opposition!

The next day, Majid Nizami telephoned Fakhar to say that Nawaz Sharif wanted to meet us, so perhaps we could drive down to the Punjab House to meet him. Nawaz, we gathered, had scooped up all the independently elected MPAs and put together a majority in the Punjab Assembly and was likely to be elected Chief Minister. While Fakhar and I were discussing the matter, Ghulam Haider Wyne, who had been elected from Khanewal, for the first time to the National Assembly, though he had been in the Punjab Assembly previously, entered our house, along with Chaudhry

Shujaat Hussain, who had been re-elected. Being the son of Zahoor Illahi, Shujaat, like his late father, had always been very courteous to me. Both Wyne and Shujaat told us that they had suggested to Nawaz Sharif to formally request me to lead the Opposition in the National Assembly: I must accept the offer, and accompany them to Punjab House. Then Javed Hashmi, who had lost his election, walked in and agreed with Wyne and Shujaat.

I said to them. 'All of you may have suffered at Bhutto's hands, but he was kind to me. He gave me my initial break in politics, and I believe that he was deprived of his life in the most horrific and unjust manner. Benazir is Bhutto's daughter. I may not be enamoured by her, but I do have sympathy for her, and great regard for her mother. Benazir offered me a Ministry last night at the dinner she hosted, which I politely declined, but to be standing in an adversarial position, and pointing fingers across the aisle at her would be difficult for me. And then Muslim Leaguers tend to cross the floor easily. If I were to accept your offer, could any of you guarantee that your back benchers would stick it out behind me?'

'Let us go to the Punjab House and discuss the matter in detail, and then you decide as you please,' Fakhar suggested. So somewhat reluctantly, I agreed to accompany the gentlemen to the Punjab House in Rawalpindi. En route I told Fakhar that I was not going to do it. I reminded him that Hakim Ali Zardari and his wife Timmy were friends and they had offered Fakhar the Governorship of the Punjab, at which Fakhar retorted that Benazir had not called him, and he had no reason to assume that Hakim Ali had sufficient clout with her to have been making serious offers. Pakistan Peoples Party circles in Multan, according to Fakhar, alleged that Naheed Khan, BiBi's political secretary, had more influence than the Zardaris.

'Fakhar, men tend to be cold blooded, more than women. I understand that becoming Leader of the Opposition would perhaps make me the alternate to Benazir Bhutto, but I do not have the capacity to pole vault in the way that she may have managed. Besides, as I warned her, she will encounter choppy waters ahead and I do not wish to be tossed about on any tidal waves. And then I have always been softer on the Bhuttos, than you. So I am going to tell Nawaz Sharif that Ghulam Haider Wyne can lead the Opposition. I will sit behind him and you can guide him along since he really looks up to you.'

'Your decision entirely,' said Fakhar as we entered the Punjab House. Nawaz Sharif had Abdus Sattar Lalika, who had been re-elected, sitting with him. I rather liked Sattar Lalika, who was a strong voice for the farm lobby, but the other person sitting there was somebody who was not likeable in the least: General Fazle Haq, who, in my opinion, had been as pernicious as General Jilani in the Zia days and was additionally reputed to be a sectarian bigot and bombastic on top of it. Having been Governor/MLA during the martial law period in the NWFP (now Khyber Pakhtunkhwa), he had tried his luck from four constituencies, lost three, and managed to win the fourth from Kohistan, polling just over four thousand votes. Unabashed by his rejection by the people, he continued to have a cocky air about him.

After the pleasantries, Nawaz Sharif asked me if I would like to lead the Opposition on behalf of the IJI (Islami Jamhoori Ittehad).

Before I could frame an answer, Fazle Haq commented, 'It will be quite a *"tamasha"* to see the two ladies taking each other on!'

'Well, General, since you managed to invade the Assembly, winning one of the four constituencies you attempted, while Benazir won from four and I from two, we would perhaps consider you a "*tamasha*" when you attempt your maiden speech in the House of the people, where I guarantee you will be heckled, not saluted!'

Nawaz Sharif was taken aback; Wyne looked troubled; Shujaat, expressionless as usual; while Lalika and Hashmi were evidently amused. Fakhar spoke in his usual quiet manner, suggesting to me that this was a political meeting, hence we should all avoid personal remarks, and focus on the issue that we had gathered to discuss.

Ghulam Haider Wyne, addressing Nawaz Sharif deferentially, informed him that Benazir Bhutto had offered me a Cabinet post which I had turned down.

'Abida Bibi has better parliamentary experience than Benazir and her concern is that our back-benchers should be looked after by you so that they do not cross floor, which is a legitimate concern. Now it is up to you to give her an assurance on that score, Mian Sahib.'

Wyne made it sound almost as if I was soliciting the position and made no mention that it was Shujaat and him who had come to me with the request of leading the Opposition.

So I responded by saying, 'Gentlemen, you know perfectly well that this is going to be a star-studded Opposition, with leaders like Khan Abdul Wali Khan back in the Assembly after a long time, Nawabzada Nasrullah Khan, Ghulam Mustafa Jatoi and several other stalwarts sitting on Opposition benches, while Benazir has a relatively less experienced parliamentary team. The Muslim League with the largest number of seats does have the right to lead the Opposition, but I am not a member of your party. I have been elected as an Independent, and want to retain my independent status. I had respect for Zulfikar Ali Bhutto and believe that he was a victim of a judicial murder. I sympathize with Begum Nusrat Bhutto who was kind to me when they were in power, and I do not believe that the National Assembly of Pakistan deserves a cat fight on the front benches. I will give Benazir Bhutto my vote of confidence, reserving the right to criticize her if she deviates from the democratic path, and will sit on Opposition benches. I thank you for asking me, nonetheless.'

Nawaz Sharif did not say anything, but General Fazle Haq winked at him and said, 'The Pushtuns would not like to sit behind a woman, so you should make Wyne sit as Opposition leader.'

Fakhar and I got up. After Fakhar had shook hands with everybody, I said a collective 'Khuda Hafiz' and we left.

On the way back Fakhar said that Fazle Haq was in the habit of baiting everybody and I should not have succumbed to his bait, I could have refused the offer as intended, but what was the sense in reminding him that he had lost three constituencies. I felt no remorse for having done so, convinced that an obvious bully like him deserved to be put in his place.

'Why did Nawaz Sharif bring Fazle Haq with him? When will he outgrow the spoon feeding? Obviously making me the offer was Wyne and Shujaat's idea and Fazle Haq must have been trying to dissuade Nawaz Sharif.'

We took Oath in the Assembly in the first week of the New Year, 1989. I went up to greet Begum Bhutto, who embraced me affectionately and asked me to sit by her side and tell her who the members were that she could not recognize.

'There are so many new faces; I do not even recognize some of our own people from Punjab.'

I provided Begum Bhutto with brief introductions of some of them and then excused myself. Malik Mairaj Khalid was elected Speaker, and I put in a request with him to be given the seat behind Ghulam Haider Wyne, which he accepted. I had stayed in touch with him over the years and we valued each other. He said that Fazle Haq and Sheikh Rasheed had both asked for the same seat but he would seat them adjacent to me, saying that he had suggested to BiBi, along with Farooq Leghari, that she try and persuade me to come back to the PPP, and had I agreed he would have seated me behind her. Now Farooq would be seated there and would be across the aisle from me.

I told the Speaker that I would be obliged if I had Sheikh Rasheed sit next to me and not Fazle Haq, at which he laughed, saying this demand was entirely expected. In the evening Ghulam Haider Wyne came to our house to solicit Fakhar's advise on helping him prepare for the opening session of the Assembly, which Fakhar did with such efficiency that the Opposition had a field day on the first day, with Benazir and her team being thrown on the back foot. Other than Foreign Minister Sahibzada Yaqub Khan, her team included Farooq Ahmed Khan Leghari, Iftikhar Gillani, Khawaja Ahmed Tarik Rahim, my friend Raafia's husband, Raja Shahid Zaffar, who was with us in the IPG, Jahangir Badar, and several others, who were friendly and decorous, but then there was Faisal Saleh Hayat, my kinsman, who was hostile towards me from the get go. Khalid Kharal was Adviser and equally hostile.

The MQM or Muhajir Qaumi Movement was a new phenomenon on our political landscape, with sixteen of their members elected from Karachi and Hyderabad, all Urdu speaking, identically dressed, and extremely disciplined. They banded under a leader by the name of Altaf Hussain, an enigmatic character that nobody seemed to know, who had opted not to contest election, and who signed a charter of numerous and difficult demands with BiBi, in lieu of which he pledged conditional parliamentary support to her. With the support of the MQM, the FATA (Federally Administered Tribal Areas) members support was secured and with her majority now in hand, BiBi moved for her vote of confidence.

Hakim Ali Zardari and Timmy dropped in to see us. Even before he asked for it, I told Hakim Ali that I was going to give his daughter-in-law my vote because I believed she deserved a chance. He was relieved because in the first few sittings of the Assembly every time I stood behind Ghulam Haider Wyne to support whatever Motion he had moved, Hakim Ali would look troubled and distressed. He suggested that when I rose in support of her I must ask for the floor and speak supportively as well, and I assured him that I would.

Quoting from the American poet Robert Frost in my speech, I commended Benazir Bhutto for the courage with which she had led the Pakistan Peoples Party (PPP) founded by her father. I then reminded her that this party stood for certain ideals, primarily justice for the downtrodden. So long as she remained committed to translating those ideals and materialized them through her governance without fear or favour, working her way diligently through the underbrush that had grown all around us, she would retain my confidence. But if she deviated from this less trodden path, I would reserve my right to withdraw my confidence.

When Benazir rose to express her gratitude for thank those who had reposed their confidence in her, she also quoted from Robert Frost, concluding her speech on 'many miles to go before I sleep'. She then went to the benches of all those not from her party who had had voted for her, to thank them. Without walking over to me, Benazir simply turned in my direction before going back to her seat and said, 'thank you' as though it were an afterthought. I could not help but feel slighted.

Sitting next to me, Sheikh Rasheed noticed this and addressing me in a raised voice, he said, 'Bibi Abida, Benazir is taller than you, better dressed than you, better made up than you, but your shoes are better than hers.' Benazir heard this and scowled at us, because in Urdu what Rasheed said carried an unflattering inuendo. Rasheed laughed, having enjoyed being provocative.

My bye-election was scheduled shortly after the conclusion of the Assembly Session. I asked Fakhar one more time if he would reconsider being my substitute candidate but he said that since he had lost to Haraj by a small margin, he did not want to give up the lien to his own constituency. I asked him if PPP and IJI did not put up a candidate and he came in unopposed, I could sustain my lien with N.A. 67 and he could maintain his base in Kabirwala, then would he consider it. He thought that if this could be managed he would. So I ran it by my friend Timmy Zardari who said she would try.

I expected Benazir to have a word with me regarding my vacated constituency, and thought of suggesting that she not put up a candidate, so Fakhar could come in unopposed, which would ensure our cooperation and neutrality, but she did not contact me and the date for filing nominations was announced. I had no option but to have a chat with Chaudhry Shujaat to tell him that

I was willing to support the IJI nominee from N.A. 67, Maulana Rahmatullah, whom I had defeated by a margin of 27,000 votes. He was a 'Barelvi'. The Barelvis in N.A. 68 had supported me, and hopefully my support to Rahmatullah would secure sectarian harmony. Shujaat said that he would inform the Chief Minister Nawaz Sharif and arrange a public meeting in the constituency at which Nawaz Sharif would also put in an appearance to launch Rahmatullah's campaign. A date was fixed shortly thereafter.

I reached Bhowana to receive Nawaz Sharif and Chaudhry Shujaat, and, seated on the dais between them, candidate Rahmatullah caused much merriment because he kept holding his head scarf to shield his face in a gesture of purdah from me! But being the good Maulvi that he was, when I threatened not to support him if he did not lower his scarf, he brought it promptly down to his chin. Beyond the stage and the gathering were lush fields of sugarcane. Nawaz Sharif asked me why I did not put up a sugar mill in this area. I answered that my late father had advised that were I to pursue politics, it would be prudent not attempt business ventures, as these could lead me into a conflict of interest, as a representative of the people. Nawaz Sharif clearly opted not to understand the import of what I attempted to gently convey. He then asked me if I had any reservations about him setting up a sugar mill in this area. And within two, years Ramzan Sugar Mill was installed near Bhowana.

Meanwhile the PPP put up the same Mohammad Ali Shah of Rajoya who did not want to wear bangles when I was elected Chair of District Council Jhang. Mohammad Ali had been defeated from the adjoining constituency on an IJI ticket, but clearly had no qualms switching sides, and Faisal Saleh Hayat was given charge by BiBi of ensuring Mohammad Ali's victory.

So he took the opportunity of arranging a visit for the Prime Minister to Bhowana, her chopper flying her into Shah Jewna for the night, and taking her to Bhowana for a public meeting the following day. Rahmatullah won the bye-election easily and Faisal Saleh Hayat was publicly embarassed. This ought to have subdued him, but instead, he strutted around even more, puffing out his chest, proceeding on a self-serving rampage as minister. He had the portfolio of Commerce and Local Government coincidentally a combination of Z. A. Bhutto's first portfolio in Ayub Khan's cabinet and Fakhar Imam's portfolio in Zia ul-Haq' s cabinet. However, he did not possess Bhutto's education or intellect, nor Fakhar's education and integrity.

Spending a childhood of relative deprivation, with sketchy education to his credit, Faisal Hayat set about feathering his nest, setting up a textile mill, which was under-collateralized, borrowing heavily from a government-owned bank that eventually made him a loan defaulter. He also took huge amounts from local government resources to have elaborate structures erected at the shrine of Shah Jewna, of which he declared himself sole keeper, in defiance of the established custom where all direct descendants of the Pir had hitherto been keepers of the shrine. He used his ministerial office to influence the Auqaf department to place the shrine in his custody. Faisal Hayat handed out lots of jobs to his constituents in corporations that came under his Ministry, without their going through due procedure. Some other ministers were similarly indulging in irregular practices and the interior minister was handing out thousands of gun licenses, which, in a violence prone society was not the best of ideas.

There was much to criticize regarding the quality of governance, the first three months. Khan Abdul Wali Khan whose Awami

National Party (ANP) had been a co-traveller with the PPP in the demand for a free and fair party-based elections, as had Nawabzada Nasrullah Khan and his Pakistan Democratic Party (PDP) had conceded a grace period to the Prime Minister and her government, being seasoned democrats. But their patience was being exhausted and both leaders started speaking out, as did Nawab Akbar Khan Bugti, who had been elected Chief Minister in Balochistan and who would visit Islamabad frequently. His younger brother, Mir Ahmed Nawaz, had stood by us like a rock in the previous Assembly.

In December 1988, at the invitation of Prime Minister Benazir Bhutto, Rajiv Gandhi, the Prime Minister of India, visited Pakistan to sign the Non-Nuclear Aggression Agreement. This was a triumph for the newly elected government. I received an invitation for the banquet hosted at the Presidency.

Rajiv was tall, fair, and exceedingly handsome. Benazir looked wonderful in an ice pink elaborate and beautiful outfit. President Ghulam Ishaq Khan was seated between the two Prime Ministers, who were conversing with each other animatedly, while the President appeared to remain silent. I was seated on the middle table, in the first row of tables situated next to the main table. I was a happy observant sitting in direct line of vision of the President and the two Prime Ministers. Khan Abdul Wali Khan was at the main table, as were Nawab Akbar Bugti, Ghulam Mustafa Jatoi, Nawabzada Nasrullah Khan, hallmarked by his red Fez cap, Farooq Ahmed Khan Leghari, Maulana Fazlur Rahman with his 'Deobandi' scarf on his shoulder. As an 'awami' touch, Jahangir Badar and Ghulam Haider Wyne were also seated on that table.

I felt pride as a Pakistani that our leadership reflected our cultural diversity, and appeared democratically matched to the Indian side, with the young and pretty wife of Rajiv Gandhi, Sonia, in a svelte silk sari, playing down her Italian identity.

As the dinner came to an end formal speeches were behind us, it was announced that at the request of the Prime Minister of India, our famous and respected singer Malika Tarranum Nur Jahan would serenade us with her songs. Nur Jahan appeared in an elaborate sari with a white scarf wrapped around her neck. She informed her audience that although she was unwell, she could not refuse the request of the world's two most beautiful Prime Ministers to sing for them. Her voice poured forth, clear as a bell as she sang ghazals of Faiz Ahmed Faiz and Ahmed Faraz.

During pauses Kulsum Apa, who was seated near me, asked whether it was true that she had come to our house with a marriage proposal for me on behalf of her son, Akbar Rizvi, and my late father had been most amused and had asked her to sing for him before he gave his response, to which she had answered that if the proposal was accepted she would sing for him whenever he wanted, if not she would not waste her breath! I confirmed the story, adding that Madam Nur Jahan had emphasized that Akbar's father, Shaukat Hussain Rizvi, was a Syed and a devoted Shia like herself, hoping that this would convince my father.

The banquet ended on a high note and a thaw was anticipated in Indo-Pak relations. But the defence establishment did not seem to be comfortable at the prospect and the political leadership seemed to make no effort to address their misgivings, which Fakhar and I thought was a mistake. We talked to Hakim Ali Zardari in all sincerity on the question but he was miffed that I had objected to his appointment as chair of the Public Accounts Committee. I reasoned with him that the chair of the PAC ought to be from the Opposition in accordance with the parliamentary norm, and my pointing this out had nothing to do with our personal friendship, but he was not appeased and my friend Timmy stopped talking to me.

On Republic Day, twenty-third March, I was invited to the Investiture. At previous Investitures I had always been seated next to Fakhar, in the front row opposite the dais when he was Speaker, alongside the Chiefs of the Armed Forces, and in the second row when he was Opposition Leader. Walking into the Presidency by myself, I missed Fakhar, and found myself oddly seated at the end of the second row, behind the Cabinet with a narrow aisle separating me from a phalanx of military officers, seated behind the Forces Chiefs. General Hamid Gul, who was now heading the ISI (Inter-Services Intelligence) was seated adjacent to me on the other side of the aisle. He leaned towards me and requested in a low voice that I send in an Assembly question asking whether the telephone hot line between the Prime Minister of India and Pakistan was being monitored.

'I am sure you would be monitoring it General, that is your job. Why would I send in such a question, it would probably be ruled out of order in any case?' was my response to him. But he had sown a seed of doubt in my mind, which in hindsight was probably exactly what he had intended.

Our Islamabad home in F-7/3 was increasingly becoming a hub of informal political gatherings. Whenever my mother visited Islamabad, Wali Khan would frequent our place, along with Nasim Wali Khan and Haji Ghulam Ahmed Bilour, who sat behind Wali Khan in the Assembly as did half a dozen of their other members. Nawab Akbar Bugti, Chief Minister of Balochistan, would drop in when he visited Islamabad, often accompanied by his friend Ardeshir Cowasjee, a prominent Karachi businessman, and now a leading columnist, who was also a friend of ours. Ardeshir tended to call everybody 'salla charya' but Nawab Bugti he would address as 'Tumandar' which is the title the British had conferred on the chiefs of major Baloch tribes. The Nawab and Ardeshir would wager with each other and make me the repository of their wagers. Sardar Ataullah Mengal and Mir Ghous Bux Bizenjo would stop by when they visited the capital. At their suggestion, I organized a multi partisan group of MNA colleagues which included Makhdum Khalique uz Zaman of Hala and Mir Hazaar Khan Bijarani from Sindh of the PPP, Haji Ghulam Ahmed Bilour from Frontier of the ANP, and Bizen Bizenjoof the BNP (Balochistan National Party), to highlight those clauses of the concurrent list in the Constitution for which we sought immediate repeal. This group would meet at our house every now and then and whenever Fakhar was in town, Haji Bilour would always insist on his joining us to give us the benefit of his advise.

Media folk congregated in our home increasingly. Prominent among them were British author, journalist, and political analyst, Anatol Lieven, Mushahid Hussain who was editor of a lively English daily, *The Muslim*, Hameed Haroon who managed the daily *Dawn*, Maleeha Lodhi who worked with Mushahid at the time, and Hussain Haqqani. Timmy's elder sister, Pappu Afzal Khan, also a good friend, declared my house to be Islamabad's only political salon, where people from all the four provinces interacted comfortably with civil servants, business executives, social activists, and journalists, sharing opinions with politicians often till late in the night, on my worn down sitting room sofas. The conversation would invariably centre on the mismanagement of the new government and the conflict of interest being perpetrated by the ministers and their stooges. Fakhar would emphasize the need to enact 'Conflict of Interest Laws' and I would make notes to feed in Assembly Questions to pin down ministers on actions being taken in violation of Rules and Procedures that were backed by Law. A consensus started emerging that all the Leaders and Members sitting on Opposition benches should coalesce into a Combined Opposition to pressure the government effectively on steering a steadier course.

I sent in an assembly question related to transparency with regard to purchases of military hardware. To my great surprise the Minister for Defence, Colonel (retired) Sarwar Cheema responded by saying that he was unable to give a comprehensive answer because 'quite honestly, Mr Speaker, I do not know'. I had never heard of Colonel Cheema before he was elected but his having defeated Hamid Nasir Chattha, who had been such a convenient tool of General Zia in replacing Fakhar as Speaker, made me think favourably of Sarwar Cheema. I had understood politics to be a game of tough choices and also an exercise in which it was always prudent to forgive but never sensible to forget. Now his candid response to my question won me over.

In 1989, Prime Minister Benazir Bhutto's visit to the United States was tremendously successful. Not only was she the Speaker at the Harvard Commencement, she was also introduced on the floor of the House of the American Congress wearing an elaborate 'Lehnga', while her spouse Asif Ali Zardari was much photographed wearing the turban of a Baloch Sardar. This caused Nawab Akbar Bugti to make caustic comments, but these photographs had hit the international and national media in a big way. My own unrecorded moment on the floor of the same floor eleven years earlier remained merely a personal souvenir, with nothing on celluloid to trigger the cherished memory. Prime Minister Benazir contracted the military hardware, a squadron of F-16 Jets, with her Ambassador-at-Large, Happy Minwalla as facilitator, while Minwalla's brother-in-law, Jamshed Marker, was Pakistan's Ambassador to US at the time. It was about this contract that I had sent in the relevant Assembly question and the minister-in-charge had come on record as having no clue about it. Little did I know at the time how badly this very contract would bedevil me and my country a few years further down the road.

The lack of transparency on fiscal matters led everybody sitting on Opposition benches in the National Assembly to group together as COP (Combined Opposition Parties). Khan Abdul Wali Khan asked me to join their first meeting which was held in Balochistan House, and Wali Khan also proposed Ghulam Mustafa Jatoi as Leader of the Opposition. Because he was from Sindh, Wali Khan suggested that Jatoi would be more effective, and also because he had been with the PPP since its inception and had a better understanding of the party in power. Mustafa Jatoi said he was honoured to be proposed by someone of the calibre of Khan Abdul Wali Khan and he would do his best to justify his trust. Nawabzada Nasrullah Khan seconded the proposal and then a phone call was received from Nawab Akbar Khan who invited us all to Quetta as his guests. He said he would also invite the Punjab Chief Minister and that we should assemble in Quetta in the following week to make a coordinated effort between two provinces, Balochistan and Punjab, with what was now a powerful Opposition in the National Assembly.

Nawaz Sharif had experienced his share of stress vis-á-vis the PPP who were his parliamentary opposition. There had been an episode of an attempt to remove Nawaz Sharif from the post of

Chief Minister, with Khalid Kharal, who, claiming unparalleled loyalty to the PPP, was now, as Adviser to the Prime Minister, tasked to supervise what came to be known as 'Operation Changa Manga' in the popular press. Nawaz Sharif survived the onslaught, continued as Chief Minister, but was obviously smarting, while Khalid Kharal, despite scoring failure in this attempt, for which he was clearly not chastised by his party leadership, proceeded to sponsor a textile mill in district Toba Tek Singh.

A large group of members of the Combined Opposition Parties (COP) arrived in Quetta. Our friend Illahi Bux Soomro, who had also lost his election, offered to accompany me to Quetta because he wanted to meet Nawab Bugti. We were driven in modest vehicles to the Chief Minister's office which was equally modest, and shown into a sparsely furnished sitting room. This was a glaring contrast to the opulence of the offices of the Prime Minister or the Chief Minister of the Punjab. As we drank our tea and exchanged pleasantries, Nawaz Sharif left the room, saying that he needed to make an urgent phone call. Nawab Bugti rose, saw him out and returning to rejoin us, informed us that Chief Minister Punjab was using the telephone sitting in the office of Chief Minister Balochistan for the first time in our history.

Nawaz Sharif seemed to be taking his time on the telephone. I was seated beside Nawabzada Nasrullah Khan, who asked: 'Where is this Chief Minister? Is he talking to GHQ? We have to begin our meeting. After lunch at which Nawab Akbar Bugti will doubtless feed us the famous Baloch dish *sajji*, which is the greatest lamb delicacy in the world, and easy to digest, even for aging people like myself, we have to catch our flight back to Islamabad in the late afternoon. Abida Bibi, would you like to go and tell him, that if he does not join us soon we will have to start the meeting without him?'

Taking advantage of my relative youth, and my facility with the written word, Nawabzada Nasrullah had also assigned me the task of recording the minutes of COP meetings. I went out of the room, informed by our host that I turn left at the end of the short passage to access his office, where I would find Saudagar, his Personal Assistant (PA) who was a settler from Jhang. Saudagar was outside the door, welcomed me enthusiastically, and informed me that Nawaz Sharif was singing on the phone! I told him to knock hard on the door, and to go in and inform the Chief Minister that the meeting had begun. I returned to the sitting room, and Nawaz Sharif walked in a minute later.

Wali Khan spoke eloquently as always, saying that the PPP government seemed to have learnt very little from their years of exile and the suffering of their workers, that they were resorting to plunder and pelf in the name of the people, and the Punjab Chief Minister would have to exert due pressure on his opposition, keeping within the limits of democratic norms of course, in coordination with the Chief Minister of Balochistan to effectively restrain the government. This would also be useful for the consolidation of the Federation; otherwise the Sindh-led government could find itself in increasing conflict with Punjab, which would only weaken the Federation. It was shaming to recall that such a staunch advocate of our Federation as him had been accused of treason, confined to prison for four years and released just a decade previous. All eyes were on the youthful Punjab Chief Minister, who was a few years younger than me. Nawaz Sharif gave an assurance that he would be available to Chief Minister Balochistan and to all COP leaders for whatever help may be required in his province and he would welcome all of us whenever we desired a meeting at Lahore. Nawabzada Nasrullah Khan spoke at length, followed by Maulana Fazlur Rahman of the Jamiat Ulema-e-Islam (JUI-F), Maulana Samiul Haq of the Jamiat Ulema-e-Islam (JUI-S), Professor Abdul Ghafoor of the Jamaat-i-Islami, and Ghulam Mustafa Jatoi who floated a breakaway faction of the PPP, as the National Peoples Party (NPP).

When Fakhar was removed as Speaker, I was very keen that we should also launch our own party. Around that time Mustafa Jatoi had called on us, suggesting that we join a party that he was launching. We flirted with the idea, but then eventually ended up remaining Independent. Ghulam Mustafa Jatoi was at least a liberal, as was Wali Khan. Nawabzada Nasrullah and the Muslim League were centrist, hence, as the only Independent I felt less uncomfortable sitting with the three religious parties, the COP evolving more or less as the parliamentary version of the erstwhile PNA (Pakistan National Alliance).

When we adjourned for lunch, under a big *shamiana* on the side lawn of the our host's office, not only was the *sajji* to die for, but so was the *kaak* bread which was baked in *tandoor*s (underground ovens) dug in the ground on the side of the *shamiana*. Nawab Akbar Khan led me to the *tandoors* to show me how his Bugti tribesmen were wrapping the dough around rounded stones, which when pulled out of the embers were lanced so skilfully that the bread was pulled off the stone in what looked like two halves of a bowl, with the *sajji* stuffed into it, so that each morsel melted deliciously in the mouth.

On our flight back from Quetta, the leaders were all snoring after the heavy meal; I was dozing off myself. I had been to Quetta the first time when Fakhar was Minister Local Government, to attend a Local Councillors Convention. The children were with us. Fakhar's friend Moeen Afzal was Finance Secretary in Balochistan. He and his wife Nighat had three daughters who corresponded in age with Umku, Shugu, and Abid, so I consigned them to Nighat's care. When the convention ended, we all set off for a two-day visit to Ziarat. The children had learnt that Ziarat was surrounded by the oldest and largest juniper forest in the world. They were also very excited that they would be visiting the Residency, where Quaid-i-Azam Muhammad Ali Jinnah had spent the last days of his life. The Residency was well maintained, with the Quaid's memorabilia in many ways representing the soul of Pakistan. The children seemed to be soaking the history lesson up and we had a happy picnic on the beautiful lawn in a remote corner of the exquisite, undulating and extensive garden of this tremendous national monument. The children would always recall their visit to Quetta and Ziarat as one of the best trips we had taken them on.

Back in Islamabad I was a diligent and hardworking member of the Assembly, fielding motions and submitting resolutions and raising topical issues from the floor. Roedad Khan commended me for being the most active member of the Parliament of 1988. An unending stream of constituents would be at my house every morning and evening and I tried my best to meet my obligations towards them. But involving as the Assembly was, my duty as a mother came into focus when Umku, who was applying to Harvard, Princeton, and Yale for undergraduate studies the following year, asked me if I would take her to Harvard for her interview. She had been interviewed by the local Harvard alumnus, and although going all the way to Harvard was not an absolute requirement for the admissions process, Umku was convinced it may earn her an extra point and, since securing admission involved extremely stiff competition, she urged that we go. Shugu joined voice with her sister since she would be applying a year later and wanted to familiarize herself with the campus. Mother was insistent that I take all three of my children to visit these great institutions and assured me that the Assembly would survive without me!

I would not have missed the experience of travelling with my children for anything in the world. We agreed that Princeton was the most beautiful campus and that Harvard and Yale were impressive and possessed old world charm. The girls both said if they had a choice they would choose Harvard because they had both read Erich Segal's romantic novel, *Love Story*, written with the Harvard Law School as the backdrop. They had enjoyed reading the novel as much as I had. Abid, who was still in junior school but truly precocious, decided on Yale. And having inherited their father's determination as well as mine, it was exactly how they planned that the children's higher education pattern gelled.

We all went to the US, and after having done the round of the colleges, I was staying, along with my brood, in my friend Samina Qureishi's ample home on Chestnut Hill in Boston when Fakhar called me to say that Ghulam Mustafa Jatoi had called him to ask for my contact number and I should expect a call for him. When he called, I was taken aback when he urged me to return as soon as possible because the COP was gearing up to move a vote of no-confidence against Benazir Bhutto.

'But is it not too early, Jatoi Sahib? She has been on the job just ten months,' I asked.

'When you return, I will explain the reason for the emergency, Begum Sahiba. We are all in agreement and Wali Khan Sahib is sitting with me, and joins my request.' After much argument the children agreed that we should head back, and on the long flight home kept quizzing me on what a no-confidence motion meant and what would I do. Would I support Benazir or oppose her? I thought I would take a decision after hearing what the COP leaders had to say. Ghulam Mustafa Jatoi dropped by shortly after my arrival. He informed me that he had lined up ten MNAs from Sindh who were deeply disgruntled with their leadership and wanted the Prime Minister to be voted out. Altaf Hussain had also pulled back his support of MQM to the Premier on the grounds that she had failed to honour the charter which she had signed with him after the elections. His support to her was conditional to her meeting all the demands of the charter. Nawaz Sharif had committed his support to the move against her and so had Nawab Akbar Bugti. So the numbers were in place and he thought that we should strike while the iron was hot. I told him that, in my opinion, it was too early and that given another few months of her misrule, we would have far more public support and anti-government rallies would give more credence to such a move inside the parliament. I further suggested that if he were elected Leader of the House in such a scenario, he could complete the term of the Assembly. And by providing competent governance, then lead us into an election, where the COP could hope to win the popular vote more comfortably. Otherwise public sympathy, which is always with the underdog, would be likely to remain on the side of Benazir Bhutto.

Ghulam Mustafa Jatoi was a sensible person, but he differed with my line of argument and said that the way the PPP government was depleting the treasury, the economy would be in disarray by the time we reached an election, and the PPP would simply try to buy their way through the next elections. Even if the PPP failed to win, the successor government would have an empty kitty to deal with. He also brought the issue of a proliferation of automatic weapons into focus and dilated lengthily on the deteriorating law and order situation in the interior of Sindh, where kidnappings for ransom had become rampant.

I met with Wali Khan. He told me there was merit in my arguments but when he had decided that Ghulam Mustafa Jatoi should lead the Opposition, then he must trust his timing of the no-confidence move, and he suggested I do the same. Makhdum Alam Anwar, MNA from Rahim Yar Khan, dropped by to see me. He informed me that along with Raees Shabbir Ahmed, MNA from Rahim Yar Khan, and Mian Ghulam Mohammad Manika, MNA from Okara, the three of them held the balance. But they were being tugged by both sides, and had decided to confer with me as to where I would be voting. They were convinced that the beneficiary of the ouster of BiBi from Premiership would strengthen Nawaz Sharif, who was not farm-friendly and, as a sugar mills magnate, used his political power to bring down the price of sugar cane for the growers. I told him he had a point but if BiBi lost the vote, Ghulam Mustafa Jatoi would win the vote of confidence and we could count on Jatoi on protecting the rights of the farm community. Hence, I would suggest that along with myself, the three of them should vote out BiBi who was young and giddy, and vote for Mustafa Jatoi who was mature and seasoned. Alam Anwar seemed to be convinced and said he would now proceed to confer with his colleagues.

Next Mian Abdus Sattar Lalika, MNA from Bahawalnagar, arrived, accompanied by Siddiq Kanju, MNA from Lodhran to inform me that BiBi's supporters had started grouping their MNAs and were going to herd them all in one place and bring them to the Parliament on the day of the vote, and therefore Mian Nawaz

Sharif had arrived from Lahore. All of Ghulam Mustafa Jatoi's key supporters were getting together in Chaudhary Shujaat's house. They queried if I could join them.

I had never been to Shujaat's house. I went there with them where some people, including Nawaz Sharif, were congregated in what appeared to be the dining room.

Nawaz Sharif was posing the question, 'What do we get out of ousting Benazir and replacing her with Jatoi, they are both Sindhis after all.' Everyone became quiet when they saw me. Shujaat then led us all into the sitting room, seating me on the sofa next to Nawaz Sharif.

Addressing Nawaz Sharif, I said, 'Mian Sahib, politics is a game of give and take. We vote out a Premier from Sindh and replace her with a Premier from the same province, so Sindh does not suffer a feeling of deprivation. Next time, it could be a Premier from our province. But for the moment, we have made a commitment to Jatoi Sahib, have we not?'

The others in the room agreed with me, and it was decided that all the MNAs who were going to vote against her be taken to Murree, which was in the Punjab and outside federal jurisdiction, so that we could all be together and keep a count, which would be reassuring to all of us. And whoever could not withstand government pressure could be kept in Murree. I did not agree with this last suggestion, reminding everyone that we were MNAs, not local councillors. To which Chaudhry Nisar Ali, MNA from Rawalpindi asserted that staying in Murree would be optional.

So the following morning, Anwar Saifullah, MNA from Kohat, along with his mother Kulsum Apa, and I drove up to Murree together. En route Kulsum Apa kept saying she did not understand why voting out a beautiful young girl like Benazir was necessary unless a handsome young man like Anwar could replace her! Anwar protested and restrained his mother form making any such observation after we alighted from the vehicle. We entered the hall of the Landsdowne Hotel, to find that attendance was somewhat thin: the MQM were there, MNAs from Balochistan were there, the ANP were there.

Ghulam Mustafa Jatoi walked in with his ten members from Sindh. And finally Mian Nawaz Sharif came with his Punjab stalwarts. I kept craning my neck to see if Alam Anwar and his two companions had arrived, but they were nowhere to be seen. As the speeches began, a head count was made. We were seven people short of a majority. At this point a member from Gujrat who was related to Chaudhry Parvez Ilahi and had been elected on a PPP ticket, started shouting that he had been befooled, given to understand that Benazir had lost her majority, and if she had not, then he was going to leave to rejoin his party. The members sitting around him tried to prevent him from leaving but Mustafa Jatoi said that although he would persevere in moving the vote of no confidence, there was certainly no coercion intended. Anybody who wished to leave was certainly free to do so. While he was speaking, a few other members slunk away.

Rana Chandar Singh, who was a Hindu minority member from Sindh, then took the floor. He made a profoundly moving speech, which made many of us hang our heads in shame. He told us that although he had many distinguished relatives across the border, one of his kinsmen being V. P. Singh, a prominent Indian politician who later became Prime Minister of India, he had opted to remain in Pakistan because his roots went very deep into the soil of Sindh, and he had been a member of several legislatures, including the West Pakistan Assembly where he had the privilege of sharing friendship with many stalwarts of the Independence Movement. He mentioned my late father among these stalwarts; as I was probably a reminder, sitting in the front row, and went on to say that he had remained a loyal citizen of the new State that he had chosen, where Jinnah had declared that all minorities would be treated equally, and would be free to worship in their own worship places. His god was Bhagwan, while our god was Allah. And Rana Chandar Singh's belief in Bhagwan demanded that he keep his word, which he had given to Ghulam Mustafa Jatoi. It was up to the rest of us to keep our word or not. Clearly we would lose the vote, and some of us could suffer as a result, but then we should derive strength from each other and assist Mustafa Jatoi in leading the opposition effectively. Rana Chandar Singh concluded his speech by stating the people of Pakistan were a wise people and we would not fall in their eyes, which was what ultimately mattered.

All of us gave Rana Chandar a big round of applause. It was decided that on the day of the vote, we would congregate in Balochistan House and drive together to the National Assembly to vote on the no-confidence motion. Before we adjourned, we were informed that the majority of the MNAs had been flown in a C-130 to Mingora in Swat.

On the day of the vote, we collected at Balochistan House as planned, and a count was made before we started piling into the coasters that were to ferry us to the Assembly and back. Nawab Bugti would host lunch and plan out further strategy. It was decided that some of us would speak before the motion was put to a vote. It was further decided that I was to be one of the speakers.

The atmosphere on the floor of the National Assembly crackled with tension. My statement emphasized that the Prime Minister, having made a courageous beginning and having received my vote of confidence at the outset of her attempt at governance, had fallen prey to a monarchical mindset, engulfed by cronyism, encircled by sycophants, with nepotism hallmarking her governance. I came down hard on the Prime Minister with whom I shared a gender status.

I may not have spoken with the intensity and passion that was long remembered by those who had witnessed and watched the proceedings of that fateful day, had it not been for the ugly incident that took place just outside the precinct of Parliament. The Parliament square was full of banners condemning us for moving against their beloved leader, Benazir Bhutto, who would be Prime Minister for life. To add to this, a crowd of a few hundred *jiyalas* (Benazir's supporters) were assembled near the entrance gate of the Parliament shouting 'BiBi, BiBi, Premier for Life!' All this I thought was the healthy sound of democracy, silly as the slogan may have sounded. But when the *jiyalas* were close to us, and our coasters were slowing down to enter the gate, I saw, as did Nur Jahan Pannezai sitting beside me, some *jiyalas* making shockingly lewd gestures in our direction. Coming from party workers of a party that was led by a woman, this was totally unacceptable. As my litany on the excesses of her government poured forth, I expressed profound regret that to defend against our motion today, the Prime Minister used public resources, commandeering a C-130 and taking MNAs, as though they were captive and criminals, to an outpost in Mingora, Swat, which did not behove the dignity of her office.

The votes were counted. Benazir Bhutto survived her vote of confidence by 15 votes. The PPP was in a celebratory mood, the COP dejected. The assembly sittings were being trivialized, with Mian Umar Hayat Lalika, of the Jamaat-i-Islami who was a gifted and natural comedian sparring with Nasreen Rao, who sounded like she was on the set of Shakespeare's 'Taming of the Shrew'.

One day Nasreen Rao decided to heckle me when I stood on a point of order. Before I could respond to her, Raja Sikandar Zaman, MNA from Hazara took the floor and reminded her that not only had I been mandated by popular vote from two constituencies, but I was also the daughter of one of the founding fathers of Pakistan, whom he had the privilege of knowing. He said, if she had bothered to hear the speech I had made when I gave the Prime Minister her vote of confidence, and the speech I delivered when I voted against her, she would have understood that I had made reference to sycophants who were damaging her and her government; with friends like this lady member, the Prime Minister needed no enemies to ensure the failure of her government, and to reduce the stature of the Assembly in the eyes of the people by making personal attacks against those who least deserved them. As I was thanking Raja Sikandar Zaman for his chivalry, Nasreen Rao went on a verbal rampage which became so embarrassing that the Speaker was constrained to expunge the entire proceedings from the record.

About this time we received the great good news that Umku had secured her admission to Harvard and would be joining in September. I accompanied my daughter very proudly to Boston and Shugu came along for an interview, because she was applying for the following year. Leaving Umku behind to start her life as a freshman at Harvard was a real wrench for me. Shugu was pleased with her interview, and a week later, we flew back. Shugu was confident that she would secure her admission as well and would return the following year, and eventually she was proven right. I was proud of my first born reaching Harvard and looked forward to both my daughters being in this great institution of learning, reputed to be the best in the world.

Shortly after my return to Pakistan, the Chief Minister of Punjab invited the COP Leaders to a meeting in Lahore. The venue of the meeting was the Chief Minister's Secretariat which was now housed in what used to be the Freemason's Hall, in the square opposite the Punjab Assembly. The building had been beautifully restored and refurbished by Lahore's most gifted architect, Nayyar Ali Dada. We were shown into a large panelled hall, with the tables arranged in a square around the hall, and a magnificent floral display of chrysanthemums in the middle of the floor. This is when I met with Altaf Hussain, leader of the MQM, for the first time. Looking straight at me, Altaf Hussain went into a rant against the 'feudals', followed by a rant against the traders and industrialists of Punjab while he now turned to look straight at Nawaz Sharif, banging on about the exploitation of the poor *mohajirs* of Karachi. Mian Nawaz Sharif had welcomed us graciously and made particular mention of the MQM leader, so he looked baffled at this tirade. I responded, 'Altaf Hussain, we were all looking forward to our meeting with you, and do not consider ourselves culpable for all the sins of the past, but we do look forward to working with you to develop a more equitable and prosperous Pakistan in which everybody gets their due share in the future. There is a great deal of poverty in Punjab also, and millions of people live in one room which is often *kaccha* made of mud where there is no electricity, no metalled road, no easy access to school or hospital, and many cities in Punjab where the slums are worse than Karachi. Our population has been growing too fast and we have to make a concerted effort to control it and to distribute our resources more efficiently.' After my statement, Altaf Hussain calmed down, and Nawabzada Nasrullah Khan suggested that the MQM stage a rally in Karachi which all the COP leaders would address this would mount due pressure on the federal government to improve its performance, and to focus on the many serious issues which confronted the nation. Altaf Hussain said that he would mount Asia's biggest rally, which would stun the entire world and take the wind out of Benazir Bhutto's sails, but he had one condition for all of us: that we come to Karachi one week before the rally and remain there, watching the preparations. Our presence would guarantee that the Sindh government temper its aggression against his workers. After some argument it was decided that we would all congregate in Karachi four days before the rally.

'Asia's Biggest Rally' was quite an experience. When we arrived in Karachi we were hosted for lunch by Ghulam Mustafa Jatoi, at his residence, from where we proceeded to Gulshan-e-Iqbal, a locality in Karachi, to a building on the main road, which we were told belonged to the MQM. We were led into a hall and seated opposite a wide screen, with Azeem Tariq, reputed to have been the real founder of the MQM, briefing us on how the money was being raised to resource the construction of a stage which would be a few hundred feet high, long, and wide enough to seat two hundred guests. The backdrop of the stage would be Quaid-i-Azam's mausoleum, and on the road leading up to the stage, there would be a gathering of a million men and women. The film showed shopkeepers handing over money to MQM activists with great enthusiasm, which later on turned into what is now termed as bhattha khori, or forced contributions. The film also showed hundreds of workers constructing the gargantuan stage, and then it gave a full and comprehensive traffic plan for those who would attend the rally as well as those who would address it.

'We may as well rename Altaf Hussain "Führer"', Malik Naeem, MNA from Khushab, who was sitting beside me, whispered in my ear.

'Veritable fascist,' I responded in an equally low voice.

The presentation ended and we were now taken to lunch under a *shamiana* in the garden outside the old Karachi Municipal Corporation (KMC) offices. The food was absolutely to die for, Lucknow cuisine at its best, with Azeem Tariq being ineffably courteous, and constantly by my side. Having eaten a vast quantity of really spicy food, I drank copious amounts of chilled 7-UP and was now looking for the facilities. I mentioned this to Azeem Tariq, who informed me that since everyone had finished eating, we would now be joining Altaf Hussain, referred by all the MQM members as Altaf Bhai, or brother, who was waiting for us inside the building.

With Nawaz Sharif and Mustafa Jatoi leading us, we entered the darkened lounge of the KMC building, the gentlemen waiting for me to enter first, as I was the only woman in the group and the age of chivalry was still somewhat with us. The room was so dark that I almost collided with the Führer himself. Stepping back, I asked if I could use the facilities. He flicked his fingers and I side-stepped my way out onto a verandah and entered the door marked 'toilet'. But I shut the door within a few seconds because the odour was unbearable, and the floor was totally wet. I re-entered the lounge and went and sat quietly on an empty chair next to Professor Ghafoor Ahmed. This was the time when the Jamaat-i-Islami and MQM were still interacting civilly despite their feud over the Karachi Municipal Corporation.

Altaf Hussain noticed me, and sent a flunkey to ask me whether I had found the toilet. Considering he looked upon me as a feudal, I marvelled at his capacity to flick fingers and order people about. I certainly could not manage it this way in Shah Jewna. I told the flunkey that the toilet was dirty and unusable. When this was conveyed to his boss Altaf Hussain, to my great amazement, he said in an audible voice to Imran Farooq, who led the MQM members in the National Assembly, that he and Azeem Tariq should clean the toilet properly themselves so that *behen*, or sister, Abida could use it. Less than ten minutes later, Azeem Tariq led me courteously out of the room and to the same toilet which now had a dry, immaculate floor and no odour whatsoever. I returned to join my colleagues immensely relieved (literally) and deeply impressed with this sense of what struck me then as total equality. When Azeem Tariq was killed, and eventually Imran Farooq, I had a vivid recollection of that amazing afternoon.

The following day brought us another MQM adventure. We were taken to see the stage which was now nearing completion. Its height was awesome. Nawabzada Nasrullah Khan exclaimed, '*wah*! *wah*!' I joined him in appreciation, and was about to start climbing up a sturdy looking steel stairway behind Altaf Hussain, when he turned around and ordered that Nawabzada Nasrullah and I should be taken up in the 'bucket' so that we could get a really good view. Not knowing what that meant, Nawabzada and I allowed ourselves to be led to a crane, which had a large container with steel bars on the edge hooked to it. We were asked to climb into the container which was not easy, but Afaq Ahmed was with us and he helped us into it, and climbed in with us himself. The container had a huge hook under it, hitched to the fork of the crane. Some fellows were now urging the crane driver to move up, and we found ourselves being lifted off the ground and zooming up higher and higher, way above the stage. Nawabzada was holding onto his fez as I was wrapping my *dupatta* around my neck, holding on to the steel bars with my other hand, with my eyes shut, praying for dear life. Afaq was saying we should open our eyes and look at the view and Nawabzada was saying he was dying '*marsoon*! *marsoon*!' he was shouting in Seraiki. The container stopped swaying momentarily and I opened my eyes. The view was indeed breathtaking. Then the fork of the crane started dipping downwards, and I shut my eyes tight once more as we lurched away and then landed with a big thud on the floor of the stage. As we climbed out of the bucket, Altaf Hussain informed us that he had tested the floor of the stage and was delighted that it was solid enough to hold even five hundred people. Nawabzada Nasrullah Khan looked at him balefully and said in his typically Seraiki-accented Urdu, that we might have suffered cardiac arrest while he was testing out the solidity of his stage. He pointed out that even Abida Bibi, who was young had become white as a sheet, never mind an old man like him! Everyone laughed and we all stood around while Altaf Hussain informed us in excruciating detail of how much steel had gone into the contraption and what the costs incurred would end up being, claiming to have over shot his budget.

'Surely he will sell the steel and recover a good bit of the cost,' Malik Naeem observed to me.

Altaf Hussain seemed to have overheard and clarified, disarmingly that the steel would be stocked at 'Nine Zero', the MQM headquarters, for Asia's next biggest rally. We were naturally amused by this reassurance, which seemed to cover some kind of guilt.

At the end of all this excitement, 'Asia's biggest rally' was something of a disappointment. The crowd appeared to me as though it was less than the lakhs that were projected, maybe even less than a hundred thousand. However, it was a responsive crowd and Altaf Hussain would walk up and down the stage, clapping with his hands above his head, and the crowd would roar with appreciation. Then the speeches started. Khan Abdul Wali Khan was cheered enthusiastically by the thousands of Pushtuns in the gathering; Nawabzada Nasrullah Khan was cheered less, about as much as me. My speech was not effective. I found it hard to holler into the mikes, and the *dupatta* kept slipping off my head, which distracted me. I spoke about the importance of women in the work place and the unity of the federation, but no catchy one-liner came into my mind.

Nawaz Sharif was clearly not much of a mass speaker either, and was cheered even less than myself, I thought. The thunderous and lengthy applause was elicited, needless to say, by Altaf Hussain, whose oratory was accompanied by shouts of 'Quaid, Quaid, Quaid-e-Tehrik!' It was somewhat disconcerting to hear the chants for some other Quaid, with the mausoleum of Quaid-i-Azam Muhammad Ali Jinnah within our view.

Finally we returned to the normalcy of Islamabad, four days later, which felt like it had been four weeks. After the rally there were shoot-outs between MQM and PPP workers in Karachi. Both parties were accusing each other of initiating the aggression, while my hands were full, moving adjournment motions on a daily basis.

Meanwhile back home in Jhang, the Sipah Sahaba were turning increasingly aggressive, with their 'Shia Kafir' (Shias are disbelievers) campaign building momentum and fresh graffiti back everywhere on the walls of the towns of Jhang. My supporters demanded that I protest in the Assembly and address the press, but I thought it would be wiser to ignore it. However, when I went down to Jhang some reporters turned up to ask me what I was doing to ensure sectarian harmony, to which I responded by saying that so long as there was no physical aggression by one sect against the other, it was best to ignore the sloganeering, as no sensible Pakistani anywhere appreciated attempts to disturb the peace. Then I was asked who I thought was behind the rise of sectarianism and I said it could only be interests inimical to Pakistan. When further questioned on whether it could be the Indians, I said the possibility could not be ruled out. As a consequence of this, although my statement was carried only in the local rags, the Sipah Sahaba filed defamation suits against me in half a dozen district courts and I had to shell out a large sum of money to defend myself in these suits, all of which were dismissed, but my pocket was lighter, and my mother became anxious.

This was only the start of the nightmare that followed. Fakhar and I were flying in from Islamabad to Lahore, routinely on a Fokker flight. Abid, now in his early teens was at the airport to receive us, which was unusual. As I hugged him, his face which was usually mischievous seemed serious. Apprehensive, I asked him what was wrong, and why had he come to the airport? 'Chando, Maulvi Haq Nawaz has been killed!' For a moment I thought he was pulling a prank. As we sat in the car Fakhar asked him who had given him this strange news. Abid said that some people had called Baji Amma (Mother) from Jhang and had given her the news. She was very anxious and had sent him to the airport to warn me to be careful. 'What will happen now, Chando?' For the first time my son, normally always insouciant, sounded worried, as he held my hand tightly. My heart was pounding with apprehension when we reached our home. Baji and Shugu were standing in the doorway, looking nervous as I hugged both warmly. I then headed straight for the telephone to call Mirza Mukhtar who was an advocate. He was a sensible person who happened to be a Shia but was free from any kind of bigotry whatsoever. I asked him what had happened, doubtless betraying my apprehension.

'Mirza Mukhtar, I hope Maulvi Haq Nawaz has not been killed by a Shia.'

'No, Bibi Sahiba, he was killed at his own doorstep, probably by one of his own followers. The shots were fired from close range. People saw Maulvi Esar ul Haq Qasimi, his young acolyte, leaving his home, as he was living there, Maulvi Haq Nawaz followed him out, was still on his doorstep when the shots rang out and got him in the head and the chest. Shaikh Iqbal reached the hospital, but Maulvi Haq Nawaz expired en route. Hundreds of Sipah activists were at the hospital and raised slogans against Shaikh Iqbal, but they are bound to accuse some Shias also. Meanwhile thousands of Sipah workers are now around Maulvi Haq Nawaz's house and around their mosque in the Mohallah Pipplianwala Markaz, where the Sipah headquarters are situated. They are pelting broken bricks on every Shia house in sight. When they were taking the body back from the hospital, they threw stones at the Shah Jewna House as well. Kindly talk to the Deputy Commissioner and the Superintendent of Police and tell them to give us protection.' Mirza Mukhtar's lucid account was corroborated by several other supporters, including my Sunni supporters, like Allama Nayyar.

I tried to talk to the Superintendent Police and the Deputy Commissioner, who said they had a serious law and order problem on their hands and were trying to do their best. My appetite had left me. Shugu worried lest I be implicated. Fakhar reassured her that my absence from Jhang was a very strong alibi. It was 23

February 1990. I tried to chat, for Shugu and Abid's sake, making a herculean effort to sound normal, relieved that at least one of my daughters was out of harm's way. The children went back to their homework after dinner and Baji took to her book on 'Hajj' by Dr Ali Shariati, while Fakhar and I retired to our rooms.

The telephone rang all night. The Sipah were on a rampage, torching Shia homes, gutting a couple of small factories of rug-weaving looms that belonged to Shias, in what was described by all my callers as a frenzy of madness. Everyone complained that the police had disappeared; the police stations had barred their gates and doused their lights. There were no street lights on either, they complained, and those that dared to peer out of their windows saw endless processions of torch bearing crowds shouting 'Shia Kaffir!' When I tried to call administration officials, their telephones failed to connect. At some point Fakhar dozed off, but I was up all night.

The children always came into our rooms to greet us before going to school in the morning, so that particular morning, they found me sitting on the sofa by the phone.

'Are you okay, Chando?' They asked me.

Hugging them, I told them to run along, and not fret, and enjoy their day at school. My head suddenly cleared. It was crucial that I scramble myself out of harm's way for the sake of my children. Maulana Fazlur Rahman and Maulana Samiul Haq could help me. I called up Fazlur Rahman first and was told he was in Jacobabad, in Sindh. I called Illahi Bux Soomro, who thank goodness, was also in Jacobabad. Informing him of my need to speak to Maulana Fazlur Rahman urgently, I shared with him my apprehension lest the Sipah Sahaba implicate me in the First Information Report with the local police at Jhang. Illahi Bux said he knew where the

Maulana was and would get hold of him right away and put him on the phone with me.

A short while later Maulana Fazlur Rahman called. Fakhar was up and sitting beside me. Both of us had a word with him, explaining our concern. He said he would talk to the Sipah folk but told us that since most of them had emerged from Maulana Samiul Haq's madrasa at Akora Khattak, we must talk to him as well, which we did and Maulana Samiul Haq reassured us that he would prevent them from taking any such step.

By this time the newspapers had arrived, and every major daily, both English and Urdu, had a black band around the front page, declaring Maulvi Haq Nawaz to be '*Rahmatullah Illeh*', the one befitting of Allah's Grace. 'Some sort of record of rapid promotions,' I said to Fakhar, 'In 1980 he was known as Maulvi Haqoo. By 1985 he became Maulana Haq Nawaz, by 1988 he was being addressed as Hazrat Maulana Haq Nawaz Jhangvi by his followers, and by 1990 he has been written about in the press as Hazrat Maulana Haq Nawaz Jhangvi, *Rahmatullah Illeh*.'

'Please be careful, Chandi. Only refer to him as late Maulana Haq Nawaz. You never know who may be listening.'

Fakhar was cautious at all times. Even he did not understand how terrified I was, so there was no question of my being rash. Illahi Bux Soomro called and said that Maulana Fazlur Rahman had spoken to Sipah leaders on my behalf who informed him that they would be naming some Shias who were present in the city at the time in the FIR, but since I had been absent from Jhang, I had nothing to worry about. But I ought to be careful when I went to Jhang, and should avoid doing that for a few days.

My employees from Shah Jewna House in Jhang town called and informed me that some policeman had arrived at the house, saying that Maulana Haq Nawaz's funeral was going to go past my house, since he was to be buried in the Deobandi graveyard located on the edge of Satellite Town. I was further informed that a loyal supporter of mine had arrived with his rifle and had joined the modest police posse at my house. When I called my employees later, they informed me that when the funeral passed by, Sipah supporters pelted stones in the driveway and some boys tried to run inside but my loyalists fired a few rounds in the air, and the urchins went away, while the police remained mere observers. I spoke with my loyalist Dilawar Khokhar to thank him and he suggested I must stay away from Jhang for a few days, but if my supporters who were feeling insecure wanted to camp in the backyard of my house, my staff should allow them to do so. I naturally agreed to this and told my manager to send grain to Shah Jewna House so that whoever took shelter there could be fed.

The news from Jhang kept going from bad to worse. The Sipah went on a killing spree. About eighty Shias were killed between the Maulana's funeral and his 'Qul', the third day of mourning. Shias started leaving Jhang city and town, taking shelter with relatives wherever they could. Some went to the adjoining districts; some even came as far as Lahore. I was so terrified I did not leave my room for four days, and kept clinging to the telephone. When my children would come, I would cheer up. Baji and Fakhar kept me company a lot of the time. Every phone call from Jhang brought news of additional violence against the Shia community.

Then I got a call from Mirza Mukhtar, my cool-headed supporter, who was strictly a man of the law. He demanded that I go to Jhang in solidarity with those who had vested faith in me and voted for me and who were now utterly insecure. As their representative, I ought to be pressing the district administration to come out of its current stupor, do its duty appropriately, restore order, and apprehend those who were flagrantly disturbing the peace. When I informed him that I was calling them and the officers in the province on a daily basis, Mirza Mukhtar felt that it would be more effective if I were to meet them along with a delegation of Shia and Sunni spokesmen who would join voice with me.

'Do not be afraid, Bibi Sahiba. Life and death are up to Allah.'

The following morning, I got a call informing me that Mirza Mukhtar had been killed. Overcoming my fear, I decided to leave for Jhang immediately. Both my mother and my son tried to stop me from going. They were scared, as was my daughter, but Fakhar said he would stay with them and be in touch with senior officers in the government.

Accompanied by one of Mother's sturdier servants, I offered a small prayer, and set off for Jhang in Fakhar's car which had a Multan number plate and thus would be less conspicuous. Entering Shah Jewna House, I was taken aback to see that almost three hundred people had taken shelter in my compound. They flocked around me, most of them deeply anxious and fearful. All my key supporters arrived and before long, there were at least seven to eight hundred people present.

What was to be done? What could be done to stop this madness and killing? As I posed the question, a thought occurred to me, which I articulated.

'Why don't we all go in procession to condole with the widow of Maulana Haq Nawaz? Our bereavement may have a calming effect on his followers, and their frenzy and fervour may abate.'

Syed Nuzhat Hussain Zaidi, a prosperous businessman of the town of Jhang whose home was in Chambeli Market in the heart of the city, countered me by saying that the rooftops of the Pipplianwalla Mohallah, where the late Maulana's home was, had rocket launchers mounted on them. And if they decided to fire on our procession I would end up creating a veritable Kerbala. He suggested that I should first telephone his widow and seek her permission, and if she agreed, then only a few of us should go. There was a consensus on this course of action. The issue now was obtaining the telephone number that the widow used. One of my migrant supporters, a gentleman who came in originally from Panipat, said he would get it from a fellow Panipatti who was a Sipah activist. It occurred to me that in our complex social fabric the bonds of ethnicity were sometimes stronger than those of creed.

The required number having been obtained and dialed, as it responded, I asked to speak to the widow of Maulana Haq Nawaz. I gave my name and stated that I wished to condole with her. I could overhear a male voice in Jhangochi repeating my name and saying Abida wished to speak with the widow, then I heard a voice speaking in Urdu and saying that there was no harm in listening to what I had to say. A young female voice then came on line and said, 'What do you want?'

'I want to offer Fateha, Bibi. You and I have nothing against each other, hopefully. I am truly sorry you have been widowed. Apparently, your children are very young and it is tragic that they should have been orphaned. May I come, along with a few people, to make a bereavement call and offer you consolation and any form of assistance that you may require?'

'No need for you to come. You can recite Sura Fateha on the phone. I do not need your assistance. My brother Osama bin Laden looks after all my needs. You must have heard of him. He is a very famous and rich Saudi, much richer than all of you *kaffirs* put together.'

Obviously she did not perceive a contradiction in asking me to recite from the Holy Quran, while declaring me a heretic. I had never heard the name of her Saudi brother hitherto, so I wrote it down, Osama bin Laden. I ran the name by the officers of the Jhang district administration, but none of them claimed they had ever heard the name. I tried the Deputy Inspector General of Police and the Commissioner, the Home Secretary as well, but no officer said they recognized the name. I rang the Secretary Interior in the federal government who pulled a blank with him as well, as I did with my friend Roedad Khan.

Over the following week or so the situation calmed down. The police arrested Tahir Sial who was known to be a rabid Shia and Kakabali, a cousin of former MNA Amanullah Sial, also a prominent Shia who was reputed to have clout, and a young Dabkar, related to my munshi, Malik Riaz. The Dabkars were an exclusively Shia community, living in Haideri Mohallah, in the vicinity of Mohallah Pipplianwala.

Close on the heels of these arrests, the Sipah Sahaba leadership announced the formation of a militant arm, 'Lashkar Jhangvi' which declared its intent to cleanse the Muslim world of all heretics.

The families that had taken shelter in my house started returning to their own homes and, as life seemed to be reverting back to normal, I returned to Lahore. My children were unusually happy to see me, and Mother could not stop offering thanks to the Almighty. Fakhar thought that I had been courageous. But in the Assembly session which had been announced, while an adjournment motion would be in order, ideally the movers ought to be the Opposition leaders Ghulam Mustafa Jatoi and Khan Abdul Wali Khan along with some PPP members in order to make the move strongly bi-partisan. But it would be wise for me not to dilate on the issue directly, except to offer Fateha for Maulana Haq Nawaz, and all others killed in my constituency, and to demand a fair and impartial inquiry into the incident by the Interior Minister. Acting on Fakhar's advise, I drafted the motions when the Assembly met and had them signed by the front and back benchers. Fateha was offered. The Interior Minister predictably said this was a provincial matter but that he would order an inquiry and report back to the House, but no report was ever made.

Seeking a meeting with Khan Abdul Wali Khan, I sought his guidance on how he viewed the situation in Jhang. With his customary clarity, he took me through the paces historically on how the British colonialists had perfected the doctrine of 'divide and rule'. He explained that they studied us carefully, understood the two major divides among Muslims, the Shia-Sunni divide and the Arab-Ajam, or Arab/non-Arab, divide. Then they used their agents to sow mischief between rulers, chieftains, tribal leaders, and potentates of all sorts in order for them to trust the British rather than each other. This method enabled the British to keep extending their Empire.

The Americans follow the same stratagems. And now with a replay of the 'Great Game' in Afghanistan, and with Shia clerics in power in Iran, it is logical that a Shia-Sunni divide be created in Pakistan, so that relations between Iran and Pakistan are adversely impacted, he explained. I followed this up with separate meetings with Maulana Fazlur Rahman and Maulana Samiul Haq. I thanked them both for interceding on my behalf with Sipah Sahaba and asked them what this Lashkar Jhangvi was about. Maulana Sheerani was with Maulana Fazlur Rahman. To my great amazement, he suggested I should join the JUI-F. He argued that this would establish that they, the JUI, were not anti-Shia and would help them to have good relations with Iran. I thanked him for considering me worthy of joining his party, but how would they reconcile with my being a modern woman, I asked. To which he answered that I carried myself with modesty, they would only request me to cover my head, and with them I would be safe, and no Lashkar would dare to come near me. I thanked him, but said I could not be a hypocrite since my belief was that religion was a private matter and ought not to be a part of statecraft. I further added that sectarian issues arose when religion became a focus of public issues, and this played straight into the hands of the detractors of the state. But the honour that Sheerani bestowed on me by making the offer was never to be forgotten by me.

I then went on to see Maulana Samiul Haq who was extremely courteous but did not offer I join his party. He did say that the formation of this Lashkar was not a good thing, and wondered who was behind it, and anticipated that it would disturb sectarian harmony.

The events and disturbances in Jhang were overtaken by a blood-let in Hyderabad, Sindh, in 1990 where an incident in 'pucca killa', a locality where there was a concentration of Urdu speaking migrants (mohajirs), led to ethnic strife which took a toll of many lives. This caused outrage among MQM Assembly members, who staged walkouts and demanded resignations of the Sindh Chief

Minister, Interior Minister, and the Prime Minister. Evidently when an entire political party was involved, the noise generated was so much more than the concerns of an individual member, even when sectarian harmony was potentially at stake.

Altaf Hussain threatened a fast unto death. The MQM members harassed Opposition leader Ghulam Mustafa Jatoi, who asked me, Haji Bilour, and Senator Behrawar Said to go to Karachi and ensure that Altaf Hussain called off his 'fast unto death'. He suggested that we fly out to Karachi in the morning and return in the evening, since the House was in session and Jatoi's presence was required at Islamabad. Our delegation would represent the COP, and my being involved in a national issue, would draw the attention of the sectarian minded lot away from me. I thought this was kind and thoughtful of Mustafa Jatoi.

We arrived at Nine Zero (MQM Headquarters), to find the alley outside their leader's office packed with men and women. All were praying for their 'Pir Sahib', which is how most of them addressed their leader. Inside the office, with huge photographs of Altaf Hussain on the walls, we were told by Azeem Tariq that his leader was in a room upstairs. It would be appropriate for sister Abida to go and persuade Altaf Hussain to drink a glass of water, or his kidney condition could cause serious problems, while brother Bilour and brother Behrawar waited in the office.

I was led out into a tiny courtyard and was told by Azeem Tariq to climb up a bamboo ladder. I had dreaded bamboo ladders since my childhood. Now being overweight and forty plus, it was terrifying, but I managed somehow to clamber up. Amazingly the great leader's room seemed to be newly and hastily built, with the bricks not even cemented and two rough looking characters guarding a steel entrance door, which opened as we entered a modest room with, bare walls, but for a large photograph of 'Pir Sahib' (Altaf Hussain) addressing his followers on the wall opposite the steel bed on which Altaf Hussain was lying, with his eyes tightly shut.

'Who has come?' he shouted.

'Abida behen [sister] is representing all the COP leaders and has come to request you to drink some water,' said Azeem Tarik in his mild voice.

'Abida, who is Abida? Famous father, famous grandfather, famous mother, famous grandmother. What will happen if Abida dies? Ministers will condole, Ambassadors will condole, the wealthy will all condole, and then there shall be silence. Altaf Hussain, who is Altaf Hussain? No known father, no known grandfather, no known mother, or grandmother. What will happen if Altaf Hussain dies? There will be blood, blood, Karachi will bathe in blood!'

As Altaf Hussain said these words, his voice rising and falling, I began to tremble and became extremely nervous.

'Please drink some water,' I managed to say. He opened his eyes and amazingly drank from the glass which Azeem held to his lips, while propping up his head. Having downed the glass of water, he sat up and fished a hair dryer from under his pillow, gesturing toward Azeem to plug it into a socket, which was embedded in the bricks beside his bed and to blow dry the sweaty and scanty hair plastered to his scalp. I could not believe my eyes. Having been efficiently blow dried by his associate, Altaf Hussain then smiled genially, and thanked me. Azeem quickly whisked me away down the bamboo stairs.

Back in the office, Azeem made me sound like a heroine, and as we left Nine Zero I found women falling on me, thanking me for helping their leader to survive. On the flight back, I told my companions that Altaf Hussain struck me as being dramatic, whimsical, arbitrary, and angry. They both seemed to agree.

During the parliamentary recess, I went to Jhang and was advised by my supporters that I should avoid sitting out in my verandah and get a wall built around my compound, with a barbed wire fence. The wall was under construction around the back and it was distressing to discover that our neighbours behind us had encroached on our land to the extent of more than half an acre. And since they were political supporters, they turned a deaf ear to my protests. Not being in a position to incur any further hostility, I had to ignore the loss, wondering how many further losses I would have to bear.

Since the weather was hot, I continued to sit on my verandah, with my usual visitors, when one of my well-wishers came running down the driveway and insisted that I move indoors. Panting away, he informed me that he had just seen Anwara Gadhi, who had killed several Shias, standing at the tea stall in the square a few yards from my house. There were a couple of policemen standing nearby, but when he went up to ask them quietly why did they not arrest this man who was wanted by the police, and there were posters up everywhere with his picture announcing ten thousand rupees head money for him, one of the cops whispered, 'Can you not see he has an automatic weapon while we have only rifles. He will kill us and nobody pays salaries to the dead, only a meagre pension.' I telephoned the Superintendent of Police and repeated all this to him, but by the time a truckload of police arrived at the tea stall, Anwara had sauntered away. That night I got a phone call for the first time from someone who identified himself as Riaz Basra, who said he was going to kill me, because I had dared to contest election against Hazrat Maulana Haq Nawaz *Rahmatullah Illeh*. The receiver fell from my hands in fear, and the line went dead. I left for Lahore the very next day, suppressing my panic as best I could and calmed myself surrounded by friends and family, making no mention of Anwara or Basra to anyone.

The Islamic Republic of Iran had an active Consulate in Lahore, which had been there since the Shah's time and now was active in promoting the writings and philosophy of the Islamic Republican Party of Iran. They often invited me to their events and now I had an invite to address a seminar, along with the Irani Consul General, Agha Sadeq Ganji. There were to be several speakers, and I was informed that I would be the last to speak. Pulling in somewhat late for the seminar at the International Hotel located on the Mall Road, my car could not access the hotel. There was pandemonium, a large crowd assembled outside the hotel. I was informed by a policeman on duty that Agha Ganji had been shot at, as he was entering the hotel and had been taken to the hospital, while his security guards had chased the killers, caught them, and handed them over to the police. The Irani Consul succumbed to his injuries on the way to the hospital. The Government of Iran lodged a strong complaint with the Government of Pakistan.

A few days later, Parvez Masud, the Chief Secretary of Punjab, accompanied by Rana Maqbool, the Senior Superintendent Police came to our Lahore residence. Fortunately, my mother had gone out and the children were at school. Fakhar was in Multan, I was alone at home, drafting assembly questions. Parvez said to me that since I was my mother's only child I should stay out of politics and stop causing her endless anxiety. He handed me the transcript of the interrogation conducted by Rana Maqbool of Riaz Basra and Akram Lahori, the main activists of the Lashkar Jhangvi, who, when asked whether they had any regret that they had killed an Irani diplomat, replied that the only regret was that they had come to kill two Shia Kaffirs, Sadeq Ganji and Abida Hussain, but the latter had eluded them. I thanked Parvez for his concern and assured him I would do my best to keep eluding these *Takfiris*. Parvez asked me what *Takfiri* meant, I told him when he had time for a history lesson I would tell him about those that made an endemic divide among Muslims during the lifetime of the Holy Prophet of Islam.

Shortly after a stormy budget session, when Benazir Bhutto's government had clocked twenty months, President Ghulam Ishaq Khan dismissed it on 6 August 1990, dissolving the Assembly under a relevant proviso of the Constitution. There was no public protest to speak of: even the *jiyalas*, the PPP activists, did not come out. Going strictly by the book, the President appointed a caretaker government in the federation, while the governors appointed caretaker chief ministers in the four provinces.

On 6 August 1990, Ghulam Mustafa Jatoi was sworn in as Caretaker Prime Minister. His cabinet comprised of a broad mix of high profile politicians from different political parties, such as Rafi Raza and Ghulam Mustafa Khar from the PPP, and veterans of Zulfikar Ali Bhutto's time, and several Muslim Leaguers. I was given the portfolio of Minister of Information. Mir Afzal Khan was appointed Chief Minister of NWFP (now Khyber Pakhtunkhwa), Zafarullah Jamali became Chief Minister Balochistan, Jam Sadiq Ali, Chief Minister Sindh, and Chaudhry Ghulam Haider Wyne, Chief Minister Punjab. Roedad Khan and Ijlal Haidar Zaidi were appointed Advisers to the President.

The President marked down a bunch of letters for me to respond to on his behalf. The letters were from several US Senators and Congressmen, protesting the ouster of Benazir Bhutto's government. I responded diligently, encapsulating the reasons cited in the Dissolution Order: poor governance, nepotism, lack of transparency in financial matters. The copies were marked to the Presidency, I received a call from the president, recording his appreciation for my effort, and informed him that I was ably assisted by my secretary and my additional secretary, who were both outstanding civil servants, I was fortunate of having a hardworking team with me, which pleased President Ghulam Ishaq Khan who believed in the capacity of the civil service, sometimes a little too much, and this bias of his was well known.

The owners and editors of all the major and minor newspapers and journals throughout the country sought appointments to see me. Invariably they demanded an increase in their newsprint quotas as it was lucrative to sell a part of the newsprint in the open market, because what the government issued to the press was a subsidized rate. I was strict on the issue and would invariably refuse, unless the secretary made a written recommendation on the basis of increased circulation, which happened only in two cases. I was therefore not a popular minister and received no accolades in the media. A large number of television producers, directors, actors and actresses would also seek appointments. One of them was a popular actress of soap operas that were telecast with high viewership. She had some scandalous stories to narrate regarding my political rival, and wanted me to send her to my constituency to make an exposé, but I told her that it was not appropriate to drag personal matters into politics. The post of Managing Director at PTV was hotly contested. To my great surprise I discovered that PTV was a strife-ridden organization, full of intrigues along ethnic/

linguistic lines, with an MQM Urdu-speaking group locking horns on a daily basis with a Punjabi-speaking mafia. Avoiding getting embroiled in their issues, I appointed as Managing Director of PTV, an Urdu speaking gentleman, Agha Nasir, who was reputed to be the most outstanding professional of his time, though this made some of the Punjabis unhappy with me.

Totally immersed in the work assigned to me, the impending elections pushed at the back of my mind, I had a reality check when I was called by Prime Minister Jatoi to attend a meeting of the COP leaders at the Sindh House. Nawabzada Nasrullah, Khan Abdul Wali Khan and Maulana Fazlur Rahman were there, complaining bitterly to the caretaker prime minister that the intelligence community was playing foul with them. All three leaders stated that a mysterious third party candidate had emerged in their constituencies, put up by these people, they suspected, with the intention of ensuring the defeat of these stalwarts. They expected Ghulam Mustafa Jatoi, whom they had given their unqualified support in the dissolved Assembly to rein them in. Mustafa Jatoi, deeply courteous as always, assured them that he would do his best, adding that not all the intelligence agencies were in his control, but he would certainly take up the matter with the Chief of Army Staff as well as with the Director General of the covert organization, and with Mian Nawaz Sharif, who was heading the IJI, the Islami Jamhoori Ittehad, whom he had invited to this meeting and who was expected to arrive any minute.

Nawaz Sharif walked in, and the complaint was addressed to him as well. Having decided to contest from the platform of the IJI myself, as an Independent, I was counselled by everybody that I should contest from my previous constituency and avoid the constituency where the sectarian strife had raised its ugly head.

This was what I had been thinking myself, and thanked the leaders for their concern. Mian Nawaz Sharif assured me that I would have his total support. He also told all the leaders that he had no control over the intelligence agencies, but he would try on behalf of Nawabzada Nasrullah Khan, Khan Abdul Wali Khan, and Maulana Fazlur Rahman who were contesting from their own platforms but for whom he had the deepest respect, that they must win their constituencies without any impediments in their path. The meeting ended amicably, and we wished each other good luck for our respective elections ahead of us. Time had come for me to wind up my affairs in the Ministry of Information, with the polling date a mere six weeks away, scheduled for 24 October 1990. I left for Jhang to file my nomination papers, stopping en route in Lahore to bid farewell to Shugu, deeply regretting that I was not being able to take her to Harvard myself. My plucky child reassured me she would be fine, as Umku was there already. Faisal Saleh Hayat had already filed his papers from N.A. 69 as a PPP candidate, as was expected. When I went to file mine, I learnt that a third candidate, Ghazi Salahuddin of Sial Sharif which was located in Sargodha district, had also filed his papers earlier the same morning. I knew Ghazi Salahuddin as he had filed his papers against me in 1988 from N.A. 67. My Bharwana supporters had informed me on that occasion that if they gave him fifty thousand rupees as a *nazrana* (gift or bribe) from adherents, he would withdraw. They had given him the *nazrana*, and he had withdrawn, and probably expected a repeat of the same.

Filing and then withdrawing nomination papers was a despicable malpractice in our political culture. Only those who possessed scant self-respect resorted to it.

Leaving the premises of the Returning Officer, an additional session's judge, I ran straight into the procession of Maulana Essar Qasmi who was filing as the Sipah Sahaba candidate from N.A. 68. Having spotted me the rank and file of the Sipah broke into their little war dance, flailing their arms about, shouting 'Kaffir, Kaffir, Shia Kaffir!' All my supporters who had accompanied me were congratulatory on my decision not to take on the Sipah, instead of reverting to my original constituency where, as an IJI candidate, I would have an easy victory. But it was crucial to obtain the withdrawal of Ghazi Salahuddin, who would eat into my Sunni votes, which would otherwise accrue to me because of the IJI platform.

I contacted my supporters who had handled him in the previous election to speak with him and request him to withdraw. They went immediately and brought back news which shocked me. Although had I applied my mind, I should have understood earlier that the 'third party' candidate the other leaders had complained about was planted in my constituency probably by the same interests. Ghazi Salahuddin told my supporters that some friends of his in Islamabad had persuaded him to file his nomination papers from N.A. 69, but he would withdraw if he were paid five hundred thousand rupees. Although my supportive friends sent him the money, he did not withdraw, and cost me my election.

I fought a hard campaign, but the situation was further complicated for me when the IJI nomination in N.A. 68 was awarded to the Sipah Sahaba candidate. This resulted in the majority of the Shia votes in N.A. 69 going to the PPP candidate Faisal Saleh Hayat, while the Sunni votes that may have come my way had the 'third party' candidate withdrawn, now went to him. Ghazi Salahuddin polled some 15,000 votes and I lost the constituency to Faisal

Saleh Hayat by 14,000 votes, losing my first ever election. The good news was that Fakhar won his election comfortably from Iqbal Haraj, who was the PPP candidate from Kabirwala, now district Khanewal. N.A. 68 was won by Essar Qasmi, who also won the provincial constituency from the town of Jhang. The IJI scored a straight majority.

Khan Abdul Wali Khan lost, Nawabzada Nasrullah Khan also lost. I derived some consolation from being in the decent company of distinguished losers, victims of 'third party candidates' and targeted by those interests who sought to rid our politics of independent minded politicians. During the election campaign, Nawaz Sharif had visited my constituency. I had put together a large public gathering for him. When I stood to speak, I was cheered enthusiastically, so Nawaz was taken aback when I told him I was losing my election. He asked me why and I told him that some people probably thought I was too independent minded, so they were orchestrating my defeat. He looked bewildered and did not seem to believe me. Ghulam Mustafa Jatoi also lost his election. It was clear that Nawaz Sharif would now be Prime Minister, and there was scant reason for me not to wish him well.

At the farewell reception which President Ghulam Ishaq hosted for the outgoing caretaker government, he came up to me, and said that he was sorry that I had lost the election, adding that he would suggest to Prime Minister Nawaz Sharif that he should appoint me as his Ambassador to Washington. Thanking him for honouring me and considering me worthy of representing my country in the world's most powerful capital, I pointed out that, not being a particularly diplomatic individual, I would prefer to wait to contest the next parliamentary election. President Ghulam Ishaq went on to tell me that my tenure in Washington would not exceed two years, after which, there would still be two years available to me to work in my constituency. Pakistan needed a totally reliable, solid Pakistani, with deep roots in the soil of our country, combined with a background of contribution to the creation of our country, to represent us in America, particularly at this juncture for sensitive strategic reasons, and someone who was articulate as well. Just a few weeks previous, the US government had invoked the Pressler Amendment, this time to cut off assistance to us, which was a fine way of rewarding us for the support we had extended to them in the covert war in Afghanistan. They were now putting pressure on us through the Amendment to abandon our nuclear programme. Ghulam Ishaq then added that he knew two women who argued persuasively on public issues: one was Benazir Bhutto, whose government he had just dismissed, and me, therefore he would discuss the matter with the Prime Minister, and if Nawaz Sharif offered me the assignment, I should seriously consider it in the call of duty to my country. I was deeply flattered because the president was not known to be generous in his complements. I felt he was being very magnanimous, almost affectionate towards me.

9

'Madam Ambassador'

When Fakhar went to take oath as Member National Assembly for the second time, I accompanied him as he had accompanied me when I won and he lost. It hurt badly that he was busy every minute of the day and I had long gaps of time to fill. The IJI (Islami Jamhoori Ittehad) had won a straight majority, and as anticipated, Nawaz Sharif took oath as Prime Minister. He asked Fakhar to join his cabinet as Minister for Education. I was happy for Fakhar and knew that he would struggle for enhancement of budgetary resources for education, which he did and with success. While time was hanging heavily on my hands, during the bye-election of the provincial constituency vacated by Essar Qasmi from Jhang city, Maulvi Azam Tariq was designated as the Sipah candidate for replacement. Within a month of the general election, while campaigning in the bye-election, Essar Qasmi was gunned down, allegedly by Azam Tariq. N.A. 68 had fallen vacant once again. When I was in Jhang, nobody pointed fingers at me; it seemed that the Sipah had become embroiled in their own war of attrition, while my supporters were flocking around me pleading for my participation in the bye-election as an IJI candidate. I was tempted, but thought it prudent to discuss the security perspective. The consensus was that I would remain inside Shah Jewna House, where voters would come to visit me rather than me visiting them for votes. There would be no rallies from our side, and on polling day, my voters would go out quietly to cast their votes. We would put up no camps outside the polling stations so the Sipah would not be able to single out or target our opponents. Since the hatred for the Sipah was at its peak, I would be elected easily by a wide margin this time. I sought a meeting with Punjab's Chief Minister Ghulam Haider Wyne (1990–1993), and ran all this by him. He suggested that I talk to Shahbaz Sharif, MNA, to obtain his support, while he would consult his Chief Secretary and Inspector General Police. We could then all meet and clinch the matter, for which the Prime Minister, of course, would need to give final approval.

This agenda was followed. Chief Minister of Punjab, Ghulam Haider Wyne; Shaikh Anwar Zahid, Adviser to Prime Minister; Chaudhry Nisar Ali, Minister of Petroleum; Mian Shahbaz Sharif; Parvez Masood, Chief Secretary; and I met at the Prime Minister's Secretariat to discuss the Jhang bye-election.

It was decided that the bye-election be pended for at least one year, to allow the sectarian feeling to evaporate altogether. Meanwhile, I should be tasked with being appointed Adviser to Prime Minister for Population Welfare, the latest politically correct description for population control. Passionate in my belief that Pakistan's population was growing much too rapidly, and would have to be arrested effectively if we were to achieve success in our economy and improve the socio-economic status of the Pakistani people as a whole, with elimination of pitiable levels of poverty, I was excited at the thought of leading the population welfare programme for my country. My supporters in Jhang would be pleased with my obtaining ministerial status as Adviser to Prime Minister, and a chilling out time would not put people's lives at risk in Jhang. With this win-win situation behind, I put my shoulder earnestly to the wheel and became deeply involved in seeking to breathe life into a moribund organization which is what the Ministry of Population Welfare was at the time. I got an incredible response from the employees of the ministry, who had many genuine issues which I sought to address while seeking to task them to improve performance on service delivery.

The Government of Pakistan allocated about eighty million US dollars equivalent in Pakistani rupees to the population ministry. Nearly all of these funds went towards establishment charges, so we were entirely dependant for contraceptive materials on USAID and UNFPA, the United Nations Fund for Population Activities. The former donated about eighty million dollars worth in technical training, publicity materials, and contraceptives, while the UNFPA grant stood at thirty million dollars. It was clear that the ministry would have to obtain more assistance from the donors to meet the demand for contraceptives, more than half of which demand was not being met. While I was emphasizing in my meetings with the ministry's officials that we had to create awareness and improve service delivery, they were emphasizing that we needed more materials to meet the demand already created. In a cabinet meeting I took up the issue and requested the Prime Minister to chair a meeting along with his team, including MNAs, Senators, and the leaders in Parliament of all the parties. I informed him that with the help of USAID, my ministry had put together a computerized slide programme, which we would like to show on a wide screen to the national leadership, on the implications of sustaining our current population growth rate of 2.3 per cent per annum. I also reminded the cabinet that during the caretaker government's tenure, US President George Herbert Bush having invoked the Pressler Amendment, which had cut off assistance to Pakistan, meaning that the USAID which gave us as much as we coughed up ourselves for this crucial issue, would now have to be substituted by the UNFPA and other countries; we would have to generate a lobby through our Ministry for Foreign Affairs, towards this end.

Despite his innate conservatism, Nawaz Sharif agreed to attend the conference, so we decided to use the State Bank hall which had served as the chamber of the National Assembly five years earlier, for this conference. This hall brought back a flood of both pleasant and unpleasant memories for me. However, the computerized slide show mounted on a large screen, impacted hugely on the entire gathering. Giving the data on the current indicators of available schools, colleges, health facilities, housing, access to roads, demand for electricity, gas, potable water, irrigation water, sustenance needs, the slides projected the data forward on an annual basis with the picture emerging succinctly that unless we were able to reduce the average family size from seven to two children per household, we would be doomed and simply sink under the weight of our population in the years ahead.

The Prime Minister gave me encouraging support and urged me to try and raise more resources, take the *ulema* or religious leaders on board with the programme as much as possible, and conduct similar presentations to all the chief ministers in the four provinces. I followed up on all of this assiduously and found that inept officers were assigned as secretaries to the population welfare departments, because this was considered to be a dead-end posting. The chief ministers were polite and reasonably responsive but none of them seemed to have the appetite to deal with population planning as a priority. Instead, all had a common baseline complaint that focused on a general lack of resources. All four of them assured me that they could only spare better officers for the population programme if I could lobby the Prime Minister to allocate more resources to their respective provinces. Similarly, the *ulema* also wanted more money. When I reported all this to the Prime Minister, he informed me that because of losing US assistance, his government was seriously cash-strapped, hence, he could not spare more resources for the provinces.

Disappointed but determined to make the best of the situation, I received a call from the British High Commissioner, Sir Nicholas Barrington. Thinking that this was an opportunity for me to solicit funds for population planning from his government, I received him most enthusiastically. Sir Nicholas heard me out politely and asked me to prepare a detailed brief which he would send through DFID (Department for International Development), the British aid agency, that provided funds to the British government for dispersal to recipient countries. Meanwhile, on behalf of Her Majesty's Government, he requested me to serve as Minister-in-Waiting to HRH Princess Diana, the Princess of Wales, who was to undertake a visit to Pakistan in a few days. He further stated that I would recall that she was to visit earlier, in October, at the invitation of Prime Minister Benazir Bhutto who lost her government just a couple of weeks prior to the visit, which was then postponed.

Pakistan's Foreign Secretary, Shehryar Khan, and Sir Nicholas mutually decided to pursue the matter with Prime Minister Nawaz Sharif, who suggested some dates, and having received concurrence from Her Majesty's Government, they had now finalized the visit for Princess Diana who would be arriving in Pakistan for a four-day visit. Prime Minister Sharif, Sir Nicholas went on to inform me, had concurred with Shehryar Khan that I would be the most suitable person to accompany the Princess during the course of her visit. His government was happy to make a formal request to me for my consent. I told him that while I was deeply honoured, I feared I would look like a cushion walking beside the world's most glamorous, tall, and beautiful princess, and would be immortalized on celluloid as such, since Princess Diana was also the world's most photographed personality. Sir Nicholas assured me gallantly that I was glamorous enough myself, leaving me with little room for not accepting his request of accompanying Princess Diana during her visit, even though it would mean defocusing from the population issue that I was deeply immersed in at the time.

The programme for Princess Diana's visit had been elaborately planned. On arrival, she would be received at the Islamabad airport by Fakhar Imam, who was Minister for Education and me along with our Foreign Secretary Shehryar Khan and his wife Minnal, and the British High Commissioner and his team of officials. The Princess would then be driven to the old cemetery in Rawalpindi Cantonment, to lay a wreath at the memorial inside the cemetery for the British soldiers buried there, who had fought in the nineteenth-century Afghan Wars, after which she would be taken to the residence of the British High Commissioner where she was to stay. I was to be seated in the limo with her, and her lady-in-waiting in the back seat, while Sir Nicholas would be seated in the front. And this protocol would be maintained throughout her visit.

Princess Diana's flight was to land at noon. She was coming in the private jet of the Queen. After spending her first day in Islamabad, she would be flown to Peshawar the next day. She was to spend the morning there and the afternoon in Chitral, returning to Islamabad for the night. On the third day, she would be flown to Lahore for the day, returning again to Islamabad for the night, and on the late afternoon of the fourth day she would fly back to London.

When I called my children, Umku and Shugu at Harvard and Abid at Lahore, to give them the news that Princess Diana was coming and I would be her companion for four days, they were thrilled to hear this, with Abid insisting immediately that he wanted to meet her. I told him that his father was hosting a lunch for her at Daaman-e-Koh, the hilltop location in the Margalla Hills in Islamabad, which offered a spectacular view of our capital, and which Mother and he could attend.

We were in April 1991, and it was already warming up. So we decided that Abid would wear a white *shalwar* and a long *kurta* like his father. Umku and Shugu telephoned me, reminding me that I had better be nicely dressed because Princess Diana's pictures would be printed all over the world and nobody would appreciate a sloppy person by her side!

When the visit was made public I was inundated with callers, all of whom wanted to meet the Princess, all of them worried what they should wear when they met her, although all these callers were mature men and women in positions of responsibility. Ironically, while my achieving ministerial rank or working seriously on a crucial national issue had made no waves; my being assigned to accompany Princess Diana did seem to, and the visit was still a week or so away.

When Princess Diana emerged from the wide-bodied Hawker Siddley jet aircraft, she looked lovely, wearing a pale green silk dress with a dashing white straw hat. She had been preceded by the arrival of sixty photographers crowding behind a rope handled by the British security, on the opposite side of the red carpet to us, flashing away their cameras. She posed nicely for them, standing at the lowest step of the jet's ladder. She then walked towards us. Sir Nicholas was beside her. He introduced her to me, and after me to Fakhar, onto Shehryar. All three of us shook hands with her while Minnal bobbed her a low curtsy despite being dressed in a sari.

The Princess smiled shyly at all of us, and as I walked alongside her. She addressed me and said, 'What is that saying about mad dogs and Englishmen in the mid-day sun? I wish I were wearing white cotton like you which looks so cool and fresh, instead of this pleated, heavy silk mid-calf length dress.'

Diana's eyes were deep blue, large, and magnificent. Her first look was her best look, I thought, she was undoubtedly a great star, glancing every now and then towards the photographers who were recording every step she took. As we entered the cool VVIP lounge of the airport, I guided her toward the sofa opposite the vents of the air conditioner, where she seemed to enjoy the cool air on her face, sipping the chilled fresh lime that was served to all of us by turbaned waiters. Sir Nicholas introduced us to Lady Sarah, the Viscountess of Campden, Diana's Lady-in-Waiting, and her Secretary, Patrick Jephson who was a senior civil servant, and who, Sir Nicholas confided in me later, was the Queen's Private Secretary. He had been spared to accompany the Princess and would be negotiating on the side-lines for our government to purchase the Hawker Siddley aircraft which was ideal for our mountainous Northern Areas, because it performed exceptionally well on short landing strips and gained height rapidly. I understood from this confession that behind the visit of the Princess was a marketing effort on the part of the British to sell expensive aircraft to my somewhat impoverished government!

Leaving the lounge a few minutes later, we entered the limo, with military police escort efficiently clearing the way for us. The roads were lined by people, I wondered whether the crowds were spontaneous or had been organized. The Princess waved at the people from time to time and they would wave back instantly. We drove slowly down the Mall, with people clapping as the limo was sighted. Entering Rawalpindi Cantonment, we weaved our way through narrow lanes that I had never seen before, people lining the lanes as well, it appeared as though everybody living in Rawalpindi had decided to come out to see the Princess, more men than women, even children. They would all clap as we passed them. It was a lovely sight. The Princess remarked on how beautiful the children were, in their lovely bright clothes, all looking so blissfully happy. She sounded almost wistful.

At the cemetery, there was a short and touching ceremony. A bugler was playing, while our soldiers brought in a large wreath, helping the Princess to lay it with such alacrity that she merely touched it, as she bent down ever so slightly. I felt quasi-colonial. It was becoming increasingly hot, with all of us wishing for the citation to end. Back in the limo, the Princess told Lady Sarah, her Lady-in-Waiting, to ask the chauffeur to turn up the air conditioning. She then turned towards me to ask her first question. I was somewhat taken aback at the question. She asked if she would have a chance to meet Imran Khan, looking at me from below her lashes, waiting for my response, with what appeared to be baited breath.

'Imran Khan is in Australia playing cricket, Your Highness. Had he been in Pakistan, of course we would have invited him to meet you, since you must know him,' I informed her.

She said she had never met him. Her sister-in-law Fergie, she meant Princess Sarah, who was married to her husband's younger brother, Prince Edward, knew him and spoke well of him, which is why she thought that if she were to have met him, she might have conveyed Princess Sarah's good wishes to him, And another thing she wanted to know was, what was the appropriate manner for her to address me, since she had gathered that I was an important personality. Again she looked at me shyly, as she said this.

'I am hardly an important person, Your Highness, merely a small cog in the wheel of my government. Please call me Abida, which is my first name.' Lady Sarah, her Lady-in-Waiting who had been quiet and expressionless throughout, spoke for the first time in a gentle voice and with a genial smile.

'But our High Commissioner addresses you by a different name.'

'Yes, Sir Nicholas often calls me Syeda, which is derived from my family name, but sometimes he calls me Abida. We have known each other for a long time, from when he was first posted to Pakistan in the mid sixties. He knows everyone here and is very well regarded by all of us.' I thought I would put in a word for my friend.

By now we had left Rawalpindi behind and were speeding down the boulevards of Islamabad, into the diplomatic enclave, swinging into the British residence, where I took leave of the Princess as she went in to rest before the President's dinner hosted her that evening.

Mother and Abid had arrived from Lahore by the time I reached home. Abid showed me the new gold *khussas*, handmade traditional shoes that curled and pointed up towards the toes, with Baji beaming proudly at her grandson, as always. Having milked all the news of her arrival from his father, Abid wanted to hear every detail about the Princess from me. Shugu telephoned from Harvard to ask if the Princess had inquired about Benazir Bhutto, and when I replied in the negative, mentioning that she asked about Imran Khan, she was very amused. Umku advised me on what I should wear for dinner, suggesting a deep pink silk outfit which would make me look less fat! Fakhar and I drove to the dinner together, but I was required to wait for her arrival in the porch of the Presidency and accompany her in, where she would first be received in the small sitting room, off the main hall to meet with the President and his family, and be led out to join the rest of the gathering. Begum Ghulam Ishaq Khan, who was seldom seen at official events, was there, along with her daughter Samina, her spouse, Anwar Saifullah, Prime Minister Nawaz Sharif and his spouse, Begum Kulsoom Nawaz, who lived in Lahore mostly but who had clearly been bitten by the Diana bug like the rest of the country.

All eyes were on the Princess; everyone in the room was riveted by her. She looked ravishing in a pale pink chiffon long dress, with a scarf draped around her neck like a dupatta. At the end of the presentation, with me introducing her to all people in power, she sat at the edge of the sofa chair, adjacent to the sofa on which the President and Prime Minister seated themselves. I was seated next to her, with the Minister of State for Foreign Affairs, Siddiq Kanju beside me. With her slender and long straight back, Diana once again looked shyly from below her lashes at the President, and then at the Prime Minister. After a brief exchange of pleasantries, both of them led her out into the hall where all the guests came up to shake hands with, or bow and curtsy to the Princess, diplomats, ministers, secretaries to government, distinguished citizens. The Princess, would give them her characteristic shy smile, casting a veritable veil of enchantment all around, but what she seemed ecstatic about were the Scottish bagpipe playing fellows, soldiers of our army and a colonial remnant we retained, who appeared to play on their bagpipes while we were eating dinner. She clapped enthusiastically for them, while the wives of our President and Prime Minister both observed that they had seldom seen their respective spouses look happier!

The following morning, Princess Diana appeared in a pink linen dress, which was fairly short, and exposed her lovely, long legs. We took her to 'Behbud', a center for advancement empowering of women, in Saidpur village. She looked at the embroideries made by the women with some interest. When she was presented with a few of them, she thanked Begum Akhtar Riazuddin, the founder of Behbud, effusively, handing everything she was presented to Lady Sarah, but she made no comment as we drove around Saidpur with me giving her a running commentary on the history of the village. I asked her if she was feeling well, she said that she was slightly queasy because she had eaten too much the previous evening, being quasi-bulimic, to which I said I would pray I turn bulimic if it would make me slender. We both laughed and drove up the Margalla Hills for Fakhar's lunch. I told her we would be walking a bit, and if her high heels did not bother her we could perhaps walk fast and work up an appetite.

Tables were laid out under garden umbrellas on the terrace which offered a spectacular view of our planned capital city on this bright sun filled day, with a gentle cool breeze tempering the heat. She wore no hat, her stylish hairdo enhanced by the sunlight, her deep blue eyes even brighter, off-set brilliantly by her pale pink dress. When Fakhar presented Begum Lady Viqarunisa Noon to her, giving my dear Aunty Vicki's distinguished background as widow of former Prime Minister, Malik Sir Firoz Khan Noon, who was Chairman of Red Cross in her own right, Princess Diana looked intently at Aunty Vicki and queried that when her husband passed away, and she stayed on in Pakistan, did she not wish to return to England?

'Your Highness, when I married Sir Firoz I felt as though I had not just married a man, I felt as though I had married a whole country,' came Aunty Vicki's reply. The Princess looked towards me then back at Aunty Vicki, whispering audibly to Aunty Vicki that she had understood completely what Lady Noon had meant!

When Diana met Abid, he put his *khussa* prominently forward for her to notice and she did, telling him they were wonderful shoes and looked like they were straight out of Alladin and his magic lamp of the Arabian Nights.

'If you really like them, you could try them on and if they fit you, I would be happy to gift them to you. They are brand new; I have worn them for the first time only this morning.' Abid was being cheeky, even flirtatious. She responded to him smiling warmly, saying that it was ever so kind of him, but if they fit her feet, and they probably would, she could never wear them, because she was used to wearing heels. She then turned her attention to my mother expressing kind words to her about me. Concerned lest our other guests feel neglected, Fakhar and I steered her towards our cabinet colleagues who were not at the President's dinner and the parliamentary members who were eager to meet her, such as our friends Makhdum Khaliquzaman of Hala and Shahid Khaqan Abbasi. Our distinguished guests also included Air Marshal and Begum Nur Khan, with the Air Marshal giving the Princess a brief lecture on the importance of literacy, a subject close to his heart. Princess Diana heard everyone intently, smiling her shy

Shah Jewna Stud Farm, Abid Hussain Imam holding and patting a Shah Jewna bred filly.

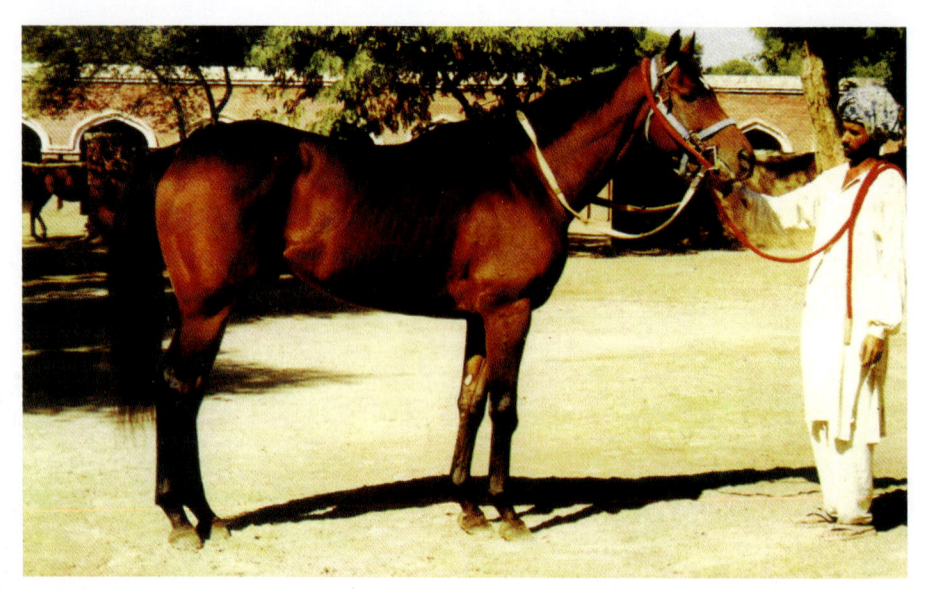

Shah Jewna Stud Farm established in 1946 by Syed Abid Hussain. Maintained since 1971 by Syeda Abida Hussain. Stallion Key Guy imported from the US by Syeda Abida Hussain, 2001.

Shah Jewna Livestock Farm. Mixed herd of pedigreed Friesians, Jerseys, and Sahiwals, along with cross breeds.

Peacocks, nurtured at the Shah Jewna Stud Farm, pecking at grain in the yard.

A Shah Jewna bred yearling in the yard of the Shah Jewna Stud Farm.

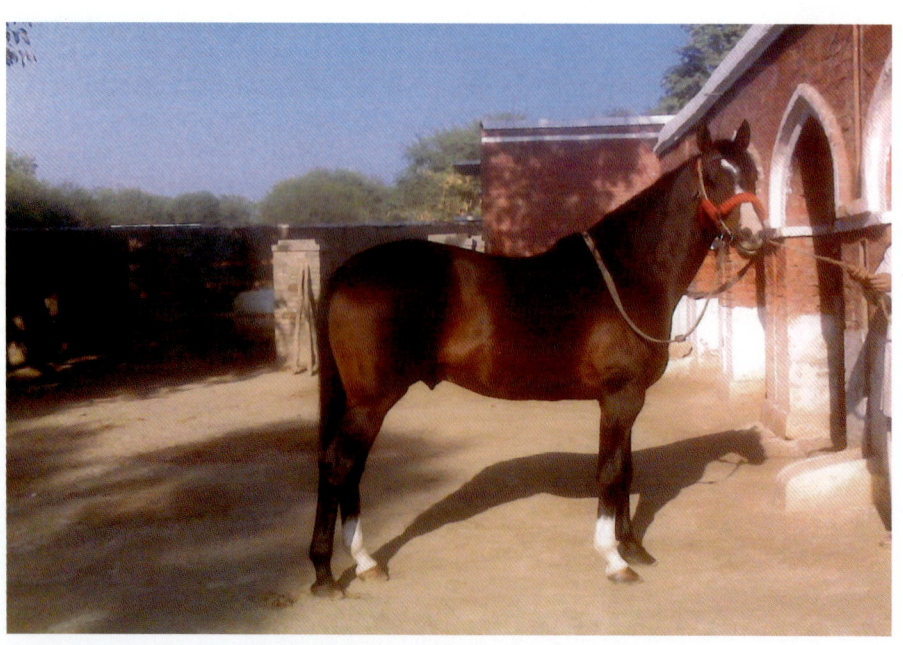

'Moohim' by 'Saddler's Wells' which stood as a sire outside his stable at the Shah Jewna Stud Farm.

smile all around, charming all the ladies and gentlemen. She did not eat a thing but drank several glasses of chilled Coca Cola. As the lunch ended, Abid ran ahead to open the door of her car, and Diana blew a flying kiss in his direction, while thanking Fakhar profusely, sending both my men straight to seventh heaven! When I said as much to her seated in the car, she remarked that my son was adorable, quite a little flirt, bright as a brass button and my husband was by far the handsomest cabinet member! Hearing this made me feel happy.

On the way back Diana lapsed into silence. We then went to the Faisal Mosque, then onto a family-planning clinic near the shrine of Bari Imam through a crowded area, where people were thronging to catch a glimpse of the Princess, and shouting 'Zindabad Diana!' She was waving and smiling, with her photographers following, clicking away, and as we entered the compound of the clinic, she nodded at all the women. Taking an infant in her arms, she seated herself on a chair for the photo-op and held the baby in her lap. The baby was without a nappy and I was terrified lest he wet her lovely dress. Clearly, sharing the thought the Princess stood up abruptly and handed the baby back to his mother in the nick of time. We then ran some of our demographic data by her and I mentioned to her that we were soliciting assistance from HMG (Her Majesty's Government), but she was not quite listening, and trying to stifle a yawn. It was time to take her back to rest. After this rather full day, Diana latticed for dinner with the Prime Minister and his spouse, wearing a dashing black and white long dress, which scored another hit with the photographers. We were scheduled to depart for the airport early in the morning the following day for our visit to Peshawar and Chitral.

Arriving at the British residence at 7.30 a.m. impressed at the Princess's punctuality, who was ready, wearing a bright red mid-calf length linen dress, we boarded the jet on time. I entered behind the Princess. The plane's cabin comprised of four seats per side, with the galley opposite. Four Royal Air Force officers stood up from the seats and the Princess, who knew them by their names, introduced them to me, and then continued into a spacious cabin which had six seats facing each other, with a short aisle between and an anterior for the facilities. There were wide tables between the chairs and a news rack at the side. The Princess picked up some newspapers, I was seated opposite her, with the self effacing Lady Sarah beside me, while Sir Nicholas and the secretary sat the other side of the aisle, facing each other. She handed me a copy of the *London Times*, and kept a copy of the *Daily Mirror* for herself. While doing so, she looked at me and saying that the *Times* was for me, because I was clever, and the *Mirror* for her because she was not!

We landed at Peshawar within half an hour and driving out of the airport to Sandy Gall's Centre for the Disabled, I was astounded to see the roads lined on either side by Pushtuns, three to four bodies deep, their lines stretching as far as the eye could see, not a woman in sight, but endless numbers of men shouting 'Sangay Shahzadi!' (Welcome, Princess!). It appeared as though the charisma of the Princess had engulfed all the Pushtuns as well, leaving no Peshawari man at home or in the work place. Looking out of the window, the Princess made a charming remark, saying she felt so humbled when she saw all these people taking time out just to see her and how she wished she could do something for them in return.

'You gladden their hearts, which is why they want to see you. You give them a return by being yourself. You are, Your Highness, the quintessential fairy-tale princess.' I said to her and she squeezed my hand warmly. At Sandy Gall's Centre the Princess was visibly moved by the disabled young men with their limbs having been severed by land mines. She listened very carefully to Sandy Gall as he described how the land mines are laid and how they can be removed, if detected. The Princess promised him that she would raise her voice against land mines, and stroked the heads of the victims with humility and affection. This was the Princess who touched the hearts of ordinary folk with her humane and beautiful face.

We then carried on to the Khyber Rifles Mess. As we were exiting out of the Mess, the car moving slowly through the narrow gates, a wonderful looking turbaned tribal elder, with a long hennaed flowing beard, tapped on the window on the side of the Princess, who directed Lady Sarah to get the car stopped and, lowering the side window, told me to ask this wonderful looking gentleman what he wanted to say. When I posed the question, the Khan promptly responded with the suggestion that if the Princess was having problems with her mother-in-law as the newspapers were suggesting, which he understood as he had similar problems in his own household, he had a solution to offer. She should tell her husband to declare himself King and to send his mother back to India and Pakistan where we would be happy to have her as Queen, because the English knew how to rule us better than we had been ruling ourselves. He concluded by saying that Diana would then be Queen of England. When he was finished, the Princess rolled up the window, and asked me to tell her exactly what he had said. I did a faithful translation for her, whereupon she threw her head back and laughed, while I felt embarrassed at his suggestion that we regress into colonial rule, at the same time I could not help being amused, sharing a laugh with the princess.

We then drove into the Governor's residence where Governor Amir Gulistan Janjua of the Frontier Province led us to an exhibit of gems mined in his province, with our friend Mir Afzal Khan, then Chief Minister standing beside him. The Princess and Lady Sarah greatly admired the Swat emeralds. Mir Afzal quietly presented the Princess with a small velvet box which she handed to Lady Sarah. We went in for lunch where the Princess was seated between the Governor and the Chief Minister. The Governor talked incessantly to the Princess, not giving Mir Afzal Khan a chance to put in a word. I was seated between him and Sir Nicholas, who informed me that the weather report indicated that we would encounter turbulence on our flight to Chitral, although the weather in Chitral was clear, so we should be able to land and take off smoothly. I suggested to Mir Afzal that he accompany us to Chitral, so I would have him to hang onto because turbulence terrified me. He said he did not care for it either, but would hate to see me die alone so he would accompany us if the Princess asked him. Sir Nicholas said it was a great idea for the chief minister to accompany us, so while we were leaving after lunch I requested the Princess to ask him, and she did so coquettishly ensuring that Mir Afzal entered the jet looking really pleased. The Princess asked him to sit next to her, so Lady Sarah and I went and sat opposite to them. As we were airborne, Lady Sarah handed the Princess the velvet box. Opening the box Diana held the gem and looked at it against the light. Even I could see that it was an amethyst, not an emerald. She hid her disappointment well, thanking Mir Afzal sweetly, but he was an extremely shrewd and observant man, so he asked me in Urdu whether he had made a mistake, I told him an emerald would have been better, to which, like a typical

Pukhtun pragmatist, he said since he was unlikely to meet her again it did not justify the expense, which he would have had to bear personally, because the emeralds belonged to the State!

The turbulence passed, and we landed in Chitral safely, driving straight from the airfield to the beautiful government residence, where we were greeted by the Kaffir women in their beautiful regalia, and elaborate headgear, standing in perfect lines on either side of us, an unusual guard of honour. As we reached the beautiful garden of the residence, they surrounded the Princess, performing their graceful slow dance with their arms on each other's shoulders. When Diana left the circle and strolled towards the sofas under the tall, magnificent 'chinar' or maple trees, with their ample shade, Mir Afzal asked his old tutor from Aitchison College, Major Langlands, to present her with a beautiful Chitrali *chogha* or short coat made of handloom wool, which fitted her so well, it looked as if it was made for her. He then handed her a Chitrali *topi* (cap) with a bird of paradise feather pinned on the middle, which the Princess greatly admired and placed it on her head at a rakish angle. The effect was stunning and the cameras went understandably crazy. This was the photograph that made it to the cover of glossy magazines worldwide. Mir Afzal also seated the old tutor next to the Princess who handed her a load of literature on our Northern Areas, and whispered in my ear that he could now die and go to heaven, having met his favourite Royal!

The return flight was uneventful. We took off as the light was fading, and caught captivating views of the mountains as we crossed over them and landed safely at Islamabad. On our way back, in the car, the Princess asked me if some turbans, such as the ones that the bearers were wearing could be arranged. She would love to take them for her sons, and I assured her that they would be arranged. The next day we were to leave for Lahore early in the morning.

Our day in Lahore proved to be as eventful as the previous day in the north of Pakistan. The Princess was dressed again in a pink short dress with pale turquoise trimmings and a long scarf to match. Seated in the car, noticing the concern on my face as I looked at her knees she asked me if her dress was too short. I told her it would be fine, she would just have to cover her head at the grand mosque with her scarf. We had a packed schedule ahead of us and would lose too much time if we were to turn around for her to change her outfit. She had opened up after the first two days and was now really friendly, calling me by my name, laughing heartily as I narrated my story to her of how I had told Nicholas Barrington that I would not like to be immortalized on celluloid as a cushion walking beside a beautiful swan! That morning Sir Nicholas and the secretary were in the other car, doubtless exchanging notes on whatever progress may have been made on their effort to market the jets, while Lady Sarah was sitting up in the front of the car.

Careful to keep her voice low, the Princess said to me if she could confide in me, as I seemed to be a wise person, and certainly did not look like a cushion but appeared to be as comforting as one. I thanked her, assuring her that whatever she said would remain with me and it did in her lifetime. She said her in-laws were very difficult, and her husband did not love her. She adored her children, and wanted them always to be with her. Willy, she said, was a lot like his father while Harry was more like her. She found it unbearable to be in a loveless marriage asking me for advise as to what she should do. I thought for a moment about what I would do in her situation and responded.

'Princess, as you have seen for yourself, you rule over the hearts of people all over the world. You have what every woman can only dream of getting. Do not throw all this away because of one individual. Try to develop an interest in horses, which may win your mother- and sister-in-law to your side. Involve yourself in issues of public importance, like land mines. Travel frequently, you would bring Britain increasing financial gain. Rejoice in your children and stop thinking about what you should do. Simply deny yourself options.' By the time my counsel ended we were at the airport, so I never knew how she might have responded.

Landing at Lahore airport, we drove straight to Kinnaird College for Women. The Lahore crowds lining the roads to catch a glimpse of the beautiful Princess were every bit as impressive as Rawalpindi or Peshawar. Women were out here more which added immense colour to the crowds. The Kinnaird College students justified their reputation of belonging to the premier women's college of Pakistan, by staging a wonderful tableau at our arrival. The hall was packed with students and alumni, many of whom surrounded Sir Nicholas as an old friend, the ceremony, concluding with the entire gathering singing our National Anthem and 'God Save the Queen' loud and lustily.

From Kinnaird College we moved on to the Mayo Hospital, to rehabilitation centre for heroin addicts, to which the DFID (Department for International Development) had contributed generously. The Princess was impressed that we had retained the old colonial names. I informed her that we had retained some old names while altering some. Many of us disapproved of renaming old names because that defaced history.

Next we visited the public sector tractor assembly plant, which was a British/Pakistani enterprise located on the outskirts of the city. As we crossed the River Ravi, I pointed the landmarks to the Princess and Lady Sarah, including the tomb of Empress Nur Jahan, when I recited the English version of her epitaph which was in Persian. Both appeared visibly moved. It was engraved:

> Upon my grave,
> When I shall die,
> No lamp shall burn,
> No jasmine lie,
> No nightingale singing overhead,
> Shall tell the world that I am dead.

Returning from the factory, we arrived at the Governor's House for lunch where Governor Mian Azhar received us. As we ascended the beautiful oak stairway, the Princess paused, sighed, and looked over her shoulder at the colourful flowerbeds in the garden with admiration. Our guests all said that the Badshahi Mosque was the most beautiful mosque they had ever seen. We then moved on to the 'Diwan-e-Khas' in the Lahore Fort that was built by the Mughals, where the Princess was entertained to tea by the chief minister and presented with glass bangles which she loved and adorned her wrists with immediately. Having had a glimpse of the history and splendour of Lahore, we left the city with her exclaiming that it had been a wonderful day.

On the day of her departure, I went mid morning to the British residence to make a farewell call on the Princess. The turbans that she had requested for were ranged in white and several colours were ranged on a table in the reception room. The Princess entered, greeted me warmly and asked which ones she should choose. I suggested the turquoise, informing her that all of them had been made to size for boys of the ages of Prince William and Prince Harry so she could take them all if she wanted. She seemed touched by this, thanking me profusely for having gone into such detail. She said she had enjoyed having me with her and hoped that we would meet again, as she presented me with a signed portrait of herself.

Princess Diana departed at noon, and I drove straight back to office to resume my work, thinking that I had seen a face of Pakistanis that I could not have imagined existed. Suffering all kinds of despots, dictators, and inept leaders, our people yearned for a fairy tale in their lives, hence, the spontaneous outpouring for the Princess wherever she went. For several days I was harassed by many from my circle of acquaintances, who all wanted me to tell them what she was really like. My summing up of her was that her beauty wore off after a few days, her best feature were her eyes, she carried her clothes well, was not stupid but not serious either, with limited focus, and basically lived for the cameras. Diana would get bored when I would seek to dilate on our dreadful demographic details, or attempt to inform her regarding our sociology and culture, all of which would only produce a yawn from her.

The population ministry officials had started pulling up their socks. The contraceptive prevalence rate started showing some improvement. I would work late hours and my officers were learning to do so as well. I made a presentation to the Cabinet suggesting that the government should restrict paid maternity leave to two for its women employees; the Cabinet agreed to three. This was some progress. I pleaded for an increase in my ministry's budget, and secured a half per cent additional resource, for which I was grateful to our Finance Minister Sartaj Aziz.

It was time for me to head out to New York to persuade the head of the United Nation's Fund for Population Activities or UNFPA, Dr Nafis Sadik, for immediate increase of grant for Pakistan from thirty to at least fifty million dollars. She was giving a hundred million dollars to Bangladesh and we deserved as much, but would have to develop absorptive capacity. Receiving fifty million from her, and an additional thirty million from USAID, which was in the pipeline, and we could be exempted from the assistance cut-off, which would give the UNFPA a year to bring our grant up to the level of Bangladesh. Hence over a two-year period I would be increasing the resource and capacity of this crucial programme. I had the documents prepared meticulously and was ready to leave by mid August.

Chaudhry Nisar Ali suggested that I join the group which was going to New York for our Independence Day Parade about the same time. Arnaz Marker, Happy Minwalla's elder sister, and an old friend, had learnt of my impending arrival from Nafis Sadik and called to say that I must stay with her and her spouse Jamshid, who was our Permanent Representative to the UN. Another old friend, Rana Sheikh's husband, Najmuddin Sheikh, was our Ambassador to the US, and Rana very kindly asked me to stay with them when I was to visit D.C.

Having arrived in New York just a day before the parade I went with the Markers to do my bit and walk down the lower end of Fifth Avenue, where all New York parades took place, ending in a park where speeches were to be made. A large crowd of Pakistanis lined the avenue, our patriotic songs blaring away on loudspeakers, with the visiting leaders, Ambassadors, distinguished Pakistanis, popular singers, Zohaib and Nazia Hassan among them, and our perennial cricket hero Imran Khan included, walking down the middle of the avenue. Initially I was as enthused as the rest of the crowd, halfway down; with my feet already aching we were asked to mount a stand which was erected on a side of the avenue, where the Mayor of New York joined us. Nisar Ali helped me up, while Najmuddin was exclusively attentive to Chief Minister Ghulam Haider Wyne, which did not go down well with Nisar Ali. I saw Dr Mahbubul Haq, who struggled to get up on the stage, meanwhile Imran Khan kept striding forward down the avenue and would therefore be walking ahead of us when we reached the park. Much of the crowd followed him and the singers. We stood still when our National Anthem was played on the loud speakers, resuming our march when it ended. Mahbubul Haq commented on the popularity of Imran, Zohaib, and Nazia with our expatriates, and I said that to be popular with Pakistanis you have to learn to swing a bat or sing songs or be a Princess like Diana! Finally the march ended with the round of speeches on a high stage in the park where Sheikh Rasheed, also there among our cabinet members, stole the march from the rest of us with his usual populist speech.

Exhausted by now, Arnaz's cup of tea was much appreciated, but when I observed to Jamshid that it was such a waste of money to send these large delegations for junkets to the US or the UN, he agreed in principle, but added that the New York parade was important because it meant a lot to our expatriate community and encouraged them to remit dollars which contributed to our economy. As I conceded the point, the telephone rang. It was Nisar Ali calling for me. He asked me what I thought of Najmuddin Sheikh. I gave my friend a positive build up, but Nisar Ali made a negative comment, asking me what my programme was. I told him I was going to be in meetings with UNFPA for a couple of days, after which I was going down to Washington for meetings with the USAID. I would be there three days, then stop in London for six days to join Fakhar and our daughters, so that we could spend a little time together before the girls returned to Harvard. I asked Nisar Ali about his programme. He said that he would stay in New York for about a week, after which he was going back to Islamabad, where he would wait for my return to discuss the issue of our Ambassador to the United States.

As the call ended, Jamshid turned on his opera music. I asked him to lower the volume, because I wanted to chat with him about the impending disintegration of the Soviet Union, where he had been our Ambassador, before he was assigned to Washington and then to the UN. To my utter amazement, he said the Soviet Union was nowhere near a state of disintegration, or collapse, only the Baltic republics would secede, which would not matter much. I told him about my visit to Tashkent a few years earlier when it was already clear that secessionist movements were rampant in the underbelly of the Soviet Union and now with the retreat of the Red Army from Afghanistan, the Central Asian Republics were already seeking independence. When Jamshid dismissed what I said as nonsense, I was truly taken aback.

My UNFPA meetings went well. I was told that we would get an additional twenty million dollars worth of assistance, so I felt somewhat relaxed. Thanking the Markers profusely for their gracious hospitality, which was Jamshid's distinct forte, I set off for Washington for meetings with the USAID, and to advise my friends Rana and Najmuddin on how to lobby to retain their assignment.

Sahibzada Yaqub Khan, as Foreign Minister in Ghulam Mustafa Jatoi's interim government, had assigned Najmuddin Sheikh to Washington. Najmuddin had not met with Prime Minister Nawaz Sharif, so I suggested to him that he should leave for Pakistan to see him as soon as possible, but before that, he should return immediately to New York and meet with Nisar Ali, who was there for another three days. Najmuddin informed me that he was leaving that very evening to accompany Chief Minister of Punjab who was visiting Texas on the invitation of the Pakistani community. I explained to my host that this Chief Minister carried less clout than the Federal Minister for Oil and Gas Chaudhry Nisar Ali. I would therefore advise him to send his Deputy Chief of Mission with Ghulam Haider Wyne and he should go to see Nisar Ali, but Najmuddin opted for Texas.

Pakistani public servants or civil servants, as they prefer to be referred to, have traditionally believed that their office makes them, as do most politicians, but those with a better understanding of power, perhaps, know that it is them who make the office. Regrettably Najmuddin dismissed my advise.

The USAID agreed to maintain what was in the pipeline. My US mission was accomplished and I flew to London to join Fakhar, Umku, Shugu. Fakhar had been in London for a four-day official visit, and we had decided to take a short one week holiday on personal expense after that. My friend Mandy arranged a short-let apartment. It was modest but centrally located.

My daughters were spending quality time together with their mother and father, when Nisar Ali called from Pakistan to say that the Prime Minister wanted to assign me as Ambassador to the US, therefore, after discussing the matter with my family, I should return home immediately, since the Prime Minister wanted Najmuddin replaced as soon as possible. Nisar also discussed this with Fakhar.

The girls wanted me to accept, saying it would be great for them, and Fakhar said that it would keep me out of sight and away from the Lashkar Jhangvi. But I had my reservations. I was really into the population issue by now, which was so very crucial for our future, and I would cause hurt to Rana who was a dear friend. Fakhar said they were going to replace her husband anyway. Moreover, it would be nice for them to have me there as replacement as their children were still studying in the US and could come and stay with me whenever they wanted. Fakhar also advised me that I should go back to Pakistan immediately, because prime ministerial summon required that, and he would stay on with the girls for some more days. Fakhar was always such a stickler for form. While I was mulling over it, my daughters called up as many of my friends in London as they could think of, all of whom also endorsed that taking up the assignment as ambassador of the United States was a brilliant idea. Before I could fully comprehend what was happening, I was on the flight from London to Islamabad with Umku and Shugu bidding farewell to me, and 'See you in D.C., Chando!' echoing in my ears.

Shortly after arrival at Islamabad, I went to the Prime Minister's office. As I waited in his ante room, Nisar Ali walked in and said that although he had been the keenest for me to go to Washington, the government had just got into a mess with the co-operative societies scam, and the President was angry, because having dismissed Benazir's government on charges of corruption, he now had corruption charges being laid at the doorstep of our government, which had greatly embarrassed him. Additionally, his equation with the premier was deteriorating, and my presence in Islamabad would be useful because I got on so well with President Ghulam Ishaq Khan. I told Nisar that unless the premier paid off his debt to the co-operative societies, the president would remain implacable, and would neither hear me nor anyone else, to which Nisar agreed. Just then the staff officer appeared to say that the Prime Minister was waiting, leading me into his office.

Prime Minister Mian Nawaz Sharif greeted me warmly, enquired after my US visit, and then addressing me as 'Abida Bibi', as he always did, he said that since I knew how to deal with the Americans, he had decided to send me to the US as our Ambassador. I would have to leave as soon as possible, if I agreed, that is.

I said to him, 'Prime Minister, Sahibzada Yaqub Khan has far greater capacity to deal with the Americans than me and yet they cut off aid to us while he was interim Foreign Minister. The Americans want us to roll back our nuclear programme, and they appear to be determined about it. So, I need to first know where you stand on the nuclear question.'

'Where do you stand on the nuclear question?' he asked me wisely, I thought.

'I am totally committed to the belief that we complete building our nuclear weapons, otherwise we will always remain under threat from the Indians. The Americans have no right to bully us, when all our pleas to them that they should take notice of India building nuclear weapons have fallen on deaf ears. So, now, either they give us nuclear cover as they give to Japan or we go ahead to build our own nuclear weapons,' I said.

To this he said that he agreed with me completely and was sure that I would argue forcefully and try to convince the Americans, visibly pleased with my emphatic response, so I felt encouraged to ask, 'What if they say that they will force you out of power if you do not agree to a roll back?'

Smilingly he observed that then he would be out of power, adding that he was not born with power, but he was born a Pakistani. This answer touched a chord in my heart, so I said to him, 'I am very happy to hear this, I would be honoured to represent you, your government, and our country, but it would be only for two years, because I would want to contest the next election.' The Constitution requires a two-year gap between an ambassadorial assignment and seeking election, so I concluded saying, 'I wish you had sent me earlier. My regret will be to leave the population ministry to which I hope you will appoint a successor who will believe as fervently in this issue as I do, which you agree is as crucial for our country's wellbeing and future. Also, I have to go to Lahore to seek my mother's permission.'

He said I must obtain my mother's blessings, and go to see her before seeing anybody else, and that I should call Nisar Ali, so that the Prime Minister's office could then issue a press release, adding that since there were several contenders for this job, therefore, the announcement must precede any speculation in the media.

'May I know who wants the job the most?' was my next question.

He answered that there were a few retired generals who were very interested, with some people suggesting the name of (retired) General Rafaqat, while others were of the opinion that the Americans may not like a retired military officer at this point in time.

'I fear then that our media will not be sympathetic to me, the PPP will also express disapproval as I will be replacing a Sindhi and a capable professional, who happens to be a friend. One of the reasons for my hesitance to agree to this appointment, until I was informed that Najmuddin was going to be replaced regardless. Prime Minister, why you did not send me earlier, when the President suggested it to you?' The premier grimaced at mention of the president, then laughed and said that he hesitated lest I start to lobby for Fakhar Imam to replace him.

Presuming he was joking, my response was quick, and precise, 'Fakhar is the wrong sect, ever since Khomeini and the hostage crisis the Americans are not too fond of Shias. They may not be too keen on me either, but what will matter to me is that I retain your trust. I hope to see you before I leave, and will remain in close touch with Nisar.'

Nawaz Sharif saw me to the door and I felt closer to him than I ever did before. He also suggested that I should take money of my own, as much as I could spare, so that I would not be entirely reliant on what the government provided. I assured him I would do so, as my resources were for the service of my country.

When I reached my mother, she was with her eldest brother, Uncle Amjad Ali, who had been our ambassador in Washington almost four decades previous. He asked me if it was true that Nawaz Sharif was replacing Najmuddin Sheikh. If so, he wanted to know who he was sending in his place. I told him he would be sending me, if Baji were to agree to my going. It seemed to take a moment for the news to sink in with Uncle Amjad. Then he said, 'Of course Kishwar will agree, Chando, and your daughters will be happy, but Washington is not an easy place to get attention in, and to be an effective ambassador you have to get attention, which you would have got ten years ago when you were in your prime, but now you are in your forties and fat, so you will have to be inventive.'

I was good friends with my uncle, so I asked him chirpily how he had managed to get attention in Washington. Honest to a fault he said, 'I failed to. I wrote to the former ruler of Bahawalpur to ship me a pair of cheetah cubs from his private zoo, with the idea that I would stroll with the cubs every afternoon along Massachusetts Avenue. That way I would be noticed and probably get a write-up in the press. But the Amir of Bahawalpur sent a fully grown cheetah, which landed at the port of Baltimore, three months after my arrival. Had I strolled with that big creature he would either have devoured me or some American, that was not the kind of news worth making, so I presented the cheetah to the Washington Zoo, and had a plaque put up and a picture taken beside it, but the press did not pick up the story. Then not long before I left, I managed to get my brother Babar Ali's wedding ceremony at the residence attended by the then Vice President, Richard Nixon, along with his wife Pat, and that got brief mention in the Press, but frankly in the early fifties, most Americans were not even aware that Pakistan existed.'

'Thank you, Uncle Amjad; if I keep narrating this charming story, I am bound to get attention.'

The news of my appointment was released the following day. I was inundated with invitations for farewells. The response from the press was mixed. The foreign office gave me a wide berth. Siddiq Kanju, Minister of State for Foreign Affairs came to call on me, informing me that his ministry officials were sulking because I was replacing one of 'them' and the generals were sulking because it was not one of them, but the Secretary General of the foreign office Akram Zaki was sympathetic because he was a political appointee and his brother, Anwar Zahid, Principal Secretary to the PM had been enthusiastic about my appointment. Next, Akram Zaki called on me, suggesting I should interact frequently with the Pakistani community who would be helpful, and rely on my Deputy Chief of Mission, Sarwar Naqvi who was solid and reliable and who he gathered that I knew well.

After these visits I was caught up in a social whirl of farewell lunches, teas, dinners and in the last few days before my departure. Even breakfast was taken up with invitations. The most elaborate dinner was hosted for me by my Uncle Wajid Ali, which was on the scale of a wedding, set out on the four-acre front garden of his home in Lahore, with tall flaming torches lining his driveway, a huge marquee under which my entire extended family, and friends of the family were gathered. Everyone telling me that they had heard that I had a new wardrobe made, and were pleased I would be dressing up instead of dressing down for a change! Even my socialist friends thought that to be taken seriously by the Mecca of capitalism, dowdiness would not do. But what touched me deeply was my Lahori breakfast with Shahbibi who was a committed PPP supporter, but had always remained devoted to me personally. She lived in an old *haveli*, off Anarkali Bazaar, and as I alighted from my car to walk through the bazaar, people were lined up on either side of the road cheering me, 'Bibi Abida Zindabad! Give the Americans hell, Bibi Abida! Tell them we will eat grass, but we will build nuclear weapons! We trust you Bibi Abida!' I was overwhelmed, tears pouring down my face.

Another breakfast that I recall which was hosted for me was in Islamabad by Kazi Abid, for whom I had been such a torment in the National Assembly of 1985, when he was in the cabinet of Mohammad Khan Junejo. A marquee had been erected in his small garden and he informed the guests that he was the first person to conceive of the idea of my going to the US as ambassador, five years previous. He had suggested it to Premier Junejo, who thought I would not agree and only presume he was trying to get rid of me!

The Ministry of Population Welfare hosted a farewell event for me, which all the ministry officials as well as lower cadre employees attended. There were several speeches, all with a similar theme, that having found a head of organization that had cared for them, and even energized them, I was now abandoning them. Some of the speeches were so moving that I embarrassed myself by weeping, assuring them I would neither forget them nor the issue that bonded us.

Ijaz Naik, a confirmed bachelor who had been a meticulous civil servant and was a dear friend, never known to entertain, had a memorable lunch. Naik Sahib who was known to be averse to drawing on his entertainment allowance, reminded me of an anecdote which my late father used to narrate. In 1954, when as Minister for Education my father had gone to Delhi for a division of the India Office Library, Maulana Abul Kalam Azad, his Indian counterpart who had also been his colleague in the Central Legislative Assembly of undivided India and was a prominent leader of the Indian National Congress, was known to never draw on his entertainment allowance. But he hosted a dinner for my father which was attended by Prime Minister Jawaharlal Nehru who told my father he should come more often to India so Maulana Azad would draw on his entertainment allowance more frequently! And now I made an amazing discovery apropos our Indian neighbours, which I thought was bound to get me attention in Washington. The Indian High Commissioner, S. K. Singh, informed me that the name of the Indian ambassador currently posted to Washington was Syed Abid Hussain. 'Excellency, you must be joking. Surely your Ambassador in Washington is Dr Karan Singh of Kashmir.'

'No I am absolutely serious. Dr Karan Singh was our man in Washington, but about a year ago my government assigned Syed Abid Hussain, when he retired as secretary commerce, having earned himself a great reputation for enhancing our volume of trade significantly, as our Ambassador to the US. He hails from Hyderabad, Andhra Pradesh, has a beautiful Nepalese wife, and I gather he is doing extremely well in Washington.' S. K. Singh informed me in the usual pompous style of the Indians when they address Pakistanis.

'Excellency, if he retired as secretary in your government then he must be a good bit older than me, and I have the advantage of two syllables extra to my name.' I said, laughing, refusing to let him get away with his pomposity. This was a windfall, I thought, confidant that it would play out well for Pakistan, I decided that my refrain would be 'Trade not Aid', while my Indian counterpart would only be focusing on 'Trade'.

The following day I called on President Ghulam Ishaq Khan, who seemed pleased that I had been given the assignment he had suggested six months prior. I complained to him that the foreign office was not calling me for any briefings. He said I should ignore that, what I needed to do was spend a day at the Pakistan Institute for Nuclear Science and Technology, where Dr Ashfaq Ahmed would brief me on our nuclear programme and tell me all I needed to know to deal with my American interlocutors. When I asked him whether I would need to see Dr A. Q. Khan, he said there was no need, as A. Q. would mostly talk about himself. I mentioned the Indian Ambassador carrying almost the same name, and he said that he was aware of it, but that would only create a healthy confusion for the Americans, and I could turn it to my advantage. I mentioned my 'Trade not Aid' idea, which he readily approved of, telling me that I should try to get our quota for fine cotton products enhanced. He went on to inform me that I needed to visit the ISI (Inter-Services Intelligence) directorate for a briefing on Kashmir. For a rundown on our diplomatic history with the Americans, Agha Shahi was the best person to brief me; for a chronology on our cooperation with them in the Afghan war with the Soviets, I should talk to Ijlal Zaidi; for our commercial links with Ejaz Naik, who along with Roedad Khan were my mentors in any case. He informed me that his office would arrange the visit to the Nuclear Institute and to the ISI directorate and he would be seeing me before I left because Reginald Bartholomew, the US Under Secretary of State was to visit Islamabad before my departure and he would like me to be present in the meeting when the visiting American called on him. Before taking his leave, I said I would only be able to do the ambassadorial assignment for two years, as I wanted to contest the next election, which he said would be fine, because I needed to keep the Americans engaged in dialogue for about eighteen months, which was the time required for us to take our programme to the level of deterrence, which would not be difficult because the Americans would know that I had his ear and that of the Prime Minister, being assigned as a political appointee. When I expressed the reservation, that having a tendency to be verbally transparent I would have a problem obfuscating, he observed that I would have to learn to be totally opaque for my country's vital interests. The trust he was placing in me was overwhelming, however, with Ghulam Ishaq Khan in the Presidency, I felt personally safe and believed my country to be safe as well.

My day at PINSTECH (Pakistan Institute of Nuclear Science and Technology) was fascinating. Dr Ashfaq took me through the paces, explaining how we had developed our nuclear process and how the Americans had looked the other way while we cooperated with them against the Soviet invasion in Afghanistan, and after Soviet withdrawal how they cut off assistance to us demanding that we roll back on the distance we had covered in the process. Since the Indians already had their weapons in place, if we were to roll back, we would need two weeks to reach their level, and would be vulnerable during that time. At the end of the day, I thanked Dr Ashfaq, telling him that he had explained the details to me so well I felt as though I had a degree in physics. He was kind in saying that I had been a fast-track student.

My afternoon at the ISI directorate was equally interesting. I was informed by the Director that the political wing which he was aware I had deep reservations about, was quite separate to the security wing that I was taken to, and given the Kashmir brief which detailed the groups we supported who had mounted a militant struggle against the Indian authorities, pinning down three divisions of the Indian army, which otherwise would be stationed along our Punjab border with India. I was asked to study the brief carefully and to commit it to memory, after which it was shredded in my presence, to emphasize the sensitive nature of the information.

Sarwar Naqvi, Deputy Chief of Mission at Washington, had earlier been our consul at New York. I knew Sarwar and Mehr quite well. Sarwar had been Fakhar's batch mate at the Finance Services Academy, but while Fakhar did not join the government service, Sarwar shifted to the Foreign Service, as did another one of Fakhar's batch mates and good friend, Aziz Khan, who was posted as our consul for the West Coast, at Los Angeles. And Iqbal Ahmed, our consul at New York was married to my childhood friend Ghazala, with whom I had shared a classroom from age six to sixteen. I could not have asked for a better team to assist me.

Rana and Najmuddin Sheikh were given six weeks to wind up, which had suited me. I made my farewell visit to Multan, Jhang, and Shah Jewna; selected my personal staff, which was to accompany me to the US. I tried to persuade Mother to come with Abid who would be joining me during his winter break from school. She said she would prefer to come for two months the following summer.

Leading up to my departure, Dennis Neil, who I gathered was our lobbyist in Washington, turned up to lobby me for an extension to his contract, and Nisar Ali called to say I must have dinner with him to meet with Saeed Sheikh who was a close friend of the prime minister, lived in Washington, and had brought Dennis Neil with him. Nisar assured me that I would find Saeed Sheikh amiable and it was important that I develop an equation with him as he enjoyed the total trust of the prime minister.

Saeed Sheikh appeared to be low key and pleasant. It turned out he owned race horses and promised to take me racing to Laurel Park. I mentioned that Dennis Neil had met me, informing me that he was recommended by Congressman Charlie Wilson, who had not been able to save his country's assistance to us at the end of the engagement in Afghanistan, while Benazir Bhutto's lobbyist, Mark Siegel seemed to have been more effective. At this Saeed Sheikh quietly responded that Dennis was his friend as well, he had brought him to meet the Prime Minister and me, and would request that we retain him.

When I called on Ambassador Nicholas Platt, who was United States Ambassador to Pakistan, he and his wife Sheila, both

Harvard graduates, told me that my having two daughters as undergraduates at Harvard would be a great advantage for me in Washington, and since the relationship between our respective countries had hit a low moment, the Harvard connection would be useful. They also said that my sharing a name with the Indian Ambassador was a blast and guaranteed to lead to amusing situations. Another advantage I would have was that Teresita Schaefer would be my immediate interlocutor in the State Department. She was familiar with Pakistan, having served here earlier and knew me well. Ambassador Platt then informed me he was leaving imminently for New York and would be missing the visit of Under Secretary Bartholomew to Islamabad, but he would return and complete his tour of duty before going on to join the Asia Society as its head. He assured me that I would do well in Washington, to which I said that my level of comfort would remain high, so long as he was in Islamabad. The Platts were likeable. It could be a setback for me with a new counterpart but since he would be returning to his current assignment for the time being, my optimism remained in place.

Other than me, the President had asked Siddiq Kanju, Foreign Secretary Shehryar Khan and his own Secretary, Fazlur Rahman, to assist him in his meeting with the US. The United States Under Secretary arrived in Islamabad just prior to my departure from home. We were seated in the President's office when the Americans walked in: Under Secretary for Political Affairs, Reginald Bartholomew, accompanied by Elizabeth Jones, the Deputy Chief of Mission from the US Embassy, and a staff officer with them.

After pleasantries had been exchanged, Bartholomew, addressing the President, urged him on behalf of US President George H. Bush to roll back our nuclear programme, if he wanted a resumption of

US assistance to Pakistan. President Ghulam Ishaq Khan picked up a file and showed the letters he had been exchanging with President Bush. Bartholomew looked at the letters, then picked out one and asked President Ghulam Ishaq to read it, in an edgy voice. The President nodded at him, picked out another letter, telling the visitor that this was what he had written in response. Having read it, Bartholomew threw the entire file onto the table in front, muttering that if we Pakistanis did not wish to understand what the United States Government was urging us to do, it was too bad for us. He then stood up, and without acknowledging his exit, he said to his accompanying compatriots, 'Let's get out of here', shutting the door hard behind them.

None of us moved or spoke. Kanju and Shehryar looked stricken. The President's face suffused with colour, Fazlur Rahman's expression remained inscrutable. The President addressed him, asking him if he had said anything out of place, but before Fazlur Rahman responded, I said, 'Mr President you have made me proud of being Pakistani. You caught him out with the letter you showed him, and he obviously had nothing to say.' Then Fazlur Rahman added that he had no right to be so rude, even boorish, and Kanju picked up the courage to agree, we sipped our tea in silence, the President's colour normalised, addressing me, he said I had a difficult time ahead of me, but I must always remain polite as courtesy was more effective than aggression. We then took our leave, and making an unusual gesture, the President stood up, patted me on the head, bestowing Allah's blessings on me.

10

Washington D.C.

With an enormous challenge ahead of me as Pakistan's Ambassador to the United States of America (1991–1993), I boarded the plane heading to the US a few days later. It was a wrench leaving Fakhar, Abid, and Baji. Abid said 'See you in D.C. soon, Chando!'

Our Consul, Iqbal Ahmed Khan, was there to receive me at the JFK airport in New York. I was to be transferred to the LaGuardia Airport for the shuttle to Washington. It was arranged that my personal staff would go to Washington with my luggage by the greyhound bus. I appreciated Iqbal Ahmed Khan's efficiency, and the privilege of travelling light for my arrival at my destination.

Quite a reception awaited me at the Washington National Airport, when I reached Washington. All the embassy officials, some with wives, children, with bouquets were there to receive me. It seemed like a classic Pakistani style homecoming. While being led into a small lounge, I tried to take in the names and faces of all of them. I expressed gratitude for their warm welcome, and said that I looked forward to working with all of them and would do my best to be a team leader who would come up to their expectations. Shahid Malik, the First Secretary, handled the required documentation while Sarwar, his wife Mehr, and our Consul Aziz Khan who had come in from Los Angeles, accompanied me out and into a large, old Cadillac limousine, introducing me to the chauffeur, a portly, middle-aged Italian who had been driving the Ambassador of Pakistan's car since a few decades.

We were on our way, and amused at the amazement of chauffeur Lido Pinneli's amazement when I greeted him in Italian, I said to Sarwar and Aziz that they would probably have been happier had it been Fakhar instead of me. They both assured me that they would be comfortable working with me and would be looking forward to 'Shahji's' visit, referring to when Fakhar would come to Washington to see me.

The residence on S Street was familiar, after all I had been there with Rana and Najmuddin Shaikh not so long ago. As we went into the sitting room for a cup of tea, Mehr told me that Rana was in Chicago with her brother-in-law, while Najmuddin had returned to Pakistan. Rana was miffed with me because she imagined that I had somehow managed to contrive replacement of her husband, not realizing that the Prime Minister had decided to withdraw Najmuddin from Washington, regardless.

Sarwar, Aziz, and I mulled out the broad contours of our strategy right away, since my energy level was still reasonable. It was early evening in D.C. and Aziz was planning to take the late night flight back to L.A. Our focus would be on developing a relationship with the Congressional representatives and Senators. Traditionally we had concentrated on the administration, which brought us economic assistance, but there was always a price attached. Now there was a suspension of assistance, so we would have to lobby the Congress.

Meanwhile, the Indians had always enjoyed support in the US Congress, especially from the Democrats, less so with the executive, which meant they asked for and obtained less assistance, while with each episode of military rule we managed to get ourselves increasingly dependant on American assistance. My own background as a representative would be useful in this regard, and would hopefully enable me to enlarge the Pak-American Caucus which had only four members, while the Indian American Caucus had more than fifty. I would also have to win over friendships in the Senate, where so far we seemed to have none. The mass of briefing documents had been placed in the study. It would take me two days to go through them, and to settle in my new abode, after which we would prepare my brief, before Umku and Shugu came down from Harvard to join me for the weekend, at the end of which I would be ready to start my conversations with American officials and representatives. We adjourned on the note that Sarwar would have to share Mehr with me, as she would need to stand in as wife of the ambassador when required, while I would be in the workplace. Mehr was attractive, well turned out and an efficient housewife, all of which would be hugely helpful. My level of confidence bolstered by the humour and bonhomie of colleagues, I looked forward to the serious preparation of my duties.

Before starting my preparation, I called Fauzia Rashid one of my closest and dearest friends, whose departure from Lahore in the late eighties to take up a job in the World Bank had been a personal loss for me at the time, but was now going to be a great advantage. Fauzia was my confidante, one of the best human beings I had the privilege of knowing. Fortunately for me, she now lived in Washington and was somebody I could totally trust, and turn to for honest advise and opinion. We took the time out for a heart to heart, at the end of which I was ready to start work. Being familiar with an environment that was new for me, she was the best guidance counsellor I could have had.

The presentation of Pakistan's case to my interlocutors, which I developed after going through all the briefing papers, was based on considerable substance, according to my colleagues, and comment obtained from our foreign office. The salient features of my arguments were:

- We had helped America to fight and win a cost-effective war in Afghanistan.
- We risked the lives of our soldiers, and gave space to about five million Afghan refugees, sharing our bread with them.
- We enabled the Americans to use our terrain for sending in men and equipment for the 'Jihad' they sponsored in our neighbourhood, whose ghosts had now begun to haunt us, with the proliferation of automatic weapons and narcotics hitherto unknown to our people.
- We put down our own money on the table to buy a squadron of F-16s, their delivery now blocked, with the Pressler Amendment having been invoked. During the period of the Jihad we had been told that the Pressler Amendment was a way around the Symington and Glenn Amendments, the Americans, therefore, were fully in the picture regarding our nuclear program. With the Soviets retreating, we were told we must not complete our nuclear program, despite Bob Gates, then Director of the CIA, having warned us that the Indians had mounted nuclear tipped missiles on the Kashmir Line of Control. Now we were told President George H. Bush could not certify to Congress that we were not crossing the 'red lines' to pursue building nuclear weapons, therefore we could no longer be recipients of US economic or military assistance in any form whatsoever. We felt, therefore that having been used we were now being discarded. We considered this short-sighted on the part of

the Americans because we were geographically placed on the crossroads of the West, Central, and South Asia, with a large population of more than 150 million Pakistanis, potentially rich in oil, gas, and mineral resources, and with about five million expatriate Pakistanis providing services in the Middle East, Africa, Europe, and around a million in North America. We were among the natural leaders of the Muslim world and were now a working democracy. In walking away from us at this juncture the US would lose credibility and goodwill with the people of Pakistan.

- We did not seek aid from the US but would value an enhancement of trade, by obtaining a consequential increase in the allocation of the textile quota sanctioned to us. We wanted OPIC (Overseas Private Investment Corporation) to encourage American investors to consider Pakistan for investment, particularly in the oil and gas sectors and with mineral development.
- We would also seek an exemption from the application of the aid embargo for the contract we had entered into with General Dynamics for the F-16s before the Pressler Amendment was invoked, failing which we would seek reimbursement of the payments we had made. US Government were guarantors to the contracts, so we would expect that a failure to secure delivery would, at a minimum, ensure a return of several hundred million dollars already paid in by us, which was a considerable amount for a relatively small economy such as ours.
- We sought to retain goodwill and friendship with the United States of America, but in view of our old bilateral dispute with our neighbour India, we were within our rights in seeking assistance from our American friends to help us

negotiate a settlement with the Indians on Kashmir. The Indians had been in a defence pact with the Soviets, from whom they had obtained a massive amount of free military equipment, and as a founding member of the Non-Aligned Movement had been considerable critics of America and its policies, while we had invariably sided with America and often been subjected to ridicule by the Indians for doing so. We failed to understand, therefore, American reluctance on urging India to settle her dispute with us. We understood that it was not an 'us or them' situation, we had also sought and maintained friendship with China, serving as a bridge for the Americans when they sought to establish relations with China, but we did feel that, as the nation that had repeatedly served America's strategic interests, we had a right to claim a strategic return in expecting America to play a role in ensuring peace between India and Pakistan.

America knew well that India embarked on nuclear development as an extension of the 'Atoms for Peace' programme donated to India by the Eisenhower administration. Pakistan had frequently agitated the issue of India building nuclear weapons with the international community, but our complaints having fallen on deaf ears, we had no option except to seek to protect ourselves. We could remain within the 'red lines' if the Americans were willing to give us a nuclear umbrella such as the one provided to Japan.

Since the Pressler Amendment was being applied to several seemingly minor issues, which included the IMET, or exchange of military officers training programme, the AIPS or American Institute of Policy Studies, and its exchange of scholars and academicians programme, the assistance for containing our population programme, the US government was in effect signalling cutting off links which would not be in America's interest in the long run. The Pakistan defence establishment would turn increasingly towards China, knowledge and interest of the intelligentsia of both countries would start dwindling, and the rapidly growing population of Pakistan would, over a period of time, be a more lethal 'bomb' for both countries, pushing increasing numbers of Pakistanis to enter the US illegally.

Meeting with my entire team at the Embassy on my first working morning, I ran all these issues by them, obtaining their consent and approval, requesting the head of each section to elaborate further on the issues concerning their section, suggesting that as a team we speak to our respective counterparts on all the issues with one voice. Assuring them of remaining available at all times, including weekends, to hear them on any matter which may require my attention, I adjourned the meeting with a positive feeling, as the wrapping up comment came from Malik Zahoor who headed the information section, that the Pakistan *muqadama*, or case, had been framed cogently, with all the officials taken into confidence, not just the diplomatic section. Reassured that a team spirit had been ignited, I set down to work the long hours which was my norm.

My very first call at the State Department was, ironically, to Under Secretary Reginald Bartholomew, who was polite and pleasant. He informed me that he was leaving imminently for Japan to take up his new assignment as Ambassador, and that this was his last day in office. He wished me a pleasant stay in Washington and handed me a paper which was a letter of credentials, allowing me to take up my duties as Ambassador before the formal presentation of credentials to the President of the United States. He explained that their president set aside a day every quarter for receiving a group of ambassadors in succession, and the last such day having been a week previous, he would be receiving the next group of ambassadors in late February, but while that was to be a formal ceremony, I would have the advantage of being able to take up the issues with him after I had had the time to understand more substantively exactly where the relationship with our respective countries stood, so the interaction could be more fruitful. He made no mention of our meeting in Islamabad. Taking his leave, I presented him with an onyx box from Pakistan, saying that the President of Pakistan was going to present him this box but since the meeting had ended abruptly I thought of presenting this Pakistani souvenir now, thereby conveying politely that the insult to our Head of State, and thereby to our country, had not been obliterated from my memory. Reginald Bartholomew thanked me, acknowledging that it had been too short a meeting, but he was required to convey a strong message, which he believed he had done.

Leaving his office, I felt relieved that we would not be encountering each other again. With my working papers in hand, Sarwar and I stopped by to see the Pakistan desk officer, who was young, enthusiastic, and overweight. Hence we ended up discussing diet plans, confiding in each other of our desire to lose weight. We then came to the seven-point agenda we would be taking up with his director and then with Assistant Secretary Schaeffer. He informed us that the officials above us would be taking up their one point agenda in detail, the summing up of which was one simple sentence, 'Roll Back your nuclear programme!' He conceded that to prepare a response to our lengthy agenda he had his work cut out for him. Thanking him for the forearming and the forewarning, we shook hands.

Leaving the State Department, my observation to Sarwar was that the Pakistan desk officer was no higher in calibre than our third secretary Sahil Abbas, and the American foreign policy establishment was supposed to be the best in the world, therefore there was little need for us to feel intimidated. However, Sarwar, being the cautious professional, asserted that we would meet stiff competition as we went to match wits with the higher echelons of their officers.

Pakistani community leaders called on me, as soon as I became operational, starting with the head of APPNA, Association of Pakistani Physicians of North America, Dr Parvez Shah, inviting me to his home in Maryland for dinner. He was followed by the head of APSENA, the Association of Pakistani Scientists and Engineers of North America, who invited me to Cleveland for their annual event. Next came, Riffat Mahmood, a successful Pakistani businessman, and real estate developer from Alexandria, who invited me to dinner to meet with the local Congressman Jim Moran. He told me his cousin Dr Ikram, a successful physician based in Las Vegas, Nevada, was a good friend of Senator Harry Reid and would be coming soon to D.C. to meet me in order to effect an introduction with his friend. The enthusiasm and the willingness to assist me in my diplomatic effort was heartwarming and I happily accepted their invitations, with my personal assistant, Jill Hall, beginning to fill in my social calendar.

The first dinner accepted where I would be meeting prominent members of the Pakistani community was to be at Parvez Shah's home, but before that my personal friends came for an informal meal at the residence. Fauzia Rasheed, her husband and World Bank colleague Larry; my childhood friend, Tehmina and her husband Imran; Mowahid Hussain Shah and his wife Daena, and Samina Quraeshi, who flew down from Boston specially just for the day. We laughed and ate heartily, as I lent an ear to their friendly advise. Before leaving, less Samina, the rest informed me that they would be seeing me next at Dr Parvez Shah's dinner.

It was raining heavily as I left for dinner, wearing a plain woollen *shalwar-kamiz*, with simple accessories. The ungainly Cadillac limo, with Lido Pinnelli at the wheel, veered dangerously as we drove for what seemed to be an endless drive. Through the rain and sleet, peering through the side windshield, it seemed to me that we were driving through countryside. When I asked the chauffeur how far out we were to go, he explained that we were nearing Burtonsville and the residence of the Shah's, which was actually not far from Laurel, and almost in the countryside. Reassured that my vision was not playing tricks with me, we swung into a driveway and a side garage, from where a door led into a small vestibule. A waiter standing inside the door led me towards a stairway leading down into a basement, and a well-lit hall with a large number of people seated on rows of chairs set out in a rectangle, with a small dais at one end. Everyone was chattering, nobody seemed to notice me, so I sat down quietly on an empty chair in the back row nearby. My friend Fauzia walked in, wearing an elegant sari, and spotted me. 'Where on earth did you come in from? We have all been waiting for you in the entrance hall upstairs,' she asked, hugging me warmly. Dr Shah appeared with his wife Birjees, who was elaborately dressed, wearing beautiful jewellery, and then Tehmina with her glamorous hairdo, sparkling clothes and amazing accessories. I felt stupidly under-dressed; embarrassed at my gaffe of coming in through what was probably the staff entrance, from the garage to the basement!

Dr Shah led me to the dais and introduced me; everyone stood up and gave me a round of applause and somebody said in a loud voice, how appropriate it was for Pakistan's first woman Ambassador to be soberly turned out. Apologizing to my host for my incorrect entry, I proceeded to say that the age of chivalry was certainly not dead and whereas I appreciated the comment on my sober appearance, the beautiful women in the room with their elegant clothes had reminded me that I must seek to showcase the wonderful fabrics of our country, and promised all those present that, in future, at all American events, I would make sure that my clothes were a statement on the beauty of the country I represented. This brought me a round of applause and encouraged me to run the Pakistan *muqadama* by those assembled, soliciting their advise on what could be added as conversation points, which they could send me in writing or take up with me verbally, as we would be interacting frequently. Recognizing many friends and colleagues in the gathering, my statement concluded with acknowledging that our country's expatriates living in the US were the true ambassadors of Pakistan, while I was a mere itinerant. Nevertheless, I would do my best to represent them to their satisfaction and would remain open to their criticism, which would enable me to improve upon my performance. The response of my audience was terrific. Fauzia came and whispered in my ear that I had hit the right notes, addressed all their reservations, and could now look forward to enthusiastic community support.

Ambassador Robert and Phyllis Oakley, good friends of mine from the time they had served in Pakistan, were now both in Washington. Bob was with the National Defence University and Phyllis was Assistant Secretary for Intelligence Coordination in the State Department. Phyllis arranged a lunch in my honour at the Cosmos Club, which was the most exclusive and elegant of

Washington's many clubs. This was also the club recommended for diplomats to become members of. It was very convenient for me to entertain my guests there since it was only a few blocks away from our embassy on Massachusetts Avenue. Phyllis had invited Nancy Rafael, widow of late Ambassador Arnold Rafael, who had been ambassador in Pakistan and had died in the crash of the C-130 which killed Zia ul-Haq in 1988. Nancy was Assistant Secretary for Human Rights in the State Department, already a friend, and Mrs Vernon Jordan, whose husband was an eminent African American attorney, powerful in Democratic Party circles, alongwith Francoise Djeridjian, wife of the Assistant Secretary for Near East, Middle East, and South Asia at the State Department. The latter two I was meeting for the first time. Phyllis also sponsored me for membership of this club.

Once I had settled in, I was ready to tackle my heavy office work load. In a detailed briefing with the officers of the defence section, with Brigadier Haroon as the defence attaché, two colonels working under him, an air attaché and a naval attaché, along with the heads of the economic section and diplomatic sections, I was apprised that we had paid US$200 million to General Dynamics on signing of contracts for a squadron of F-16s, and a further US$300 million as first instalment. Our next instalment of US$200 million was now due for payment, once we paid this in, half the aircraft contracted would be ready. However, if we failed to pay further, we would forfeit US$150 million as a fine. To my question regarding what the suppliers would pay as fine if we failed to get an exemption from the Pressler Law, I was horrified when told that we had no fine written into the contracts, since the US government were guarantors for the suppliers. In other words, the Government of Pakistan had entered into one-sided contracts, obviously with someone spinning a quick buck. This was nauseatingly outrageous. Arshad Farooq, the economic minister, said that while he shared my outrage, he would advise me against probing the matter, because the quick buck spinners would thwart my political career. Not doubting his sincerity, and aware that none of the officers present were in Washington when these wretched contracts were signed, my response was that it was our national duty to establish the details. We would not perhaps be able to repair the damage done, but at least we had a right to know the details, and could take a collective decision on how to handle the situation. The first step to take obviously was to meet with the guarantors and to find out what our chances of getting the aircraft were before we sought further funds from our cash-strapped government. We requested a meeting with Carl Ford, the relevant Deputy Assistant Secretary in the Department of Defence.

On my first visit to the Pentagon, I was accompanied by Air Commodore Shahid and Sarwar Naqvi. We drove to the front entrance, were given full protocol, received on the steps by Carl Ford himself, and led smoothly through a labyrinth of corridors till we reached the Deputy Assistant Secretary's office, which was a small room. Ford was well prepared, brought out his pad, saying what we needed to discuss was simple arithmetic. We ought to, in our own interest, pay in the due instalment of US$200 million, and take the payment up to completion of half the jets in the squadron, which would be 'moth balled' in Arizona, and if we failed to step back form the 'red lines', then the US government would try to make an onward sale of these jets to another buyer, and the South Koreans would be happy to take delivery of this half squadron, reimbursing our money, less the one hundred and fifty million for the fine plus thirty million deducted for administrative charges. 'What would the administrative charges be for, Mr Ford?' was my question. He informed us casually that this was the amount deducted from the down payment, by our people.

'Wait a minute, are you suggesting that our people took this money for our own administrative charges, why would we do that? This is beyond my comprehension. We paid half a billion dollars, now you want us to pay a further two hundred million from which you deduct one hundred and eighty million, so we get five hundred and twenty million back. Is this fair? And you were guarantors so we did not have a reciprocity clause on fines put into our contract.'

Ford's response left me speechless. He said the US government would have had no issue with our putting in a reciprocity clause on fines. This was an oversight on our part and the administrative charges were what a few individuals on our side had taken to give the sanctions and approvals. The penny had dropped with me.

'Are you suggesting that a few individuals on our side were taking what we call commissions or kick-backs from out of our own money? Would the suppliers not be paying that money?'

Smiling indulgently, he replied that I was clearly not familiar with how commercial deals were transacted. But essentially I was right, if we made an onward sale of the jets, we would be incurring a loss of one hundred and eighty million dollars for our treasury. He therefore advised that we lobby the Senate to get exemption from the Pressler Law, and the suppliers would help us to access the senators from Texas who would be helpful to us, and Senator Pressler himself could be accessed by the edible oil exporters from his state, South Dakota, from where we could procure much of our edible oil imports. His apparently friendly advise brought home to me, as we left the Pentagon, the nexus between

American business interests, their system of representation, and their contingent public policies. The American military industrial complex was even more powerful than ours, more fine-tuned. We had probably set up ours guided by the British and the Americans in the first place.

Thanksgiving is a particularly American ritual. Umku and Shugu had a week off from college. We were invited for Thanksgiving to the extraordinarily beautiful Rosen estate in the vicinity of Sound, beyond Baltimore. Rachel Rosen, the daughter of the house, was a classmate of Shugu's and a cousin of Congressman Ben Cardin. Entering the estate we were welcomed, as it were, by scores of deer, who raced besides our limo as we drove through the woods which led to a large sprawling mansion, with the interior decorated to perfection. The Rosens welcomed us warmly. Rachel was large and lovely, the mother svelte and elegant, the father short and portly. They seemed like simple folk, and very proud of Rachel being at Harvard. They informed me that they had tried to get hold of Mr Rosen's cousin, Ben Cardin for supper, and although he sent his regrets but said that he would be happy to receive the Ambassador of Pakistan when Congress resumed after the current recess. We invited the Rosens for dinner I was hosting a couple of evenings later; Mrs Rosen, while accepting the invitation, informed me that she had never been to an ambassador's dinner before. This would be a rare privilege which she would always cherish and would tell Cousin Ben that he must help Ambassador Hussain in every possible way.

We gorged ourselves on gourmet turkey and pumpkin pie supper. Rachel was full of questions on our issues with her country, but her parents looked bored and sleepy, hence, we took our leave just as the sky was reddening with the early evening sun, lights glinting on the waters of the ocean, and filtering through the woods. My daughters and I agreed that there was so much wealth in America that people like the Rosens were totally unaffected by their wealth, which was refreshing and charming.

Back at my residence, we were in time to receive my first house guests, Mussarat and Ijazul Hassan, who were dear friends. Ijaz, one of Pakistan's most gifted painters at that time, had brought a collection of his own work, and that of several other leading painters for an exhibition in the IMF gallery. He was also an active member of the Pakistan Peoples Party, his presence in the residence would lend credence to Pakistan being a working democracy, I thought. When I mentioned this at the opening of his exhibition, it seemed to resonate with the audience, the Pakistanis working in the IMF who were present, including old friends from Lahore, along with people of other nationalities.

My meetings in the State Department had been continuing. I had met with Teresita Schaefer, my immediate interlocutor, and Edward Djeridjian, the Assistant Secretary of State for the Middle East, Near East, and South Asia bureau. I took a real liking to Ed Djeridjian, who was of Armenian extraction, utterly charming, with a humorous, winning style. He made me feel at ease, assured me that the Americans did not like to be seen as fair-weather friends, but they were a law-abiding nation and the law could not be circumvented. When I reminded him that the timing of their interpreting the law, in the way they were currently doing, made us feel as though we had been used and dumped. He assured me that the timing was coincidentally fortuitous, from the American point of view, because their economy had entered recession and they would be cutting back on assistance to many countries, which may be of little comfort to us, but America valued its relationship with us and all was not lost as yet, we would have to work hard and seek to find mutually acceptable solutions.

Ed Djeridjian was a consummate diplomat, who made me feel that the door was not being shut in my face. He also told me that my meeting with Deputy Secretary of State Lawrence Eagleburger, which would be after Thanksgiving, would be crucial. Before meeting the Deputy Secretary, I was to call on the Under Secretary for Political Affairs Arnold Kantor.

The visit to Kantor's office turned out to be singularly unpleasant. As rule of thumb, I never met with any official or representative of the host country alone. Sarwar Naqvi always accompanied me. We walked into Kantor's large office which had a beautiful view of the river. As he rose to greet us, I was pleased to note that he was as short and overweight as myself, and was about to start discussing diet plans, as we had done with his junior officer, when Kantor spoke in a stern voice, with a furrowed forehead. Addressing me, he said he had to take up an unpleasant but very important issue with me. In the opinion of US government, my country's persistence in seeking to develop nuclear weapons was bad enough, but we were now compounding it by harbouring some deadly terrorists as well. He went on to state, with considerable emphasis, that he had proof of Osama bin Laden being in our country. At the mention of this name a shiver went down my spine as I recalled the words of Maulana Haq Nawaz's widow, but I somehow managed to maintain my composure. My response to Arnold Kantor was that this was an unfair accusation, given the reality that we were victims of terrorism ourselves because of our cooperation with the US-sponsored resistance to the Soviets in Afghanistan. I went on to question how he asserted with such certitude that a particular individual was present in our country, surely their satellite over our space could not identify one individual. He responded to my question in embarrassing detail, the gist of which was that he had human intelligence sources to corroborate the information. To this I reacted by suggesting that it was not particularly moral to buy information. My observation produced a physical reaction, making him go puce in the face as he said, almost shrilly, that he did not appreciate being preached at. With not much more left to say, we took our leave, and he appeared relieved to be rid of us. Eventually, he was vindicated, but at that point in time I genuinely believed this Saudi character, Osama bin Laden, to be in Saudi Arabia.

Not surprisingly, many years later Arnold Kantor emerged as a prominent neoconservative in the American political landscape, as did Paul Wolfowitz, Under Secretary for Defence, whom we next called on at the Pentagon. As the discussion proceeded on our issues, he informed me that ambassadors did not make policies. He felt confident that the Pakistan government had attempted eyeball to eyeball conversations with the US government in the past, but had always ended up blinking first. I assured him that this time it would be different. Our economy was surviving without assistance from the US, we were growing enough cotton to have become the third largest producer in the world of a commodity with an increasing demand, and were close to becoming food sufficient. We did seek an amendment to the Pressler Law to be able to get the F-16s we had contracted to purchase, or at least obtain our half billion dollars back, but abandoning us at this stage would alienate the people of Pakistan, and with the Soviet Union crumbling, if there were a strategic requirement from us in the future, dealing with us would not, perhaps, be that easy. Wolfowitz was dismissive of my argument, saying that since neither of us had a crystal ball, there was nothing more to my contention than pure speculation. He was not as abrasive as Kantor, but it was a relief when he informed us that he had been assigned as US Ambassador to the Philippines, and his successor Ambassador Frank Wisner, who had just completed his tour of duty in Egypt, would be resuming the conversation with us after he had settled in.

Walking into the Deputy Secretary's office, after the holidays, I felt better immediately. Lawrence Eagleburger had a plaque on his desk with the words: 'Feel Free to Smoke'. As I seated myself, he offered me a cigarette, telling me that my reputation preceded me. He was affable and jolly, trading jokes on smokers and smoking. Becoming serious, he told me how hard he had argued for us before President Bush, but despite his best effort, State Department lawyers had won the day. He agreed with me that we had given crucial support to America in the covert war in Afghanistan, his country owed us and he shared my crystal ball. His country could need us again, when we may have no reservoir of goodwill left for them in our closet. I understood from his observations that not only did the US government speak with one voice, they also kept each other informed on language and content of all conversations made from our side, running their government tightly and competently, with no loose ends. He apologized for Under Secretary Bartholomew's abrasive conduct with the President of Pakistan, and for Under Secretary Kantor's less than polite conversation with me. However, he emphasized that harbouring terrorists would not serve our long term interests and he expected me to urge Prime Minister Nawaz Sharif to ensure that tolerating terrorists ceased, as this would cause us damage in the long run. He was sympathetic on the issue of the F-16s and wished me well in my lobbying effort with US lawmakers, adding that he had enjoyed the privilege of working with the greatest expert of international relations of our times, Dr Henry Kissinger, who had great regard for Pakistan. When we took our leave, my level of comfort had been significantly bolstered by the Deputy Secretary's persuasive display of friendship. Between Ed Djeridjian and Larry Eagleburger, maybe we could find our way through the thicket of American indifference, which rankled with us.

The first formal dinner I was invited to by an American was in the home of Mrs Katherine Graham, owner of the *Washington Post*. I first met Mrs Graham in Atlanta, Georgia, at the Democratic Party Convention which I attended in 1988. Her daughter, Lally Weymouth, had visited Pakistan a few years previous, where we had met, become friends and stayed in touch. Lally invited me to a reception her mother was hosting on the sidelines of the Convention, where Mrs Graham had thanked me for the hospitality extended by me to her daughter in Pakistan, and suggested she would be happy to see me whenever I visited Washington. Shortly after my arrival as Ambassador, we had met at her office, she not only remembered our previous meeting, but was gracious enough to say that I was now her friend as well, and that she liked to be addressed as 'Kay' by her friends and henceforward I should call her 'Kay'. She was known to be the most sought after woman in Washington, a veritable power house, who had single handedly brought down Richard Nixon from the office of President of the US for having told a twisted truth to the American people.

Kay was hosting a dinner for the newly appointed President of the World Bank. Kay's father, Eugene Meyer, had been the founding President of the World Bank, and the new appointee, Lewis Preston, was clearly from her large circle of friends.

Driving to her Georgetown mansion, Lido, the chauffeur, informed me that Ambassador Yaqub Khan and Ambassador Jamshid Marker, were the only two Ambassadors of Pakistan ever invited to Mrs Graham's residence; I was the third. This clearly put me a notch higher in Lido's opinion! Kay's guest list was star-studded, which included the Secretary Treasury, and the Secretary for the Environment, and the new Under Secretary for Defence, Frank Wisner. Kay led me straight to the guest of honour, 'Lou, meet my friend Abida from Pakistan. She has recently arrived as Ambassador for her country; I expect you to look after her.' Preston was really tall, as I craned my neck to chat with him, mentioning that we had several senior bankers from Pakistan in the institution he was now heading, including Moeen Qureshi, he informed me affably that, having found his new institution overloaded, he had gone in for some downsizing, and Qureshi had forfeited his job that very morning. Trying to hide my surprise, I was relieved when the Secretary Treasury joined us, putting his arm around Preston, who told him that he should be downsizing US government or the recession would deepen. Hearing this, it occurred to me that such a conversation taking place in Islamabad was unimaginable, although we needed downsizing in our government perhaps far more than the Americans did.

Five round tables, to seat eight people at each table, had been laid out in the dining room, with beautiful white chrysanthemum circlets around candelabras holding tall white candles, suffused indirect lighting of the high ceiling, made the ambience very European. I found myself seated next to Ed Djerijian, with his beautiful wife Francoise seated opposite. Ed told me that it was a true honour for them to be sharing friendship with Kay Graham and that a great deal of the business of government in this town was informally transacted at her dining table. The four-course meal was beautifully served. Kay stood up to speak before the dessert was served. She welcomed her chief guest, and then went on to recognize the Secretaries to US government, concluding by acknowledging not only Under Secretary Frank Wisner, the son of her closest personal friend, Mrs Wisner, but also her friend, Ambassador Abida Hussain from Pakistan. Ed squeezed my hand and whispered that no Ambassador could ask for a better social introduction in this town. Tough as the story largely was for me in the workplace, the warmth of friendship at a personal level had begun to engulf me in Washington D.C.

The Pakistani community in Atlanta, Georgia was hosting a dinner for Senator Wyche Fowler and were barraging my office with phone calls asking me to attend the dinner. Accompanied by Sarwar, we flew down for the dinner, arriving at the hotel dining room just ahead of the Senator. The dinner was well attended. About two hundred Pakistani men and women seated around the dinner tables. Placed beside the Senator, whose demeanour was casually friendly, he opened the conversation by confessing ignorance on South Asian questions, proceeding to inform me that it was good of the Pakistani community in Georgia to contribute ten thousand dollars to his 'war chest' for the coming year's election, when he would be making his bid for a second term in the United States Senate. He added that in the following week he was being hosted by the Indian community who were donating twenty thousand dollars for his war chest, therefore, if re-elected, he would seek to apprise himself of South Asian issues. Following this statement, the Senator stood up to for a brief acknowledgement speech. Ploughing through the meal, before the dinner ended, when our hosts called on me to speak, I said that the Senator would have to bear with me while I sang for my supper, by briefing him on the nature of the time-tested friendship between our two countries, which currently required nurturing by the representatives of the American people. The Senator became attentive, laughing heartily at the suggestion that while Pakistan was the gateway to Central

Asia, Atlanta was surely the gateway to America. With the dinner concluding on a pleasant enough note, and the Senator accepting the cheque for the campaign contribution and departing, our community leaders joined Sarwar and myself for a discussion, during the course of which I emphasized to them that there was no sense in their wasting their hard earned money on candidates who would lean towards India, because of their community dishing out the fatter cheque. To serve the interests of Pakistan they would need to target candidates who were being neglected by the Indian community, and our embassy would send a list of such hopefuls to our kind and supportive hosts.

On the flight back to D.C., Sarwar asked me how we could conjure up such a list. I assured him that Umku's classmate, Jeff Livingstone, an exceptionally bright African American whose home was in Atlanta, would give us some ideas. We would have to tap into whatever resources we could muster to provide guidance to our community, in order to maximize their contribution to our diplomatic effort. Sarwar reminded me that I had several invitations pending to speak at leading think-tanks that Washington D.C. was famous for, starting with the Brookings Institution, to be followed by Carnegie, then the Centre for Security and International Studies (CSIS) and the Asia Society. To this I added that the centres for international studies at Georgetown, John's Hopkins, and George Washington universities were also awaiting responses for lectures to their students, World Affairs Councils in different cities, and a long list of members of Congress and Senate that we had asked to see. There was so much work at hand and really not enough time, even though my hours of work were lengthy.

For any Ambassador newly arrived in Washington, other than the state and defence departments, the crucial coordinating institution to be visited is the National Security Council (NSC). Sarwar and I had called on the Afghanistan/Pakistan Deputy Director, Bruce Riedel, who informed us shortly after we had begun our discussion, that he had been seconded to the NSC as a specialist for our region by the Central Intelligence Agency (CIA). Taken aback momentarily, I laughed and said to him that whenever I met his compatriots, this question, that they may be working for the CIA, often came to mind. Therefore, in his case, the confirmation was appreciated. We commenced with our discussion with Riedel making what sounded like sympathetic observations. He then set up a meeting for us with Dr Richard Haass, Director for Asia in the NSC, after which we would be meeting the National Security Adviser, General Brent Scowcroft.

Dr Richard Haass was scholarly and detached. He was deeply interested in my view and vision regarding the impending break-up of the Soviet Union. My thought that the Central Asian Republics would emerge as independent new states, Kazakhstan, Kyrgyzstan, Uzbekistan, Tajikistan, and Azerbaijan, all with Muslim majority populations. Adding to this assessment my opinion that these Central Asian states, after achieving sovereignty, were likely to remain under the influence of Russia, for the foreseeable future, because of their dependence on the Russian language, their official language for about a century, and the Russian bureaucracy that handled all their issues. This seemed to intrigue Dr Haass. He asked multiple questions, to which my response was brief and precise, but I could not resist telling him the story of my visit to Samarkand three years previous , after a conference hosted by the Soviet Women's Committee in Tashkent.

After the two-day conference was over, my mother and I, who had both been delegates at the conference, tried to rent a car which was to drive us to Samarkand before our return home to Pakistan. Failing to find a car to rent, we were offered an expensive six-seater coaster, whereupon my mother asked four Indian delegates, with whom she had interacted during the conference, if they would like to join us for the excursion, sharing the fare. They agreed, so we left early in the morning, driving through endless fields of cotton, and then the low hills which led us through an extraordinary natural rock formation, like an enormous arch, known as Tamerlane's Gateway, beyond which lay Samarkand, a jewel of a city, that all of us agreed was breathtakingly beautiful. We saw the Registan, which housed the seat of governance of the Timurid dynasty, the Gur-e-Mir Mosque, the ancient observatory, the Sufi shrines reminiscent of Mazaar-i-Sharif, all stunning, and all with a strong Islamic presence. While Mother and I were rapturous everywhere we went, the Indian women kept mumbling 'nice', 'quite nice', their body language uncomfortable while Mother and I were identified as Muslims and embraced warmly by Uzbek women. Some parts of the bazaars we walked through reminded both Mother and me of Quetta, which was, in a crow's flight, only as far from our Baloch capital as Islamabad; our articulation of this reality seemed to put the Indian women's noses truly out of joint. At this point in my narrative, Dr Haass interrupted with the observation that even he was not aware of the proximity of Samarkand to Quetta.

Apologizing to Dr Haass for taking so long and encouraged by him to continue, I raced to reach the coup de grace in my story. Three of the Indians were Hindu and vegetarians, the fourth was a Parsee. We sat for a meal at an open verandah eatery in the bazaar. Mother, the Parsee lady, and I gorged on fresh large pieces of roti, accompanied by soft, salted roasted lamb, just like the Baloch *sajji*, while the Hindu ladies contented themselves with equally delicious chick pea curry. By the time we boarded the coaster, we had fallen into an easy camaraderie, the satisfying meal having helped, and in agreement that it had been a fascinating day. We sang a few popular Indian and Pakistani songs, traded Sikh jokes, and my mother reminisced about her school days with her friends who now lived in India. We lapsed into brief silence, which was broken by the Parsee lady asking me curtly what economy Pakistan had other than American charity. To which my response was that she should get off the coaster, find her way to Balkh, cross the Oxus river, wend her way to Mazaar-i-Sharif, bus her way through the arid land of the Afghans, who had managed to chase out the Soviet friends of India, then drive down the Khyber Pass to Peshawar, from where she could bus her way further, through the verdant land of the Punjabis, all the way to the Wagah border, and her precious India. En route she would also perhaps notice some of the sugar and textile mills of my country that I was proud to belong to. The journey would explain to her exactly what economy we had other than American charity!

When I finished my narrative, Dr Haass seemed greatly amused, which gave me the courage to tell him that when his diplomats told me that for the US, friendship with India and Pakistan was not mutually exclusive, it failed to resonate with me, specially when it was emphasized that Kashmir being a bilateral dispute between our two countries, the US really could not intervene. What, therefore, had been the benefit to Pakistan for collaborating with the US in the covert war in Afghanistan when the Indians had got away with their defence treaty with the Soviets and a whopping amount of free military equipment, without even forfeiting American friendship? Dr Haass responded that he had been provided with considerable food for thought and would apply his mind to some of the issues raised, when he prepared his brief for the consideration of the National Security Adviser.

Getting into my stride in the workplace, I realized my housekeeping was in a mess. Mehr Naqvi did her best to help, but she had a lot on her plate, so I called Pappu Afzal Khan to ask if she could fly out to help me organize my household. She agreed to come, and set to work: rearranging the furniture, improving the menu, training my staff to cope with the endless stream of house guests who had had begun to descend, starting with my Uncle Babar Ali, who gave me sound advise on how to cut our losses on the F-16 aircraft deal, followed by my late father's erstwhile colleague from the pre-Pakistan Legislature, Yusuf Haroon, who lived in New York at the time, and was accompanied by his brother, and my husband's former ministerial colleague, Mahmood Haroon. The paintings which I had brought with me from my various homes in Pakistan, were shifted around by Pappu to maximum effect. These included the portrait of Mohammad Ali Jinnah by Askari, which my father had commissioned just after the creation of Pakistan, my pair of Shahid Jalals, Ijazul Hassan's magnificent painting of Lilies, and the best Gulgee I owned. I was now prepared for the impending visit of the Chief of Army Staff, General Asif Nawaz Janjua who was coming at the invitation of the head of the Central Command of the US army, and would be in Washington for a few days.

Because of the importance of an Army Chief in Pakistan and because at the core of US-Pakistan relations was the connect between the Pentagon and our GHQ, I was on my toes for the visit, arranging two formal dinners in his honour at the newly spruced up residence—the first one for eighteen people, all Pakistanis, embassy personnel and a few community leaders—

and the second one for Asif Nawaz to meet with forty friendly Americans, which would include Kay Graham, the Wisners, the Djeridjians, the Oakleys, the Schaeffers, Congresswoman Patricia Schroeder, who chaired the Defence Committee, and Congressman Jim Moran.

On arrival, General Asif Nawaz spent two days with the US army central command in Florida, after which he came to Washington D.C. Brigadier Haroon received him at Fort Myers airbase and drove him to the embassy. He was accompanied by Lieutenant Geneeral Sardar Ali and his military secretary, Brigadier Shami. We chatted comfortably over a cup of tea in my office, after which there was a short formal briefing, during which I informed him that he would have a meeting with Under Secretary Arnold Kantor at the State Department and Secretary Defence Dick Cheney at the Department of Defence. Kantor would be assisted by Assistant Under Secretary for South Asia, Teresita Schaeffer, who would also assist Secretary Cheney, while I would accompany Asif Nawaz and assist him.

We had requested a meeting with Secretary of State James Baker but were bound by the protocol of our hosts who set up meetings for our highest ranking personnel to suit their convenience. I warned General Asif Nawaz that the Under Secretary would not be very forthcoming. About Secretary Cheney, I had no anticipation, not having met him as yet. He carried the reputation of being a tough nut to crack, would probably try to meet the General on his own, which would be wise to avoid. Both these Americans would mount verbal pressure on rolling back our nuclear programme, for which they would offer many incentives, but my advise was that the General's response should be brief. He should indicate to them that neither the government nor the people of Pakistan would accept such a decision. He should dwell as lengthily as he pleased on the strategic assistance we rendered in the Afghan war against the Red Army, and how our being dumped unceremoniously when the job was done had cost the Americans a loss of popularity with the Armed Forces of Pakistan. General Asif Nawaz listened to me attentively, and then said that he could here a metallic sound and suspected that our conversation was being recorded by some bugging device. I said this was more than likely, but no new or classified information was being revealed, only repeat of stated positions, so the bugging made no difference. The meeting concluded with my sharing the gist of all the conversations that I, always accompanied by Sarwar Naqvi, had held with American officials and representatives. General Asif and his officers thanked me warmly before leaving. We were to meet the following day for the two meetings and then again in the evening for dinner at the residence.

When General Asif Nawaz and I alighted from our limousine on the porch of the State Department, we noticed a crowd of cameramen just outside the building. The General observed that he was getting quite a reception from the media. When informed by me, as the cameras moved away, that they were probably here to cover the Israeli and Palestinian delegations who were starting their conversations in the State Department that morning, the General grimaced, asking me how I knew. I told him that the story was front-page headlines in the newspapers; he confessed that he had not seen the newspapers that morning. To get us through the security clearance, as we entered the vast entrance hall, Asif Nawaz was most offended at being frisked. Assuring him that this was the routine here, I was leading the General to the bank of elevators towards the right side of the hall, when the cameramen we had seen outside appeared from the left side of the hall, walking backwards and clicking away at the Israeli and Palestinian delegations, with someone shouting 'out of the way' and pushing us towards the elevators. Luckily the first elevator door was open, the General and I were unceremoniously pushed into it. As the elevator doors shut, and I told the elevator boy to whiz us up to the Under Secretary's office, the general complained to me in Urdu that our hosts were shockingly rude! When I reminded him that they were a working democracy, the general said so were we, to which I said, 'sometimes' and laughed. By the time we emerged from the elevator, the General was looking more relaxed.

Ambassador Teresita Shaeffer received us in the outer office of the Under Secretary, with a courteous Islamic greeting, *Salaam Alaikum*, and going on to expressing to Asif Nawaz how happy she was to welcome him at the State Department, and how fond her memories were of Pakistan when she was there on her tour of duty. Under Secretary Kantor received us perfunctorily, seating us on a sofa while he sat on an adjacent chair. It was a dark early December morning, with a storm brewing on the horizon. The lights had been turned on, but just as we started our conversation, the lights went out, the room plunging into semi darkness. Kantor became deeply agitated, wondering out loud whether this could be the warning of a nuke attack, to which Tezi, as Teresita was popularly known, with her customary serenity, observed that there were lights across the river visible through the windows, so it was probably just a blow out. Kantor, however, responded nervously, declaring that in all his years at the State Department, he had never experienced a blow out. General Asif Nawaz, at this point, said that Washington was probably undergoing a bit of load shedding, which made Kantor ask what he meant by that. Shaeffer explained that in Pakistan load shedding was what the Americans called a blow-out. Kantor then fished in the drawer of his side table for a torch. He attempted to make it stand on the table but failed in doing so. At that moment General Asif Nawaz applied his soldierly skills and arranged the torch at a perfect angle, at which point Kantor's demand on roll back and terrorism began to sound limp and unconvincing. We left the meeting feeling pleased.

The Pentagon put up quite a show. We were accompanied by General Sardar Ali. After the saluting and clicking of heels at the entry, we were escorted to Dick Cheney's office on the main floor. The outer office had a pleasant seating arrangement to a side, where Sardar Ali was requested to sit, by an attractive personal assistant, while she led me and General Asif Nawaz into Secretary Cheney's office. It was a large rectangular room, with an enormous desk at the end of the room, a huge American flag on a shiny brass pole standing beside it, and a working table near the entrance door where the secretary was sitting, along with Ambassador Schaeffer. Both stood up to receive us. General Asif had brought with him a fairly large carpet, tightly rolled in green felt cover to present to Dick Cheney. This was brought in by the young officer it had been handed to at the entrance. General Asif had it opened promptly and unfurled. It was indeed a beautiful carpet, with a silk finish, and deep colours, classic Persian design, and made in Pakistan. Secretary Cheney ran his fingers through it admiringly, enquiring what it might have cost. Asif Nawaz was about to reply when I interrupted him, and addressing the secretary I said, 'Excellency, our army chief being apprised of your US$5,000 gift limit, chose this from our embassy's collection of gifts, the price of this carpet precisely US$4,500.'

Dick Cheney stared at me through his cold blue eyes. Turning his attention to Asif Nawaz, he said in that case, he would accept the gift. He thanked us, adding, that his wife would love it. As we proceeded to sit down, General Asif embarked on a lengthy statement, as briefed, on our role in Afghanistan, while Cheney observed him closely. When he finished, Cheney asked if he could have a word with the General alone. My misgivings were correct. I kept sitting, while Tezi stood up to leave. General Asif Nawaz asked me in Urdu what we should do. I suggested that he should insist that his Ambassador shall remain with him, at which the General commented that it would seem that we were expressing mistrust, since the lady there to assist their top gun had departed. So dragging my feet a bit, I walked out of the room.

General Sardar Ali was upset, as I went out to sit beside him, saying that I should not have left his boss alone, and ought to return to rejoin the discussion. I refused to do that as it would now be much too awkward. The doors re-opened a few minutes later, with General Asif looking pleased. Cheney walked out with him, shook hands with Sardar Ali and me and we left. In the car, General Asif suggested that he would brief his colleague on what Cheney had said to him alone, and would come with his wife to the residence half an hour earlier for the dinner, in order to apprise me of the conversation as well.

Keeping his word, my chief guest, and Begum Nuzhat Nawaz, arrived at the residence early. She was a simple lady, who reminded me of Begum Zia. Her spouse asked me if I would hazard a guess on what Cheney had said to him. 'He probably suggested that if it made it easier for us to step back from the red lines on our nuclear program, then a military takeover of the government in Pakistan would be tolerated by the Americans.' General Asif Nawaz confirmed that this is exactly what had been said, commending me for being perceptive, he added that he had refused and stated firmly that the government in Pakistan would never accept it, and the army was in no mood to take over. He went on to add that Nawaz Sharif was not necessarily indispensable and maybe if the Prime Minister changed, because after all he did not have a large majority, a few members switching loyalties would do the job, this could buy us time with the Americans. I told him that it would make no difference to the American attitude, to which Asif Nawaz asked me if Fakhar Imam had the majority lined up behind him, would it not make a difference. I told him it would make no difference, explaining that the Americans were not interested in individuals, only in compliance, which is always the requirement of the powerful, adding that this was no different to what the Pakistan Army required from Pakistani politicians. This last observation made General Asif Nawaz laugh heartily.

His Military Secretary walked in, and told his boss that General Hamid Gul had refused to take up his assignment as the head of Ordinance at Wah cantonment. In a cold voice, General Asif Nawaz curtly ordered the Military Secretary to fax the order to the GHQ immediately for Hamid Gul's retirement. He emphasized to me that in the army resisting orders meant risking your job, so wise politicians must not play games with army generals, whereupon I assured him that none of this was any of my business.

Both my dinners for General and Begum Asif Nawaz Janjua went off really well, specially the second one. At that dinner, Kay, Frank, and Christine Wisner, Ed and Francoise Djeridjian, Congresswoman Pat, Mr Schroeder, General Asif Nawaz and General Sardar Ali on the main table. The conversation flowed easily.

Kay asked General Asif if he would like to visit her office, which, again, against my advise, he did, and was quoted in *The Washington Post* affirming that we were on the verge of completing our nuclear programme. His name was withheld in the news story, but it stated, *senior military officer on a visit* had confirmed that we would shortly be in readiness with our nukes. This caused a furore at our foreign office, with Shehryar asking me repeatedly how it had happened. I told him that the General went against my advise to the office of *The Washington Post* and did not take me with him. Shehryar said that this was in violation of protocol, and while agreeing with him, I told Shehryar that restraining an army chief was quite beyond my mandate, wondering if it was a part of his.

General Asif Nawaz remained in Washington D.C. for a week, for the treatment of his wife. When his official visit came to an end, I was able to resume my normal diplomatic duties.

Dr Parvez Shah hosted a second dinner, this time in honour of Senator Harry Reid. I made an impassioned speech on Kashmir, reminding the Senator that in 1948, Admiral Chester Nimitz of the US Navy had been sent by the UN accompanied by James Korbel, in 1948 to supervise the Referendum in Kashmir and had reported back to the UN authorities that the Indian government had prevented the conduct of the Referendum. This detail seemed to stick with the Senator, who asked me to write up a note for him so he could move a discussion on the floor of the Senate. Presenting the Senator with Alastair Lamb's book for background reading, I promised to send him a note as well. Nevada had a small congressional delegation, a pair of Senators and a pair of Congressman and thanks to Dr Ikram and Dr Javed Sheikh, a plucky pair of Pakistani Americans who made home visits for the medical care of their representatives, Senator Reid assured me of support, along with his colleagues, on all our issues, except the nuclear proliferation question, because he was a committed pacifist and argued for the US to reduce its own arsenal. But on Kashmir, if adequately briefed, he would speak in the Senate and this would be the first time that Kashmir would be raised on the floor of the US Senate. This produced a big cheer from the gathering for both the Senator as well as for me. Senator Harry Reid kept his word and took up the Kahmir issue on the floor of the Senate.

Going to speak at the Brookings Institution, I was singularly honoured when Pamela Harriman, one of Washington's icons and the Chair of the institution at the time, came to hear me speak. She informed me that her son, Winston Churchill junior, had called her to say that I was friend of his and she must look after me in Washington, so she was hosting a lunch for me and would ask some leading intellectuals, for me to present my country's case in an informal setting. Her home was about an hour's drive from the residence. It was a freezing cold day, I draped myself in my best Kashmiri *jamawar* shawl and looked forward to meeting her friends, who quizzed me intensively, especially Ambassador Abramovich, who was a highly regarded international relations expert and opinion maker, and David Ignitius, who was one of the senior editors of *The Wahington Post*. Pamela walked me through the mist to the stables of her estate where she kept some wonderful looking horses, and said that in the springtime I should come and ride out with her.

By now I was ready for my first encounter with Ambassador Abid Hussain of India, from whom I had received an invitation for dinner in honour of his outgoing consul at Los Angeles, Satti Lambah. The invite was followed by a phone call from the Ambassador, who, speaking in chaste Urdu, informed me that he could no longer contain his curiosity about the Ambassador of his neighbouring country who was so active that wherever he went, he heard that I had already been there. I told him that all of this was entirely true of him as well and that I looked forward to meeting him and his beautiful wife. No conversation could have been more redolent of hypocrisy, but I looked forward to the evening nonetheless.

When I arrived at the Indian Ambassador's residence, Abid Hussain, looking elegant in his Nehru jacket, with trendy longish grey hair, oozing charm, his attractive Nepali wife beside him, was greeting his guests in an ample hallway which had Hindu deities in well lit cornices inset in the walls. The spacious lounge was full of people. I was led to the group where the guest of honour was standing.

As we exchanged pleasantries, an American corporate big gun, leered at me, saying, 'You Paks should get on the right side of the Indians and bury the hatchet, as we are doing with the Russians.'

Feeling affronted, I reacted by reminding him politely, perhaps with an edge to my voice, that we were known as Pakistanis, not 'Paks', just as they were known as Americans not 'Ams', and the Indians were not 'Inds'. This made the guest of honour laugh, while the American mumbled that some names could be more easily abbreviated than others, and abbreviations saved time. It was impossible to anticipate at the time that further down the years, we would be glibly referred to as the 'AfPak region'.

At the dinner table, I was seated next to a youngish Congressman Mike Kopetski from Oregon. Presuming the Congressman to be a friend of India, I tried to turn on my bit of charm to spin for my country, but the Congressman informed me that he was deeply committed to nuclear non-proliferation and wanted to lobby with both our countries to roll back on our nuclear programmes.

Assuring him that if he pulled his weight to lean on India as hard as he leaned on us, he could be confident of retaining my friendship and I would be happy to have him over to have a meal with us, but before that, he should expect a call from me in his office. Before the dinner ended, engaging with the host, I gathered that his best relationship in D.C. was with Carla Hills, the US Trade Representative, during whose tenure, Indo-American trade was in an impressive upward trajectory.

My meeting with Carla Hills got stuck on the issue of expansion of our quota of cotton. Hills was emphatic that since our quota for coarse counts remained unsubscribed; there was little justification for her to increase our quota for fine counts. It was distressing that the textile manufacturers in Pakistan did not bother with coarse counts because the profits there were smaller, while the Indians were willing to fulfil that demand because they were willing to work for smaller profits to enlarge their volume of trade. We were focused on the higher levels of profit, backed by our military and civilian bureaucrats, our textile manufacturers had the view that our strategic involvement with the Americans should give us a spin-off benefit in their direction. We had a case, of course, but we simply were not as hard-headed in business matters as our eastern neighbours, and at the end of the day it would be clear to us that this increased volume of trade would become a useful strategic tool for India. We could try to focus on widening exportable commodities that were marketable in the US, the trade section in our embassy headed by Naseem Qureshi, would have to work harder, with his team.

Meanwhile, Christmas was approaching and I looked forward to having all three of my children with me. The last social event which made a serious impression on me, was a large buffet lunch hosted by another well known Washington hostess, Esther Coopersmith. It was a bright sunny day but very cold. The large lounge was crowded and over heated. I was chatting with Ed Djeridjian, asking him whether it was by default or design that we were invited to the same social events, when he suggested that we step out for a breath of fresh air so he could explain to me that the State Department availed of the hospitality of wealthy American women who enjoyed entertaining and meeting with diplomats, and this was a way for state department officials to return the hospitality they received from the diplomatic corps, as with the long hours of work they put in, it was not easy for them to entertain in their often modest homes.

At this point I noticed two men standing nearby, with their arms around each other, laughing their heads off. When I asked Ed who they were, it came as a shock when he informed me that the tall dark heavy-set man was Prince Bandar bin Sultan bin Abdul Aziz, the Ambassador of Saudi Arabia and the slimmer fair man was the Ambassador of Israel. Ed led me up and introduced me to them, but they clearly did not want to be interrupted, so while Ed lingered with them, I quietly walked back to the heated rooms, where the buffet was now being laid. Prince Bandar was supposed to be extremely well connected, and reputed to have an 'in' with Secretary of State James Baker. But despite several efforts to invite him for lunches and dinners at my residence, I had failed to access this powerful Ambassador, even though in Pakistan we assumed that the Saudis were our good and generous friends everywhere and at every level.

Bob and Phyllis Oakley invited Umku and Shugu who had come down from Harvard, and Abid who had flown in from Pakistan to join their family for Christmas lunch in their home, which was on Cathedral Avenue, Foxhall, one of the most expensive residential areas of D.C. The Oakley's had a daughter, recently married and with a baby, who was there along with her husband along with their son, who was a cadet at a military academy, and Bob's mother who had flown out from California for Christmas. Phyllis was not only an outstanding diplomat, she was also a great cook. We had a wonderful meal, with my children being made to feel at home by the Oakley family. Phyllis was a helpful guide for me throughout the time that I was in Washington, never imposing her opinions, merely informing me on how her government coordinated its policies. She also suggested helpful material to read for effective discharge of my duties. She informed me that a new bureau was likely to be voted in, during the ensuing session of Congress. Congressman Steve Solarz had done most of the leg work to establish the South Asia Bureau, which would work to our advantage in the long run, as this new bureau would include Afghanistan, but it would take about a year before the bureau actually became operational.

Congressman Solarz was known to be India-friendly—I wondered how this new development would pan out—and in the meanwhile, an assiduous effort to cultivate him was required. He was considered to be an intellectual, a popular New Yorker with wide travel experience of our region. He had visited Pakistan several times, and India even more often. We had met in Pakistan.

Solarz's office was one of the first congressional offices I visited, along with the office of Congressman Robert Torricelli, who was from New Jersey and Pakistan-friendly. The Indians had a 'friends of India caucus' in Congress with about fifty members, while Pakistan could count only four members, who were overtly friendly: Democrat Charlie Wilson from Texas; and Dan Burton, a Republican from Indiana, among them.

Solarz was the moving spirit of the Indian caucus. I tried to persuade him to join our Pakistan caucus which he agreed to do, provided I could get more democrats on board, which I managed, starting with Bob Torricelli, Jim Moran, Mike Kopetski, Ben Cardin, Patricia Schroeder, Lee Hamilton, Nancy Pelosi, and the list kept growing. I was the first politician from Pakistan with an electoral background to be appointed as Ambassador to Washington D.C., therefore working the corridors of Capitol Hill was not much of a chore for me. Managing to take our caucus up to thirty-eight members by the time my tour of duty ended was the best reward for my effort on behalf of my country. In the Senate we had been singularly lacking in friendship, but I managed to add Senator Harry Reid and Senator Bill Bryan, with the help of Dr Ikram and Dr Javed Sheikh, to our list of friends.

As the holiday season ended, Abid returned to rejoin his school at Lahore, while the girls went back to Harvard. Umku had become the student representative in the Institute of Politics, along with her friend Jeff Livingstone, who organized for me to speak at the Institute on Pakistan as a working democracy. Jeff had become my friend as well. We would chat regularly on the phone, Jeff guiding me towards the African-American delegation in the Congress to stimulate an interest in our Pakistan caucus, where we obtained several members, including Congressmen Wheat and Charles Rangel. Jeff was also at the airport to receive me on my arrival at Boston, and drove me to the Institute for my first speaking engagement at Harvard. Umku emerged out of Winthrop House and Shugu out of Lowell House just in time for my speech. I could tell that both my girls were nervous lest I fail to measure up to the high speaking standard at Harvard, but they relaxed when the applause broke out among the audience every now and then, and at the end of the talk, they introduced me to all their friends. Kitty Galbraith had come and was delighted to meet my girls. Samina Quraeshi was there, of course, as was my dear friend Emily MacFarquhar. It warmed up my heart to see my girls radiant and happy in their setting, and to be there with their friends and mine. Kitty asked me if her son, Peter, had organized a visit for me with Senator Claiborne Pell who headed the Senate Foreign Relations committee. The meeting had been arranged, was due shortly, she whispered that I should target Senator Al Gore, who could emerge as the presidential candidate for the Democratic Party. The year 1992 was to be election year in the US, and tracking law-makers was not going to be easy, but the Harvard connection would stand me in good stead, even though I had to rush back the same evening to catch the State of the Union Address of President George Herbert Bush the following morning. Before leaving, my second public-speaking engagement at the Harvard Institute of Development was arranged for late spring. Umku and Shugu were immensely pleased that in a few weeks, they would be flying down to Washington to accompany me for presentation of credentials at the White House. Nothing brings mothers more solace than the pride they may engender in their children. Leaving my girls that evening made me bask in their glow.

The diplomatic corps being seated on the floor of the House of Representatives was a surprise for me, when I arrived at Capitol Hill for this annual Presidential Address. I found myself squeezed between the Ambassadors of Oman and Qatar, in the fifth row from the front, the seating in alphabetical and regional order of the countries we were representing. The floor was packed, as were the galleries. When President George Herbert Bush ascended the podium, he got a standing ovation. At the start of his address he announced a formal end to the Cold War, and received another standing ovation. He thanked the American people for remaining resolute during the past five decades to ensure victory for democracy over dictatorship, for capitalism over communism, eliciting a prolonged round of applause and another standing ovation. He recognized the contribution of the Pope, of the allies of America, but he made no specific mention of Afghanistan and Pakistan, which disappointed me. As victors of the Cold War, it was to be expected that the representatives of the American people would be proud of their country's achievements, and would then become that much more difficult to deal with.

Although my friend Peter Galbraith had come to visit me shortly after my arrival, telling me what a great appointment my country had made in sending me to Washington, when he took me in to visit Senator Claiborne Pell, he sat quietly as the Senator lectured me on the importance of non-proliferation to maintain peace. Agreeing with the Senator, I reminded him that the same ought to apply to India, which he opted not to hear. As Peter saw Sarwar and me out of the Senator's office, we mentioned to him that we were now heading towards the offices of Senator Jesse Helms, the ranking member of the Foreign Relations Committee, whose staffers called his boss 'Stillborn'. Peter was not amused, chastising me for hanging around Republicans too much. The political rivalries in Washington were clearly every bit as intense as ours in Islamabad.

Senator Jesse Helms who was elderly, like Senator Pell, told us in his deep southern drawl, which I loved, that he was really not interested in the world outside of America, the world could go to hell for all he cared. And within the world, Asia could certainly go to hell, and so could South Asia, but within South Asia, he wished greater hell to India than to Pakistan, because we had been on the right side. This made me get up and hug the old man! However, our visit with Senator John Glenn was most unpleasant. He accused all Pakistanis of lying to him about our nuclear programme, which we took exception to, with Sarwar speaking out, which he was normally not prone to doing. No amount of effort on my part to charm the former astronaut worked. Our meeting with Senator Al Gore, on the other hand, turned out to be quite hilarious. As we walked in, the Senator got up to greet us, smiling pleasantly, he put his hand out to Sarwar, saying, 'Ambassador, welcome to my office.'

Moving forward, I floored him by speaking up and saying, 'Excuse me Senator, I am Ambassador, Mr Naqvi is my Deputy Chief of Mission. My office did send your staff my profile but perhaps, you did not have time to look at it.'

The Senator was embarrassed and apologetic—said he had been running all morning—not having had the time to look at the papers on his desk.

'Senator, may we profit from this by getting an extra few minutes of your time?' His response was warm and friendly, he said we could take all the time we wanted. I told him how much I had enjoyed reading his book on Environment, and how the rapid increase in world population would lead into equally rapid environmental pollution. Since we were among the guilty nations whose population growth rate was too high, we needed to retain American assistance for our population programme, reminding him gently that his nation's share of exhaling pollutants was extremely high. While agreeing with the latter half of my statement, saying that this was recorded in his book, he differed with my suggestion on any compromise on assistance to countries pursuing nuclear programmes, as nuclear non-proliferation would be one of the main points of his Party's platform of issues during the elections coming up in November of that year. Although we drew something of a blank, at least the meeting was pleasant and certainly it seemed to me that we had dented Senator Gore's pro-India bias marginally.

While I struggled with the representatives of my host country, India stole a stealthy march over us by downgrading her championship of the Palestinians, and recognizing Israel, promptly proceeding to set up diplomatic relations with the bastion of the Jewish people in the world. Calling on Senator Orrin Hatch of Utah, a committed Mormon, I was taken aback when he said that on behalf of his good friend Senator Joe Lieberman and himself, he would urge me to persuade my government to follow the Indian example and recognize Israel, which would enable my country to solve many of its problems. Returning to the Embassy, I was accosted by a Sri Lankan reporter of a local South Asian newspaper asking if Pakistan would also be recognizing Israel. Telling him that Pakistan's commitment to Palestine was obviously deeper than that of India, Pakistan could only recognize Israel if the process of talks between the Israelis and Palestinians concluded successfully. We did not have a quarrel with the Israelis independent of the Palestinian question.

Sadly, I was quoted out of context in the Pakistani press and the religious parties went ballistic, demanding my removal. In trouble with some of my countrymen, I went through a rough patch, which was disheartening, but the moment passed, with many of my compatriots and our expatriate community agreeing with what had been stated.

A steady stream of delegations and visitors from Pakistan kept pouring in to Washington, as I entertained, worked Capitol Hill, and prepared for my first meeting with President Bush. Presenting credentials is ceremonious in Washington. The family of the ambassador is invited; in my case, it was my daughters. We sat in a grand limo sent by our host government, with the flag of Pakistan on one side of the front of the car, and the US flag on the other side, and three uniformed Americans on motorbikes, leading the vehicle, in formation, with our own limo following.

We walked into the White House, a trio of proud Pakistani women, and were led into a dining hall, where other ambassadors and their families were waiting their turn, sipping their tea or coffee, helping themselves to cakes and cookies. The Ambassador of Pakistan was announced within five minutes, and we were now taken by the Chief of Protocol into a sitting room, where President George Herbert Bush, along with his National Security Advisor, Brent Scowcroft and Ambassador Teresita Schaeffer awaited us. Teresita introduced us to her President, telling him that my daughters, Umku and Shugu, were undergraduates at Harvard. President Bush, shook my hand warmly, apologized for his wife's absence, who was away in Texas, hugged the girls warmly, saying he was sorry they were not at Yale, his alma mater. A photographer appeared to take pictures of the three of us, standing together with President Bush, after which he sat me down on a sofa beside him, handed me my letter of credentials, receiving from me a letter from the President of Pakistan, with the photographer taking more pictures before we left the room. Both letters also contained formal statements encapsulating the aspirations of our respective countries.

Umku and Shugu were taken for a tour of the Oval Office and the public rooms of the White House by his Secretary, while President Bush asked Teresita and General Scowcroft to join him and me for a conversation. Addressing me, he said that he valued enormously the contribution made by Pakistan to the Cold War victory and wanted to help us, but the law of his country could not be countermanded, therefore he sincerely hoped that some solution would emerge to address the current impasse between us. I responded by saying that since politics, not diplomacy, was my actual metier, I sought his permission to make a forthright statement. On his go ahead, I said, 'very respectfully Mr President, if you meant what you said about Pakistan having rendered assistance to your country in achieving victory in the Cold War, then you owe us, not merely financial assistance, but a strategic return for the strategic support we provided. You owe us a Referendum in Kashmir. The Soviet veto of the 1948 UN Resolutions, as you would well recall, denied the people of Kashmir their right to self-determination for four decades. Today, the gross violations perpetrated against the Kashmiri people suffer benign neglect of the international community, your own concern for human rights ignored by the Indians. However, as the world's greatest power, surely you could intercede with the Indians to agree to a Referendum.' With the conclusion of my statement, President Bush smiled kindly, telling me that I may not be diplomatic but was certainly politically persuasive. However, since he had a genuine fondness for my country he must warn me that the Indians would have tilted the demography in their favour by now. To which I responded by mentioning that this was why we had suggested a district-by-district Referendum throughout Kashmir, which would effectively mean that Jammu and Ladakh would opt for India; the Kashmir we held would remain with us;

and the Srinagar valley would either come to us, or seek to remain independent, which would be acceptable to us and should be so for the Indians as well. At the end of my clarification, President Bush turned towards General Scowcroft, asking him if he had anything going on Kashmir. Brent Scowcroft replied that he had recently engaged with the Foreign Secretary of India during the latter's visit to Washington, and did spot a slight softening. To which President Bush said that it was positive feedback, and he should continue working on this issue.

Thanking President Bush, very sincerely, I took my leave, exiting as the next ambassador was being lined up for his presentation. My daughters rejoined me in the hallway, flushed with excitement for having stepped inside the Oval Office, as we sat in our own limousine to drive out, waving to the crowd outside. I recorded the exact words of my conversation and those of the US President and his National Security Adviser, for the telegram to be sent to my President and Prime Minister, on my return to our embassy. After this, I told my girls that they must never forget that they owed this privilege to Pakistan. They returned to college the next day, and I took my first flight back home in five months.

Arriving in Islamabad, my first call was on President Ghulam Ishaq Khan, who had already read my telegram. He had, in fact, been reading all my telegrams, and in acknowledgement of his satisfaction with my performance, he made the rare gesture of hosting a dinner in my honour in the residence of the Presidency. His wife was there, as were my mentors, Ijaz Naik, Agha Shahi, Roedad Khan, Ijlal and Shireen Zaidi, Fakhar and myself. He said he had kept the gathering small, so that we could speak confidentially, asking me to encapsulate the conversation with President Bush for the benefit of all his guests. He then asked

Agha Shahi for his comment, who said that we would have to wait and see, as the power of the Israeli lobby during election year was not to be underestimated. Shahi added that my effort was in the right direction, and ought to be sustained. At the end of dinner, Begum Ghulam Ishaq asked me to ask her husband to sanction some money for the re-upholstering of the sofas in the sitting room, because when wives of diplomats came to call on her they noticed the frayed silk of the sofas. Broaching the subject with the president cautiously, his response was expectedly impressive. He told his wife that he could sanction funds for heavy cotton fabric, made in Pakistan, as he had done for his office, but silk was too expensive, justifying his reputation for being ultra careful with public money.

Seeing Fakhar after the longest gap we had since our marriage twenty-two years ago, and my mother from whom I had never been separated for so long since my European school days, was pure pleasure, as was seeing Abid after two months. Making a dash down to Jhang to offer prayers at my father's grave and to look in on the farm, inundated by a large number of visitors, I returned to Islamabad for my call on the Prime Minister, who laughed at my attempting the American drawl, asking when he should expect to visit Washington, to watch me in action. My answer, regarding it being election year, with the Americans tending to postpone most high level visits till after their elections, seemed to disappoint him. He encouraged me to pursue the Kashmir issue and agreed that since we had paid in our third instalment on the F-16s, we should proceed to cancel the deal and get at least our half billion dollars back as soon as possible. My next visit was with the Army Chief General Asif Nawaz, who had the Air Chief Air Marshal Farouk Firoz sitting with him. The latter informed me that he would be visiting Washington in the coming month, whereupon General

Asif was complimentary about my hard work and hospitality. After an extended chat with Nisar Ali, I returned to Washington, my eight days at home having flown by much too quickly.

Leaving the beautiful spring of my country, I returned to the wet weather of the US capital, to await my honoured house guests, Sahibzada and Begum Yaqub Khan, whose guest I had been in the same residence sixteen years previous. The Yaqub Khans were very well remembered in Washington. Meanwhile, the Government of Pakistan got embroiled in another mess with the US government. The Pakistani government had placed an advertisement in international newspapers, in an effort to encourage Pakistanis to bring their capital back into Pakistan, had worded the advertisement, that *were they to do so, no questions would be asked regarding the source of the funds*. The clumsily worded advertisements indicating that no questions would be asked regarding the sources of this capital, were linguistically misconstrued by the nit-pickers on the American side, who said that this was an attempt at money laundering by our government, and threatened to revoke our sovereign guarantees. I was at my wits end with the issue, when Sahibzada Yaqub managed a rescue. Accompanying me to visit with his old friend Brent Scowcroft, through his personal goodwill with him, Sahibzada Yaqub got us off the hook.

At all social events in Washington by this time, all discussion focused on the coming elections, with the Democrats floundering in their search of a candidate, while President George H. Bush looked initially like an easy winner for his second term. The conventional wisdom of Pakistanis had been that while Republican administrations were good for us, the Democrats favoured India, but the current administration had not favoured us, the cozy days of the Reagan administration and the Zia regime being buried in the past of both our countries. It no longer mattered to us which side won in the Presidential contest or in the House and Senate. Non-Proliferation was a favoured bi-partisan mantra, and we were on the wrong side of the issue, but Sahibzada Yaqub Khan thought that nonetheless the Republicans would be better for us in the long run.

Esther Coopersmith had attended several events at our residence, and now relocated herself in a grand house around the corner from S street, where she invited me for a quiet lunch to meet with Dr Madeleine Albright and the presidential candidate for the Democratic Party, the governor of Arkansas, that both women were both hoping would emerge. There would be just the four of us and it would give me a chance to make his acquaintance well in time, in case he was elected President.

Full of curiosity, I arrived at Esther's. Dr Albright was there, but the candidate, Governor of Arkansas, William B. Clinton, had called and regretted, but asked Esther to communicate to me that he would catch up with me at a later point. Expressing my disappointment, I focused on Madeleine Albright, whom I had met earlier at Harvard with Emily MacFarquhar, and learnt how familiar she was with the Kashmir issue because her late father James Korbell, had accompanied Admiral Nimitz to Kashmir to supervise the aborted Referendum, using her, when she was in her early teens, to type his notes. Esther informed me that if Bill Clinton were elected, he would make Madeleine his Secretary of State. In the weeks ahead Bill Clinton's candidature did start emerging.

Meanwhile, since a spate of popular movies had contributed significantly to India's positive image with the American people, starting with 'Gandhi' and several Hollywood successes, I contacted my friend Sara Suleri, who taught English literature at Yale, and was the only tenured professor of Pakistani extraction at an Ivy League institution, while India had more than a score of them, to ask if she would agree to her wonderful novel, 'Meatless Days' being made into a Hollywood movie. Sara was excited at the prospect, but commented that a producer, director, and screenplay writer would need to be identified. I contacted Waris Habibullah, whose late father, Sonny Habibullah, had occupied a significant place in my earlier years. He was my late father's dearest friend and his adviser on horse breeding. Waris Habibullah was a successful Hollywood film director. He seemed very interested in my proposal, suggesting that a financier would need to be located, which made me get hold of Akram Chaudhry, an extremely successful Pakistani American businessman, whose brother had an interest in making films. He said that they could organize the funding of the movie but it would have to be after the American elections. He was also contributing towards the election campaign of Bob Torricelli, a consistent supporter of Pakistani issues. My other target was to get a pictorial exhibit mounted of Parvez Ahmed's spectacular photographs of the Hindu Kush Mountain Range which was shared by Afghanistan and Pakistan, and to which belonged the second highest peak in the world, Mount Godwin Austin, popularly known as the K-2, which was marginally shorter than Mount Everest. And also the Nanga Parbat and the Himalayan foothills. The exhibition would be held at the Sackler Gallery of the Smithsonian Museum, which was the cultural pride of America. I thought we would ask Senator Al Gore to inaugurate the exhibit, which would take a year to prepare. Dr Milo Beech, curator of the Sackler Gallery and his understudy, Francine Berkowitz, were bombed by Parvez Ahmed's (called Patti by his friends), work and put the process for the exhibition in motion. But more than anything else, I extended Pakistani style of hospitality to a large number of Americans, playing host to academics, journalists, students, prominent social workers, authors, and as many Senators and Congressmen as it was possible to get hold of.

Chief Justice of Pakistan, Justice Afzal Zullah and his wife visited Washington. This offered an opportunity to invite and interact with the Deputy Attorney General of the US and other prominent Washington attorneys.

Among others, I played host to Abdul Hafeez Pirzada, a prominent framer of the 1973 Constitution, Yahya Bakhtiar, who had been Attorney General in the outgoing Benazir administration, S. M. Zaffar, former law minister of the Ayub era, and Chairman of the Senate Waseem Sajjad. This enabled me to bring diverse groups of people together: lawyers, bankers, World Bank and IMF personnel, and prominent Pakistanis. My personal funds came in handy for the residence to remain amply supplied with food and flowers. Waseem Sajjad made a spirited effort to persuade Senator Larry Pressler, whose contemporary he had been at Oxford, to move the required amendment exempting the F-16 contract, made before the law moved by him was invoked. But he said such an attempt would not be fruitful before the coming elections, but could be considered in the year ahead.

Sylvat Sher Ali Khan, my dear friend, came to stay with me, as did Agha Shahi, who wanted to meet Katherine Graham. Makhdum Khaleequzaman of Hala and his wife Shamsi were also staying with me, so when I invited Kay for an impromptu dinner with my house guests and she did me the honour of coming, Shahi Sahib was quite amazed at how informal Kay was with me. He engaged with her lengthily on a variety of subjects: the Non-Aligned Movement, the Organization of Islamic Countries, Non-Proliferation, Palestine, and Kashmir. When Kay was leaving, she thanked me for a fascinating evening, saying that she found informal evenings, such as the one we had shared, far more productive than formal ones.

11

America Elects a New President

As we moved into late spring, I had an increasingly hectic time, the American electoral process started picking up steam, and more high profiled visitors from Pakistan were arriving. The Democratic Party had narrowed the field of candidates to Senator Albert Gore, and Governor of Arkansas, Bill Clinton, While President Bush was likely to retain Dan Quayle as his running mate even though he had spelt potatoes incorrectly, providing the American media with canon fodder to try and shoot him down with. I had been invited to lunch at the Vice President's residence by Marion Quayle his spouse, who was an attorney, modest and impressive. She heard me attentively on how important it was for us to get continued technical assistance for our population program. The American Vice President's residence was further down from where we were just off Massachusetts Avenue, sitting on top of a small hillock, with a beautiful garden all around the house, gardens on gradients always show beautifully and the late spring in Washington was even more spectacular than the spring of Lahore, feeling somewhat disloyal when thinking it.

Air Marshal Farooq Firoz and his wife, Farzana whom I really liked, arrived in Washington at the invitation of the US Air Chief, General Merrill McPeak. I hosted an elaborate dinner for them, at which the general's wife seemed to be quite overawed with what she described as the splendour of our residence. She and her husband had invited us to their home for dinner the following evening, and she said their place was a shack compared to our residence. I queried whether she had dined at the British Ambassador's residence, suggesting that ours was a shack compared to that grand edifice built by the great 18th century architect Sir Edwin Lutyens, who was instrumental in the layout and design of New Delhi and other wonderful buildings in British India. Mrs McPeak said although the colonnade of the British residence was indeed outstanding, the dining table was too small for the big dining hall, and the food was just three modest courses, as had been at their house too, whereas our table was laden with food. Farzana put her somewhat at ease saying that because of our laden tables we all had weight problems and were in a constant struggle with diets. The home of the US air chief was modest, but well appointed. Our hostess served the dinner herself, with one helper.

Air Marshal Farooq Firoz was quiet. The conversation geared towards the Gulf War. I observed that this was probably the first high-tech war the world had seen, to which our host responded that this was the first modern war, the next one America would engage in would be a high-tech war. When asked what would be the difference, he explained that what involved a hundred pilots in the gulf war, would be managed by a few folk sitting before a bank of panels who would press buttons to send unmanned electronic devices to knock out whoever was perceived to be America's enemy. I was riveted and asked whether individuals could be perceived as enemies or installations. He explained that it was individuals that were behind installations. So, if for instance, sitting on my ranch in Pakistan, America for some reason perceived me to be an enemy, something would hit me and I would cease to exist. The suggestion made me break out in a sweat, this was an early warning of what further down the road emerged in our airspace as 'predators'. When the dinner ended Air Marshal Firoz said that while we would never get the F-16s we wanted. We had, of course, a couple of squadrons given to us by the Reagan administration, which we valued, but had now decided per force to buy Mirages from the French. General McPeak, while seeing us off, asked me if I was enjoying Washington, assuring him it was a great experience, I mentioned that the only snag was the flight home was too long, and I dreaded turbulence, which invariably hit at some point en route. Whereupon he said casually that 'flight' really applied strictly to fighter jets, what I was referring to was just 'transport', if I thought of it that way the turbulence would not bother me. He was proven right on this count as well.

Our Air Marshall's visit was followed by that of our Naval Chief, Admiral Saeed, accompanied by his wife Raana. Our Navy, at the time depended heavily on three vessels which we had leased from the US Navy. We were told that the lease was also hit by the Pressler Law and we would have to surrender these vessels, which would render us substantially vulnerable to India with twice as many equally efficient vessels contributed to their fleet by their Soviet friends. But our American friends, impervious to our needs, suggested that Admiral Saeed call on Dick Cheney. This was clearly to bear weight down on our Admiral and emphasize to him that we could face a naval embargo by the Indians if we were to lose the American vessels, but if we rolled back our nuclear programme, everything would fall into place, the lease on the vehicles included. We went through the same ritual, Admiral Saeed and me, with our visit to the office of Secretary Defence at the Pentagon that I had experienced with General Asif Nawaz. The difference being, that when Dick Cheney said to Admiral Saeed that he wished to have a word with him alone, the Admiral responded that his Ambassador would remain in the room to assist him. Close on the heels of these two visits, with neither our Air Chief nor our Naval

Chief blinking, US government wrote to Prime Minister Nawaz Sharif a letter threatening to put us on the 'Watch List' of States sponsoring terrorism. I sought a meeting with Ed Djeridjian to protest having been bye-passed, with the letter being sent directly to the Prime Minister. Ed was embarrassed, proffered friendly advise suggesting that a visit for our Foreign Minister be organized and we use the opportunity to argue the point with the Secretary of State, whose office had sent out the letter.

In this background, Minister of State for Foreign Affairs, Siddiq Kanju, the Prime Minister still not having assigned the portfolio to a full Minister, reached Washington. Kanju was accompanied by Foreign Secretary Shehryar Khan. We secured a meeting with Secretary of State James Baker. We found ourselves facing four forbidding looking Americans, James Baker, Dennis Ross, Samuel Berger and Teresita Schaeffer; while at our end there were four cheery faced Pakistanis, me, Kanju, Shehryar Khan, and Sarwar. Both Ross and Berger worked closely with James Baker, the former from the State Department, the latter from the National Security Council. Both carried a reputation for being sympathetic to Israel and to India.

We were seated opposite each other. Baker sat in front of Siddiq Kanju, who was sandwiched between me and Shehryar. Baker fixed his cold blue eyes on Kanju, reminiscent of Dick Cheney, minus the rimless spectacles that Cheney wore. Under his breath Kanju observed to me in Seraiki that he was disconcerted by Baker's cold stare, I responded in Jhangochi, which is very close to Seraiki, that he should ignore the chill, disarm him with his naturally warm style, but should make his points brief and precise. But of course Siddiq Khan did not hear me.

Substituting unctuousness with warmth, he opened his statement by informing James Baker that Lahore, the capital of Punjab, land of the five rivers, once known as the Paris of the East, essentially a city of parks and fountains, enjoyed good fortune when Prime Minister Nawaz Sharif, during his tour of duty as Chief Minister Punjab, who had sought to revert Lahore to its original glory, restoring the old buildings, developing new parks for a rapidly growing city, and acquiring a reputation throughout the country for being a development oriented public figure. As Prime Minister, his focus again was on developing highways and motorways for our country, so why would he encourage terrorism. James Baker, unfazed, responded to our man Kanju by congratulating him for finally making the point via a verbal tour of the city of Lahore, which he must make an effort to visit. He then went on to grill us for leaking terrorists into Indian held Kashmir. Kanju dismissed the allegation as Indian propaganda, suggesting that Secretary Baker use his considerable skill in becoming an arbitrator between India and Pakistan and help to resolve the Kashmir dispute between the two countries. James Baker did not respond but Dennis Ross did ask some questions and Shehryar made an efficiently worded response. Baker concluded that we would remain on the 'watch list' for a while, but after the elections the new administration would review the list.

We were being squeezed by the Americans in every way possible. I was quite certain by now that the next squeeze would come on our loans and credits obtained from the World Bank and the Asian Development Bank. Meanwhile, Bill Clinton was by now the front-runner for the Democratic Party nomination as Presidential candidate, with Senator Albert Gore as his running mate for Vice President. We had only a small presence in American Academia. Fakhar decided to visit the US before getting caught up in the budget session of the National Assembly at home, planning a visit to the University of Arkansas to set up a linkage with the University of Agriculture in Faisalabad and to discuss setting up a Chair for Indo-Muslim studies at Harvard as suggested to us by our friend Dr Annemarie Schimmel, the well known German scholar who wrote extensively on Islam and Sufism. It was also suggested by our old friend and historian Dr Barbara Metcalf, whose area of expertise was the colonial period of the subcontinent, that a similar one should be set up at the University of California, Berkley.

Fakhar and I spent two happy days in Washington, flew to Boston, saw our girls, met with the President of Harvard Dr Neil Rudenstein and Dean Jeremy Knowles, who said that if we could raise half a million dollars, Harvard would match it to set up the Chair. Zara Aga Khan was a classmate of Shugu, at whose suggestion her father, Prince Karim Aga Khan, invited Fakhar to stop over in Paris to have lunch with him, on his way back from America, to discuss the matter further.

From Boston we flew to Los Angeles. At Berkeley we were told that we would need to put up a quarter million dollars, the university would match it and the Chair would be established with half a million. We stayed with Ayesha and Aziz Khan in our Consul's residence. They invited Safi Qureishi who had been very successful in a tech company, who pledged an endowment for the purpose.

After a couple of days we flew to Arkansas, facilitated by Dr Afak Haider, originally from Pakistan, who managed to get the university president to host a lunch for us, where I was seated next to a charmingly quaint lady, known to be a close friend of Virginia Kelly, Bill Clinton's mother. She regaled us with stories of the future American President's childhood in her prominently southern drawl, assuring me that she would take me to the White House with her since I was the first Ambassador that she had ever met. She concluded her narrative with the observation that 'she loved her friend Virginia Kelly, who had all that history of husbands, but she did not kill them, they just died!' Hearing this the academics at the table looked uncomfortable, but I assured them that American folk were lovely, as they often said it like it was, without pausing to consider that what they said could ever be misconstrued. This new world culture was different to our own old world culture, where we seldom said what we thought, except in our rural communities where candour was equally prized. We then visited the cotton farm of the university and Fakhar was able to establish the linkage that he was seeking for our premier agriculture university at Faisalabad and our cotton institute at Multan.

Dr Henry Kissinger was now heading a firm of consultants with his office located in New York. I had sought an appointment with him to seek his advise on how to deal with the pressure that the US government was mounting on us. He gave the appointment on the day that Fakhar was to fly out to Paris before his return home. Umku was to start her senior year at Harvard after the summer break, so I asked Dr Kissinger's office if my spouse and daughter could accompany me. His secretary informed me that Dr Kissinger would be honoured to have the Minister for Education from Pakistan and a Harvard undergraduate in his office along with me. We fetched Umku from the train station and the three of us arrived at Dr Kissinger's office on Park Avenue. We were received by Ambassador Bremmer, whom I had met earlier in Washington. He escorted us to the office of the one individual whose opinion was sought after by the corporate sector as well as by many governments worldwide, on strategic issues that inevitably impacted on world economy.

The first comment of Dr Henry Kissinger to us, as we sat down on his comfortable sofa, was that the last time he had met a father from Pakistan with his Harvard undergraduate daughter, was Z. A. Bhutto and Benazir Bhutto, and he was heavily misquoted. He emphasized to us what he had said to Bhutto was: 'if Pakistan pursued the nuclear route our country would be in trouble.' It was not a personal attack on Bhutto. Addressing me, he went on to say that he was not proven wrong, and the trouble we were now encountering in Washington was a natural corollary of our past decisions. To this my response was that the Glenn and Symington Amendments being in place, the Pressler was brought in clearly to facilitate our cooperation in the covert operation in Afghanistan against the Soviets. But with America victorious in the Cold War, walking away from us would perhaps not prove to be smart in America's own interest in the long run. Dr Kissinger responded by saying that he thought there was merit in what I had said and he hoped I was telling my interlocutors in Washington the same. In his opinion President Bush was misguided, but it would take America at least a decade to develop an effective post Cold War policy and in the meanwhile relations with Pakistan would remain rocky. Therefore we were wise to stick closely to China. China would emerge as a great global player further down the road. He then regaled us with a lovely vignette, telling us that while he did not dislike Bhutto, the South Asian leader that he found impossibly arrogant was Prime Minister Indira Gandhi. She telephoned him when he was Secretary of State to protest against the American naval build-up in Diego Garcia, to which he assured her that the island was at quite a distance from India, so she had little cause to worry. Her response was that she differed with him, because the island was after all in the Indian Ocean, to which he had said that then they could think of changing the name of the Ocean! He had no real suggestion to make on policy, but he did advise that I seek a meeting with General Colin Powell who commanded the American armed forces at the time, and whose strategic sense he thought was sound.

Before we left, he asked Umku what her major was at Harvard. Umku informed him it was 'Government', the American academic term for Political Science. He responded to that by saying that she could have taken lessons on it from her parents. He had of course taught the subject at Harvard, and wondered whether politics would ever really qualify as a science, and she ought to have read history. Umku told him that that is what her mother had advised also, to which he responded that everyone should listen to their mothers. Giving a hug to Umku, Kissinger declared that he had not, and had regretted it!

My meeting with General Colin Powell materialized. Pleading with the US Joint Chief, that dumping us would lead to an unbridgeable chasm between our two countries, and whatever weapons we may be trying to put together would, in any case, remain buried deep in the ground, and only help us in achieving a balance of terror with our Indian neighbours, I obtained a response which was direct and disarming. Stating it with warmth and friendship, General Powell reminded me that America and Russia were cutting back on their own lethal weapons, the Ukrainians and the Kazakhs were likely to surrender theirs, we should consider it in our interest to surrender ours, and would be adequately compensated with conventional weapons which would be so effective that the Indians would be envious. My response was that no amount of conventional weapons would render us safe from nuclear blackmail at the hands of India, unless we were given nuclear cover like member countries of NATO (North Atlantic Treaty Organization). To this the general replied that this was a decision which only the political leaders of his country could take. He ended the conversation by telling me he appreciated my spirit, and I should intensify my lobbying effort after the election year in his country ended.

For part of their summer vacations, Umku obtained internship at the National Democratic Institute (NDI), and Shugu, at the office of Congressman Dante Fascell, who chaired the Foreign Affairs Committee of the House. Harvard interns were always in demand in Capitol Hill and in the Democratic as well as Republican Institutes, and of course them majoring in 'Government' helped.

The girls arrived towards the middle of June 1992 and fell into their work routine, going off to work using public transport, and coming home late afternoon every working day. Umku got on well with Jean Dunn at the NDI, who told her that she would be one of the volunteers at the Convention of the Democratic Party in New York in July and would get to meet all the party leaders; a prospect that was obviously exciting for her. Meanwhile Shugu got on well with the Congressman's staffers and found the Congressman himself an 'adorable halwa', as she described him, because of his being elderly! Abid and Mother arrived towards the end of the month. It was a great comfort for me to have Baji by my side, to give me the benefit of her wisdom and sound advise. She had an unimpeachable character and her humanity made her endearing to whoever she encountered. She loved the Cosmos Club and the tea room of the Four Seasons Hotel. I invited Kay Graham and Ed and Francoise Djeridjian to have lunch with us at the Cosmos. Mother was widely read, her profound conversation at lunch impressed Kay and Ed so much that Ed asked her if she would consider working for him, to which she responded by saying if he was serious she would consider it, provided she could work on the Middle East which was important because of being such a vast source of energy, whereas South Asia only had people. And she doubted if the US had any interest in people with traditional customs and practises when it was involved in new discoveries all the time, which was precisely what made America important to the world. Kay complimented her on her astuteness, for catching Ed out, and was kind to me as always, telling my mother that the apple did not fall far from the tree. Mother's dear friend and my surrogate mother, Vicki Noon arrived for her open-heart surgery. The operation was successful. We all pitched in to look after her, and she felt she was given new lease of life, but kept complaining about the cost, and was very excited about expensive health-care emerging as an important issue in the American election campaign. We were all increasingly engaged in observing the campaigns through the profusion of electronic networks and the print media, with mother fascinated by the plucky outsider Ross Perot, while Aunty Vicki was a solid Bush supporter, and the children favoured the Democrats. I was amused to observe that with our embassy personnel included everyone was as involved in the US elections as we are during election time.

Fakhar arrived, and we set off for New York to attend the Democratic Party Convention. Umku was already there, camping with her colleagues. Most of the diplomatic corps were staying at the Plaza Hotel. We were amused to be received by her as an NDI volunteer, as she introduced us proudly to her colleagues, suggesting which of the many events around the Convention we should attend. The Democratic National Committee formally nominated William B. Clinton as their Presidential candidate, with Senator Albert Gore as his running mate for Vice President. Hillary Clinton and Tipper Gore were a major focus of attention. The Democratic ticket was going to be carried by two young, attractive couples in their forties, around the same age as Fakhar and myself. For us, the focal point of the activities was going to be a lunch hosted for the diplomatic corps, where the Vice Presidential nominee would be introduced to the ambassadors and their spouses, followed by a reception where the presidential nominee and his spouse would meet with us. In the line-up for presentation at the lunch, the chief of protocol, an officer of the State Department, announced the Ambassador of Pakistan and Minister Imam. Fakhar and I were alongside each other, Senator Gore, straightening his tie, put his hand out to Fakhar, photo-op smile on his face, as he said 'Ambassador, what a pleasure.' Fakhar smiled back, while I spoke up, not smiling, 'Senator, I cannot believe you have forgotten me.' The Senator looked at me, smile still in place, and he said, a little nervously, making a quick recovery nonetheless, addressing me as Ambassador, that he could not believe he had done it again. He requested me not to tell the media; otherwise they would pound on him. Then turning to Fakhar, he told him he had an amazing wife, and could he please make sure she would keep his cover. At this I spoke up again, 'Of course, I will keep your cover, Senator but then you will have to promise to visit Pakistan when you are elected Vice President of the United States of America.'

'I promise that Pakistan will be one of the first countries I shall visit. It is a promise I will have to keep, otherwise Madam Ambassador, you will catch me out again!' he responded. All three of us laughed, and as we moved on, a bunch of reporters surrounded us, wanting to know what the relatively lengthy conversation we were having with Senator Gore was about. I kept his cover, telling them that while I had met him before in Washington, he was meeting my husband who was in the Cabinet of Pakistan, for the first time, and since he had come specially to attend the Democratic Convention, the Senator was thanking him. As events proved later, I kept my word but Albert Gore failed to keep his. He never visited Pakistan. Our meeting with the Clintons was less eventful. Both of them shook hands with us, making deep eye contact, and we were moved on.

I flew back to Pakistan with Fakhar for a quick round of talks and debriefings, while Mother and the children remained in Washington. My meetings with President Ghulam Ishaq Khan and Prime Minister Nawaz Sharif were pleasant. When I told them that the US election results were unpredictable at this stage, both observed that it mattered little to us which side would come on the top, but both encouraged me to continue my lobbying effort with the law makers in my host country, and both agreed that now that we had paid in more than half a billion dollars for the F-16s, we should cut our losses and try to salvage as much of our money as we could. However, there was a change of Director General of the ISI (Inter-Services Intelligence). General Javed Nasir was appointed officer in charge.

My meeting with him was slightly disconcerting, he sported a longish beard, refused to look up at me, scrutinizing his finger nails as I spoke, and he had the classic appearance of what the Americans would describe as a 'Fundo'. They would have twigged into this by now, which would make my task harder in Washington, although what he had to say was not unreasonable, and strictly in Pakistan's interest. He informed me that he was sending me one of his best cover officers, and hoped he would be useful.

After a dash down to Shah Jewna for a prayer at my father's resting place, and a quick look at my horses and cows, having been home barely a week, I said goodbye to Fakhar, telling him my next visit home would be after the American elections, winging my way back to Washington, in what I now described to myself as 'transport'.

On my return, I found that Mother had taken the girls, who had concluded their internships, and Abid, for a week to Disneyworld in Florida, because this had been her promise to her grandson. Meanwhile, the General Dynamics representative in D.C., having heard that we were terminating the F-16 deal, pestered the air attaché, Air Commodore Shahid, to fly me down to Texas for the day, doubtless to make a last minute effort to influence me into changing my mind. Shahid and I flew down in a G.D. small jet, which landed on a short airstrip outside the factory floor, covering one square kilometre. Very impressive it was, bars of steel entering the factory on a conveyor belt, at one end, with a fully completed F-16 being rolled out into an adjacent hangar, at the other end. Shahid and I were driven around in a tiny vehicle and shown the fighter jets in tidy rows at different stages of completion. The largest factory floor I had seen before was that of the packaging factory of my family, which would fit into a small corner of this gargantuan enterprise. At the end of the tour, we were led into the Board Room, meeting with the top executives of the company. The head-honcho among them turned towards me and asked what he could do for us. Nothing could now be done, was my response, since G.D. had failed to lobby their law makers effectively, a failure I shared with that of their company, therefore we had decided to terminate the contracts, having paid in half the money, we had now requested US government to make an onward sale of the aircraft, which we gathered were in readiness, and sought our funds to be reimbursed to us. At this point Shahid was asked by the person sitting next to him if he would like the feel of sitting in the cockpit of one of the completed jets, and rejoin the meeting in fifteen minutes. Shahid looked at me, I nodded saying he should not take too long, because we had along flight back. No sooner was he out of the door, when the head-honcho turned to me again saying that his sources in Islamabad led him to believe that I was influential with the Prime Minister, and could make him change his mind to continue with the deal. So what could G.D. do to make me change my mind, perhaps they could buy me a nice house in D.C., which could be rented out to cover the costs of the expensive Harvard fee I was paying for my two daughters studying there. Shocked at his blatancy, I responded curtly, telling him that my daughters had obtained a grant from their college and availed of the student loans facility as well, and we could afford the fee that we were required to pay. Besides, none of us was extravagant, our needs were therefore modest. To which he responded by stating that it was a pleasure for him, at last, to meet a Pakistani with modest needs. I had rebuffed him but he had verbally slapped me back, as it were. There being little left to say, I stood up, exiting the room, as soon as Shahid returned, we shook hands with everybody and departed. General Dynamics was then bought out by Lockheed, and we did not get our money reimbursed until several years later.

Ambassador Abid Hussain of India called to inform me that he had been recalled back to India by his government and would be leaving shortly. I immediately asked him for a date to host a farewell dinner for him. It was a convivial evening, with Ambassador Harvey Schaeffer, now retired from the State Department, while his spouse Tezi was still serving, among the many guests. Harvey was writing a biography on Chester Bowles, with whom he had served in India, and observed that history was being made that evening when the Ambassador of India was being dined out by the Ambassador of Pakistan in Washington for the first time, with both Ambassadors sharing a name to confound the simple American people! Mother enjoyed the evening, inviting the chief guest to Pakistan to dine with her in our home in Lahore, and contribute towards peace between our two countries, but he never availed of her offer. Ambassador Abid Hussain informed me that his successor was going to be Siddharta Shankar Ray, a well known Bengali lawyer, who had taken the brief of the Muslim community in their case to fight for retaining the mosque which had been built on the temple at Ayodhya. It occurred to me that his curriculum vitae would sell well in Washington, beefing up the secular image of India, a Hindu lawyer pleading the case of Muslims, taking on Hindu extremists. The Indians were certainly cerebral when it came to making political appointments, always looking to maximize their strengths and draw focus away from their limitations.

My colleagues and I were now preparing for our Independence Day reception on the 14th of August. I had prepared a star-studded guest list. My friends Pamela Harriman and Kay Graham did us the honour of coming, which was amazing because all my guests from the State Department, the Defence Department and the National Security Council, were all represented at the level of Under Secretaries and Assistant Secretaries. Our hard work was truly rewarded, with Ambassador Kandemir of Turkey complimenting me on achieving a turnout that he had never managed, even though Turkey was a NATO ally, while Pakistan was quasi sanctioned. The Ambassador of China said he would host a lunch for me to share assessment on the likely outcome of the American elections.

The forthcoming elections and the likely results were the exclusive topic of conversation by now, with barely three months to go, Bill Clinton was becoming mired in personal scandals, while the Perot factor was hitting President Bush, the presidential elections appeared to be wide open, while Republican supporters became increasingly confident of securing a majority in the Senate, Democrats seemed certain of retaining a majority in the House of Representatives. As a political worker, soaking up all these conversations, I felt fortunate in being in the US during election year. The snag was that meeting with Congressmen was increasingly difficult, and only those Senators were available who were not up for re-election.

Congressman Tom Lantos agreed to see me at the end of the summer recess. Since he headed the Human Rights Caucus which had nearly two hundred members, this was to be an important meeting in which we would be taking up the issue of human rights violations in Kashmir, but to my great dismay, the congressman told me that earlier that year, when it was still quite cold, a group of Brahmins from Kashmir, had walked into his office, shivering in their cotton clothes, and explained to him that the Indian Army was in Srinagar valley to protect the Hindu minority from persecution at the hands of the Muslim majority. Sarwar and I were both aghast at the Congressman believing what was clearly a set up, and decided to task Shuja Khanzada to counter this propaganda. Shuja was a recent arrival, who fitted well into our team. He put a clever plan in motion which somewhat neutralized the damage done by the visit of the Brahmins, but we were all jolted by how gullible some representatives in our host country could be. Senator Warner who chaired the Select Intelligence Committee received us shortly thereafter. He heard me out, before we took our leave, he said I reminded him of one of his former wives, in fact his most famous former wife; he added her name was Elizabeth Taylor! Assuring the Senator that it would be more flattering if he were to be supportive of our issues, we were reassured by him in all seriousness that he would like to help Pakistan, because we had been with America against Russia, but everything would be on hold until after the elections. Leading up to the elections, my agenda was filled with speaking engagements, at the 'think-tanks', addressing students of international relations at the Universities of Virginia, Maryland, Pennsylvania, Michigan, Boston University, Tufts, Columbia, and Cornell. At all these Institutions, Pakistani students were warm and welcoming, but it disappointed me that most of them wanted to work in America, although, they would invariably say that eventually they would return to Pakistan.

Pakistan was hit by serious floods in September; Jhang was badly affected, with the Jhelum and the Chenab rivers both in high flood. Sitting at a distance, the motivation for a fund-raising effort to mobilize resources for those affected became a crucial priority. Sartaj Aziz came to the World Bank to obtain a soft loan of two hundred million dollars for rebuilding the infrastructure which had been wiped out. Accompanying him, it was upsetting to encounter a disinterested Board of Directors. Endorsing the Ministers' statistics, I pitched in with a narrative on what the fury of the rivers was like and how it impacted cruelly on hundreds of thousands of lives. The loan was sanctioned and Sartaj Sahib promised that the main arteries of my district would get due priority. Nusrat Fateh Ali Khan happened to be in America.

Our Embassy arranged a Qawwali concert for him at the Kennedy Centre. This was the first time that the great Nusrat was to perform in a prestigious location. The concert was a sell-out. We were able to avert disaster, when shortly before the curtains went up, the main *tabla* player of the performing group hopped into a taxi, with a view to disappearing in the American wilderness, but was hauled by a patriotic Pakistani taxi driver back to the Kennedy Centre. Nusrat told me cheerfully at the end of the concert that whenever he performed in America, he lost a player or two, who would join the ranks of illegal immigrants. We raised sixty thousand dollars, and when Chief Minister Punjab Ghulam Haider Wyne received this contribution, he was pleased, telling me that since my district was one of the worst affected by the calamity it would get a generous portion of this contribution.

In November 1993 the Americans went out in large numbers to vote. William B. Clinton was elected President of the United States of America, with Albert Gore as Vice President. The Democrats retained their majority in the House and the Republicans theirs in the Senate. The period of a ten-week transition started, with now the favourite guessing game being regarding the team he would pick, the diplomatic community focusing on the possible choice of Secretary of State. One of my colleagues in the Embassy informed me that he had a sound tip from some friends that Congressman Peppers from Florida who had been a Congressman since a long time, a veteran democrat, was the dark horse candidate. Conferring with Sarwar, we concluded that asking for an appointment would be worth a try. When we obtained the appointment within a couple of days, both of us thought that our colleague's tip could be a winner, otherwise why would such a quick response have come from this particular congressional office. The Congressman looked ancient, greeted us warmly, heard me out, then turned to Sarwar, addressing him as Ambassador, he told him he had a lovely wife, but she talked too much! Informing him that I was the Ambassador, Mr Naqvi my Deputy Chief of Mission, we were told by the Congressman that he was retiring from politics, not because he was too old but because his constituency had been redistricted, and he was not pleased with his party, so he would not be able to do anything for us. We left his office in a hurry and were not pleased with our colleague for sending us on a wild goose chase.

Since the Ambassador of Pakistan in the US is concurrently accredited as High Commissioner to the West Indies, I availed of this time to go to Jamaica to present credentials to the High Commissioner. Umku, Shugu had their Thanksgiving break from college, so they accompanied me, along with Shireen Safdar, who was head of chancery in our embassy. Kingston was not beautiful, but the markets were lively, the four of us kept singing Harry Belafonte's great calypso song Jamaica farewell, 'down the bay, where the nights are gay', and 'this is my island in the sun' but the music shops belted forth the new rage of popular music in the Caribbean, reggae, which my daughters loved but what I really could not get into. The Governor General's residence was reminiscent of a governor's house in Pakistan, typical early nineteenth century colonial architecture, except the wood was mahogany instead of teak. The Governor General was elderly and affable. After the exchange of formal letters of credentials and photo-ops, we sat down to a comfortable chat on the major connection between Pakistan and the West Indies, which was, of course, cricket. His government provided us with a car and we drove across the island to Montego Bay the next day, staying in a lovely cottage of the resort hotel for a couple of nights. The girls had a blast, saying this was the best Thanksgiving break they could have had, while I found it hard to believe that a whole year had whizzed by.

In early December, Fakhar's younger brother, Hassan Imam had passed away, so I flew home to be with Fakhar and my in-laws in

Qatalpur. Hassan and I had been the same age, and we all felt his loss deeply. He left behind a young widow and five small children, who were now to be Fakhar's responsibility to nurture, educate, and settled. Their mother being a housewife would need to be looked after. Fakhar fulfilled this duty admirably.

After a few days, I went to Islamabad for a visit with our leadership for review meetings on what the change of administration could portend for us. The consensus was that nuclear proliferation being a big issue and the Republican administration having walked away from us, we should not expect the Democrats to raise the bar of friendship, but keep trying to engage the new government as best we could and work towards exchanges of high level visits. The day before my return I got a call from the office of General Asif Nawaz inviting Fakhar and myself for dinner. When we walked into Army House, it turned out that the general was celebrating his birthday. He came up to Fakhar and me and introduced us to a large gentleman whom we had never met before, who our host informed us was President Ghulam Ishaq Khan's brother-in-law, and an old friend of his, now living in Australia. He chided his friend for being over-weight and said to Fakhar that he, too, was putting on weight and ought to get himself a treadmill, which was what helped the general to stay fit, and on which he walked for an hour every day. Seeing us off, our host informed me that he was going to visit Washington in March, and since Fakhar would not join him in any intrigue, he had decided to replace Nawaz Sharif by Mir Balakh Sher Mazari. Fakhar said to me in the car that we must keep mum on what we had heard, for all we knew he may just be joking.

On the morning of my departure I sought permission from the Prime Minister for Fakhar to attend the inaugural Ceremony of

President Clinton as my spouse's presence would be a requirement. Fakhar was listed up for another foreign visit, as Minister for Education, so he could spare less than a week for Washington. Along with him came Haji Javed, who was in the Cabinet of our dear friend Mir Afzal Khan, Chief Minister in the Frontier province. Haji Javed, as member of the international Rotary Club had visited Arkansas, met and made friends with Governor Clinton, with whom he sustained a correspondence as a result of which he was invited to the Inaugural, and had a seat on the Mall in the box reserved for the 'F.O.Bs', or Friends of Bill Clinton', as they came to be referred to, or 'Friends of Bill'. The media said that President elect Clinton would spend some time engaging with his friends who came from all over America and the world. Haji Javed expected a chat but failed to manage even a handshake, as the box for the F.O.B.s, in the end had an estimated ten thousand people in it!

Fakhar and I watched President William B. Clinton take oath as President of the United States from the overhang balcony of the Rotunda on Capitol Hill, where the diplomatic corps was seated. The Mall was filled with a crowd estimated to be around a million folk. As Bill Clinton stood, with Hillary Clinton beside him, with Al and Tipper Gore just behind them, to take his oath, a roaring cheer broke out from the crowds below and all the way down the Mall. As our friend Ambassador Nicholas Platt had observed to me earlier, emerging from the great mess of the elections, when the newly elected President stood to take his oath, there was almost a mystical quality to the moment. The entire ceremony was unquestionably impressive, but when I noticed a couple of Indians prominent in the second row behind the guests of the president, and was informed that these were the Hinduja brothers who were among the mega donors to the Clinton campaign, my heart sank a little. Fakhar consoled me by saying that we were not getting anything from the Americans in any case, so it made little difference except that we should be prepared for the commercial links between America and India to consolidate and should focus on our own economy. At the Inaugural Ball the diplomatic corps was again seated together. Ambassador Ray of India had called on me in my office a few days earlier, pretending friendship, he and his wife now joined Fakhar and me at our table, which we were sharing with Ambassador Mahar of Egypt and his very attractive wife. Not surprisingly, Ambassador Mahar, a skilled diplomat, went on to become the foreign minister of his country. We were seated at tables on the overhanging gallery of this beautiful, vast hall. Below us was the dance floor, with a live band playing great music. When President Clinton and his First Lady Hillary Rodham Clinton entered, the band played the American National Anthem, 'Star Spangled Banner', and the First Couple opened the dance with a waltz. All of us at our table were keen to reach the dance floor to share the waltz, but by the time we made our way down the stairs to reach the floor, it was so packed that all we could manage was to stand beside the dance floor, with Fakhar and me holding hands and humming with the music.

Newspapers back home blowing this event out of proportion, wrote that neglecting our Islamic ethos the Ambassador of Pakistan was dancing at President Clinton's Inaugural Ball; some papers even suggested that I was dancing with President Clinton! None of them mentioned that my husband was by my side, reporters called my poor mother and harassed her, she ended up saying she was not there, but she doubted that her daughter would be dancing because she was too fat to dance, the most popular Urdu daily front paged the story in bold. The following afternoon, to wind up the Inaugural ceremonies, there was a live concert by Aretha Franklin, and a host of great American singers, on the Hill, which the Clintons and the Gores attended. Again, the diplomats were seated towards the side of the terrace, with the new young leadership, senators, congressmen and their supporters being in the front. We had to walk quite a bit from our cars and back, which Fakhar found bracing, but being weighed down by my heavy fur coat, I found exhausting. Fakhar left the next day, a few days later the diplomatic corps was invited to Georgetown University for formal presentation to the new President and Vice President of our host country.

Recalling being weighed down by my fur coat, having been informed that we would be bussed in to the university from the State Department, I decided to wear a lighter cloth cape over my turquoise raw silk *shalwar-kamiz*, presuming that the presentation would be in a heated hall. On our arrival at the venue, we were led into an open quadrangle, and I was seated next to the Ambassador of Poland who was wearing a heavy top coat, so I leaned towards him to borrow some warmth, on the other side was the new Ambassador of Kyrgyzstan, Rosa, who became my friend from the get go, as she was wearing a heavy coat with fur trimming and encouraged me to snuggle with her, telling me she was the first Muslim woman to come as Ambassador to Washington D.C. When I corrected her saying that I had been Ambassador here more than a year and was very much a Muslim, so she was the second, she scowled and then laughed, saying that second was good enough, because she had been foreign minister of Kirgysia, but since nothing happened in Bishkek and everything happened in Washington she had appointed herself as Ambassador. So at least in that she was probably the first. She was greatly reassured when told that I had not been foreign minister and had not appointed myself, so in that way she was unique, Rosa hugged me, and our friendship lasted down the years. She returned to her country and became foreign minister again and eventually ended up contesting election for the Presidency of Kyrgyzstan, although sadly she did not win the contest.

President Clinton was not known to be punctual. We waited in the freezing cold for nearly an hour before he walked in, apologising for being late, he made a brief and eloquent speech, introduced his secretary of state, Warren Christopher, a wizened old gentleman, former state department hand, pulled out of his retirement from California, and concluded by saying it was much too cold for us to be outdoors, retreating into the building from where he had entered. We were all then led through a corridor, to cloak rooms where we handed in our coats, and finally into a warm hall, where we were asked to queue. I managed to get myself into the middle of the queue, which moved reasonably rapidly, with each Ambassador's name and nation being announced by the chief of protocol, the Ambassador then shaking hands with President Clinton, the First Lady, Mrs Gore, and Vice President Albert Gore, the four of them standing in a row, close to each other. Soon enough it was my turn, President Clinton held my hand briefly, making direct eye contact, Hillary Clinton likewise, onto Tipper Gore and the Vice President who held my hand in both his and addressing me as 'Ambassador Hussain', he said he was not making the same mistake a third time. As I congratulated him, I added that there was no gentleman beside me today so he could not repeat the mistake even if he tried, he laughed, while Tipper Gore addressed me said that her husband had told her about his repeated gaffe, and how I had kept his cover and the promise he had made to me. She said she was dying to visit Pakistan, and hoped he would take him with her. At this point Hillary asked Tipper what we were laughing about, Tipper told her, to which Hillary, addressing him as 'Al', asked him how he could have made the same mistake twice. She went on to say that he had better visit Pakistan or Ambassador Hussain was bound to catch up with him again somewhere! We all laughed again, and now Hillary passed the story to President Clinton, who joined the laughter and I moved on, while the Ambassador behind me was announced. Moving towards the tea and coffee table, where the diplomats were milling around after meeting the leaders, several colleagues asked me how I was able to engage the President, Vice President and their spouses in conversation. While narrating the incident, I noticed Warren Christopher standing nearby listening, moving up to me he told me he would like to see me sometime soon, as there were many issues to discuss, particularly non proliferation, and no American leaders would visit Pakistan, regardless of promises made, unless we rolled back our nuclear program. This was such a dampener, after my moment in the sun, watching the queue again, it brought me satisfaction that no other colleague of mine was being able to engage the dynamic new leaders of the American people, except of course the British Ambassador but then the British were 'cousins' of the Americans while Pakistan was quasi sanctioned.

The new administration was getting bogged down in controversy, starting with the appointment of Attorney General, whoever was named was found to have an illegal immigrant working in their homes as nannies, so the names of three appointees were announced and withdrawn, with the popular press describing this as a scandal, naming it 'nanny gate'. Holding the administration accountable in American political culture started from the get go. There seemed to be nothing like the 'honey moon' period which hallmarked British political culture or ours. Despite this I was summoned by the new Secretary of State, whose confirmation hearings had gone through without a glitch, Warren Christopher, and put on the mat again for my country harbouring terrorists. My response was that these former Mujahideen had been turned into professional killers because of the positive symmetry clauses in the Geneva Accords. Afghanistan was littered with weapons, which was the responsibility of the Americans to buy out, but with America pleading poverty, we simply did not have the capacity to deal with the monsters which the War in Afghanistan had created. Christopher reminded me that President Clinton had to fix the economy before dishing out more money to clear the Afghan debris, while I reminded him that a day would come when these ghosts would haunt the American people. Warren Christopher said I was being ridiculous in making such a suggestion.

Early the following morning, end of the first week of January, it was freezing cold, while still in bed, I got a phone call from Pakistan, from President Ghulam Ishaq Khan's office, informing me that our Chief of Army Staff, General Asif Nawaz Janjua, had passed away of a heart attack and the Embassy flag should fly at half mast. I sat bolt upright, thinking that all the tread milling he had mentioned to us so recently must have done it, when my phone rang again. This time it was my friend Phyllis Oakley, asking me if I had heard the news and if it was true. I confirmed it, telling her I had just received a call from our Presidency. My third caller was the defence attaché, Brigadier Khalid Maqbool, who had replaced Haroon about a year earlier. Khalid was an ambitious type, unlike his predecessor, who had been a quiet professional. Khalid sounded quite upset, offering my sympathy to him; I ordered the Embassy flag to be lowered to half mast and the one at the residence as well. Khalid stopped by in my office, along with two Americans he introduced as being from the department of defence, one of whom asked me as to who would be the likely new army chief in Pakistan. Before hearing my response, Khalid said it would be General Farrukh, who was an outstanding officer, the senior most and posted as chief of general staff, from which position the rise to chief of army staff was traditional. Irritated with his speaking out of turn, and coughing up information which was ostensibly not the business of the Americans, I said the Prime Minister would take a suitable decision and the American defence attaché in Islamabad would surely brief his government on the issue. After the departure of the Americans, my quiet reprimand was not lost on Khalid, who explained that one of the two was from Langley, and very friendly to us on our issues. I reminded Khalid that Bruce Riedel, the Pakistan specialist in the NSC was as well, but had any of them been able to get us a reprieve on our issues. And did we have the privilege of asking them who would command the US army next. We were of course a younger, smaller and weaker state than America, our land area equal roughly to that of Texas, our population about half of America's, and our economy as large as that of one county in California, but that did not mean that we abdicate from jealously guarding our sovereignty as best we could. Khalid was quiet, momentarily; he then asked me what my thought on the subject was, promising to keep it to himself. I said I hoped it would be General Farrukh, his wife was my Aunty Tahira's niece, from one of the founding family's of Pakistan, but since background was no longer a qualification in our country, I had no idea who the Prime Minister would appoint. Khalid then took his leave. He was ambitious, my assessment was that he would rise in his career, but there was no way to predict that he would eventually become the longest lasting Governor of Punjab.

Nisar Ali called me a couple of days later, sounding extremely anxious. He said they were in trouble with the Presidency, and I should fly out for a couple of days to talk to the President.

Disturbing as this news was, Warren Christopher's scolding was weighing on my mind, so I said I would come if it would help, but since we were in trouble with the new administration in Washington as well, I would come if he promised that he would then visit Washington to help me out with the task assigned to me, and my staff would start lining up high level meetings for him. He agreed, so I flew in to Islamabad, before my visit to the President, Nisar Ali and Shahbaz Sharif, the Prime Minister's younger brother, came to see me to tell me that General Farrukh did not suit them because they had picked issue with him over the Irfan Marwat, Veena Hayat tangle, which had hit the Press and become a national scandal, reverberating even in Washington, with Tezi Schaeffer, summoning me to the State Department to express concern. I had told Tezi that my counterpart in Islamabad had not been summoned to protest the Smith case, a scandal in which one of the young Kennedy's was involved, so why was I being summoned, and Tezi had responded that she did not anticipate a different response from me, but this was for the record. Running the story by Shahbaz and Nisar, I pointed out that Marwat being President Ghulam Ishaq's son-in-law, the friction, if any should be between him and the general. At this my visitors responded that our government would be safer with General Ashraf who was Corps Commander at Lahore, and with whom they had a good understanding.

My visit with the President drew a blank. He was not willing to discuss the subject, saying simply that General Farrukh was the best officer and deserving of the appointment. He expressed deep interest in my narrative of Washington, amused by the story of my meeting Clinton and Gore and how I managed to catch their attention. Spending a day with my mother and Abid in Lahore, and a day with Fakhar in Islamabad, I returned to the chill of

Washington, with flu and fever, and with a sense of apprehension in my heart. Mir Balakh Sher Mazari had driven into our house at Lahore, just as I was driving out on my way to the airport. He sat in my car, so we could speak en route, asking me if anyone had mentioned his name to me regarding Premiership. Pretending ignorance, urging him not to fall prey to any intrigue as it was crucial for us to remain stable, in order to withstand the American onslaught, but even as I spoke, deep inside myself, there was no escape from the realization that we were on the brink of major instability.

Seeking to make the most of my time in the 'world capital' as my friend Rosa described Washington, I undertook visits to Nevada, Oregon, Ohio, Missouri, and Texas. In Las Vegas I was guest of Dr Ikram and Dr Javed Sheikh, who not only hosted an event for me to meet Congresswoman Vucanovich and Senator Bryan, but also took me to an amazing ranch which boasted the largest collection of pure bred Arab horses in the world. At Portland Oregon, I was received at the airport by Congressman Mike Kopetski, driven through the most beautiful countryside, vaguely reminiscent of Switzerland, to a dairy farm, owned by Mike's friends: three generations, grandpa, dad and teenaged son, working the family farm together. We had a lovely time, pitching in with the trio, Mike, his staffer, and myself, with hay forks, to feed the cows, with Mike telling me that my credibility with him had improved, I was a real farmer, and on his next visit to Pakistan he would like to visit my farm, and introduce his son, Matt, to my son, Abid, as they were the same age. Eventually Matt and Abid did meet and became friends. We had dinner in Portland with Dr Anita Weiss who had researched extensively on rural women in Punjab and had several publications to her credit.

In Cleveland Ohio, I was guest of the Association of American Pakistani Engineers and Scientists, at their annual event, and was delighted to run into so many young engineers who seemed to be doing really well. The Pakistani American community congregated wherever I made an appearance and would extend warmth and solidarity and assure me of running Pakistan's issues by whichever influential Americans they encountered. In St. Louis, Missouri, my visit to Monsanto, an agriculture corporation that excelled in cutting edge agriculture technologies and were developing the BT gene cotton seed, was an unforgettable experience, as was my dinner interaction with the spirited Pakistani community. Houston, Texas was the boom city of America at this time, glamorous and exciting. Texans were in clover because their President had won the Cold War, and Charlie Wilson the Congressman celebrity who shared the laurels. My friend Joanne Herring Davis, our Honorary Consul, hosted a grand lunch at which Prince Bandar bin Sultan bin Abdul Aziz, the Ambassador of Saudi Arabia was a joint chief guest along with myself. Joanne seated us beside each other, but Prince Bandar hardly spoke to me; his attention almost exclusively focused on a gorgeous blonde, with a deep décolleté seated on his other side.

In between my travels, Nisar Ali called to inform me that their tangle with the President had been amicably resolved, and General Abdul Wahid Kakar had been appointed Chief of Army Staff. He would be ready to visit Washington in April. It was a pleasure for me to have Nisar Ali in Washington. Several ministers had been to Washington already, as had several delegations of MNAs, Senators and even MPAs I had entertained them all, but Nisar Ali's visit was consequential because he would be meeting Warren Christopher to help me allay the fears of the US government that we were not a bunch of retrogrades, sponsoring terrorists and endangering the world. However, the day Nisar Ali arrived, our Defence Minister Mir Hazar Khan Bijarani resigned.

A few of days later, Anwar Saifullah also a minister, resigned. Nisar and I were both distraught. It was clear that the President and Prime Minister were on the war path with each other again. The meeting with secretary of state was a neither here nor there affair with the secretary asking us why our minister's were resigning and with both of us framing answers that did not sound particularly persuasive, even to ourselves. At my dinner for Nisar Ali, I confided in my young friend, Vali Nasr, that the Nawaz Sharif government was likely to be dismissed and my stint in Washington may be even shorter than the expected two years. Vali was an American of Irani extraction, with a deep interest in Pakistan, where he had lived more than a year, pursuing his doctoral thesis, and keenly followed events in our country. Based in San Diego, Vali was currently on a visit with his parents, who lived in Washington. Vali agreed that we could undergo yet another mid term election, to which my thought was that if Nawaz Sharif challenged the dismissal order in the Supreme Court of Pakistan, his government could even be reinstated, but I would quit my Ambassadorship and return home, in order to be in readiness to contest the next election.

In late May, President Ghulam Ishaq Khan dismissed the National Assembly of Pakistan. Four days before the dismissal order was signed, I asked Khalid Maqbool to find out from his friends at Langley what their read out was on events in Islamabad. Khalid got back to me within a few hours, telling me we had only a few days to go. I told my staff to start packing, and rang to inform Fakhar, who was sitting in Illahi Bux Soomro's house. Fakhar came on the line, was not surprised to hear the assessment and handed the phone to Malik Naeem who was sitting with them and wanted to speak to me. He did not sound surprised either and said that along with Ilahi Bux, Fakhar and he had visited the President, who was implacable, and at this very moment they were watching television, with the President sitting with Benazir Bhutto in the Presidency, both smiling nicely at each other! Four days later the dismissal order was signed.

Umku and Shugu came down for the weekend from Boston, with Shugu repeatedly stressing that I had joined the wrong party and should always have been with Benazir Bhutto who would be Prime Minister again.

I tendered my resignation immediately, hosted a farewell lunch for my Embassy colleagues, and a reception for all my American friends, bade farewell to my daughters, promising Umku that come hell or high water, I would be there for her graduation, which was barely a month away, with my packing all completed at a cracking pace, just about eighteen months after I had arrived in Washington D.C. as Ambassador of Pakistan, I flew back home to Pakistan, having spent thirty-five thousand dollars from my personal pocket, and possessed with a much deeper understanding of the American political system. And having found friendship with Americans from diverse backgrounds, some who had their roots in Pakistan and who remain friends to this day, and others belonging to different ethnicitywho have also remained my friends over the passage of years.

As my airplane took off for Pakistan, I understood that, regardless of what lay ahead, there would always be a fond recall in my memory of my days in the USA as Ambassador. I will miss the Washington spring, the New England fall, and the laughter shared with so many people, some of them I might never meet again but their wit would remain with me. I have yet to meet people who can match in wit and humour than the people of the United States of America.

12

Back to Basics

Within a few days of my return home in 1994, America had become a distant dream. I flew into Lahore for a brief catch-up with Abid, Baji, close friends and family, and then joined Fakhar in Islamabad for the court drama that all of us were caught up in a few days later. Just as I had anticipated, Nawaz Sharif had filed a petition with the Supreme Court of Pakistan, challenging the dissolution order of President Ghulam Ishaq Khan. Mir Balakh Sher Mazari had been appointed Caretaker Prime Minister, the ball that late General Asif Nawaz had set in motion had clearly reached its goal. While Fakhar and I both had personal goodwill for President Ghulam Ishaq, as well as for Mir Balakh Sher Mazari, we honestly felt that the dissolution of the Assembly was legally not appropriately justified, it was a test for the court, which in the past had sided with the executive, and now it was time for it to endorse legislature, if we were to avoid the image of being a sham democracy.

We would be in the court diligently every morning, Nawaz Sharif would make the occasional appearance, but Shahbaz Sharif attended the hearings more regularly, with Chaudhry Nisar Ali always by his side. The court upturned the verdict, after days of gruelling hearings, and restored the government. We felt this was a great triumph for democracy, and hosted a dinner at our Islamabad residence to celebrate the occasion. Ambassador

John Monjo, who had replaced Ambassador Nicholas Platt as US Ambassador in Islamabad, and his wife Sereca, were among our guests, as were several of Fakhar's cabinet colleagues. When I observed to Ambassador Monjo that this could lead to a new beginning for Pakistan, providing us with the opportunity of enshrining more of a democratic culture in the way we governed ourselves, Ambassador Monjo observed that to mark the new beginning perhaps it would be appropriate for Prime Minster Sharif to remove from his cabinet those ministers who were not transparent about the dual nationalities they held, since the law in Pakistan did not allow dual nationals legislative representation. Fakhar asked him whether he was sure that there were such individuals in the cabinet, and if so, how many could there be, to which the ambassador cautiously replied that he was certain about those who carried the passport of his country, but it was for us to find out who and how many they were.

We were considerably dampened to hear this, and I asked to see the prime minister to apprise him of this infringement of the law at the highest level of government, to suggest the matter be investigated, and such ministers be dropped from the cabinet. I also wanted to give him a final wrap-up of my yatra in Washington.

Prime Minister Nawaz Sharif asked me if I would like to return to Washington as Ambassador. Declining the offer, I told him that it would be prudent for me to be in Pakistan since I was planning to context the next elections. There was a bar on ambassadors seeking electoral office for a period of two years between the foreign assignment and representation, and absenting from my constituency for a longer period could cost me another election. But I told the Prime Minister that if he so desired, it would be possible for me to work informally on Population Welfare, as my replacement, Rana Nazir Ahmed was relatively lax on the issue and could do with some help, but for the time being I would have to return to the US for a some weeks to attend my daughter, Umme Kulsum's graduation at Harvard. Nawaz Sharif said that if I was not interested in returning as Ambassador, he would assign Akram Zaki who was keen on the assignment, but it would take him a few weeks to wind up at the foreign office, and since I was going to the US, perhaps he could send me as Special Envoy, so that after attending my daughter's graduation I could go down to Washington and gauge how the restoration of his government was being viewed. We could discuss how I could be adjusted back on my population welfare assignment when I returned from the US. I agreed, telling him that I would do my best to be persuasive on his behalf in Washington D.C.

Although Harvard was the Mecca of liberalism, it was also a campus which was big on nationalism, so the Commencement Speaker chosen was General Colin Powell, hero of the Gulf War. The graduation ritual involved the family of the graduate walking beside themin the parade, where the graduating class lined up behind the banner of their House, in Umku's case it was the Winthrop House. They entered Harvard Yard in formation, with the most beautiful music playing through enormous speakers placed at the four corners of the yard. The graduating class sat in the front rows while the three undergraduate classes, sat in rows behind, on the left, facing the dais. There were four thousand undergraduates. Parted down the middle by a wide grassy aisle, on the right hand side sat the faculty members, and behind them the families of the graduating class. About eight thousand chairs were laid out and if more people came, they either stood or sat on the steps of the Widener Library.

The speakers were all lustily cheered: the loudest cheer was for General Colin Powell, with pink balloons in thousands released in the air. The graduating class then lined up to receive their degrees from the Dr Rudenstein, shaking hands with Colin Powell and the deans, walking out in formation, and finally throwing their caps up in the air. By the time I met up with my girls, we were all truly exhausted, and elated. The girls were going to wind up, and fly back home together in a few days, while I went down to Washington for a week.

In Washington the senior most official I met was Sandy Berger in the NSC (National Security Council), who gave me the impression that we were heading towards another mid term election. Nobody appeared to be overtly impressed by our judiciary having endorsed our legislature, Frank Wisner stating it succinctly, when he said that the real connection between the US and Pakistan being via the Pentagon and our GHQ (General Headquarters), his government would wait and watch carefully the reaction of all our institutions, and would be supportive of whatever was constitutional. Obliquely, he said what Berger had observed, that we could face yet another mid term election.

During my absence in the US, events in Islamabad took another dramatic turn. The restored Prime Minister Nawaz Sharif addressed the nation on television and said he would take no further orders from the Establishment, and put up with no further palace intrigues, after which he took a train journey to Lahore, pulling crowds at all the railway stations en route, and a very large crowd at Lahore. He was hailed now as a leader in his own right.

Before I could call on him and apprise him of my observations in Washington, Fakhar and I were both called to attend an emergency meeting at the Prime Minister's residence. When the

Prime Minister walked into a very crowded room, he stood to inform us that he had returned from the Presidency a couple of hours earlier, where it had been decided between him, the Army Chief and President Ghulam Ishaq, that the President and the Prime Minister both resign, and under a new non-partisan caretaker government to be headed by Moeen Qureshi, with a technocratic team of Ministers, oversee a mid-term election, after dissolution of the national and the provincial assemblies. The Americans had been right.

The two-year gap required under the law between my ambassadorial assignment and the elections being legal requirement, dejected me, because I was going to miss another Assembly, but my spirits lifted when the interim government published a list of people who had defaulted on their bank loans, and Faisal Hayat's name featured prominently in these lists. Since bank defaulters were not qualified under the law to seek representation, my opponent Faisal Hayat would not be qualified for the contest either. My thought was that if my mother agreed, her nomination papers could be filed, I would campaign on her behalf, and she would probably make a wiser representative than myself, and if she felt like withdrawing after a couple of years, I could come in on a bye-election. On the other hand, if she wanted to see the term through, I would have more time for Fakhar and the children, and work in the constituency, and manage the farm.

Mother was reluctant, and suggested I file my papers and she would be my covering candidate. If my papers got rejected, then she would stand in for me for two years. She argued that having spent more of my personal money than what government had allocated to me for my ambassadorial assignment in the US, the court would surely take this into account. My lawyers thought I would have a slim fighting chance of getting my papers through, but Faisal Hayat's would definitely be rejected.

The Returning Officer did reject my papers and those of Faisal Hayat, but my mother's papers got through. Faisal filed an appeal in the election Tribunal, as did I, but the page on which his name was listed was nicked out of the voluminous bank records placed before the Tribunal, which rejected my papers and passed his!

I campaigned vigorously on Mother's behalf—who appeared only at the rallies—while the canvassing was almost entirely handled by me. When she was cheered at the rallies, I saw the tears rolling down her face. She would look at me endearingly, and say that all the cheering was due to my hard work and sweat. I would embrace her, and assure her that it was she who gave me the impetus to learn how to sweat. The campaign ended on a high note for us. When general elections were held on 6 October 1993, my anguish was profound when the votes were counted and Baji lost by about eight thousand votes. To compound my misery, Fakhar lost his election as well.

On 19 October 1993, Benazir Bhutto took oath as Prime Minister for a second time. She did not get Ghulam Ishaq Khan re-elected as President of Pakistan, as was expected in some quarters. Instead Sardar Farooq Ahmed Khan Leghari, the Secretary General of the Pakistan Peoples Party (PPP) was elected as President.

Fakhar and I were happy for our friend Farooq, but found ourselves out of the corridors of power for the first time in more than a decade, which disappointed our children, who were used to seeing their parents in the thick of national events. Umku was home after her graduation, mulling out different projects, seeking to avoid the heart aches that politics brought and determined to set up a business project of her own. Interested in the energy sector, she would say that she was attracted not to political power but to electric power. Shugu was gearing up to graduate from Harvard, while Abid was in his final year of High School, and applying for college, aiming to get to Yale.

Fakhar and I focused on our farming and nursing our constituencies, which was uphill because Benazir Bhutto managed to keep the PML-(N) out of power in the Punjab as well, collaborating with the breakaway faction of the Muslim League to form government in Punjab. Faisal Hayat was announced Advisor to Chief Minister Punjab, with the home and local government departments assigned to him.

After my return from the US, I had not heard from the Lashkar Jhangvi for a while. But now suddenly their threatening telephone calls were reactivated, and a home department functionary appeared at my house in Jhang to inform my employees there, that while heading towards Jhang, which I was planning to do that day, my car had hit an improvised explosive device, or IED, of the kind that were frequently found in Afgahanistan, and the car, my driver, my bodyguard and I had been blown up. My distraught employee telephoned our house in Lahore to break the news to my mother. I happened to pick up the phone and hearing my voice, he became quiet. When I pressed him to tell me why he had called, he came out with what he had been told. Reassuring him that there must have been a mistake, I decided to probe the matter a little before setting off for Jhang. The phone rang again, this time it was the superintendent of police of Jhang. He, too, paused a moment when he heard my voice, informing me that he had been given information regarding a disaster en route to Jhang in which I had been involved. When told about the functionary's message delivered at my house, he confirmed that the he was informed by the same source.

With the threatening phone calls from the same person who identified himself as Riaz Basra, and now with this disturbing message, I decided to consult my lawyer. I thought it prudent to write a letter to Prime Minister Benazir Bhutto, regarding the threat to my security. A few days later, an additional secretary from the Prime Minister's office called me, saying that the Prime Minister had received my letter and would be responding to it, but when the letter came, it was disappointingly sterile, with no mention of any remedy for my predicament. Instead it contained a lengthy paragraph on the achievements of her government and the initiatives taken for the welfare of the public. It read as though it was the standard letter sent out to everyone who sent any correspondence to her.

Riaz Basra had grown into a veritable monster and took credit for killing Shias in different localities of the country; he seemed to be beyond the reach of the law enforcers, the only remedy available to me, therefore was to have two loyal retainers as my body guards accompanying me everywhere, which was cumbersome.

Pakistan was beginning to run short of energy, a private power generation policy was announced by the government and Umku started developing a project for a small ten megawatt power plant, becoming totally immersed in learning as much as she could about the power sector. But shortly after, a series of scandalous revelations started hitting the media on how Benazir Bhutto and Asif Zardari's cronies had started floating projects of hundreds of megawatts, costing hundreds of millions of dollars that were blatant scams. Umku would go to the offices of the newly established private power board and come home wide-eyed and horrified to learn first hand of what was going on. I was disappointed that Benazir's second administration seemed to have learnt little from the errors of her first term, and were emptying the kitty of the state as the had done during their previous term.

When I went for Shugu's graduation, some people at Harvard also seemed to be aware that Benazir was being criticized again. The Commencement Speaker this time was Vice President Albert Gore, himself a Harvard graduate. It was impossible for me to reach him to remind him about his visit to Pakistan, though I made a vain effort to do so at the reception which Professor John Kenneth and Kitty Galbraith held for him in their home in Francis Avenue. Kitty tried to lead me towards him but we were pushed away by his security men. Shugu wanted to stay on in the US and work for a year. She slotted into the Council for Foreign Relations, a prestigious think-tank which published *Foreign Affairs*, a journal read by foreign policy framers worldwide.

Shugu became Programmes Assistant, working in the office of Ambassador Richard Murphy, who chaired the Council at the time. Abid made it to Yale as he had intended, making his unilateral declaration of Independence from his sisters, as he put it.

Meanwhile, in Afghanistan a dramatic new development started taking shape. Emerging out of the Wahabi centre of religious learning resourced by the Saudis, and located at Akora Khattak, near the entree to our Frontier province, known as the Madrasa Haqqania, a half blinded Afghan Mullah, named Omar, returned to his homeland heading a new phenomenon described in our media as the 'Taliban', or religious students, who swept through our neighbouring country, making people lay down arms, overtaking the warlords that had been fighting fierce internecine battles after the Cold War had ended, reducing Afghanistan into a strife torn and ravaged land.

General (retired) Naseerullah Babar, Benazir's Interior Minister, claimed credit for having supported this new phenomenon that was bringing peace to Afghanistan. While some analysts, experts, and commentators in our country sounded sceptical, others believed General Babar was doing a great job. General Babar also claimed credit for restoring peace to Karachi, by cracking down on the MQM, and forcing Altaf Hussain to flee the country seeking political asylum in Britain. Most people in Karachi seemed to feel a sense of temporary relief, for which the kudos went to Benazir Bhutto with her hard core Sindhi supporters.

Not having visited Iran since the Khomeini revolution, I was excited to receive an invitation to attend a Conference on Afghanistan being hosted in Tehran by the Foreign Minister of Iran, Dr Ali Akbar Velayati. Ambassador Moussavi the Iranian envoy to Islamabad at the time came to our residence in Islamabad to deliver the invitation personally. Before accepting the invitation, my question to him was whether my Pakistani dress code of *shalwar-kamiz* would be acceptable. I would cover my head with a *dupatta* (scarf), as a concession to the conservative values prevailing in his country, but in my view, as a visitor to his country, there was no obligation for me to adopt the Iranian 'hejab' or head-to-toe outer garment.

The ambassador appreciated my concession to covering my head, and proceeded to give me a list of the other Pakistanis invited to this conference. This included the two Shia clerics, Allama Sajid Naqvi and Maulana Iftikhar Naqvi, from district Attock, who were leading a political organization that had emerged largely as a reaction to the Sipah Sahaba, funded by the Iranians, named the Thereek-e-Fiqh Jafaria or movement for propagation of Shia law. Agha Murtaza Poya, who had been publisher of the English newspaper, *The Muslim*, and Mushahid Hussain, editor of the newspaper, were also among the invitees.

President Hashemi Rafsanjani opened the conference, convened in the Iranian ministry of foreign affairs. After the formal opening, a young woman in hejab, came up to me, uncovered half her face, and in Americanized English, introduced herself as an officer of the ministry, assigned to me for the duration of the conference. She informed me that Dr Ali Akbar Velayati would chair the first working session of the conference, after the prayer and lunch break. I was requested to chair the afternoon session. She also informed me that she was a graduate of Boston University in the US where her father had worked as a medical doctor, but was now a committed member of the Islamic Republican Party of Iran. This explained her accent. Her name was Fatimeh.

Majority of the speakers in the session that I chaired were mostly from the five Iranian-backed groups of the Afghan Mujahideen. When the session adjourned for *Asr*, or late afternoon prayer, Fatimeh led me to Dr Velayati's office, who informed me that while I was in the chair, the 'Maulaneh' (plural of Maulana in Persian) Naqvi, had questioned why Abida Hussain was being honoured and not them, whereupon they were informed that 'Khanum Abideh', the Iranian way of acknowledging me, was not on anyone's payroll!

During the concluding session of the of the first day of the conference, Fatimeh seated me next to another young woman in hejab who introduced herself as Fatimeh Hashemi, whispering in my ear that she wanted me to meet her mother. I whispered back that I would be happy to meet her, if she could take me to her home at the end of this session. She said to me that since she would be working late, her friend Fatimeh would take me. Exiting from the ministry my escort now led me to a black Mercedes parked right in front. Seating myself in the car with dark tinted glasses, with Fatimeh beside me, finally exposing her full round and perky face, Fatimeh told me that it was Jamraan where we were going and where Ayatullah Khomeini had lived before settling in Qom, and where President Rafsanjani now lived. She told me that it would take us at least half an hour, way up the hillside beyond Shimraan, therefore I should relax. Somewhat confused, I asked Fatimeh whether her friend and colleague's full name was Fatimeh Hashemi Rafsanjani. My escort nodded, telling me that the president's daughter was a good friend and her namesake, but they worked in different departments of the ministry. She was working in the Political Department, while Fatimeh Hashemi, being an outstanding sportswoman, worked in the Department for the Promotion of International Sports. She then proceeded to tell me that Jamraan was a village and the car would stop outside the entrance to the village so she hoped I would not mind walking through the village alleys. Reassuring her that I was used to walking in village alleys since my own home was in a village, at which she queried how I had gone to the US as Ambassador if I came from a village. My narrative had barely begun when the car came to a halt and my escort quickly covering her face, hopped out of the car informing me that we had reached Jamraan.

The narrow, paved alleys we walked through made me feel as though we were in Shah Jewna: lots of children running around, young lads loitering about, the chatter. We came to a low stone wall, with a wide iron gate, sentry boxes on either side, with the sentry's slouching and smoking, Fatimeh showing her Identification Card card to them. One look at her card and they straightened up, opened the gate smartly, letting us in with a 'Salaam, Khanum'.

Walking through a couple of really narrow lanes, we now faced a higher wall, with barbed wire rolls atop, a simple iron gate and sentries, two on either side, more alert, I.D. check and gates opened, immediately beyond which we entered a well-lit room, as it was dark outside by now, with two men and two women to run a security check. The women did a thorough probe of Fatimeh's handbag, but did not look at mine, saying 'Chashm Khanum Abideh Mujahideh'. Dr Velayati had also introduced me similarly when I had taken the chair at the conference, mentioning my electoral victory over the killers of their diplomat Aghae Sadegh Ganji. As Fatimeh and I stepped out of this room, with our shoes having been removed and bagged neatly by the security women for us to carry, we went in through an immense doorway in front of us, entering what was clearly an Imambargah. Beautifully carpeted with large, well-worn rugs, and the lovely smell of incense emitting from long thin incense sticks in ornate brass stands along the walls painted with exquisite calligraphy, and a series of large blown glass chandeliers, we walked through the large hall, at the end of which we exited out of a small door into a tiny courtyard, at the end of which was a modest and plain house. A lady was standing in the doorway. Taking my shoes out of the bag and quickly slipping them on, I saw that the woman in the doorway was middle aged, taller and fatter than myself, with short hennaed hair, wearing a plain, knee length black dress and black stockings. She greeted me with a '*khush amideed*' (Persian for 'welcome'; literally, 'happy arrival').

This was my first encounter with the First Lady of Iran, Khanum Hashemi Rafsanjani. She embraced me, and led me by the hand through her tiny hallway, into a small sitting room with deep upholstered sofas, and low brass tables. Seating me on a sofa, she asked Fatimeh to remove her hejab and to sit beside me while she brought her 'honoured guest', Iranian '*quehwah*', or green mint tea. She returned from her small kitchen, balancing two trays on her hands, one with three small glasses of tea, and three bowls of pistachio nuts on the other, and seated herself on the sofa opposite us. She then made a formal statement welcoming me, not only because of my courage in contesting elections, but also because my husband had been Speaker of Parliament, as her own husband was before he was elected President. Very candidly, I told her how impressive the simplicity of their lifestyle was, and how it reflected the true spirit of our faith. Being a Shia, it made me feel even more proud. It made me hopeful that in Pakistan we would make good progress if we were to follow the example of Iranian leadership and make our own lifestyles more modest. To this her response was that it was wrong for us to be divisive in faith, in Iran there were no Shia nor Sunni, only Musulmaan, and that modesty was an Islamic requirement, along with simplicity. She added that while the Islamic Republic of Iran had made good progress, they had a great deal that needed to be done, especially for women, and she admired Pakistan for the progress of its women.

My four-day visit to Iran was inspirational. It had included a one-day visit to Meshed, where I felt my father's presence acutely, and dreamt of him for the first time in many years.

However, in the meanwhile, Benazir Bhutto had run into trouble with her brother, Mir Murtaza Bhutto. After the elimination of their father, Zulfikar Ali Bhutto, Murtaza and Shahnawaz, Bhutto's sons, had hijacked a plane that was diverted to Kabul. After spending some time in Eastern European capitals, the brothers had eventually landed in South of France. There, Shahnawaz had lost his life somewhat mysteriously, but Murtaza had eventually returned to Pakistan just before the 1993 elections. He was elected member of the Sindh Assembly, had a falling out with his sister, and had floated his own faction of the Pakistan Peoples Party (PPP), which our friend Makhdum Khaliquzaman of Hala had joined.

Khaliquzaman and Murtaza were both in Islamabad, when the former called me to ask if they could drop by for a cup of coffee. I told him that Fakhar had left for Multan, but I was home and would be happy to meet the son of my late benefactor. Umku was home and joined us, when Khaliquzaman and Murtaza arrived. Murtaza was tall and handsome, and blossomed when Umku told him that one of his classmates at Harvard had been her teaching fellow and always spoke about him and said he was a very good student. Murtaza emphasized that he had been a better student than his sister, she had always had a threat perception from him and although he loved her dearly, he felt she really did not know how to govern and had become intolerant hence they had politely parted company. Since then she had him followed around by her intelligence hounds. Murtaza asked me why I had left the PPP and heard me out patiently. It was a short and pleasant meeting. He hoped that we would meet again, and he would be really happy if I would consider joining his party, because in his opinion, Mian Nawaz Sharif was much too conservative, and in the long run, I could find it difficult to work with him. Seeing him out, I noticed several intelligence vehicles parked on the road outside our house.

Benazir Bhutto's government had logged close to three years, during which time it had lost most of its gloss, when my mother, Fakhar, and I received wedding invitations for the marriage of

Awais Leghari, Farooq Leghari's younger son. The wedding was held at the Presidency. It was segregated, with the men in one hall and the women in the other. As Mother and I entered the women's hall, Farooq's eldest sister received us, and led my mother to the front row, to seat her next to her own mother. Benazir was seated on the raised dais, next to the bride, facing the gathering of women. Farooq's younger sister was my age, and who had been a playmate of mine in our childhood in the 1950s, when our respective fathers served in the same cabinet, we were allotted houses next to each other. She seated me next to Nilofer, spouse of Ali Kuli Khan, now a general in the Pakistan Army, who had been a classmate of Fakhar's at Aitchison College, before Fakhar had left for school in England. He and Ali had always remained friends. Farooq was a year senior to them at Aitchison, with the three of them having bonded down the years. Nilofer had the Army Chief's wife sitting next to her. We were introduced and were chatting away when I noticed that it seemed to cause discomfort to some of the women who were a part of Benazir Bhutto's team. As we walked to the dinner tables, with these women shadowing me and the wives of the generals, Nasreen, Farooq's wife came up to hug me, and said that I should visit her at the residence of the Presidency some time. This was overheard by the women shadowing me, who looked positively dismayed. Nasreen noticed, and turning towards them said that politics aside, I was like a sister to her and to Farooq, and our families went a long way back.

Not long after this, my good friend and also my lawyer, Shahid Hamid, who had been a batch mate in the civil service with Farooq Leghari and was now his lawyer as well, met me and said that the president wanted to see me, but the visit, would have to be kept under wraps. The newspapers had been reporting that Benazir Bhutto had locked horns with President Farooq Leghari over the appointment of the new army chief. General Abdul Waheed Kakar had completed his three years as Chief of Army Staff. The prime minister offered him an extension, but being a principled officer, General Kakar refused, earning wide respect for himself as well as for his institution. The senior most general after the outgoing chief was General Jahangir Karamat, who was well reputed, a good soldier, and apparently considered to be something of an intellectual in military circles. Benazir Bhutto allegedly had a threat perception from him and wanted either one of two junior generals, considered to be more malleable, to be appointed by the president. This seemed like a repeat of the Nawaz Sharif/Ghulam Ishaq tussle over the appointment of Army Chief, which I had chatted earlier with Shahid Hamid about, assuming that Farooq Leghari would have the persuasive capacity to convince Benazir that senior most general would be safe; a secondary choice could always turn out to be another Zia against another Bhutto. Shahid mentioned that in all probability Farooq would have suggested just this, but the press indicated that the appointment issue had complicated the relationship between the President and the Prime Minister.

On the appointed day, Shahid Hamid drove me in his own car to the Presidency. At the gate he gave his own name, and the second name given was Bahadur Khan, which was not the name of the driver, but Shahid said this was the name that Shamshir Khan, the secretary to the President, also a batch mate of theirs, who had stuck to the civil service, had decided to confer on me, this being his idea of a joke. Shahid and I entered the Presidency laughing, with Shamshir there to greet us, addressing me, not as Bahadur Khan mercifully, but as Begum Fakhar Imam. Farooq Ahmad Leghari was formal, yet warm, as always, telling me how happy he was that my mother had come especially from Lahore to attend his son's wedding, and how my presence had set the cat among the pigeons, according to his wife. He suggested that his wife would welcome a visit from me sometime soon. After this we talked about the faltering economy, with me expressing concern lest our loans be recalled. He shared my concern, saying that the leader of the opposition, Mian Nawaz Sharif should attend the assembly more often and exert due pressure on the government, which would give democracy some meaning. He also said that Nawaz Sharif kept sending messages that he wanted to meet with him, but it would be more suitable for him to first meet with Shahid Hamid at my house, and in the presence of Fakhar and myself to iron out some issues, before he could receive the opposition leader in the Presidency.

The meeting was arranged at our house. Shahid Hamid, Fakhar and I were sitting together when Nisar Ali and Sartaj Aziz walked in, accompanying Mian Nawaz Sharif. Shahid told Nawaz Sharif that Majid Nizami, editor of the leading Urdu daily, *Nawaiwaqt*, had called on the president and requested him that he receive the leader of the opposition, but while the president felt that it was the right of the opposition leader to call on the president and be received by him in all courtesy, in accordance with parliamentary norms, nearly three years had lapsed and previous to this the opposition leader had never requested such a meeting. The resident had then asked to see Abida Bibi, who was a close family friend, to visit with him, and suggested that we have this meeting today to work out the modalities for the visit, as Prime Minister Benazir Bhutto would not look favourably on such a meeting, which would certainly be covered by the media and lead to all sorts of speculation. Mian Nawaz Sharif told Shahid Hamid that the Prime Minister having brought in a new and completely incompetent Chief Minister in the Punjab, Sardar Arif Nakai, was putting the PML-(N) MPAs backs to the wall and they were pressing him, their party leader, to resign from the assemblies and force a fresh election. Also, with the federal government running the economy into the ground, the chambers of commerce in Punjab were mounting pressure on him as well to quit the assembly and launch an agitation. He wanted to bring all this to the notice of the president. Shahid Hamid being the clever lawyer that he was, suggested to Mian Nawaz Sharif that he should take a well-drafted Memorandum for the consideration of the President, but it should not appear as though the opposition leader were making a threat, as the President obviously would not take kindly to that.

Mian Nawaz Sharif asked Sartaj Aziz to draw up the Memorandum and run it by all of us, including Shahid Hamid, after which, perhaps, a date could be fixed for him to meet with the President. Shahid said he would discuss the matter with the president who would let Abida Bibi know, in whom he reposed great trust, and who would be calling on the president's wife in the next few days. Shahid went on to add that it was prudent to be cautious, and in everybody's interest to use a bridge, which would perhaps provoke less curiosity.

Feeling slightly queasy, because of really not knowing who Riaz Basra and his ilk might be working for, I thought of telling Nasreen Leghari, when calling on her, that perhaps the president could arrange some security for me. Nasreen was not convinced of the wisdom of Farooq's decision to meet Nawaz Sharif, as she passed on his message regarding the meeting, but being the decent person that she was, she assured me that she would sensitize him to my concern regarding security. Her worry was that Farooq Leghari had been on the side of the Pakistan Peoples Party for a long time, had suffered for it, then been rewarded by it, and although Benazir no longer listened to him, this leap into the unknown that he was taking could backfire. I did my best to assure her that Farooq Leghari having a sturdy head on his shoulders, would never do anything without careful thought, a great deal would depend on how his meeting with Nawaz Sharif proceeded, and on what the president perceived to be in the best interest of Pakistan.

At the beginning, the meeting was fairly stiff, then eased up when the president assured us that he would examine our Memorandum carefully, and although he had a concern for the economy, he was on record for being against the Article 58-2(b) of the Constitution. All of us who accompanied Nawaz Sharif were of the opinion, when we mulled over the meeting, after leaving the Presidency, that despite having expressed his reservation, the president's mention of the relevant Article meant that at least he was thinking about it.

Not long after our visit to the Presidency, Chaudhry Nisar Ali called to say that Mian Sharif, father of Nawaz and Shahbaz Sharif had invited me up to Murree for lunch. It was mid September by now, and the Sharif family usually spent this month in their house in the hills. Never having met the gentleman popularly referred to as 'Abbaji', I was naturally curious. Nisar Ali said he would drive me up himself. It was a surprise for me to see that he had Shahid Hamid with him, neither of them forthcoming on why we had been invited. The drive up from Islamabad to Murree was consumed by the amusing bits of my narrative of our abortive no-confidence against Benazir's first administration, with Nisar telling Shahid that this time around the only remedy was dissolution of the assemblies, and Shahid laughing away, saying he could not promise anything. We reached Murree and went up to the Kashmir Point. Driving in the direction of the Mall; Nisar Ali veered the car sharply left, down a steep curve, and stopped.

We alighted, and went further down a bank of stairs, and the house was right before us. It was a bland and newish bungalow. A short, elderly gentleman was standing in the doorway. This could only be our host, Mian Sharif, who, surprisingly, kissed me on my forehead and holding on to my arm, led me into the house, saying what a fortunate day it was for him that late Colonel Syed Abid Hussain Shah's daughter was gracing his home. Beyond the small hallway, in a large sitting room with enormous windows and a stunning view of the hills, Mian Nawaz and Shahbaz Sharif appeared, nattily turned out in their customary starched *shalwar-kamiz* and waistcoat. They lifted themselves out of ornate sofas, which looked a little out of place in this setting, and came forward to greet us. Mian Sharif seated me next to himself, and after the customary exchange of pleasantries with Nisar and Shahid; he narrated the story of when he had first met my father, riveting in his simplicity.

It was way back in 1954. A tall, handsome suited-booted gentleman entered what was then Mian Sharif's small foundry. Syed Abid Hussain Shah was a minister in the central government at the time. He asked him to drive down with him to his estate in Shah Jewna, to install a tube-well, which he agreed to do. Abid Hussain Shah sat on a simple cot to supervise the installation himself, and was most gracious in every way. A year or so later Abid Hussain visited his foundry again, this time accompanied by an equally tall and handsome gentleman, also suited-booted. He introduced the gentleman as his brother, Sardar Mohammed Khan Leghari, requesting Mian Sharif to install a tube-well at Choti Zareen, located in the Dera Ghazi Khan district, and the ancestral town of the Legharis. Mian Sharif went on to emphasize that Sardar Mohammed Khan and my father were truly like brothers. Therefore the present President of Pakistan, Sardar Farooq Ahmed Khan Leghari would be looking upon me as a sister and would never refuse me a favour. And the favour that Mian Sharif requested me to ask was that the president put aside whatever grudges he bore against his sons, and he, Mian Sharif, a humble and God fearing man, would always remain beholden to Sardar Farooq Ahmed Khan Leghari and Syeda Bibi Abida Hussain.

This statement of Mian Sharif, premised on disarming humility, was so compelling that I promised him I would seek to persuade the president that he extend an invitation to Mian Sharif to visit with him, because his direct approach would be more persuasive than my advocacy on his behalf.

President Leghari was as charmed by Mian Sharif as I had been a few days earlier, when he called me for another visit to the Presidency. He was also deeply concerned about further deterioration in the economy. Benazir was ballistic with him since he had received Nawaz Sharif, and kept sending him rude messages. Leghari was in a dilemma, and suggested that Shamshir Khan and Shahid Hamid meet with Shahbaz Sharif and Nisar Ali at my place and discuss with them whether they had a deadline on resignations, or whether this was a mere threat to provoke a reaction from him. Nisar and Shahbaz were due to arrive, when Shahid appeared telling me that caution demanded that we meet in the home of a friend, which was around the corner from my house, on the main Margalla Road. He also suggested we take a detour, in case we were being tailed, mentioning that Masood Sharif, Director Intelligence Bureau, was monitoring telephones, suspecting something, and had code named me 'Slim Jim'. I had never met Masood Sharif, but now had a curiosity about him because clearly this was someone with a sense of humour.

The friend in whose home we met was Farouk Majeed whose sister was married to my mother's cousin, and whose uncle was our friend, Khwaja Rahman. Farouk was extremely hospitable, seated us in his sitting room, served us an elaborate tea, and withdrew. Shamshir explained that our host was very reliable, totally discreet, and had no interest in our conversation. He asked Nisar Ali whether there was a time-line on the resignations, to which Nisar answered that their members of the Punjab Assembly would be resigning within a week. Shahbaz looked a little taken aback. We adjourned shortly thereafter, and drove back to my house, where Nisar Ali explained to Shahbaz that in this game of poker that we were playing, the president had shown his hand by sending Shamshir, who was, after all risking his job, because the Prime Minister could suspend him, or at a minimum transfer him.

Fakhar had joined us and concurred with Nisar. My thought was that having said it, Nisar and Shahbaz would now have to deliver and make sure the resignations of the MPAs were obtained and submitted within the week. Shahbaz said that he and his brother would get to Lahore immediately and try to manage it in less than a week, provided this would ensure dissolution. Nisar and I thought it was a risk worth taking, as it would force the hand of the president, who was on the brink, but needed a solid justification for dissolution of the assembly, and a week or two after the MPAs, the MNAs would also need to resign, as such a large number of bye elections would be logistically difficult, though not impossible. Benazir, we thought was capable of taking the risk of announcing bye-elections, but if the president dissolved the legislature in such a scenario, the Supreme Court would uphold the dissolution order.

The fat was in the fire, and we would not have to wait long for events to unfold.

The 22nd of September was Mother's birthday. The previous year I had a birthday dinner for her followed by a musical evening of Abida Parveen, our great Sufi singer, in the garden of our home at Lahore. It was attended by Frank and Christine Wisner coming in from Delhi, since Frank was now the US Ambassador to India. I had taken Frank to meet Mian Nawaz Sharif at Islamabad. Frank had come to my house, expecting to meet Nawaz Sharif there, but the venue of the meeting was Chaudhry Shujaat Hussain's house. En route Frank asked me why we were relocating, to which I mentioned that being from a back ground with wealth achieved by his father not that long ago, Nawaz Sharif found my house in Islamabad too modest and the home we were going to was much larger, belonging to another nouveaux colleague, where Nawaz felt more comfortable. When Frank saw Shujaat's ornate, gargantuan entrance door, he observed that this was not nouveaux, it was 'yesterday'!

Nawaz Sharif had Mushahid Hussain and Akram Zaki in attendance, along with the host, Chaudhry Shujaat. Frank was seated beside Nawaz Sharif whose hand he held and in his typical southern and courtly style, kept addressing him as Prime Minister, which obviously appealed to Mian Nawaz Sharif, who felt so prime ministerial that when Frank conveyed to Nawaz Indian Foreign Minister I. K. Gujral's greetings, Nawaz responded by saying he really liked Gujral and was thinking of inviting him to Pakistan. With a dismayed expression, Frank told Nawaz that it may be awkward for the Indian Foreign Minister to accept the invitation of the opposition leader of Pakistan, to which Nawaz confessed ruefully that for a moment he had forgotten he was not the prime minister!

A year later, we were plotting to get Nawaz back as prime minister, persuaded that he would fare better than Benazir. To achieve this end, Shamshir, Shahid Hamid, Chaudhry Nisar, Shahbaz Sharif and I were meeting in Farouk Majeed's house. Nisar was saying to Shamshir that it had already been several days since the resignation of the MPAs, and what must the president now be contemplating. Before he could respond, Farouk Majeed burst into the room to inform us that the television had just announced that Murtaza Bhutto had been shot in the street outside his home in Karachi, and had been taken to the hospital. It was 20 September 1996. Shamshir went out to make a phone call and then left. We sat in silence for a bit, sobered by the dreadful news, and then adjourned to our respective abodes.

When I reached my house, Umku was sitting riveted to the television on which the horrific details of Murtaza's murder were being highlighted. Murtaza Bhutto's vehicle was ambushed and fired at near his home, 70 Clifton, in Karachi. Bhutto was taken to a private hospital nearby. Ghulam Mustafa Jatoi's nephew, Ashiq Jatoi, who was sitting next to Murtaza was shot as well and died on the spot. Prime Minister Benazir Bhutto was at the Islamabad airport leaving for Karachi. The President was also at the airport.

Mother called me and asked me to cancel her birthday dinner that I was planning. Although she did not know the young man, she said to me, the Bhutto family had suffered enough tragedies already, and she could not bear the thought of a celebration in her house in the wake of such a calamity. Umku was crying. I tried to reassure my mother and my daughter, but was very confused when the television announced that the Prime Minister had reached Karachi, and had first gone to the Bilawal House, her residence, and then to the Mid-East Hospital where her brother had been taken. Murtaza breathed his last, just as she was entering the hospital.

The question that all our friends who were dropping in by now, were posing was: why did the Prime Minister not order for her brother to be moved to Jinnah Hospital which had far better emergency facilities, as soon as she got the news, and why did she not go straight to the hospital from the airport. I kept insisting that it was because Murtaza's wife Ghinwa Bhutto was there. She and Benazir's relations were strained. With Ghinwa in charge, what could Benazir have done. After all prime ministers are human, and to err is human was my thought, while my friends were less charitable, as were most people who did not care for Benazir Bhutto or her spouse Asif Ali Zardari.

Murtaza Bhutto's gruesome death sent a wave of horror throughout the country. The newspapers reported that his body was flown to Larkana for burial, and he was laid to rest beside his father Zulfikar Ali Bhutto and brother Shahnawaz Bhutto. The only surviving male of Z. A. Bhutto's lineage now was Murtaza's baby boy, named after his grandfather i.e. Zulfikar. Conspiracy theories on who may have been behind this tragedy abounded and there was little talk of anything else for days. Benazir returned to the capital and held a prayer for her brother. She was crying while giving her speech that was watched by millions of Pakistanis. She, more or less, laid the blame at the doorstep of the Establishment, her finger seemingly pointing towards the Presidency.

It was November 1996. Chaudhry Nisar Ali and Shahbaz Sharif dropped by to mull over the situation with me. We concluded that the president now had little option but to hold whatever he may have been contemplating in abeyance. However, to our great surprise, within a relatively short span of time, Shahid Hamid asked us to join him and Shamshir at Farouk Majeed's house where they informed us that the President had signed the order to dissolve the National Assembly of Pakistan, and would be appointing Malik Meraj Khalid, former Speaker of the National Assembly, as the Caretaker Prime Minister.

Late at night, Mian Nawaz Sharif telephoned me to say that the president had called him and suggested that he nominate me for a cabinet position in the Interim Government, and that he would also take one member of the PPP in the cabinet, the rest of the cabinet would be comprised of technocrats. My response to him was that since I wanted to contest election I would have to withdraw from the cabinet, when the election schedule would be announced, to which he said that if that were my decision, he would not deter me when the moment came, but for the time being I should take the cabinet position as he trusted me to protect our common interests, to ensure a level playing field for the elections.

Malik Meraj Khalid was a dear man, and I was happy to serve under him, as I took oath for the second time in the caretaker government, confident that in the forthcoming election I would win my constituency back. It was a small cabinet in which several ministries were clubbed together, with the portfolios of education, culture, sports and tourism, science and technology, coming to me. Although this was a holding operation, I was snowed under a mass of files and asked to head several sub committees of the cabinet, which were holding inquiries into cases of graft and mal practises of the outgoing government. I found myself working long and late hours once again and tried my best to discharge myself of my duties adequately. A month flew by; a controversy developed regarding loan defaulters, with the law minister proposing that anyone on the board of a company with loan defaults be disbarred from contesting. The Prime Minister and the rest of the cabinet took the view that anyone holding beyond thirty-three per cent shares should be disbarred, but minority share holders be exempted. On this issue the law minister, a well reputed lawyer and former judge of the Sindh High Court, tendered his resignation from the cabinet, as a result of which the dissolution order of the President pended in the Supreme Court for several weeks, upheld finally a fortnight before the polls. Just before the election schedule was announced, I called on the President, to request him to allow me to withdraw from the cabinet as he had announced that members of the interim government would not be eligible for contesting the election.

President Leghari told me that he was worried for my security, and if Mian Nawaz Sharif was willing to give me a Senate nomination, it would be prudent for me to continue in the Cabinet. But I told the President that my desire to vindicate my defeat was a paramount consideration which would enable me to win my constituency back, my rival's popularity being at an all time low, and it would be preferable for me to carry my own weight politically, instead of being obliged to my party leadership, as a nominee. With the President finally agreeing I tendered my resignation to the Prime Minister who told me he would miss me and I knew he meant it, our regard for each other having endured for twenty-five years, when we were on the same side of the political divide, as well as when we were on opposing sides.

It was a blistering campaign. My rival seemed to have accumulated considerable wherewithal, and threw resources into the campaign which were not possible for me to match, but the Pakistan Peoples Party's popularity was at an all time low. The buzz was that the PML-(N) was going to form the next government. My campaign picked up considerable steam when the President's Dissolution Order was upheld, because the PPP had been propagating that this would not happen and the elections would not go through. The final swing came in my favour in a big way, delivering my constituency back to me by a margin of twenty-four thousand votes. The PPP was routed in the Punjab, and even fared relatively poorly in Sindh. The PML-(N) ended up winning a two-third majority, first time in our sketchy political history, a grand victory was scored by PML-(N).

As the results poured in, my haveli in Shah Jewna became choked with my supporters and the drums were beaten through the night, heralding my victory. Elated and exhausted, sharing my triumph with my daughters, cousin Maryam, and my friend Bunny, I finally passed out in the early hours of the morning, to be roused by the drums just a few hours later with constituents arriving from everywhere with boxes and baskets of *mithai* (sweets) and everyone joining in a *bhangra* in my courtyard throughout the day. The celebratory mood of my supporters engulfed me for several days, but there was a large fly in my ointment, as during the campaign there had been a serious disaster in Fakhar's constituency. Ziaur Rahman Farooqi, who was the Secretary General of the Sipah Sahaba, had filed his papers in Kabirwala as candidate for the National Assembly, was visiting Lahore for a court appearance during the campaign, when he was blown up in a bomb attack, and the election was held in abeyance until March. Fakhar won his constituency back, but we were denied the pleasure of walking into the assembly together to take oath.

During the polling week, for security reasons, Fakhar was grounded in Lahore, so before going to take oath in Islamabad I stopped in Lahore to see him and Mother, whose favourite brother, Uncle Amjad Ali, was seriously ill. Mother herself was not keeping well, and had not been with me during my campaign.

Fakhar and I called Mian Nawaz Sharif to congratulate him, who sounded overjoyed on the telephone and asked us to visit him early the following morning as he wanted to consult with us on some issues. When we entered his house in Model Town, he hugged both Fakhar and me warmly, saying that he did not doubt that Fakhar would soon be with us in the National Assembly. But at this moment he had called us to get our feedback on a scheme that someone had suggested to him. It was regarding launching a scheme to urge overseas Pakistanis as well as those of us who lived in Pakistan to contribute generously toward a debt retirement fund he planned to announce right after his oath taking ceremony. Fakhar said that he should announce a fund but it would yield only a few hundred million dollars, while given the state of the economy, we needed a moratorium on our foreign debt, or at a minimum a serious rescheduling. Agreeing with Fakhar, I suggested that if he were to visit the World Bank and the IMF (International Monetary Fund) in Washington, immediately after taking oath as Prime Minister, with his massive victory not lost on the lenders nor on the US government, he was bound to be conceded massive relief. But Nawaz Sharif's view was that he would only go to the US when he was officially invited. He then said that he planned to initially form a small Cabinet, and that I would be part of it. If Fakhar's election had not been stuck he would have been the natural choice for Speaker. My comment to him was that it did not matter who he appointed, as long as the key positions were given to those who were honest and competent and fiercely patriotic, and he should consult with President Farooq Leghari who had great goodwill for all of us now, and understood governance issues well. My statement produced an displeasure on Nawaz's face, noticed by both Fakhar and me, making us wonder why he should look unhappy at mention of Farooq's name.

My daughters were in the gallery for my oath taking, looking ever so happy, which warmed my heart. We took oath, and the register signing started. When the leader of the opposition, Benazir Bhutto, led her mother towards the dais to sign the register of membership, holding her by the hand, I went up to pay my respects to Begum Nusrat Bhutto. Begum Bhutto had a vacant look in her eyes. Benazir told her my name, asking her if she remembered me, to which Begum Bhutto said that she remembered nothing. Benazir then informed me that her mother was suffering from early Alzheimer's, which is what Ghinwa Bhutto had said when I had gone to 70 Clifton, in Karachi to condole with her for Mir Murtaza Bhutto, prior to the elections. A wave of sadness swept over me, while expressing my sympathy with Benazir, and hearing from her that her mother had mercifully not quite registered the latest tragedy that had befallen their family. This encounter momentarily took away the triumph of the moment from me. But my colleagues did not appear to share my sentiment.

After installation of the assembly and a short session, we adjourned for a few weeks, during which time, I went down to Lahore to see my Uncle Amjad Ali whose health, my mother informed me, had taken a turn for the worse. By now he was in his late eighties. Standing by his bedside, I recalled his visit with me in Washington, in the residence which he had occupied all those years earlier. He was with me for his eighty-fifth birthday and I had organized a birthday dinner party for him. Knowing his penchant for pretty young girls, inviting all the lovelies available, including a stunning young Afghan woman who worked in Congressman Charlie Wilson's office, and had been crowned 'Miss Nebraska' a couple of years earlier, I earned a big 'thank you, Chando' from my favourite uncle who was delighted, making the Afghan/Nebraskan sit beside himself the entire evening. The recall made me smile, as he opened his eyes, to tell me in a fading voice, that he was very happy to hear that I was back in the National Assembly, and now would Nawaz Sharif make me foreign minister? My response to his question was that it was rumoured he had decided on Gohar Ayub, which seemed to disappoint him.

The following day, Nawaz Sharif, who was on very friendly terms with Uncle Amjad Ali's youngest son, Yawar Ali, came to inquire after his health and asked me what my travel plans were. Not having completed my rounds of gratitude in my constituency I mentioned my intent of remaining in Jhang till his summoning of the National Assembly. He responded that my presence in Islamabad would be required sooner, as the Cabinet would be sworn in within a few days. My response was that since he was taking Gohar Ayub as foreign minister according to rumours circulating, my interest would be either to head the Accountability Bureau he had pledged he would establish, or a Population Welfare Commission which he could consider establishing. He made no response to my suggestion, only said that he would be seeing me soon.

Mother, with her own health deteriorating, was very anxious about her brother, so after spending a couple of days with her in Lahore, I returned to my constituency, as I had organized a big feast for my supporters at my farm, after which my gratitude rounds in homes of my key supporters began. During the first day of these visits, I was sitting with my constituents in a remote community near the River Jhelum, when my assistant from Shah Jewna House arrived to inform me that the Prime Minister's office had been calling to say that he had sent his own aircraft to Faisalabad, the closest airport to Jhang, to fly me into Islamabad to take oath in the Cabinet which was being sworn in that evening. The entire community seemed to be thrilled to hear this news, hustling me into my car without further ado, refusing to hear me express my disinclination, many of the folk suggesting that joining the Cabinet was a must, subsequent to which a resignation could be considered at a moment of my choosing.

As I boarded the Prime Minister's jet, the pilot informed me that he had been receiving anxious calls from the premier's office wanting to know our arrival time. The oath had been scheduled for 7 p.m., but since it was already close to 7 p.m., the oath taking ceremony was rescheduled for 9 p.m.

As we landed I requested the pilot to give the control tower the telephone number of my house and leave a message for my daughters to drive straight to the Presidency, and wait for me at the gate, to join me in my car and accompany me for the ceremony. No sooner had I taken position at the cabinet table, with Nisar Ali saying that having missed the 7 o'clock news, it was just as well we were going to feature in the 9 o'clock bulletins, when President Farooq Ahmad Khan Leghari and Prime Minister Nawaz Sharif walked onto the dais to administer oath to the eight of us: with four each standing on either side of the table. My assignment was population welfare, women's development and social welfare, environment, and rural development. Nobody seemed to have been assigned food and agriculture.

The oath having been taken, my query to the Special Assistant to Prime Minister, Anwar Zahid, was regarding who had been given food and agriculture. He confessed that food and agriculture had been forgotten, which was a terrible oversight on his part, and since I was the only cabinet member actively engaged in agriculture, he would have to assign it to me. My protest that this would be an overload brought forth the reassurance from him that the cabinet would be expanded in a few weeks, and my work load would be considerably reduced, so as a trusted member of the Prime Minister's team, I would have to grin and bear it.

There were congratulations all around. Then the President and Prime Minister led the way to the reception hall for tea. Both of them asked me to share the moment with them which was recorded by a photograph, with me holding a cup with the President pouring the tea; and the Prime Minister concurrently pouring milk into my cup. And in that moment, my cup literally and figuratively, flowed over.

13

Winner Turns Loser

With a plethora of ministries to cope with, I asked for and obtained an office in the premises of the cabinet division, the most beautiful of the triad which constitutes our capital, the Presidency at the apex, with the Parliament and Cabinet Division buildings below it and parallel to each other. While my office was being set up, I went to Lahore. Uncle Amjad Ali's health condition was precarious.

I found out via newspaper headlines that the Government of Pakistan had recognized the Taliban government which had just assumed power in Afghanistan. This news was upsetting to the extreme. The Taliban turned out to be virulently anti-women, anti-history, anti culture, with a narrow Wahabi vision, why would we want to recognize their government and make such an obvious mistake at the very start? A cabinet meeting, our first after our installation, was called the following day. After recitation of the Holy Quran, I immediately raised the issue of recognizing the Taliban government in Afghanistan, reminding Prime Minister Nawaz Sharif that since 'government' in a parliamentary system meant the cabinet, that was meeting as of right now, hence, which government had recognized the Taliban government in Afghanistan? Before the Prime Minister could respond, Gohar Ayub Khan who was Foreign Minister spoke up, saying that the Prime Minister had discussed the matter with him, which made me observe that the Prime Minister and Foreign minister did not constitute the entire cabinet. The Prime Minister then informed us that General Hamid Gul had telephoned him to suggest that it would be in Pakistan's interest to be the first government in the world to recognize the Taliban government as this would pay our country rich dividends in the future. The Foreign Minister who was of the same view. He was now requesting the cabinet to endorse the decision, but in the future, he would consult the cabinet first. He then asked Gohar Ayub which other governments had recognized the new Afghan government, who said that Saudi Arabia and Kuwait were the only ones so far.

The Ministry of Food, Agriculture, and Livestock (MINFAL) consumed the major portion of my time, with a looming shortage of wheat potentially pitting our new government into a crisis. The orders for import of wheat were booked normally in November, but in this case because the caretaker minister was new to the assignment, as was his secretary, and the orders had gone into a crucial four-week delay, the ships bringing in the grain would not be docking at the Karachi port before late May. Our reserve stocks had been depleted by the previous government, and because of a late cycle of spring rain, the new crop would not start coming in before late April or early May. We were already in early March, and could hit a fortnight in April with no wheat available in our country. This ghastly nightmare was staring me in the face, when Secretary Mahbub placed the data before me. I was wondering who we could turn to when my private secretary informed me that the agriculture attaché from the US Embassy, to whom an appointment had been given, had arrived and was waiting. He was shown in, a young African American, Maurice House, who informed me that the World Food Programme (WFP) folk kept a reserve from which we could borrow a few hundred thousand tons, and replenish their stocks as our own wheat crop came in. He also suggested that he could help through satellite imagery to give me an idea of exactly when our crop would be ready for harvesting, provided his Ambassador gave him permission.

Obtaining the telephone contact of the local WFP contact from my helpful visitor, I was connected telephonically to their headquarters for me to seek sanction from the executive head of their programme, who agreed to release us three hundred and fifty thousand tons. This would be an adequate buffer, if we could prevent our flour millers from hoarding local stocks. Meanwhile, permitted by his Ambassador, Maurice House brought the first laptop computer I had ever seen into my office. I was stunned by the visual capacity of the satellite imagery beamed onto the screen of the laptop placed on my desk. He asked me if I knew the precise location of a wheat field. I gave him the location of a field on my farm, he fed the data into his computer and within a few minutes, the image of a wheat field appeared on the screen. As he zoomed onto it, I saw that it was precisely the field that had been indicated. An acre of the field was shown on screen, the focus was then narrowed onto one-twentieth of the field, enabling me to count the number of plants, concentrating on the colour and size of the ears, it was easy to assess when the field would be maturing. Secretary Mahbub and I were thus able to calculate, precisely to the day, when the harvesting in Sindh would start, followed by Punjab a fortnight later. This was so much more efficient than the cumbersome route of getting reports from the provincial food secretaries, who would be seeking the data to be collected by the district food officers who would be relying on chronically absent field assistants. I was really grateful to the US Embassy for their cooperation and my having served in their country not so long ago clearly helped.

We managed to avert the crisis by a hair's breadth. What shocked me was the blatant corruption of our food departments in the provinces, and their collusion with the flour millers. Information of an impending shortage leaked to the media by the personnel of the departments, and possibly at lower levels in MINFAL, led to hoarding by the flour millers now manipulating the price of wheat, which persuaded me to seek the Prime Minister's intervention for cracking down on this corrupted and rotten way of disrupting something as basic as wheat supply, at an affordable price fixed by the government. Presenting the Prime Minister with a precisely worked out action plan, I obtained his permission to start organizing for an Agriculture Conference which could be convened in April, and would be chaired by him. By the 20th of March, MINFAL matters were sufficiently under control for me to take up a new duty which had been assigned to me, this time by the Presidency.

On 23 March, President Leghari was hosting a celebration to which all the Heads of Governments of the OIC (Organization of Islamic Cooperation) had been invited. I was assigned to be Minister-in-Waiting to President Süleyman Demirel of Turkey, who was coming accompanied by his wife. The Turkish delegation would be in Islamabad for three days and then Lahore for a day before departing.

I got on really well with the Demirels who were utterly devoted to each other. I gathered they had no children but had remained committed to their marriage for half a century and Madame Demirel informed me that her dear friend Madame Kandemir had asked her to convey her warmest regards to me. President Demirel mentioned, during the course of our first conversation on the day of their arrival, that he had tasked himself to arrange a détente between Crown Prince Abdullah of Saudi Arabia and President Hashemi Rafsanjani on the sidelines of our Summit of the OIC which Pakistan was so generously hosting. This thought really appealed to me and I shared with the President of Turkey and the First Lady my impressions of my recent visit to Iran and the utter simplicity of the lifestyle of the Iranian leadership, as well as my memories of the Islamic Summit convened at Lahore in 1974 by Zulfikar Ali Bhutto. President Demirel complimented me and said I was a great raconteur; and that he would thank President Leghari personally for assigning me to accompany him and his wife.

The new Convention Centre was the venue for the conference, which was inaugurated in great style: with army bands in full regimental regalia playing outside, and our very impressive mounted President's Bodyguard escorting the visiting heads of state and their retinue from the entry gates to the porch, where they alighted from their limousines. Inside the rotunda of the centre, the arrangements were immaculate. The defining moment came when Pakistan's national anthem was played through the powerful public address system and the entire gathering rose to pay tribute to our proud nation, recording a half century of our life as Pakistan. On the dais stood our leaders of the day, President, Prime Minister, Chairman of Senate, Speaker of the National Assembly, the four Governors and Chief Ministers, my only spasm of regret being that Fakhar was not among them as Speaker. My cabinet colleagues and I were in the first box on the right hand side of the dais, while the ornate front desks in the ellipse of the rotunda had the visiting heads behind them.

After recitation from the Holy Quran, President Farooq Ahmad Khan Leghari paid tribute to the founder of our nation, Quaid-i-Azam, Muhammad Ali Jinnah, and briefly encapsulating the struggle for Pakistan, underscored the importance of the 23 March 1940, and the passage of the Pakistan Resolution in which the leaders of the All-India Muslim League formally demanded a separate homeland for the Muslims of India, which is why this day was designated as our Republic Day, while 14 August was our Independence Day. Nisar Ali, sitting next to me asked sotto voce, why our president was giving us this basic lecture, making us stifle our yawns. I reminded him that this was for the benefit of our visitors, since many of them were not exactly historians and were probably being informed of our history for the first time. The prime minister dwelt on our poet philosopher, Allama Iqbal, with a speech which was crisp compared to that of the president, which followed the style of the localities they belonged to, central and south Punjab. It struck me then that all the power posts of the federation had swung to Punjab, which was perhaps not such a good thing, and likely to breed a reaction further down the road.

The second important moment of the conference came when President Süleyman Demirel of Turkey made Crown Prince Abdullah of Saudi Arabia link hands with President Hashemi Rafsanjani of Iran, and lead them into one of the side rooms of the conference centre. If this could lead to a cessation of the surrogate war that the Saudis and Iranians had launched in Pakistan by providing resources to sectarian groups, then all the costs incurred on the conference, which included the import of thirty armour plated Mercedes limousines, would stand amply justified. The conference concluded, and President Leghari hosted a grand banquet for all the equally grand visitors who had come to celebrate Pakistan's fiftieth birthday, during the course of which I gathered that he had invited Queen Elizabeth II, as Head of the Commonwealth to celebrate our fiftieth Independence Anniversary on the 14 August, four months later.

Shortly thereafter, Uncle Amjad Ali passed away which saddened me. Although he was in his late eighties and had lived a full life, I would miss my occasional tête-à-têtes with him. My mother was heartbroken. For twenty-seven years he had helped her to keep her spirit up and relieved her of some of her loneliness. I had a horrid feeling that she would not last long after him. While announcing his demise, the media: television, radio, and newspapers, along with the positions that he had held, also mentioned that his niece was in the federal cabinet, as a hallmark of our 'kursi' culture, so I was inundated with bereavement visitors, phone calls, telegrams, and letters from all over. The courtesy of our culture demanded that I juggle my time between my ministerial office and my personal obligations to family, which kept me in a state of perpetual exhaustion, bringing home to me that crossing into my fifties made me tire more rapidly.

President Turgut Özal of Turkey, immediate predecessor to President Süleyman Demirel, had instituted a group of the eight most populous Islamic countries of the world, under the auspices of the United Nations, and this grouping had the nomenclature of D-8. At the start of the month of May, there was to be a meeting of the D-8 in Istanbul. The Prime Minister's Secretariat informed me that I was to accompany him and his wife to this meeting in Istanbul. This was the first foreign visit that Mian Nawaz Sharif was undertaking, since his elevation as Prime Minister the second time around, and it was to be a small delegation, with Foreign Minister Gohar Ayub; Advisor Mushahid Hussain; Nawaz's younger daughter Asma; and the editor of the Urdu news daily, *Nawa-i-Waqt*, Majid Nizami, who was a friend/guide/philosopher of the Sharif family; and a few staff members.

Istanbul being one of the world's most beautiful cities motivated me, as did the thought that I would have more time to sleep, and also get to know Begum Kulsum Nawaz, the premier's wife, better. Above all I looked forward to meeting the Demirels again. President Hashemi Rafsanjani of Iran would be attending the conference, although, the recently conducted elections in Iran had favoured Ayatollah Khatami, who would be installed as President of Iran about a month later. The thought of encountering Mahathir Mohammed of Malaysia interested me as did the prospect of meeting Dr Hermano, who, the briefing papers indicated, would be accompanying President Suharto of Indonesia. One of the sessions was to be dedicated to demographic issues, during which I would be making two interventions on behalf of Pakistan, one on demography, the other on agriculture. The Bangladeshi, Nigerian, and Egyptian heads of government would also be attending this important conference, completing the frame of the eight most heavily populated Muslim nations.

Entering the aircraft, I was led to the bulkhead seat on the left of the aisle and seated next to Majid Nizami, with Gohar Ayub and Mushahid Hussain seated behind us. The Prime Minister and Begum Kulsum Nawaz entered and were seated across the aisle, adjacent to Majid Nizami and myself, with Asma Nawaz and Begum Kulsum's secretary behind them.

Not long after we were airborne, Nawaz Sharif asked me to swap my seat with his, saying that he wanted to chat with Majid Nizami, while his wife wanted to chat with me. Begum Kulsum and I had a long and animated conversation. She told me that she had admired me from a distance, even when I was opposed to her husband. I gave her a rundown on the Demirels and also described my visit with Khanum Hashemi Rafsanjani. We laughed and joked with each other, and at some point Mian Nawaz leaned across the aisle to say he was happy I was getting along with his wife.

We stayed at a former grand palace of the Ottoman rulers, right on the Bosphorus. It was a spectacular building, with a breathtaking view, and dinner was to be in the suites, although, Mian Nawaz took Mushahid Hussain and me, along with his family, to a fancy restaurant, behaving quite like a tourist.

The following morning President Suharto called on Prime Minister Sharif in his suite, accompanied by Dr Hermano who informed us that he had used the model developed for Pakistan and successfully brought down the population growth rate of Indonesia, because President Suharto saw him every morning for half an hour to obtain a daily progress report. Since I was present in the meeting, our premier told his visitor that he would do the same, but as soon as the Indonesian's left, he light-heartedly told me since his first visitor every morning was the ISI chief, I could only be his second visitor of the day. The plenary session was in the afternoon, where all eight heads of state spoke, the most cerebral speech was made by the Malaysian Prime Minister, Mahathir Mohammed.

During the course of the afternoon working sessions, we broke up into groups, while I made my interventions to two separate groups. The banquet hosted by President Demirel was on the lawns of another Ottoman palace, where I finally met Madame Demirel, who embraced me most affectionately, as did President Demirel himself. The following morning when President Rafsanjani called on Prime Minister Nawaz Sharif, he was urged by the latter to buy our basmati rice. Rafsanjani responded by saying that he was returning to Iran in the evening, and since we would be spending another day in Istanbul, he invited us to stop over in Tehran, and meet with his colleagues, as well as with the incoming President

Ayatollah Khatami. Prime Minister Nawaz Sharif agreed. Hence, after a wonderful day spent on a short cruise around the bay and a visit to the Aya Sofia grand mosque, we left Istanbul and its splendour to land in Tehran for an unscheduled stop. We were warmly welcomed by both the outgoing as well as the incoming Presidents of Iran.

Suitably dressed in a plain black *shalwar-kamiz*, with a black chiffon *dupatta* covering my head, I was seated next to our Prime Minister with President Rafsanjani facing him on the table opposite, while Rafsanjani's top aide was facing me. Mian Nawaz asked me to make the presentation for marketing our entire crop of basmati rice to our hosts, a topic which was alive during the first Sharif government, but the second Benazir government had managed to lose the Iran market, incurring losses for Pakistan. While pitching the case for our commodity, I noticed the gentleman opposite me was doing an *istekhara* (asking for divine guidance) on his *tasbih* or worry beads. Our premier asked me in a whisper why he was rolling his *tasbih* in a particular manner. I told him that he was seeking divine guidance. Just then, the person doing the *istekhara* informed President Rafsanjani that permission had granted, after which Rafsanjani told Prime Minister Sharif that Iran would buy all the surplus long-grain rice from Pakistan as it had done in the past.

We then went to visit Ayatollah Khatami, the President-elect of Iran. Khatami, whose father had also been an Ayatollah, was a celebrated orator. He received us with great warmth, addressing me, he emphasized that he owed his victory to the women of his country; he sounded like a progressive and scholarly individual. Prime Minister and Begum Sharif, along with their entourage were then received formally at the Saadabad Palace, by both President

Rafsanjani as well as President-elect Khatami. Begum Kulsum Nawaz was in hejab, and I was wearing a black outfit with my head covered. Both of us escorted to an adjoining building for an early supper with Khanum Rafsanjani, who greeted us effusively. She introduced us to the wives of the outgoing and the incoming cabinet members. She was still in her standard black dress, while many of the other women were in colourful dresses; the majority of them were young and either francophone or English speaking. We had an animated discussion on women's rights and the importance of family planning. It seemed to me that women's power was well and truly emerging in Iran, which would inevitably have a liberalizing effect on their social order.

The same evening we flew to Pakistan. Not long after our return to Islamabad, Nawaz made a sudden move in order to further strengthen his power. He decided to move a Constitutional Amendment to repeal Article 58-2(b) from the Constitution, so that the president would no longer have the power to dissolve legislature; this power would now vest only with the prime minister. None of us held any brief for this particular article, and we all looked forward to a five-year term in parliament, but the emerging danger would be that if at any point, Nawaz started turning autocratic, we would lay ourselves open to yet another military intervention. But it was too early since Nawaz had assumed power, and so far he was on track, hence, there was little sense in fretting about it.

Nawaz Sharif expanded his cabinet just after the budget session, adding about twenty ministers. All my portfolios were taken away, he even forgot to leave health and population together, but at least I was not lugged with a minister of state, and could turn my exclusive attention to family planning. At the end of the budget session, I flew to the US for a week, back to UNFPA headquarters in New York, to raise a further twenty million dollars for meeting a demand for family planning which was increasing, while service delivery was lagging behind. Visiting Washington for a couple of days, with the diplomacy bug not entirely out of my system, I got the sense that the American love affair with India was intensifying, while there was lesser interest in Pakistan. An empowered Nawaz Sharif did not seem to excite much interest. Meeting with Congresswoman Connie Morella, who had an interest in the Population Council, the leading international NGO on demography, I managed some useful technical assistance, returning home to throw all my energy behind our effort to bring down the population growth rate.

Meanwhile, Fakhar had been asked to chair a Commission on Government Reform, which kept him very busy and in Islamabad, while I was touring the country to infuse more energy into our effort to improve our demographic contours. My visit to Quetta landmarked the consolidation of my friendship with the family of Nawab Akbar Bugti. The Governor of Balochistan at the time was Miangul Aurangzeb of Swat, who insisted I stay at the governor's residence as his and his wife Nasim's guest. Nasim was the daughter of General Ayub Khan and eldest sister of Gohar Ayub and Tahir Ayub and a great beauty of her time. Much photographed when she accompanied her father to the US when John F. Kennedy was President and Jackie his First Lady, the consensus in Pakistan of the sixties had been that Nasim was far more beautiful than Jackie. Miangul and Nasim accompanied me to to Nawab Bugti's house for dinner.

On arrival we were ushered by Nawab Bugti into his *hujra* or men's reception room. I was surprised to see Chaudhry Shujaat

Hussain, my cabinet colleague there. We were seated on the floor on carpets as was the custom with the Bugtis. Nawab Akbar Bugti told Shujaat Hussain that our government would not complete its course and we would probably be ousted halfway through the tenure of our government, since we were a bunch of predatory Punjabis. We were bound to pick a fight with Chief Justice Syed Sajjad Ali Shah, who was an incorruptible and non compliant judge, but we would win. We will then pick a fight with the Punjabi army, the prospect of which did not displease him. Turning to me, he said that Nawaz would eject me out of his cabinet the moment I differed with him, which would happen sooner or later, because my worldview was different to his, and because he hated anyone who owned land. Shujaat attempted to mumble in defence of Nawaz, of which our host was scathingly dismissive. Taking leave of Miangul Aurangzeb for a few minutes, he escorted me into his home, where Nasim was seated, along with the women of his family, again on carpets, backed by comfortable bolsters. He introduced me to his senior wife, who coquettishly semi-covered her face with her *dupatta*, then to his daughter, Baby, and his daughters-in-law. He left me there and withdrew to his *hujra*. Baby and I bonded immediately, we devoured the delicious dinner and laughed a lot, spending a happy, comfortable time together. We were what our social scientists and city folk described as a bunch of 'feudal' women.

In my opinion, feudalism is a mindset: anybody powerful can come under the ambit of 'feudal'. The bourgeoisie in our country often behave like autocrats with their domestic employees or even their subordinates in the workplace. Feudal, in the context of rural Pakistan, only means flowing from a tradition, often upholding values of courtesy and kindliness, caring for those less privileged, sharing your bread, and nurturing relationships that are not always transactional. My late father may have been a feudal to the extent that he owned a large quantum of inherited land, but he was protective and benign and generous to a fault. My maternal grandfather, on the other hand, was a self-made man, who generated a lot of wealth, remained humble throughout his life, spawning a large and reasonably talented brood; he had the wit to marry four of his five daughters into feudal backgrounds. None of his sons-in-law encroached on his resources but the son-in-law who was his nephew quarrelled constantly over money with his sons. Two of his sons became part of the corporate culture with its endless advertising of philanthropy, while giving away of resources brought them substantial tax relief.

Nawab Bugti was accused relentlessly of being feudal by our bureaucracies if he demanded an increase in the stipend paid to his tribe for the natural gas fields at Sui near his home in Dera Bugti. Miangul Aurangzeb was lampooned if he mentioned the emerald mines in the Swat Valley being nationalized to pander to swindling employees of the state-run gem stone corporation, and I was considered vulnerable to threat from government because of maintaining a stud and livestock farm on my hereditary property, arbitrarily converted to leased land under a martial law regulation. Any commentator could take swipes at us for being 'feudal'! To assert on behalf of people to whom we connected through the generations was made out to be sinful, while it was kosher to buy land at low prices from small landholders, to build palaces and develop farms as corporate entities, as Shujaat Hussain or Nawaz Sharif had done. This attempted defacement of history flowed from the syndrome of what my father used to describe as 'small people filling big shoes'.

On my return from Quetta, Fakhar informed me that the British High Commissioner had indicated to him that he had put in a request with our government for me to serve as Lady-in-Waiting to Her Majesty Queen Elizabeth II, who was to visit Pakistan for our Independence Day celebrations. While on my next trip to Lahore, my friend Shahid Hamid, who was Governor of Punjab, mentioned that Nawaz Sharif had informed him that Shahid's beautiful wife Sarwat had been assigned as Lady-in-Waiting to the Queen of England on her visit to Pakistan. Making no mention to Shahid and Sarwat of what the British H.C. had told Fakhar, I asked Nawaz Sharif, when we met a few days later for a discussion on population issues, whether the British High Commissioner had mentioned me in the context of the Queen's visit. He affirmed that he had, but since Sarwat was keen to be Lady-in-Waiting, and it would not matter one way or the other to me, he had decided to give me another portfolio instead, the Ministry of Science and Technology as compensation. Assuring him that no compensation was required, with population as well as science and technology being under resourced ministries handling crucial issues, I could end up doing justice to neither. But the answer I received was that it would give me an opportunity of ensuring fiscal discipline, which was always my emphasis in cabinet meetings. Something seemed to be irking him, and I noted it in my diary.

Queen Elizabeth arrived in October 1997 and was given a royal reception by the President's Bodyguard at a majestic ceremony outside the Presidency. After she took salute on the dais, President Leghari led her down the red carpet where the cabinet members had lined up. While introducing me, he informed her that not only was I a senior and respected member of the Cabinet, I was also the leading horse-breeder in Pakistan. Upon hearing this, the Queen's bright blue eyes lit up.

'What do you breed? Thoroughbreds? Any British bloodstock?'

'Yes, your majesty, I stood a stallion sired by your great horse Aureole.'

'Really? Which one?'

'Gold Jet, your majesty.'

'I remember him. Bay horse, out of an Umidwar mare, was he not? We must talk more about him and his performance at stud.'

Flashing her bright smile and a kindly look, she moved on. I was the only minister she had stopped to chat with, which seemed to cause heartburn among some of my colleagues. The following day, at the reception of the British High Commissioner who had been conferred a knighthood, as per their tradition, Sir David Dain, led me up to her, telling her that population was my portfolio. The Queen observed that this was a most crucial assignment, adding that we had been about thirty million at Independence, and she had been informed that our population was well over eighty million now. She then enquired how much time was I able to for horse-breeding, given the important nature of my official assignment. Before I could frame a coherent answer, one of my jealous colleagues cut in to speak, so I took my leave, suggesting courteously that since we would be meeting in Lahore the following day, we could talk at length about horses, but for the moment I ought not to monopolize her. The Queen said that we would talk about 'Gold Jet', obviously taking pride in informing me that she had retained the name.

At the governor's lunch at Lahore the following day, the Queen was flanked by Governor Shahid Hamid and Chief Minister Shahbaz Sharif. Lady Norfolk, who had accompanied the Queen, was seated next to Shahid and I was seated next to her. Lady Norfolk was herself a keen horse-breeder and informed me that Her Majesty had mentioned that I had an Aureole sire standing at my stud farm which was presumably in Punjab, at which point the Queen entered the conversation, and we managed to chat about Gold Jet's success as a sire at last.

Our anti-feudal commentators were never derisive of large estates of thousands of acres of land in Britain, nor did they ever mention that Winston Churchill was a Marlborough and born to a huge estate, yet he was a great politician and as much a leader of the working classes as of the middle classes of Britain. My late father had placed in his study in Lahore an autographed photograph of Sir Winston Churchill with my father, alongside Premier Zhou Enlai of China, and one of Gamal Abdel Nasser of Egypt whose Minister-in-Waiting he had been in 1954. In his view these three twentieth century statesmen stood in very high esteem: Zhou Enlai for consolidating the People's Republic of China; Nasser for bringing awakening to the Arabs; and about Churchill he would say that had he not lost election to Clement Attlee after the Great War, he would never have allowed Mountbatten to do a hatchet job in the partitioning of India because, having been born to an estate, he would have known how to deal with carving land causing minimum distress to the people who lived on it.

About two months after the royal visit, what had irked Nawaz Sharif spilled out. He summoned a meeting of the National Assembly and informed us in a party meeting prior to the first day's session, that he had decided to replace the Chief Justice of the Supreme Court, Justice Sajjad Ali Shah. I had stuck up for the Justice in a cabinet meeting when he was accused of being obstructive on a move made by the Attorney General for the setting up of Special Courts. Marvelling at Akbar Bugti's accurate sense of anticipation, I was dismayed to listen to Justice (retired) Rafiq Tarar, who was invited to address the party meeting as a special guest of the Prime Minister, make an unbecoming verbal assault on the Chief Justice of the Supreme Court that was televised live by PTV, the government-owned television channel. Fakhar sitting next to me whispered that the Chief Justice would haul up everybody in contempt of court, if he were watching and hearing this speech on television. When Rafiq Tarar concluded, a colleague moved a resolution on behalf of PML-(N) demanding the removal of Syed Sajjad Ali Shah from the post of Chief Justice of the Apex Court of Pakistan. The resolution was passed around for all of us to sign. Fakhar and I refused to sign, along with a handful of other colleagues, but not enough to mount any pressure, as democratic restraint was trashed before our very eyes.

Predictably, Sajjad Ali Shah hauled up Nawaz Sharif for contempt of court. He summoned a meeting of his parliamentary party, on receipt of the contempt notice, at which it was decided that we would all accompany him when he appeared before the court, and it would become difficult for the court to enter into a collision course with a leader who commanded a two-third parliamentary majority. Some of us counselled that he personally tender an apology to the court; others were of the view that the Attorney General tender the apology on his behalf.

President Leghari called me to the presidency, expressing his regret at the unfortunate turn of events. He asked me to muster all my diplomatic skills to urge the Prime Minister to tender an outright apology, and learn to live with an independent chief justice. He kept emphasizing that an independent judiciary was an integral part of the democratic process, till he had my assurance that I would do my best to convince Mian Nawaz Sharif of the same, although he no longer really listened to me.

On the date fixed for hearing of the contempt case, we all arrived in full force with our party leader. Nawaz stood politely, along with everyone else in the courtroom when the judges entered. If he had bowed his head low and mumbled a brief apology it may have worked better than the arduous and circuitous apology tendered on his behalf by the Attorney General. The court adjourned, reserving judgement. It was clear by now that before completing our first year of governance; we had entered a full blown crisis, with the frequent reference to our 'heavy mandate' weighing us well and truly down. But a worse moment was yet to come.

The day the judgement was to be announced, arriving at my office fairly early in the morning; I was informed by my staff that the Supreme Court had been attacked. Unbelievable as it was, craning my neck out of the office window I could see a crowd on the avenue outside the Supreme Court, and then a heavy contingent of police arriving. The images on television which had been switched on were so upsetting that I burst into tears, much to the consternation of my staff, who probably found it hard to reconcile the image of the tough taskmaster minister constantly bossing them around, with that of the dejected woman weeping before them. My staff could not understand my lamenting the fact that we had lost the moral right to rule. I called my mother, who was whimpering, watching the horrible saga on television. Always deeply concerned with the issues of her country and with her eldest brother no longer there for her to talk to, I decided to fly down to Lahore to see her, for her to share her thoughts with me, and for me to share my time with her. Prescient as always, she told me that the ugliness would not end here, that Nawaz would now try to influence the judges and force Sajjad Ali Shah to resign, which in a nutshell was more or less what transpired.

In the view of thoughtful Pakistanis, Sajjad Ali Shah stood taller, while Nawaz Sharif's stature diminished. My mother had been convinced that the only real justification for Farooq Leghari's removal of Benazir's government was her intolerance of an independent-minded Chief Justice, and she now felt that the only honourable course for Leghari, Shahid Hamid, Fakhar, and me to take would be for all four of us to resign, and provide the people of Pakistan with a leadership premised on integrity and capacity. In hindsight I so regret that all of us missed the moment.

Mother's liver had been acting up. She had developed Hepatitis-C because of the rich food and sedentary lifestyle that she had been living. Her doctors counselled that she walk regularly for an hour everyday and limit herself to a fat-free diet. Persuading her to follow her doctor's instructions, I returned to Islamabad to discover that Nawaz Sharif had sent his current confidantes to persuade Farooq Leghari to resign from his office of President. Calling on Nawaz, I sought to remind him that Farooq Leghari had risked his reputation, amputated his connection to a party he had dedicated the best years of his life to and had suffered for it, and had facilitated our return to power. Why should we break our ties with him especially at this juncture when the events around the Supreme Court were being critically viewed by the intelligentsia?

Nawaz went into a litany of complaints against the 'arrogant' attitude of President Leghari, very similar to the complaints that he harboured against President Ghulam Ishaq Khan. I went on to inform him that my mother was in poor health, and it was my duty to look after her, so would he kindly accept my resignation from the cabinet, to enable me to nurse my mother to regain her health. To this Nawaz responded that my mother's health was doubtless of great importance to me, therefore, the remedy for that was to continue operating my ministry from Lahore, which would enable me to be closer to my mother. He added that since we had walked into government together, we would walk out together, but Farooq Leghari would be well be advised to resign.

Leaving his office extremely unhappy and disturbed, it came as no surprise to me when a few days later, on 2 December 1997, President Farooq Ahmad Khan Leghari's resignation was announced. He had been forced out of office—just as Justice Sajjad Ali Shah had been—causing a great deal of unhappiness and apprehension in me.

In December the same year, I was listed up to attend a conference at Dhaka. Never having forgotten my visits to the Intercontinental Hotel in Dhaka as a girl, I was now looking forward to the conference on family planning being convened twenty-six years later, in the same hotel, in what was now the independent state of Bangladesh. Checking with my mother's doctor as to whether it would be alright for me to be away for about ten days, as I planned also to avail of Dr Hermano's invitation to Djakarta after Dhaka, I was shocked when the doctor advised me not to be away for long as Mother's condition was deteriorating rapidly. Sitting by her bedside the very next day, I tried to cheer Mother up by reminiscing about the visit that we made to Dhaka in early 1967. It was a time when the Ayub administration was entering its twilight. The visit was to attend the Democratic Action Committee (DAC) meeting convened by Bengali leaders for all the consequential political leaders of West Pakistan of the time. We had stayed in the newly operational Intercontinental Hotel.

Maulana Mufti Mahmood, leader of the Jamiat-e-Ulema Islam had flooded an entire floor of the hotel because he kept flushing the toilet for his ablutions before offering his prayers! Mother smiled sweetly at me, recalling what good health my father was in and how handsome he was on that last visit of ours to Dhaka. She then told me that she had dreamt of him: he had kissed her, and she could feel the sensation even after she had woken up. In the dream he was calling her, and she was missing him now more than ever. She said to me that she was going to join him in March. Hugging her close, I asked if she was going to abandon me, to which she answered that I no longer needed her, what with my children grown up, and my being immersed in work.

'Baji, if you abandon me, I will have nobody to pray for me, or give me wise counsel.'

Mother stroked my hair gently, and I felt somewhat comforted.

January and February of 1998 were difficult months for me, shuttling between visits to my ailing mother at Lahore and my workplace at Islamabad, with quick visits to Jhang in between, where I would be assailed by my constituents. Shugu was helping out with the management of the farm and earned my admiration for so rapidly learning the basics of farming, while Umku was caring for her only surviving grandparent, to whom she was profoundly attached. She would call Abid at Yale and make him speak to his grandmother, which would cheer her up. Her speech was becoming slurred, and the doctors had a hospital bed moved into her room, with all the contingent equipment, because Mother resisted hospitalization, just as my father had done. She would say that she wanted to die on her own bed; in the same room from where my father had gone.

I happened to be in Islamabad on 17 March 1998. Very early in the morning, the telephone by my bedside rang. It was Mother calling.

'Happy Birthday, Chando! May you have a long life!'

Her voice was distinct and normal, and I was thrilled to hear it, offering my thanks to Allah. Umku called mid morning to wish me, telling me that her Baji Ammah had made a special effort of celebrating my birthday by sitting out in her front garden, admiring her gladioli. She really wanted me to be with her. I left for Lahore immediately, and was with her by the afternoon to cut the cake she had so lovingly ordered for me from her favourite confectioner.

My mother, Syeda Kishwar Sultana, known as Begum Syed Abid Hussain subsequent to her marriage at age seventeen, passed away on the 21 March 1998, ever so peacefully in her own bed, as she had wished, at age seventy-six. She outlived my father by twenty-eight years, having endowed the Syed Abid Hussain Memorial Hospital for women and children at Jhang, and also the Abid Hussain Foundation School to provide quality education to children of low income families. She sponsored the Lahore Grammar Schools system, chairing the eight-member board of directors, which included me, two of her nieces and four of our close women friends. The Lahore Grammar Schools system evolved as the most successful private school system in Pakistan, winning academic accolades throughout Asia. Like her father, she did not propagate herself as a philanthropist, adhering to the Islamic, as well as Christian notion of the left hand not knowing what the right hand was giving away. She opted to avoid being a part of the corporate culture of her siblings in many ways, and was often heard saying that while her body remained capitalist her mind had turned socialist! She read and valued greatly, the writings of Dr Ali Shariati, the Irani scholar killed by the SAVAK, the Shah of Iran's secret service. His murder became a rallying point for the Iranian Revolution of 1978. Marrying into a family flowing from a Sufi tradition, she developed a mystical quality of her own. Prone to premonitions, she would often mention her dream of tall towers tumbling and the world changing, whenever that happened.

Her funeral prayers were offered in the front garden of our home in Lahore. I stood alongside all the men; emboldened enough by this time to lead the funeral procession out of Lahore. We drove to Jhang and on to finally Shah Jewna, where I carried the bier from the front, through the portal of the *Imambarah* which Mother had built, to her grave site beside my father's. Burying my mother myself, having wished to do the same for my father, without the courage at the time to break with the tradition of burials being an exclusively male task, I was now joined by my daughters and my surrogate mother, Vicki Noon, along with the men of the family.

Mother's memory was honoured by most of the leaders of Pakistan. Those still in office flew in on helicopters to pay their last respects. Thus a helipad had to be prepared on the flat space across the road to Shah Jewna. Others drove from all over the county. Prime Minister Nawaz Sharif, Governor Punjab Shahid Hamid, Chief Minister Punjab Shahbaz Sharif, Chief Minister Balochistan Akhter Mengal, Chief Minister Sindh Liaquat Jatoi, former President Farooq Leghari, former Prime Ministers Ghulam Mustafa Jatoi and Balakh Sher Mazari, Chairman Senate Wasim Sajjad, Speaker Illahi Bux Soomro, former Chief Justice Sajjad Ali Shah, most of my Cabinet colleagues, Begum Nasim Wali Khan, former and serving Senators, MNAs, MPAs, former governors, chief ministers, former ministers, ambassadors, and federal and provincial secretaries to government crowded into the *Imambarah* at Shah Jewna for several days. All the landowning clans of Jhang, with no exceptions, came for condolences, as did at least a hundred thousand humble folk from our own as well as the neighbouring districts, along with Fakhar's entire clan, our common aunts, uncles, cousins, and a host of personal friends, many coming from as far away as Karachi, Quetta, and Peshawar. Abid arrived from Yale, managing to make it for Mother's 'Qul', or third day prayer and was desolate to leave us to return to college after a few days. Several newspapers paid her glowing tributes, the most moving one sent in by her surrogate daughter, my friend Bunny. Although I had the satisfaction of knowing that my mother was well remembered as the daughter of a distinguished family; widow of a great man; as well as for her own achievements, I was disconsolate at my loss, as I had been on losing my father, no longer feeling like a winner, but as a complete loser. I was heartbroken.

After twenty-one days of mourning, with three Thursday special prayers having been offered in the traditional manner for my mother at Shah Jewna, Fakhar, Umku, Shugu, and I moved to Lahore for her 'Chehlum' prayer (held after forty days of demise). There we were invaded by friends and those relatives who could not make it to Shah Jewna, with a large contingent of my daughters' friends, who often brought their families along.

Meanwhile Local Elections had been announced and Shugu decided to contest for the Shah Jewna Union Council. I thus headed back to hold the fort in my hometown, as in a fundamental sense, the baton had to be passed on. Exactly one month later I returned to Islamabad. There also our house was constantly filled by bereavement callers. President Rafiq Tarar came to condole, as did the Chief of Army Staff, General Jahangir Karamat, who complained that the Prime Minister had gone with Dr A. Q. Khan to test-fire a missile in the Cholistan desert, which was likely to provoke a reaction from the Indians. As it turned out, General Karamat's apprehension was not out of place. In May, the Indians tested their nuclear device with contingent fanfare. An emergency meeting of the cabinet was called. Prime Minister Nawaz Sharif informed us that he had met with the Defence Committee of the Cabinet; the army chief was non-committal and said it was up to the cabinet. The first to speak was Foreign Minister Gohar Ayub who vociferously advocated that we follow suit and should test our weapons. Most colleagues agreed with him vehemently. But I differed, arguing that it was the first time that international opinion was strongly against India. Japan had frozen the three billion dollars of assistance it had pledged to India, the five nuclear states had unanimously condemned India, whose economy at this point was in better shape than ours. Why should we allow our traditional opponent the opportunity to dictate the timing of our test, when we could conduct our test at a moment more convenient for us, I argued, recommending that the premier visit Japan and secure the same three billion for Pakistan, which would be a shot in the arm for our economy. We could also use the moment to solicit some state of the art defence equipment from the Americans, which our defence forces could do with. I concluded my statement suggesting that we review the matter six months later and for the moment, enjoy witnessing the world heap further blame on India. I was supported in my view by Nisar Ali and Mushahid Hussain.

The Prime Minister concluded the meeting by informing us that President Clinton had telephoned him to say that he was sending his director for Asia in their National Security Council, Bruce Riedel, who was bringing a letter and detailed message from him. The emissary was due to arrive and he would call a cabinet meeting to take a final decision after a visit to Saudi Arabia, who could give us more than Japan. As we adjourned, I approached Nawaz Sharif for permission to leave for the US, after presentation of the budget in June, to attend my son's graduation. Granting permission, he asked me to go down to Washington once again as his special envoy, to assess the lay of the land, and to return as soon as possible to give him my assessment. His office, he said, would send me a shopping list of the strategic equipment to be put up to the relevant American officials that our ambassador would take me to meet.

In the meantime, the local elections had picked up steam, and Shugu wanted me to be with her for the last week's slug out of her campaign. As rule of thumb, the smaller the electoral unit, the harder the fight. I found my child's voice hoarse with constant speaking, sleepless, and zipping in and out of the alleys and homes of our Qasbah, mastering the local accent and intonation of our dialect. Shugu was every bit as impressive in Shah Jewna as she was in Lowell House at Harvard, Cambridge, Massachusetts. Shugu sailed through her first round and was pouring over the list of her electoral college for Chairmanship of the Jhang District Council that she was natural aspirant to, when I left her and Umku, who was there to help her, along with cousin Maryam, to attend Abid's graduation.

Unable to attend the graduation of either Umku or Shugu at Harvard, Fakhar could make it for Abid's graduation at Yale. During our flight he mused as usual, whispering to me that Nawaz Sharif would detonate during our absence. I argued that Nawaz would mull over it until our return, otherwise there was no reason to have armed me with a hardware shopping list. By the time we reached New Haven, we got the news that Pakistan had detonated a nuclear device at Chaghai, in Balochistan. Fakhar's prediction had proven better than mine.

Yale had a tradition whereby the graduating students were expected to wear comical hats when they entered the yard in parade. I had suggested a turban to Abid, who differed, saying a turban was our formal headdress in the Punjab, not a funny hat! He chose a funny little felt cap with an elongated feather popping out of it. The Commencement Speaker was Tom Brokaw, the leading NBC television anchor. Although it had been pouring and we were all huddled under umbrellas, the sun burst through the clouds just when all the hats were thrown up in the air. We stood there as proud parents when Abid was presented with his degree. He was surrounded by friends, but disengaging from them, he came and hugged me, and when he said that he was missing his Baji Amma today, tears rolled down my face. Abid had decided to go to Morocco to teach at the American School at Tangiers in September, but for the time being was going to stay in New Haven to pack his mass of books and belongings, while we went down to Washington D.C.

In Washington, we stayed with our friends, the Parvez Shahs. Ambassador Riaz Khokhar was unenthused as he accompanied me to a few meetings on Capitol Hill. Although I was nervous about the state of our economy, and thought we might have waited, now that we had detonated, as a Pakistani I was proud of our achievement, nonetheless. This sentiment was shared by most Pakistanis whom we met, who, while living in the US, had hearts that beat largely for Pakistan. Most of the Americans I talked to were disapproving and reserved. Reminding them that India had initiated was not an argument that carried any particular weight.

Fakhar and I returned home to find a proud and happy country, despite the scorching heat of summer. By mid summer, however, a fly appeared in our ointment. The government decided to put a freeze on all the foreign currency accounts, to prevent an outflow of dollars, contradicting its own policy of economic liberalization. This decision did not sit well with anybody, least of all our expatriate community, as a result of which the national euphoria began to fade away. Nawaz Sharif made an attempt to push through the construction of a water reservoir at the controversial location of Kalabagh, but despite his popularity graph still showing a high, he failed to persuade the representatives of the smaller provinces, suffering a setback with his base of Punjabi support. He was disinterested in my briefings on my observations in Washington, and more concerned about the findings of the accountability process he had earlier set in motion, zeroing in on his political adversaries, the PPP leaders, including Benazir Bhutto and her spouse, Asif Ali Zardari.

The conclusive round of the local elections was approaching, I went to Jhang, where the distinct majority of those elected to the Union Councils collected at Shah Jewna House, and unanimously decided to nominate my daughter, Syeda Sughra Hussain Imam, as their candidate for Chairmanship of the Jhang District Council. It was a proud day for me, when I drove out accompanying my daughter to the District Council Hall for the vote, looking forward to seeing her installed as Chair. It would be the third generation to hold this position, with my late father and me having preceded her. It therefore came as a bit of a shock when I learnt from the Deputy Commissioner that he had received informal instructions from the Chief Minister's office that the election should be scuttled, but since there was no provision in the law to postpone voting when all the voters were assembled, he had ordered the start of the balloting.

Shugu won with a strong majority, and drums started to beat at Shah Jewna House once again. We had them silenced to offer a prayer for my mother. I wondered at the last minute glitch before the vote, because the Deputy Commissioner was transferred out of Jhang that very evening. I went to meet Chief Minister Shahbaz Sharif to find out what may have caused this loss of confidence; he suggested I meet his brother. Nawaz Sharif was not particularly forthcoming either, making a vague complaint regarding some random observations I had made at a private dinner. My conversation was repeated to him somewhat out of context. My visiting him, though, seemed to have cleared the air between us.

Abid settled in at Tangiers in Morocco as a high school English teacher. He sent us photographs of his class. Most of his students looked older than him!

After attending the Cairo Plus 5 Conference on population control in Egypt, I planned to visit Morocco for the first time to see my son working at his first job. My visit to Cairo was unusually exciting. The city was fascinating, especially the old Fatimid part. The Cairene were friendly, charming, and easygoing. My counterpart, their Minister for Health went out of his way to extend great courtesy, arranging a visit for me at my request with the great Egyptian writer, Naguib Mahfouz, and accompanying me to their Vice President and close associate of Hosni Mubarak who kept lauding Pakistan for having become a nuclear state and, consequently, the pride of the Muslim world. Having spent a fruitful five days in Cairo, where on the basis of my presentation at the conference, additional resources were pledged by the donors for our population control programme, I flew to Casablanca, to join my son.

Morocco is God's own country, endowed by all the bounties of nature: a comfortably mild climate, fascinating cities that include Casablanca, Rabat, and Tangiers, each with a flavour of its own, mountains, desert, endless beaches, fertile orchards of citrus, handsome people, strong and ancient culture, different to us, yet with flashes of similarity, highlighted by the call to prayer permeating the atmosphere five times a day. The casbah of Tangiers was captivating and Abid and I fantasized about buying a little house in this locality as a holiday home, a fantasy, that to date is awaiting fulfilment. My five days with Abid were precious for me. My son was rapidly developing social skills. He had made friends in Tangiers, and was spending fun times with them. We dined at the elegant home of a couple. The wife was an interior decorator while the husband was an antique dealer. It was a memorable evening. Our days together went by all too quicky, and it was time for me to depart from this unique country.

Shortly after returning home from Egypt and Morocco, the political air around Rawalpindi and Islamabad became heavy. General Jahangir Karamat, the Army Chief, while addressing senior officers of the Pakistan Navy, was cautiously critical of the performance of government. His address was released to the press, which created something of a furore, and led to the Prime Minister demanding his resignation four months before he was due to retire. He was expected to be replaced by General Ali Kuli Khan, who was the senior-most general at the time, serving as Chief of General Staff, from which post, according to military tradition, the next position normally was that of army chief. However, in a move that surprised and disappointed many, including Fakhar and me, since Ali Kuli was not only a good friend of ours, but also because we knew him to be widely respected in military circles for his professional competence, Prime Minister Nawaz Sharif anointed General Pervez Musharraf from the third position, who did not come from a military background. Musharraf's father had worked in the Ministry of Foreign Affairs, while Ali Kuli's father had retired as a senior general in Ayub Khan's era, and a military background was cherished in our army. General Musharraf was also reputed to be a hot-headed commando, prone to knee-jerk reactions, and capable of irresponsible conduct.

Encouraged by Fakhar, I called the Prime Minister on the green phone, the ministerial hotline to our premier, urging him that since Musharraf had been announced as Army Chief, perhaps he should make a follow-up announcement for Ali Kuli as Joint Chief. The two officers would not only be an effective check on each other such an appointment would also appease the Pushtuns in the army. Nawaz Sharif's response disappointed me. He said that the appointed Army Chief would be calling on him in the morning, and he would discuss the matter with him. It was obvious to me that having been elevated to the most coveted position in the strongest institution in our country, Musharraf would not want to be restrained by an officer better regarded in the military than him.

The following evening, General Ali Kuli Khan resigned from the Pakistan Army. First Sajjad Ali Shah, then Farooq Leghari, and now Ali Kuli Khan—all three individuals of high calibre—lost prematurely to serve Pakistan, made me feel very sad for my country and the government. People of calibre often stood their ground, but were seldom treacherous, while mediocrity more frequently lent itself to treachery, as Nawaz Sharif would eventually discover, at great cost to himself as well as to our country.

On 1 December 1998, Nawaz Sharif arrived in Washington for his first three-day official visit to the United States. He was accompanied by his wife, along with Shahbaz and his wife, another brother Abbas Sharif, and several of their children. Nawaz had commandeered a wide-bodied jet from PIA for the visit. The cabinet members included Sartaj Aziz, who had been appointed Foreign Minister; Ishaq Dar, who was now Finance Minister; Nisar Ali, Minister for Oil and Gas; Information Minister Mushahid Hussain; Fakhar and me; several secretaries to government; cronies, a retinue of staff; and a large press party. The prime minister and his family stayed at the Blair House, while the rest of the members of this large delegation were housed at the expensive Willard Hotel. Considering the state of our economy which continued to be in dire straits, this was extravagance we could ill afford, since the hotel bill was being paid by the public exchequer.

President Clinton hosted a working lunch for Prime Minister Nawaz Sharif, his brother Shahbaz Sharif, and the ministers of finance and foreign affairs, while Hillary Clinton hosted a lunch for the women at Blair House, where much of the conversation was sustained between her and me, with Kulsum Nawaz complaining afterwards that she and her family had found Blair House too old fashioned and uncomfortable! I was not surprised when Assistant Secretary for our region, Rick Inderfurth, whispered to me on our last day in Washington, that the visit had not gone well.

We flew from D.C. to New York, where the aircraft disgorged us, and carried the Sharif family on to Niagara, where they spent two days. We were lodged again in an expensive Upper East Side hotel in Manhattan, with Fakhar and me grumbling with Nisar

Ali about all this extravagance at the expense of the public. The first official visit of Nawaz Sharif ended as something of a visit with much fanfare achieving little result, and I was relieved that I was not ambassador at the time.

Having exploded their respective nuclear devices, and under pressure from the international community, the leadership of India and Pakistan entered into a tentative process of détente. Easing up on travel restrictions as a first step, a train service was to be initiated from the Khokhrapar border of India, down to Karachi, and a bus service was to ply between Amritsar in India into Lahore, through the border at Wagah. The first bus was to cross over in February 1999, Prime Minister Vajpayee of India sent an emissary to his counterpart at Islamabad seeking permission for what came to be known as 'bus diplomacy'. The cabinet was called to meet, and Nawaz Sharif informed us of Vajpayee's request. My asserted opinion, being the first minister to speak, was that the time had come to make a break from the past, having achieved a balance of terror, we could now afford a pursuit of friendship with our eastern neighbour and should suitably welcome our visitor. The entire cabinet was in agreement, with several colleagues emphasizing that we must protest the Kashmir issue effectively with our visitor. One of our colleagues even suggested that we allow some agitation on our visitor, including a light brick-batting of his vehicle, to effectively convey to the Indians about our commitment to the people of Kashmir. Not everybody agreed with this, of course, but since this particular cabinet member was known to be well connected in military circles, it was easy to deduce that the military would mount some kind of resistance. Brick-batting would be taking the matter too far, however. Some federal ministers, along with the governor and chief minister

Punjab were designated to receive the Indian Prime Minister at Wagah.

Vajpayee was bringing a bus full of prominent Indians, including top businessmen, a famous movie star, a celebrated cricketer, leading journalists, and his adopted daughter. After their arrival in the afternoon, and a rest from their journey, they were all to be feted at a banquet in the Lahore Fort. I received a phone call from Governor Shahid Hamid to say that Vajpayee and his officials were going to have a working lunch the next day with our Prime Minister, who wanted me to host a lunch for the rest of the Indian Prime Minister's delegation, and that the chief of protocol would be in touch with me to apprise me of the logistics. The chief of protocol then called to say a lunch had been organized at the Village Restaurant that served all kinds of *desi* dishes, and he would send me a guest list of the local MNAs and MPAs, to which I could add about thirty people, whose particulars would have to be faxed to him for security clearance. I composed a list of people who could converse appropriately with prominent Indians and faxed it to protocol for due clearance, before leaving for the banquet.

Agha Shahi, who was quite frail by now, had been invited to the banquet and was our house guest. Shahi was seated in the front, Fakhar and me in the back of the car as we set off for the longish drive from our Gulberg residence to the Lahore Fort. Our police escort informed us that he had been radioed by traffic police that there were demonstrations en route so we should take a route which would enable us to avoid the demonstrators. Hence we wove our way through the traffic smoothly, until we swung into the road with the main entry to the fort in sight. Suddenly, from out of the shadows, a volley of stones splattered the front and side windscreens of our vehicle, the shards covering Agha Shahi and the chauffeur, and to a lesser extent Fakhar and me. The car veered somewhat, but the chauffeur managed to steady it, as we drove up the main driveway of the fort to the Dewan-e Aam. Fakhar helped Shahi to dust all the bits of glass off his head and his suit, as I dusted the shards off me and from Fakhar's *achkan*. Climbing up the steps of the Dewan, the first person we encountered was Khalid Maqbool, my former defence attaché at Washington, now a Major General and posted in Lahore. He looked amused at our discomfiture; it almost appeared as though he might have put up his boys to do a 'little mischief'. Everyone entering behind us was meted the same treatment, even the diplomats were not spared, with the Saudi Ambassador and the Australian High Commissioner complaining audibly. Led by a protocol officer to receive Vajpayee's adopted daughter, I chatted with her spouse and young daughter who accompanied her, until the arrival of the Prime Ministers in horse drawn carriages, and bugles started to blow from the balcony of the Dewan. National anthems of both countries were played when they reached the gathering.

Dinner was served in the Dewan-e Khaas. The two prime ministers, our foreign, finance and defence ministers, along with an Indian minister, our governor and chief minister, were seated up under the marble canopy of the Dewan, while the rest of us were at tables on the grassy area below. It was a chilly winter's night, but the warmth of Indo-Pak friendship seemed to have been kindled with the speeches of both Prime Ministers which reflected a desire for peace and a resolution of contentious bilateral issues, Nawaz Sharif dilating on Kashmir and Vajpayee conceding a mention of it.

The next day, accompanied by Fakhar, I reached Village Restaurant well before the guests, to have a quick look at the arrangements and go over the menu. Everything appeared to be in order, but I noticed an inordinate number of waiters, probably more than half of them intelligence community. As the guests started arriving, I was there to receive them, to effect introductions, help the Indians mingle with their Pakistani counterparts, and to make sure the fruit juices and the food were within easy access of everybody. I noticed Ahmed Rasheed and Fakhar chatting with Aroun Shourie, the celebrated Indian journalist, our level-headed civil servant and cricket buff buddy, Moeen Afzal, along with another cricket buff and gifted artist Shahid Jalal conferring on this popular South Asian sport with Kapil Dev, captain of the Indian team. Shabana Azmi, the Bollywood star, known to be a beauty with brains, surrounded by my dear friend and Lahore Grammar School partner Samina Rahman, Cousin Popety, Aunty Tahira Mazhar Ali Khan, and Afsar Qizilbash. The businessmen from India were deep in conversation with their Pakistani counterparts that I had invited, while Premier Vajpayee's adopted family seemed to enjoy sampling all the Punjabi vegetables and the flat buttered corn bread. The atmosphere remained convivial, and when our Indian guests departed, all the Pakistani guests began to thank me copiously, and I clarified that we had all been guests of the Government of Pakistan. On our way back Fakhar congratulated me on my smooth handling of the event, but I was preoccupied with the image of the spooks that had been hovering everywhere, trying to overhear conversations, that would doubtless be reported. Had our Premier been on a visit to India, doubtless Indian spooks would have done the same; mutual suspicion being an intrinsic part of Indo-Pak relations.

In the afternoon, we attended a reception on the front lawn of the Government House. We gathered that Nawaz Sharif had taken Vajpayee to visit the Pakistan Memorial, and were asked to sit in the rows of chairs laid out in the vast garden before the Prime Ministers arrived. When they entered, we gave them a standing ovation. General Ziauddin Butt, Director General of the ISI (Inter-Services Intelligence) was there, with General Khalid Maqbool beside him. Neither officer raised his hands to clap, both appearing to be noticeably tense.

Known for his outstanding oratory skills, Atal Behari Vajpayee excelled himself that afternoon in Lahore. Speaking off the cuff he said that when Prime Minister Nawaz Sharif asked him to visit the Minar-e-Pakistan, where the Pakistan Resolution had been passed, his people said that he should think about it because his going there would mean that he would be conferring the seal of approval to Pakistan. Unhesitatingly he told them that Pakistan existed, it had become a reality and half a century later it did not need Vajpayee's approval, and went. Turning towards Nawaz, he said that many people of India as well as Pakistan, some overtly and others covertly, would be unhappy with the steps of friendship that both countries had taken towards each other, and in the time ahead, these steps could be pushed back, but eventually friendship between our countries would also become a reality. Quoting from the contemporary Indian poet Sardar Jafri, he went on 'and then we shall ask; which enemy did we refer to?' The speech, intoned to perfection, was etched into my mind. Nawaz Sharif made a brief reply, confessing that he was no orator, and that the Prime Minister of India had spoken for him as well and he thanked him profoundly for his visit.

February 1999, In the same month, Benazir Bhutto announced that she going into exile to Dubai, in protest against what she described as a selective process of accountability that Nawaz Sharif had initiated against her, her family, and some of her supporters. This did not bode well for the democratic process. In her last appearance on the floor of parliament, addressing the Speaker, she described the government of Nawaz Sharif as a government of 'ganjas', or bald men. Her pronunciation of 'ganja' was unusual and hilarious. Rattling off the names of those who were balding, which included Nawaz, Shahbaz, ministers Sartaj Aziz, Mushahid Hussain, Khalid Anwar, Siddiq Kanju, Majeed Malik, Chaudhry Shujaat Hussain. Nisar Ali and Shaikh Rashid, who, she alleged, wore wigs to hide their baldness, at which point Speaker Illahi Bux Soomro interjected that he could vouch for his crop of hair on his head as his own, at which the whole House had a hearty laugh. Benazir concluded her statement on an angry note warning us of disaster ahead. When she was walking out, many of our colleagues shouted 'go, go, go'. I, for one, was unhappy that she had left, and hoped she would change her mind at some point and return to the House in which it was her right to lead the Opposition.

Seeking to improve the economy, Nawaz had taken note of the inefficiencies in the state-owned corporations such as the Steel Mill, PIA, and the Water and Power Development Authority, popularly known as WAPDA. He decided to hand over the correction of line losses, popularly described as theft of electricity, to a General from the corps of engineers of the army, who had been highly recommended by the new Army Chief. Chairing a meeting of the cabinet to seek approval for his decision, he informed us that he had recommended that the private connections of everyone in government, including himself and his cabinet members be checked. A heated discussion ensued, with some colleagues arguing that since it was the metre readers that caused the losses, they may well be bribed by our local political rivals to scandalize us, while the majority of the members, including me, concurred with the Prime Minister that to lend credibility to the process, nobody ought to be exempted. My bills were always paid on time, so I felt I had nothing to fret about. But the Ides of March it seemed were upon me. As soon as we entered the month, the newspapers ran headlines of the prominent names of those who had been declared as electricity thieves, and horror of horrors, my name was among them. I counter-checked with my domestic and farm employees who informed that the metre reader had sent no detection bill, which was the legal requirement when a discrepancy was detected. In spite of this, a case had been registered against me.

Extremely perturbed, I drove down to my farm at night, defying all security instructions, and asked the local WAPDA officials what the precise issue had been. They informed me that one of the metres on my farm was running slow and had caused a loss of two thousand three hundred rupees worth of electricity, and that they had been ordered by the army officer, a major in charge of the area, to register the case.

Taking all my electricity bills of the previous five years with me, I returned to Islamabad and met with General Zulfiqar Ali, who had been appointed Chairman WAPDA. When I asked him why would I slow one metre on a tube well on my farm, where I had eight tube wells and no billing issues on the remaining seven, and why would I steal two thousand three hundred rupees? He informed me that the first reading had not been correct, the second reading indicated a line loss worth of two hundred and sixty thousand rupees, that being the amount of all my bills on my farm for the previous month, which had been duly paid and receipted. When I produced these bills, he refused to concede his error, whereupon I said that since no detection bill had been served, the case registered against me was without lawful authority, so I would have to take the matter to a court of law. The Prime Minister was on a visit to Bangladesh, meanwhile I requested Begum Shahida Ejaz Azim, whose son-in-law was a staff officer of the army chief to provide an opportunity for me to meet him. She very kindly put together a dinner post haste to which she invited several people, among them Sahibzada and Begum Yaqub Khan. When General Musharraf entered the room, our hostess led me up to him and introduced us. Addressing Musharraf, I told him that we lived in a country which was full of all kinds of thieves, but I was certainly not one of them, and if his general chair in WAPDA did not tender a public apology, I would be constrained to take him to court. We seated ourselves in an ante room, at the suggestion of our kind hostess. I was carrying my file of bills with me and placed it before him. He asked me what he could do: I suggested that he tell his officer to tender an apology, which could be sent to the press and the matter would be ended. He said he would discuss it with General Zulfiqar and then made a reference to my being a feudal. I reacted to his remark by asking him if Allah had *asked* him which home he wished to be born in, proceeding to suggest that Allah had not *asked* me either. Nevertheless, I was responsible for my conduct, not for my circumstance of birth, which in any case caused no embarrassment to me. After an awkward silence, we joined the rest of the gathering where Musharraf went up to Fakhar, was polite and pleasant to him, while I chatted with Musharraf's wife and Begum Yaqub Khan.

When the Prime Minister returned to Islamabad, we met, and I requested him to accept my resignation, so that I could take the Chairman of WAPDA to court. He said he was perturbed about this whole electricity issue. The Chairman of WAPDA had not even spared President Rafiq Tarar and extorted a huge bill from his private residence at Lahore. He needed a little time to think about what he should do, to which I suggested that removing General Zulfiqar from WAPDA, and appointing another General would be one way of resolving the issue. He wondered whether he could do that, while my observation was that, since there were more than a hundred generals in our army, surely another one could be seconded to what was, after all, a civilian post. I further mentioned to the premier that, having met the army chief at a private dinner, my instinct was that he was up to some mischief. Nawaz Sharif ignored the comment, and said he would get back to me in a few days. He did, at the end of a cabinet meeting. In April 1999, the Prime Minister sent me a message through his principal secretary to say that he was ready to receive my resignation. I gathered that at the end of a briefing in the GHQ, General Musharraf had demanded from the Prime Minister that I be dropped from the cabinet, I lost no time in filing a lawsuit against Lieutenant General Zulfiqar Ali, Chairman of WAPDA. My writ petition was admitted by the Lahore High Court. Nonetheless, I was deeply hurt that Nawaz Sharif had failed to take a stand on my behalf, and had allowed himself to be bullied by military officers who were his appointees, I understood that his heavy mandate continued to be used for personal aggrandizement, but perhaps loyalty had ceased to beget loyalty according to what was appearing to be a behaviour pattern. I was also quite certain that Musharraf was testing the waters with my resignation, and would now oust Nawaz at a moment of his own choosing.

My instinct was proven right. In May 1999, the story broke out in the international media, as well as in our media, that the Pakistan Army had occupied Indian bunkers in the Kargil sector, just inside the boundary of Indian-held Kashmir, according to the foreign media on the boundary itself, according to ours. The implications were extremely serious: it seemed that India and Pakistan were once again on the brink of a war. The bunkers occupied by our soldiers were being pounded by Indian artillery fire while we were firing back at the Indians casualties in hundreds claimed on either side. Both countries being nuclearized, alarm bells were ringing worldwide. The Assembly was called into session; all of us were nervous. The budget was presented, the ensuing debate lacked lustre, with Kargil the primary topic of discussion. Had the Prime Minister sanctioned this manoeuvre? This was the big question posed by everyone, with the majority opinion being that he must have done so.

It was clear with the passage of each day that we were sustaining heavy casualties, and now looking for some form of saving face. Foreign Minister Sartaj Aziz called me to his office for consultation. He said that the Prime Minister had mentioned that I had tried to warn him, and asked me the basis of this knowledge. I clarified that it was not knowledge, mere instinct, regrettably turning out to be more like a premonition. Sartaj said he was going to China with the Prime Minister, and stopping in Delhi briefly on the way back. My thought was that these visits would neither hurt nor help, but in order to achieve a ceasefire we would have to approach the Americans. Nawaz kept trying to do so, until finally, US President Bill Clinton agreed to see him on 4 July 1999. It being a holiday would allow a few hours of discussion. Nawaz ought to have taken Pervez Musharraf along to face the Americans who would doubtless have given him the earful he deserved for bringing us to the brink of a major war. Musharraf was guilty of sacrificing the lives of about four thousand soldiers and at least as many poor civilians of Gilgit-Baltistan, but Nawaz let Musharraf off cheap, and went to plead with the Americans himself. President Clinton used his great skill to get us off the hook from the Indians, and Nawaz returned to Pakistan, with a ceasefire being announced in the wake of his US visit. Needless to say, we had to surrender the bunkers back to the Indians. At this point, Nawaz ought to have used his brute parliamentary majority to summon the Army Chief to parliament, and to obtain a parliamentary sanction for his dismissal, but he missed his cue again, and now it was a question of time before circumstance decided who would pounce on whom first.

Playing his cards close to his chest, trusting no one but his son, Hussain Nawaz, the Prime Minister clearly mulled his action plan incrementally. Nisar Ali stopped by to see us, disturbed about the downturn in civil and military relations. It was too late now to take the parliamentary route, as that was feasible only in the heat of the moment, now, we thought it was best to sit tight and focus on providing good governance to the people.

By now it was September. Nisar Ali drove into our house once again, and hustled us off the breakfast table, informing us that he had come to take us to see the Prime Minister, for us to give him some sound advise. We asked Nisar why he assumed that we would be heard, as we had gathered that Mian Nawaz was not listening to anyone these days. Nisar was candid, observing that Nawaz may or may not hear us, but if democracy were to fall casually, at least we would not regret that we did not counsel the Prime Minister to take appropriate measures to prevent a disaster. We understood, though Nisar did not spell it out, that the Prime minister was going to replace the army chief, who would retaliate, and we could end up with a military intervention, so we agreed to accompany Nisar to the Prime Minister's residence.

Seated in the Prime Minister's office, at his residence, from one of the windows of the room, we could see the chopper landing on the helipad, further down the compound. A cavalcade of vehicles sped towards the helipad, out of which emerged some of Nawaz Sharif's most established sycophants. We could see Nisar push his way through the cordon surrounding the premier, and hop into his limo. Nawaz's frequent jetting from Raiwind and Lahore had increased. He had acquired several hundred acres of land there and his family had built a series of elaborate homes. Hence the Prime Minister's jet was flying from one airport to another; his helicopter would bring him in from his private residence to his official residence every other day. We used to scoff at Benazir for this extravagance not too long ago, so it was embarrassing that our premier should be following the same pattern as that of Arab potentates.

A few minutes later, accompanied by Nisar, the Prime Minister walked into the room where we were waiting, and greeted us affably. I opened the conversation with the plea that either he ought to have dismissed General Pervez Musharraf immediately after the Kargil fiasco, but having missed the moment, he should now carry on with sobriety and with measured governance, and provide no opportunity for Musharraf to pounce. To this, Nawaz responded by saying there was no need to worry, because he was in frequent contact with Bill Clinton, to which I reminded him that Clinton could not prevent a military intervention in Pakistan. Having elevated Musharraf and tolerated him thus far, he should now not be given any excuse to expiate his pettiness in any way, or he would turn on all of us, most of all on the Prime Minister. Nawaz Sharif diverted the conversation to Fakhar, asking him what he anticipated for the current year's cotton crop, shook hands with him, smiling at us enigmatically as we left. Nisar Ali seemed pleased with the meeting, although I got the feeling that our advise had had no impact on Nawaz. Nisar continued to be nervous, which became apparent when Musharraf was given the rank of Joint Chief as well.

At the end of September, Fakhar and I were lunching with friends at the Islamabad Club, when Pervez Musharraf walked in accompanied by a phalanx of hangers on. He looked cocky and confident. Driving back home, Fakhar agreed with me that the body language of the Army Chief betrayed his intentions of soon staging a coup d'état. Not having the stomach to witness another military intervention, the thought of escaping to Washington for a couple of weeks, to be at a safe distance from a situation that could turn ugly, I contemplated leaving Islamabad the day after my Umku's birthday, on 4 October 1999. The Lashkar Jhangvi threat had reared its ugly head yet again and with the tension mounting in the corridors of power, the level of comfort regarding my personal security had been dwindling.

Fakhar and my daughters thought that I should distance myself from my milieu for a while, as did a few friends and well-wishers who were aware of my security predicament. Having been well protected while in the cabinet, reliant now on my personal security, I felt somewhat nervous, when informed by the minister for religious affairs that the Lal Masjid (Red Mosque) cleric in Islamabad had accused me by name of getting a mosque razed to the ground, an allegation which had no basis whatsoever.

The fall season in Washington is as beautiful as spring time; just as it is in Islamabad. But while Washington spans great swathes of generous space, our capital is as crowded as dictated by our demography. Flying out towards open spaces brought me a sense of relief, similar to what I felt when driving away from the cheek by jowl environment of our cities, commuting every now and then to my farm. Being in the countryside never failed to uplift me; just as it never failed to amuse me when my urban relatives and friends, when visiting the countryside would feel a sense of discovery of nature. My timing was perfect. Planning to be away for a fortnight leaving my country at a time when anything could happen, I returned according to schedule.

A great deal had occurred during my absence. The optimist in me yearned for us to enter a period of reform, a period of correcting course, allowing the best within us to surface and flourish.

14

Musharraf Usurps Power

Being in Washington brought me no cheer. My friend and kind hostess, Birjees Shah, and her son, my young friend and acolyte, Zeeshan Shah, sat up with me two nights in a row, as I kept discussing my anticipation of an intervention and my conviction that we could end up on a heap of junk, with the latent possibility of ushering in some amount of improvement, the odds as per my calculus, were even. Birjees thought it would be the former while her son shared my optimism, and opined that it could be the latter. Three days later, the fateful call came from home that Nawaz Sharif had announced General Ziauddin Butt as the new Army Chief. Through a series of phone calls to friends and family, the picture of the dramatic events taking place in Islamabad emerged. General Ziauddin Butt failed to take command.

General Pervez Musharraf on a visit to Sri Lanka managed to stage his coup d'état from the aircraft flying him in from Colombo to Karachi on 12 October 1999. Nawaz Sharif allegedly attempted to prevent the aircraft from landing but failed. The triple one brigade, known as the coup-making brigade, attached to the corps headquarters at Rawalpindi, moved to Islamabad, encircled the television station, the radio station, the Prime Minister's residence, arrested Nawaz Sharif and Shahbaz Sharif who were together in this residence, while all the top commanders of the army reached Karachi, and were closeted with each other for seventy-two hours.

Before they made their crucial announcement, as word spread regarding the military takeover, people were shown on television distributing sweets, welcoming the usurpation of power, with no counter demonstrations protesting the demise of the government installed democratically two-and-a-half years earlier. I was deeply upset for Nawaz and Shahbaz and prayed for their safety. The events that had unfolded were extremely sinister and could be repeated again, or whenever politicians fell short of expectations. Bonapartism was as enshrined in our military as the Constitution was in the minds of politicians worth their salt.

World reaction, by and large, was muted. George W. Bush, elected President of the United States a year later, when asked to comment by the television networks on the recent development in Pakistan, let the cat out of the bag, as it were, by saying that although he did not know the name of the general who had assumed power in Pakistan, his sources informed him that he was on the American side! Sitting in Washington, watching this bulletin, the thought struck me, which I noted in my diary, that if Bush were to be elected to the world's most powerful Presidency in a year's time, Musharraf would inevitably seek to hang on to power. President Clinton on the other hand, condemned the derailment of democracy in Pakistan, as well as the detention of Prime Minister Nawaz Sharif. Since we were not receiving assistance from the Americans or Europeans after our nuclear test, and had been managing by piling up our national debt, the new authority in Pakistan did not face any threats from any country, only pleas for a restoration of the democratic process, as soon as possible. The government of India, however, reacted strongly cutting off the bilateral talks which had been in process between our two countries.

Hedging their bets, the commanders of the Pakistan armed forces announced a suspension of the power related articles of the Constitution of Pakistan, suspending Parliament, conferring the title of 'Chief Executive' on General Musharraf, as opposed to a departure from the previous three coup makers in our country who had declared martial law and themselves as chief martial law administrators. Musharraf's usage of language was contemporary, sounding more like a sugar-coated pill, but a bitter pill nonetheless, with the military returning to rule our country for the fourth time in five decades. Benazir welcomed General Musharraf's intervention, demanding that he hold a fresh election in a short time frame. When BBC asked my comments on the situation, my suggestion was that the suspended Parliament be restored as soon as possible. To sum it up, the reaction of everyone was self-serving, and Musharraf was a beneficiary.

Shugu had been chairing her District Council enthusiastically as well as effectively and, for a few days after the intervention, the local councils were left in place. Assuming this to be an oversight, and sensing that the elected officials would be removed sooner rather than later, I did not want my daughter to suffer the humiliation of being called by some official and told she need not come to office, so I urged her to join her father and sister at Islamabad and decided to fly back home myself, although Fakhar called to say there was no need for me to rush back, as it would take a while for the contours of any new road map to emerge. However, my apprehension having materialized, there was no reason for me to stay away and tax my hosts any further, therefore I flew home within a week of Musharraf installing himself as the new reality, after exactly a fortnight of absence from home. Even the Lashkar Jhangvi seemed to be awaiting fresh instructions.

Hence my security issue faded away for the time being, and I felt refreshed and relaxed, worrying now for my country.

Our home appeared to have become a hub of foreign and local journalists, along with diplomats serving in Pakistan, seeking analysis from Fakhar, our daughters, and me. Many of our fellow 'suspended' colleagues kept dropping in as well; we would spend a jolly time together in our state of suspended animation. One of them from Karachi who had known Pervez Musharraf from his school days, and was in touch with our new 'Chief Executive', took me aside and said Musharraf was wondering who to send to Washington as Ambassador, and may want to know of my willingness to return to that assignment. Musharraf must be a real simpleton to consider making such an offer, I told our friend. Presenting my credentials as a suspended MNA to the world would be a colossal embarrassment for our country, likely to make the international media even more derisive of Pakistan. Besides, my priority at the moment was to remain at home, and struggle along with my colleagues for restoration of the Parliament. Then a journalist dropped by to ask me the same question, indicating that rumours were circulating in Islamabad faster than the speed of sound, the atmosphere permeated by queues of self-serving eavesdroppers, many of them looking for jobs for themselves or their cronies.

General Zulfiqar Ali, Chairman of WAPDA, called to say that he apologized for his mistake and would agree to withdraw the case instituted by his organization against me, if I were kind enough to withdraw my lawsuit against him from the Lahore High Court. Conceding to the reality of military authority, I accepted his apology. Both cases were withdrawn, and I stood vindicated that I had stolen nothing, including electricity, but this unfortunate episode had succeeded in removing my strong voice from Nawaz Sharif's side, when he, perhaps, needed it most.

A few days later, the PML-(N) met at the Muslim League House, which was around the corner from our house on the Margalla Road in Islamabad. The working committee, a large number of suspended legislators, office bearers of the party assembled at short notice. The meeting was chaired by Raja Zafar ul Haq, seniormost vice president of the party. By now it was established that Mian Nawaz Sharif was being detained in Attock Fort, which cast a pall of gloom over the meeting. A twenty-member 'enabling committee' was constituted, Fakhar being one of the twenty, which decided to request former law minister, Barrister Khalid Anwar to petition the Supreme Court for restoration of the Parliament. On the date fixed for hearing, Khalid Anwar failed to show up. Fakhar and I attended the hearing. The strategy that had been mulled out by the enabling committee was that the Supreme Court would have no reason to turn down a request for restoration of the Parliament and once the Parliament convened, General Musharraf would be squeezed into a trade-off, stepping down as Army Chief in lieu of amnesty for his intervention. Release of Mian Nawaz Sharif would be secured. Of course, the party would have to nominate a Prime Minister to lead the National Assembly during the passage of the required legislation, after which the party could re-elect him back as Leader of the House. But in contravention of this strategy, and in the absence of Khalid Anwar, the former Attorney General, Chaudhry Farooq, stood at the Bar, pleading for a restoration of the deposed government. Chief Justice Saeed uz Zaman Siddiqui kept urging Chaudhry Farooq to 'show him a way out'. It was obvious to us that if the plea had been made for a restoration of Parliament, 'a way out' would have been shown to the Court. But it was equally obvious that Mian Nawaz Sharif was not willing to trust his own party at that crucial juncture, which caused resentment among many in his party.

The reality of military authority caught up with everybody. The Supreme Court judges were required to take fresh oath and the court was thereby virtually reconstituted. To his credit Chief Justice Siddiqui refused to take fresh oath and was replaced by Chief Justice Riaz. The new Attorney General Sharifuddin Pirzada, the architect of the 'Law of Necessity', pleaded for three years of free hand to be conceded to the 'chief executive', for an even-handed process of accountability to be launched, and for the economy to improve. The Supreme Court started to hear the case, while the Parliament remained suspended. By December, a National Accountability Bureau was established with the interesting acronym, NAB. It was announced that anybody that had defaulted on repayment of more than five hundred million rupees of bank loans was being nabbed and would remain under detention until repayment of their debt. The list included some leading businessmen, along with some politicians, such as my nemesis from Jhang, Faisal Saleh Hayat, who remained in the lock-up of Lahore cantonment police station for several months, while some businessmen were released by the recently appointed finance minister, reducing the credibility of the exercise.

Meanwhile, as the world entered the new millennium, President Clinton announced a five-day visit to India, with a brief refuelling stop over at Islamabad airport, where he intended to have a meeting with General Pervez Musharraf. Our press started speculating whether General Musharraf would go to the airport himself or send his newly appointed Foreign Minister. I did not doubt for a moment that he would go himself, and said as much to our friend Badaruddin who had taken retirement as a major, and, after working long years in the Gulf, was now living in Lahore. Badaruddin told us that he had been senior to Musharraf when he served in the army, knew him well, and occasionally met him. A few days later, Badaruddin stopped by at our house in Lahore, to say that Musharraf wanted to see me for a consult regarding the Clinton visit. Observing my reluctance, Badaruddin assured me that it would be an off-the-record discussion, with no publicity, and held in a safe location. Moreover, he would be with me.

Badaruddin drove me to a safe house, near the ISI offices on Lawrence Road, where Musharraf arrived in a modest black Japanese car, with heavily tinted windscreens, jumped out of the vehicle, saluted Badaruddin, then greeted me respectfully. His demeanour was quite different to when we had last met in Begum Ejaz Azeem's home; he was obviously focused on converting hostility to support. It was ironical how military despots in our political culture invariably yearned for popularity, which they never managed to achieve, because coming in the name of reform, they ended up perpetuating not only their power but also the status quo. They all ended up using all institutions and all individuals for their personal aggrandizement. Moreover, they never failed to surround themselves with sycophants, eventually ending up deeply deluded towards the end of their stint in power. This had been the previous paradigm and it did not seem to me that Musharraf was cast in the mould that would depart from that pattern.

The discussion revolved around Pakistan-US, relations, with me suggesting that he should have his meeting with Bill Clinton at the airport, and not insist on bringing him to Islamabad for a few hours, as that would serve no purpose. I counselled that he crack down on terrorism which was increasing, and address our issue of an exploding population growth rate, which not only were our country's urgent requirements, but also our focus on these issues would be viewed, for added measure, with respect by the Americans. He heard me, but perhaps did not properly understand, and certainly showed no interest in discussing these issues. My suggestion that Parliament be restored was parried by the response that the economy needed to be fixed and his Finance Minister Shaukat Aziz had begun to do a commendable job. The Americans, he declared were interested only in the economy. When I argued that if he reined in the terrorism, the economy would improve, he responded that there was no link between the two. Every now and then, he would grind his teeth and push his right shoulder up in a slight vertical movement. Musharraf struck me as being opinionated, insecure, and dangerous. This was not a forthright soldier in the style of an Ayub or a Yahya, nor was he flinty yet unctuous like Zia. This one would more readily destruct than construct, since he had absolute power. We had to be careful, and hopefully he was not reading my thoughts.

General Musharraf went on to institute a case of attempted hijacking of his aircraft against Nawaz Sharif, Shahbaz Sharif, and some colleagues, that included the former Defence Minister Ghous Ali Shah, and Chairman PIA Shahid Khaqan Abbasi, along with a couple of civil servants. A special court was constituted at Karachi to hear the attempted hijacking case. The detainees were held at Landhi jail in Karachi, where, ironically, Asif Asif Zardari, Benazir Bhutto's husband, was being held in a corruption case that had been instituted against him by the Nawaz government.

When the hearings in the special court began, I flew down to Karachi for one of the hearings. My friend Hamida Khuhro and I obtained passes for the special court being convened in a public building of the Karachi Development Authority (KDA), near

Clifton beach. The auditorium of this building was being used as the courtroom. We went and sat in the row where Kulsum Nawaz was seated. The entire scene and situation was deeply troubling; this was the classic 'kangaroo court'. When the under-trial prisoners were brought in, Nawaz Sharif looked a picture of misery, having lost a considerable amount of weight, with his clothes hanging limply on him, his face drained of colour. At the end of the hearing, I scrambled to reach him. When he saw me, he asked how I was, and my eyes brimmed with tears. His wan smile faded and he was led away. Shahid Khaqan had been standing beside Nawaz Sharif. He urged me to do something to get them out of this hideous situation. Shahbaz Sharif, who was behind Shahid Khaqan Abbasi, echoed the same. I leaned forward and whispered that the only way out would be to talk to the odious Musharraf. Both men whispered their agreement before being whisked away.

The PML-(N) leadership met again. Amidst a heated argument, it was suggested by some of us that instead of appointing Begum Kulsum Nawaz as Chair of the party, as proposed by a few colleagues, Mian Azhar should act as Party Chair. Mian Azhar was from Lahore; former governor; now a suspended MNA; and was a close friend of the Sharif brothers. It was mandated by us to begin talks with Musharraf, with a view to securing, first and foremost, a release of our party leadership from the ridiculous hijacking case of which he, himself, was prime beneficiary. The meeting ended inconclusively.

Summer and the hijacking case dragged on. A year of turbulence was close to passing, usurpation of power increasingly justified by multiplying vested interests, while our eyes remained fixated on the Supreme Court of Pakistan. Would Musharraf get a judicial endorsement for the three years he was asking for? Before and after every hearing, the multiple satellite channels now in place, resulting from global technological breakthroughs, would telecast footage of Nawaz Sharif supporters attacking the Supreme Court. The propaganda took its toll. Musharraf got his three years from the superior judiciary.

Fakhar called me in Washington to give me news of the verdict. Abid had completed his year of teaching in Morocco and had relocated himself in Washington to work with a consulting firm, and I was assisting my son with settling down in his new location, where he was likely to remain for two years. When I returned to Islamabad, Musharraf had already survived beyond his first year in power. The judicial verdict extending his term for three years meant that he would get at least as much time as a President obtains in America when he is elected into office, while we would be stuck with arbitrary governance for the same length of time. In December 2000, perhaps unwittingly, Nawaz Sharif conferred more time in power to Pervez Musharraf by making a deal to secure a release from prison for his brother Shahbaz and himself. This deal, brokered by some Arab rulers, remained a closely guarded secret, revealed to the public and to members of his party through the media. Via the press, we gathered that Nawaz Sharif had agreed to exile in Saudi Arabia for an indefinite period of time, taking with him his entire family, the only family member left behind being Hamza, the eldest son of Shahbaz Sharif, who would look after their business interests in Pakistan, while remaining strictly neutral in the political sense.

On television screens we obtained glimpses of footage of Nawaz Sharif boarding the special jet, smiling and waving as he left Pakistan, and smiling as he landed at Riyadh, where he seemed to be well received. Our leader walking away from us, for what was speculated to be a minimum of ten years, caused deep disappointment among many of us in the party, a party that despite strains and stress, did not split until Nawaz Sharif left for Saudi Arabia.

Mian Azhar became the front running candidate to lead the PML, with Fakhar and me helping him to try and keep the party united and together, and failing miserably. The Muslim League factionalized once again, with those in a minority deciding to wait for Mian Nawaz Sharif's return from Saudi Arabia, continuing to be referred to as PML-(N), while the majority of the suspended Members of Parliament, seeking to pursue lobbying for restoration of the Parliament or an early election. They grouped themselves under the banner of Pakistan Muslim League, Quaid-i-Azam Group, with the acronym PML-(Q). At a party convention of the newly established PML-(Q), Mian Azhar was endorsed as President of our latest political reality, naturally backed by the establishment. Having created a National Reconstruction Bureau, or NRB, engaging consultants through the United Nations Development Program (UNDP), the Musharraf regime launched a consultative process for establishing a local government system that would devolve the government down to the grass roots. Shugu was very excited at the prospect of being able to participate in the new process, and hoped she would be re-elected to chair the district-level institution, and resume from where her development work had been interrupted. I went to call on the Chairman of NRB General (retired) Tanvir Naqvi who Fakhar and I happened to know.

My interaction with General Naqvi was illuminative and troubling. He informed me that while a directly elected head of district government, as laid out in the devolution plan, was what he had favoured, the bureaucrats got hold of Musharraf's ear to a greater extent and the head of district government would now be indirectly elected. Informing me that the 'Chief' had tasked him to develop a list of prospective Prime Ministers, since the local election was to be followed by a parliamentary election, Naqvi wanted to know who I would recommend for this position. Appalled by this simplistic approach, and attempting to test the waters, naturally, my response was that after the conduct of a free and fair election, the members of the National Assembly would elect their majority leader, so what was the use of my making a premature recommendation. He laughed at the suggestion of a no-holds-barred election, informing me that General Yahya Khan had foolishly ordered such an election and split the country as a consequence. Post the dismemberment of Pakistan, all elections had been managed, some more, some less. But I was in any case in the party that was likely to win the election, so there was no need for me to worry. He laughed again, after which there was little reason to continue with this conversation.

Umku had been tracking her power generation project with little success, because the Musharraf regime had little interest in the power sector. She therefore applied for a highly competed for grant and obtained it, to study for a Masters' in Business Administration from the Business School of the Imperial College for Science and Technology in London. We thought this was plucky of her, while Shugu started focusing on the local elections which she was convinced were round the corner. She was proven right.

The devolution programme was announced by 'Chief Executive' Pervez Musharraf in May 2001, concurrently ordering a Presidential Referendum, which turned out to be as bogus an exercise as

General Zia ul-Haq's Referendum had been, and equally self-serving. Musharraf had managed to secure a resumption of dialogue with the leadership of India. Before he flew to Agra for a meeting with the Prime Minister of India, Musharraf addressed the nation and actually dared to say that he had hitherto never sought any benefit for himself.

Presuming us to be a gullible nation that would believe that Musharraf was an altruist, the General informed us that it was in order to maintain the prestige of Pakistan that he had decided to declare himself President. As his first edict, he announced the dissolution of the Parliament. This was a blow for us, somewhat cushioned by the second edict, which assured the nation that in 2002, he would order a fresh election to the Parliament. Meanwhile, he gave assurances that he would focus on making friendly overtures towards India but on equal footing, thus, upholding the dignity of Pakistan, implying that all previous attempts had been at the cost of Pakistan.

All these were bitter pills to swallow, but shorn of options, Fakhar and I decided to concentrate on the local elections, where in the case of district Khanewal, Fakhar's younger brother was a candidate, while in district Jhang it was our daughter, Shugu. In light of my conversation with General Naqvi, hoping that this would not be a manipulated election, my usual sangfroid when contesting elections abandoned me. A last minute change in the electoral rules made me further nervous. This change dictated that the head of the district, with the new nomenclature, 'Nazim' instead of chairman, would be elected not in the usual first past the post way of the parliamentary norm, but through a run-off between the first and second, unless the first got more than fifty per cent. Shugu did much of her own strategizing, both of us working hard, with the first round going well for her, although Fakhar's brother did less well in Khanewal. Shugu picked up enough support, more than fifty per cent, to be elected Nazim.

The hallmark of military authority in our political culture had become synonymous with a change of nomenclature, rather like recycling old wine in new bottles, or as in the case of the army and business elite, passing off vodka as water. It was therefore not unexpected when the Corps Headquarters of the Army at Mangla, where Musharraf had served as Corps Commander before being elevated as Army Chief by Nawaz Sharif, called me up to say that since the elections were being monitored by the Mangla Corps, the Corps Commander General Ghulam Mustafa wanted to see me. I was required to reach Mangla the following day by noon.

It was a six-hour drive from Jhang to Mangla. I left really early, changing cars to dodge my Lashkar Jhangvi stalkers, which for me had become routine by now. I took my maid along with me, as two women in a car caused less suspicion. During the long drive, the sheer affront of a summons by folk who had no legal right to this monitoring remained uppermost in my thoughts. My electricity theft allegation had also originated by the monitors of WAPDA from the Mangla Corps. The increasingly devious Pervez Musharraf clearly used his subordinate officers to assume power and then to cling to it. Events in our country were going further and further off-track, instead of coming back on to some reasonable track.

Finally reaching my destination, I was captivated by the beauty of the setting, and was stunned by the prosperous appearance of the cantonment itself. Our enormous defence budget clearly helped contractors of all sorts to line their pockets. We had a huge army with a command that seemed to have developed wasteful spending habits; no corrective measures seemed forthcoming. Naturally they would be inclined to favour the greedy and compliant politicians.

My car was guided to a pretentious chalet. A major received me who guided me into an overly decorated little lounge, where my maid was asked to take a seat next to me. This was viewed by me as a democratic gesture. The major was followed by a colonel who sat with us while tea was served. My maid hesitated when the sandwiches and cakes came around, but encouraged by me, she helped herself to a plateful. The colonel then said to me that before the brigadier joins us, he would like to tell me that he was honoured to share a cup of tea with the renowned daughter of a colonel, now with a famous daughter of her own, and he hoped his own daughters would end up as famous. Thanking him for his compliment, wishing his daughters well, I informed the colonel that my late father's rank had been of an honorary nature and that he had not served in the military as such, but the colonel did not seem to understand and kept repeating this, when the brigadier entered the room. He looked at me, then at my maid, who was just a few years younger than me and homely looking, but as well dressed as me. He asked me if she was my daughter, the candidate for Nazim, since the colonel had informed him that my daughter would be accompanying me. When I told him that Bakhaan was my maid and no Nazim candidate, it was not pleasant to witness the rough manner in which poor Bakhaan was removed from the room by the colonel and the major breathing down her neck—the veneer of what appeared initially to me to be democratic conduct having fallen away—while the brigadier disappeared to escort the general in to meet with me.

The general was extremely courteous, led me to the lunch table, and informed me that his intelligence reports indicated that

Sughra Imam and Hamid Sultan were going neck to neck, so their teaming up with each other, with him as Nazim and her as Naib (Deputy) Nazim would be suitable. I told him that his intelligence information was inaccurate. Sughra was well ahead of Hamid Sultan and therefore Sughra heading the District Government and Hamid Sultan as her Deputy could have been a possibility, but it was a little late for that now. His next statement revealed what was actually in his mind. He asked me whether I would be willing to stand by General Pervez Musharraf under all circumstances. I gave a very cautious reply—telling him that our family harboured democratic values—and if General Musharraf stood by his commitment to the restoration of a democratic order, we would then stand by him. General Mustafa thanked me for giving him an honest answer. After lunch the general saw me off, wishing Shugu best of luck in the forthcoming contest. I returned to Jhang and hoped that the visit would not have adverse consequences.

Shugu had stitched up her votes extremely efficiently. On polling day, I was confident of her winning by more than fifty per cent of the votes. While driving to the polling station I received shocking news. Maulana Azam Tariq, the top gun of the Sipah Sahaba, who was under trial for killing more than a dozen Shias in a bus not far from Rawalpindi, was released on bail that very morning. The news was blaring from the loudspeakers of a mosque nearby, and pamphlets with the news were being handed to the voters as they were entering the polling station. It had a distinctly intimidating effect on some of our supporters. Was the timing a coincidence? I wondered.

Shugu led the field by 245 votes from Hameed Sultan, who pulled 100 votes ahead of Qaisar Shaikh. But unfortunately, Shugu scored 49 instead of 51 per cent of the total votes, so she could not be declared an outright winner. There would be a run-off round between Shugu and Hameed Sultan. We had about a week at our disposal. Fakhar joined us because his brother was out of the contest, and it was obvious that, first and foremost, we needed to woo Qaisar Shaikh, who immediately became difficult and threw his lot in with Hameed Sultan. We now needed only a little over fifty votes to ensure victory for our Shugu who struggled hard but she lost by about forty votes. In the end Hameed Sultan's Sunni credentials, emphasized through a lethal covert campaign, launched effectively and professionally, got the better of us. In the new political era being launched by Pervez Musharraf, Pakistan's fourth military dictator, who had usurped power touting accountability, the fact that Shugu had a brilliant incisive intellect, unimpeachable integrity, and an unmatched work ethic mattered not. The patterns of the past were being repeated again.

Quite heroically, Shugu refused to budge out of Jhang. We tried unsuccessfully to persuade her to attend her best friend's wedding in Lahore, so that she was diverted. Her priority was to go to thank all the folk who had voted for her, and she asked us to attend the wedding on her behalf. Shugu assured us that she would galvanize her group to lead the opposition within the district government, and keep herself locally engaged until the parliamentary elections that had to be held sooner or later, Fakhar and I reluctantly left for Lahore. Extremely disturbed by the hurt caused to Shugu, the question uppermost in my mind was the timing of the release of Maulana Azam Tariq and the pattern of Shia-Sunni conflict raising its ugly head whenever any of us would be close to victory. This pattern was being repeated in the third generation. My father had been its victim in the late sixties; Fakhar and I through the eighties; and now Shugu at the start of the twenty-first century. Will this fundamental injustice ever stop? Will this pattern never be broken? Who and what were the insidious forces that pulled the invisible strings that kept the pattern going? Multiple conspiracy theories kept swirling in my mind. I was now beginning to tire of it all.

Then an odd accident occurred. General Ghulam Ahmed Alizai, the Chief of Staff, was killed while driving from Islamabad to his home in Dera Ismail Khan. He was said to be the institutional check of the Army on Musharraf, a well-reputed officer, known to be honest and competent. It was rumoured that the accident had been designed and calibrated by those that wanted Musharraf to be freed of all constraints.

Fretting about Shugu in Jhang, Umku in London, and Abid in Washington, and apprehensive about a dictator turning rogue on us, I had been sleeping fitfully and having strange dreams, a deep sense of apprehension mounting in me. Telling Fakhar that there was something happening around Abid that was making me nervous, I was encouraged by him to take a break and visit Abid and Umku. He had understood how deeply hurt I was on account of Shugu and felt a change would do me good.

Arriving in Washington on 7 September 2001, seeing Abid and my friend Fauzia at the airport was reassuring, but the feeling of nervousness was with me the following day as well. Abid told me to stop fretting, call my friends, get around, walk to Georgetown, try and lose weight, cheer myself up. But my energy seemed to have abandoned me. Umku called from London to say she was looking forward to seeing me on my return from Washington, asking how long my visit to D.C. was going to be. I told her it would mot be more than ten days and I would be with her for about a week, and then get back to Shugu, and convince her to abandon Jhang for a while.

The two friends that I did call in Washington were Phyllis Oakley and Tezi Schaefer. Both were retired from the State Department: Phyllis was teaching and Tezi was working in a think tank, with an office which was less than five minutes walk away from Abid's apartment. Tezi and I were to have lunch together in a nearby restaurant on the 11th while Phyllis invited me to lunch at their home on the 13th. Our Pakistani American friend Sajjad Chaudhry had come up on the 10th from Houston, Texas, where he lived, and was to take me out to tea the next day.

Abid left for work as usual at 8 a.m. on the morning of the 11th, while my inertia kept me in bed, awake but uneasy. The telephone rang, it was Sajjad, telling me to put the television on. The World Trade Centre in New York had been hit. By the time I switched on the TV, the second tower of the World Trade Centre was being hit by what looked like an aeroplane going straight for the tower. Tezi rang me up and asked if she could come to Abid's flat to watch the events since the one television in her office was crowded by shocked people. She raced down the two blocks and joined me within minutes, and watched silently and intently. Television commentators gabbled on. As I got us some coffee, Tezi finally spoke, saying that she hoped for our sake that this entire mess would not lead close to our doorstep, to Afghanistan, which sadly had become a sanctuary for terrorists.

After she had left, a good while later, my energy suddenly restored, I started to call Pakistan but all telephone lines were jammed. Abid returned from work early, since his office had been shut. Had he not come, my anxiety would have been boundless.

Reaching Bob and Phyllis Oakley's home for lunch was not easy because President George W. Bush was going to the Cathedral for the memorial service, and the roads were choked with traffic. As we agonized together over the extraordinary events of two days previous, Bob Oakley quite accurately predicted that his former state department colleague, Paul Wolfowitz would join voice with the 'hawks' in the Pentagon and get America embroiled in war. Phyllis informed me that General Mahmood, the Director General of our ISI (Inter-Services Intelligence) was in Washington, and would be getting an earful from his counterparts as Musharraf's role would be crucial in the times ahead.

Fakhar was able to get through to me on the telephone the same evening. I suggested to him that he must somehow get word across to Musharraf that when President Bush called him, he must ask for a debt write-off for Pakistan in lieu of the support he would be asked to render to the United States. But Fakhar said it was fanciful of me to think he could get across to a man who would not even allow our daughter to win a local election. In any case, Fakhar informed me that our media was suggesting that Bush had already called Musharraf and obtained from him his unqualified support, without setting any terms and conditions. We had clearly blown another opportunity for our country.

Spending a few days in London with Umku, my return home marked the rise of Pervez Musharraf as the leader of Pakistan, being courted and wooed by dozens of high profile visitors arriving from all over the developed world, and droves of international media people installing themselves in Islamabad. Interviewed through satellite by BBC world, along with Richard Perle, the prominent neo-conservative close to the Bush administration, I was taken aback by the blatant Muslim bashing which Perle articulated without hesitation. Meanwhile Musharraf conceded several bases to the Americans in multiple localities inside Pakistan, and having been declared a crucial ally of the countries that mattered, he entered 2002 with great aplomb, clearly determined to have an election that would bring forth 'suitable' results. To ensure this, he set aside his fellow coup makers, replacing the corps commander Karachi, the Director General of the ISI (Inter-Services Intelligence) and the Chief of General Staff, implanting himself as dictator who was now internationally acceptable, a Hosni Mubarak in the making.

In December 2001, Musharraf dictated a change in the electoral laws, requiring all potential candidates to hold a Bachelor's degree in order to qualify for contest to Parliament, further announcing that elections would be conducted in July and August of the ensuing year. Obtaining the schedule for examinations to achieve the required qualification, I decided to sit for my BA examination in early summer that same year, so that my degree would be in hand in time for the elections. Many colleagues in the same situation decided to petition the Court on the grounds that this dictate was in contravention of the Constitution, but having no trust in the dodgy dictator, I counselled several of them to give the BA exam and get the degree just as I was doing.

As the next obstacle in our path, the newly appointed Director General of ISI spoke with Fakhar and me, asking us to persuade Mian Azhar, the President of the PML-(Q) to withdraw from his position in favour of Chaudhry Shujaat Hussain, which we flatly refused to do. We argued that Shujaat was the man who had nominated Azhar. Moreover, Azhar's reputation was sound: he was well-rooted in the politics of Lahore, and was suitably filling the vacuum that had been created by Nawaz Sharif's departure. On the other hand, several cases were pending against Chaudhry Shujaat in the Accountability Bureau. The General agreed with us, but said that he had been given orders. We discussed the matter with Shujaat, who agreed that Azhar ought to continue in his position.

In late spring of 2002, I was visiting Bangladesh to attend a conference, returning to Dhaka as I had stayed earlier with my late parents, I was assailed with memories of them and what was once East Pakistan. Dhaka seemed far more prosperous and immense my visit land marked by my encounters with a few Bengali friends, including Rahman Subhan who had visited Shah Jewna in the early sixties, accompanied by Hamza Alvi, a lecturer at Sussex University in Britain, who preached land reforms to my father, and was reminded by him that he ought to persuade the British to carry out land reforms, since most of his friends there farmed tens of thousands of acres on their estates! Dr Kamal Hossein and Rahman Subhan had been the ideologues of Bangladesh but seemed disappointed with its current condition under General Ershad. My friend Hasna's husband, Modoud, who was law minister, on the other hand was bullish about the economic progress their country was making.

On my return to Islamabad, Fakhar and I, along with a dozen colleagues were invited to meet with Musharraf to discuss a legal framework order he was proposing to announce. Azhar asked Fakhar to make a presentation on our behalf, which Fakhar did admirably, suggesting several amendments to the proposal. He emphasized that there was no need to expand the size of Parliament, nor was there any need to add to the required criteria for qualification as elucidated in Articles 58-(2b) sub sections 62 and 63 of the Constitution. All the former lawmakers concurred with the proposal while I contributed the thought that having just returned from Bangladesh, where the progress of women had been outstanding, they had done away with quota seats for our gender, and we ought to do the same, encouraging women to contest general elections. Musharraf looked quite at sea, not knowing how to respond to the hard-nosed advise he was being given, when Zafarullah Jamali bailed him out, saying that the army chief could do as he pleased it would be acceptable to most people, which made Musharraf look visibly relieved. As we were leaving the meeting, I told Zafarullah Jamali that he would probably become Prime Minister, while Fakhar and I would be ruled out, as we were perhaps a little too democratic-minded for the dictator's taste and he was clearly wary of us.

The Legal Framework Order (LFO) was declared. It was a triumph for Musharraf that all the major political parties of Pakistan decided to contest elections, without objecting to it. The National Assembly was enlarged by about an additional one-third number of seats, which led to a re-delimitation of constituencies. Fakhar decided to contest from two constituencies of Khanewal district, one in Kabirwala, where Qatalpur was located, the second one from Khanewal itself. Shugu picked two provincial constituencies for herself around the town of Jhang where the Sipah Sahaba was not a factor, while I was going to contest the new constituency which would be partially in Chiniot, and partially in Jhang. My rival would be Faisal Saleh Hayat, from whom I had won the last election, having previously lost to him. All three of us seemed to have easy elections ahead of us, and our campaigns moved smoothly, but when the results were announced Faisal Saleh Hayat had won from me by around twelve thousand votes. Raza Hayat Haraj won from Fakhar Imam by about fourteen thousand votes. However, Shugu won one of her constituencies and was now a member of the Punjab Assembly. Although we were deeply disappointed to be out of legislature, at least Shugu was there to keep our flag flying in the political arena. The elections had, of course, been heavily manipulated, with nearly every politician with conviction and a sturdy political base kept out of the legislature. Musharraf had it going all his own way. The powerful nations of the world acknowledged his elections as a legitimate process, and elected by the Parliament he had created, the world recognized him as a legitimate President! Living with this travesty made many millions of Pakistanis deeply unhappy, but not angry enough to spill out into the streets for the time being—the South Asian belief in the ballot continuing for the moment to be deeply ingrained among the public at large. People hoped that having voted in a government, the problems of deteriorating basic services, worsening law and order situation, and rising unemployment would be addressed and mitigated.

Within a few days after election results had been announced, it was clear that the hung Parliament would require further manipulation, since the PPP had pulled in a large block of seats. It came as no surprise to us that the twenty-two members of the PPP that announced a breakaway faction were led by Faisal Saleh Hayat, followed by Raza Hayat Haraj, calling themselves the 'patriot' group, who joined up with the PML-(Q), as did Maulana Azam Tariq, head of the Sipah Sahaba, who had been elected while under detention; and with these additions, Zafarullah Jamali was elected Prime Minister by a one-vote majority. This explained, we were convinced, the stuffing of the ballot boxes of our rivals. Mian Azhar fell by the wayside like us. And in subsequent years Musharraf authored a book in which he claimed having sponsored the PML-(Q) with Chaudhry Shujaat as the leader of this party. Clearly the episode of the rump of the PML-(N) breaking away of its own volition, and Azhar being elected by the majority of suspended Parliamentarians was not even noticed by Musharraf as in classic dictatorial style, he simply ordered the intelligence community to have some people elected and some eliminated, by the time elections were held in the third year of his rule.

Fakhar and I were in Lahore where we watched on television Zafarullah Khan Jamali take oath as Prime Minister. The following day, two journalists came to visit us, to say that they were coming straight from the airport, having just flown in from Dubai. They informed us that they had been with Benazir Bhutto, who had requested them to visit us and to urge me to contest from the constituency vacated by her party member from Bahawalpur who had also contested from Lahore, and had retained the Lahore constituency. She felt that my presence in this National Assembly would be salutary and sitting on Opposition benches, I would be effective in ensuring that more and more of her members did not join up with the renegades. I told our visitors that while it was nice of her to repose confidence in me by making such an offer, it was an unrealistic suggestion, because having had me eliminated in my own constituency, the covert apparatus of the Musharraf regime was not likely to allow me to get in through a bye-election. In any case this was a rigged Assembly, and would eventually come down like a house of cards, but it would be interesting for her and me to meet and we could set up something whenever it would be mutually convenient.

Shortly after receiving Benazir's message via the journalists, Qasim Zia, the President of the PPP in Punjab, who was also Leader of the Opposition in the Punjab Assembly, came to call on me to say that Benazir Bhutto invited me to visit her in Dubai. I told him that it would not be appropriate for me to undertake a visit especially to Dubai, which was not a locale familiar to me. I would rather meet his party leader in London or Washington whenever her travel plans concurred with mine.

Meanwhile, Fakhar, Azhar, and a few of our other associates who had our elections stolen from us were going to caucus to decide a collective course of action, and Fakhar and I were also going to file election petitions to try and establish that our elections had been rigged. As we started networking with our political friends from different parts of the country, we decided to set up an Independent Democratic Group, to tour different towns and cities, address Bar Associations in the High Courts and the District Courts, and to mobilize public opinion against a sham democracy, against corrupt practices multiplying in government, against a compromised foreign policy, and above all, against covert support to militancy. Musharraf had tasked his covert apparatus to ensure a fusion of the religious political parties which included the Jamaat-i-Islami, the two factions of the Jamiat Ulema-e-Islam and the Jamiat Ulema-e-Pakistan, to enter into a coalition called the Muttahida Majlis-e-Amal, or united front for action, with the acronym MMA, which many people described as the Mullah Military Alliance.

The MMA had formed government in the NWFP (Khyber Pakhtunkhwa) bordering Pakistan, and while the Americans were duped into believing that the MMA would contain the militants, it was actually only strengthening them. The bombing of Tora Bora by the NATO forces in Afghanistan drove more militants into Pakistan, where it was easy for them to obtain sanctuary, given the friendly nature of the provincial government. This duality was obviously going to spread militancy throughout Pakistan. We were persuaded that unless people came out in the streets to challenge Musharraf's military dictatorship, Pakistan's fundamental interests would be increasingly jeopardized. And those who were sitting in the assemblies but not supporting the government could only perform effectively as opposition if some pressure built up, with some amount of restlessness reflected in the streets of urban centres of the country. Musharraf had also undertaken a reckless programme of privatization, leading to non-transparent and sketchy deals.

During the course of the year, the IDG, our Independent Democratic Group, picked up some steam but not enough for us to launch a movement. Meanwhile, Shugu was inducted by Chief Minister Punjab, Parvez Ilahi, in his Cabinet. We were proud of our daughter, she was much too outstanding to have been ignored, but we knew that her elevation would not last long, as she did not really fit into the paradigm of corrupt practices that had become the hallmark of Musharraf's political arm. Some of those who had earlier been locked up as a part of the short-lived accountability process initiated by Musharraf were now important ministers in the federal as well as provincial governments, while Asif Zardari, Benazir Bhutto's spouse remained under detention on charges of corruption.

Umku was back in Pakistan, continuing to track her small ten megawatt power project, relocating it in Jhang, while Abid decided to sign up at the Columbia Law School in New York. In September 2003, I went to visit him. Before my departure, Qasim Zia informed me that Benazir Bhutto was going to be in Washington at the same time, so he coordinated a meeting between the two of us. Flying down from New York to Washington, Benazir and I decided to have brunch together at the Hay Adam's Hotel. She apologized to me for not having reached out to me earlier, saying that since all politics were essentially local, it was her fault in giving precedence to my local rival, who had ended up being a shameless turncoat. She reminded me that her mother remained fond of me, and her father had held me in high esteem, as did her father-in-law, so she hoped that now we would be friends. Assuring her that the air between us would clear if she could explain to me why she had failed to be transparent in her financial dealings, given that even her father's worst enemies could not lay financial misdemeanours at his doorstep. Had she followed that part of his legacy as well, nobody would have been able to displace her from her position as Prime Minister. Her answer was almost poignant, though not quite excusable. She explained that her mother, being a simple person, before her father's brutal elimination, gave away whatever cash they had to whoever said they could help, so that by the time they were allowed to leave the country, they had to ask Shaikh Zayed of Abu Dhabi for assistance. Although he was generous, it was not pleasant to incur this kind of obligation; so on becoming Prime Minister, her priority was never to be in a situation where she would have to ask anyone for money again. Appreciating her for giving an honest answer, I made her promise that if she became Prime Minister for a third time, she would run government transparently, and whatever she had which were surplus to her own and her children's requirement for a reasonably comfortable life, she would spend on the people of Pakistan. She made the promise with generosity of spirit, and we settled down to a discussion of how Musharraf could be got rid of before he caused irrevocable damage to our country. Both of us agreed that he had caused great damage already.

While informing her about the IDG, and of the curtailments for mounting a mass movement to oust the dictator, it was our view that her return to Pakistan would make a meaningful difference, but first and foremost Benazir would have to get her spouse out of the clutches of the Musharraf team. She wondered how that would be possible. I told her that the two people whom we gathered had Musharraf's ear, his Principal Secretary Tariq Aziz and his Military Secretary Nadeem Taj, should be contacted by her and a negotiation for the release of her husband initiated. She said that her factotum Rahman Malik seemed to know Tariq Aziz, so a negotiating process could be launched, but she wondered what the trade off would be? Probably the same as the one that Nawaz Sharif had used with Farooq Leghari: resignations of her party members from Parliament, was my suggestion. This threat might secure Asif's release, after which it would be in order for Asif and her to go to Saudi Arabia for pilgrimage and a meeting with Nawaz Sharif, in coordination with whom she could mull out a plan to formulate a common strategy for the ouster of Musharraf.

Our first meeting lasted well over two hours, and we agreed to meet a couple of days later in the home of Riffat and Shaista Mahmood for dinner. Shaista arranged a friendly dinner, inviting my friend Fauzia and her husband Larry, our common friend Peter Galbraith, a friend of Peter's from the State Department, and another couple who were friends of Benazir and mine, Dennis and Marie Kux. Everyone at this dinner wanted to know how Benazir and I had managed to smoke the peace pipe, without anyone finding out. She responded by saying that when two people have a common perception regarding the damage being caused to their country, they come together. My explanation added that both of us had a mutual understanding of what would trigger a military dictator's downfall, a dictator who had, for the time-being, the unqualified support of the international community. When asked if we would be willing to share the perception, Benazir looked towards me, and I explained that we were in agreement that a collaboration between Nawaz Sharif and Benazir Bhutto would have enormous impact on the people of our country, as it would bring the conservative and liberal communities together which was the standard requirement for taking on a military dictator in our political culture. And if appropriately publicized, this would, in all probability, trigger a chain of events that could eventually lead to a popular movement against our fourth military dictator. Even President Bush would have to pull back support from Musharraf and allow a popular upsurge to result in a fresh election. Not everyone at the table was entirely convinced by my prognosis, which elicited further questions, with Benazir fielding some of them while I handled others. As dinner wound up, Peter observed that he was happy to see that the capacity to hold forth, which was a characteristic shared by his only two women friends from Pakistan, had been contained by both! Benazir then took me aside, saying that we had set a ball rolling. But since she had to leave the following day and would want to see me again as soon as possible. I told her that ARY Television wanted me to come to Dubai to record a programme, hence, I will visit her there towards the end of the year.

When I met Benazir Bhutto in Dubai a few months later, I asked her if I could meet her mother, but she said her Alzheimer's had advanced to such an extent that she really did not allow anyone but her doctors to meet her, although she would like me to meet her children. So we had a meal together—it was pleasant for me to see Benazir in the role of a devoted mother. She was living in an unwieldy house in Jumairah, large but not palatial. Her children did not say much, the one that I was most attracted was Bakhtawar, who, as the classic middle child, had the strongest personality out of the three, rather like my Shugu. Benazir told me that Rahman Malik had set up contact for the release of Asif Zardari, but progress was slow, and that Musharraf was a harder nut to crack than we had assumed. Taking an optimistic view, assuming that Asif would be released sooner rather than later, we went into detail regarding their visit to Jeddah. Benazir was uncertain about Nawaz Sharif's response if they tried to visit him, but I assured her that the response would be positive and they would probably find him very cooperative at the suggestion of collaborating to bring down the man who had treated him so shabbily.

Asif Zardari was finally released from detention within three months after my visit to Dubai. Fakhar and I had gone to Karachi to speak at an event, and met with Asif for dinner in the home of his father Hakim Ali Zardari and his stepmother and my friend Timmy. We found Asif warm and friendly. We complimented him on his steadfastness in putting up with seven years of confinement. He invited us to Bilawal House, the name given to his residence in Karachi, which was constructed when Benazir became Prime Minister the first time, and had been at the centre of considerable controversy for being vast and luxurious. The architecture was not easy on the eye, a portion of the house served as the public domain and served as the party secretariat. The private quarters were housed in a large compound, surrounded by high walls. The house did not strike me as being inordinately luxurious. Asif informed us that he was going to tour Sindh and visit Lahore before he left for Dubai to spend some time with his wife and children. His tour of Sindh was well-received by the people of our second largest province. In Lahore, although a large number of PPP workers visited his house that he had acquired in Lahore cantonment, the city remained largely disinterested in his presence as most Punjabis tended to pin the blame for Benazir's failure on her spouse, Asif Zardari.

Episodes of terrorism were on the rise throughout the country. In markets, in mosques, in *Imambarahs*, remote-controlled bombs were being detonated, often resulting in the killing of scores of men, women, and children. In fear, well-off Pakistanis had begun to transfer their resources to other countries, and obtaining dual nationalities in Canada, United States, Australia, Britain, Greece, Italy, Spain, the Nordic countries, and most of all Dubai. Meanwhile, the population of the country was rising without any check and balance. No one in government seemed to be interested in addressing this very crucial issue. With assistance from NATO countries, billions of dollars were pouring into our defence establishment and the public sector. Banker turned Finance Minister Shaukat Aziz introduced consumer banking in a major way, with consumer goods such as cars, motorcycles, air conditioners, refrigerators, washing machines, etc. all being sold on easy instalments. Hence a sense of artificial prosperity was created but little money was spent on improving the infrastructure. Private television channels proliferated, and while the regime tolerated criticism, the increasingly commercialized media by and large tilted in favour of the regime. Drone attacks which eliminated a few militants, were heavily publicized episodes, and gave a fillip to the election campaign of George W. Bush as America entered the serious phase of its contest for President.

Benazir Bhutto and Asif Zardari did go to Jeddah and seemed to have had a convivial meeting with Nawaz Sharif and his family. She messaged me to ask when it would be possible for us to meet. Abid was graduating from Law School in June, and I messaged Benazir that me along with Fakhar and Umku would stop in Dubai en route to the US and meet her. Shugu had resigned from her ministry but was going to remain in Lahore for the budget session of the Assembly. Benazir asked us to join her and Asif for dinner at a restaurant around the corner from her house. She said they had got on well with Nawaz Sharif and Kulsum Nawaz. They had decided on framing a charter of democracy together. Fakhar suggested that the charter include the setting up a truth and reconciliation commission, taking a leaf out of Nelson Mandela's book. Benazir requested Fakhar to frame the chapter along with some of the proposals he had written up for the Independent Democratic Group, of which I had sent her a copy, which he might consider relevant for inclusion in the charter. She claimed that she had managed the PPP through the internet in the last six years as her phone calls continued to be monitored and intercepted. Her filing system was not up to the mark as she had little help of any competence and had misplaced the papers we had sent her, but she recalled that when she had read them, she was impressed with most of the ideas which had been succinctly framed, and she hoped that the charter that she drew up in cooperation with Nawaz Sharif would inspire and motivate the people of Pakistan to come out to fight for their democratic rights.

Nawaz Sharif had managed to use his influence with the Saudi rulers to allow his brother, Shahbaz Sharif to relocate to New York for treatment of his health issues, close on the heels of the demise of their father, Mian Sharif, and it was reasonable to assume that soon enough Nawaz would be able to move to London from Riyadh, where he and Benazir could sit together to sign their charter. She wanted all the paperwork to be in place as soon as possible. The death of Mian Sharif and his burial in Lahore without the presence of his sons had caused sympathy among people throughout our country, and Nawaz Sharif was likely to cash in on the sentiment. His followers had thronged their homes in Raiwind, in suburban Lahore, for the Qul, or third day prayer after the burial, which Fakhar, along with Mian Azhar had attended.

We reached New York to share Abid's proud moment when he obtained his Juris Doctor degree from the Columbia School of

Law to enter a profession that he was eminently suited for, being argumentative by nature and a gifted debater. He had decided to join a prestigious law firm in New York and planned to live in the city for at least two years. We spent a happy time together, but when we returned home after a few weeks, a nasty episode had erupted in Sui, in the Bugti area of Balochistan. A woman doctor posted at the local hospital was raped and had accused a military officer of the Frontier Corps as the perpetrator of the crime. This heinous crime was vociferously condemned by Nawab Akbar Khan Bugti who was in Dera Bugti at the time, in the vicinity of Sui. General Pervez Musharraf was quick to jump to the defence of the military officer; the complainant doctor was shifted to Karachi and silenced by her employers who were executives of the government-owned gas company. But Nawab Akbar Bugti kept the issue alive in the media, and a war of words thereafter ensued between the great Baloch leader and the self-appointed President Pervez Musharraf, which caused widespread tension in the Baloch areas, which made up, territorially the largest province of Pakistan.

The tide of public opinion was definitely turning away from Musharraf but, revelling in his circle of cronies, Musharraf was clearly oblivious to his lack of popular acceptability. Nor did the increasing episodes of terrorism, combined frequently with sectarian killings, seem to disturb him. Having survived five years as dictator, he seemed confident of securing his decade. But a great deal depended on how the American elections would unfold. Senator John Kerry emerged as the presidential candidate of the Democratic Party. Fakhar and I were invited by the National Democratic Institute (NDI) to attend the Convention of the Democrats in Boston. En route we stopped in London. There we met Benazir who agreed that if Senator Kerry won the contest,

Musharraf would face more difficulty, but her sense was that Bush would be re-elected.

Fakhar and I enjoyed the Democratic Convention; particularly the speeches of Presidents Jimmy Carter and Bill Clinton and the new star of the Democratic Party, Barack Obama whose oratory swayed Fakhar into predicting that he would be elected US President in 2008. I was more concerned with whether Senator Kerry would pull through, feeling deeply dejected when he failed. The re-election of George W. Bush was an unquestionable shot in the arm for Pervez Musharraf. Most of our American friends were also dejected, complaining to us that the war that Bush had embroiled the US in was not going well at all. Saddam Hussein's trial had made even veteran Saddam critics feel embarrassed, and the war in Afghanistan had begun to look increasingly like a nightmare, and a bloody one at that. Musharraf was successfully making a fool out of Bush by constantly going back on his assurances of fighting the militants, while he was clearly protecting them at the cost of thousands of Pakistani lives. Weapons manufacturers in America were obviously profiting from their relationship with Bush, while arms dealers were enriching themselves through Musharraf. Despite all that was being written on these issues, the elimination of half a dozen terrorists in Afghanistan and Pakistan seemed to secure victory for Bush, and concurrently prolong Musharraf being in power.

In the summer of 2005, local elections were announced by the Musharraf regime, with endless propaganda on how successful the four-year term of 'devolution' had been. The visible success, of course, was that corruption had devolved down to the grass roots. Stealing public money was no longer even commented upon; financial honesty becoming a rare virtue. It came as a surprise, therefore, when, while sitting in my home at Jhang, I received a telephone call from someone who identified himself as a colonel from the ISI, saying he wanted to visit me. I told him that since local elections had been announced, there were many visitors at my residence, but if he wanted to join the gathering he could come. He said he would need to talk to me in private for a few minutes, and if that was possible he would come right away. I answered him in the affirmative.

Two brand new land cruisers (doubtless resourced by coalition support funds provided by the Americans for our assistance to them in the failing war against terrorism) swung into the driveway of Shah Jewna House. A colonel and a major alighted from the vehicles. I politely shook hands with them while my visitors were seated in the verandah. With equal politeness I asked them to seat themselves, and continued my lecture to my visitors on the importance of honesty in the utilization of public resources. As expected, within a few minutes the colonel said he wanted to speak to me privately. I took him and the major into my sitting room, pointing out to them the historic photographs of my late father with all the great leaders of the Independence Movement, both, of the Indian National Congress, as well as of the All-India Muslim League.

Both the young officers seemed to be duly impressed, with the colonel repeating several times, that what they were seeing was history. He then asked if he could proceed to inform me regarding the nature of his visit, to which I said that he was probably wanting me to stay out of the local elections. 'On the contrary, Madam, we have come to request you to become the candidate for District Nazim, because according to our survey you are the only person here who can manage this district.'

'Thank you colonel, while I am flattered to hear this, there is no remote interest on my part to do a job which I did a quarter of a century earlier. Why must I limit myself to Jhang, why should I not aim to be Chief Minister or even Prime Minister?'

'Sure, Madam, it is your right to aim. But do not mind my saying so, Madam, there is only one problem in the way. You do not own textile mills and sugar mills and to aim so high you really have to have a lot of money and mills.'

'Colonel, I must thank you for making me understand finally why my husband and I stand disqualified from leadership.' He tried to persuade me that the district was the appropriate level for me. I thought he was refreshingly honest, and shook his hand warmly as he proceeded to take his leave, certain that in Musharraf's Pakistan, he would never be elevated to senior positions. The nexus between money and power had started during the Ayub regime, which launched the military industrial complex in Pakistan, and appeared to have come full circle in Musharraf's realm. Cloaked in some layers of pretence in the past, it had now come to be the prevailing reality of the day. The attributes of capability, integrity, and a strong work ethic were not what leadership in Pakistan needed to be based on. Sugar mills, textile mills, and manipulative skills were now the formula for leadership. Fakhar and I would continue our struggle but there remained little doubt in my mind that the exercise of power would remain elusive to us.

The local elections went through with most of the districts throughout our country getting more of the same, while the majority of folk were by now persuaded that Musharraf was becoming an increasing liability not only for our country, but for the entire world. However, it would take America a bit of time to find out. Public opinion against America had also reached down to the grass roots, with those availing of American assistance the most, cursing America the most. An ill-wind was blowing through our land and likely to culminate in some great natural disaster in the opinion of soothsayers and forecasters of all manner and types.

15

Nawab Akbar Bugti's Assassination

In September 2005 I went to Dubai, needing to buy a stallion for my stud farm. Having procured some sales catalogues, I had earmarked a few horses that were well bred and had broken down on the Dubai race track. A trainer, who was in touch with me, suggested that these animals would be available for sale at affordable prices, but would require me to have a look at them and then strike a suitable deal. Timmy Zardari, Hakim Ali Zardari's wife, was visiting her niece in Dubai and asked me to stay with her. It was the month of Ramadhan (fasting), and the day after my arrival, Timmy invited Benazir for Iftar (first meal to open the fast at sunset).

That morning (8 October 2005) I set off for a stud farm owned by one of the Maktoums to inspect a potential stallion for my farm. The trainer met me at the stables, which were in an immense centrally air-conditioned barn. While we were looking at the horses, a Pakistani groom came running up to us and in a deeply agitated voice, informed us that Pakistan had been hit by a devastating earthquake. Azad Kashmir, the NWFP (Khyber Pakhtunkhwa), and some parts of Punjab had been badly affected. Thousands of people had been buried under collapsed structures. My heart lurched up to my mouth, and I immediately left the stud farm, telling the driver to speed me back to my lodgings in the Arabian Ranches enclave. Thanks to the modern miracle of the mobile phones, I was able to speak to Umku at Lahore, Shugu at Jhang, and Fakhar at Multan, and they all reassured me that our family, friends, and employees were all fine, and that our homes and buildings were all intact. When I reached Timmy's niece Poppy's home, both of them were glued to the television, watching gruesome shots of the apartment block which collapsed in Islamabad. The death toll in Azad Kashmir was frighteningly high.

Benazir arrived shortly before Iftar. She loved the delicious savouries prepared by Timmy, and helped herself to a moderate amount, but none of us could do justice to the delectable dinner because of the sad news. After dinner, Benazir and I settled ourselves in front of the television, and sat for eight hours straight to follow the dreadful news that was being telecast from home. Timmy discreetly ensured that nobody disturbed us.

I told BiBi about my visitors from the Intelligence, informing her that since she owned several sugar mills in Sindh, she qualified for leadership at least by this measure and criterion of our intelligence community. Benazir told me to stop pouring salt on injuries, her party having been battered in the local elections even in Sindh this time, and assured me that once back in power, she would dispose off the mills and spend the money on the people of Pakistan, as per her promise made to me. Asif Zardari was in New York receiving treatment for the heart condition he had developed. Benazir told me that they had agreed that Asif would not return to Pakistan if she was able to regain power. He would live in Dubai with the children and keep an eye on their schooling, while her time would be exclusively devoted to Pakistan. She went on to say that he had also promised to stop dabbling in business if they returned to power. All this was a good idea, and I told Benazir as much, adding that if Asif was in Pakistan he would be the 'fall guy' again. She asked me to explain what that meant. I told her with brutal frankness that if she made compromises allowing her party people to indulge in financial excesses, while keeping herself clean, Asif would be blamed for it all, as his reputation had been so sullied that even seven years in prison had not succeeded in redeeming his image.

On hearing this, Benazir seemed disturbed. Suddenly she said if she could ask me a very personal question. When I answered in the affirmative, she asked me whether my husband had ever been unfaithful in our marriage. I told her that like any wife who had clocked thirty-five years with her spouse, I had certainly had my moments of suspicion, but in all fairness to Fakhar, there was nothing that could ever be seriously pinned on him. Whereupon, Benazir said with ineffable sadness, that perhaps she had not been as fortunate, but she loved Asif very deeply, so she forgave him, even when he hurt her. She then said that I was lucky to have the best marriage in politics in our country and she envied me for it. My response to her was that, in fact, she was the one who had the best marriage in politics, she made most of the errors and her husband was the one who went to jail and incurred the bad name! My husband would never take the rap for me; he would tell me that if I had done something wrong then I must pay for it. This explanation seemed to cheer her up.

Benazir and I talked till the early hours of the morning. She was curious about the clans and prominent families of the Punjab, telling me that I was a mine of information, and how she would be happy to have me working with her or at least be available to her for advise and guidance. When she was leaving we embraced each other fondly, The call for *fajr*, early morning prayers, drifted through the windows of Poppy's home. We had been together from *Iftar* till *Sehr* (early morning meal before the start of the fast)! We promised to meet again, perhaps next time in London, as early as possible in the coming year.

News on television was becoming progressively worse. Thousands were declared dead; tens of thousands rendered homeless. Musharraf's appeal to people and to the world at large for earthquake relief was met with huge response in the form of money and other aid. This only meant that the ill wind had blown against the people but had left Musharraf unscathed. Benazir and I agreed that he would ride out the year comfortably and cash in on the calamity.

Not having the heart to examine horses after hearing about the havoc the earthquake had wrought in the lives of so many, I returned home to Pakistan to my family and friends, and to make my own contribution towards the relief effort for the victims of the earthquake. Generous aid was received from world over: with the Cubans sending in medical teams, and the Turks, Japanese, Europeans, and Americans all donating generously. The people of Pakistan all stood up and donated in all manner: from money to food to shelter to water. No one held back, be it the corporate sector, political parties, school children, people with modest means, and the wealthy. And indeed one of the success stories in Pakistan has been the construction of homes and the resettlement of the earthquake victims within three to four years. In the short run, it gave Musharraf enough of a sense of power for him to deepen his dispute with the Baloch, most particularly with Nawab Akbar Khan Bugti, which also enabled him to take the focus away from Nawaz Sharif relocating to London from Riyadh, with lots of people going to visit him from Pakistan, along with the Pakistani diaspora living in Britain.

By early 2006, when the dust began to settle on the earthquake calamity, talk of a Charter of Democracy being signed between Benazir Bhutto and Nawaz Sharif started doing the rounds. Benazir was now in regular touch with me. Pakistan Peoples Party's (PPP) office-bearers would come to call whenever we were in Lahore, with Jahangir Badar, Secretary General and Qasim Zia, the President of the Punjab wing of the PPP, being our most frequent visitors. Fakhar sent Benazir a two-page document on the Truth and Reconciliation Commission as he conceived it in the context of our situation, along with what he had put together as the agenda for the IDG (Independent Democratic Group). She sent Makhdum Amin Fahim, the senior Vice President of her party to visit us in Lahore to thank Fakhar for his contribution towards the Charter of Democracy which she was now finalizing and planned to sign it with Nawaz Sharif, who had accepted her draft, making some nominal additions, in mid May. We told Amin Fahim that we would like to sign the charter as the IDG. He said he would pass on the message to her. He got back to us to say that while she had readily agreed, Nawaz had not agreed to include us when the party heads met to sign the charter since IDG was not a party, but Benazir would be happy to have us sign the charter, with her as head of the PPP, with ourselves as the IDG.

Fakhar and I reached London just after the charter was signed between Benazir, Nawaz Sharif, and several other regional and smaller party leaders on 14 May 2006. We met with Shahbaz Sharif and Nisar Ali for lunch, and expressed our disappointment at not having been included in the signing of the charter, along with everyone else, so we were now going to sign it bilaterally with Benazir Bhutto. I tracked with them the story of my meetings with her over the last three years, of how we developed a friendship, and of how I was now even thinking of teaming up with her and was on the verge of joining her party. They asked Fakhar what he was going to do, and Fakhar responded that he was so far undecided. Nisar Ali thought that my joining the PPP and Fakhar remaining independent was not a bad idea. I would serve as a bridge between Benazir and them, and he knew me to be an effective bridge-builder, referring to my having brought them together with Farooq Leghari. We adjourned on a comfortable note, and a few days later we signed the Charter of Democracy with Benazir Bhutto at her Queensgate flat in London, in the presence of Amin Fahim, Jahangir Badar, and Qasim Zia, and a large number of media people from the television as well as journalists.

After we had spoken with the media, Benazir took us aside into a small lounge of her flat. She asked Amin Fahim to join us. She told us that she was excited to learn from Timmy that I was thinking of rejoining the PPP. While answering in the affirmative, I told her that Fakhar was undecided, and that she should try and persuade him, to which she said that perhaps I could join first and Fakhar Sahib (as Fakhar was addressed by Benazir, while she called me Abida) could consider joining later. I told her what Nisar Ali had said, and at the mention of Farooq Leghari she frowned, but went on to say that I was welcome any time, while she hoped that my 'better half' would not remain independent for too long. Amin Fahim said that Fakhar Imam was like his brother and he would keep seeking to persuade him. She then came out to see us off, which we were told was a courtesy she extended to very few people.

My friend Patsy's husband, David Maude Roxby had kinship with Francis Maude who was shadow Chancellor of the Exchequer. Patsy and David organized a dinner party at my request for Maude and Benazir to meet and chat informally. Blair was becoming progressively unpopular and it would be useful to acquaint ourselves with Conservative party leaders. Patsy had a beautiful and spacious ground-floor flat in a gated community of Kensington. Benazir was very taken in by Patsy's hospitality and the warmth and elegance of the ambience, complimenting me in Urdu that I had wonderful friends. At the dinner table Maude asked Benazir how a military autocrat in power in Pakistan could be displaced, causing minimum damage to the country. Benazir said that Fakhar Imam had an interesting proposal to make on the subject. Fakhar explained to Maude that the coming year would be the run-up year to parliamentary elections in Pakistan, and Musharraf would want to be re-elected President but an Article of the Constitution of Pakistan would be an impediment, because as Chief of Army Staff he was holding an 'office of profit', and unless two years elapsed, he could not seek re-election. Musharraf would then seek a waiver from the Supreme Court, which would be impossible for him to obtain because the bar associations of our country were active, and politicians like ourselves were out there addressing these associations, sensitizing them to the issue that would inevitably arise regarding Musharraf's re-election. And if the political party leaders, opposed to the regime, activated their supportive lawyers and parliamentarians, sending them regularly and consistently to address the bar associations, a lawyers movement would be catalysed which would effectively render it impossible for the court to grant a waiver, in view of a robust nexus between the bar and the bench which was part of our institutional practices. Maude observed that this was a fascinating hypothesis.

When we met Benazir after this dinner, she picked Fakhar's brain further on the issue; we were impressed with her capacity to examine every possibility in minute detail. Benazir agreed that a lawyer's movement, if effectively orchestrated, could turn into Pervez Musharraf's Waterloo.

In the last week of July, we flew back to Lahore. Mir Balakh Sher Mazari stopped by to see us. Nawab Akbar Bugti had left his home in Dera Bugti and was living in a cave in the arid hills nearby, in what was Bugti tribal territory. Balakh Sher was in touch with him via satellite telephone. He informed us that the Nawab was keeping good health, and by living in the caves he was not only stressing himself, but his life was now in serious danger. Balakh Sher had gathered from the local intelligence community stationed at Rajanpur, in the Mazari tribal area, that Musharraf had ordered the elimination of Nawab Akbar Bugti. He suspected that some ploy would be engineered to force Akbar Bugti to come out of the caves. He would then be assassinated. We were horrified to hear this and thought that the Nawab should somehow be persuaded to return home. He could then somehow come to Karachi where he would be relatively safe and also be able to get proper medical care. When we said as much, Mir Balakh Sher told us that we could cautiously suggest the same to the Nawab on the satellite phone, and he hoped that we are able to persuade Bugti although he had refused to listen to his family.

We called Akbar Bugti on the number that Balakh Sher gave us and managed to get through. Fakhar spoke first, offering a prayer for his brother, and our good friend, Mir Ahmed Nawaz Bugti, who had passed away during our absence from the country. Fakhar then handed me the telephone. After telling Akbar Bugti who I was I said to him, 'Nawab Sahib, will you please come out of this cave of yours and go down to Karachi to get yourself properly treated. You need to look after your health. Your daughter Baby is certain to take good care of you, and your family and many friends are extremely anxious about you.'

Nawab Bugti's voice came across loud and clear, 'Abida Bibi, good to hear your voice. Ahmed was younger than me and he has gone. I have clocked nearly eighty years and it is time for me to go. And your Punjabi army is going to kill me, which will convert me into the spirit of liberated Balochistan. That would be a befitting end for me with no regrets.'

'Nawab Sahib, our army is not that stupid. Musharraf may be, but not the entire army, surely. There have been commanders like Generals Abdul Waheed Kakar, Ali Kuli Khan, Salahuddin Tirmizy. Many of them are Pushtuns and they hold you in high esteem.' My voice did not seem to be reaching him, subsequently fading away, and finally the line went dead. Mir Balakh Sher, Fakhar, and I sat in silence for a while, gradually pursuing discussion on what could be done. Eventually, we decided to draft an open letter to Musharraf for release to the media.

A civil society group had written an open letter to Musharraf which had obtained good coverage in the media a few days earlier. This letter had mentioned some of the fault-lines emerging in our body politic, and we hoped that our letter would be similarly publicized. We decided to obtain the signatures of two widely respected former chief justices of the Supreme Court, Syed Sajjad Ali Shah and Saeed uz Zaman Siddiqui, who had refused to take fresh oath after Musharraf's intervention in October 1999. As former Ambassador to the United States I was also among the signatories, along with former Speakers, Fakhar Imam and Ilahi Bux Soomro; former Deputy Speaker Wazir Ahmed Jogezai; former Chief Minister Balochistan, Mir Taj Mohammad Jamali; and former Caretaker Prime Minister Mir Balakh Sher Mazari.

The letter was a strongly worded plea for Nawab Akbar Khan Bugti's life to be protected, for the best health-care for him to be ensured, for his demand for an enhanced royalty for gas for the Bugti tribe from the gas fields of Sui, and royalties for the Marri tribe from the Marri gas fields. This was imperative for diminishing the alienation of the two largest tribes of Balochistan, and for the strengthening of the federation of Pakistan. Despite our best effort, only one television channel telecast the news in one bulletin regarding our open letter, and only one newspaper, the English daily *Dawn*, printed it on their back page. Musharraf's media managers successfully managed to kill the news of the open letter at a wider level. There was little else we could do, hence, Fakhar returned to Multan to tend to his farming and I returned to Jhang to tend to mine.

On 26 August 2006 Nawab Akbar Khan Bugti was assassinated. Shugu was with me when we got the news. He had come out of the caves in the Bugti area and was on his way to the Marri area when he was attacked, sheltering himself in a compound with the help of Balach Marri, the heroic son of Nawab Khair Bux Marri, Akbar Bugti's lifelong friend and classmate at Aitchison College in Lahore. Shugu and I mulled over what this brutal assassination would portend for Pakistan, and were both quite clear that Balochistan was likely to remain a troubled part of our federation for a long time to come. It did not make any sense to me that Musharraf, supposedly a partner of the Americans in their war against terrorism and religious extremism, should have a secular Baloch leader allegedly assassinated.

The Pushtun localities of Balochistan were bristling with militants and terrorists. Most notably, my old stalkers, the Lashkar Jhangvi, and the Jaish-e-Muhammad, headed by Mullah Azhar, who had been held in an Indian jail for four years, and released at Kandahar airfield from a mysteriously hijacked airplane, which took off from Delhi, landed at Lahore, then equally mysteriously, through the personal prowess of commando Musharraf, diverted to Kandahar in Afghanistan. And Jundullah, the notoriously anti-Iran militia; all these Wahabi religious extremists had their sanctuaries in these Pushtun localities, while the Baloch tribes were all predominantly secular. So why was Pervez Musharraf so preoccupied with Akbar Bugti was the key question? Could he still be bearing a grudge over the woman doctor who had been raped at Sui and in whose defence Nawab Akbar had spoken up? If this was so, it would be absurdly petty of Musharraf. Moreover, it did not make sense for the already sensitive Baloch issue to be widened into an open fissure. No patriotic Pakistani could condone this senseless act. All this could lead to disastrous consequences for our federation. The spilling of more Baloch blood would certainly not help in controlling the alleged insurgency. All of this was happening under Musharraf's watch, whose slogan was 'Pakistan first'. None of it made any sense at all.

The Quetta airport was sealed along with all the highways leading from Sindh and Punjab into Balochistan. Both Fakhar and I could not forget how Nawab Akbar Bugti had driven alone from Dera Bugti all the way to Shah Jewna on the death of my father, and we were wondering how we could reach Quetta to make our bereavement call on Nawab Akbar Khan's grieving family.

We called Mir Balakh Sher who informed us that he had obtained special permission because of his kinship with the Nawab to attend his Qul, third day prayer, and was driving from his home in Rojhan to Quetta where the family were located after the funeral. He was informed that Quetta airport would be de-sealed on day five after the burial, so we could take a flight from Islamabad. In the meantime, he would inform Nawab Bugti's family of our arrival. We took that flight, and were received at the Quetta airport by Tarik Khetran, Mir Balakh Sher's nephew and former classmate of Fakhar's late brother at Aitchison College.

Tarik drove us to the Bugti House located in the older parts of the city. Jamil Bugti, one of Nawab Akbar Khan's surviving sons, received us in the narrow alley which led to the house. His older brother, Talal was in the *hujrah* (sitting room for men) receiving the bereavement callers, where Fakhar was escorted. Making my way to the women's quarters, walking past hundreds of Bugti women inside the compound, I entered the familiar porch and verandah of the house, and into the drawing room. The women of the family were seated on the carpeted floor, wailing and mourning in the traditional manner for the man who had been pivotal to their lives. The ritual of mourning for the Bugti women was similar to the way it is for Bokhari women, when our Pirs pass on. One woman begins the wailing in a rhythmic tone, calling out the name of the mourner and the relationship of the mourner to the departed soul, after which all the women join in the wailing in unison. The immediate family sit straight backed and restrained, with relatives rocking backwards and forwards and their weeping getting louder.

All the women of Nawab Akbar's family were there. Each one of them embraced me: his surviving sisters, wives, daughters, daughters-in-law, their daughters, Mir Ahmed Nawaz's widow and daughters. The only one missing was my friend Baby. Rehan's widow and Brahmdagh's mother informed me that her husband was on his deathbed and she had left after the Qul to tend to him in Karachi. Durdana, Baby's sister, put me on the mobile phone to her and we wept together on the air waves. I condoled with all of them separately. Durdana then took me to her brother Jamil's lodgings which was situated at the opposite end of the compound for a cup of tea. Durdana was married to our friend Humayun Marri, Nawab Khair Bux Marri's nephew. She insisted that we visit their home later in the day. We first visited her and carried on to have dinner with Senator Fasih Iqbal, who was the owner and editor of the *Balochistan Times*, an English language daily.

Fasih was an Urdu-speaking settler of Quetta and was friends with several tribal leaders. He took us for dinner to the Quetta Club, where he had invited a few friends. We were a sombre group, all sitting and grieving, reminiscing about Nawab Akbar Khan, in the garden of the club. It was a balmy evening, a buffet dinner had been laid out, and many families were around, mostly army folk, attacking the food, appearing to be enjoying themselves, as though nothing had happened. I felt the nausea rising, finding it difficult to sit out there, with laughter from the other diners wafting through the air. We did not stay long at the club, with Fasih apologizing for having taken us there, as upset as we were at the lack of sensibility of the officers, who, regrettably, appeared to be predominantly Punjabi.

In protest of Nawab Bugti's murder, Humayun Marri and Akhter Mengal were taking out a procession down Jinnah Road the next day. Humayun had asked us if we would care to join in the protest, and of course our answer was in the affirmative. We asked Fasih if we could visit Sardar Ataullah Mengal after the protest. He said that he would gladly take us and would also inform the Sardar that we were coming.

Driving to Jinnah Road, we were really angry with the lack of any consequential reaction anywhere else in the country, according to television channels and the press. Not surprisingly, when we reached the square at the beginning of Jinnah Road, the slogan rising up was, 'Answer you Punjabis, account for the blood!' But the moment we appeared, the innate courtesy of the Baloch made Akhter Jan Mengal and Mir Humayun Marri stop the chanting. The next chant that that went up through the amplified sound system was, 'Answer you Pakistanis, account for the blood!' I did not know which slogan was worse for our federation. Akhter Mengal and Humayun Marri positioned us between themselves, with each of them holding the edges of the same banner, while we held up the middle. The slogan then became 'Akbar Bugti Zindabad!' (Long live Akbar Bugti). This slogan was sustained all the way down Jinnah Road. The banner was now held ahead of us, while the four of us walked in a row. As the pace of the march quickened, Fakhar moved me to the side as he held my elbow and kept inquiring if my feet were hurting. They were because my shoes were not sensible but I was so charged up that I had not paid attention to the discomfort. A large number of men lined the divider between the roads, the shops were shut but men were standing on their steps. Every now and then, we heard people calling out our names in tones of respect, even admiration. Clearly we were identified as friends of the Baloch, our Punjabi ethnicity overlooked. We marched down the length of Jinnah Road at the end of which Fasih Iqbal was waiting. We got into his vehicle and drove to visit Sardar Ataullah Mengal at his house.

The Sardar was waiting inside his gate to receive us, and walked with us to the entrance of his house, opening the door for us himself. His sitting room was plainly furnished, we were seated on frayed sofas, he sat beside us and as we munched on the pistachios and almonds laid before us, drinking the hot green tea, the best thirst quencher. He told us that his heart, despite his pacemaker, still beat for Pakistan. He hoped that the heart of his sons and grandsons would beat in the same way, but he suspected that their hearts were souring and the assassination of Akbar Bugti was a wound inflicted in the hearts of all Baloch, including himself. He asked us why Musharraf had allowed this to happen. Our only explanation was that we were deeply baffled ourselves, and saw him as mindlessly irresponsible. It was a dastardly act, which played straight into the hands of the detractors of Pakistan. Musharraf was drunk on power and we saw him as the most destructive of the rulers that had grabbed power in Pakistan. He had caused the death of thousands of soldiers and civilians, making no serious effort to rein in the militant groups that had proliferated under his watch. He had marginalised all those politicians in the Punjab that had some respect in the smaller provinces. He had broken the back of the civil administration and introduced a culture of theft of public resources down to the grass-roots levels. He had allowed ethnic strife, sectarian bigotry, and societal disharmony to increase at every level. He reduced taxation for the wealthy, increased our debt burden, and wasted the foreign assistance coming to Pakistan, with no enhancement of our power-generating capacity. We had to free Pakistan from his cursed stranglehold on power, and our best bet was the Supreme Court of Pakistan, now headed by a Chief Justice who owed his career in the judicial service to Akbar Khan Bugti.

Sardar Ataullah Mengal agreed with all of this, and then Akhter Mengal and his Baloch National Movement (BNM) colleagues joined us, with their march having concluded.

Shortly thereafter we took our leave, as we were to fly back to Islamabad the following morning. The flight out of Quetta was difficult. While we were airborne, the aircraft developed some trouble and returned back to the Quetta airport. After a long wait, we were finally flown into Karachi in the evening and on to Islamabad the next day. We were told by Baloch senators that this happened frequently as the most run-down aircraft were used by PIA for Quetta flights. The Baloch seemed to have every possible kind of grievance, and our Balochistan province had become the Achilles heel of Pakistan. This deteriorating state of affairs had been predicted by scholars in the past, but despite all the crises down the years, it continued to be the largest province of our country, and we needed Balochistan to be a part of Pakistan. Musharraf's act had made us apprehensive for the federation of Pakistan but we had no idea that what lay ahead of us was actually going to be much worse.

After considerable discussion between me and Fakhar, we decided that the time had come for us to join the only mass party, the Pakistan Peoples Party (PPP), whose leadership was from our second largest province, i.e. Sindh, and which was popular with the people of Punjab. We wanted to lend our shoulder to the wheel for restoration of democracy through a party platform. The PPP had no sectarian or gender bias, our children were keen on it, and Benazir was keen to have us. She seemed committed to good governance, given a third chance, and we could help her steer steady course.

Back in Shah Jewna in October, my cousin Maryam, who was living there at the time, became seriously ill. Benazir Bhutto called me from New York to say that she was there with Asif Zardari and wanted us to come to New York to join them there and to consider announcing our joining of the PPP in New York. I told her that my cousin, who was like a sister to me, was seriously ill and it would be impossible for me to get away immediately, but

Abida Hussain as a student at Montreux, Switzerland, 1963.

Syeda Abida Hussain in 1968, a few months before her marriage.

Karachi Race Course, 1965: Syeda Abida Hussain, recently returned from Florence, Italy, leads her filly 'Firenze' with Jockey Arif Rasheed astride. 'Firenze' was bred by Syed Abid Hussain Shah at his Shah Jewna Stud and Livestock Farm.

Syed Abid Hussain Shah and Begum Kishwar Abid Hussain at their Shah Jewna Haveli (1968).

Washington D.C. Aug. 1992: Ambassador Abida Hussain with her mother, Begum Kishwar Abid Hussain. Photographed by Didi, spouse of Ambassador Walter Cutler.

Shah Jewna House in Jhang town. Built c.1900 by Makhdumzada Pir Raje Shah Bokhari, grandfather of its current owner Syeda Abida Hussain.

'Kachi Kothi'. Pir Raje Shah's bunglow on Syed Abid Hussain Shah's farm at Shah Jewna, district Jhang.

Syed Abid Hussain Memorial Trust Hospital, Saddar, Jhang.

Syed Fakhar Imam Shah Bokhari dressed as bridegroom at his wedding to Abida Hussain, February 1969 at Lahore.

Syeda Abida Hussain Shah Bokhari as bride at her wedding to Syed Fakhar Imam, February 1969 at Lahore.

Syed Fakhar Imam in 1970, shortly after his marriage to Syeda Abida Hussain in 1969.

Syeda Abida Hussain, shortly after being elected MPA in 1972, in Lahore to attend a session of the Punjab Assembly.

Syeda Abida Hussain and Syed Fakhar Imam, newly elected Members of National Assembly of Pakistan and the latter subsequently elected Speaker, National Assembly, outside their residence at Islamabad, 1985.

Syed Abid Hussain Imam, son of Abida Hussain and Fakhar Imam, watching tent pegging at Shah Jewna, March 2012.

Syeda Umme Kulsum Imam, daughter of Syed Fakhar Imam and Abida Hussain, 2012.

Syeda Sughra Imam, daughter of Syed Fakhar Imam and Abida Hussain, 2012.

if she stabilized, we could travel after a couple of weeks. Benazir informed us that by then she would be in London and we could join her there to make the announcement. Fakhar was unable to travel by the time Maryam was out of hospital, so we decided that I should go to London and make the announcement on his behalf as well.

I reached London in late November. Naheed Khan, Benazir's secretary told me to come to Rahman Malik's town-house on Edgware Road. When I reached, I was shown into the sitting room where Benazir was sitting along with some PPP office-bearers. On seeing me, Benazir stood up and greeted me warmly, welcoming me into the PPP fold. She reminded me that I had been in PPP when it was led by her father Zulfikar Ali Bhutto. She always referred to him as Bhutto Shaheed. Benazir then turned towards Shah Mahmood Qureshi, who had replaced Qasim Zia as President of the Punjab wing, and said that Fakhar Imam and I would be her candidates for National Assembly from the PPP platform in the coming years' general elections, with running mates of our choice, along with our daughter, who would also be the PPP candidate from a constituency of her choice. She then asked for the media people who were waiting outside to be called in and the announcement was made. Benazir seemed to be delighted, although some of her party people looked a trifle disconcerted, not altogether comfortable with the importance she was giving us, who they probably viewed as a new entrant.

Before we adjourned, she informed me that she was leaving for Dubai the following evening, but would like to visit me wherever I was staying. Mention of my location, which was in Ennismore Gardens and was a short walk from her own flat pleased her. She said that would be able to spend more than an hour with me. Her sister, Sanam Bhutto, would be with her and perhaps I could invite Naheed Mirza (Iskander Mirza's widow) and her daughter Safia. They also lived at Ennismore Gardens and had been thrilled to learn, when Benazir had spoken to them earlier and had informed them that Fakhar and I had decided to join the PPP.

My one-room flat that I had rented for a week was nicely decorated. Benazir loved it, and we spent a happy hour together chatting and laughing. On a serious note, I said to her and the others present that having had Akbar Bugti allegedly assassinated, Musharraf was bound to make elaborate arrangements to rig the coming elections. My son, Abid was going to turn thirty on the 9th of December, I would be flying to New York to be with him for his birthday, and could then go down to Washington to discuss the matter with a few friends. Benazir thought this was a good idea and suggested a few common friends who should be sought out, and sensitized to the predicament that Pervez Musharraf was in, and the danger his continuing in power was posing to the federation of Pakistan. The matter of her personal security, when Benazir returned to Pakistan, would be raised in my discussions. Her presence in Pakistan that was scheduled for the end of the coming summer would pose a direct threat to Musharraf's hubris.

Being with my son in New York for his thirtieth birthday was pure pleasure for me. He had rented a cosy one-bedroom apartment in the fashionable lower south-west side of Manhattan. Being more familiar with the upper-east side, I was able to see an entirely different part of New York. Abid vacated his bedroom for me, parking himself on his commodious sofa-bed in the lounge. With the help of his friends he had decorated his apartment artistically. He had his old maps nicely framed, some of them collector's items, on the walls. Abid appeared to be enjoying his work at the law firm and had an interesting set of friends, all of whom we entertained on separate evenings at restaurants serving delicious food.

I hosted a birthday brunch for Abid at the Yale Club, to which he invited a few of his close friends, allowing me to include Lally Weymouth. He also allowed me to attend his birthday bash that evening, since I was paying for it, he said! Abid was earning good money, was quite in his elements, but I was desolate when he told me that he really did not wish to return to Pakistan. We argued away, my point being that not only did he owe his family his presence there, he owed it to Pakistan. Moreover, I told him that New York had a few hundred thousand well trained lawyers, while Pakistan had only a handful of lawyers who were as well trained as him. Abid had signed a two-year contract with his law firm, and had completed his first three months with them. Both his father and I wanted him by our side when this contract ended. His siblings had returned to Pakistan, and he ought to as well. My week with him in New York was timely, and my impression was that some of my arguments did have some impact on him. His ability with the written and spoken word made me feel extremely proud to be his mother. In due course he would hopefully take Fakhar and me to be his mentors as well.

I then journeyed on to Washington D.C. There I did my rounds with friends. All of them were of the opinion that dislodging Musharraf would be monumental as 'W', which is how most Americans described their President, George W. Bush, was still pro Musharraf. Several individuals in the US Administrationand on Capitol Hill were beginning to sense Musharraf's reluctance to take the militants head on. But Musharraf'spaying lip-service tobeing America's partner in the War on Terror continued to weigh with the White House, and the fact of his having conceded bases was counted as a major plus in his favour. Akbar Bugti's assassination drew much less interest than the realization that Quetta was increasingly a sanctuary for the Taliban, but most people believed that NATO (North Atlantic Treaty Organization) was winning the war, so any suggestion that the Taliban were in fact gaining ground was simply not heard. On Benazir's security, the comment was that there was no sense in crossing bridges before they were reached, but there was some muttering that came my way on Asif Zardari's frequent presence in New York and his lavish lifestyle when he was there, articulated by some well connected Republicans sources.

Back in Pakistan by mid December, Fakhar and I were invited to attend the Asian Racing Conference in Dubai in the last week of January 2007. We had entered election year, and Benazir who was in Dubai was keen to meet Fakhar. Hence it was opportune for us to attend the conference with follow-up visits with her. We were involved in the Conference for three days, which enabled me to acquire a stallion for my stud farm, my earlier attempt having been aborted by the earthquake in Azad Kashmir.

We got in touch with Benazir and went to visit her in her new home in Emirate Hills. She had lined up Shah Mahmood Qureshi, her party president from Punjab, and her party divisional coordinators from Faisalabad and Multan, for us to discuss each constituency in our respective districts. Wazir Jogezai, former Deputy Speaker, who had transitioned along with us from the IDG (Independent Democratic Group) to the PPP, joined us at the tail-end of our fairly thorough discussion. Benazir adjourned the discussion and her party members left. We were to carry on for dinner at the home of Ijlal Haider Zaidi's daughter. I told Benazir that Ijlal had lost his wife, my friend Shireen, who had passed away the previous year. Ijlal Haider had served as Benazir's Advisor during her second term as Prime Minister. He had complained that BiBi had not condoled with him. When I told her so, Benazir was contrite. I informed her that he was currently in Dubai, staying with his daughter Anjum; she immediately called him, and he invited her to the dinner. Wazir Jogezai was also invited.

We left her house together. Since Benazir's daughter Bakhtawar had taken her car, Benazir asked us if she could come with us. Wazir Jogezai and we both had our cars. Benazir suggested that Fakhar accompany Wazir in his car while she would sit with me. A young man lurking outside her front gate darted forward to open the car door. It was a young Niazi who had been Abid's classmate at the Lahore American School. Benazir said he was always hanging around her house and occasionally she would send him to do errands for her, but she did not know quite who he was. Marvelling at her naiveté, I mentioned that his mother was a good friend of the Chaudhries of Gujrat, while his aunt was an equally good friend of the Sharif's of Lahore, and he was hanging around her house in Dubai. This was what in the parlance of bankers would be described as 'hedging'. Benazir laughed, informing me that he was in fact a banker, but the diversity of his political credentials demanded that she pass him onto Makhdum Amin Fahim, so that he would stop hanging around her house. Neither of us could imagine the mega scam this kid would pull further down the road, peddling her name, nor how many people he would get into trouble, including Amin Fahim.

It was a short drive to our destination. En route, Benazir observed that Fakhar did not seem to approve of her. It was a sharp observation, I told her so, adding that he was worried lest she repeat her past performance, so she would have to convince him and charm his doubts away. She promised to try. After offering a prayer for late Shireen Zaidi, Benazir focused on Fakhar and succeeded in breaking through his reserve. Ijlal told her how happy he was that we had come together politically. It was a comfortable evening, old and new friends bonding together, enjoying the delicious meal prepared by our hostess, who was as accomplished a cook as her late mother. Benazir asked Fakhar and me what we thought of Ishaq Dar, and on hearing our positive comments, she also said that she received good vibes from him when he called on her, as they were near neighbours. She requested us to meet him and run matters of common interest by him, essentially probing him on whether Nawaz wanted an electoral adjustment with her party or whether they would go into adversarial mode during elections and form a coalition government perhaps after elections. We met Ishaq Dar for lunch a couple of days later, and agreed that a post election coalition would be more feasible than an electoral alliance. Benazir invited us for dinner the following evening, where we discussed in depth, not only what had transpired between us and Ishaq Dar, but also the broad contours of a wider coalition in which the Pushtun and Baloch nationalist and progressive parties would be included, to make it a federal, liberal, centrist coalition, in order to secure a five-year term of democratic and stable governance for our country.

Before we adjourned, she asked me whether my children had bothered me when they were younger about their mother and father carrying different names. I told her they used to, not so much my daughters as my son, and eventually it was he who found the solution by declaring himself as Abid Hussain Imam. When I said this, Benazir leaned towards me and hugged me. Thanking me, she said she had found the solution to the issue.

Henceforward, her son would be called Bilawal Bhutto Zardari. By the time we left Dubai, even Fakhar had fallen into an easy camaraderie with Benazir, and we told each other that we would remain in close touch, and meet in London by early summer.

As we had assessed, the issue of Musharraf seeking a reprieve from the Supreme Court from the Constitutional requirement of two years elapsing before the holder of an office of profit could seek electoral office, came up, as we entered the spring of this crucial year in our history. For Musharraf it meant that he would want to retain the office of Chief of Army Staff, which was how he had assumed power, and yet he would want the new Parliament to re-elect him as President, but the Constitution would need to be favourably interpreted by the Court. He probably saw this as a minor issue that needed a minor adjustment. His minions clearly did not view the matter any differently. Chief Justice Iftikhar Chaudhry whose family had been Punjabi settlers in Balochistan was summoned to Musharraf's residence in Rawalpindi where his minions broached the subject with the Chief Justice in his presence. The Chief Justice pointed out his inability to do so, since a full court judgement on the issue was on the record. The dictator had been defied, the consequences were inevitable.

On 9 March 2007 Chief Justice Iftikhar Mohammad Chaudhry was suspended by President Pervez Musharraf. It was for the first time in the history of Pakistan that the highest judicial authority of the country had been removed. Reasons given by Musharraf for this move were that Iftikhar Chaudhry had violated the norms of judicial propriety, was corrupt, and was seeking illegal favours. Iftikhar Chaudhry decided to challenge Musharraf and filed a petition against this unconstitutional move.

Iftikhar Chaudhry was prevented from entering the Supreme Court and confined to his residence. At that time we were at our house in Islamabad, and news spread rapidly. Senator Sadia Abbasi, who was also a Barrister, came by our house, to give us the news and to tell us that if we went to the residence of the Chief Justice, we may be allowed to meet him, since Air Marshal (retired) Asghar Khan had been allowed to meet the Chief Justice. Wazir Jogezai was with us, so taking him along, Fakhar, Sadia, and I arrived outside the Frontier House, to find a police cordon and barricades, which prevented vehicles from driving further forward towards the Judges Colony where the Chief Justice and Judges of the Supreme Court resided. We got off our cars and walked up to the barricade. We argued with the young magistrate on duty that we could not be prevented from visiting the Chief Justice. The officer was in a quandary, very respectful towards Fakhar, conceding that he could not prevent us from proceeding for a visit but he could not let our vehicles through. We could walk up the hill to the colony, but it would be a long and tiring walk. Joking with him that the exercise would do us all some good, we thanked him, as he told the sentries to open the barricade so we could our go through. It was a long brisk walk. By the time we reached the Chief Justice's residence, we were completely out of breath.

We rang the doorbell and were shown in by a staff person into a large sitting room. The Chief Justice entered a few minutes later, seemed really happy to see us, embraced Fakhar and Wazir, shook hands warmly with Sadia and me, and apologised for the trouble we had to undergo in reaching him. Addressing Fakhar, he said that he had always desired to meet us in person because he respected Fakhar for his Rulings as Speaker. Moreover he had heard Nawab Akbar Bugti speak about us with great affection on several occasions. He informed us that the late Nawab had been his benefactor, and had given him the opportunity to serve as a law officer when Akbar Bugti was serving as Chief Minister of Balochistan, and what a great blow Bugti's loss had been for all of us and for the federation. We assured him that we, along with the bar associations, democratic minded leaders, and the people of Pakistan were with him.

Within the next few days a lawyers' movement had been catalysed, with back-up support from the political parties. Regular strikes were called by bar associations on the premises of the courts. Lawyers, politicians, political workers, and the general public thronged in the periphery of the Chief Justice's residence where he was confined. In the current affairs programmes on television channels, discussions were being held, and experts were being invited to highlight various aspects of the articles of the Constitution of Pakistan that dealt with power. Hence, pressure was mounting slowly but surely on the Musharraf regime. The President was left with no choice but to lift the ban on Iftikhar Chaudhry's movements.

The Chief Justice aggressively began to campaign against Musharraf's suspension orders by addressing bar associations in the provincial capitals, rapidly gaining in popularity and sympathy from people of all cadres.

I had gone to Karachi to appear in some television programmes. It was during that time that Iftikhar Chaudhry had planned to address gatherings in Karachi. A welcome rally was organized by supporters of Iftikhar Chaudhry. I went along with my friend Timmy Zardari and Zia Ispahani, and we joined the PPP procession that was collecting outside Lyari, a densely populated area of old Karachi and a traditional PPP stronghold. The procession was to go to the airport to receive Iftikhar Chaudhry.

We proceeded in a long cavalcade of buses, four-wheelers, cars, and motorcycles, all flying party flags, holding up party banners. Our procession was joined en route by an equally large and impressive procession of the ANP (Awami National Party), with their bright red party flags and banners.

As we entered the road that led to the airport, firing broke out on the procession from the buildings on either side of the road, the Ayesha Bawany Academy building was on one side, and a multi-storeyed block of flats on the other. Several workers of PPP and ANP were badly injured. They were rushed to the hospital where many succumbed to their injuries. We were fortunate to have escaped unscathed.

The Chief Justice was bundled back into the airplane and prevented from proceeding towards the Sindh High Court. The MQM (Muttahida Qaumi Movement) was accused of being involved in the firing, which they denied. Some token arrests were made, but events hurtled along and it was difficult to keep track of the cases. The lawyers' movement rapidly gained momentum and regular protests began to be held outside the Supreme Court.

Fakhar and I joined in the processions whenever we were in Islamabad. The leaders would sit on top of buses and trucks, but Fakhar and I preferred to walk with the workers and found much solidarity and support among them. The weather was heating up. We would squat in front of the Supreme Court and roadside vendors would appear, selling drinks and fruits the atmosphere increasingly like that of a street party. Having a weakness for coconut, someone handed me a slice of coconut, and as I bit into it, one of my teeth got wrenched out. I ended up with a mega dental issue. For the next few weeks my time was divided between the street party and the dental chair!

The Chief Justice was now gearing up to do road tours through Punjab, and the finale would be his long march or drive from Islamabad to Lahore. He had been warned by the Musharraf regime not to pursue his intent to drive to Lahore in a cavalcade as there was a threat to his security. But Iftikhar Chaudhry and his supporters were not to be deterred. Fakhar went to Khanewal and when the cavalcade of the Chief Justice drove through Khanewal town, Fakhar was there with a large crowd to cheer him along, while I did the same at Chiniot.

Before he set off from Islamabad, we visited Iftikhar Chaudhryat his residence. A large crowd had gathered in his sitting room, but on seeing us, he got up and greeted us warmly. We sat with him as he concluded an interview with a foreign journalist, after which he took us aside and showed the letter of warning from the administration which had been faxed in to him. We suggested that he pay no heed to it, the public was energized and would ensure his security. He thanked us for coming, and we said we would be waiting among the crowds to receive him at Lahore.

In the procession we sat up all night on top of a PPP trawler. Jahangir Badar was sitting next to us. The PML-(N) leaders were on an identical trawler beside the main entry gate of the Lahore High Court; we were opposite it; the Jamaat-i-Islami was trawler in between us. The crowd below radiated so much energy that we sat on uncomfortable straight-backed steel chairs from dusk to dawn. Even Fakhar remained wide awake which was singularly rare for him.

The High Court judges had been required to take fresh oath, which some of them had refused to do, and they were considered to be heroic with lawyers and politicians endorsing them, speaking and writing in their support and cheering for them. The concept of the rule of law had become nothing short of a popular demand, like a slogan. Even children were seen shouting for rule of law. It was an inspiring time, and the Musharraf regime was unquestionably cornered. It was a new beginning for Pakistan. Fakhar and I, now aging protagonists of the rule of law, were excited to be part of what was becoming a popular movement in favour of the rule of law, which would hopefully be a precursor to a more rooted form of democratic governance than what we had experienced in the past. We hoped that the rule of law would also lead to a cessation of the plundering of public resources by the salariat (salaried class) of the state, as well as by those who claimed to be representatives of the people.

Despite the partnership with the Americans in the War on Terror, Pervez Musharraf appeared to be lackadaisical about curbing various militant groups emerging out of the Wahabi/ Ahle Hadith/ Deobandi religious schools, popularly known as Madrassahs, which were proliferating throughout the country, particularly in south-west and south Punjab. He was also reluctant to take back a children's library near the Lal Masjid (Red Mosque) in Islamabad, which had been taken over by the mosque's preachers and proselytisers and converted into a women's hostel. Investigative reporters claimed that this was done because the women's hostel that was within the compound of the Red Mosque was being used as a storage centre for a vast cache of arms and lethal weapons, hence the takeover of the library to house the women students of the Red Mosque seminary.

There was a huge uproar by civil society groups to get the library vacated and restored to its original function. The federal administration was cornered. Everyone expected Musharraf to order the administration to act but no action was forthcoming.

Till now Pervez Musharraf had been successful in dodging the Pakistanis as well as the Americans, and while the people of Pakistan had seen through his tactics, there were few signs that the Americans had reached the same page.

16

Benazir's Assassination

In early June, 2007, Fakhar, Umku, Shugu and I arrived in London, and were joined by Abid from New York, his law firm having assigned him a task which required him to work with a London based law firm for a few weeks. We hosted a lunch for Benazir Bhutto at our club, the Royal Overseas League, booking rooms that overlooked Green Park. We invited Sanam Bhutto, Naheed Mirza, Safia, several British friends that included two former High Commissioners who had served in Pakistan, a top-ranking BBC anchorperson, some personal British friends that included Lady Mary Gaye Curzon and her partner David McDonough, who had known Benazir from her Oxford days, and who BiBi was really pleased to see after many years.

We were twenty-four people in all. Before going in for lunch we introduced Benazir to our guests. She was meeting Shugu for the first time and complemented her on her looks which pleased Shugu immensely. Fakhar mentioned to Benazir that we had gathered before leaving Pakistan that the Chief Justice would be restored in a few days, but she said her sources informed her that it would take a while. Abid was sitting beside Sanam; both were chatting and laughing. Benazir leaned towards me and said that she had not seen her sister laugh so heartily in a long time. Abid must be very amusing and she should seek him out for a good laugh as well. Food was good, with a lot of chatter and laughter going back and forth. I had to clink my glass several times for a moment of quiet, so that we could formally welcome Benazir and our other guests, and to request Benazir to say a few words and to answer any questions that our friends may have for her.

Benazir Bhutto spoke graciously and succinctly, making a strong pitch for restoration of democracy to Pakistan, thanking Fakhar and me for bringing so many Pakistani experts together. She welcomed us as distinguished members of her party, the Pakistan Peoples Party (PPP).

A few days later Iftikhar Chaudhry was restored as Chief Justice, as Fakhar had anticipated. Benazir invited us for dinner to her flat the same evening. She had four other guests, and when we were sitting down for dinner, I noticed that two chairs were empty. I thus asked Benazir if Shugu and Abid could join us after dinner, as they had been very keen to talk to her, while Umku was in the countryside visiting her friends. At this Benazir told us that we should have brought them along with us and that they should come right away. When I called them, they were in a restaurant having dinner with their friends, and said that they will join us after dinner.

Benazir had a long tête-à-tête with Abid, and he seemed to have impressed her. She asked him if he would like to work with her. Abid said he was in a contract with his law firm till the end of the year, but when that ended he could consider her offer, depending on the terms. Amused with this answer, Benazir responded that she could offer him no terms unless she became Prime Minister again. She had been looking for someone with Abid's credentials but had not come across anybody so far. She told Abid that he came from a political family, and also that as his parents had done, he should serve his country not for monetary gains! Abid's reply to

Benazir was that his parents had been emptying up all the family resources, and on top of it, they were also control freaks. On hearing this, Benazir went into peals of laughter and said that she hoped Abid would not say this to her children since this would only endorse what they said about her! They both exchanged email addresses, and Benazir asked Abid to write down his ideas that they had discussed, and send them to her.

Turning her attention towards Fakhar and me, Benazir asked us what we anticipated would now ensue after the restoration of the Chief Justice. Fakhar said the lawyers' movement would obviously conclude, but the next crisis for Musharraf would be dealing with the Lal Masjid (Red Mosque) issue. Before adjourning, Benazir told us she had completed her first round of discussions on candidature with her Sindh parliamentary board; after the weekend, she would start on Punjab, and would like us to be present, and that we would have to spare a week for the task.

We arrived at the same town-house, off Edgware Road, where we had gone when our joining the PPP had been made public. It was raining heavily and Fakhar opened his large umbrella as we stepped out of the cab. Scores of people were standing around, many of them without umbrellas or raincoats, getting nicely soaked. There were many familiar faces among them, but we were hustled indoors by someone designated to wait for us, who informed us that the meeting had begun. We entered the main room which had a table placed at one end behind which Benazir Bhutto, Party Chairperson, was seated with her office bearers beside her. In front, about fifty people were seated in five rows. We went in and sat down quietly. A young man in the front row vacated a seat for me. Fakhar was in the last row. When Benazir saw me craning my neck, she asked Naheed Khan to escort me to the table where she was sitting. She then sent Safdar Abbasi to escort Fakhar up to the table, loudly saying that both of us were very senior and had come to the meeting at her request. This put many noses out of joint, but nobody dared to counter the Chairperson. Benazir pored over the file in front of her, while Safdar Abbasi briefed her on each constituency, giving the results of the two previous elections, and the names of those who had applied for PPP tickets for the forthcoming election. Qasim Zia, the Punjab President, would then add a comment, followed by Chaudhry Ghulam Abbas, the Secretary General. The applicants present in the room, and some waiting outside would then be asked to speak, if they had anything to say. Occasionally, more than one candidate appeared, and a vociferous argument would break out.

The political culture of the PPP was very different to that of the Muslim League. We had sat in the parliamentary boards of the PML-(N), as well as the PML-(Q), where candidates were always polite, even when they had competing interests, but they were sycophantic towards the leadership. The PPP was more of a rough and tumble, where Benazir showed great patience, remained friendly, particularly with her old workers, was tough only when a cell phone rang out, when she would raise her voice to say she did not want any telephonic sounds and all phones must be put off. One poor blighter did not know how to put his phone off fast enough, and was asked to leave the room. Her focus and concentration were acute, and her experience revealed itself. Rawalpindi division was being discussed, and was to be followed by Sargodha division. Around 1 p.m., lunch boxes were brought in and passed around. Benazir was given a separate tray with Harrods salad, and seemed to enjoy what she was eating, while the food in our lunch boxes was almost inedible. She noticed this, and chastised Rahman Malik, ordering him to have the catering improved. Rawalpindi division went on till an hour before we adjourned, covering the districts Attock, Rawalpindi, Jhelum, and Chakwal. When Sargodha division started, Mianwali had few applicants, with several constituencies that had no applicants at all. Khushab was somewhat better, not contentious; Sargodha likewise; Bhakkar again had some constituencies with blanks. Before the meeting was adjourned, Benazir announced that we would have to make faster progress the next day, and would be covering Gujrat, Gujranwala, Lahore, and Faisalabad divisions. On day three Sahiwal, Multan, Dera Ghazi Khan, and Bahawalpur divisions would be addressed, and on the fourth day, the pended constituencies would be finalized.

Lahore was exhausting for everybody as was Faisalabad. The urban constituencies were clearly the most contentious and it seemed to me that that was where the PPP would score the least. When it came to Jhang, the only controversy was over Chiniot. I was the only applicant for my constituency. Benazir observed that everyone must have been scared of me, and therefore did not dare put in an application against me. Saying this, she winked at me and laughed. When it came to Shugu's constituency, the younger brother of Faisal Saleh Hayat appeared. She shooed him off saying his brother, on whom he was dependant, was a turncoat, and she was awarding the ticket to Sughra Imam who had resigned from ministerial office in the Punjab. There were no applicants on two constituencies of Jhang, where she delegated me the responsibility of finding suitable candidates. On Fakhar's constituency there was no discussion either; he had applied for two constituencies, but she said she was not doubling for anybody, not even herself because then the bye-elections became a problem, and he could choose the one out of the two which he wanted. Fakhar opted for N.A. 156, in which Qatalpur, his home, was located. The third constituency of Khanewal had no applicant, for which I recommended Faisal Imam, Fakhar's younger brother, clarifying that he may not win the constituency, but would put up a fight. Benazir agreed, but some people were unhappy that four nominations were going to the same family.

Benazir left for Dubai, while we scouted around for a flat that we wanted to buy. We had intended to do this ever since it became legal to own property overseas, provided one could justify the source of the money, and pay tax on it, which we certainly would do.

Meanwhile the Red Mosque saga reached a gory conclusion, with hundreds of lives being lost because Musharaf had neglected to address the issue at the appropriate time. When Benazir returned to London, she called another round of meetings to finalize her party nominations and also discuss the schedule and logistics for her return to Pakistan. There were fewer people attending these meetings, but while the atmosphere did not unduly disturb me, Fakhar never really took to it. Her party members who had been with her since long, especially those who had been in the party led by her late father, were civil and friendly, but those who had drifted towards her from the Muslim League before we did, or those who were relative newcomers to politics, felt visibly threatened by our presence. Fakhar and I had logged more years in politics as independents than we had in the Muslim League, and had gone from the local to the national level in politics, which enabled us to score more than fifty thousand votes upward, even when we lost elections, which gave us secure bases in politics. But while Benazir viewed this with respect, many of her colleagues were discomfited by it. The consensus in the meetings was that she should plan her return for September, and land in Islamabad; all ticket holders should mobilize a few hundred supporters from their constituencies to be at the airport to guarantee a crowd of a hundred thousand, who would then accompany her to Golra Sharif and Bari Imam, the two significant shrines located in the suburbs of Islamabad. This would be a deterrent to any thought Musharraf may have of arresting her upon arrival. The following day, she could then address a mega rally at Liaquat Bagh. While we were absorbed in this planning, Benazir got a call from Shaikh Khalifa, the Ruler of Abu Dhabi. She spoke to him from another room after which she came back and said that she was adjourning the meeting, and that all party members would assemble again after three days.

Fakhar and I deduced that a meeting between her and Musharraf was likely to be arranged by the Ruler of Abu Dhabi. The story was out in the media the very next day, with some commentators alleging that a 'deal' had been struck between Benazir Bhutto and Pervez Musharraf. On her return, she gave us no details, but explained that she met Musharraf briefly at dinner hosted by the Ruler of Abu Dhabi, after which Musharraf called on her at her residence in Dubai, where it was settled that the cases against her and her family would be withdrawn before she returned home, which would be closer to the end of September. We were in August by now, and had chosen a modest two-bedroom flat off Sloane Square which we put an offer on. After meeting Benazir Bhutto one last time at a reception at Zia Ispahani's flat, where Abid handed her the two-pager he had promised her, we said our goodbyes, and returned with our daughters to Pakistan, while Abid went back to his law firm in New York.

Late August, I was back in Shah Jewna, having been away from my farm for a longish spell, while Fakhar was in Qatalpur to survey his cotton crop. Over the years Fakhar had become one of the most successful cotton growers in our country, having applied his academic knowledge acquired at Davis admirably, to plant an extensive mango orchard and produce high-yielding varieties of cotton. For both of us, losing elections had been financially beneficial, as we had more time to attend to agriculture and to making beneficial financial investments on our assets, with Umku, who had a sharp nose for lucrative buying and selling of stocks and shares, as my guide.

One late monsoon evening I was sitting outside in the verandah of my *haveli* with pedestal fans stirring the still air and visitors dropping by, when Abid called from New York to say that Benazir had telephoned him to commend him for what he had written and she seriously wanted him to work with her. Hence Abid was now thinking of returning home when his contract ended in December. Both Fakhar and I were very happy to hear this. We owed Benazir a vote of thanks for motivating our son to return home. Not long after, we got a message from her asking us to come to London for a few days at the end of September. Since Fakhar's cotton crop was at a critical stage, it was easier for me to go. I would also be able to close the deal on the flat we were going to buy.

Back in London in September, I arrived at the same location to find that only twenty people had been summoned. Asif Zardari was there, and discussions were already underway. The decision was that Benazir Bhutto would return to Pakistan in mid October, after seven-and-a-half years of absence from the country. The precise date would be announced about four days ahead of her arrival. She would land at Karachi, as it was anticipated that a couple of hundred thousand supporters would pour in from Sindh, and another hundred thousand from Karachi itself. The Sindhis present in the room said there was no need to mobilize from the other provinces, but some of us felt strongly that every ticket holder must bring in their key supporters, as this would energize the entire party, and become an epoch-making event. Asif informed us that he had commissioned a container, which would contain a capsule at the bottom of the vehicle, equipped with a bed, chairs, table, a small fridge, television, a tiny bathroom, and a narrow stairway up to the roof of the container. The design of the container had been made in Germany and it would be armour-plated and absolutely secure. It was being built at Zulfiqar Mirza's sugar mill in Thatta and would be ready when BiBi arrived at Karachi, and she would ride on it from the airport to Quaid-i-Azam's mausoleum and onto Bilawal House at Clifton. She could then travel in this container to tour the country during the election campaign. Benazir said her party leaders would announce the date of her arrival a few days prior. Her arrival date would be announced simultaneously from Islamabad, Lahore, Karachi, Peshawar, Quetta, and Muzaffarabad ensuring maximum media coverage. She assigned Islamabad to Amin Fahim, Lahore to Jahangir Badar, Karachi to Aftab Shaban Mirani, Peshawar to Masud Kausar, and Quetta to me.

By the time I returned home, the news of Benazir's impending arrival was dominating the media. In an attempt, perhaps, to pre-empt her, Mian Nawaz Sharif decided to fly into Pakistan first. His flight landed at Islamabad airport where about thirty thousand people tried to congregate, but the police prevented them from being able to access the airport. Had it been ten times that number, the police would not have been able to succeed.

Mian Nawaz Sharif was bundled back into the aircraft and flown to Saudi Arabia. Before Benazir's arrival, the regime was clearly sharpening their knives to prevent a mega reception for her. Attempts were made to scare her. Musharraf advised her not to return as her life was under threat by militants. When I arrived at Quetta airport five days before her arrival, there was a whiff of the trouble that lay ahead. Lashkari Raisani, PPP President of Balochistan, who was to fetch me from the airport, was stopped en route several times, pulling in late. Our friend Tarik Khetran was there to receive me, and Raisani made it to the airport just as I was sitting in Khetran's car.

My arrival at Raisani's residence, Sarawan House, was quite disconcerting. The Raisani brothers, Lashkari and Nawab Aslam, who was older, were not on speaking terms with each other, and were refusing to join the gathering of PPP office bearers and the media, who had gathered in the front garden of their house asking questions. Everybody was urging me that both Raisani brothers would agree to come out if I requested them personally, invoking the Baloch custom of not denying a sister. I requested both the brothers individually, finally managing to secure their presence in the gathering. The date and time was announced by me, on receiving a call from Benazir on my mobile, with the speaker on, a mike attached to the phone amplifying the sound. She was heard in pin-drop silence, telling her Pakistani audience that she would arrive on the 18th of October at Karachi, via an Emirates flight and would hope to land in the morning. She looked forward to stepping foot on Pakistani soil and on being with all of us again. Everyone stood up and cheered, 'Benazir will rule again!' She called me later in the evening, and wanted a blow by blow account of the announcement event at the Sarawan House, asking how enthusiastic the response had been.

Returning from Quetta to Lahore, ranked now among the senior leaders of the PPP, receiving calls from PPP workers from everywhere, telling me so, I left for Jhang immediately to start rounding up my two hundred supporters who were to be mobilized to Karachi for her arrival. Shugu was already there lining up the same number of her supporters, Fakhar and his brother carrying out an identical exercise at Kabirwala. Within a short while after my arrival, the US Embassy called, with Ambassador Nancy Powell inviting Fakhar and myself to dinner the following evening to meet Dr Richard Haass who was visiting Islamabad and had asked specially to see us. We decided to drive up the next afternoon, attend the dinner and drive back late in the night. Dr Haass seemed pleased to see us and asked how Benazir and Musharraf would coexist. We said it would depend on how strong an election the PPP would win, and if Musharraf ceded power, she would probably allow him to carry on as a figurehead, after the required constitutional amendment, and consensus among the other political parties, adding that an amendment would also be required for her to become Prime Minister for a third term. The best solution would be for Musharraf to bargain for Constitutional indemnity and bow out gracefully. After our chat with Dr Haass, we proceeded to mingle with the other guests when I was taken aside by a leading television anchorman, Dr Shahid Masood, who asked me if Benazir was really going to arrive, since Musharraf was making a desperate last minute bid to stop her. I told him she was certain to arrive, to which he said I should try to stop her, as he feared there would be blood spilt on her arrival; he had been hearing that a dreadfully treacherous plan was afoot. Driving out of Islamabad, I told Fakhar what Shahid Masood had said, so we decided it would be prudent to telephone Hakim Ali Zardari in Karachi, and run the information by him in the morning.

When I called Hakim Ali Zardari the next day from Shah Jewna, he said that Musharraf was a treacherous man, but his daughter-in-law was unlikely to listen to anybody at this stage. The entire PPP had been mobilized, and hundreds of thousands of people were going to be pouring in from Sindh. The container that Asif had commissioned was secure and at least two thousand members of the Zardari tribe were going to be surrounding the container to protect her with their lives. Our supporters, eight hundred of them from four different constituencies, were to be despatched to Karachi. Shugu and I were sending our lot by train, while Fakhar and his brother rented coaches for their lot. We flew into Karachi, and were going to camp with Zia Ispahani. We visited Hakim Ali Zardari and Timmy who suggested that I send a message on my Blackberry to Benazir for her to alert our American friends regarding the threat to her security. Sending a long message to Benazir, I mentioned that we had learnt at Karachi airport that Musharraf had sent in a detachment of Commandos to Karachi, those who had been trained in the US to combat terrorists, but for Musharraf we were probably more threatening than the terrorists, so she must urge the American leadership to restrain him.

We tied up with Kamal Azfar to ride in his car to the airport the following morning, on 18 October 2007. As former Governor of Sindh, his car would be able to follow close behind Benazir's truck, and it was large enough to accommodate Shugu, myself, Fakhar, and Zia, along with Kamal. But we got a call from Bilawal House at 8 a.m. asking Fakhar and me to leave for the airport immediately, as the roads were already clogging up and Benazir had messaged from Dubai to ask us to be there to talk to the international media that were already thronging the airport. We left within a few minutes, and sure enough, by the time we reached the airport, we were surrounded by television cameras and journalists, both local and foreign, all asking what the 'deal' was between Musharraf and Benazir, how would they coexist, and why had he tried to prevent her from coming at the last minute. Our responses were that there was no deal, other than the National Reconciliation Order (NRO) that Musharraf had announced, according to which all politically motivated cases against political leaders stood withdrawn. All political leaders were beneficiaries of the NRO, and Benazir Bhutto would do whatever was in the interest of Pakistan, and in accordance with the aspirations of the people of our country. The sun was beating down on us, it was already hot, and giving a series of short interviews was an exhausting task, particularly when our focus was not to rise to any provocation, or make any observation that our detractors could describe as politically incorrect. Benazir was to enter through the old airport of Karachi, and party leaders were already crowding the entrance to the VIP lounge where she would be entering after disembarking from the aircraft. We tried to get to the lounge as well, but Safdar Abbasi spotted us and told us that Benazir had not left Dubai as yet, where a huge crowd had gathered to see her off, and the flight was delayed. She messaged him the list of people she wanted with her on the truck, and made particular mention of both our names. The truck was parked already, not far from the building, and he suggested that we climb up the ladder attached to the back of the truck, or container, and wait, pointing to Aftab Shaban Mirani, who was already sitting on top of the truck. He said that she would not be stopping in the lounge, so there was no sense in our trying to get in there.

At this point we saw Timmy arrive, who suggested we go into the lounge, but as we were conferring on what to do, Kamal Azfar, Zia, and Shugu arrived. Shugu said we should climb up on the truck, but Kamal said it would be hours before the truck would begin to move, so we should do that later. He suggested that we go to Sindh Club for a meal, where we could follow Benazir's disembarkation from the aeroplane on television, and join up with her on the stage at the Quaid's mausoleum, after which we stand with her on the container. From the mausoleum, it would still be a long way before we reached Bilawal House. This sounded like a sensible plan, and Fakhar and I were hardly the sort to relish riding on top of the container, so we piled into Kamal's car to follow his plan.

Weaving our way through the cheering crowds, we left the airport. Our vehicle moved slowly in the direction of the Sindh Club. We had just finished eating, and were sitting with our cups of coffee in front of the large television screen in the hallway, when we saw Benazir's aircraft touching down at Karachi airport. Even Shugu was now pleased to see what we would have missed watching had we remained all this while at the airport. We saw her stand on top of the steps, dressed befittingly in green, with her signature white *dupatta* on her head, waving to the sea of people that had broken through the security cordons below. We saw her hold her hands up in prayer, doubtless thanking Allah for her homecoming after eight years in exile. We watched her bend down, as her feet reached the ground to kiss the soil of her homeland, and as the camera caught the tears rolling down her face, our own eyes moistened. Other people had joined us to watch her arrival on the television screen, among them two important members of the Musharraf regime, whose faces were suddenly drained of all colour.

We drove to the Quaid's mausoleum, wondering how Musharraf would be taking all this. The area all around the mausoleum was already packed with people, mostly from the interior of Sindh. Drummers, colourfully dressed women, children, all dancing away as we joined the crowds, I joined the women in an enthusiastic bhangra, and the women pushed Fakhar, Kamal, and Zia in the middle of the circle, with a dear old woman making Fakhar hold up his hands and pushing him to join the bhangra, making Shugu and Zia go into screams of laughter. It was all lovely and festive and utterly spontaneous, with everyone shouting, 'Benazir will rule'!

By now it was late afternoon and the sun had begun to come down. We were all eager to get to Zia's place, quickly freshen up, and join the rally. Zia had sent for his car, and when we reached his house, his niece and some of his cousins were watching television. It was already dark, and Benazir's truck was moving at snail's pace, with the commentators saying that she was still an hour away from the Star Gate, the landmark that highlights the entrance road to the old airport, from the main artery that goes to the city.

My mobile phone was ringing. It was Timmy. She said that BiBi was about to strangle Safdar Abbasi for having failed to get us up on the container with her and wanted us to come immediately. Hakim Ali would send his car, his driver knew all the Zardari security guards, and would be able to get us through to the truck. Telling Timmy that I would come, while Fakhar and Shugu would join us on the stage at the Quaid's mausoleum, and then Fakhar would carry on with us to Bilawal House, which would probably be at dawn, I got myself ready to hop into Hakim Ali's vehicle as soon as it arrived. Khan Mohammed, Hakim Ali's driver, was a sturdy fellow who drove me through a labyrinth of back alleys and side roads and managed to get me through onto the main airport road where the container, brilliantly lit and now in sight, had just rounded the Star Gate and entered the main road.

Getting out of the vehicle, which the driver managed to park, wedged between two well-lit trucks with people from Punjab on top of them, clapping and shouting slogans in Punjabi, with Khan Mohammed walking protectively behind me, I joined the best street party of them all. There were trucks parked on either side of the road, as far as the eye could see, both sides of the road packed with people, men standing on the road divider, body-to-body, women and children present in large numbers. Hundreds of drummers were beating drums, and people of all ethnicities and both genders were dancing away. Bulbs of high wattage were put up in strings, flags were seen in abundance ... lots of light, colour, sound, and movement.

I stood momentarily by the edge of the road savouring it all, when I heard my name being called, 'Abida Bibi, join us, join us!' Looking up at the truck from where the shout was coming, I saw old Mr Bajwa from Faisalabad, a PPP enthusiast from Z. A. Bhutto's days, waving at me, sending young men from his truck to help me climb up onto it. Unable to refuse him, I managed to clamber up the bamboo ladder placed beside the truck. The view from that height was even better. Benazir's container did not seem to be that far away. Hugging Bajwa Sahib, and thanking him, I shouted into his ear that BiBi was waiting for me to join her on the container and taking leave, I struggled down the ladder. Back on the pavement, where Khan Mohammed was waiting, I told him that we should start making our way towards the container; he agreed, saying that we would now be able to reach it in about twenty minutes. Walking along the pavement, watching the enthusiastic crowds, I noticed three lads popping betel leaves into their mouths, whispering to each other. Stopping by them, I asked if they were from Karachi or elsewhere. They told me they were local and offered me a betel leaf thanking them, I asked if they had heard anything unusual, to which they said, they had heard that something was going to happen near 'Karsaaz', so they had moved away from there and were going to watch her passing by from here, which was at a safe distance.

I took this in, hoping it was merely a random observation, and walked at a faster pace toward the container. Khan Mohammed moved towards the lads surrounding the truck, which was very noisy, as it had its own generator with it making a racket, lighting up the truck with blindingly bright lights. Several young men, along with Khan Mohammed, encouraged me to put my foot on the ladder attached to the rear end of this huge vehicle, which was moving very slowly. I did so, climbing up, one step at a time, with television cameras appearing and my hoping they would not be telecasting my rear end, with my climbing up the steps, slowly and cautiously! Timmy had been alerted atop the truck, and reached down to me as I negotiated the last steps, hefting me up to a shaky arrival. The container seemed to have lots of people on it. Benazir was no longer standing in the front and Fehmida Mirza had taken her place. With a white *dupatta*, from a distance she could pass off for Benazir since she had a striking resemblance to the latter. BiBi had paused to take a rest and was sitting on a chair at the back.

When I reached up to Benazir, she pulled me down close to her and whispered that she had messaged Condoleezza Rice after getting my message. It seemed to her that there was substance in what I had written, so she wanted to go down to the capsule and discuss with me what was to be anticipated. She sent for Naheed Khan, whispering that she would climb down first into the capsule, and Timmy and I were to come down a few minutes later to avoid attention. We quietly went down. When we entered the capsule, we saw that Benazir was lying down on the sofa bed, with Naheed ministering to her. Timmy sat down on a chair near the entrance, while Naheed pulled the other chair up for me to sit beside Benazir's bed, and offered me a glass of chilled water. Gulping the water down, having to talk loudly to be heard through the din of the container, I told her of my apprehension that she would be attacked, and suggested that she get out from the side exit of the capsule. Naheed said she could go out first and get Fehmida's land cruiser for her which was following the container. But Benazir was resistant to my suggestion that she leave the capsule, exclaiming that it would be callous of her to abandon all the people. According to television reports, about half a million strong had gathered to receive her. I told her that a large part of the crowd had seen her, everyone knew she had arrived, so she could now drive in another vehicle to the mausoleum; surprise everybody, and after a quick address, carry on to Bilawal House and safety. The best security, I reminded her, lay in the element of surprise. She thought for a moment, then said that while she was still at the airport, a white pigeon kept circling above her head, and even left droppings on her white *dupatta*. She had seen it as an omen of peace, but on reflection, the pigeon could have had some electronic devise attached to it. Just before she had sat down on the chair above on the truck, and minutes before I reached her, at a quarter past ten, she had seen the time on her wrist watch when I had arrived, a baby was being passed by some fellows over the heads of the crowd as though this baby was being passed up towards her. The baby was close enough for her to see that its face was totally expressionless, which scared her momentarily, and that is when she moved away and went to sit down on a chair. Pausing again, she then said to Naheed that maybe the cruiser should be moved up, but first she should go up and fetch Fehmida Mirza, since it was her vehicle, and then the five of us could get away.

Naheed brought Fehmida down quickly, much to my relief. The two of them stepped out to bring the vehicle. However, my relief was momentary. Benazir suddenly jumped off the bed, saying that her cousin Laleh, and her young son, had come especially from London via Dubai with her for her homecoming, and were up on the truck, sitting in the end corner near the entry to the capsule where she had seen them before coming down. She would climb up for a minute, bring them down and take them with us. Timmy stood up and said she would go, but was too tall and may attract notice, as would BiBi. So I offered to go up and Timmy could stay with BiBi. I clambered up, whispered to Laleh that her cousin was calling her and her son down. As they were going down, I stopped briefly to look down at the crowd.

There was very bright lighting, and the container moving still so slowly, that some folk below spotted me and were calling out my name. Victoria Schofield, Benazir's great friend, and Christina Lamb, the journalist, were standing right there, looking down on the crowd. We exchanged greetings. They said I should wave back at my fans who were cheering me, while my anxiety made me pull them back. Then, there was a small blast, and the container shook a bit; the Englishwomen went down, prostrating themselves towards the capsule exit, myself doing likewise behind them, while the men started jumping over our heads, making for the stairs down the external exit. Aitzaz Ahsan and Raja Parvez Ashraf missed my head by a fraction, while Victoria and Christina managed to slip down the capsule exit. Scores of people atop the truck clambered down the external exit with great speed, impeding my movement forward to the capsule exit, which I had just managed to reach. At that moment the big blast came and a huge flame beside the truck reached skyward. It seemed as if it would swallow everything in its fury. The container was soon engulfed in flames. I glimpsed Amin Fahim as the last man going down the external stairway, while the spiral stairway down to the capsule had disappeared. I was left hanging on to the ledge. Looking down the dark hole, I saw some fellows below shouting up at me, 'Jump, Addi (sister), jump!' The flame seemed about to devour me. I flung my bag that I was stupidly clutching on to, and somehow God gave me the strength to jump. As I came down, I was partly caught by the men below who pushed me along with themselves off the container. As my feet hit the road I felt excruciating pain, my face contorted in agony. I managed to yank one foot off the ground. By now the bright lights of a television camera that had appeared out of the dark were blinding me. Some men threw me into a white four wheeler, banged the door shut, and shouted something to the driver. He drove full speed but had to slow down when the traffic became heavy. My foot was hurting badly. Convinced that my bones were smashed, I urged the driver to get me to a hospital, asking him whose car it was. He told me that it belonged to Zulfiqar Mirza and Fehmida Bibi. They had gotten away with Benazir Bhutto and others in the vehicle ahead of this one; and none of them was hurt, by the grace of Allah. Though relieved to hear this, a moment later I felt the life ebbing out of me and fell into a swoon.

The vehicle jerked to a halt and my eyes opened. I saw a huge black gate in front of me: the gate of Hell, or so I thought at the time, with that devouring flame still burning in my mind's eye, resistant to the notion that I was being consigned to an eternal fire. It was reassuring when the gates opened and the car swung into what was unmistakably the Aga Khan Hospital, stopping in front of its Emergency. I was pulled out of the vehicle, placed on a stretcher, carried past a large crowd outside, and taken inside into the hospital building through a corridor, where doctors and nurses were running around with people on stretchers all around, and the dreadful stench of blood. I heard someone shouting that more patients were being brought in, and they had run out of stretchers. Sitting up, I grabbed the doctor who was shouting. He was in green overalls, his head covered up to his forehead, and a white mask was covering his face. I urged him to take me off the stretcher and put me on a wheelchair. Then I said to him that I feared that my foot had been smashed. He pulled the sheet off me, poked and prodded, checked my foot and shouted, 'This one is not bleeding, bring a wheelchair and take her to the X-ray Room.' I was transferred on to a wheelchair, and pushed forward inside the emergency area. There was an injured person in every cubicle of the emergency. Screams of agony were coming from all directions. I just sat in a stupor with my own foot in intense pain.

Realizing that I had nothing on me, except my pale pink cotton *shalwar-kamiz*, my *dupatta* having fallen probably when I jumped down what must have been twenty feet. I was without anything on me: no wallet, no mobile phone. There was no way for me to inform Fakhar or Shugu of my whereabouts. I was well and truly bereft. Suddenly, someone rushing past stopped, and looking closely at me, asked if I was Abida Hussain. On my nodding in the affirmative, he pushed my wheelchair into an enclosed cubicle, where a young girl was undergoing dialysis. He told me this was his daughter who had recently suffered a renal failure. She was only fourteen years old, and could I please pray for her, because I was a Syeda Bibi. Holding my hands up in prayer, I prayed fervently for the girl, and all the injured around. She smiled at me sweetly and whispered to her father that she was my fan, and he should take my autograph. The father produced a scrap of paper and a pen. Managing to scrawl my signature, I asked the father if he could go out and call my husband from his cell phone, but he said he had no mobile as they did not allow them inside Emergency. I asked him to wheel me out for a moment, maybe somebody else would be carrying a mobile phone; he had just popped me out when a familiar face appeared. It was Talat Tyabji. She had been at school with me decades ago. We recognized each other, and she enquired what had happened. After giving her a brief rundown, I suggested to her that she examine my foot and get it X-rayed. Talat said that she was not a doctor and worked in the hospital's administration. She then summoned a nurse who wheeled me towards the X-ray Room while Talat took Fakhar and Shugu's mobile numbers, assuring me she would go out and call them, and would return as soon as my foot had been examined by the radiologist. She would wait for me outside the examination room. Talat had appeared out of nowhere and acted like an angel of mercy for me!

As my wheelchair was wheeled into the room outside the X-ray area, it seemed as if we had entered a morgue. Dozens of dead bodies were lying on stretchers; a hysterical doctor was hollering in perfect cockney at a police officer that the families of the dead had a right to being informed and how dare any cop prevent it. The nurse hurried me past and into the dark room, where my foot was finally X-rayed, with the radiologist washing the picture, and clipping it on to the lit board. He told me there was no fracture at all, but as he examined my toes with a pencil light, he spotted the cut between my big toe and second toe, which he cleaned out carefully. I flinched with pain as he poured antiseptic into the cut, then bandaged my foot, and gave me an injection which he said would relieve me of my pain.

When I came out, the bodies were still there, but the cop and the doctor had disappeared. Talat was by the door as I was wheeled out, with a big bandage on my foot. The radiologist came out and told her that since dirt had seeped into my cut, it needed to be cleaned up properly and I would have to do a course of antibiotics. Moreover, I needed to keep my foot elevated for a week. Since I was mildly diabetic, the doctor added that there was a small chance of the injury turning gangrenous, but if due care was taken, the injury would heal in about a week or so.

Talat had failed to establish contact with my family, but said her car could take me to wherever they were. At that moment, Rahat Javed drove up and found me. Her son worked at the TV station nearby, and had just learnt that I was taken to the Aga Khan Emergency. Rahat was a political worker who had known me since the eighties; she said that the television footage of me being injured and thrown into a vehicle was being repeatedly shown on all television channels, including the BBC and CNN, and my family was extremely anxious. She had spoken to Shugu, who, along with her father, had been to Jinnah Hospital and Liaquat National Hospital. Having failed to locate me, they were frantic with worry. Rahat had informed Shugu that her son had just learnt that I was in the Aga Khan Hospital, and they would bring me to Zia Ispahani's house, as they had established that my injury was not serious enough to cause alarm.

I hobbled into Zia's house. My Shugu looked stricken and just kept hugging me. She then called up her siblings, Umku in Islamabad and Abid in New York, and made me talk to them, while Fakhar thanked Rahat profusely and helped me sit comfortably on a sofa. He then gently informed me that 184 party workers had been blown up in the explosion along with at least two dozen policemen as well. We had much to be grateful for that I was more or less alright. Timmy arrived, having retrieved my sandals which had fallen when I had jumped, and my bag which had been flung away, both picked up by PPP workers and deposited to the Bilawal House where Timmy had found them. There was nothing missing from my bag, proof of the devotion of PPP workers. On Shugu's insistence, Timmy took me to the Ziauddin Hospital for a re-examination. The prognosis was the same. My wound was cleaned again, more antiseptic was poured which brought back the pain, and oral painkillers were prescribed. By the time we returned to Zia's house, dawn was breaking. Fakhar helped me up the steps and I was finally tucked into bed. I slept for a few hours.

Lally Weymouth called me from New York, saying she had seen the horrible television clip, in which she thought I was dying. She called Abid, who reassured her that he had spoken with me. She wished me safe recovery and informed me that the *Washington Post* would be doing a story on the attack. Lally was my first overseas caller, followed by many others from different countries and from all over Pakistan. Fakhar's mobile along with mine simply would not stop ringing. I was deeply moved by all the prayers and good wishes, but now the urge to get away from Karachi was gripping me. Fakhar also felt that we should take the evening flight to Multan, where his medical friends from Nishtar could examine my injury. The word 'gangrenous' was weighing as much on his mind as it was on mine.

We flew into Multan and the doctors came the moment we reached home. There was no difference of opinion, I was getting my wound cleaned and re-bandaged when Asif Zardari telephoned from Dubai to say how sorry he was that this should happen the first time I went out among the crowds after joining their party. Reminding him that I had been in many PPP demonstrations when we were protesting in support of the judiciary, although the scale of the crowd at Karachi was, of course, incomparable, I now had a bond of blood with the party, quite literally. At this he laughed and asked me where I was because BiBi would be coming to express her gratitude for having saved her life, and he wanted to beat her to it at least on the telephone. When he learnt I had left Karachi and was in Multan, and would be going to Jhang after a day's rest, he said that BiBi had not been informed, but he would let her know. When the call ended, Fakhar observed that Benazir, in her first telecast had mentioned that Abida Hussain was with her and had saved her and was injured in the process, so she could have asked where I was. It was typical of the PPP second line to be jealous even at a time like this, as none of them had called or bothered to come before we left Karachi. We were in agreement that while the PPP workers were wonderful, some of the second-line leaders were tremendous self-seekers and would not give a hoot about anyone but themselves.

After a day of rest in Multan, with a large number of Fakhar's supporters coming to call, Shugu and I headed out to Jhang where Umku joined us. Our constituents whom we had sent to Karachi for the airport reception had returned home safe and sound, which was a relief. Shugu remained at Jhang while Umku and I went home to Shah Jewna to offer our prayers and thanksgiving at my father and mother's graves.

Benazir telephoned me the following day, telling me, during the course of a long chat, what had been happening at her end. So many of her devoted workers had lost their lives, Amin Fahim and I had been injured, and nobody had told her of my having left Karachi. Her security had become a nightmare. She was unable to sleep, as every time she dosed off, her curtains would start rustling, and she would rush to the glass doors, pull the curtain aside, and watch two guys disappear into the shadows. She would call her security guards, who would say they had seen nobody.

The party had decided to lodge a First Information Report (FIR) with the local police. Aftab Shaban Mirani and others were being sent every day to the police station, but even their simple FIR was not being entertained. BiBi enquired about my injuries, and why had I not come down with Laleh. On hearing my narrative, she said it was a mistake not to precede the English girls who were both athletic and would have jumped more easily. Showing concern about my foot, she asked if I had a capable doctor on hand for dressings. I informed her that my doctor from the Abid Hussain Memorial Hospital drove in from Jhang for the dressing every morning. She was satisfied with the healing and was confident that I should be able to walk in about a week's time. Benazir expressed satisfaction, and told me that she would be going to Islamabad after a week and that Fakhar and I should join her there.

We went to Islamabad. There was a steady stream of friends and well-wishers visiting us at our house. Benazir called a meeting in Zardari House in F-8/3, and seemed to be really pleased when she saw us there, observing that my hair appeared to have greyed a little more. When I said it was caused by my presuming that I was being consigned to hell the day of the attack, she laughed heartily, assuring me that I had done more than my bit to secure a place in heaven. She sat out on her driveway, under an awning, with the party workers around her. There was adequate security at the gate, and no strangers were allowed in, but when one of her MNAs from Sindh brought some *mithai* (sweets), which he had bought in the local market, she popped some immediately in her mouth. Sitting next to her, I whispered that she should be careful with what she ate, and avoid eating foodstuff from the bazaar, because poisoning should not be put past her enemies. She called Naheed and asked her to take note of what I was saying.

Benazir decided to address a *jalsa* (large gathering) at Liaquat Bagh in Rawalpindi, and to mobilize all her parliamentary support from the provinces and the capital, along with party office bearers and leaders, and party workers from the adjoining districts. She thought that fifty thousand people would collect quite easily. Mian Nawaz Sharif was also returning to Pakistan, with her having paved the way, the atmosphere was conducive to the launch of pre-election activity. With the attack on her arrival having aborted, the government would have to ensure her security. Some of us felt that it was perhaps too early, but the majority agreed with the Chairperson. She told her staff to inform members of PPP's Central Executive Committee (CEC), to which Fakhar and I were also nominated, and her party office bearers, Senators, MNAs and prominent media persons to meet the day after next at Naheed Khan and her husband Safdar Abbasi's farmhouse at Bani Gala, just outside Islamabad.

Naheed and Safdar had quite a spread laid out. A large marquee was set up in the garden and Benazir was sitting on a dais. Spotting Dr Azra, Asif Zardari's sister, sitting beside Fehmida Mirza, I went to sit beside them, telling them that I was concerned about BiBi's security. She was poorly protected, even at this event. The government circles were rattled by her popularity, and we should make sure in every possible way for her safety to be ensured. They agreed, saying that BiBi was strong-headed and took her own decisions, but they appreciated my concern, and thanked me for the timely warning on the day of her arrival. They enquired after my injury. It was decided at this meeting that a day later we would all accompany her to her rally at Liaquat Bagh in Rawalpindi, and would collect here, and then drive out to Rawalpindi in a cavalcade, while local workers would fill the grounds inside the fenced off area of the Bagh.

On the morning of the rally, we got a message from Benazir to say that very few people were being called to her F-8 residence. We were among them, and should reach immediately to accompany her to the rally. When we reached her house, our vehicle was stopped at the entry to her street, and we had to walk past a series of roadblocks, through rows of policemen with helmets and padded jackets, and anti-riot squads. Many of them who belonged to our home districts greeted us as we walked by them. The other end of the street, closer to her house, was totally blocked, with rolls of barbed wire, and huge roadblocks, like an impregnable wall, behind the wires. A large number of television cameras and reporters had assembled on the main road where our vehicle had been stopped, but none of them had been allowed to enter the street.

Benazir had called about forty people, everyone saying that the government was obviously sabotaging the Liaquat Bagh rally by preventing her from reaching it. However, she seemed determined to make an effort. So she sat in her vehicle, driving out of the house slowly, while we followed the vehicle on foot. She told the driver to turn left and halted just before the barbed wire barricade. Putting her head out of the side window she asked the men to try and remove the barbed wire. For a moment nobody moved, then she called out again and this time Zulfiqar Mirza and Mehreen Raja, who was a hefty woman, moved forward to make an attempt. They were then joined by the other men, including Fakhar, to make a fruitless attempt. I went up to her vehicle and suggested to her that we were not going to succeed at this end, but since the media were lined up on the main road on the right side of the street, I could walk there, and tell them that they should position their cameras, and she would be coming towards them and would address them from her vehicle. She thought for a moment and asked how I would get through, since that end had also been barricaded by now. I told her that I had spotted a police officer whose home was in Jhang, perhaps I could persuade him to let me through to return home, and if I managed, en passant I could tell some of the tele-journalists to position their cameras, and perhaps one of them could get hold of sound amplifiers from the market nearby, and a mike which could be passed to her. If the local channels, BBC, and CNN recorded her and telecast her live, since they had their OB vans parked on the road, she would reach a wide audience and expose the administration's crude effort to block her.

Benazir accepted my proposal. Several women offered to accompany me but Benazir told them that only I should handle it along with Fakhar. We managed. Within an hour, she was standing on the seat of her vehicle and through the sunroof aperture addressed the people, with television cameras on top of their respective vans ranged on the road opposite and two large amplifiers on tall stands nearby, picking up her voice effectively. She made a furious speech, chastising the government for separating her from the people who awaited her for hours at Liaquat Bagh, demanding a free and fair election, and allowing the people to decide who they wanted as their representative government. A large crowd collected behind the camera vans and as she was being cheered by them, the police resorted to a baton charge, the crowd pelting stones at them. We managed to reach our vehicle, and drove to the safety of our home. Benazir left for Karachi, and called us to a meeting at

Bilawal House the next day. Before our departure from Islamabad, a senior civil servant came to inform us that Musharaf was going to declare Emergency, but some articles of the Constitution were going to be suspended again, so it would be virtually a second military intervention.

When we reached Bilawal House, the meeting had already started. Spotting us, Benazir had a couple of chairs vacated for us near her. She informed the gathering that she was going to Dubai for four days to see her husband and children and her mother whose health was deteriorating, and would return to Islamabad to plan a visit to Lahore, followed by a visit to Balochistan. When she paused, I whispered to her that we had gathered that Musharraf was going to make a second intervention imminently. A few minutes later she adjourned the meeting for the lunch and prayer break. While leaving, she asked Fakhar and me to follow her into a smaller room where lunch had been laid for her. We told her what we had heard, whereupon she asked Naheed to fetch a copy of the Constitution and suggested that Fakhar read out the relevant portions to clarify what our source had indicated.

Resuming the meeting in the committee room, she indicated that if Musharraf declared Emergency or went even beyond that, what could be anticipated as the immediate consequences. A heated discussion ensued. The majority opinion was that the Bar and the Bench would fight it out, and Musharraf would be forced into dissolving the Parliament and conducting election. The campaign would have to be vigorously led by 'Mohtarma BiBi' which would secure victory for the PPP. My opinion was different. I suggested that she remain in Dubai, and lead a virtual campaign, the way she had done in 2002, or with the advancement in technology, addressing crowds on big screens like Altaf Hussain of the MQM managed, as there would be a serious threat to her life. Some of the Sindhi stalwarts supported me, but most of the Punjabis opposed my suggestion vehemently, shouting that they would guard her with their lives and her presence in Pakistan was crucial or her party would be decimated. The dye was cast. Benazir announced that she would return to Pakistan on the fifth of November, leave quietly and return quietly, and proceed with her tours, campaigning vigorously, and if she was arrested, which was likely, it would only ensure a PPP victory.

On 3 November 2007, Musharraf made his second intervention: the High Court Bars did put up a stellar resistance, there were vicious battles fought between the lawyers and the police in the precincts of the courts, which more or less stopped functioning. Benazir returned from Dubai a couple of days later, flying into Islamabad. We were asked to be there for a round of discussions. The Chief Justice was not being allowed to receive visitors at his residence. We suggested that, accompanied by all of us, she drive up to the road that led to his residence, opposite the Marriott Hotel, but before that, she visit the journalists protest camp, to buck them up for defying the restrictions that were being imposed on them, and then have some of them accompany us to visit the Chief Justice. Some friends and colleagues had stopped by to see us. We missed her visit with the journalists, but when we reached the road opposite the Marriott, Benazir had attracted a crowd. We got out of our car and walked to the road leading to the Chief Justice's residence. Her four-wheeler was just reversing out of the road when she saw me and came out of her vehicle, asking me what I was doing standing by the roadside. Linking arms with me, she suggested we stroll across to the hotel for a cup of coffee, reminding me that I had told her that the best security was the element of surprise. Naheed and I virtually had to push her back into her vehicle with my saying that some risks were not worth taking. The next day, all of us left for Lahore by road.

By the time Benazir reached Lahore, the atmosphere was charged, electric with tension. She was staying in the home of Barrister Latif Khosa. When I reached his house, with scores of policemen around it, and hundreds of workers outside the gate, it was difficult to secure entry into his compound. By the time I entered the hallway, it was packed with party stalwarts. Chaudhry Ghulam Abbas took me up a spiral staircase and into the room where Benazir was sitting with half a dozen of her office bearers. She welcomed me affectionately, telling me that they were making a plan to court arrest. She was going to try and get herself arrested at Lahore, with Jahangir Badar and Qasim Zia beside her, Shah Mahmood would go to Faisalabad to be arrested, and she wanted me to go with him. Although Faisalabad was my divisional headquarter, my preference was to court arrest at my district headquarter, Jhang. She agreed to that and then turned to Rahman Malik, calling him 'Dr Malik'. She said he would never be arrested, and then asked him to tell us what his doctorate was in, since he was the only doctorate holder amongst us. When he responded that his degree was in 'craminolgy' she went into peals of laughter, correcting him, enunciating 'criminology' with precision, which she said she was doing for the umpteenth time and he never got it right! Rahman Malik was her tool, but she cut him down to size whenever she wanted, making me wonder why he took it, never reacting, always smiling politely.

Getting arrested in Jhang was not easy. I called a few lawyers and supporters to my house and we marched, mid morning, out of Shah Jewna House and onto the road with a couple of policemen, who had been lurking around outside my front gate, following us at a polite distance. As we turned the corner to proceed towards the district courts, about a dozen more policemen appeared, a few of them now walking like an escort besides us. We reached the bar room, had a cup of tea with the President of the Bar Association, who sent a few young lawyers to round up their colleagues, and as the hall of the bar room filled, we went in, escorted by the president who led me to the dais, where I made as aggressive a speech as I was capable of, got enthusiastic rounds of applause, left the bar room with some more lawyers joining us, walked past the Deputy Commissioner's office, shouting angry slogans, and then started heading towards the district jail. En route we passed a tea stall, where a policeman was digging into a plate of *halwa*, a local sweet dish. There were a couple of television cameras, and a few reporters recording our demonstration. I paused in front of the policeman, chastising him for gorging himself on *halwa* when it was mid morning instead of tending to his duty, and picking up the plate in front of him, I flung it at the wall behind the tea stall. The camera caught the moment, my arm in motion made it look as though I had slapped the policeman. Seeing the video clip, I was embarrassed, although a lot of people called to congratulate me for slapping the policeman, because the police are never popular with the public. We reached the gates of the jail, I was now pleading with the police to arrest me, but they would look away, so I sat in my car and arrived at the police station. Walking into the police inspector's office, I requested him politely to arrest me, congratulating him on the nice new building of the Kotwalli police station of Jhang town, and informing him that this was the first time in my life that I had actually come inside a police station, and was happy to see how clean and orderly it was. Having driven past the old Kotwalli building over the years, the thought of entering it had never occurred to me. I had never consciously transgressed the law. But this was a political protest and it was important my arrest was recorded.

The deputy superintendent then arrived and informed me that he had orders for me to be house-arrested. He sounded deeply apologetic, and persuaded me to drive back to Shah Jewna House in my own vehicle; he would follow, and post two policewomen inside the house and a few policemen at the gate. Visitors would be allowed but would be required to obtain permission from him; he would be obliged if offence was not taken if he did not allow more than four at a time. I requested him to make it eight, to which he readily agreed, anticipating that there would be hundreds of visitors to see me daily. He added that the permission for each batch would need to be limited to no more than ten minutes at a time. Fakhar arrived from Qatalpur. The news of my house-arrest was all over the electronic media. Three women had been placed under house-arrest: Benazir Bhutto, human rights activist Asma Jahangir, and me. Thousands of PPP workers courting arrest, along with party leaders and office bearers, were detained in police station lockups. All our friends from everywhere were telephoning and joking that the real sufferer was Fakhar for being caged with me for an indefinite length of time!

The house-arrest lasted only three days. Fakhar, Shugu, and I quite enjoyed the time spent together. We chatted and joked with our endless stream of visitors during the day, and spent quality time together in the evenings, watching television to keep track of events. Benazir called in the morning of our release and asked me to reach Lahore as soon as possible, as she wanted to talk to me before she left for Karachi that night.

Reaching Latif Khosa's house in the late afternoon I found Benazir surrounded by party workers and stalwarts; she pulled me into the bedroom off the hallway, in which she had been staying, asking Qasim Zia and Jahangir Badar to join us. She told Naheed to bring in her food on a tray as she was famished, and wanted to eat the partridges, which an old supporter had brought for her, before she left for the airport. I asked her whether she had raised the issue of her security with John Negroponte, the US Under Secretary for Defence who was on a visit to Pakistan, and whom she had spoken with telephonically, according to the media. She said she had, but his response was indifferent. It seemed to her that we were not being facilitated by the Americans. She had told Negroponte that the government had neither provided her with a bullet-proof car, nor did it have jammers of the kind that had helped Musharraf survive two terrorist attacks, but he made no assurance of raising the issue with Musharraf. She had therefore concluded that we were on our own, with our backs to the wall, but the people were with us, and we were going to fight a hard campaign. She would see me next when all PPP candidates were called to Islamabad for allotment of party symbols and wished me luck for my election.

Fakhar and Shugu had already launched their election campaigns. I returned from Lahore and plunged into mine, seeking to visit at least twenty communities everyday. The response of my constituents was enthusiastic, and each time we spoke on the phone, Fakhar and Shugu would assure me that their campaigns were going well. Umku was sometimes with me in my constituency and sometimes with her sister, helping out with the paperwork and logistics planning and budgeting. Abid would call from New York. He was in regular email contact with Benazir and had told his law firm that he would not be extending his contract with them after the first week of December. Occasionally he would copy me the emails he was exchanging with Benazir. Lally

Weymouth called me at the end of November to say she wanted to interview Benazir Bhutto for a cover story she was doing on her for *Newsweek*, so when should she come to Pakistan. Messaging BiBi, I got an immediate response that she would be in Islamabad on 13 December, and I could bring Lally over that evening for the interview and dinner. She would be allotting party symbols on the 14th and 15th, so I could get mine on the 14th and head back into my campaign for a week, because after that she would be doing rallies in the Punjab and would want me to be with her in some of them.

Hurtling through my constituency, stopping at some roadside gatherings, changing routes for reasons of security, I managed to reach my house in Islamabad just before Lally, accompanied by her *Newsweek* International editor, Rod Nordland, walked in. We drove to Zardari House immediately. I was exhausted, with Lally telling me I looked like hell, but better than when she had seen me on television the day we were bombed at Karachi! We entered Benazir's sitting room, with Lally and Nordland starting the interview, Naheed and I listening quietly. Lally's first question was that after the great reception that the people of her country had given her, when she returned home after all those years in exile, how she had felt about being attacked by bombs and who did she hold responsible for the attack. Benazir's reply was cool and measured. It was a classic terrorist attack, but there was clearly a lapse of security, and she had lodged a complaint with the police, but was not apprised of the follow-up investigation. Answering a few further questions, she asked Naheed to have the dinner laid, and we adjourned to the dining room, next to the sitting room, with the interview continuing while we ate. Benazir complained about the indifferent level of government security provided to her, which prompted Lally to question whether, if elected to power, she could coexist with Pervez Musharraf. Benazir answered that if in the interest of Pakistan she was required to do so, she would. Lally and Nordland left after dinner. Seeing them off, Benazir stopped to have a word with her press secretary, Farhatullah Babar and her personal secretary, Brigadier (retired) Aman.

Addressing both of them, I said that BiBi must not address a rally at Liaquat Bagh. She could address rallies at Mochi Gate, Lahore, at the stadium of Faisalabad, at the fort of Multan, but she must avoid Rawalpindi. Benazir differed, saying she had been in Nowshera on that day, had a really good day, stopping by the roadside to buy apples just near the Madrassah Haqqania of Maulana Sami ul Haq, where she was lustily cheered by the Pushtuns. She said we were likely to pull in just behind the ANP (Awami National Party) and would probably end up forming a coalition government with them in the NWFP (Khyber Pakhtunkhwa), while the mullahs would have to sit on Opposition benches, less possibly Maulana Fazlur Rahman who always cooperated with her government. A rally at Liaquat Bagh, Rawalpindi was necessary to establish with the public that her party was now strong enough to be unstoppable, as this would secure the swing vote for her candidates, but this would be her last one in Punjab. Her first one would be in Multan, followed by Lahore, and then Faisalabad, where I would join her and ride in her vehicle with her and we could discuss, en route, alternate locations in Rawalpindi or Islamabad for her finalé in Punjab.

She then asked me to stay and help her finalize the last lot of party nominations, about thirty-five of them in Punjab still pending. As we settled down her on her comfortable sofa, with Naheed and Safdar opposite, she said that it was a while since we had chatted. She asked me if I had read the last email which Abid had sent her regarding the Chinese Politburo, in which he had copied me as well. 'You must be so proud of your son Abida. He is truly gifted, and do you know the mails in which he does not copy you are full of jokes which make me laugh heartily and relieve me of my tension. When is he coming? I cannot wait for him to start working with me.' I told her he had concluded his contract with Pillsbury Winthrop on the 3rd of December, and was booked to fly back on the 3rd of January, would help out at our polling stations on the 8th and would report to work with her by the 15th of January. She responded by paying him another compliment—saying that, as always, his sense of timing was sharp—that is precisely when she would need him to start researching and writing for her. She added that we would have to start moving amendments to the Constitution which had been so severely mauled by the current government. First and foremost, we would have to withdraw the bar on third-time Prime Minister, which had been inserted into the Constitution by Musharraf, specifically designed to prevent her and Nawaz Sharif from becoming Prime Minister again. Aftab Shaban Mirani would stand in for her as Prime Minister till such time if our party won a majority.

She then settled down to work over the list of pending applicants in Punjab. The big surprise for me was Hina Rabbani Khar, who had been understudy to Shaukat Aziz when he was Prime Minister. Benazir said that Hina's sister was Wajid Shamsul Hassan's daughter-in-law. Hina had been refused a PML-(Q) ticket at the last minute by Chaudhry Shujaat, and had contacted Wajid, who had been at BiBi's beck and call for years in London, and seldom asked her for favours. Now that he had asked her for one, she could not refuse him and was thinking of giving Hina the ticket because she had no real applicant from this constituency. Asking me for my comment, I told her that Hina would bring in the constituency. As long as BiBi was sure that Hina would remain loyal to her, who else Hina worked for did not really matter. The next one she asked about was Mansur Hayat Tamman, who had my strong recommendation. We adjourned at 2 a.m., with BiBi informing me that she had no applicants for almost one hundred constituencies because the number of national and provincial constituencies had been so absurdly enlarged. The PML-(N) had twice the number with no applicants, she had gathered from her sources, and the constitutional amendment she would move, perhaps closer to the end of the tenure of the next parliament, would pare the number down to the previous size, although the enlarged number of women's seats could be maintained. She asked me if I would like a nomination for a reserved seat for women for myself or my daughter, since she was keeping one for herself, and nobody ever knew what hurdles could come up during a general election. I thanked her for her generous thought, adding that there was already resentment in the party regarding her giving four tickets to one family, and another one would only compound this resentment. She saw me to the door; we hugged each other warmly; and she said we would meet in Faisalabad in about ten days time. That was the last time I saw Benazir Bhutto.

The following day Fakhar and Shugu drove in to get their party symbols, and the three of us drove to the party office together, Fakhar's brother was coming later. When we returned home, I was planning to return to my constituency, having fallen behind on my schedule and now knowing that I would be taking another three days off joining BiBi's rallies. Lally called to ask if she could swing by as she wanted to talk to me before she left to return to New York. Lally and Rod Nordland had interviewed Musharraf that morning, and told us that when they asked him the same question they had posed Benazir regarding how he would coexist with her, he had turned ballistic, and nearly walked out of the interview. When he had regained his composure, he sat on the edge of his chair, fulminating in his mouth whenever he took her name, and had trashed her like anything. Lally said she had really liked Benazir, and wanted me to warn her that she should be extra careful regarding her security.

We returned to our constituencies, all three of us campaigning as hard as we could. It was the 25th of December, expecting a call from Benazir any minute, when my eye fell on a news item of the morning's papers which said that Benazir was entering her campaign in the Punjab and would address a rally at Liaquat Bagh on the 27th morning. Feeling immediately apprehensive, I tried to reach her to find out why she had changed her plans. Getting no response, I left for my own campaign, and was in the upper end of my constituency, at a community called Langar Makhdum, sitting in the home of one of my supporters, when Benazir called. She said that she really regretted she was not able to address a rally in my constituency, but had told Makhdum Amin Fahim to visit my constituency on the 31st, so he would have to sacrifice his New Year's Eve. Wishing me luck, she handed the phone to Amin Fahim. I told him that if he set off from Islamabad on the 31st morning, he would be in Lalian in just over two hours, exiting from the motorway at the Makhdum interchange, address a rally, and return to Islamabad by the evening to join his New Year's celebration. He said that was a kind thought, but elections were a priority, and we would celebrate after polling day on the 8th of January. That was the last time I heard Benazir Bhutto's voice.

On 27 December 2007, I was addressing a small gathering at the lower end of my constituency, not far from Shah Jewna, when a friend called from Karachi to say that Benazir Bhutto had been attacked just outside Liaquat Bagh, and had been rushed to the hospital. Hastily adjourning my corner meeting, I jumped into my vehicle and told the driver to get back to Shah Jewna as fast as possible. A few minutes later, Umku called me, sobbing away, informing me that it had just been announced on television that Benazir Bhutto was dead.

There was no question of any sleep for any of us that night. Abid called from New York, asking me in a choked voice what he should do. I told him he must return home. We needed him to be with us. He agreed to return, saying he could not stand the thought of being alone in New York and would reach us on 3 January as planned. I would never forget that I owed Benazir Bhutto my son's return to Pakistan, for it was she who had ignited the spark of patriotism lying latent inside him. She had inspired so many, and just when she had matured enough for proper governance, she was gone, leaving her country the poorer and many millions of its people bereft.

Early the following morning, I left for Multan to join Fakhar in order to drive down with him to Larkana for the burial. At Multan we kept getting calls, telling us that the bridge near the border of Sindh had been blocked and no traffic was being let through. With our vehicles bearing the PPP flag we set out in a retinue of four, along with friends and supporters and a few security guards. Driving out of the city, we kept encountering crowds of people, mostly young men, who were burning tires, and pelting stones at the nominal number of cars or buses plying on the roads. All shops had their shutters down, but the moment our PPP flags were spotted, we were cheered and let through by the crowds. It was the same story whenever we passed through a town en route, crowds by the roadside, tires burning, cheering at the sight of PPP flags, until we entered Sindh, and came to the bridge which had been blocked, with a huge tree trunk across it, which was smouldering at one end. A small crowd of young men came towards our halted vehicles, a couple of them waving banners, and recognized me, shouting my name, wailing and sobbing they said, 'Addi (sister) Abida Hussain! Where were you? Why did you not save our BiBi, why did you not save our treasure, our diamond of Sindh? You saved her when she arrived, why did you not save her now?' I got out off the vehicle and hugged them all, one by one, as did Fakhar, who had joined me. Eventually one of them shouted that Addi Abida should be allowed to go to her sister's funeral, and all the manpower heaved the log to a side. We returned to our vehicles and drove into Sindh, stopping every now and then, wherever there were crowds and demonstrators, I would call out 'Jeay Benazir!' and the demonstrators would yell back 'Jeay (Long Live) Benazir!'

Although Benazir was dead, through the slogan, her spirit lived on.

Epilogue

Through my supporters from Mandi Shah Jewna whose family members lived in Sukkur, we had booked rooms in the Forum Hotel in Sukkur. At the hotel entrance we encountered Brigadier Aman and Farhatullah Babar, both of them embraced me. We all grieved for Benazir, and both acknowledged that I had tried to prevent Benazir from going to Liaquat Bagh, and they wished she had listened to me. Since we were told that the funeral was over, we decided to stay overnight in Sukkur and drove to Naudero the following morning.

The roads were in a state of disrepair, the fields around with crops of much poorer quality than Punjab, greater poverty in evidence. It was amazing how this humble land had produced the brilliance of Zulfikar Ali Bhutto and the grace of Benazir.

Bhutto's house in Naudero was teeming with people. Fakhar was escorted to where Asif Zardari was sitting, and I was taken to Sanam, now the only surviving child of Z. A. Bhutto. We remained with the family for three days, and were present when the baton of leadership was passed to Asif Ali Zardari and Bilawal Bhutto Zardari. The new leadership decided that we would contest the polls scheduled for 8 January 2008. Probably apprehending a landslide in favour of the PPP, Musharraf postponed the polls.

Postponing the elections, Pervez Musharraf bought more time for himself. After Benazir's assassination, my heart was really not in the election. I also understood that Fakhar and I would be targeted. Musharraf and his cohorts would not want Asif Ali

Zardari to have anyone with capacity, who had old links with the Bhutto family, to be elected from Punjab. Fakhar understood the same. We hoped Shugu would come through but the election was stolen from her as well. Benazir was dead, and we were politically shipwrecked.

A year later, Asif Zardari gave Shugu a PPP nomination to the Senate. Before that, he was elected President of Pakistan, with Musharraf finally easing out in September of 2008. Had Benazir Bhutto lived, she may have been able to run the government with a better team, and might have managed to pull our country out of the morass we had begun to sink into. Asif Zardari managed to play the survivors game, and a civilian government was able to complete a five-year term in office for the first time since 1977. But his five years in power were rocked by a series of financial scandals as he fielded an absurdly poor team. The coalition government, which Asif Zardari sponsored, failed miserably in its attempt to deal with the power shortages gripping the country, and with the deteriorating economic situation that Pakistan was engulfed in, nor was it able to cope with the escalating incidents of terrorism.

By the time 2013 general elections came, the mass appeal that the PPP had enjoyed had diminished drastically everywhere: in Punjab, NWFP (renamed Khyber Pakhtunkhwa), and Balochistan. Although in Sindh, the PPP retained a majority.

The PML-(N) won the 2013 elections and was comfortably able to form the government. Pakistan Peoples Party was now leading a friendly Opposition, just as the PML-(N) had led a friendly Opposition during the PPP's tenure. Imran Khan, a later entrant into politics, emerged as a third force through his party, the Pakistan Tehreek-e-Insaf (PTI). He scored well enough to lead a coalition government in Khyber Pakhtunkhwa, sharing the rightist space with the religious parties and the PML-(N). The liberal, progressive space remains with the PPP for the time being, but its space has shrunk into it being a Sindhi party only.

Friends stop by to ask what my current preoccupation may be. They are often surprised to learn that having dedicated my life to politics, I am now resigned to my retirement from active politics, and seek only to comment on issues that I feel qualified to speak or write on from time to time.

The problems gripping Pakistan continue unabated. Population is on the rise; acts of terrorism and bombings have become part of daily life; levels of unemployment of the educated youth, both in rural and urban areas, is alarming; robbers, dacoits, and killers are running free; inflation is breaking the backs of all; bribery and corruption have become so rampant that it is now a way of life. The government seems unable to expand the number of direct tax payees, and continue to rely on indirect taxation, resorting to increase in our internal as well as external credits. Enveloping themselves in corporate garb, countless are becoming richer, while the government and the general populace are getting poorer. There is an energy crisis, our rivers are drying up, and with India continuing to build dams on the two rivers left to us, Rivers Jhelum and Chenab, there is a serious water shortage staring us in the face. The outlook for our future remains bleak, and the thought that keeps recurring to me is that had we avoided being proactive in the wars in neighbouring Afghanistan, we may have lived up to the promise that did originally reside in us: of becoming a more prosperous and balanced nation. The 'might have been' of history is the story of all peoples everywhere, and everything is relative, but it is sad and troubling for me that millions of young Pakistanis are willing to jump into the unknown and seek to leave their country in search of a more prosperous and peaceful life.

Many of the young I encounter want to know what Pakistan was like during my youth. Without hesitation, I tell them it was a much better place. It was far less crowded and there was greater hope for a better future. But then I recall my meeting with Mohtarma Fatima Jinnah, and the understanding comes that life is a series of bittersweet memories for all of us. What is important is that when we look back upon our lives, we should be able to feel that we have spent it meaningfully, that we had made some sort of contribution towards the betterment of the country and alleviating the sufferings of others. When old age approaches, what is consequential is to be in readiness to depart from the world with fewer regrets and greater satisfaction, a sense of the spiritual combined with a sense of peace, and to remind ourselves that it is never too late to make amends for any hurt we may have caused to our fellow human beings. Life flows from humanity and we keep learning until the very end. Many are resistant to the notion of mortality, but then as many reconciled to it. Where and who we are born as is an accident, as is where and when we die, the passage of the years in between, shorter for some than for others. What is important is how each one of us negotiates that passage and what we contribute to life as we go along. My young listeners sometimes seem to value what they have heard; sometimes I observe them stifling a yawn, a signal for me to end.

My father used to say that each person has an inherent right to live till at least age fifty, after which it is God's Grace. By his own yardstick he exercised his due right, passing away at age fifty-five. My mother used to say everyone ought to pray for their ultimate release without being a burden on anyone. She was walking a mere six hours before she was gone, at the age of seventy-six. Both my parent's lives were well spent.

What awaits us all around the corner is the mysterious unknown, but we all have a right to our dreams. My dream is that my country achieves a leadership of unimpeachable integrity and considerable capacity: a leadership that is able to frame and implement policies so that further failure is ceased; a future for Pakistan is planned that moves it towards improvement and success.

That is my dream ……

Index

A

Afghanistan 1, 14, 153, 155, 161–3, 193, 215, 217, 268, 271–2, 285–7, 295–7, 365, 377, 402, 41–14, 420, 433, 435, 440, 442, 448, 455, 458, 467, 477, 496, 510, 512–13, 538, 603, 610, 619, 633, 696

Aitchison College 2, 12, 14, 130, 131, 395, 519, 632, 634

Albright, Dr Madeleine 466

Ali, Amjad 13–14, 52, 54, 103, 118, 131, 156, 191, 198, 407–8, 533–5, 538, 544

Ali, Babar 9, 95, 155, 220, 408, 443

Ali, Chaudhry Nisar 346, 379, 400–4, 406–7, 414, 465, 497–8, 500–1, 504, 521, 523–9, 536, 543, 563, 570, 576, 581–3, 627–8

Ali, Tariq 11

Altaf 329, 344, 351–6, 367–9, 513, 681

Avery-Jones, Sir Francis 40, 44, 60, 65

B

Balochistan 95, 97, 101, 125–6, 136–8, 157, 205, 210, 226, 229, 235, 278, 333, 335–6, 338–40, 342, 347–8, 371, 549, 561, 565, 618, 631–3, 635, 638, 645, 647, 661, 681, 695

Barelvi(s) 305, 331

Basra, Riaz 370–1, 511, 522

Bhutto, Benazir 104–6, 109, 111–14, 118, 123, 154, 160–1, 214, 270, 292–5, 300, 305, 318–30, 333, 337–8, 343–4, 346–7, 349–50, 352, 371–2, 377, 382, 388, 404, 414, 468, 477, 502, 509–13, 517–23, 525–6, 528–9, 534, 547, 557, 566, 576, 582, 587, 592, 609, 611–18, 623–9, 638–40, 642–5, 652–71, 673–95

Bhutto, Nusrat 25, 79, 91–2, 94, 96, 97, 103, 118, 153–4, 158, 160, 214, 322, 327, 488, 534

Bhutto, Sanam 640, 652, 694

Bhutto, Shahnawaz 201, 517–8, 529

Bhutto, Zulfikar Ali 14, 16, 25, 51, 53–5, 71, 77–8, 81, 88–90, 95, 104–6, 125, 127–8, 135, 149, 152–3, 156, 158–9, 183, 201, 321, 327, 371, 517, 529, 542, 639, 694

Bilawal House 529, 615, 660, 663, 665–6, 669, 675, 681

Bizenjo, Mir Ghous Bux 95, 152, 164, 336

Bugti, Nawab Akbar Khan 27, 74, 97, 152, 333, 335–7, 339, 341, 344,

348–51, 555, 618, 626, 630–2, 634–6, 640, 642, 646–7

C

Chandi 8, 10, 20, 23, 25, 34, 36, 47–8, 56, 65, 75, 91, 96, 115, 121, 139–40, 167, 202, 236, 297, 315, 360
Clinton, Bill 466, 470, 474–5, 486, 491, 580, 582, 591, 619
Clinton, Hillary 481, 491–2, 494–5, 570
colonial 2, 10, 104, 120, 124, 193, 389, 394, 397, 475, 489
Combined Opposition Parties (COP) 12, 338–40, 341, 343–4, 350–2, 367–8, 373

D

Dhaka (Dacca) 25, 40, 78, 153, 558–9, 606

E

East Pakistan 2, 12, 15, 28, 34, 53, 59, 66, 77, 80, 118, 151, 210, 222, 606
Eighth Amendment 249–52, 255, 280, 317

F

Fahim, Makhdum Amin 627–8, 643, 660, 671, 676, 691
Farooqui, Salman 230–1

G

Gandhi, Rajiv 333–4
Gul, General Hamid 215, 271, 300, 335, 449, 539

H

Hamid, Shahid 123, 177, 290, 519–23, 525, 528, 530, 552–3, 557, 561, 572
Haq, Dr Mahbubul 220, 231, 243, 245, 251–2, 300, 401
Hashmi, Javed 149, 213, 250, 260, 290, 304, 324, 326
Hayat, Faisal Saleh 129–30, 134–5, 140, 160, 177, 313, 328, 331–2, 374–5, 508–10, 590, 607–8, 656
Hussain, Chaudhry Shujaat 324, 326–7, 330–1, 346, 527, 549–51, 576, 605–6, 608, 689
Hussain, Mushahid 336, 514, 527, 544–6, 563, 570, 576
Hussain, Syed Abid 8, 12, 17–18, 34, 40, 56, 63, 65, 70–1, 85, 98–9, 122, 146–7, 175, 187, 524
Hussain, Syeda Abida 43, 89, 92, 99, 101–4, 116, 121, 137, 139, 146, 168, 170, 173–5, 181, 186–8, 191, 195, 209–10, 225, 233, 259, 264, 294, 297, 300, 303, 320, 323, 326, 330, 339, 354–5, 363, 367–8, 371, 387, 405, 409, 437–8, 514, 521–2, 525, 527–8, 631, 667, 672, 676, 689, 693
Hyderabad Conspiracy Case 125–6, 150, 188

I

Imam, Abid Hussain 14, 27, 28, 33, 36, 42–3, 55–8, 98, 203, 313, 384, 387–8, 390–1, 414, 417, 454, 456, 464, 479, 483, 498–9, 504, 510, 512, 559–60, 562, 565, 567–8, 594, 602–3, 611, 616, 640–1, 644, 652–4, 658–9, 674–5, 686, 688, 692

Imam, Fakhar 20–6, 31, 40, 49–50, 55–8, 61, 65–6, 68–9, 71, 74–5, 77, 79–81, 86, 95, 97–9, 104, 117, 119, 124–5, 127, 130, 142, 145, 149, 154–5, 159, 165, 170, 174, 178, 181–2, 189–90, 192, 19–6, 198–207, 209–10, 212–14, 218–21, 223–4, 226–38, 240, 244, 246–49, 253–4, 256–58, 260, 262–3, 265–72, 275–83, 285, 289–93, 298, 300–4, 306–9, 314–16, 318, 323–8, 330, 332, 334–7, 341–3, 357–62, 365, 370, 376, 378, 383, 385, 388–91, 401, 403–4, 407, 413, 417–18, 449, 463–4, 474–6, 480–3, 489–3, 498, 501–2, 504–5, 507–10, 518–21, 526, 532–4, 542, 549, 552, 555, 557, 562, 564–6, 568–70, 572–4, 578, 582–3, 587–9, 594–5, 597–8, 601–2, 604–7, 609–10, 615–19, 621, 624–5, 627–34, 636, 638–46, 648–50, 652–9, 662–3, 665–6, 672–81, 685–6, 690, 692–5

Imam, Syeda Sughra Hussain 83, 566, 600, 656

Imambarah (Imambargah) 70, 73, 178, 516, 561–2, 615

Independent Democratic Group (IDG) 611–12, 627, 642

India 2, 6, 9, 11–12, 14, 17–18, 31, 35, 63, 101, 119, 121–2, 155, 162, 191, 251, 273, 319, 333–5, 347, 393, 405, 410, 413, 421–2, 439, 442, 451–3, 455, 458–60, 462–3, 465, 467, 471–4, 477, 479, 484–5, 492, 527, 543, 549, 554, 563, 565, 571, 574–5, 580, 586, 590, 597, 696

Islamabad 79, 86, 91, 124, 137, 199–201, 203–4, 207–9, 211–15, 226–7, 230, 233, 252, 268, 275–6, 291–2, 299–301, 304, 306, 316, 318–21, 333, 335–6, 339, 342, 356–7, 367, 375, 383–4, 387, 395, 402, 404, 409, 412, 415, 424, 437, 441, 458, 463–4, 484, 490, 497–8, 501, 504–5, 507, 513, 518, 523, 527–8, 533, 535–6, 541, 548–9, 557, 559–60, 562, 568, 571, 577–8, 583, 585, 587–91, 594, 602, 604, 606, 624, 634, 637–8, 646–50, 658, 660, 662, 674, 677–8, 681–2, 686–8, 691

Islami Jamhoori Ittehad (IJI) 304, 308, 313–14, 316, 325, 330–1, 373, 375–6, 378

J

Jamaat-i-Islami (JI) 134, 139–40, 144, 149, 241–42, 250, 280, 282, 304, 315, 341, 350, 354, 610, 649

Jamali, Zafarullah Khan 204, 371, 607–9
Jamiat Ulema-e-Islam (JUI) 214, 315, 341, 366
Jamiatul Ulema-e-Pakistan (JUP) 308, 250
Jatoi, Ghulam Mustafa 142, 214, 326, 333, 338, 341, 343–8, 352–3, 365, 367, 371, 373, 376, 402, 528, 561
Jhang 9–10, 12, 22, 36, 50, 52–9, 61–5, 69–70, 78–9, 83–4, 86, 87, 89–92, 98, 103, 116–17, 120, 128–30, 133–5, 140–1, 146, 155, 159–61, 165–6, 170, 175, 177–9, 181–6, 189–91, 196, 198, 201, 203–5, 213–14, 216–17, 219–21, 230, 285, 287–8, 290, 303, 305, 308, 310–11, 331, 340, 356–66, 369, 374, 376, 378–9, 414, 464, 487, 510, 535–6, 559–62, 564–7, 590, 597–8, 600–2, 607, 611, 620–1, 624, 632, 656, 662, 676–7, 680, 683–4
Jhang District Council 165, 175, 196, 213, 564, 566
Jhangvi, Haq Nawaz 314, 360
Jhelum (river) 11, 146, 184, 487, 536, 656, 696
Jinnah, Fatima 7, 12, 15, 55, 697
Jinnah, Muhammad Ali (Quaid-i-Azam) 12, 17–18, 28, 51, 54, 59, 63, 241–2, 348, 356, 542, 595, 635–6, 660
Junejo, Mohammad Khan 227, 236, 238, 240–1, 246, 249, 252, 259, 261, 275, 279–80, 282, 289, 291–2, 294–6, 300, 303, 323, 409

K

Kabirwala 130, 145, 155, 214, 219, 290, 330, 376, 532, 607, 662
Kaffir 59, 64, 162, 288, 311, 359, 364, 371, 375, 395
Kalabagh, Nawab 3, 12, 27, 139
Karamat, General Jahangir 520, 562–3, 568
Karbala 67
Kashmir 9, 11, 15, 96, 119, 191, 410, 412–13, 420, 422, 442, 450–1, 462–4, 466, 469, 474, 486, 524, 571, 573, 580, 623–4, 642
Khan, Air Marhsall Nur 110, 115, 225, 227, 250, 277–8, 293
Khan, Air Marshall Asghar 139, 142–5, 214, 646
Khan, General Ali Kuli 519, 568–9, 631
Khan, Ghulam Ishaq 205, 238–9, 307, 315, 318–23, 333, 371–2, 376–7, 388, 404, 411–12, 416, 463–4, 482, 490, 496, 498, 501, 504, 508–9, 520, 557
Khan, Gohar Ayub 144, 535–9, 544–5, 549, 563
Khan, Khan Abdul Wali 53, 77, 97, 125–6, 131, 152, 162, 164, 187, 209, 214, 326, 332, 333, 338, 356, 365, 373–4, 376
Khan, Nasim Wali 131–3, 137, 139–40, 142–3, 146, 150–1, 154, 335, 561
Khan, Sahibzada Yaqub 9, 119, 191, 221–2, 236, 296, 298, 300, 323, 328, 402, 405, 465, 466, 578
Khan, Tahir Ayub 3, 549

Khomeini, Ayatollah 154, 515
King's Party 242–3, 260, 279, 286, 289
Kissinger, Henry 122–5, 299, 435, 476–8

L

Lahore Fort 93–4, 285, 398, 572
Lal Masjid 583, 650, 654
Landowner(s) 121, 130
Lashkar-e-Jhangvi 364, 366, 371, 403, 510, 583, 587, 598, 632
Leghari, Farooq Ahmed Khan 154, 292–4, 328, 333, 509, 519–20, 522–3, 525, 531, 534, 536, 541–3, 552, 555, 557–8, 561, 569, 613, 628
Liaquat Bagh 658, 678–80, 688, 691–2, 694
London 5, 17–20, 25, 31–2, 35, 40, 43–5, 50, 53, 59–60, 67, 75, 155, 214, 263, 269–70, 272, 275, 304, 384, 392, 401, 403–4, 596, 602, 604, 609, 617–18, 626–8, 639, 645, 652, 657, 659, 670, 689

M

Mahmood, Maulana Mufti 97, 102, 139, 559
Mahmudabad, Raja 17–19, 42, 75, 321
Majlis-e-Shoora 222, 225
Mazari, Mir Balakh Sher 81, 104, 105, 106, 107, 108, 131, 250, 490, 499, 504, 561, 630, 631, 633, 634

Mazari, Sardar Sherbaz 131, 139–40, 142–4, 149–51, 164
Meshed 41, 43, 45–6, 48, 72, 517
Mirza, Iskander 17–18, 60, 640
Mubarak, Hosni 567, 605
Muharram 67–9
Mujahideen 215, 272, 287, 296–7, 496, 514
Multan 26, 86, 88, 98, 117, 130, 165, 170, 174, 181–2, 192, 194–6, 198–9, 209, 213, 260, 306, 316, 324, 362, 370, 414, 476, 518, 624, 632, 642, 656, 675–6, 688, 692
Murree 3, 6, 33–5, 86–7, 124, 142–4, 189, 215, 225, 240, 346, 523
Musharraf, Pervez 569, 578–83, 585–619, 621, 626, 629–33, 637–8, 640–1, 645, 647, 649–51, 654, 657–8, 661–5, 681–2, 686, 688–90, 694–5
Muttahida Majlis-e-Amal 610
Muttahida Qaumi Movement (MQM) 315, 329, 344, 347, 351–6, 366–7, 373, 513, 648, 681

N

Nasrullah, Nawabzada 27, 139, 142–4, 214, 323, 326, 333, 338–41, 352–6, 373–4, 376
National Awami Party (NAP) 53, 97, 126, 131, 152, 270
National Democratic Front (NDF) 16
National Democratic Institute (NDI) 479–80, 618

National Democratic Party (NDP) 131, 137, 139–40, 144, 146, 150–2, 154, 164–5, 295
NATO (North Atlantic Treaty Organization) 479, 485, 610, 616, 642
Noon, Malik Sir Firoz Khan 3, 30, 390
Noon, Vicki 3, 124–5, 189, 208, 214, 229, 236, 389–90, 480, 561
North-West Frontier Province (Khyber Pakhtunkhwa) 30, 157, 239, 325, 371, 610, 623, 688, 695–6
Nuclear 122, 125, 377, 405, 409, 411–12, 415, 420, 422, 424, 433–4, 448, 450, 452, 459–60, 472, 477, 479, 490, 495, 563, 565, 567, 571, 586

O

Ojhri Camp 300–1, 303

P

Pahlavi, Raza Shah 154
Pakistan Democratic Movement (PDM) 16, 24–5
Pakistan Muslim League (PML) 53, 280, 510, 522, 532, 555, 589, 593, 595, 605, 608, 649, 655, 689–90, 695–6
Pakistan National Alliance (PNA) 131, 133–6, 138, 142, 146, 149–52, 341
Pakistan Peoples Party (PPP) 51, 53, 77–8, 90, 92, 105, 120–1, 128–33, 136–7, 140, 142, 146, 149, 154, 156, 158, 160, 214, 292–4, 304, 308–9, 313–15, 317, 328–31, 333, 336, 338–41, 344, 347, 350, 356, 365, 371, 374–6, 406, 409, 509, 518, 530, 532, 566, 608–9, 615–17, 627–8, 638–40, 642, 647–9, 653–6, 661–3, 667, 675–6, 678, 681–2, 685–6, 692, 694–6
Pir Pagaro 139, 240–1
Pirzada, Abdul Hafeez 94, 104–5, 142, 156, 468
Pirzada, Sadia 92, 94, 104, 109, 111
Powell, Colin 478, 506–7
Punjab 2, 6, 9, 11–12, 15, 18, 30, 36, 50–2, 74, 78–9, 81, 89, 98, 100, 116, 124, 131, 137, 138–9, 142–3, 153, 157–8, 171, 177, 181, 184–7, 190, 205, 208, 210, 215, 220–1, 230, 235, 248, 254, 273, 278, 282, 291, 310, 315, 317, 323–5, 328, 338–40, 346–7, 351, 370–1, 379, 403, 413, 474, 488–7, 499, 510, 521–2, 526, 532, 540, 543, 552, 554, 561, 565, 572, 607, 609, 611, 623, 625, 627, 633, 637–9, 642, 649–50, 654–6, 667, 687–9, 691, 694–5
Pushtun 30, 131, 162, 242, 263, 286–7, 322, 327, 356, 392, 569, 631–3, 644, 688

Q

Qatalpur 20–1, 26, 117, 145, 316, 490, 607, 657, 659, 685
Qul 74, 361–2, 617, 633–4

Qureshi, Shah Mahmood 639, 642, 683

R

Rahman, Sheikh Mujibur 16, 28, 34, 40, 53
Rasheed, Sheikh 317, 328, 330, 401
Rawalpindi 34, 40, 65, 92, 121, 124, 150–1, 199, 229, 250–1, 293, 298, 300–1, 321, 324, 346, 383, 386–7, 397, 568, 585, 600, 645, 655–6, 678–9, 688
Republican(s) 6, 370, 456–8, 465–6, 479, 486, 488, 490, 514, 642
Revision of Constitution Order (RCO) 248, 280

S

Saifullah, Kulsoom 121, 230, 321, 322, 323, 334, 346
Shah Jewna 9–10, 14–15, 20, 24–5, 30, 33, 54, 56–8, 61–2, 64, 68, 70–1, 73, 78–9, 86–7, 91, 98, 100, 128, 131, 133–4, 136, 141, 148, 159–60, 166, 169–70, 173, 175–6, 178, 184–5, 203, 290–1, 305, 311, 313–14, 332, 354, 358, 361, 362, 378, 414, 483, 515, 524, 532, 536, 561–2, 564, 566–7, 606, 620, 633, 638, 659, 663, 676, 683, 685, 691–2, 694
Shah, Mubarik Ali 13, 51–2, 55, 61, 69, 71, 74
Shahi, Agha 103–5, 114, 116, 189–90, 192–3, 204, 412, 463–4, 468, 572–3
Shaikh, Najmuddin 227–8, 400–3, 406–7, 414, 418
Sharif, Mian Nawaz 182, 209, 220–1, 290, 300, 303, 308–9, 316, 323–7, 331, 338–40, 344–7, 351, 353, 356, 373–4, 376–8, 381–2, 388, 402, 405, 407, 435, 449, 473–4, 482, 490, 501, 504–7, 518, 520–3, 525, 527, 530–1, 533, 535–6, 538, 544–9, 551–2, 554–7, 561, 563–4, 566–7, 569–71, 573, 575–6, 579, 582–3, 585–6, 589, 592–5, 598, 605, 613–14, 616–17, 626–7, 660–1, 678, 689
Sharif, Mian Shahbaz 379, 498, 504, 523–6, 528–9, 553, 561, 567, 570, 576, 585–6, 592–4, 617, 627
Shia(s) 48, 59, 61, 63–4, 72, 82, 133, 163, 288, 300, 310–11, 334, 356, 358–62, 364–5, 369, 371, 375, 407, 511, 513–14, 517, 600–1
Shugu 86, 95, 97, 113, 124, 127, 133, 136, 145, 155, 198, 200, 259, 313, 342, 350–1, 357–9, 374, 384, 388, 403–4, 419, 431, 454, 456–7, 461–2, 475, 479, 489, 502, 510, 512, 559, 562, 564, 567, 587, 595–8, 600–2, 607, 611, 614, 616, 624, 632, 652–3, 656, 662–6, 672–6, 685–6, 690, 695
Sipah Sahaba 285, 287–8, 303, 305, 308, 311–14, 356–61, 363–4, 366, 375, 378–9, 513, 532, 600, 607–8
Soomro, Ilahi Bux 204, 212, 227, 228, 233, 293, 502, 631

Soviet Union 103, 105–6, 108–10, 112, 114, 116, 161–3, 215, 268, 271–2, 285, 296–7, 402, 412–13, 420, 422, 433–4, 440, 442, 462, 472, 477
stud farm 15, 25, 172–3, 273, 551, 553–4, 623, 642
Sunni 59, 63, 72, 305, 358, 362, 375, 517, 601

T

Taliban 512, 538–9, 642
Tarar, Rafiq 555, 562, 579
Tehran 43–5, 49, 513, 546–7
Timmy 7, 75, 160–1, 295, 324, 329–30, 335, 615, 623–4, 628, 647, 663–4, 666–70, 674–5

U

Umme Kulsum (Umku) 75–6, 78, 83, 86, 95, 97, 113, 124, 127, 133, 136, 145, 155, 198, 200, 259, 313, 342, 350, 374, 384, 388, 403–4, 419, 431, 439, 454, 456–7, 461–2, 476–80, 489, 502, 506, 509, 511, 518, 528, 559–60, 562, 564, 583, 596, 602, 604, 611, 616, 624, 652–3, 659, 674, 676, 686, 692
United Nations (UN) 13, 189–93, 197–8, 400–2, 450, 462
United States of America 21, 118, 191, 193, 215, 377, 417, 422–3, 432, 435, 439, 458, 467, 471, 475, 477–8, 480–1, 487, 488, 491–2, 496–7, 500, 503–4, 594, 604, 616, 619, 621–2, 641
United States of America (USA) 502

V

Vajpayee, Atal Bihari 571–5

W

Wahabi 305, 512, 633
Washington D.C. 118–19, 162, 194, 376, 401–2, 404, 407–8, 410–11, 413–15, 417–19, 421, 423, 425, 427–9, 431, 433, 435–9, 441, 443–5, 447, 449–51, 453–4, 455, 456–9, 461, 463–5, 467–70, 473, 475–7, 482–3, 485, 490–1, 493, 498–502, 505–7, 533, 549, 564–5, 566, 570, 573, 583, 585–6, 588, 594, 602–4, 609, 611, 641
West Pakistan 2, 3, 6, 15, 27–9, 53, 77, 87, 110, 118, 153, 188, 283, 348, 558

Z

Zardari, Asif Ali 295, 315, 337, 511, 529, 566, 592, 611, 614–16, 624, 638, 642, 659, 675, 678, 694–5
Zardari, Hakim Ali 295, 315, 324, 329, 334, 615, 623, 662–3, 666
Zardari, Timmy 160, 315, 336, 624
Zia ul-Haq 141, 144–6, 149–52, 154–6, 158, 161–3, 165, 171, 188, 193–7, 199–201, 204–7, 212, 214, 216–18, 221–2, 225–7, 229, 231–3, 235–8, 240–2, 248–

9, 251–3, 255, 276, 278, 279–82, 289, 292, 294, 297–300, 302–4, 306–7, 325, 332, 337, 428, 448, 466, 520, 592, 597, 609, 611, 627–8, 639, 655, 658, 663–4, 666, 674, 683, 686